Athletic Training

The Contributors

Thomas D. Fahey, Ed.D.
California State University, Chico
Chapters 4, 5, 24, 25, 26, 27, 28

Michael F. Cembellin, B.S., A.T.,C.
Santa Clara University
Chapters 20, 22

Paul L. Christensen, M.S., P.T., A.T.,C.
Director, Athletic Rehabilitation and
    Physical Therapy Associates, Inc.
Los Gatos, California
Chapters 8, 18

Donald A. Chu, Ph.D., R.P.T.
California State University, Hayward
ATHER Sports Injury Clinic
Dublin, California
Chapters 14, 15, 16

Gary Delforge, Ed.D., A.T.,C.
University of Arizona
Chapter 9

Jeffrey Dwyer, Ph.D., R.P.T., F.A.C.S.M.
Supervisor, Cardiac Rehabilitation
Santa Clara Valley Medical Center
San Jose, California
Chapters 6, 17

Richard A. Eagleston, R.P.T., A.T.,C.
Orthopedic and Sports Physical Therapy, Inc.
Portola Valley, California
Chapter 19

**Frank C. Egenhoff, Jr., M.S., R.P.T.,
    A.T.,C.**
Mesa Community College
Chapter 23

Joseph J. Godek, M.S., A.T.,C.
West Chester University
Chapters 1, 2, 11

Stanley A. Herring, M.D.
Team Physician, University of Washington
Washington Sports Medicine and
    Orthopedics Associates
Kirkland, Washington
Chapter 19

Jeffery B. Hogan, A.T.,C.
University of California, Davis
Chapters 20, 22

Charles J. Redmond, P.T., A.T.,C.
Springfield College
Chapters 3, 10

John A. Romero, M.A., R.P.T.
Sports Medicine Center, Inc.
Chevy Chase, Maryland
Chapter 12

Jeffrey A. Saal, M.D.
Team Physician, Santa Clara University
Consultant Team Physician, San Francisco
    49ers
Chapter 7

Terry L. Sanford, M.A., P.T.
University of Utah
Chapters 3, 10

Richard V. Schroeder, M.A.
Director, Exercise Physiology Laboratory
De Anza College
Chapter 23

Martin Trieb, M.D.
Orthopedic Consultant, Men's and
    Women's Athletic Departments
San Jose State University
Chapter 21

**Susan Anthony Trieb, P.A.C., R.P.T.,
    A.T.,C.**
Chapter 13

Athletic Training

Principles and Practice

Thomas D. Fahey

California State University, Chico

Mayfield Publishing Company

Mountain View, California

RD97
F34
1986

Library of Congress Catalog Card Number:
85-062619
International Standard Book Number:
0-87484-582-3

Manufactured in the United States of America
10 9 8 7 6 5

Mayfield Publishing Company
1240 Villa Street
Mountain View, California 94041

Sponsoring editor: James Bull
Developmental editor: Janet M. Beatty
Manuscript editor: Eva Marie Strock
Managing editor: Pat Herbst
Art director: Cynthia Bassett
Designer (interior and cover): Randall Goodall
Cover photograph: Michael Zagaris
Illustrators: Valerie Winemiller, Jeanne Koelling,
    and Paula McKenzie
Production manager: Cathy Willkie
Compositor: York Graphic Services
Printer and binder: Malloy Lithographing, Inc.

The most up-to-date research in the field of athletic training forms the foundation of this text. The publisher and contributors disclaim responsibility for any adverse effects or consequences from the misapplication or injudicious use of the information contained within the text.

Contents

PART FOUR: FACTORS AFFECTING PERFORMANCE

24. *Disease and the Athlete* 441

25. *Environmental Stress* 455

"Putting It into Practice" Tips

Preface

ATHLETIC training is the "front line" discipline of sports medicine; its practitioners are most closely involved with the day-to-day health problems of athletes. More than other health care practitioners, athletic trainers must have a thorough knowledge of most aspects of sports medicine to successfully treat, rehabilitate, and condition athletes. They must be familiar with basic medical procedures to communicate well with physicians and understand the implications of medical treatment. To best promote conditioning and therapeutic exercise, they must learn exercise physiology. To assess mechanisms of injury and prevent future disability and to understand physical therapy in order to better appreciate the application of therapeutic modalities, they must understand biomechanics. They must also be familiar with psychology, to help athletes cope with the emotional stress of injury, and with nutrition, to assist athletes with their dietary requirements. In short, athletic trainers serve athletes best when their knowledge is broad based.

Approach and Audience

Athletic Training: Principles and Practice is a compendium of practical information on preventing, evaluating, and treating injuries. The collaboration of athletic trainers, physicians, physical therapists, and exercise physiologists makes this book a wide-ranging source of information for students who are interested in athletic training. Each chapter was written by a specialist with extensive expertise, which assures a state-of-the-art presentation on each topic. Chapters on professional preparation, injury prevention, injury evaluation, and emergency treatment of injuries, for example, were written by athletic trainers with years of experience. The chapter on internal medical disorders was written by an internal medicine specialist, and the chapters on modalities, philosophy of rehabilitation, and inflammation were written by physical therapists. Chapters on conditioning, nutrition, and environmental stress were written by an exercise physiologist. All these experts have combined their specialized knowledge with their extensive work with athletes to present information that is both theoretical and practical.

Students in courses in athletic training and prevention and care of athletic injuries will find this text illuminating; it will also serve as a useful primer on sports injury management for students interested in becoming coaches, physical educators, nurses, and physical therapists. Those students who are looking for an easy-to-use reference book for athletic injury management will find that this book meets their needs.

Franklin Henry, a pioneer in the concept of physical education as an academic discipline, once said that the theoretical man is the practical man. For Henry, proper practice depended on a sound theoretical underpinning. In this book, we have attempted a marriage of the theoretical and the practical. Our chapters on injury management abound with concrete and practical procedures for injury evaluation and treatment. However, we have also taken great strides to ensure that students know *why* injuries occur. With this approach, students will learn to base a treatment program on sound scientific principles derived through research rather than blindly following a treatment program as if it were a recipe in a cookbook of athletic injuries. Students will see the processes and consequences of athletic injuries before they learn the step-by-step procedures for dealing with them.

Organization

We've divided *Athletic Training: Principles and Practice* into four parts. Part One introduces students to the responsibilities of contemporary athletic trainers and to the equipment and facilities with which they work. Part Two devotes eleven chapters to the principles involved in preventing and managing injuries. These chapters enable students to better understand the reasons behind injuries, treatment, and rehabilitation. In Part Three, we present a head-to-toe look at specific injuries and how they can be prevented and managed. The final part, Part Four, covers the factors that can affect an athlete's performance, including disease, environmental stress, nutrition, body composition, use of drugs, and youth and age.

Features

Athletic Training: Principles and Practice contains a number of features that make this book a valuable learning tool for students. We have attempted to make the text as self-contained as possible. There are *background chapters* on soft tissue, bone, synovial joints, inflammation, and conditioning to help students understand the processes involved in athletic injuries, their treatment, and rehabilitation. There is an *extensive discussion of anatomy and physiology* in almost every section. Therefore, students lacking formal courses in these basic sciences can gain an appreciation for the basics of injury prevention and management, while students with more extensive backgrounds are furnished with a thorough review that will make the injury management material more relevant.

To help students learn and remember the vocabulary of athletic training, we have included a *running glossary* that defines each new term in the margin on the page where it first appears. Summaries of treatment protocols called *Putting It into Practice* appear frequently throughout the book so that students can effectively remember basic athletic training procedures. For convenience, a separate listing of these protocols appears in the table of contents. The *Johnson & Johnson taping guide* is included as an appendix to provide students with precise and easy-to-follow instructions on basic taping techniques. *Boxes* that provide additional information on specific topics are included throughout the text. The book is *extensively illustrated* with *photographs and anatomical drawings* to visually explain procedures and injury phenomena, and *references* are listed at the end of each chapter to provide students with additional sources of information. Finally, the book is designed to be pleasing to the eye and easy to use.

Acknowledgments

A book such as this is not possible without the help of many people. First of all, I would like to thank the contributors; it has been an honor to be associated with such a talented group of professionals. I would also like to thank the people at Mayfield for their hard work and diligence—particularly Jan Beatty, Eva Marie Strock, Cynthia Bassett, Pat Herbst, Elaine Wang, and Jim Bull. The text was extensively reviewed by athletic training professionals who examined the manuscript for errors and relevance. These reviewers include

Dennis Aten, M.S., A.T.,C., R.P.T.
Eastern Illinois University

Bill G. Bean, M.S., A.T.,C.
University of Utah

Gerald W. Bell, Ed.D., P.T., A.T.,C.
University of Illinois

Edmund J. Burke, Ph.D.
Springfield College

Louis R. Osternig, Ph.D.
University of Oregon

Ron Pfeiffer, Ed.D., A.T.,C.
Boise State University

Michelle E. Piette, A.T.,C.
Arizona State University

John W. Powell, Ph.D., A.T.,C.
The Pennsylvania State University

William E. Prentice, Ph.D., A.T.,C., L.P.T.
The University of North Carolina, Chapel Hill

Dale A. Rudd, M.S., A.T.,C.
Purdue University

Kent Scriber, Ed.D., A.T.,C., R.P.T.
Ithaca College

Patricia Troesch, B.S., M.A., A.T.,C.
Miami University

Richard K. Troxel
University of Oregon

This project would not have been possible without the support of my family—my wife Kilty, sons Tommy and Mikey, mother and father Barbara and Tom, and mother-in-law Babs. I am also indebted to my former laboratory staff at De Anza College—Rich Schroeder, Martha Rowe, Ron Freeman, Jim Ratcliff, Greg Peterson, Robert Andrews, Betsy Jasny, and Sharon Haugen—for their comments on the manuscript and their moral support. I would also like to thank colleagues at Chico State, such as Don Scott, Bill Colvin, Steve Henderson, Dick Trimmer, Don Lytle, and Ed Miller, for providing an atmosphere that allowed me to work effectively on this book.

A project of this magnitude almost literally consumes one's life for several years. Such a commitment of time would not have been possible were it not for the love of sports science instilled in me by professors such as G. L. Rarick, F. M. Henry, Frank Verducci, Jack Wilmore, and Bob Lualhati. Perhaps most of all, I am indebted to my friend, co-author (*Exercise Physiology: Human Bioenergetics and Its Applications*), and former professor George Brooks of the University of California, Berkeley. I am honored to have worked with Dr. Brooks, and I deeply appreciate the encouragement and support he has given me over the years.

Thomas D. Fahey

PART
ONE

The Athletic Trainer and the Training Room

The Modern Athletic Trainer

THE JOY of sport draws most people to athletic training. **Athletic training** is a profession that allows you to be part of the action. As an athletic trainer, you will find excitement, intellectual stimulation, and the opportunity to help athletes. By taking an active role in the prevention, recognition, and management of injury, you will play an integral part in athletic practices and competitions, and the decisions you make will often determine an athlete's future success and well-being.

The athletic trainer has the opportunity to become a sports medicine problem solver. **Sports medicine** is a branch of medicine concerned with athletes' medical problems. Disciplines often considered part of sports medicine include exercise physiology, athletic training, **biomechanics,** sports physical therapy, kinesiology, sports psychology, motor learning, and sports chiropractic. As an athletic trainer, you will be a team's "front-line" medical professional. In athletic training, learning about and observing the many possible types of athletic injuries, treatments, and rehabilitation measures will provide unending intellectual stimulation. Consider the athletic trainer presented with an athlete with a knee injury who needs to maintain good physical condition without aggravating the injury. The athletic trainer devises a conditioning technique involving deep-water sprinting that allows the athlete to continue building fitness without irritating the injury. As an athletic trainer, you will always find new problems to solve and intriguing challenges to face.

Responsibilities of an Athletic Trainer

The modern athletic trainer is a qualified health professional and a vital member of the sports medicine team, dedicated to making sports participation a safe, positive experience. As Robert Murphy, M.D., Ohio State University, has said:

> You can have the best team doctor in the world, but if you have a poor trainer you will have a poor program. [Cited by W. Shapiro in Sports pages, *The Physician and Sportsmedicine.* 7:86, 1977.]

The qualified athletic trainer plans and organizes physical conditioning programs, gives advice on sound nutritional habits, and strives to prevent athletic injuries. When injuries do occur,

Athletic training: An allied health profession involved in the health care of athletes.

Sports medicine: A branch of medicine dealing with medical problems of athletes.

Biomechanics: Study of the physics of motion in humans or animals.

Athletic trainers are part of a team of support people who help athletes achieve their best. Here, Kathy Johnson, a member of the 1984 U.S. Olympic team, is congratulated for her winning performance on the balance beam at the National Sports Festival.

an athletic trainer can give first aid and evaluate the injury so that proper medical care can be obtained. An athletic trainer plays an important role in the rehabilitative process following an injury and is qualified to administer tests that help evaluate an athlete's readiness to return to physical activity.

Among the athletic trainer's professional responsibilities are preventing and managing injuries (includes evaluation, first aid, management procedures, and rehabilitation); communicating with athletes, parents, physicians, and other professionals; participating in research; managing the athletic training room; and distributing sports medicine information to interested athletes.

Preventing and Managing Injuries

The athletic trainer is responsible for continually monitoring the health of each athlete. To fulfill this responsibility, the athletic trainer must be thoroughly aware of each athlete's condition prior to participation, know each athlete's **history** and personality, know the

correct methods of injury **evaluation,** and be able to properly determine the athlete's readiness to return to sports participation following an injury.

The athletic trainer is typically the most qualified health professional to deal initially with an athlete's injuries and illnesses. Although physicians, physical therapists, nurses, and emergency medical technicians are often involved in giving health care to athletes, most of the day-to-day burden falls on the athletic trainer, and at the onset of a problem the athletic trainer is responsible for obtaining appropriate medical attention. Because the optimal outcome of an athlete's injury often depends upon the athlete's correct placement in the health care delivery system, the athletic trainer must be careful to not abuse his or her position as the primary health care provider.

In addition to monitoring an athlete's health, an athletic trainer strives to prevent injuries by designing physical conditioning programs, devising and administering physical fitness tests, rendering sound nutritional counseling, and organizing preparticipation medical

Evaluation: Assessment of an injury; the process typically includes past and present history, inspection, and testing.

History: Review of present health status, past injuries and illness, or circumstances surrounding a specific injury.

examinations. The athletic trainer should also assume a role in selecting and fitting equipment and conducting safety surveys of athletic facilities so that hazardous conditions can be identified and corrected (Figure 1-1). The athletic trainer should scrutinize drills and techniques that may cause injury. In some circumstances, tape, wraps, or braces may be used to prevent an injury, help an existing injury from getting worse, or thwart the recurrence of a condition (Figure 1-2).

When an injury does occur, the athletic trainer's job is to ensure that the injury receives proper medical care. As part of that care, the athletic trainer provides the initial evaluation, first aid, treatment, and rehabilitation.

Box 1-1 (p. 6) is an interesting overview of a football athletic trainer's duties and impact and how they have changed with time. This excerpt is from a Father Koestler mystery about the death of a pro football player. Jack Brown, the team's trainer, is reminiscing about his profession. Brown was a team manager in high school. In 1951 he received his college degree in physical education and got a job as assistant trainer for a New York hockey team. While in New York, Brown learned how to tape from boxers' trainers. Brown then became a college football trainer at various schools whose teams were coached by the man who eventually became the owner of the pro football team Brown now works for.

Initial Evaluation. The ideal time for evaluation is immediately after an injury has occurred because many diagnostic tests are difficult or impossible to duplicate even a relatively short time later (due to swelling, apprehension, pain, and inflammation). The athletic trainer often conducts this initial evaluation because most athletic injuries occur during practice time, when no physician is immediately available (Figure 1-3).

Correct evaluation depends upon a

Figure 1-1 By recognizing individual differences in physical characteristics when fitting equipment, an athletic trainer can help prevent injury.

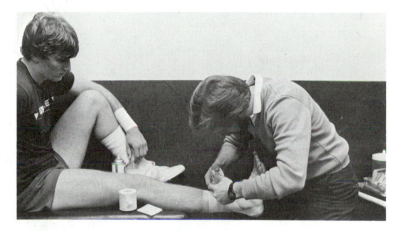

Figure 1-2 Taping is an important component of both prevention and treatment of injury.

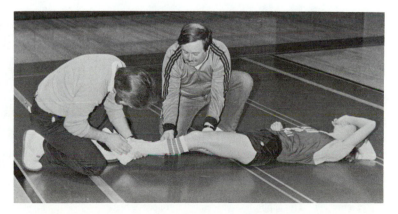

Figure 1-3 An athletic trainer and a coach evaluate an on-court injury.

BOX
1-1

The Athletic Trainer

Jack Brown watched his profession evolve over the years he practiced it. In his early days, it was carrying water and fixing bandages over cuts. Then it moved on to ice packs, towels, hot packs, and massages. Trainers were expected to acquire something of a pharmacist's expertise in pills and liniment.

Then came the National Athletic Trainers Association and its board of certification. At one time, the title, Certified Athletic Trainer, was, in an exercise of cronyism, passed on to a very few veteran male athletic trainers. Now, the initials ATC after one's name were highly sought after and awarded only after long and demanding scholarly study and practice.

Those associated with Jack Brown professionally knew that he admirably fulfilled the responsibilities of an up-to-date athletic trainer, whose functions were to prevent athletic trauma and treat any conditions that might adversely affect the health or performance of an athlete. Such functions included management—first aid, evaluation, treatment, and rehabilitation—of athletic trauma or other medical problems that affected the athlete, as well as counseling the athlete in such health-related areas as nutrition, relaxation, and tension-control and personal health habits.

Trainers were expected to be able to manage and operate such therapeutic agencies and procedures as hydrocollator, hydrotherapy, diathermy, ultrasound, cryotherapy, cryokinetics, contrast bath, paraffin bath, and infrared, manipulative, and ultraviolet therapy.

In short, Jack Brown exemplified the modern athletic trainer who has made the long journey from water-bucket brigade to just this side of a medical degree.

But of all the expertise he had acquired in his years as trainer, that of which he was most proud was, oddly, taping. No mean skill, it involved not only the routine taping of ankles—required even for practices—but the building of castlike pads, made of fiber glass, covered with a protective layer of foam rubber and held together with tape.

SOURCE: Kienzle, William X. *Sudden Death.* Fairway, Kan.: Andrews, McMeel & Parker, 1985, pp. 120–121. Copyright © 1985 by GOPITS, INC. Reprinted with permission of Andrews, McMeel & Parker. All rights reserved.

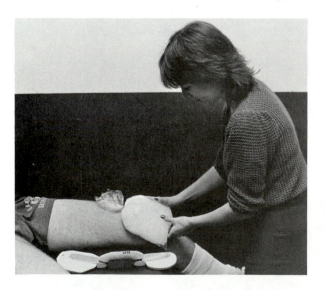

Figure 1-4 The application of ice and a protective brace may stabilize an injured knee until further aid is available.

Figure 1-5 Palpating the athlete's wrist helps the athletic trainer determine how serious the injury is.

meaningful account of how the injury occurred; thorough understanding of anatomy, the mechanism or cause of an injury, and the body's reaction to **trauma;** comprehension of the athlete's state of mind; and the ability to perform various evaluative tests. These skills determine whether the athlete receives the necessary first aid, appropriate medical attention, and subsequent injury management. (Evaluation is discussed in detail in Chapter 9.)

First Aid. The athletic trainer is responsible for administering **first aid** after the initial evaluation (Figure 1-4). These procedures range in complexity and seriousness from **cardiopulmonary resuscitation (CPR)** to cleaning and bandaging a minor wound. The athletic trainer must be an expert in advanced first aid because the early management of the injury may have a significant effect upon the athlete's subsequent condition and well-being.

Management Procedures. As mentioned, the athletic trainer is most often the first provider of treatment for the injured athlete regardless of whether he or she is acting on personal initiative or executing the direct orders of a physician (Figure 1-5). After evaluating an injury and rendering first aid (when no physician is present), the athletic trainer must decide the appropriate treatment and determine whether medical attention is needed. If the injury does not require medical assistance, the athletic trainer must initiate appropriate follow-up procedures.

Treatment and management techniques include immobilization, taping and wrapping, application of protective padding, and therapeutic **modalities.** The available modalities vary with the situation and legal circumstances. In some instances the application of modalities such as ultrasound and electrical stimulation may be restricted by legal statute. In cases where an appropriate treatment is available from some

other health care practitioner, such as a physician or a physical therapist, the athletic trainer's duty is to procure that treatment for the injured athlete.

Rehabilitation. Injured athletes should not participate in sports again until they have achieved optimum levels of flexibility, strength, endurance, and skill. Injury **rehabilitation** is the application of therapeutic techniques that are based upon the scientific application of exercise for restoring the function of an injured body part (Figure 1-6, p. 8). To plan a successful rehabilitation program, the athletic trainer must have a thorough knowledge of rehabilitation equipment and therapeutic exercises and be proficient in their application.

Once the athlete begins the process of rehabilitation, the athletic trainer must perform evaluative tests to ensure the appropriateness of the exercises, monitor and document the athlete's progress, and make adjustments as the need arises. Finally, the athletic trainer must be able to recommend functional tests that can be used in determining an athlete's readiness to return to participation (Figure 1-7, p. 8).

Communicating with Athletes, Parents, and Professionals

Successful athletic trainers must develop friendly, trusting relationships with athletes and cordial, businesslike relationships with parents, coaches, physicians, media personnel, sales representatives, and other professionals such as educators.

Athletes. The athletic trainer's most important relationship is with the athlete under his or her care. This relationship must be based upon confidence and trust, which are essential if the athletic trainer is to effectively serve as a mediator among athletes, coaches, and medical personnel.

Good rapport with athletes is based upon professional competence, leader-

Trauma: Injury or damage.

Rehabilitation: Restoration of normal function through the use of therapeutic exercise and modalities.

First aid: Emergency treatment administered before professional medical care is available.
Cardiopulmonary resuscitation (CPR): Mechanically compressing the heart of a pulseless, nonbreathing person to increase cardiac output and blowing air into the mouth to increase the lungs' oxygen content.

Modality: A physical technique or substance administered to produce a therapeutic effect.

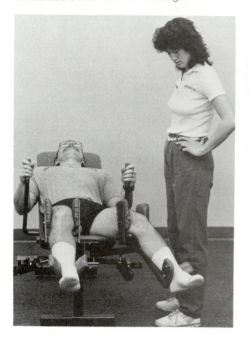

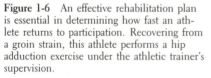

Figure 1-6 An effective rehabilitation plan is essential in determining how fast an athlete returns to participation. Recovering from a groin strain, this athlete performs a hip adduction exercise under the athletic trainer's supervision.

Figure 1-7 Functional field tests provide an extra measure of confidence that the athlete is ready to return to play. Following an ankle sprain, this athlete hops on the injured extremity to determine functional ankle stability.

ship, and the ability to maintain confidentiality (expected of any health care professional). The athlete has the right to assume that personal information will be kept in the strictest confidence. The astute athletic trainer must devise methods of using such information for the best interest of all involved parties without betraying this all-important trust. The athletic trainer should be perceived as a person who considers the health and well-being of each athlete as the paramount concern. However, this does *not* imply that the athlete should be overprotected.

It is difficult to generalize about the ideal relationship between the athlete and athletic trainer because of the many factors involved, including level of competition, differences in personality, and numerous other psychological factors. One fact, however, is absolutely certain: The successful athletic trainer must be capable of developing positive relationships with athletes.

Parents. The athletic trainer should never underestimate the importance of good relationships with parents. Parental relationships are most significant in dealings with younger athletes, although they can be important at all levels of competition (including professional sports). The key to successful relationships with parents is realizing that, regardless of the athlete's age, the parents still think of the athlete as their child. The emotional ties between parents and children are extremely strong and should never be underestimated. Parents must always be treated with respect and in a manner that clearly establishes them as special people in the athlete's life. Perhaps the best single strategy for developing good relationships with parents is for the athletic trainer to think about how he or she would like to be treated as a parent of an athlete in a particular situation. Given the diversity in family circumstances and philosophies, an athletic trainer must learn to be flexible when dealing with parents.

Coaches. A good relationship with coaches is critical to the athletes' health and the success of the athletic program. Athletic trainers and coaches can become frustrated with each other. The athletic trainer's frustration sometimes stems from a coach's adherence to practices that seem unjustified. On the other hand, the coach sometimes feels that the athletic trainer is overstepping bounds and meddling in coaching affairs.

Lack of communication between the coach and athletic trainer can often be minimized by developing clearly defined job descriptions. The athletic trainer should represent the physician as the primary authority on health and safety in the athletic department. However, the athletic trainer is not a coach and should not be directly involved in coaching matters. The coach, on the other hand, must yield to the athletic trainer's expertise in health and safety matters. A clearly defined and understood policy is essential to a good athletic trainer-coach relationship. Coaches and athletic trainers who understand each other's role and who respect each other's areas of authority and expertise are less likely to find themselves in an adversary relationship.

One particular point of contention between coaches and athletic trainers is the return of an injured player to competition. Many athletic trainers mistakenly regard this matter as their decision, when in fact it is a coaching matter. Although the physician and athletic trainer will decide whether an athlete is *medically capable* of returning to play, the coach has the responsibility for deciding if the medically cleared athlete will play. Coaches and athletic trainers who function together successfully in this important phase of their relationship seem to have a better understanding of each other's respective responsibilities and professional exper-

tise and fewer problems in other areas of their relationship.

Physicians. Athletic trainers must be able to interact professionally with physicians. Most athletic trainers enjoy excellent relationships with those physicians with whom they regularly work. These successful relationships evolve over time as the physicians come to know and respect the athletic trainer's capabilities. Far too often, the student athletic trainer who has witnessed this positive rapport between his or her supervising athletic trainer and the team physician enters the profession expecting to be immediately treated in an identical fashion. But often this does not happen.

Athletic trainers realize that the physician is at the top of the medical hierarchy and is the final authority on all medical matters. They should be very careful not to practice or pretend to practice medicine but to assist the physician in providing the best possible medical care for the athletes. There must be a clear understanding of the physician's and athletic trainer's duties and responsibilities. This understanding is the foundation for a gradually evolving, strong, dynamic relationship that will maximally use the attributes of the athletic trainer and physician in providing optimal health care to competitive athletes.

Those athletic trainers who must deal with many different physicians (often the case in secondary schools) must apply these same principles to each separate physician-athletic trainer relationship. Each separate relationship will develop at a different pace and have its own unique characteristics. Whenever possible, the athletic trainer should strive to have a single team physician appointed to expedite the medical communications that are important to proper athletic health care.

The Media. Athletic trainers must often deal with people in the media.

These contacts can often yield beneficial rewards for the athletic program, but they can threaten the confidentiality that must exist among athlete, physician, and athletic trainer. Athletic trainers must treat their relationships with athletes as confidential and should not be pressured by the media to reveal the status of an athlete's treatment.

Sales Representatives. Athletic trainers are often deluged by sales representatives wanting to sell athletic training supplies and food supplements. Trainers must very carefully ensure that they make purchases based upon need rather than personal rapport with a particular salesperson. Most athletic programs operate on limited budgets that cannot accommodate money being wasted on dubious products.

Other Professionals. The athletic trainer must deal with a variety of other professionals, including educators, lawyers, researchers, and technical representatives. It is beyond the scope of this text to specifically discuss each relationship, but there are two principles for dealing with other professionals: (1) All professional relationships must be based upon mutual respect. (2) All satisfactory personal and professional relationships rely upon adequate communications. People who have difficulty with interpersonal relationships probably should not become athletic trainers.

Participating in Research

Participation in research is vital to maintaining professional competence and helping the field of athletic training to progress. Research need not be formal, large-scale experiments that result in publication in a medical journal. Research may involve nothing more than systematic observations of how various exercises and treatment techniques affect the healing process. The results of such "informal" research can then be passed on to colleagues at regional athletic training meetings.

Managing the Athletic Training Room

The athletic trainer has significant administrative responsibilities, including budget management, inventory control, and record keeping. Records must meet institutional requirements and comply with medical and legal guidelines. Administrative procedures must be practical and efficient because of the athletic trainer's many time commitments. However, all methods should be thorough and records well documented. The athletic trainer incapable of devising and implementing a sound administrative structure is less valuable to the institution's athletic program.

Acting as Information Resource

The athletic trainer is frequently perceived as a sports medicine expert and is often asked questions about nutrition, conditioning, injury care, and rehabilitation. He or she should be willing to share information or refer the inquirer to an appropriate source. The athletic trainer must remain informed about the latest sports medicine information because many athletes establish lifetime health practices based upon what they learn from the trainer (see Box 1-2).

Becoming an Athletic Trainer

Perhaps even more important than the educational and certification requirements for becoming an athletic trainer are the numerous personal characteristics successful athletic trainers need, including a sharp intellect, good communication skills, enthusiasm, and adaptability.

BOX 1-2

Keeping Informed in Sports Medicine

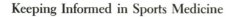

Hundreds of scientific journals are published every month, many of which contain information of interest to the athletic trainer. Pertinent articles may appear in unusual places: A law journal may publish an article about the legal aspects of athletics; a veterinary medicine journal may publish information about wound healing; a medical journal may present a clinical study about a promising new orthopedic appliance. Subscribing to all possible sources of information in sports medicine is expensive and inefficient. Information services provide a relatively painless way to keep up with the scientific literature.

Most university libraries subscribe to information indexes such as Index Medicus and ERIC, which list published articles by subject and author. Although these services are valuable, it is usually inconvenient for the practicing athletic trainer to use them.

A number of inexpensive personalized literature search services that provide ready access to most of the world's scientific journals are available to individual athletic trainers. Two such services are *Current Contents* and *Automatic Subject Citation Alert*, both published by the Institute of Scientific Information. *Current Contents* is a weekly journal that contains the tables of contents of journals published in a specific subject area. In the back of *Current Contents* are lists of the names and addresses of the senior authors of papers named in the tables of contents. These authors typically send a reprint of a paper to those who ask for it. The athletic trainer can have postcards preprinted to facilitate writing for reprints.

Automatic Subject Citation Alert (ASCA) is a computerized, customized list of articles that appeared in journals during the past week. More expensive than *Current Contents*, ASCA lets the athletic trainer scan a listing of pertinent literature and write for reprints in a much shorter period of time.

We are in the midst of an information explosion. The athletic trainer who does not keep up with the scientific and clinical literature in sports medicine will rapidly lose ground to better-informed colleagues.

Desirable Personal Characteristics

Athletic trainers must be intelligent and articulate. They must have the intellectual ability to successfully complete a rigorous college curriculum that heavily emphasizes basic and applied sciences. Furthermore, the student trainer must perform well in this course work while engaging in the hundreds of hours of clinical experience that are so vital to professional preparation. Intellectual demands are likely to increase in the future as the knowledge and level of sophistication of sports medicine increase.

The athletic trainer must be proficient in both verbal and written communication. Writing skills are required for such day-to-day chores as record keeping and injury reports. Adept oral communication facilitates productive discussion of injuries with physicians, coaches, athletes, and parents. Athletic training students should systematically develop speaking skills; otherwise, they will be severely handicapped in their professional careers. Communications allow people to convey their thoughts to each other. Successful communications require tact and the willingness to cooperate.

Athletes and coaches tend to be enthusiastic, fun-loving people. An unenthusiastic and humorless athletic trainer will have difficulty fitting in with the athletic community and probably will not be happy in the profession. The ability to appreciate the humorous aspects of various situations and to communicate that humor in a friendly manner enhances the athletic trainer's rapport with others. Devotion to the ideals of athletic participation and dedication to the athletes' safety and well-being are critical personal philosophies. Successful athletic trainers must truly believe in what they are doing and thoroughly enjoy their vocation; this positive attitude should be obvious to the people with whom they work.

Stamina and adaptability are prime prerequisites for the job. Typically, the workday begins several hours before a game or practice session and ends sometime after the conclusion of the activity. The duties may be combined with other responsibilities, such as teaching or educational administration. This rigorous life-style is possible only by practicing the principles of regular exercise, sound nutrition, and prudent living. Although this profession requires stamina, the payoff is a vital, stimulating, and rewarding life-style.

Athletics and athletic training are worlds of fluctuating circumstances. Athletic trainers must be able to accommodate to such circumstances as last-minute schedule changes imposed by the coach or to improvise when a desired piece of equipment is unavailable. The person who cannot think clearly and quickly under stress and amid changing circumstances will find the duties of athletic training very trying. The adaptable athletic trainer must have confidence, poise, flexibility, and the ability to focus upon an objective.

Sound judgment and sterling ethics are also important personal characteristics. The athletic trainer must be emotionally stable to make sound judgments under varying and sometimes extremely adverse conditions. The athletic trainer must keep situations in their proper perspective regardless of any existing confusion and emotionalism. The welfare of the athlete must be placed above all other concerns, and the athletic trainer must have a strong enough conviction to not let this principle be violated. The athletic trainer must maintain an air of calmness, tranquility, and

control when others may find it extremely difficult to do so. Inability to exercise emotional control may result in the failure to gain professional and personal respect from others. The athletic trainer must provide an unquestionable example of fairness and moral courage in the performance of all duties.

The rules and standards governing the behavior of the athletic training profession are similar to those that govern other professions, such as medicine and physical therapy. Since 1957, the National Athletic Trainers Association (NATA) has had a Code of Ethics to guide its members. Based upon the premise that athletic trainers must conform to the highest standards of behavior in the execution of their duties, the NATA code adheres to the principles of honesty, integrity, and loyalty. Persons not capable of living up to these standards are not likely to possess the personal qualities required for a successful career in athletic training.

Educational Requirements

Recent guidelines developed by the Professional Education Committee of the National Athletic Trainers Association require that approved athletic training curriculums include formal instruction in the following subjects:

- Prevention and care of athletic injuries and illnesses
- Evaluation of athletic injuries and illnesses
- First aid and emergency care
- Therapeutic modalities
- Therapeutic exercises
- Administration of athletic training programs
- Human anatomy
- Human physiology
- Exercise physiology
- Kinesiology and biomechanics
- Nutrition
- Psychology
- Personal and community health
- Instructional methods

Table 1-1 *Competencies Required in Athletic Training*

Prospective athletic trainers should be competent in the following areas, which are covered in the NATA written examination:

Preparticipation

Knowledge of specific sports (risks, physical requirements, etc.)
Fitness evaluation
Protective devices (recognition, selection, and fitting)
Equipment maintenance
Environmental conditions (precautionary procedures)
Trauma or reinjury (physiology and risk factors)
Preexisting physical conditions (diseases and predisposing conditions)
Conditioning programs

Recognition and evaluation of injury

History
Inspection
Palpation
Range of motion
Ligament stress testing
Assessment of neurological, sensory, and motor function

Management, treatment, and disposition

Applying protective devices
First aid
Athletic training procedures
Medical referral

Rehabilitation

Restoration of function
Criteria for return to activity
Theory of physiology and processes of rehabilitation

Organization and administration

Record keeping
Facilities
Purchasing and procurement
Health care services system
Policies and procedures
Emergency support services

Education and counseling

Previous injuries
Health (alcohol, smoking, drugs, sexually transmitted diseases, etc.)
Social and personal problems
Role of the physician
Instruction of student athletic trainers
Continuing education

SOURCE: Modified from *Certification Information for Athletic Trainers*, Board Certification of the National Athletic Trainers Association, Inc., 1001 E. Fourth Street, Greenville, NC 27834.

Presently, over seventy institutions of higher learning offer NATA-approved undergraduate curriculums, and several offer approved graduate programs. For complete listing of approved athletic training education programs, write Chairperson, Professional Educational Committee, National Athletic Trainers Association, Inc., 1001 E. Fourth Street, Greenville, NC 27834.

The student should be familiar with the NATA role delineation study that identifies the specific tasks athletic trainers perform. Table 1-1 lists identi-fied competencies and the approximate degree of emphasis each competency should receive during academic preparation.

Certification Requirements

Since 1970, the NATA has administered a certification examination that measures specific competencies in athletic training. Most authorities consider certification by the NATA the standard of qualification for the practice of ath-

What Does It Take to Become an Athletic Trainer?

- *The role of the athletic trainer:* Works to prevent, evaluate, provide first aid for, treat, and rehabilitate athletic injuries. Acts as sports medicine resource person for the institution and community.
- *Personal characteristics:* Relates well to others; is enthusiastic, physically fit, cooperative, tactful; has good communication skills; is adaptable, mature, ethical; has moral courage and a sense of humor.
- *Educational requirements:* Courses in basic sciences (e.g., anatomy, physiology, chemistry, physics, biomechanics, exercise physiology, biochemistry), therapeutics, and evaluation and management of injuries.
- *Clinical experience:* Work with NATA-certified athletic trainer.
- *NATA certification:* Pass written and practical examinations.

letic training. Certification requires that the prospective athletic trainer have educational preparation and clinical experience and pass a practical and written examination. Putting It into Practice 1-1 and Figure 1-8 summarize the steps to becoming an athletic trainer. The American Athletic Trainers Association (AATA), a relatively new athletic trainer's association, also has a certification program.

In 1973, the Texas state legislature passed a law to license athletic trainers. Because of increasing legal complexities and the significant degree of overlap among various health-related professions, the NATA announced at the 1976 national meeting a nationwide effort to encourage state credentialing in the form of licensing, registration, or state-regulated certification. To date, several states have implemented or are close to implementing some form of state-regulated certification. Indications are that this trend will continue and that most states soon will have rules and regulations regarding the practice of athletic training. With this in mind, you should be aware of all pertinent regulations in each state in which you might wish to practice athletic training. Your state board of medical quality assurance can tell you whether licensure to practice athletic training is required in your state.

Figure 1-8 Steps to becoming an NATA-certified athletic trainer.

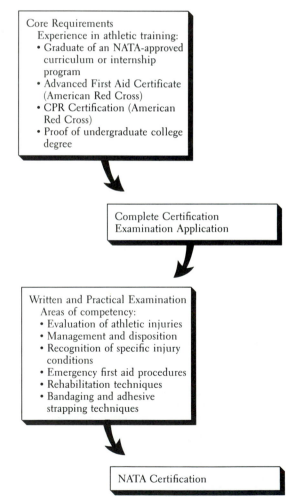

Core Requirements
Experience in athletic training:
- Graduate of an NATA-approved curriculum or internship program
- Advanced First Aid Certificate (American Red Cross)
- CPR Certification (American Red Cross)
- Proof of undergraduate college degree

Complete Certification Examination Application

Written and Practical Examination
Areas of competency:
- Evaluation of athletic injuries
- Management and disposition
- Recognition of specific injury conditions
- Emergency first aid procedures
- Rehabilitation techniques
- Bandaging and adhesive strapping techniques

NATA Certification

Joining a Professional Organization

Professional organizations serve the common interest of their members and are a mechanism for the exchange of ideas pertinent to the profession's activities. The organizations also develop and promulgate appropriate standards of formal education and norms of behavior that systematically lead to the ongoing development of knowledge in the profession. There are several professional organizations for people who deliver health care to athletes.

The National Athletic Trainers Association

The National Athletic Trainers Association (NATA) is the principal professional organization for athletic trainers. It was founded in 1950 and is presently headquartered in Greenville, NC. According to its constitution, the association pursues the "advancement, encouragement, and improvement of the athletic training profession in all of its phases" and attempts to "promote a better working relationship among those persons interested in training." The NATA is the sole certifying agency of athletic trainers in the United States, sets standards for academic programs in athletic training, and enforces a code of ethics relevant to the profession.

Beginning in 1969, the NATA adopted a set of standards for college curriculums that prepare athletic trainers. Over the years, these standards have been revised and updated so that today they are recognized as the standard by which professional-preparation curriculums in athletic training are judged. Also, since 1970, the NATA has administered a written and oral/practical examination.

In addition to holding an annual national meeting and symposium that offers an outstanding selection of speakers and topics related to the prevention, recognition, and care of athletic injury, the NATA actively supports other educational activities concerning athletic health care. *Athletic Training*, the NATA's journal published quarterly, keeps members abreast of the latest developments in their profession. Although a relatively young professional organization, NATA has over 5000 members nationwide and maintains an active part in shaping the professional knowledge of today's athletic trainers.

State Athletic Training Organizations

State athletic training organizations are becoming rather common. Most of these local organizations were originally formed to help achieve state credentialing of athletic trainers; many have evolved into viable professional organizations that serve the special needs of local members. It is very likely that the importance of these local organizations will increase dramatically as the trend toward state regulation of athletic training continues.

The American Physical Therapy Association

The American Physical Therapy Association has long had an important influence on health care delivery in the United States, but not until recently has the association exerted any influence on the prevention and management of sports injuries. With the emergence of the Sports Medicine section of this association in the 1970s, the organization has begun to exercise a role in the improvement of health care for athletes. The Sports Medicine section is designed to meet the needs of physical therapists who want to specialize in

BOX
1-3

Minimizing Liability Through Informed Consent

In 1980, in a sports liability case in Seattle, Washington, a school district was found negligent in the injury of a high school football player. The court ruled that the athlete was not properly warned of the dangers of the sport or adequately instructed in techniques to avoid serious injury. With today's climate of frequent and sometimes frivolous litigation, coaches and athletic trainers should probably obtain written informed consent from athletes involved in hazardous sports or extensive rehabilitation programs. Written informed consent is a signed statement from the athlete that he or she understands the nature and hazards of the activity or rehabilitation program. This practice may save the coach, athletic trainer, and institution from paying financially draining legal damages. Here is an example of a consent form.

Centralia (Wash.) High School's Safety List*

Football is a contact sport and injuries will occur. The coaches working in our program are well-qualified, professional people. Fundamentals related to playing football will continually and repeatedly be emphasized on and off the field. The information contained within this list of rules and procedures is to inform the young men in our football program of the proper techniques to practice for maximum safety in the contact phase of the game.

*SOURCE: *Interscholastic Athletic Association* magazine, Fall 1982. Published by the National Federation of State High School Associations. The list was developed by Coach George Potter.

Tackling, Blocking, and Running the Ball

By rule, the helmet is not to be used as a "ram." Initial contact is not to be made with the helmet. It is not possible to play the game safely or correctly without making some contact with the helmet when properly blocking and tackling an opponent. Therefore, technique is most important in preventing injuries.

Tackling and blocking techniques are basically the same. Contact is to be made above the waist but not initially with the helmet. The player should always be in a position of balance, knees bent, back straight, body *slightly* bent forward, *head up*, target area as near to the body as possible with the main contact being made with the shoulder.

Blocking and tackling by not putting the helmet as close to the body as possible could result in shoulder injury such as a separation or a pinched nerve in the neck area. The reason for following the safety rules in making contact with the upper body and helmet is that improper body alignment can put the spinal column in a vulnerable position for injury.

If the head is bent downward, the cervical (neck) vertebrae are in a bind and contact on the *top of the helmet* could result in a dislocation, nerve damage, paralysis or even death. If the back is not straight, the thoracic (mid-back) and lumbar vertebrae are also vulnerable to injury with similar results if contact again is made to the *top of the helmet.* Centralia's daily workout includes isometric type exercises; the development of strength in the neck muscles is one of the best methods of preventing head injury and enabling an individual to hold his head up even after getting tired during a workout or contest.

Basic Hitting (Contact) Position and Fundamental Technique

If the knees are not bent, the chance of knee injury is greatly increased. Fundamentally, a player should be in the proper hitting position at all times during live ball play and this point will be repeated continually during practice. The danger is anything from strained muscles to ankle injuries or serious knee injuries requiring surgery. The rules have made blocking below the waist (outside a two-yard by four-yard area next to the football) illegal. Cleats have been restricted to no more than $\frac{1}{2}$-inch to further help in preventing knee injuries. A runner with the ball, however, may be tackled around the legs.

In tackling, the rules prohibit initial contact with the helmet or grabbing the face mask or edge of the helmet. These restrictions were placed in the rules because of serious injuries resulting from noncompliance to these safety precautions. Initial helmet contact could result in a bruise, dislocation, broken bone, head injury, internal injury such as kidneys, spleen, bladder, etc. Grabbing the face mask or helmet edge could result in a neck injury, which could be anything from a muscle strain to a dislocation, a nerve injury or spinal column damage causing paralysis or death.

The illegal play by participating athletes will not be tolerated and all players are repeatedly reminded of the dangers of unsportsmanlike acts.

Fitting and Use of Equipment

Shoulder pads, helmets, hip pads, pants (including thigh pads and knee pads) must have proper fitting and use.

Shoulder pads that are too small will leave the shoulder point vulnerable to bruises or separations; they could also be too tight in the neck area, resulting in a possible pinched nerve. Shoulder pads that are too large will leave the neck area poorly protected and will slide on the shoulders, making them vulnerable to bruises or separations.

Helmets must fit snugly at the contact points: front, back, and top of head. The helmet must be safety "NOCSAE" branded; the chin straps must be fastened and the cheek pads must be of the proper thickness. On contact, too tight a helmet could result in a headache. Too loose a fit could result in headaches, a concussion, a face injury such as a broken nose or cheek bone, or a blow to the back of the neck causing a neck injury, possibly quite serious such as paralysis or even death.

This report does not cover all potential injury possibilities in playing football, but it is an attempt to make the players aware that fundamentals, coaching and proper fitting equipment are important to their safety and enjoyment in playing football at Centralia High School.

The above information has been explained to me and I understand the list of rules and procedures. I also understand the necessity of using the proper techniques while participating in the football program.

_____
Athlete's Signature

_____
Date of Signature

_____
Witness

treating physically active patients. Presently, a national boarding procedure similar to that employed by various medical specialties is being developed to certify competency in sports physical therapy.

In 1978, the NATA and the American Physical Therapy Association formed a joint task force to work to achieve professional standards and scope of practice. In Pennsylvania, state associations representing athletic trainers and physical therapists have jointly brought about a state credentialing process for athletic trainers. This type of cooperation benefits the public by providing a more effective system of health care delivery.

The American College of Sports Medicine

The American College of Sports Medicine (ACSM) is dedicated to the generation and dissemination of knowledge of human participation in physical activity. ACSM serves medical professionals, basic scientists, and educators who are interested in physical activity and sports. Although the organization is primarily research-oriented, with emphasis upon exercise physiology, its activities are relevant to people interested in the prevention and care of athletic injuries. Some of the most authoritative researchers in the world publish in the ACSM's journal (*Medicine and Science in Sports and Exercise*) and speak at its various meetings and symposia.

Avoiding Legal Problems

As more and more people have taken up sports, the number of legal entanglements pertaining to sports participation has increased, most often when injuries result (see Box 1-3). In Washington, an athlete won a judgment against a school district because an improperly fitted helmet was judged partly responsible for a neck injury he sustained in football that resulted in him becoming a quadriplegic. It is imperative that the athletic trainer understand the legal aspects of his or her profession (see Putting It into Practice 1-2).

Understanding Laws, Contracts, and Institutional Policies

People involved with the delivery of health care to athletes are accountable for their actions. Sports medical personnel are accountable for failing to carry out a legal duty or performing some duty not legally theirs to perform (for example, a trainer prescribing medication). A person may be held liable for unreasonable or imprudent action or failing to perform actions that would be expected of a reasonable and prudent person. A person may be in legal jeopardy for not taking actions that should have been, for taking actions that should not have been, and for taking actions that were performed in an unacceptable manner. Courts determine the prudence of a person's behavior by comparing the propriety of actions in a given situation with accepted standards of performance. The sports medicine professional must be aware of accepted standards and perform accordingly to avoid legal difficulties.

Although no suggestions can ensure that a sports medicine practitioner will not be sued, there are several that reduce the likelihood (also see Box 1-3). First, know the state laws. All parties who deliver health care services to athletes must be certain that they are operating within the scope of pertinent laws. Each party must be sure to not engage in any practice that is legally restricted to some other profession. Of special consideration is the fact that many states' laws expressly prohibit anyone other than a licensed physical ther-

PUTTING IT INTO PRACTICE 1-2

Preventing Lawsuits

- *Liability:* An athletic trainer may be held legally liable for unreasonable or imprudent acts and failure to perform certain acts.
- *Standard of conduct:* An athletic trainer should act in a reasonable and prudent manner.
- *Preventive measures:*
  1. Practicing scrupulous professional conduct
  2. Knowing thoroughly the pertinent laws
  3. Being aware of professional and personal limitations
  4. Obtaining a written contract and job description specifying duties and responsibilities
  5. Maintaining an adequate professional liability insurance policy
  6. Being aware of institutional policies
  7. Maintaining current knowledge of sports medicine and athletic training

apist from using therapeutic modalities. Any nontherapist who engages in such an act is guilty not only of violating the law but of performing an act not legally within his or her domain and is likely liable for imprudent behavior.

Next, ask for an explicit contract and job description. Individuals who provide health care for athletes should have a *written* contract with the institution for which they work. A specific job description that outlines specific responsibilities should be included in this contract or in a separate document. For example, athletic trainers should understand precisely which therapeutic modalities they are expected or permitted to use. *Oral* agreements are unsatisfactory because one or both parties can misunderstand them. Also, reconciling differences in the parties' recollection of spoken agreements can be very difficult, and the difficulty may work to the advantage of the plaintiff during litigation.

Finally, study the institution's policies. It is important for everyone in sports medicine to know and operate within the policies of the institution for which they work. Procedures that do not correspond to existing policies should be halted, or efforts should be made to change the policies. Many athletic trainers have found it useful to obtain a written document of agreement with the school physician regarding the trainer's specific duties, options, and procedures.

Insurance Coverage

Both athletic trainers and athletes should carry adequate personal liability and health insurance. Insurance protects the athletic trainer from having to pay negligence damages in the event that he or she is ever involved in a lawsuit. Even if there is absolutely no basis for the suit, legal fees can run many thousands of dollars. An athlete adequately insured is less likely to pressure the athletic trainer into injury-management procedures that rightly belong in the medical domain.

It is absolutely necessary for the sports medicine practitioner to be covered by *personal liability* insurance (similar to medical malpractice insurance). The policy should specifically cover an individual during the performance of his or her assigned professional responsibilities related to the prevention, recognition, and care of sports-related injuries. Personal liability policies associated with homeowners' insurance and similar coverage are insufficient. Both professional and student members of the NATA are eligible for excellent liability coverage through the association. Other health care professionals should contact their professional organizations for effective, low-cost coverage.

All participants in sports programs must be covered by acceptable *health insurance* policies. Many lawsuits arise out of financial burdens caused by injury. For example, often a parent of an injured athlete who bears no malice toward the institution sues because of the high cost of medical treatment. Waivers that state that the institution is released from financial liability for injury are not sufficient for preventing litigation. These waivers do nothing to prevent the financial hardships that often cause parents to initiate lawsuits, even when the waivers are legally acceptable.

References

Moore, W. E. *The Professions: Roles and Rules.* New York: Russell Sage Foundation, 1970.

National Athletic Trainers Association. National Athletic Trainers Association Code of Ethics. *Athletic Training* 17(1), 1982.

National Athletic Trainers Association. *Professional Preparation in Athletic Training.* Champaign, Ill.: Human Kinetics Publishers, 1982.

National Athletic Trainers Association (Professional Education Committee). *Guidelines for Development and Implementation of NATA Approved Undergraduate Athletic Training Education Programs,* 1980.

National Athletic Trainers Association (Professional Education Committee). *Guidelines for Development and Implementation of NATA Approved Graduate Athletic Training Education Programs,* 1981.

The Athletic Training Room

COLLEGE and high school athletic training rooms have come a long way since the early days, when typically the only equipment was a table used for taping and massage. Today, well-equipped training rooms contain sophisticated equipment such as **isokinetic dynamometers** to analyze functional capacity, advanced devices such as electrical muscle stimulators and ultrasound to facilitate healing, and computers to store information.

The athletic training room should be the main facility for the prevention, first aid, and rehabilitation of athletic injuries. Preactivity taping, wrapping, and padding are the most common preventive activities performed in the training room and account for most patient traffic. The majority of the injury-prevention physical conditioning program is conducted in gymnasiums, weight training rooms, or on playing fields, but still the athletic training room is an important center for design of the prevention program and the evaluation of the success of the program.

The second most common activity in the athletic training room is rehabilitation, which includes therapeutic modalities and therapeutic exercise programs. The room is also often used for the more involved injury-management follow-up procedures to the first aid administered at the site where injuries occurred. **Splinting** and immobilization are performed here, and often physicians use the athletic training room for **suturing, joint aspiration,** and injections.

Physicians frequently use the athletic training room for medical evaluations. Ideally, a separate, private examination room should be part of the athletic training room. This area can also serve as a consultation room for the physician and athletic trainer. The room should also have space for storing records such as medical histories, preseason medical examinations, and athletic training room records (i.e., injury information, records of treatments and rehabilitation procedures, and pertinent progress notes).

Facilities

Usually the athletic training room is already established before the athletic trainer is hired, so he or she has little influence upon the room's design. However, the characteristics discussed in Putting It into Practice 2-1 should

Splinting: Immobilization of a joint or body part with a rigid device.

Suturing: Application of a surgical stitch or suture to unite soft tissue surfaces.

Joint aspiration: Removal of fluid from a joint.

Isokinetic dynamometer: A device that measures isokinetic power output (force exerted at constant speed) for testing and rehabilitative resistive exercise purposes.

be stressed when the athletic trainer's opinion is sought. In any case, certain aspects of design and content must be considered in even the most modest athletic training room. Access, size, and safety concerns are among the factors that must be planned for. The quality of the athletic training program varies according to the nature of the facility in which it is conducted: The better the facility, the better the athletic training program can be.

Access

We must state the obvious: The athletic training room must be accessible to the athletes. Because both men and women will use the facility, the room should be located adjacent to the men's and women's locker rooms. Ideally, athletes should have direct entry into the training room from the locker room. The room should also be readily accessible through an outdoor entrance. Multistory buildings should have ramps or elevators because stairs are a significant obstacle when transporting injured athletes. The doors to the room should be wide (double doors or a single door at least forty-four inches wide) to accommodate stretchers. To safeguard the facility, only authorized personnel should have keys.

Size and Construction

An athletic training program may serve anywhere from 10 to over 1000 athletes. The training room must be able to accommodate the number of athletes who typically use the facility in the short time before a practice or game. The training room should also be large enough to provide patient comfort and privacy when therapeutic modalities are being applied and storage for patient records and athletic training supplies. In short, the space allocated to the athletic training room must take into account equipment, patient load, and staff size (Figure 2-1, p. 22).

PUTTING IT INTO PRACTICE 2-1

The Athletic Training Room

- *Activities*: Injury prevention, first aid, injury management, rehabilitation, medical examinations, storage of medical records, dissemination of sports medicine information.
- *Location*: Must be accessible to the athletes from inside and outside the locker room and to medical personnel in case of an emergency.
- *Size*: Large enough to accommodate the patient load (varies with the situation).
- *Construction*: Sturdy, easy to clean, well lighted, sufficient power and electrical outlets, allows for constant supervision.
- *Principal fixtures*: Ice machine, refrigerator with freezer, whirlpools, sinks, shelves, cabinets, cold and hot water taps, taping and treatment tables, office equipment.

Ankle injuries sustained during volleyball matches can send players to the athletic training room for rehabilitation.

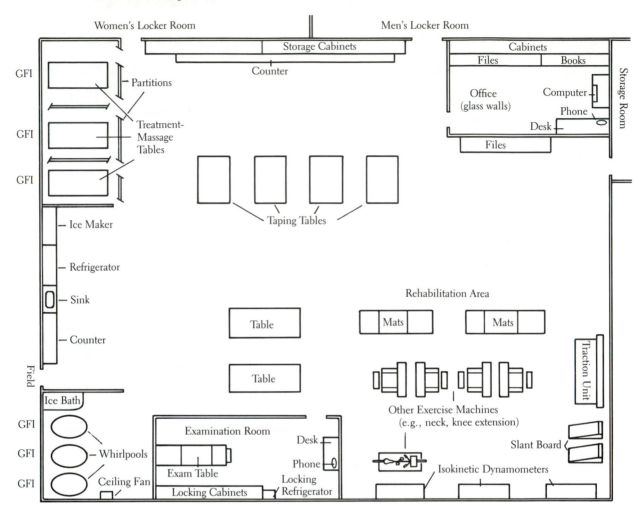

Figure 2-1   Floor plan of an athletic training room.

There are several important specifications for a well-planned athletic training room. The training room walls should be of painted concrete block or plaster, and for sanitary reasons they should be washable. Acoustical tile ceilings are recommended for a degree of noise control. Ceilings must be at least ten feet high so tall athletes can stand on the top of three-foot-high taping tables. Floors should be concrete with a non-slip finish and graded to slope toward floor drains located throughout the room. Carpeting should not be used because fabric holds moisture and can be a potential breeding ground for infectious organisms.

Lighting should be natural; windows must be positioned to provide privacy but prevent shadows that might interfere with athletic training procedures. Natural illumination should be augmented by nonglare lighting; fluorescent lighting with diffusers is an excellent source of artificial light. Windows provide natural ventilation, but a supplementary ventilating, air conditioning, and heating system is essential.

Safety Precautions

Safety is a primary concern in the design of the athletic training room. The room must allow for constant supervision, unobstructed traffic flow, and proper electrical specification. Ideally, the whirlpools and ice machine should be isolated from the rest of the training room by a three- to four-foot concrete or block wall. But because of the dangers associated with **hydrotherapy,** the area should not be so isolated that constant observation (see Box 2-1, p. 24) is not possible. This area should be adequately ventilated to reduce humidity. Excessive humidity can cause mold to form and speed the deterioration of the athletic training room's equipment.

Treatment stations should be situated so that they do not interfere with athletes entering or leaving the training room. For example, an athlete performing knee extensions following knee surgery could be severely injured if he banged his leg into a passing athlete. Isolated treatment areas give the athletes privacy and safety.

The athletic training room must have sufficient power supply and electrical outlets to support the numerous electrical appliances that are used. The number of outlets will exceed the number typically installed in other similarly sized rooms, so careful planning is necessary. All outlets should be located three to four feet above floor level and equipped with **ground fault interrupters (GFI).** Recent regulations dictate that all outlets that service whirlpools be equipped with these safety devices.

Permanent Fixtures and Furnishings

Certain fixtures and furnishings are critical to training room operations, including ice machine, refrigerator with freezer, hydrotherapy tubs (whirlpools), shelves, cabinets, hot and cold water taps, sinks, and taping and treatment tables. Most athletic trainers agree that a supply of ice is essential. The ice machine must produce enough crushed ice or small ice cubes to provide for first aid needs, treatment of injuries, and cool water.

A standard-size refrigerator with a freezer compartment is a valuable item. Besides providing the cold environment some liquids must be kept in, the refrigerator can be used to store wet elastic bandages necessary in certain first aid procedures. Cups of frozen water for ice massage can be stored in the freezer compartment.

Hydrotherapy tubs are used for cold water, hot water, or alternating hot water–cold water immersions. Most training rooms use stainless steel whirlpools for these treatments.

Sufficient shelf and cabinet space with easy access to supplies allows more efficient operation of the training room. The more hazardous materials (e.g., physician's drugs) and more expensive supplies should be kept in locked cabinets.

The training room must contain a sink with running hot and cold water to facilitate cleanliness—of both the athletes and the equipment. It is not critical that showers and toilets be within the training room; however, if they are not within the room, they should be located in an immediately adjacent area.

Finally, no training room is complete without the proper number of taping and treatment tables. As a rule of thumb, there should be one taping table for every fifteen athletes who are taped regularly (e.g., six taping tables for a ninety-athlete football team). Specifications for these tables can vary, provided the tables are of a size and structure suitable for use by athletes. Some institutions have found that taping tables one-half the length of normal treatment tables are an option when space is limited. For sanitation, separate tables should be used for treatment and taping whenever possible.

Hydrotherapy: Use of water as therapy.

Ground fault interrupter: An electrical safety device that interrupts current when output does not equal input. Should be used with all modalities requiring electricity.

BOX 2-1   **Safe Whirlpool Treatments**

The whirlpool is a common fixture in most schools because of the popularity of hydrotherapy treatments. In many cases, however, coaches and administrators are untrained in whirlpool use, and could therefore be exposing their athletes to dangerous situations, including electrocution.

In those rare cases where the generalized effect of full-body immersion is deemed to be beneficial, particular care must be taken to keep the water temperature within acceptable limits, and the duration of treatments must be monitored. The water temperature may be as warm as 110°F for treatment of extremities, but it should not exceed 104°F for full-body immersion. Duration of full-body immersion should not exceed 10 minutes! An accurate temperature gauge and a clock (or preferably a timer) are absolutely essential.

If these precautions are not observed, two serious problems can result. First, the athlete may faint. As blood vessels throughout the body dilate, blood is drawn away from the only body part not submerged, the head. If the athlete is unsupervised, he could drown. The other problem is that the body may become overheated. With almost all of the body surface surrounded by water that is warmer than normal body temperature, heat cannot be eliminated from the body by evaporation, conduction, convection, or radiation. Body temperature can reach an exceedingly dangerous level, especially if the athlete gets into the whirlpool immediately after vigorous exercise. A cool-down period is needed to dissipate the internal body heat accumulated during exercise.

Another very serious danger associated with whirlpools is the possibility of electrocution. Resistance to the flow of electrical current through the body is greatly reduced when the body is wet; a shock received at that time can be five times as great as when the body is dry. In many schools, whirlpool motors are old, poorly maintained and not properly grounded.

Even if the motor is properly grounded, failure of the motor insulation can still result in electrical current being received by a person in the water. A conventional fuse or circuit breaker will not interrupt current flow until leakage far exceeds a fatal level.

The solution for this problem is the installation of a ground fault circuit interrupter. This is a relatively inexpensive device that continually monitors the amount of electrical current flowing to the motor and the amount returning from it. If there is any discrepancy, the flow of electrical current is immediately interrupted, preventing electrical shock.

The death of a Kentucky high school athlete in 1980 was sobering proof of the importance of proper grounding mechanisms. The athlete apparently was electrocuted while using a whirlpool bath at his school; the cause was determined to be a defective grounding receptacle. The Board of Directors of the NATA subsequently passed a resolution urging any institution using whirlpools to install ground fault interrupters to prevent such tragedies in the future.

Although installation of a ground fault interrupter should provide adequate protection from shock, additional precautions might be considered. The whirlpool motor should be turned on and off by someone outside the water. Situations will invariably arise in which the athlete is in the whirlpool and is tempted to flip the switch himself. For this reason, there should also be a sign posted warning people not to turn the whirlpool on or off while they are in the water. A rubber insulating cover over the switch will add still more protection.

SOURCE: Reprinted from Wilkerson, G. B. Safe whirlpool treatments. *The First Aider* (a publication of Cramer Products, Inc.) 52:1, April–May 1983. Used by permission.

Storage and Office Space

In addition to the space for the basic treatment equipment, there must be ample room for storage and office operations. Short-term storage space for frequently used, expendable supplies must be located within the training room. These supplies are typically kept in the available cabinets and shelves mentioned in the previous section. A large, long-term walk-in storage facility close to the training room can house bulk supplies and expendable items, bulky equipment, and specialized devices not used daily. This area must be large to provide easy accessibility and cool and dry to prevent rapid deterioration of items such as adhesive tape.

Within the athletic training room, the office must be located in a spot where constant supervision of the entire facility is possible. Many institutions use glass walls so that the athletic trainer can see all operations from the office. The office should have a chair, filing cabinets, bulletin board for posting important notices, and, most important, a telephone with a direct outside line for emergency communications and professional consultations.

Computers

As computers become more common, many functions will be performed via a microcomputer or computer terminal. Whenever possible, provisions for a computer should be included in the athletic trainer's office. If a computer terminal is used, there should be two phone lines to the athletic trainer's office: one for the computer and one for normal telephone requirements. Computers can ease training room administration and be used to automate instruments, such as isokinetic dynamometers. Many successful athletic training programs, such as those at the University of Santa Clara in California, have used computers for several years.

Presently, computer technology provides hardware and software for such procedures as inventory control, storage of medical histories, storage of injury and treatment records, and even testing and exercising of specific body parts (see Box 2-2, p. 26). Few computer programs are specifically designed for athletic training room requirements, but many relatively inexpensive medical and business programs can be adapted for this purpose. For example, data base programs can be used to store athletes' treatment records and medical histories. Any instrument with analog or digital output can be interfaced with a computer, allowing instantaneous acquisition of data that the athlete and athletic trainer can immediately observe and interpret.

Equipment and Supplies

The specific equipment on hand in the athletic training room depends upon the scope of operations, budget, and philosophy of the athletic trainer and athletic department. However, overall guidelines can be applied.

First Aid and Injury Management

Table 2-1 (p. 27) lists the equipment and expendable supplies that should be available for first aid and injury management. Quantities are not given since individual requirements vary according to circumstances, such as level of competition, specific sports served, institutional policies, and size of the athletic training staff. For example, one institution, a typical NCAA division II athletic program with ten men's and women's teams, uses 150 speed packs of $1\frac{1}{2}$-inch adhesive tape each year. The beginning athletic trainer can receive valuable advice about the required quantities of specific items by consult-

BOX 2-2

The Microcomputer in Athletic Training

A large-capacity (large-memory) microcomputer costs about $2000. A small system consists of the microprocesser (the actual computer), monitor (video display), one or more disk drives (stores information), and printer. Other devices, such as an analog-to-digital converter (translates information from a measurement instrument to the computer) and a graphics tablet (translates graphic information to the computer), are useful auxiliary items.

Computers serve the athletic trainer in several ways:

- *Record keeping:* Patient records such as medical histories, preparticipation physical examinations, and progress reports can be stored on magnetic disks. Computer storage facilitates access to records and makes it possible to render statistical profiles of the program or specific populations. An athletic trainer could easily obtain information about injury patterns in particular sports and recovery rates for specific injuries.
- *On-line instrumentation:* Instruments such as isokinetic dynamometers, gas analyzers, force plates, and underwater weighing scales can be directly linked to computers via low-cost analog-to-digital converters. Computerized instrumentation allows the trainer to find information that would be otherwise impossible or impractical to obtain.
- *Budgeting and inventory control:* Carrying out these usually tedious chores is much easier through software currently on the market (e.g., Database II). Many software packages can be customized to fit a specific situation as well.
- *Information retrieval:* The computer can be used to catalog sports medicine articles or tie directly into various information-retrieval services, such as Medline, that are presently available. Soon, a university medical library will be available in every athletic training room.
- *Data manipulation and statistics:* Complex calculations such as body composition from skinfold regression equations and windchill factors can be calculated almost instantly with microcomputers. The athletic trainer can also chart information trends that are unique to his or her institution.
- *Athlete profiles:* Fitness and injury-susceptibility profiles can be rapidly prepared by comparing an athlete's physical performance results with established norms. Individualized computer reports that summarize the athlete's strengths and weaknesses can be printed.

---

ing with experienced athletic trainers who work in a similar situation.

A well-stocked field kit is essential because the athletic trainer often must perform services outside the training room. The carrying case for the kit should be portable but large enough to carry the necessary supplies. Cases and the contents of the kits are available from athletic training supply companies. Table 2-2 (p. 28) is a list of items that should be included in the kit.

Rehabilitation: Therapeutic Modalities

Several factors, particularly state laws and institutional policies, determine the specific therapeutic **modalities** available for the rehabilitation of injured athletes. The modalities used in the athletic training room include cryotherapy, hydrotherapy, thermotherapy, electrotherapy, mobilization, and massage. Each modality requires specific equipment (e.g, electrotherapy requires a device such as an electrical muscle stimulator).

Cryotherapy. The essential ingredient in **cryotherapy** is ice. Cups of ice to be used for ice massage can be stored in the training room freezer. An ice maker that supplies crushed ice for ice bags and an ice bath are also important components of the cryotherapy program.

Modality: A physical technique or substance administered to produce a therapeutic effect.

Cryotherapy: Use of cold as therapy.

Wraps and splints

Abdominal binders (assorted sizes)
Acromioclavicular splints
Air splints: one-half arm, one-half leg, ankle, full leg
Ankle wraps
Back brace
Cervical collars
Cockup forearm splints
Elastic wraps (2, 3, 4, 6 in; 4 and 6 in double length)
Finger splints ($\frac{1}{2}$ and $\frac{3}{4}$ in)
Heel cups
Knee splints
Posterior leg splints
Rib belts (male and female)
Skin closures
Slings (cradle)

Cloth items, bandages, pads, and applicators

Bandage (knuckle)
Band-Aids (assorted)
Cast padding
Cotton applicators
Felt adhesive ($\frac{1}{2}$, $\frac{1}{4}$, $\frac{1}{8}$ in)
Felt donuts (assorted)
Felt heel pads
Felt long arch pads
Felt metatarsal pads
Felt sheets ($\frac{1}{2}$ and $\frac{1}{4}$ in thick)
Foam rubber (assorted sizes and densities)
Gauze (3 × 3 sterile and nonsterile, 4 × 4 sterile, sterile nonstick 3 × 3, 2-in gauze roller)
Heel and lace pads
Moleskin
Padding material ($\frac{1}{2}$, $\frac{1}{4}$, $\frac{1}{8}$ in)
Stingkill swab
Stockinette (3, 4, 6 in)
Tampons
Tape, adhesive ($\frac{1}{2}$, 1, $1\frac{1}{2}$, 2 in)
Tape, elastic (2 and 3 in)
Tape underwrap

Liquids and medications

Acetaminophen (e.g., Tylenol)
Adhesive foam
Alcohol
Ammonia capsules
Analgesic balm
Antacid tablets
Aquasonic gel (ultrasound)
Aspirin tablets
Cold sore ointment
Collodion
Debrox ($\frac{1}{2}$ oz)
Eyedrops
Eyewash
First aid cream
Foot powder (bulk and 4 oz)
Massage lubricant
Oil of cloves (1 oz)
Ointment (antibiotic)
Ophthalmic dye
Orthoplast (18 × 24 in)
Petroleum jelly
Skin lotion
Soap (solid and liquid)
Sphygmomanometer and stethoscope
Whirlpool disinfectant

Equipment

Blankets
Coolers
Crutches (assorted sizes)
Eye irrigator
Forceps
Hydrocollator pack covers
Hydrocollator packs (extralarge, regular, knee, neck)
Sandbags (assorted, 0.5 to 5 kg)
Scalpel blades and handles
Scissors (straight and curved surgical)
Sling psychrometer (relative humidity)
Stretchers (regular, scoop)
Tape remover
Thermometers (oral, rectal, environmental)
Water caddy (4 gal)

Miscellaneous supplies

Bottles (plastic, assorted)
Calestone (for abrading calluses)
Cups (plastic, assorted)
Pill bottles (plastic)
Plaster of Paris
Plastic bags (ice)
Tongue blades
Travel trunk
Water bottles

Table 2-2 *Contents of the Athletic Trainer's Field Kit*

Adhesive items

Adhesive felt and foam rubber
Adhesive wound closure (butterfly
  strips)
Band-Aids (assorted sizes)
Butterfly strips
Cloth tape ($\frac{1}{2}$, 1, $1\frac{1}{2}$ in wide)
Elastic tape (2 and 3 in wide)
Moleskin

Cloth items

Ankle wraps
Combine roll (cloth wraps)
Felt (orthopedic, $\frac{1}{4}$ and $\frac{1}{2}$ in wide)
Gauze (2-in rolls)
Gauze pads (nonsterile and sterile)
Tampons

Elastic items

Elastic bandages (regular length: 3 and
  4 in wide; double length: 4 and 6 in
  wide)
Pretape underwrap material
Rib belt

Liquids and medications

Alcohol (isopropyl)
Ammonia capsules
Analgesic balm
Antacids (tablets or liquid)
Antiseptic
Aspirin

Eyewash
First aid cream
Foot and body powder
Insect sting kit
Liquid soap
Petroleum jelly
Skin cream
Skin lubricant
Tape adherent
Tape remover

Equipment

Contact lens kit (including suction
  device for removal of lenses and small
  mirror)
Fingernail/toenail drill
Forceps (tongue and splinter)
Nail clippers
Plastic airway
Safety pins
Scalpel and blades
Scissors
Sling/cravat bandage
Tape cutter
Tongue depressor

*Items that should also be close
  at hand*

Cooler with ice and ice bags
Crutches (different sizes)
Splints
Stretcher

Cold compression units for treating athletic injuries (Figure 2-2, p. 29) have recently been introduced. These units automatically supply cold and compression simultaneously. However, they are not yet widely used.

Hydrotherapy. Whirlpools are the most frequently used apparatus for hydrotherapy treatments. Whirlpools, stainless steel tanks with a motor for agitating water, come in many different sizes. Since the primary physiological effect of hydrotherapy comes from the temperature of the water rather than from the massaging effect of the agitated water, almost any type of tank or tub large enough for the submerged affected body part can be used. Laundry tubs, galvanized trash cans, and similar containers have been effectively used in place of commercial whirlpools. However, these makeshift whirlpools are less than ideal and should not be used if at all possible.

Cold compression unit: A device that simultaneously applies compression and cold for therapy.

Whirlpool: Hydrotherapy tub or pool of cold to hot aerated water used to supply a therapeutic effect.

Thermotherapy. Many types of **thermotherapy** equipment deliver surface, deep, moist, or dry heat to a given area of the body. Superficial heat can be provided by such simple equipment as a heating pad or a **hydrocollator pack;** both devices are relatively inexpensive and readily available. More sophisticated devices that use **ultrasound,** shortwave **diathermy,** or microwave diathermy provide deeper penetrating heat. Heat lamps and paraffin baths are being used less and less in the athletic training room.

Electrotherapy. The sophistication and availability of **electrotherapy** have dramatically increased in recent years. Muscle stimulators are used to strengthen muscles and prevent **atrophy.** Many athletic trainers use a **neuroprobe** to locate trigger points for pain and to subsequently stimulate cu-

taneous nerves (**transcutaneous electrical nerve stimulation**) as a significant step in pain control. As more is learned about the effects of electrical stimulation, these modalities may become second only to cryotherapy in rehabilitation. Electrical stimulation equipment is expensive, so the athletic trainer should shop for it carefully and judiciously.

Mobilization. Mobilization techniques are being used more and more in the rehabilitation of athletic injuries. Many of these techniques are accomplished through manual manipulation of the patient; others are achieved with machines. Some athletic training rooms contain a traction device that can be used for treating certain types of neck and spinal injuries. A traction table with electronically controlled tension that can be used for traction of all spi-

Thermotherapy: Use of heat as therapy.
Transcutaneous electrical nerve stimulation: Therapeutic application of electrical nerve impulses to decrease pain.
Hydrocollator pack: Canvas pack filled with silica gel, used to apply superficial moist heat.
Ultrasound: Use of high-frequency sound waves (greater than 20,000 hertz) as deep-heating therapy.
Diathermy: Use of high-frequency electrical current as heat therapy.
Mobilization: Manual manipulation of a joint or soft tissue.
Electrotherapy: Use of electrical energy as therapy.
Atrophy: Decrease in size and function of a muscle.
Neuroprobe: A device that decreases pain by using electrical energy to stimulate trigger points along the pathways of nerves sensitive to stimulation.

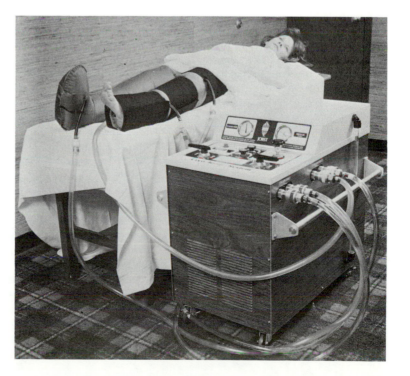

Figure 2-2 An expensive but useful addition to the athletic training room, the cold compression unit simultaneously administers cold and compression to injured areas.

nal segments may be a sensible purchase, provided that trained medical personnel to perform the procedure are available.

Massage. Massage as a treatment for athletic injuries is decreasing in popularity. Many modern athletic trainers feel that massage is a waste of time because it is not as beneficial as other modalities. However, massage has several benefits if performed by a qualified individual. Numerous hand-held, electrical massage devices are now available for the athletic trainer who wants to include this modality as one of the available treatments.

Training Room Administration

Most athletic trainers are people-oriented and often dislike the administrative aspects of the job. Yet these administrative duties are vital to a sound program. Handled efficiently, these duties need not drag on the time devoted to actual athletic training. For maximum efficiency, the athletic trainer must ensure training room decorum, good time management, and proper training room maintenance.

Decorum

The athletic trainer should maintain professionalism at all times in the training room, and the training room staff should always behave and dress accordingly. Rules of behavior should be established and posted for athletes who use the training room (rules will vary according to the philosophy of the athletic training program and the type of institution). In general, except in emergencies, athletes should be required to report to the training room properly dressed and should receive treatments only after showering. Language and

behavior should be exemplary, and athletes should not be allowed to loiter in the training room.

Time Management

Athletic trainers who do not master good time-management skills will be swamped with the minutiae of administration and unable to devote sufficient time to athletic training. For example, athletic events and practice sessions are frequently scheduled simultaneously. All these events may be at home or require travel. The training room schedule must then be adjusted so that the best possible health care is available to athletes; this juggling of schedules can be quite a feat.

As we saw in Chapter 1, there are numerous and complex demands on the athletic trainer's time. In addition to the normal athletic training duties, the athletic trainer may be required to teach classes, serve on committees, and perform other duties required of school faculty members. The athletic trainer may also be required to select, care for, and issue athletic equipment. Each duty must be given a priority based upon available time and the relative importance of each task. The athletic trainer should establish these priorities by consulting with the department chairperson or appropriate administrator. The athletic trainer must realize that one cannot be all things to all people; trying to perform too many jobs results in overall poor performance or job burnout.

Assistant athletic trainers and students can help ease the athletic trainer's load and effect better time management. Professional assistants should be given an opportunity to share in the performance of all aspects of the athletic training program. By creating an atmosphere of shared governance and equal opportunity, treating associates as professional equals, and delegating specific administrative and service-oriented

Massage: Manipulation of soft body tissue by rubbing, kneading, and tapping to induce therapeutic relaxation.

duties, trainers can increase each assistant's feeling of being a productive member of the staff. Many institutions have found it feasible to assign each professional assistant as the head athletic trainer for certain sports, with the head athletic trainer as the ultimate authority in all cases.

Student athletic trainers can be helpful in managing activities, but they should not be assigned duties and responsibilities for which they are not prepared. Institutions should always evaluate the competencies of students prior to assigning specific duties. Inappropriate assignments may result in injury to an athlete and subsequent legal liability for the athletic training staff and the institution.

In institutions with only one athletic trainer, particularly in secondary schools, effective time management is critical. A single athletic trainer cannot provide equal services to all sports. The athletic trainer, athletic director, and coaches must arrive at a logical plan for covering practices and athletic events that will permit a sensible and adequate level of health care for the athletes. This plan should be based upon available resources and the specific nature of each sport. Some secondary schools have made the athletic trainer a full-time position or given the athletic trainer release time from regular school-day duties in recognition of the job's many time demands. Whatever the level of work, the key to success is to learn to manage your time rather than let your work manage you.

Maintenance

In most institutions, the custodial crew and training room staff share the responsibility for training room maintenance. Each group must understand its specific responsibility. Generally, those duties associated with general cleanliness of the room (emptying the trash receptacles and cleaning the floors, walls, shelves, and so on) are best assigned to the custodians; maintenance chores specifically related to athletic training equipment (e.g., disinfecting and cleaning whirlpools and therapeutic equipment) should be performed by the athletic training staff. Each member of the athletic training staff should be responsible for specific maintenance duties so that the "someone else will do it" syndrome does not take root. A clean and orderly athletic training room is essential if it is to be perceived as a place in which professional health care is administered.

References

Baker, B. B., and C. A. Rode. Legal implications concerning the use of modalities by athletic trainers. *Athletic Training* 10:208, 1975.

Giek, J., R. S. Brown, and R. H. Shank. The burnout syndrome among athletic trainers. *Athletic Training* 17:36–40, 1982.

Laird, D. E. Practical guidelines for health care management in secondary school athletics. *NASSP Bulletin* 65:4–11, 1981.

National Athletic Trainers Association. *Professional Preparation in Athletic Training.* Champaign, Ill.: Human Kinetics Publishers, 1982.

Powell, J. W. Safety in the athletic training room. *Journal of Physical Education, Recreation, and Dance* 54:50, 1983.

Vergamini, G. Professional burnout: implications for the athletic trainer. *Athletic Training* 16:197–198, 1981.

PART TWO

Principles of Injury Prevention and Management

Injury Prevention

THE RISK of injury accompanies participation in almost all sports. It has been estimated that two out of three runners and as many as 50 percent of high school football players are injured each year. As the number of participants in both competitive and recreational sports has increased, there has been a corresponding increase in the number of injuries. Those individuals directly or indirectly involved in sports (coaches, athletes, physicians, athletic trainers, sport therapists, paramedics, physical education teachers, athletic administrators, parents) must better understand the factors that can cause athletic injuries and actively follow a consistent, systematic, and well-defined injury-prevention program to control them.

Athletic injuries can have profound, long-lasting effects on athletes. Injuries, particularly those not properly cared for, may develop into conditions that can last a lifetime, such as **lateral epicondylitis** (tennis elbow), **subpatellar chondrosis** (runner's knee), or **osteoarthritis** (inflamed joints). Figure 3-1 (p. 36), which depicts the many injuries the great football player Jim Otto sustained, graphically illustrates this fact. Although now retired from athletics, Otto is still plagued by chronic

pain from his injuries. A systematic injury-prevention program might have spared him some of his residual pain. For example, his statement "I've never been carried off the field" implies a disregard for the possible additional damage caused by "walking off an injury." An injury-prevention program includes a written protocol defining when athletes should be carried off the field and when they can walk off by themselves. It is indeed a tragedy that the wonderful experience of athletic participation is so often spoiled by injuries that are preventable.

The specter of athletic injuries has even affected the very existence of some sports. Athletes involved in trampoline, for example, have sustained so many catastrophic injuries that it is now virtually impossible for schools to obtain insurance for the activity. The possibility of litigation arising from sponsorship of boxing, scuba diving, and skiing programs has drastically affected the existence of these programs in some high schools and colleges.

A strong prevention program will effectively reduce some athletic injuries. For example, in football, the combination of improved helmets, preseason medical examination, more emphasis on physical conditioning, and banning

Lateral epicondylitis: Pain and tenderness of the tendons near the lateral epicondyle of the humerus, caused by microtrauma and tendinitis. Commonly called tennis elbow.

Subpatellar chondrosis: Degeneration of the cartilage on the under surface of the patella. Commonly called runner's knee.

Osteoarthritis: Disease of the joints characterized by degeneration of joint (articular) cartilage and increase in the size (hypertrophy) of local bone.

Flexibility training is an important part of injury prevention. The athletic trainer must be careful to see that preventive exercises do not cause injuries. It is difficult to determine here if the flexibility exercise is preventing or inducing injury.

"I've never been carried off the field, though."

Concussion
12 Broken Noses
Facial Cuts Requiring 100 Stitches
Cauliflower Ear
Injury-induced Arthritis
Shoulder Pointer
Calcium Deposits
Injury-induced Arthritis
Torn Ribs
Cracked Ribs
Bruised Ribs
Crystallized Joint Fluid
Hip Pointer

Detached Retina
Cauliflower Ear
Cracked Jaw
Cervical Bone Protrusion
Shoulder Pointer
Calcium Deposits
Injury-induced Arthritis
Torn Ribs
Cracked Ribs
Bruised Ribs
Injury-induced Arthritis (back)
Crystallized Joint Fluid

1975 AFC PRO BOWL

Dislocated Fingers
Broken Fingers

Broken Fingers
Dislocated Fingers

Charley Horse
Four Knee Operations
Broken Kneecap
Torn Cartilage
Torn Ligaments
Injury-induced Arthritis
Plastic and Stainless Steel Knee Joint

Charley Horse
Three Knee Operations
Broken Kneecap
Torn Cartilage
Torn Ligaments
Injury-induced Arthritis

Shin Splints

Shin Splints

Sprained Ankle
Broken Ankle
Injury-induced Arthritis

Sprained Ankle
Injury-induced Arthritis

Figure 3-1 During a fifteen-year career as an Oakland Raider, all-pro football player Jim Otto incurred all these injuries. How many could have been prevented is open to speculation. He was a symphony in survival as he started 210 league games in a row. The action is all over now, but Otto's battered body is still hurting. (From *California Today* [*San Jose Mercury*], Nov. 7, 1976.)

butt blocking (spearing) and **face tackling** has led to a pronounced decrease in head and neck injuries and fatalities (see Figure 3-2, p. 38). There has been an 81 percent decrease in football fatalities between 1968 and 1978.

Incidence of Injury

A study commissioned by the United States Congress noted that there were more than 1 million athletic injuries in high schools and colleges in 1975 to 1976. Of these injuries, more than 100,000 (10 percent) were classified as major—serious enough to prevent participation in athletics for more than

twenty days. The highest rate of injury occurs during unsupervised sports and physical activity. Nicholas's (1974) and Wright's studies suggest that lack of physical conditioning is the most important factor predisposing people to athletic injury.

The rate of serious sports injuries in high school athletes has been estimated to be approximately 11 to 27 injuries per 1000 participants. Girls have a slightly higher rate of serious injury than boys, possibly because girls tend to be less conditioned and use inferior equipment. Contact and collision sports, such as football and basketball, account for the greatest number of serious injuries in both sexes. Table 3-1 compares injuries of high school boys

Butt blocking: In football, an illegal blocking technique in which the blocker's head is the first point of contact with an opponent. This technique has caused many serious head and neck injuries. Also called spearing.

Face tackling: In football, an illegal tackling technique in which tackling is initiated with the head.

Table 3-1 *Injuries Sustained by High School Boys and Girls Participating in Similar Sports*

Boys	Girls
Sprains	Sprains
1. Ankle	1. Ankle
2. Knee	2. Knee[a]
3. Foot, wrist, elbow	3. Foot
Strains	4. Hip
1. Leg and thigh	5. Shoulder
2. Shoulder	Strains[b]
3. Back	1. Back
4. Foot, hip/groin, elbow	2. Leg and thigh
Fractures	3. Shoulder
1. Hand	4. Foot, hip/groin
2. Leg and thigh	Fractures
3. Foot	1. Ankle
4. Head and face	2. Hand
5. Ankle, wrist, arm, shoulder	3. Leg, thigh
Contusions	4. Elbow
1. Head and face	Contusions
2. Foot, leg, thigh, knee, hip, groin, shoulder	1. Hand, wrist, leg, thigh
3. Hand	2. Knee, elbow
	Dislocations
	1. Hand
	2. Elbow
	3. Patella

NOTE: The sports were track, cross-country, swimming, tennis, volleyball, soccer, basketball, baseball/softball. Injuries are listed in order of frequency.

[a]Girls incur knee sprains almost three times more often than boys do.

[b]Strains are less prevalent in girls than in boys.

SOURCE: Derived from the data of Shively, R. A., W. A. Grana, and D. Ellis. High school sports injuries. *The Physician and Sportsmedicine* 9:46–50, 1981.

and girls in similar sports. Table 3-2 (p. 39) outlines the principal injuries occurring in various sports. Lower extremity injuries predominate, suggesting the need for an injury-prevention program concentrating on the lower area of the body.

Athletic injuries are not restricted to high school or college athletes. Middle-aged participants in exercise and sports are also experiencing an array of **traumas** and overuse injuries. An overuse injury results from continually stressing a body part beyond its tolerance, for example, tennis elbow and shin splints. The stress may involve too much volume or intensity (excessive for the level of fitness). A poll *Time* magazine conducted among various age groups estimated that 75 percent of people who jog will experience an injury serious enough to curtail their exercise program for seven days every year. Overuse injuries occur most often in urban recreational athletes, with the greatest percentage of injuries resulting from jogging, basketball, tennis, and dancing. Nicholas and Friedman observed that increased leisure time and better recreational facilities have allowed middle-aged and older adults to become more physically active. Unfortunately, the health benefits of an exercise program are sometimes overshadowed by the injuries that result.

As briefly mentioned in the opening sentences of this chapter, active injury prevention involves people other than the participants. Athletes should report injuries and follow through with the prescribed rehabilitation. Coaches should be skilled in prevention techniques and qualified in first aid and injury management. Physicians and therapists should communicate clearly with those involved concerning an athlete's risk of injury and prognosis for recovery if the athlete is injured. Parents should help injured athletes follow through with conditioning, injury awareness, and rehabilitation. Parents should also be the liaison among the

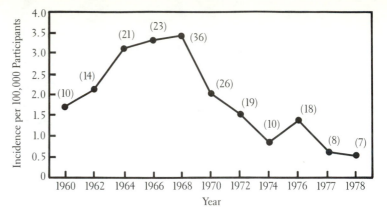

Figure 3-2 Head and neck fatalities from football in the 1960 through 1978 seasons. The fatalities decreased dramatically after 1968, most likely because of a vigorous nationwide injury-prevention program. (From Mueller, F. O., and C. S. Blyth. Catastrophic head and neck injuries. *The Physician and Sportsmedicine* 7:71–74, 1979.)

family physician, athletic trainer, and coach. School administrators must be taught the importance of maintaining quality and high standards even in the face of declining budgets. Physical education teachers should stress the importance of safety to their students. Paramedics should be involved in coordinating plans for transporting athletes to the hospital following injury. Only when all the individuals directly and indirectly involved in athletics understand the principles of injury prevention and actively apply them will the incidence of sport-related injuries decrease.

Trauma: Injury or damage.

Variables Affecting Athletic Injuries

Many injuries athletes suffer are preventable. But an effective injury-prevention program is not easy to achieve. It must (1) be aggressive; (2) follow high standards of quality and maintenance of equipment and facilities; (3) use qualified coaches, athletic trainers, and physicians for practices and games; (4) teach proper sports technique and sportsmanship; (5) emphasize year-round conditioning; and (6) include a pervasive awareness of the injury process.

Table 3-2 *Major Injuries in Popular Sports*

Sport	Most Frequent Injury	Serious (Life-threatening) Injury
Football	Sprains: Ankle, knee Strains: Leg, thigh Contusions: Hip and lower extremities	Head and neck trauma
Baseball	Sprains and strains of elbow and shoulder	Head and chest trauma
Basketball	Lower extremity strains and sprains (foot and ankle not common)	Head trauma
Boxing	Upper extremity strains and sprains	Head and neck trauma
Gymnastics	Foot, ankle, knee sprains Upper extremity and back strains	Head and neck trauma (from trampoline)
Soccer	Lower extremity sprains, contusions, strains	Rare
Wrestling	Sprains: Knee and ankle Strains: Shoulder and back Contusions: Head and face	Rare
Tennis	Elbow and shoulder strains	Rare
Racketball and squash	Lower extremity strains and sprains, facial lacerations, eye injury	Cardiac arrest (recreational participant)
Swimming and diving	Shoulder strains	Drowning (recreational participant) Neck injury (from diving)
Alpine skiing	Knee sprains, fractures	Head trauma
Jogging and running	Lower extremity strains	Cardiac arrest
Cycling	Back and lower extremity strains	Automobile accidents

Most sport injuries are caused by one or more factors (Figure 3-3, p. 41), including

- Inadequate preparticipation screening
- Poor coaching
- Inadequate conditioning
- Improper equipment use or fit
- Inadequate or poorly maintained facilities
- The athlete's psychosocial problems
- Inadequate field care
- Inadequate rehabilitation
- Premature return to participation

Except for such unforeseen circumstances as injuries that occur from high forces generated in athletics (e.g., broken bones and dislocated joints), the athlete or those responsible for the athlete's health and training can reduce the risk of injury from any of these nine factors. The following discussions elaborate these factors; see Putting It into Practice 3-1 (p. 40) for an overview of ways to prevent injuries.

Any effort to prevent injuries must involve systematic consideration of each factor. Priorities and guidelines for minimizing the risk of athletic injuries must be established. As examples, if the environmental temperature and humidity exceed the established safe levels, cancel practice or reschedule it for a cooler time of day. If a piece of equipment is broken and places the athlete at increased risk, do not use it until it is repaired. Athletes develop their prowess most quickly and safely when their training program is controlled, and this

PUTTING IT INTO PRACTICE 3-1

Strategies for Preventing Injuries

Preparticipation Screening

- *Evaluate injuries reported on the medical history form.* If the injury is not adequately healed, institute a rehabilitation program.
- *Anticipate and prevent potential injuries.* Compare the athlete's muscular strength, endurance, power, flexibility, etc., with normal and optimal values of similar athletes. Disqualify a "deficient" athlete from participation, remedy deficiencies, or rechannel the candidate into more appropriate activities.
- *Watch for athletes who "hide" or "cover" injuries.* Previously injured athletes face increased risk of reinjury. Encourage athletes to be candid about their injury status.
- *Maintain communication* among athletes, parents, physicians, coaches, and athletic trainers about temporary or permanent medical disqualification.

Coaching

- *Maintain hiring standards.* Hire only experienced and qualified coaches.
- *Keep current.* Conduct regularly scheduled in-service workshops on first aid, sports medicine, proper sports technique, and injury prevention. Encourage coaching staffs to attend clinics, workshops, and college classes in physical education and athletic training.
- *Communication.* Have the coaching staff collaborate with athletic trainers and physicians to set strategies for preventing injuries.
- *Consistency.* Insist that all athletes obey the rules and exhibit sportsmanship.
- *Supervision.* Always adequately supervise all practices and games.
- *Proper techniques.* Teach biomechanically correct techniques that will result in fewer injuries.

Conditioning

- *Planning.* Maintain systematic, year-long conditioning plans that allow for individual differences in fitness, motivation, and ability.
- *Knowledgeable athletes.* Teach athletes the importance of conditioning for preventing injury and attaining maximal performance. Knowledgeable athletes are better able to follow a long-term conditioning program.
- *Injury versus conditioning.* Ensure that the design of the conditioning programs for injured athletes does not jeopardize healing.
- *Access to conditioning facilities.* Make sure athletes have ready and convenient access to conditioning facilities. If possible, structure and supervise off-season conditioning programs.

Equipment

- *Inspections.* Regularly inspect equipment; if it is found unsafe, remove it from service. Delegate responsibility for equipment inspection, and conduct regular and systematic inspections.
- *Proper fit.* Equipment must be properly fitted; be sure the coaching staff and athletic trainers are skilled in this aspect.
- *Proper use.* Never teach or tolerate techniques that use equipment as weapons.

Facilities

- *Maintenance standards and inspections.* Always adequately supervise and maintain facilities. Make sure inspections occur regularly and are systematic. Correct deficiencies immediately.
- *Proper equipment.* Maintain facilities with all necessary safety equipment, such as pads and mats, to cushion incidental collisions.

Psychosocial Considerations

- *Injury proneness.* Be aware of possible psychosocial problems, such as injury proneness, that could result in injury. Take effective steps, such as counseling, to remedy problems.
- *Fear of reinjury.* Be aware of an athlete's excessive preoccupation with the possibility of reinjury.

- *Alcohol and drugs.* Discourage the use of alcohol or drugs. Attempt to discover the athlete's motivation for using these substances. Refer problems to an alcohol-abuse counselor.

Field Care

- *Emergency procedures.* Establish and practice specific procedures for dealing with serious injuries. Make sure all necessary equipment is nearby.
- *Education.* Be sure responsible personnel are trained in first aid and injury procedures.

Rehabilitation

- *Systematic rehabilitation.* Institute systematic programs for rehabilitation, and closely monitor injured athletes throughout their courses of rehabilitation. Rehabilitation programs should use objective measures such as power output on an isokinetic dynamometer to gauge their success or failure.

Return to Participation

- *Objective criteria.* The decision to return to practice should be objective, based on the criteria listed in the "Premature Return to Participation" section later in this chapter (see p. 51) and consultation with the team's or the athlete's personal physician.

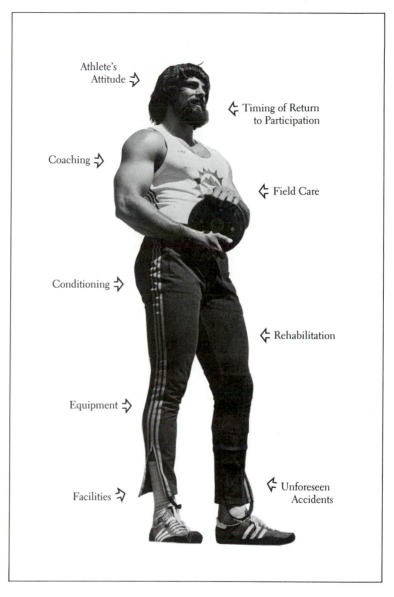

Figure 3-3   Factors associated with athletic injuries. Pictured is Mac Wilkens, 1976 Olympic gold medalist and 1984 Olympic silver medalist in discus throwing.

is most easily accomplished when athletes, athletic trainers, and coaches know what is expected of them. Guidelines should be written down and adhered to.

Preparticipation Screening

Preparticipation screening determines the existence of any factors that may make the athlete more·susceptible to injury. For example, the participation of an athlete with an enlarged spleen due to **mononucleosis** is **contraindicated** in contact sports. Similarly, an extremely obese, physically immature individual with little muscle mass faces increased risk of injury in a contact sport like football. When factors affecting an athlete's health, structure, or maturity are discovered, the course of action involves restricting the athlete from the activity, modifying the activity, and/or eliminating or controlling the physical problem. The decision to restrict an athlete should involve information from the physician (medical contraindications), the coach (the athlete's ability to be competitive), the athletic trainer (the athlete's past injury status and susceptibility to injury), and the parents (the athlete's emotional well-being).

The traditional preparticipation medical examination (discussed in detail in Chapter 11) includes medical history (written summary of the athlete's health history); examination of eyes, ears, nose, and throat; assessment of blood pressure and pulse; and **hernia** examinations. As sports medicine professionals gained more experience and emphasized **musculoskeletal/orthopedic** problems more than **systemic medical disorders** (athletes incur more orthopedic than systemic medical problems), more appropriate screening methods developed. Today, the ideal preparticipation medical examination places more priority on such factors as

strength, **joint laxity,** posture, and a detailed history of past injuries. To supplement the physician's efforts, the examinations require the active involvement of physical education teachers, athletic trainers (Figure 3-4), physical therapists, and nurses. Schools that use preparticipation medical examinations and screenings can effectively implement preventive and corrective programs that will lead to a decrease in such injuries as strains and sprains (see Chapter 11).

Coaching

Coaches play important roles in preventing athletic injuries. They are responsible for the structure and administration of the physical training program and the athlete's conduct on the playing field. Most athletic programs, particularly those at the high school and youth level, do not have the services of a physician and an athletic trainer at games and practices. Therefore, coaches must develop a high level of expertise, enabling them to recognize and care for injuries as well as prepare athletes for competition (see Putting It into Practice 3-2).

Unfortunately, many coaches, particularly of youth and high school sports, have no training in the care of athletic injuries, physical education, or athletics. In a 1983 survey of sixty-two youth coaches, Hackworth and coworkers found that only one person had a degree in physical education and only seven coaches had completed a first aid course within the past three years.

At the high school level, coaching positions are increasingly filled by noncredentialed or unqualified people. These volunteers are well intentioned, but they usually lack the necessary specific knowledge of **exercise physiology, biomechanics, motor learning,** athletic administration, and the nuances of the sport to be effective coaches.

Joint laxity: Abnormal movement of the joint when the joint is manipulated.

Mononucleosis: Infectious viral illness characterized by fever, sore throat, enlarged spleen and lymph nodes, and abnormal amount of lymphocytes in the blood.

Contraindicated: Not appropriate or recommended.

Hernia: Protrusion of an organ through the tissue wall that normally contains the organ. In athletes, hernia most commonly occurs in the groin or low regions of the abdomen.

Musculoskeletal: Pertaining to skeleton, muscles, and tendons.

Orthopedics: A branch of medicine dealing with the skeleton and related structures, e.g., muscles, joints, ligaments, tendons.

Systemic medical disorders: Internal diseases.

Exercise physiology: Study of physiological function during exercise.

Biomechanics: Study of the physics of motion in humans or animals.

Motor learning: Study of how physical skills are learned.

PUTTING IT INTO PRACTICE
3-2

Preventing Injuries Through Knowledge and Communication

Knowledge of Technique and Body Mechanics

- Provide athletes with reading material and advice about techniques that prevent injury.
- Be aware of fundamental injury-prevention techniques by attending clinics, taking courses, and reading the sports medicine literature.

Open Communication

- Provide athletes with a rationale for their training program.
- Establish methods and objectives for training and rehabilitation programs. Professional staffs should regularly discuss their methods and procedures.
- Establish an open, professional, and trusting relationship with the physician.

Figure 3-4 Musculoskeletal evaluation accompanied by an active program to correct deficiencies can reduce the risk of injury. This athletic trainer is evaluating the passive range of motion of an athlete's ankle joint.

Blyth and Mueller found that the high school football teams with the lowest injury rates were those whose coaches were older, had both high school and college playing experience, and had been coaching longer. They also found an inverse relationship between the number of assistant coaches and injuries. This study reinforces the importance of adequate funding and continuity in the athletic program. Professional standards can be raised among part-time coaches by offering them workshops and supplementary courses in athletic training, exercise physiology, and coaching techniques.

Other factors that contribute to injuries, such as poor technique and lack of consideration for rules and sportsmanship, are primarily the coach's responsibility. In most sports, proper technique requires the use of major lower body muscle groups rather than the weaker muscles of the upper extremities to initiate a movement. Failure to follow this fundamental principle leads to injury. For example, tennis players who attempt to hit a backhand without stepping into the ball frequently develop tennis elbow. Many young football players spend hours working on the bench press at the expense of the muscles in their lower body because they mistakenly believe that the muscles of the upper body are the most important for football. The knowledgeable coach stresses the fundamental techniques that lead to success on the playing field and a reduction in injuries. Coaches should study the techniques found in the biomechanics literature and coaching manuals; these techniques are based upon sound kinesiological principles.

Coaches should always insist that athletes follow the rules and observe proper etiquette on the playing field. For example, coaches should not allow football players to spear block (an illegal technique) because serious injury may result. Rules were established to ensure fair play and minimize the risk of injury. There is no place for coaches who let their players violate the rules or who encourage poor sportsmanship.

Conditioning

Athletes must be conditioned to perform well and withstand the stresses of competition in both contact and noncontact sports (see Putting It into Practice 3-3). To repeat a time-honored phrase: "Get in shape for sports; don't use sports to get in shape." General conditioning is beneficial for almost all sports, but an athlete should be especially prepared for the rigors and stresses of his or her specific activity. For example, the football linebacker who is blocked below the waist must have strength in the thigh and leg muscles to support the knee when it is stressed. The gymnast must have flexibility in the hamstrings and lower back to withstand the stresses of mounts and dismounts. The recreational runner must develop muscular endurance in the lower extremities to avoid the inherent risk of overuse injuries.

Regardless of the activity, the athlete's front line of protection is proper conditioning. Conditioning for injury prevention is an active, year-long process and should include all the components of fitness development: cardiovascular endurance, flexibility, speed, muscular strength, muscular endurance, agility, and coordination. Too often, fitness programs emphasize strength development at the expense of equally important components such as flexibility and endurance. The coach and athletic health care professional must understand the nature of the activity and condition the athlete accordingly. Training for performance and injury prevention must be based on scientific principles (see Chapter 4).

Systematic progression is one of the most important principles of conditioning for injury prevention. The development of any type of fitness is based upon a countless number of biological adaptations (see Chapter 8). For exam-

Systematic progression: A conditioning technique in which muscles are repeatedly stressed to gain high levels of strength. Progression should be achieved slowly over time.

ple, an athlete does not attain high levels of strength all at once. First the athlete stresses the muscles and gains a small amount of strength. Then he or she stresses the muscles again, gaining more strength. The athlete repeats this process many times until she or he attains high levels of strength. The athlete must be encouraged to develop fitness slowly and progressively, particularly early in the season. Failure to progressively develop fitness is probably the cause of early-season overuse injuries such as **arthralgia** of the patella (kneecap) or femur (thigh or thighbone), **anterior tibial periostitis** in runners, or **medial epicondylitis** in pitchers

and other throwers. Regular and progressively tolerable conditioning programs provide a measure of defense against overuse injuries.

The coach and athletic trainer are critical to the conditioning process. They must have an artist's feel for maximizing the rate of biological adaptation. If they work athletes too hard, there will be injuries. On the other hand, if they do not work athletes hard enough, the athletes will not be adequately conditioned. The coach and athletic trainer must also consider the environmental temperature when designing the conditioning program—a workout easily tolerated one day may be

Arthralgia: Pain in the joints.

Anterior tibial periostitis: Inflammation of the periostium (outer surface of the bone) of the anterior tibia.

Medial epicondylitis: Pain and tenderness of the tendons near the medial epicondyle of the humerus. More common among skilled tennis players than among novices.

PUTTING IT INTO PRACTICE 3-3

Preventing Injuries Through Conditioning

The components of fitness should be objectively measured and deficiencies systematically corrected.

Endurance

- *Examples of tests:* Treadmill, field tests (e.g., 12-min run, step test), swim test.
- *Endurance development:* Overdistance (jogging, lap swimming, etc.), interval training.

Body Composition

- *Examples of tests:* Skinfolds, underwater weighing.
- *Principles of weight loss:* Limit weight loss to 1 to 2 lb per week. Emphasize proper diet and exercise.

Flexibility

- *Examples of tests:* Sit and reach, measurement of

range of motion using a goniometer (a device that measures joint angles).
- *Developing flexibility:* Static (stationary) stretching exercises.

Strength and Power

- *Examples of tests:* Isokinetic dynamometer, weight lifts (bench press, power clean, squat, etc.), pull-ups, standing long jump.
- *Developing strength and power:* Weight training, plyometrics (see Chapter 4 for a discussion of plyometrics), manual resistance exercise, calisthenics.

Muscle Endurance

- *Examples of tests:* Sit-ups, pull-ups, push-ups, wall sitting (phantom chair—leaning up against a wall with knees and hips flexed

at 90°, as if sitting on an invisible chair).
- *Developing muscle endurance:* High-repetition resistive exercises.

Speed

- *Examples of tests:* Sprints (land or water), maximum work tests (10 to 16 s) on a bicycle ergometer (a stationary bike used to measure work capacity).
- *Developing speed:* Sprinting, strength training, high knee sprinting.

Agility

- *Examples of tests:* Specific agility tests that approximate the agility requirement of the sport, such as run and cut tests for football.
- *Developing agility:* Specific agility drills, resistive exercise, sprinting.

intolerable on a day when the air temperature is extremely high. Part Three (Chapters 14 to 23) discusses exercises for preventing specific types of injuries.

Equipment

After physical conditioning, the athlete's next line of defense against injury is equipment (see Boxes 3-1 and 3-2). In sports such as football, ice hockey, and lacrosse, athletic equipment shields the athlete from mechanical shock and trauma and provides a vehicle for participation in the sport. Athletic programs should use only properly fitting and good-quality equipment (see Putting It into Practice 3-4 and 3-5, p. 49, for discussions about fitting football helmets and shoulder pads). Poorly maintained or substandard equipment could cause a serious injury.

Protective equipment is becoming popular in sports such as cycling and racketball. Even casual cyclists are wearing helmets to protect themselves from head injuries. Racketball players should wear eye protectors to prevent eye injuries (Figure 3-5, p. 50).

In recent years, sports equipment manufacturers have lost a number of product liability suits and been forced to pay millions of dollars in damages. These lawsuits have resulted in an effort to increase the safety of athletic equipment. However, even the safest equipment can become dangerous if improperly used or fitted. It is the coaches' and athletic health care professionals' responsibility to make sure the equipment fits and is used according to the manufacturer's recommendations.

Another associated issue is the use of the equipment itself to cause injury. For example, the change in the football helmet's composition from leather to

BOX 3-1   **Results of Damaged Equipment and Poor Facility Use**

During a preseason football practice, a blocking sled accidentally struck a player's leg. Evaluation of the injury by the athletic trainer revealed a deep laceration of the mid-Achilles tendon with almost complete severance. After the athlete was taken to the hospital, the piece of equipment was found to have developed a crack on the normally smooth, curved portion of a runner. The cracked runner struck the player and caused a career-ending injury. Two preventable problems led to the incident: (1) poor maintenance of the equipment and (2) poor supervision in that the player should not have been in a position to be struck by the sled.

BOX 3-2   **NOCSAE**

In 1969, The National Operating Committee on the Standards of Athletic Equipment (NOCSAE) was formed to examine safety standards for football helmets. By 1974, NOCSAE had developed voluntary standards to decrease head injuries in football by establishing minimum impact-attenuation standards for football helmets. All football helmets, whether new or reconditioned, used in secondary schools, colleges, and universities should have the NOCSAE seal on them and a warning label about improper tackling technique and not using the helmet as a weapon. In the near future, NOCSAE will examine and set standards for other pieces of protective equipment, such as baseball helmets, for the direct purpose of preventing injury associated with equipment failure.

Fitting a Football Helmet

Despite recent improvements in the area of football safety, head injuries still seem to come with the turf in this collision sport. Thanks to rule changes prohibiting butt blocking and face tackling, and to industry helmet standards, the incidence of such injuries has been greatly reduced. However, even more head injuries could be prevented if more care were taken in fitting the helmet to the individual player.

In too many instances, the athlete fits himself, the coach or equipment manager does not give enough attention to each individual fit, or an entire team is fitted in a haphazard approach that consists of each player trying on various helmets until he finds one that "feels good." The end result is a poorly fitted helmet, which could be a contributing factor to a serious head injury.

Severe damage can be done to the brain whenever the head strikes (or is struck by) an object with great force. The impact of the brain against the irregular projections on the interior of the skull can cause hemorrhaging within the brain. A properly fitted and maintained helmet can minimize the force transmitted to the brain from blows to the head through absorption of kinetic energy. An improperly fitted helmet may not adequately dissipate the force of such blows.

Coaches should follow specifications for helmet fitting as provided by the manufacturer. In general, however, there are a few ground rules to follow.

When the coach fits a helmet, the player's hair should be at normal length and should be wet, to best simulate the hair's condition during actual play. Measure the perimeter of the head exactly one inch above the eyebrow. Make sure the measuring tape is pulled snug. Convert the measurement in inches to hat size (see chart). Arrange helmets from small to large. In some cases, it may be necessary to go one or more sizes smaller or larger than the determined hat size for a good fit. An individual with an irregular head shape may get a better fit with an air helmet because this type of helmet conforms better.

When fitted correctly, the front edge of the shell should rest approximately $\frac{3}{4}''$ (one finger width) above the eyebrow, and the athlete's ear and the shell's ear-hole should match up. There should be at least $\frac{3}{4}''$ space between the athlete's head and the plastic outer shell and not more than a $1\frac{1}{2}''$ space.

The best fit resists motion of the helmet on the head. Remove the jaw pads and ask the athlete to flex his neck, resisting your efforts to rotate the helmet from side to side. Although any helmet will rotate on the head if enough force is applied, use enough pressure to determine whether or not the skin on the forehead moves with the helmet. If the skin doesn't move, the helmet is not snug enough. Also, rotate the helmet up and down to be sure that the front edge of the shell does not come down on the bridge of the nose and that the rear edge of the shell does not impinge on the nape of the neck. All helmets should have a nose bumper pad.

Jaw pads of proper thickness will help minimize side-to-side rotation of the helmet. There should be no space between the jaw pads and the jaw and cheek. A properly adjusted chin strap will help minimize forward and backward rotation of the helmet. Always use a four-point chinstrap, with equal tension on all four attachments and no slack in the straps. Also, be sure the cup is centered on the chinstrap.

Helmet Fitting

	Head Measurement (in Inches)	Hat Size
Small	$19\frac{3}{8}$	$6\frac{1}{8}$
	$19\frac{3}{4}$	$6\frac{1}{4}$
	$20\frac{1}{8}$	$6\frac{3}{8}$
	$20\frac{1}{2}$	$6\frac{1}{2}$
	$20\frac{7}{8}$	$6\frac{5}{8}$
Medium	$21\frac{1}{4}$	$6\frac{3}{4}$
	$21\frac{5}{8}$	$6\frac{7}{8}$
	22	7
	$22\frac{3}{8}$	$7\frac{1}{8}$
	$22\frac{3}{4}$	$7\frac{1}{4}$
Large	$23\frac{1}{8}$	$7\frac{3}{8}$
	$23\frac{1}{2}$	$7\frac{1}{2}$
	$23\frac{7}{8}$	$7\frac{5}{8}$
	$24\frac{1}{4}$	$7\frac{3}{4}$
	$24\frac{5}{8}$	$7\frac{7}{8}$
Extralarge	25	8
	$25\frac{3}{8}$	$8\frac{1}{8}$
	$25\frac{3}{4}$	$8\frac{1}{4}$
	$26\frac{1}{8}$	$8\frac{3}{8}$

SOURCE: Reprinted from Wilkerson, G. B. The fine art of helmet fitting. *The First Aider* (a publication of Cramer Products, Inc.) 52:8–9, April–May 1982. Used by permission.

(continued on next page)

Fitting a Football Helmet (*continued*)

The athletic trainer should be sure the football helmet is neither too small nor too large. The helmet should be above the eyebrows, pressure should be on the crown of the head, not the brow, and the player should not feel any other pressure points. Jaw pads should feel firm against the face, and the helmet should not twist from side to side.

The chin strap should be snug enough so the helmet does not move up and down. The athletic trainer should adjust the strap for the player's comfort.

The athletic trainer should check to see that the back of the helmet is not too low; if it is, it could injure the vertebrae of the neck.

plastic resulted in blocking and tackling techniques in which the helmet was used as a weapon rather than as a protective device. The coach and athletic trainer should always be wary of practices that may injure their athletes or the athletes' opponents.

Facilities

The physical environment in which athletes participate must be free of un-necessary hazards. Most activities have enough inherent risks without adding a hazardous or improperly utilized playing area. Both practice and competition facilities must be actively and continually monitored and maintained. They must be well lighted and free of uneven surfaces. The walls, bleachers, and poles close to playing areas must be padded to cushion incidental contact. When multiple activities are occurring in the same facility, such as basketball

---

PUTTING IT INTO PRACTICE 3-5

Fitting Shoulder Pads

The two styles of shoulder pads used in American football are *flat pads* (also called "pro-style" or quarterback pads) and *cantilever pads* (named for the bridge that extends over the shoulder). Flat pads provide less protection than cantilever pads but allow more mobility. Large, double cantilever pads, called "big boys" or linebacker pads, provide the most protection but allow less mobility because of their bulk.

Shoulder pads should protect the sternum (breastbone), clavicle (collarbone), acromioclavicular joint, deltoid (shoulder joint) muscles, and scapulae (shoulder blades). In the event of shoulder contusion (bruising of shoulder tissue), the shoulder pads can be supplemented with a rubber donut pad. Properly fitting shoulder pads are

important for preventing injury. If the pads are too loose, they may slide and cause an injury to the acromioclavicular joint or neck. If the pads are too tight, they impinge on the player's neck or cause the deltoid flaps (epaulets) to dig into the deltoid muscle when contact is made with another player.

Determine pad width for each player. The pads should extend to the end of the acro-mioclavicular joint. (This width can be precisely measured with anthropometric calipers, a device that measures skeletal diameters). The neck opening should be large enough to allow mobility without impinging on the neck yet not so loose that it lets the pads slide around. Straps should be firmly adjusted but not so tight that they are uncomfortable. Inspect shoulder pads regularly.

Shoulder pads should fit snugly so there is no space between the pads and the shoulders. When the player raises his arms above his head, the pads should not pinch his neck; the ends of the pads should cover the tips of the shoulders and the deltoid muscles. Shown here are cantilever pads.

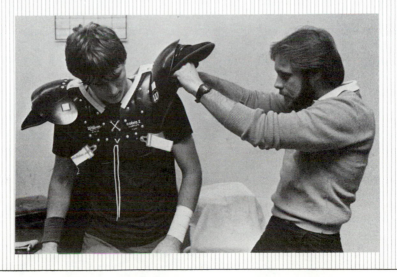

practice on one court and softball pitching practice on the adjacent court, precautions must be taken to prevent a ball from one activity from rolling across the floor onto the other court.

Coaches and athletic trainers must develop a sense of awareness and be alert to unsafe equipment or facility design and use. They should take appropriate steps to eliminate problems before injuries occur. As is the case with other injury-prevention strategies, those in charge must ensure that all activities are properly supervised (see Putting It into Practice 3-6).

The Athlete's Psychosocial Problems

Researchers in performance and injury prevention are increasingly studying psychosocial factors. Since self-motivation and attitude affect performance, it seems logical that the athlete who is experiencing some emotional difficulty may be functioning at an increased risk of injury. Bramwell's study of high school football players found that those who scored highest on a life-adjustment scale (more life stresses) modified for athletes had significantly higher incidences of injury than those who scored lower. The study concluded that high school football players who have experienced serious emotional and personal disruption were at greater risk of injury.

Currently, psychological testing is widespread only at the professional sports level. With the increasing emphasis upon the holistic approach to medicine (prevention of disease through a life-style based upon proper diet, exercise, and emotional well-being), which includes the prevention of sport injuries, it is crucial that those responsible for athletes get to know their emotional and psychological needs and behaviors and counsel the athletes if necessary.

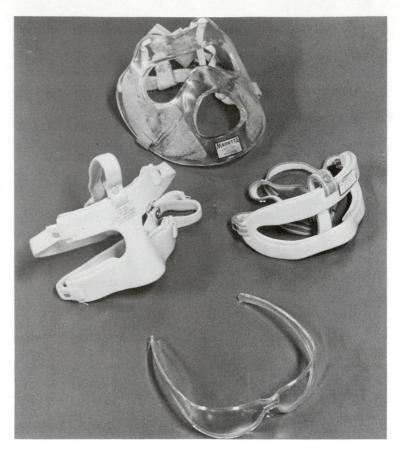

Figure 3-5 Racquetball players often wear eye protectors similar to the one at the bottom of the picture. Eye and nose protectors are also worn in sports such as football and hockey to protect injured areas.

Inadequate Field Care and Rehabilitation

Many reinjuries are often the result of poor initial management and rehabilitation. Kent reported that F. S. Lloyd and J. L. Marshall surveyed 450 amateur athletes and found that 50 percent waited five days or longer after they were injured before seeing a physician. Lloyd and Marshall stated, "There was a tendency for the athletes to minimize the painfulness of the injury and to disregard serious symptoms such as swelling, stiffness, instability, locking, and limping." Many of these unreported injuries develop into chronic conditions when the athlete continues to participate. This attitude is exemplified by Jim Otto's statement (Figure 3-1, p. 36).

Improper initial management and rehabilitation could conceivably be grounds for litigation against an institution or athletic trainer.

Pain and soreness are indisputable factors in sports participation. However, the coach and athletic trainer should not establish an atmosphere where injuries go unreported. They should be capable of recognizing a significant injury because athletes tend to not report painful symptoms. Coaches and athletic trainers should be just as acutely aware of signs of overtraining and injury as they are of signs of improved fitness. Overtraining and injury symptoms include sudden decrease in performance level, irritability, limping, change in attitude, sluggishness, insomnia, increased susceptibility to illness, and nonspecific pain. Each factor equally affects performance. When injuries do occur, all involved individuals must be prepared to handle them intelligently and quickly. Correct emergency care must be administered, and then rehabilitation must be applied.

1. *Emergency action plan*: Athletes, coaches, and the athletic trainer should write and understand a protocol for dealing with injuries. Emergency procedures for serious injuries sustained on the field should be practiced regularly (see Chapter 10). These procedures should detail individual responsibilities for tasks such as phoning the ambulance and physician, criteria for moving an injured athlete, and crowd control. Injury procedures should ensure that athletes receive necessary and competent medical attention as soon as possible.
2. *Rehabilitation*: Once an injury has been recognized, the next step is to rehabilitate the injured part to a point that allows an athlete's safe return to participation. Too often

PUTTING IT INTO PRACTICE 3-6

Preventing Injury Through Proper Athletic Administration

- *Supervision*: Members of the athletic training and coaching staffs should have clearly defined responsibilities.
- *Consistency*: Define and enforce rules.
- *Equipment maintenance*: Regularly inspect and repair or replace damaged equipment.
- *Proper fit*: Fitting should be performed only by experienced personnel. Issue no ill-fitting equipment.
- *Emergency procedures*: Establish and often practice the guidelines.
- *Rehabilitation*: Let no injured athlete return to play until he or she is rehabilitated.

athletes feel that the day the sling or cast is removed they are ready to return to participation at preinjury levels of ability and intensity. The rehabilitation must be scientifically applied and supervised by a trained professional (athletic trainer or sports physical therapist) working under the direction of a physician. Only when the risk of reinjury has been reduced can the athlete be returned to participation. (See Chapter 12 for a discussion of principles of rehabilitation.)

Premature Return to Participation

The athlete's premature return to practice or a game when the injury is not fully healed increases the risk of reinjury or injury to another body part. An athlete's readiness to return to participation should not be guessed at; the determination must be as objective as possible. Here are five criteria for return to participation:

1. *Full, pain-free range of motion (ROM)*: Incomplete and/or painful **range of motion** indicates that the injury may still be acute. An in-

Range of motion (ROM): Movement of a joint through its normal range of motion.

jury can be totally healed, but a residual loss of motion may be present. However, this reduced ROM may increase the risk of reinjury. ROM should be restored both actively and passively. Active ROM is an athlete's ability to move a joint through its normal range; passive ROM is the range a joint can be moved by other people.

2. *Normal or average strength and power:* Strength can be tested by **bilateral comparison** using manual muscle tests or measured objectively by an **isokinetic dynamometer** (Figure 3-6), **cable tensiometer,** or weights. Because strength is proportional to the cross-sectional area of a muscle, circumference measurements are useful for establishing the extent of rehabilitation. If muscle weakness in one limb predisposed the athlete to injury, then an acceptable level of strength in both limbs should be developed before the athlete is allowed to return to participation.

3. *Excessive emotional concerns:* If an athlete seems excessively concerned about injury, he or she is not likely to concentrate on the activity. Extreme anxiety about the activity or movement that caused an injury could lead to reinjury or a new injury.

4. *Functional stability:* The evaluation should include an assessment of the athlete's ability to perform the skills of the sport. The athlete should have normal, coordinated patterns of movement, with all injury-compensating movement patterns, such as limping, eliminated.

5. *Relative freedom from pain:* Pain may indicate that the injury is still acute.

Failure to meet any one or a combination of these five criteria should pre-clude athletes from returning to participation. The decision to return to active participation should be based upon input from the athlete, coach, athletic trainer, and physician and objective criteria, such as the results of strength, power, flexibility, and endurance tests. Once athletes return to participation, they should be closely monitored to prevent relapse.

The severity of the injury is also an important consideration in predicting a successful **prognosis** (see Chapter 4). Some injuries, particularly those repaired by surgery, take a considerable amount of time to heal. Even though the injury is apparently healed, the athlete may not have sufficient tissue strength to avoid reinjury.

Preventing Specific Injuries

The cause of specific injuries varies according to the sport. The three principal measures for preventing injuries are conditioning, which strengthens vulnerable body parts to withstand the rigors of athletics; proper technique, which maximizes the athlete's biomechanical efficiency so that the body's strongest muscles are bearing most of the load; and adequate supervision, which ensures that athletes are participating in a controlled environment. However, even if these guidelines are rigorously followed, injuries will still occur. The following discussions briefly summarize injury-prevention strategies for the major athletic injuries. Part Three of the book (Chapters 14 to 23) details exercises to improve specific body segments.

Foot Injuries

Foot injuries are particularly common in running and basketball. Proper footwear is the best preventive measure for foot injuries. Athletes should be fit-

Prognosis: Expected outcome of an injury or disease; the prospect of getting better.

Bilateral comparison: Comparison of a body part on one side of the body with the identical part on the other side.

Isokinetic dynamometer: A device that measures isokinetic power output (force exerted at constant speed) for testing and rehabilitative resistive exercise purposes.

Cable tensiometer: A device that uses cables and strain gauges to measure isometric strength.

ted with shoes that meet individual anatomical characteristics. The athletic trainer should watch the athlete walk and run and note any abnormalities that might affect the biomechanics of the foot. Athletes with significant anatomical deviations, such as severely pronated (flattened longitudinal arch) feet, should be referred to a podiatrist for possible fitting of **orthotics.**

Specific foot exercises such as rolling up a towel or picking up marbles with the toes may help prevent injury in athletes prone to foot problems. Shock-absorbing inserts may help reduce shock to the feet and lower extremities. The amount and intensity of the training should not be excessive (taking into consideration the athlete's fitness). Injuries of the feet are discussed in Chapter 22.

Ankle Sprains

Ankle sprains are extremely prevalent in sports such as basketball, gymnastics, soccer, tennis, and football (see Chapter 22). Properly fitting shoes are important for preventing injury. Shoes should provide adequate lateral stability (shoes of the correct width help provide more stability that those that are too narrow). High-top shoes may help prevent ankle sprains, particularly when used in conjunction with tape support (see the appendix). Whether tape support is effective is debatable. Tape does provide some support, but the support diminishes with time, so the wrap should be reapplied daily.

Strengthening the plantar (calf) dorsiflexor (shin) muscles gives the ankle a measure of functional stability. All athletes playing sports with a high rate of ankle injuries should practice ankle eversion (turning the ankle outward) exercises (**isometric** and manually resisted). Statically stretching the calf and Achilles tendon is also an important part of preventing and treating ankle injuries.

Scrutinize playing surfaces for irregu-

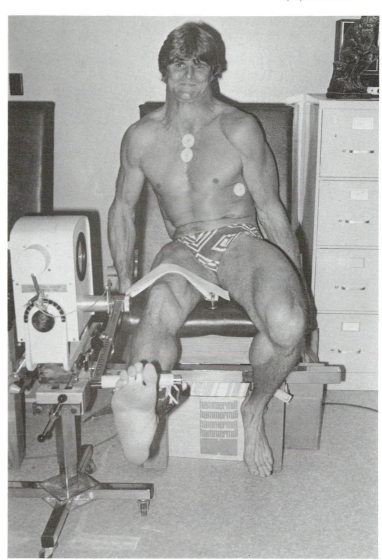

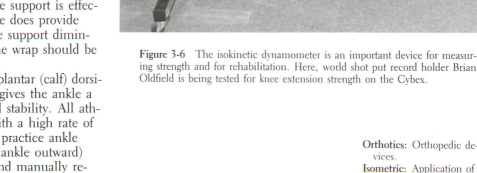

Figure 3-6 The isokinetic dynamometer is an important device for measuring strength and for rehabilitation. Here, world shot put record holder Brian Oldfield is being tested for knee extension strength on the Cybex.

Orthotics: Orthopedic devices.

Isometric: Application of force without movement. Also called static.

larities such as gopher holes and protruding sprinkler heads. Runners who want to run on soft surfaces to prevent overuse injuries should very carefully watch for potential hazards on the grass or the sides of roads.

Injury of the Achilles Tendon, Calf Muscle Strains, Shin Splints

These overuse injuries are particularly common in runners, especially deconditioned (previously inactive) beginners. Hard or irregular running surfaces contribute to these injuries. Shock-absorbing shoe inserts sometimes help prevent these injuries.

The best preventive measures for Achilles tendon–calf injuries are **dorsiflexion** stretching exercises (see Chapter 22), **plantar-flexion** strengthening exercises (heel raisers or manually resisted plantar-flexion exercise; exercise machines, such as the Orthotron, also provide plantar-flexion resistance), and running shoes with a slightly raised heel. Also very important is a proper training program, with the right amount and intensity of exercise.

Shin splints are caused by a number of factors, including weak, inflexible muscles, running on hard surfaces, overuse, and malalignment **syndromes.** An excellent way to prevent shin splints is to perform exercises that strengthen the ankle dorsiflexors. The best exercise is to apply manual resistance to the athlete's foot during active dorsiflexion. Resistance can also be provided with surgical tubing or with machines (e.g., the Orthotron or Cybex) designed for that purpose.

Knee Injuries

Knee injuries (see Chapter 21) are most common in contact sports, but they regularly occur in almost any kind of physical activity. The three most common injuries are **sprains,** meniscus (fibrocartilage of the knee joint) damage, and patellofemoral disorders. Increasing the strength and flexibility of

the calf and thigh muscles is the best measure for preventing knee injuries (see Chapters 20 to 22). Strengthening exercises should include heel raisers, knee extensions, hamstring curls, squats or leg presses, hip **adduction** (manual or machine resistance), and hip **abduction.** Some of these exercises are contraindicated for patellofemoral disorders (see Chapter 21 regarding the patella-protection program).

Serious knee injuries are particularly prevalent in football. Preventive measures include the use of turf shoes or soccer shoes with smaller cleats (cleats reduce friction between the shoe and turf), lateral-protection braces in linemen, and enforcement of the rules. Spear blocks to the lateral flexed knee have been implicated as a cause of the "unhappy triad" (rupture of the medial collateral, anterior cruciate ligaments, and medial meniscus; see Chapter 21). Unsafe blocking and tackling techniques should not be tolerated.

Patellofemoral disorders, such as **chondromalacia,** are common problems, particularly among female runners (see Chapter 21). People who are prone to these disorders should avoid conditions that produce excessive patellofemoral compression, such as climbing or descending stairs or hills, full range of motion knee extensions, and squatting. Preventive measures include short-arc knee extension (last twenty degrees of the range of motion using light weight and high—twenty to forty—repetitions), properly fitting shoes, appropriate training schedules (not excessive), avoiding recreational sports such as snow and water skiing (if possible), and anti-inflammatory medication (under direction of a physician). Stopping when pain is present will help prevent serious inflammatory flare-ups.

Back Injuries

Back pain, extremely common in the general population, is also a problem among athletes. Back injuries occur in all sports, but they are most common

Adduction: Movement of a part toward the midline of the body.
Abduction: Movement of a part away from the midline of the body.

Dorsiflexion: Upward flexion of the ankle by pointing the toes toward the shin.
Plantar flexion: Downward flexion of the ankle by pointing the toes away from the shin.

Chondromalacia: Softening of the patella's (kneecap) cartilage. Not necessarily painful.
Shin splints: Pain between the knee and ankle, mainly from overuse. The course of the injury may include strain, stress fracture, and vascular entrapment.
Syndrome: A group of signs and symptoms that appear together in a predictable manner.

Sprain: Disruption or injury of a ligament.

in those activities that involve twisting, such as discus throwing, pitching, golf, gymnastics, and diving, and placing heavy loads on the back muscles, such as weight lifting and rugby. The most common causes of back strain are weak and inflexible back and abdominal muscles and poor body mechanics. Chapter 16 describes back exercises and proper body mechanics.

Body mechanics must be stressed to athletes with back problems. Improper sitting, sleeping, and driving postures can undue the good achieved from the most judicious back-strengthening program. All athletes should be taught to lift correctly to prevent back injury.

Tennis Elbow

Lateral epicondylitis (tennis elbow), injury to the common extensor tendon of the forearm, occurs most often from racket sports. This injury is caused by a combination of poor technique during the backhand by bending the elbow, hitting the ball late, and not stepping into the ball; muscle weakness and inflexibility; and overuse. Inappropriate equipment, such as a heavy racket strung too tightly or with the wrong grip size, may also contribute to the problem.

Preventive techniques are extensively discussed in Chapter 18. Briefly, tennis players should work on upper body strength and flexibility. Emphasis should be upon good technique. Convince the athlete that he or she can generate much more power by initiating the shot from the legs rather than from the arms (and thus avoiding overstressing the smaller upper body muscles). A tennis elbow brace may help prevent this problem in athletes prone to lateral epicondylitis.

Shoulder Strains

Shoulder strains are common among throwing athletes, such as pitchers and javelin throwers, and among swimmers. The muscles of the shoulder are rela-tively small and easily injured from overuse. Athletes should diligently maintain shoulder strength and flexibility, particularly in the often-neglected rotator cuff muscles (muscles that rotate the humerus). Chapter 17 discusses shoulder strength and flexibility exercises. Encourage athletes to report any signs of shoulder pain or weakness so that they may be rested and actively rehabilitated.

Head and Neck Injuries

Head and neck injuries are the most potentially dangerous injuries the athletic trainer will encounter. These injuries account for the majority of sports fatalities. Fortunately, the fatality rate for these injuries in football has fallen from 3.4 cases per 100,000 participants in 1968 to today's rate of approximately 0.5 per 100,000. The drop in fatality rate corresponds to a national effort to reduce serious football accidents through improved equipment, safer playing techniques, and better conditioning of the athletes.

Head injuries occur most often in contact sports such as football, boxing, and hockey, but they can also occur in noncontact sports such as alpine skiing. The head and neck injury rate in boxing is 6 per 1000. Preventing head injuries involves minimizing exposure, protecting the head, and not tolerating unsafe sports techniques. Minimizing exposure is an important consideration in boxing. Almost 100 percent of boxers experience some degree of trauma to the brain after a fight. Limiting the number of fights may lessen the long-term consequences of boxing.

Many fatal head and neck injuries occur from unsupervised diving. Warn athletes about exposing themselves to unnecessary risks of diving in shallow pools or natural streams.

In sports such as football, the helmet is an important protection against head injuries. Always use properly fitted, high-quality helmets in sports carrying a high risk of head injury (Putting It into

Practice 3-4, p. 47). However, improper use of the helmet can increase the risk of these injuries; never teach or tolerate spear blocking and tackling. Likewise, improperly fitting shoulder pads can increase the risk of neck injury (Putting It into Practice 3-5, p. 49).

Measures to prevent neck injuries include ensuring proper physical conditioning, avoiding dangerous techniques, and supervising potentially dangerous activities. Athletes in sports with a high rate of neck injuries, such as rugby, football, wrestling, and judo, should participate in a year-round neck-conditioning program. The program should work the neck in all its ranges of motion (flexion, extension, lateral flexion, and rotation) through the use of manual resistance, a weighted neck harness, neck machines (e.g., Nautilus), and neck bridges. Never permit dangerous techniques such as grabbing the face mask and spearing. Carefully supervise potentially dangerous activities, such as trampoline. Never let athletes attempt techniques for which they are not ready.

References

Blackburn, T. A. (ed.). *Guidelines for Preseason Athletic Participation Evaluation*. Washington, D.C.: American Physical Therapy Association, 1979.

Blyth, C. S., and F. O. Mueller. Injury rates vary with coaching. *The Physician and Sportsmedicine* 2:45–50, 1974.

Blyth, C. S., and D. C. Arnold. *Forty-seventh Annual Survey of Football Fatalities 1931–1978*. National Collegiate Athletic Association and American Football Coaches Association, 1979.

Bramwell, S. T., et al. Psychosocial factors in athletic injuries. *Journal of Human Stress* 1:6–20, 1975.

Califano, J. A. *U.S. Department of Health, Education and Welfare News*. Washington, D.C., Feb. 25, 1979.

Fairbanks, L. L. Return to sports participation. *The Physician and Sportsmedicine* 7:71–74, 1979.

Garrick, J. G. Determinants of return to athletic activity. *Orthopedic Clinics of North America* 14:317–321, 1983.

Garrick, J. G., and R. K. Requa. Injuries in high school sports. *Pediatrics* 61:465–469, 1978.

Hackworth, C., K. Jacobs, and C. O'Neill. A coaches' clinic for injury management in youth sports. *The Physician and Sportsmedicine* 11:59–64, 1983.

Jackson, D. W., et al. Injury prediction in the young athlete: a preliminary report. *American Journal of Sports Medicine* 6:6–14, 1978.

Kent, F. Athletes wait too long to report injuries. *The Physician and Sportsmedicine* 10:127–129, 1982.

Kraus, J. F., and C. Conroy. Mortality and morbidity from injuries in sports and recreation. *Annual Review of Public Health* 5:163–192, 1984.

Lloyd, F. S., G. G. Deaver, and F. R. Eastwood. *Safety in Athletics: The Prevention and Treatment of Athletic Injuries*. Philadelphia: W. B. Saunders, 1939.

Lysens, R., A. Steverlynck, Y. van den Auweele, J. Lefevre, L. Renson, A. Claessens, and M. Ostyn. The predictability of sports injuries. *Sports Medicine* 1:6–10, 1984.

Marshall, J. L., et al. Joint looseness: a function of the person and the joint. *Medicine and Science in Sports and Exercise* 12:89–94, 1980.

Nicholas, J. A. If we understand sports injuries we can prevent them. *Modern Medicine* 42:48–54, 1974.

Nicholas, J. A. Risk factors, sports medicine, and the orthopedic system: an overview. *Journal of Sports Medicine* 3:243–259, 1975.

Nicholas, J. A., and M. Friedman. Orthopedic problems in middle-aged athletes. *The Physician and Sportsmedicine* 7:39–46, 1979.

O'Donoghue, D. H. *Treatment of Athletic Injuries*. Philadelphia: W. B. Saunders, 1984.

Shaw, J. Will sports survive the product liability suits? *The Physician and Sportsmedicine* 5:19–23, 1977.

Stanish, W. D. Overuse injuries in athletes: a perspective. *Medicine and Science in Sports and Exercise* 16:1–7, 1984.

Strauss, R. H. (ed.). *Sports Medicine and Physiology*. Philadelphia: W. B. Saunders, 1984.

Taerk, G. S. The injury-prone athlete: a psychosocial approach. *Journal of Sports Medicine* 17:187–194, 1977.

Witman, P. A., M. Melvin, and J. A. Nicholas. Common problems seen in a metropolitan sports injury clinic. *The Physician and Sportsmedicine* 9:105–110, 1981.

Wright, D. Prevention of injuries in sport. *Physiotherapy* 55:114–119, 1979.

Physiological Adaptation to Conditioning

4

P HYSICAL capacity, including such factors as speed, strength, endurance, flexibility, and agility, limits an athlete's ability to perform in sports. For example, an athlete must have the physical prerequisites to throw a discus 235 feet, sprint 100 meters in 10.0 seconds, or run a marathon in 2 hours and 10 minutes. Likewise, an injured athlete must regain his or her necessary level of physical conditioning before being allowed to return to the field. Empirical evidence and numerous studies have demonstrated the importance of conditioning in preventing injuries. Athletes must develop the physical fitness characteristics their particular sport demands by following a systematic and progressive program of applied scientific conditioning principles.

Physiologically, the purpose of a physical training session is to stress the body so that it adapts to the rigors of physical effort. If the stress is not sufficient to overload the body, no adaptation occurs. If a stress cannot be tolerated, injury or overtraining results. The greatest improvements in an athlete's performance will occur when the appropriate exercise stresses are introduced into the training program.

Many athletic injuries result from inappropriate application of the training stimulus. Too severe a training program invariably causes injury. Just as the physician is involved in the prevention of disease, the athletic trainer should be involved in the prevention of athletic injury. The results of the conditioning program should be gradual development of an appropriate level of fitness and minimal risk of injury (see Chapter 3 for discussion of injury prevention). This chapter explores the principles of the body's physiological adaptation to physical stresses of conditioning.

Physical Training and Conditioning Elements

The conditioning principles include stress adaptation, overload, specificity, individual differences, progression, and warm-up. First we discuss the techniques and then survey the athletic trainer's role in the application of these elements to the rehabilitation of an injured athlete.

Physical conditioning is a critical factor in preventing injury. This crew team trains for over eighteen hours a week, perfecting technique with both long and short rowing movements and building up cardiovascular endurance and strength by running and working out in the weight room.

Stress Adaptation

In the late 1940s, Hans Selye formulated the theory of stress adaptation that has had a profound effect upon medicine and has tremendous implications in conditioning for sports and physical activity. Selye called his theory the **general adaptation syndrome (GAS)** and described three processes involved in response to a *stressor* (a stressor is something, such as exercise, that upsets the body's **homeostasis** or balance):

1. Alarm reaction
2. Resistance development
3. Exhaustion

Every athlete, coach, and athletic trainer should be extremely familiar with each process. (See Figure 4-1.)

During the initial response to the stressor, the alarm reaction, the organism mobilizes its resources. During running, for example, the body combats stress by increasing the transport of oxygen. The body accomplishes this increase by augmenting cardiac output, redistributing blood to active muscle, and increasing the rate of **metabolism.** Because the body's capacity to adjust to various stressors is limited, the body adapts its capacity so that the stressor is less of a threat to the body's homeostasis in the future.

The body adapts its capacity or builds its reserves during the resistance-development stage. This stage is the goal of physical conditioning. Unfortunately, the optimal attainment of **physiological resistance** (more commonly referred to in athletics as "physical fitness") does not result from just any random stressor. For example, if the stress during physical training is below a critical threshold, there is no training effect. On the other hand, if the stimulus is above the threshold and cannot be tolerated, injury most likely results.

The effectiveness of a stressor in causing an adaptive response depends upon the individual and is relative to any given time or place. For example, running a ten-minute mile may exhaust a sedentary forty-year-old man but essentially cause no adaptive response in a world-class distance runner. Likewise, a training run that can be easily tolerated one day may be completely inappropriate after a prolonged illness. Environment can also affect an individual's performance. An athlete's performance capabilities typically decrease in extreme heat or cold, at high altitude, or in polluted air (see Chapter 25).

When stress becomes intolerable, the organism enters the stage of exhaustion (sometimes called **distress**). This stress

Physiological resistance: Development of the body's adaptation of its capacity to respond to a stressor or build its reserves. Also called physical fitness.

General adaptation syndrome (GAS): Selye's theory describing the body's three-phase response to stress: alarm reaction, resistance development, and exhaustion.

Homeostasis: The body's balance or its physiological equilibrium.

Metabolism: The sum of all the chemical reactions that occur in the body.

Distress: Injury. Another name for the exhaustion stage in Selye's general adaptation syndrome. Distress occurs when the body cannot tolerate a stressor.

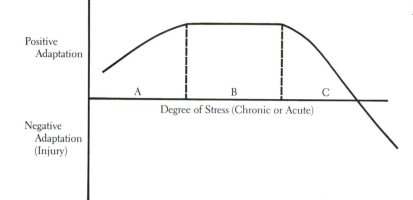

Figure 4-1 The effects of exercise stress on adaptation and breakdown. (A) Stress causes positive adaptation. (B) Increasing stress causes no additional adaptation. (C) Stress cannot be tolerated, and injury results.

can be either *acute* (applied all at once) or *chronic* (occurring over a period of time). Acute exhaustion includes fractures, **sprains,** and **strains;** chronic exhaustion is more subtle and includes overtraining, stress fractures, and emotional stress.

Stress Adaptation and the Injured Athlete. Selye determined that the body has difficulty adapting to several stressors that occur at once, such as overtraining or disease or injury. In such a circumstance, the body may experience a variety of other injuries in response to workouts that previously may have been easily tolerated. Preventing these distress injuries in already injured athletes is obviously extremely hard to do because of athletes' natural enthusiasm for heavy training and the difficulty in determining at what point the training stimulus is becoming excessive. The athletic trainer can work with or prevent distress injuries by developing a thorough understanding of common diseases and the physical conditioning process and through related experiences over time.

Overload

The basis of the general adaptation syndrome is that a body stressed at a tolerable limit adapts and improves its function. A positive stressor is sometimes called an **overload,** the components of which are repetition, rest, and frequency.

Load is the intensity of the exercise stressor. In strength training, the load is the amount of resistance; in running or swimming, load is speed. In general, the greater the load, the greater are the fatigue and required recovery time. Of all the components of overload, load is probably the most important.

Repetition is the number of times a load is administered. More favorable adaptation tends to occur when the load is administered more than once. Generally, experts agree on the ideal number of repetitions in a given sport. However, these empirical maxims are in a constant state of flux as athletes successfully use overload combinations different from the norm. For example, in middle-distance running and swimming, interval training workouts (repeated bouts of high-intensity exercise) have become extremely demanding due to the success of athletes who have performed repetitions far in excess of those commonly practiced. Sebastian Coe, the great British middle-distance runner, sometimes runs forty repetitions of 440 yards in sixty seconds, which is considerably more than the average world-class runner performs.

Rest is the amount of time between

Overload: A positive stressor that subjects the body to more stress than it is accustomed to. Its components are load, repetition, rest, and frequency.

Sprain: Disruption or injury of a ligament.

Strain: Disruption or injury of a musculotendinous unit. A serious strain is often called a pulled muscle.

repetitions or sets (a set is a group of repetitions). Rest is vitally important for adaptation and should be applied according to the nature of the desired physiological outcome. For example, a weight lifter who desires maximum strength is most concerned with load and as a result requires a considerable amount of rest between exercises. A short rest would impair the weight lifter's strength gain because he or she could not then exert maximum tension because of inadequate recovery. A mountain climber or endurance runner, on the other hand, is more concerned with muscular endurance than with peak strength, so he or she would use short rests to maximize endurance.

Frequency is the number of training sessions per week. In some sports, such as distance running, there has been a tendency toward more frequent training sessions. Unfortunately, this often leads to increases in overuse injuries (see Chapter 3) due to overtraining. More severe training regimens have indeed improved performances in many sports, but such workouts must be tempered with proper recovery periods or injury may result (see Table 4-1).

Overload and the Injured Athlete.
When an athlete is suffering from injury, the affected muscles and joints should be overloaded only with caution because inappropriate stimulus may intensify the problem or cause new injury. Injury rehabilitation should consider such factors as degree of **inflammation,** joint rheology (joint lubrication), and joint and soft tissue integrity (soundness).

Salminen and Vihko, among other researchers, showed that vigorous exercise causes some cellular necrosis (death) of skeletal muscle and local inflammation. In soft tissue that is already inflamed, vigorous exercise may cause further necrosis damage and increase the severity of inflammation. Inflammation must be arrested before skeletal muscle can be significantly conditioned. (Chapters 5, 8, and 21 discuss inflammation and conditioning.) Local swelling stimulates **Golgi tendon organs** to inhibit muscle contraction, which dampens any conditioning effects.

When articular (joint) surfaces are disrupted, either from injury or during surgery, normal joint lubrication may also be hampered, which can damage

Inflammation: Tissue's reaction to trauma, irritation, or infection, characterized by swelling, pain, redness, local temperature increase, and loss of function.

Golgi tendon organs: Receptors within skeletal muscle that sense and inhibit tension.

Table 4-1 *Workouts Designed to Overload the Bodies of a Runner and a Weight Lifter*

Runner	Weight Lifter			
Distance (load): 400 m	Monday and Friday of a 4-day workout			
Speed (load): 65 s	Squats	5 sets	8 reps	300 lb
Repetitions: 10	Pulls (cleans or snatch)	5 sets	5 reps	175–200 lb
Rest: 200-m jog	Heal raises	4 sets	10 reps	250 lb
Frequency (days) per week: 2	Knee extension	4 sets	10 reps	100 lb
Other days: overdistance	Knee flexion	4 sets	10 reps	80 lb
	Sit-ups	4 sets	20 reps	40 lb
	Tuesday and Saturday: Work shoulders, chest, arms			

NOTE: These are generalized plans. The amount of the loads, the number of exercises, and specific exercises will vary according to sport, level of fitness, time of year, and purpose of workout.

articular cartilage if the athlete's exercise rehabilitation program is too severe. And as discussed in Chapters 5 and 8, **adhesions** formed following injury affect the normal gliding actions of soft tissue and create focal weaknesses at the point of injury. An exercise program that is too severe may easily cause reinjury. Similarly, severely injured ligaments need time to heal (see Chapter 7). Prematurely exercising an injured joint will delay healing or cause permanent joint damage.

Specificity of Training

The body adapts specifically to the stress of exercise. The adaptation to endurance exercise (e.g., distance running or swimming) is different from that to strength exercise (e.g., weight lifting) and power exercise (e.g., sprinting). Any training program should reflect the desired adaptation; the more similar the training is to the requirements of the sport being prepared for, the more valuable will be the outcome.

Training has to be specific partly because different motor units perform tasks that require endurance, strength, or power. A muscle contains numerous **motor units,** each unit consisting of a motor nerve and muscle fibers (also see Chapter 5). The muscle fibers are classified as **slow-twitch** (type I) or **fast-twitch** (types IIa and b), depending upon the type of contractions they must perform. Which particular type of fiber in a muscle is called upon (recruited) depends upon the contraction requirements. Endurance activities recruit slow-twitch fibers (type I); strength and power activities recruit fast-twitch fibers (types IIa and b).

Muscle fibers produce different forces and vary in their resistance to fatigue. Slow-twitch fibers are relatively fatigue-resistant but have a lower capacity for tension than the fast-twitch fibers. Type I fibers are smaller than type II ones, and their **threshold to stimulus** is lower. They have a greater blood supply, which enables them to call upon the more fatigue-resistant aerobic (requiring oxygen) metabolic pathways. Type I fibers have a higher capacity to burn fats, which also gives them greater endurance. Low-threshold, slow-twitch fibers are recruited for low-intensity activities such as jogging and also for most tasks of human motion.

Fast-twitch fibers contract more rapidly and forcefully than slow-twitch fibers but fatigue faster. Glycogen, their main fuel, is rapidly depleted during high-intensity exercise. Type II fibers have a less prolific blood supply than type I fibers, which makes them more dependent upon endogenous fuel supplies and less capable of converting energy through aerobic metabolism. High-threshold, fast-twitch fibers are recruited for high-intensity activities such as weight lifting or sprinting.

An athlete trains muscle fibers in proportion to their recruitment. For example, to improve speed, the athlete must recruit and train the fast-twitch fibers through high-intensity exercise. High-repetition, low-intensity exercise, such as distance running, relies on the recruitment of slow-twitch fibers and improves the fiber's oxidative capacity. Concurrently, physiological capacities that facilitate oxygen transport, such as cardiac output and blood volume, are also developed. Low-repetition, high-intensity activities, such as weight training, cause **hypertrophy** of fast-twitch fibers, with some changes to the lower-threshold, slow-twitch fibers. Because the oxygen transport system is less important in these activities, it will experience little or no effect from training.

Different training stimuli can actually interfere with each other. For example, simultaneous participation in a training program designed to stimulate both strength and endurance apparently will interfere with the ability to gain strength (strength training may not interfere with the ability to gain endur-

Adhesion: The binding of adjacent tissue surface, caused by the formation of fibrous (dense) connective tissue.

Motor unit: A structure composed of a motor nerve and many muscle fibers. When the unit is stimulated, all the muscle fibers contract.
Slow-twitch muscle fibers: Fibers well suited for endurance exercise. They have high oxidative capacity, prolific blood supply, many mitochondria, high myoglobin content, relatively small fibers and motor nerves, well-developed ability to use fat as fuel.
Fast-twitch muscle fibers: Fibers well suited for high-intensity exercise. They have a high glycolytic capacity, large fiber diameter and motor nerve, limited blood supply and mitochondrial density, high glycogen content.
Hypertrophy: Increase in size of a muscle fiber; usually stimulated by muscular overload.
Threshold to stimulus: The electrical energy of the nerve impulse required to contract the fibers of a motor unit.

Principles of Injury Prevention and Management

ance—up to a point). Hickson found greater than 20 percent difference among subjects in a strength-endurance training program compared to subjects who trained only for strength (Figure 4-2). He suggested that athletes training for strength may inhibit their ability to gain strength by participating in vigorous endurance activities. Hickson also hypothesized that muscles may be unable to optimally adapt to both forms of exercise.

Motor skills are very task-specific. Henry was among the first to describe the specific development of motor skills, a process he called the **memory drum.** The precise patterns of movement are imprinted on the brain (much as data are imprinted on a computer's magnetic disk) and can be recalled and performed by the athlete. The aim of practice and coaching is to ingrain the correct motion; if an incorrect motion is inscribed on the memory drum, an inappropriate technique will be executed during competition. The more an athlete practices a movement (up to a certain point on a learning curve, depending upon the sport), the more the movement is reinforced on the memory drum. Therefore, the practiced movement *must* be as correct as possible. Henry's research demonstrated that the imprint on the drum was extremely specific: If the speed of the movement was altered, the execution of the movement was much less precise. Therefore, an athlete must not only practice difficult movements but must execute them at the speed to be used in competition.

Specificity and the Injured Athlete. Many athletic injuries are often classified as a single syndrome but actually may result from a combination of unrelated factors. For example, jumper's knee (patellar tendinitis) may be confused with patellofemoral arthrosis, a meniscal tear, an infrapatellar fat pad inflammation, or bursitis of one of the numerous bursae around the knee (see Chapter 21). Improper recognition of

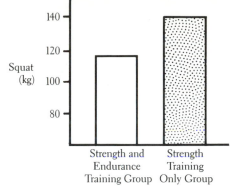

Figure 4-2 Strength changes in response to two types of training. Simultaneously training for strength and endurance interferes with strength development. This study reinforces the importance of specificity of training. (Adapted from Hickson, R. C. Interference of strength development by simultaneously training for strength and endurance. *European Journal of Applied Physiology* 45:255–263, 1980.)

the injury and a subsequent inappropriate rehabilitation program may cause further injury. For instance, some experts recommend a load and stop eccentric exercise program (stopping suddenly during a squatting motion) as part of the treatment for patellar tendinitis. If this program were instituted and the problem was actually patellofemoral arthrosis, the resulting increase in patellofemoral compression might actually increase the irritation of the articular surface of the patella. The physician or athletic trainer must properly identify the problem before instituting rehabilitation.

Strength deficiencies should be identified according to the requirements of the sport. For example, research has shown that throwing speed in baseball is directly related to the strength of the upper extremities, particularly the muscles involved in external rotation, flexion, and extension of the shoulder. The specific muscles involved in a sport's motion should be analyzed and tested. The rehabilitation program should be designed to condition deficient muscles to optimum levels.

Each injured anatomical component should be considered in the condition-

Memory drum: Henry's theory of motor performance: Motor skills are imprinted in the brain; when a motor skill is being performed, the imprinted data are retrieved and played back.

ing process. For example, fast-twitch muscle fibers are trained best through higher intensity resistive exercise; slow-twitch muscle fibers require an exercise regimen involving more repetitions and lower resistance. According to Curwin and Stanish, tendons may be better strengthened through eccentric rather than concentric exercise. As discussed, injured articular surfaces should be protected during rehabilitation. For example, if a kneecap is dislocated and its articular surface damaged, the quadriceps may be strengthened by isometric and hip flexion exercises.

Individual Differences

People who can organize and process thoughts more quickly and uniquely than the rest of the population are labeled geniuses. Mental processes are nothing more than the transmission and organization of nervous impulses. The processes are very similar to those used to accomplish complex movement patterns in sports. In a biological sense, superior athletes can also be called geniuses. Their natural talent enables them to translate nervous impulses into the most efficient and economical movements required for their sport; their transition from thought to athletic action is superior to the process "normal" people use. Based upon these criteria, a Jesse Owens, a Jim Thorpe, or a Mildred "Babe" Didrikson has to be considered as superior as an Albert Einstein.

There are large individual differences among people's ability to perform and learn sports skills. These differences are based upon the components of training and genetics, both of which are important for superior performance. A naturally talented athlete is seldom successful if he or she does not devote sufficient time to training. Likewise, an athlete sparsely endowed genetically is hard-pressed to perform at a superior level, even if subjected to the most arduous training regimen.

The determination of the effect of genetics on performance usually involves a comparison of identical and nonidentical twins. Identical twins have the same genetic material, so variability in their performances is caused solely by environmental considerations. Variability in nonidentical twins results from a combination of genetic and environmental factors. Most studies indicate that genetics is the most important factor affecting individual differences in performance. In relatively sedentary populations, there are slight if any differences in **maximal oxygen consumption** between identical twins, whereas the differences between nonidentical twins are often considerable.

Genetic studies are important for emphasizing the trained state as a temporary level of adaptation. Training studies with identical twins do demonstrate that the active twin improves while the sedentary twin does not. But when the levels of activity are similar, heredity asserts itself, and physiological characteristics in the genetically identical individuals move closer together.

The adaptability of the human body is limited. Maximal oxygen consumption, for example, can be improved by about only 20 percent. Thus an endurance athlete must start with a high **oxygen transport capacity** if she or he is ever to reach Olympic levels of performance. Studies of athletes' characteristics reinforce this idea.

Many of an athlete's performance characteristics are determined by the relative percentages of fast- and slow-twitch muscle fibers present. There is a high correlation between the percentage of slow-twitch fibers and maximal oxygen consumption. Studies of athletes with outstanding endurance reveal a disproportionately greater amount of slow-twitch fibers in the muscle groups they use in their sport (Figure 4-3, p. 64).

These same results apply to fast-twitch muscle fibers for sports requiring speed, such as sprinting. A high percentage of fast-twitch fibers is a prereq-

Maximal oxygen consumption: The best measure of the fitness of the cardiovascular system; the heart's maximum capacity to pump blood and the tissues' maximum extraction and use of oxygen.

Oxygen transport capacity: Capacity of the cardiovascular system to deliver oxygen to tissues.

uisite for performing fast muscle contractions. However, it has been shown that many world-class discus throwers and shot-putters have a normal balance between fast- and slow-twitch fibers (approximately 50-50). So, in many sports, particularly those demanding exacting technique, training may overcome the lack of certain genetic prerequisites.

Individual Differences and the Injured Athlete. Athletes respond in various ways to an injury-rehabilitation program (see Chapter 12). Factors such as motivation, responsiveness to training, and anatomical characteristics will affect the success of the program. For example, athletes with pronated feet, a large Q angle (see Chapter 21), or on overambitious training programs may receive differing degrees of success in a rehabilitation program for shin splints than athletes who are anatomically "normal" and willing to scale back the intensity of their exercise program.

Progression

Most sports require a good fitness base involving general conditioning exercises to develop cardiovascular strength and power, endurance, and flexibility. Adaptation to the stress of training occurs most readily when the stress is applied gradually. High levels of fitness require many years of training and involve small stages of progression. The fitness of an athlete in championship form represents the culmination of numerous small gains. The body cannot be forced to adapt rapidly; to attempt to do so will only cause injury. Progression is best applied by following a year-round training program, generally divided into preseason, in-season, and off-season regimens.

General conditioning is developed during the off-season. Specific muscle groups to be used in the sport are emphasized by concentrating upon the amount rather than the intensity of the training. Although the particulars of the

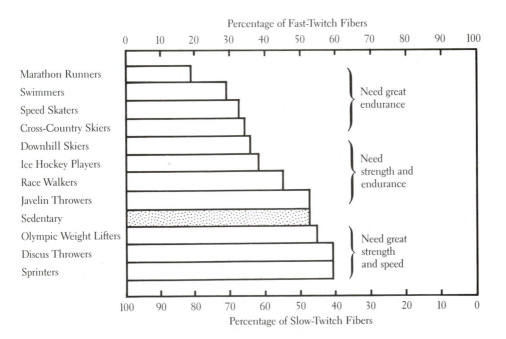

Figure 4-3 Typical distribution of muscle fiber for selected male athletes. There are sometimes large individual differences among muscle fiber types within a given sport.

base program are different for each sport, the nature of the program is the same. The football player, for example, works on strength by weight training, endurance by running, and flexibility by stretching exercises. Short sprints and contact are not emphasized during this period of the base program. Similarly, the distance runner works on general conditioning, placing little emphasis upon interval training techniques, which are more important during the competitive season (see Putting It into Practice 4-1).

The pre- and in-season programs involve gradual transition from the base period's high-volume, low-intensity training to high-intensity training. The transition is from the general to the specific, from quantity to quality, a change in concentration from the parts to the whole of a movement. The football player begins to concentrate upon execution and high-intensity fitness. The distance runner gradually begins to incorporate more and more high-intensity interval training into the workouts.

During the peak (competitive) season, the volume of training decreases dramatically, with the focus upon maximum performance for a few specially selected contests. Empirical evidence suggests that peak form can be maintained for only a short time; the body must have sufficient rest to completely recover from the stresses of exercise training. However, this rest eventually causes deconditioning, with a subsequent loss of form. Long-term planning is necessary for the body to be in peak condition and achieve top performance. In general, an athlete who has been through an intense and well-planned base and pre- and in-season conditioning program will be able to stay in peak condition for a longer time.

Athletes in team sports usually do not have the luxury of resting for a particular contest; they must be physically prepared over an entire season. The pre- and in-season conditioning programs are particularly important to

PUTTING IT INTO PRACTICE 4-1

Maintaining a Training Diary

You can most readily physically condition yourself by following a program of regular, progressive, and systematic exercise. During your pre- and in-season, your regularly scheduled athletic practices will be structured this way, but in your off-season your training program may be more haphazard. The training diary, a written record of your future and past training sessions, is one of the best techniques for ensuring a systematic conditioning program.

Your training diary does not have to be elaborate. Use a school notebook to maintain a record of such factors as body weight, diet, duration and intensity of the workout, and future goals. By faithfully recording entries and frequently using the diary as a reference, you can evaluate your program, determining how and when to motivate yourself and making sure your conditioning procedures are well planned and systematic.

Example of a training diary entry for a discus thrower during the off-season.

date: 10/17/86
weight: 245 lb.

weight training:
    power cleans
        5 × 5 225 lb.
    squats 5 × 8 380 lb.
    sit-ups (45 lb)
        2 × 25 reps

discus:
    25 south africans
    2/3 effort

running: jog 1½ mi.
    + 6 × 100 yd. strides

these athletes for optimum performance and injury prevention. Deconditioning during the peak season is often a problem for team-sport athletes; the conditioning process must be continued throughout the entire season.

Progression and the Injured Athlete. As discussed in Chapter 12, an athlete's rehabilitation can be hampered by working too hard and/or not working hard enough. The athletic trainer should advance the program from one stage to another as systematically as possible. However, progression in training load or volume (frequency and repetitions) can be made only if the healing of injured tissue is keeping pace. Increased inflammation from inappropriate progression will only hamper recovery.

All through rehabilitation, the athletic trainer should measure and keep track of each athlete's gains in such factors as strength and power, endurance, and flexibility. Optimal progression will have been gained when the athlete's recovered capacity equals that of the training level.

Warm-Up

Warm-up is preliminary exercise that optimizes muscle and joint performance, decreases the risk of soft tissue injury, reinforces motor skills, and maximizes blood flow to active muscles and the heart. Although warm-up is a time-honored ritual in almost all sports, its biochemical and physiological benefits are uncertain. Research studies have not yet effectively revealed the effect of warm-up on sports performance or its ability to decrease the risk of injury. Thus, warm-up is a gray area in sports medicine. Nevertheless, most authorities recommend that athletes practice it (see Putting It into Practice 4-2), although they disagree about the best way to carry it out.

Some experts suggest that warm-up should include static (isometric) stretch-

ing, gentle range of motion exercises, and low-intensity preliminary exercise; other experts feel that static stretching prior to activity may actually contribute to athletic injuries. In any event, warm-up probably does not hinder performance, and it indeed may be an essential component of athletic participation. Athletes are psychologically attached to warming up before competition; if the opportunity to warm up is removed, their performances might suffer because of psychological considerations.

Conditioning Techniques for Sports

As discussed, physical training should be specific to the demands of the sport. Athletes should devote sufficient time to optimally developing strength and power, endurance, and flexibility. Here we survey the principles of developing each fitness characteristic; detailed descriptions are beyond our scope and left to specific texts.

Developing Strength and Power

Strength is the ability to exert force; *power* is work per unit of time. In most sports, power is more important than strength. Fortunately, there appears to be a transfer of effect between the two characteristics: Training exercises that require little rapid motion have been proved effective in developing power. For example, discus throwers perform weight lifting exercises (e.g., the bench press) at a speed much slower than that required in their activity. The strength gained in the relatively slow weight lifting exercise increases the power required in the faster discus-throwing movement.

There are three categories of strength exercises: **isometric** (static), **isotonic,** and **isokinetic.** Isometric exercise is applying force without movement; isotonic exercise is applying force with

Warm-up: Low-intensity exercise prior to participating in full-effort physical activity.

Isometric exercise: Application of force without movement. Also called static exercise.
Isotonic exercise: Application of force with movement.
Isokinetic exercise: Application of force at constant speed. A form of isotonic exercise.

Purpose

Warm-up stimulates the flow of blood to muscles and coronary arteries and acts as precompetition practice; it may also prevent injury and enhance performance. The subject of warm-up is very controversial. Although research on its effectiveness has rendered conflicting results, most sports medicine experts recommend warm-up before vigorous physical activity. Warm-up can be either general, utilizing large muscle groups in preliminary exercise such as running or calisthenics, or specific, involving specific muscles that are to be used in the sport or activity.

Types

• *Stretching and joint mobilization*: Stretching should be static (isometric). Bounce (balistic) stretching stimulates stretch receptors in muscle, which has the short-term effect of actually decreasing flexibility. Isometric stretching maximizes joints' range of motion and helps disperse synovial fluid over the joints' surfaces. This clear liquid lubricates and provides nutrients to joints, bursae, and tendon sheaths. Some experts no longer recommend stretching before activity as part of the warm-up, feeling that this may actually increase the risk of injury by initiating stretch reflexes that contract the muscles.

• *Low-intensity*: Such specific exercise includes jogging before sprinting in track, football, or basketball; easy throwing before hard throwing in baseball, discus, or javelin; easy rallying before competition in tennis, handball, or racquetball. Low-intensity exercise increases muscle temperature (muscles' biochemistry is more efficient when muscles' temperature is slightly higher than at rest) and increases the flow of blood to skeletal and heart muscle.

• *Precompetitive practice*: These specific exercises reinforce the motor patterns necessary for the sport. Examples include a receiver running pass patterns before a football game or volleyball players practicing a spiking drill before a competition.

---

movement; and isokinetic exercise is exerting force at a constant speed.

Although isometric exercise received considerable attention in the late 1950s, it is now less popular as a primary means of gaining strength. Isometric exercise does not increase strength throughout a joint's range of motion (unless practiced at various points in the range of motion); it is specific to a joint angle at which the training is practiced. Likewise, isometric training does not improve (and may hamper) the ability to rapidly exert force (power). Athletes sometimes use isometrics to help overcome "sticking points" in an exercise's range of motion. For example, if an athlete has difficulty lifting a weight from his chest during the bench press, he may perform this exercise isometrically at the point where he is experiencing his greatest degree of difficulty (Figure 4-4).

Figure 4-4 Isometric exercise is especially effective in developing strength at a particular point in the range of motion. Here, Olympic discus thrower Art Burns is performing an isometric squat on the power rack.

Isometric exercise is valuable during the early stages of rehabilitation from injury, particularly when joint mobilization is contraindicated. Exercises such as quad sets may be used to prevent **atrophy** from disuse during immobilization. Isometrics have been proved valuable for developing strength in a single muscle that has been found weak during manual muscle testing.

Isotonic exercise is the type of strength training most popular with and familiar to athletes and coaches. Isotonic techniques include constant, variable, eccentric, plyometrics, and speed loading.

Constant resistance exercise employs a constant load, but the relative resistance varies with the angle of the joint. For example, in the free weight squat, it is easier to move the weight at the end of the range of motion than when the knees are almost fully flexed. Maximal loading can occur only at the weakest point in the range of motion. Barbells and dumbbells are the most common devices used in constant resistance exercise and are the most popular with the majority of athletes who are seriously involved in strength-training programs. (See Figure 4-5, p. 69, and Putting It into Practice 4-3, p. 70.)

Variable resistance exercise is increasing the load throughout the range of motion so that there is a more constant stress on the muscles. This form of exercise requires the use of machines that change the relationship of the fulcrum and lever arm as the arm moves (Figure 4-6). Variable resistance places more stress on the muscles at the end of the range of motion, a position of increased mechanical advantage. Thus far, studies have failed to consistently demonstrate that variable resistance training is superior to traditional constant resistance training techniques.

Eccentric loading, sometimes called negative resistance, places tension on the muscle as the muscle lengthens. For example, in the bench press, eccentric training could be used by resisting the movement of the bar as it approaches the chest. Several studies have shown that negative resistance is an effective way to gain strength, although it is not superior to other isotonic techniques. One drawback of eccentric loading is that it seems to create more muscle soreness than other methods. Strength athletes do not widely practice this method as a primary training technique but often use it as an adjunct to other training methods. Eccentric exercise is being increasingly used in rehabilitation for such injuries as tendinitis. Curwin and Stanish suggested that eccentric exercise overloads the tendons more effectively than concentric exercise, which focuses the load on the belly (the contractile unit) of the muscle.

Plyometrics, sometimes called implosion training, is the sudden eccentric loading and stretching of muscles followed by their forceful concentric contraction. The sudden stretch causes the muscle stretch receptors to perform a stretch reflex (see Chapter 5) that results in a more forceful contraction. An example of plyometrics is jumping from a bench to the ground and then jumping back onto the bench (Figure 4-7). Plyometrics should be practiced to develop the desired type of power. For example, for vertical power, conduct the plyometric exercise in a vertical direction. Practicing multiple-repetition plyometrics will develop specific muscle strength and endurance.

It has been shown that plyometrics training increases strength and jumping ability, but it may subject the athlete to an increased risk of injury (vigorous plyometrics certainly should not be used during the early phases of injury rehabilitation). Plyometric loading has become very popular with many athletes, but more research is needed to assess its effectiveness and safety.

Speed loading is moving a load as rapidly as possible in an attempt to simulate the contractile velocities employed in athletic movements. Most studies

Atrophy: Decrease in size and function of a muscle.

Constant resistance exercise: A resistive exercise technique involving a single amount of resistance.

Plyometrics: Rapid stretching of a muscle group undergoing eccentric stress followed by a rapid concentric contraction. Also called implosion training.

Variable resistance exercise: Application of an increasing load during exercise. Generally, resistance is increased toward the end of the range of motion.

Eccentric loading: Placing a load on a muscle as it lengthens. The muscle contracts eccentrically in order to control the weight.

Speed loading: A strength-training technique involving the performance of a resistance exercise as rapidly as possible.

Figure 4-5 Olympic lifts, such as the power snatch, are an important kind of isotonic exercise practiced by "strength-speed" athletes such as throwers and football players.

Figure 4-6 Variable resistance exercise machines, such as the Nautilus pullover machine, stress the muscles uniformly.

(A)   (B)   (C)   (D)

Figure 4-7 Plyometrics. This type of isotonic exercise overloads the muscles' elastic component, which results in a forceful muscle contraction. The technique is practiced to improve strength and power. A technique for developing leg power involves (A and B) jumping off a low bench, (C) landing on the floor and absorbing the shock with legs, and (D) jumping back up onto the bench.

Exercises for Developing Strength and Power

Every weight-training program designed to increase strength and power in athletes should be composed of three basic types of exercise: *presses*, *pulls*, and *squats*. Although other exercises are important for developing muscle groups necessary in a specific sport, these three types are central to a good strength-training program. Press exercises include bench press, incline press, jerk, dumbbell press, dumbbell incline, and behind the neck press. Pulling exercises include the clean, snatch, high pull, and deadlift. Squat exercises include hack squat, front squat, leg press, back squat, and "ram rack" squat. Following is a description of basic weight-training exercises. Beginners should perform three sets of ten repetitions for each exercise. Programs for more advanced athletes vary with the purpose of the programs (e.g., to build strength and endurance and power) and time of season (e.g., off-season, peak phase).

Power clean

Pulls

Power clean: Place the bar on the floor in front of your shins. Keep your feet approximately one foot apart. Grasp the bar with your hands at shoulder width, with your palms down, and squat down, keeping your arms straight, your back at a thirty-degree angle, and your head up. Pull the weight past your knees to your chest while throwing your hips forward and shoulders back. The main power for this exercise should come from your hips and legs. Return the bar to the starting position.

Presses

Bench press: Lying on your back on a bench with your feet on the floor, grasp the bar at shoulder width with your palms upward, away from your body. Lower the weight to your chest, and then return the bar to the starting position.

Dumbbell incline press: Lying on your back on an incline bench and with your hands spaced shoulder width, rest the dumbbells on your chest and then press the dumbbells overhead. Return to the starting position.

Squats

Squat: Begin in a standing position, with your feet shoulder width apart and the bar resting on the back of your shoulders, with your hands holding the bar in that position. Keep your head up and low back arched. Squat down (under control) until your thighs are approximately parallel with the floor. Drive upward toward the starting position, keeping your back fixed throughout the exercise.

Selected Other Exercises

Biceps curls: From a standing position, grasp the bar with your palms upward, with your hands shoulder width apart. Keeping your upper body rigid, flex your elbows until the bar reaches a level slightly below the clavicle (collarbone). Return the bar to the starting position.

Bench press

Dumbbell incline press

Squat

Biceps curls

(continued on next page)

Exercises for Developing Strength and Power (*continued*)

Knee extensions: Using a knee extension-flexion machine (some machines are dedicated solely to knee extension or to flexion), place both feet under the lower pad and flex your knees. Fully extend your knees, and then return to the starting position. People on a patellar-protection program (see Chapter 21) should perform this exercise using the last twenty degrees of the range of motion.

Knee flexion: Using the knee extension-flexion machine, assume a prone position, with your heels resting on the under side of the flexion pad. Fully flex your knees and then return to the starting position.

Abdominal curl: Assume a supine position on the floor or mat, with your knees bent, feet flat on the floor, and hands behind your head; lift your head and shoulders while flexing at your trunk. Continue the movement only until your shoulders are lifted from the mat. Be sure to keep your lower back on the floor or mat. Return to the starting position.

Toe raises: Perform this exercise while resting a bar on your shoulders or with a "calf machine." Plantar-flex your feet and raise up on your toes, and then return to the starting position.

Bar dips: Assume an upright support position on the dip bars or parallel bars. Lower your body by flexing your elbows until the bars are approximately level with your sixth ribs. Return to the starting position.

Knee extensions

Knee flexion

Abdominal curl

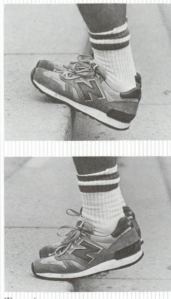

Toe raises

Bar dips

have found that constant resistance isotonic exercise is superior to speed loading for gaining strength. Speed loading may not permit the muscles to create sufficient tension to cause a training effect. Strength athletes often practice this technique at various times in their training schedule in the hope of maximizing power.

Proprioceptive neuromuscular facilitation (PNF) is manual resistance exercise that uses a combination of stretching and isotonic and isometric loading (Figure 4-8, p. 74). Physical therapists and athletic trainers widely use this technique for primitive neurological patterning and to develop strength and flexibility during the prevention and treatment of athletic injuries. Unfortunately, there is little data available comparing PNF with traditional loading techniques.

Isokinetic exercise involves muscle contraction at a constant speed. It is sometimes called accommodating resistance exercise because the exerted force is resisted by an equal force from the isokinetic exercise machine (Figure 4-9, p. 75). Isokinetic exercise has become extremely popular with athletic trainers and physical therapists because it permits the training of injured joints with a lower risk of injury. Exercises can be practiced at faster speeds than can other forms of isotonic exercises; this places less torsional stress on the articular surfaces. Also, isokinetic dynamometers provide a speed-specific indication of the absolute torque (force around a point of axis) created by a muscle group because maximum power can be assessed at velocities from 1 to over 300 degrees per second.

Training at slower speeds using isokinetic exercise (sixty degrees per second or less) produces the greatest strength gains. Training at fast speeds increases the ability to exert force rapidly, but no more than traditional isotonic techniques. Although isokinetic exercise appears to be a promising technique of loading, more research is

needed to establish its role in strength training and to determine the ideal isokinetic training protocol.

Endurance Training

Endurance is the ability to exercise for sustained periods and is an important fitness component in many sports. As with strength (and any fitness characteristic), endurance is specific to the activity. For example, the endurance required during a sustained hold in wrestling is fundamentally different from the endurance required for running the length of a soccer field, which is different from the endurance required in a marathon. Each activity induces a specific physiological adaptation.

Activities lasting more than a minute increasingly rely upon the body's capacity to deliver and extract oxygen. This ability is called cardiovascular endurance; it also involves marked improvements in cellular metabolism. Training to develop endurance fitness can be divided into overdistance training and interval training. Using the target heart rate (THR) is a valuable technique for helping the athlete select the proper intensity of endurance exercise (see Putting It into Practice 4-4, p. 74).

Overdistance training develops maximal oxygen consumption and increases **cellular respiratory capacity**. The process involves exercising at distances considerably greater than those required during competition. Distance runners have been known to train in excess of 150 miles per week, and 20,000-meter swimming workouts are not unheard of. By necessity, the pace of these overdistance workouts is slower than those of competition. However, although overdistance training develops an important type of fitness, it is not specific to race pace and therefore does not constitute the entire endurance-training regimen. Interval training is a means of achieving this endurance overload.

As discussed, **interval training** involves periods of intense exercise inter-

Proprioceptive neuromuscular facilitation (PNF): Sustained muscular contraction in selected, repetitive motions: Initial muscle stretch is followed by sustained resistance through a range of motion.

Overdistance training: Exercising at distances greater than those required in competition. Also called long, slow distance (LSD) training.
Cellular respiratory capacity: The capacity to produce adenosine triphosphate (ATP) through oxidative metabolic pathways.

Interval training: Repeated bouts of exercises that manipulate speed, distance, repetition, and rest. Typically used to provide intensity overload.

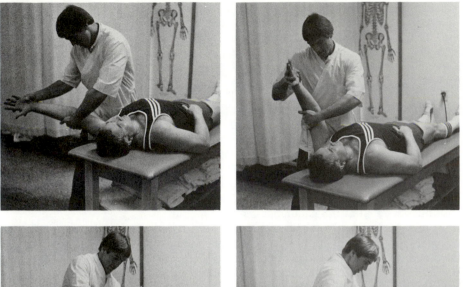

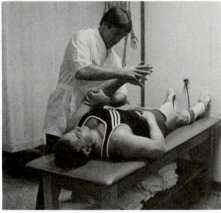
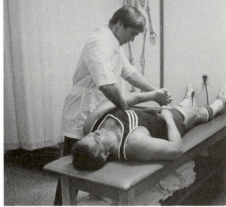

Figure 4-8 Proprioceptive neuromuscular facilitation (PNF). This type of exercise employs manual resistance and a combination of stretching and isotonic and isometric contractions using concentric and eccentric loading. PNF is used mainly during injury rehabilitation and is thought to develop strength, power, range of motion, and neuromuscular patterning. In this four-stage sequence, the athletic trainer is using PNF as part of a shoulder-rehabilitation program.

PUTTING IT INTO PRACTICE 4-4

Calculating the Target Heart Rate

Research shows that a person must exercise at between 60 and 80 percent of cardiovascular capacity ($\dot{V}O_2$ max) to achieve a conditioning effect. Heart rate can be used to predict metabolic rate during endurance exercise. The target heart rate (THR) is the heart rate that corresponds to the exercise intensity (metabolic rate) that results in a training effect. Unfortunately, a given percentage of maximum heart rate (HR) is not equal to the same percentage of $\dot{V}O_2$ max (for example, 60% HR max = 43% $\dot{V}O_2$ max).

You can accurately assess proper training intensity by using the heart rate reserve (HR max − HR rest) and the Karvonen formula:

THR = 0.6 to 0.8 × (HR max − HR rest) + HR rest

where 0.6 to 0.8 is a range of percentages of HR reserve (choose one for each calculation), HR max is the measured or predicted maximum heart rate, HR rest is a typical resting value for heart rate.

Maximum heart rate can be measured as the highest heart rate achieved during a maximum treadmill test or estimated by subtracting the athlete's age from 220. In young, healthy athletes who are warmed up, maximum heart rate can be more precisely estimated by measuring heart rate for ten seconds immediately after an all-out 300- or 400-meter run.

spersed with relief or rest periods. This training varies the distance, speed, number of repetitions, and rest intervals. The event determines the nature of the interval training routine. A sprinter repeats shorter distances performed at high intensities; a marathoner runs longer distances.

Interval training helps the athlete learn pace and provides a potent cardiovascular stressor. This type of training is known to help the athlete better use lactic acid, which is produced in large quantities during high-intensity exercise, as fuel. The presence of high levels of lactic acid in muscles is thought to be associated with the pain experienced during intense effort.

Excessive interval and overdistance training can cause overuse injuries. As with strength training, it is vitally important that the athlete be given adequate time to recover between interval training sessions, to allow the athlete to be ready for another quality workout when he or she is again subjected to interval training.

Endurance Training and the Injured Athlete. Studies prove that deconditioned muscles rapidly lose their oxidative capacity, so both cardiovascular endurance and specific muscle endurance must be developed during rehabilitation from injury. Cardiovascular endurance can be developed through relatively non-weight-bearing exercises like stationary cycling and running in a swimming pool. Specific muscle endurance can be developed by performing a high number of repetitions of an exercise. For example, ten repetitions per set are commonly prescribed to develop strength in exercises such as knee extensions. An athlete performs 30 to 100 repetitions to develop local muscle endurance.

Flexibility Training

Stretching exercises are an important component of the conditioning process for most sports (see Putting It into Prac-

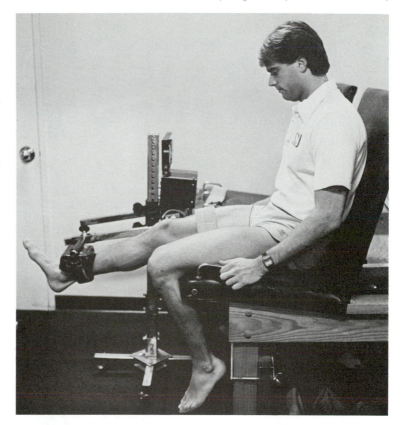

Figure 4-9 The Orthotron is an isokinetic device designed for training rather than testing; the Cybex in Figure 3-6 (p. 53) is used for training and testing. The athlete here is exercising the extensor and flexor muscles of the knee.

tice 4-5, p. 76). Unfortunately, there is little scientific proof of stretching's effectiveness in improving physical performance or preventing injury. However, most sports medicine experts highly recommend including this training in the conditioning and injury-prevention program.

Static stretching is considered superior to **balistic** (bounce) **stretching** because balistic stretching stimulates stretch receptors within muscles, which in turn causes a reflex muscular contraction. This contraction counteracts the desired "lengthening" effect that stretching exerts on muscles, and it may cause an injury by placing a sudden load on a muscle that is experiencing a reflex contraction. Stretching exercises usually involve holding the stretch ten to thirty seconds. The

Balistic stretching: Stretching initiated by suddenly loading muscle's elastic component during a relatively rapid movement. Also called bounce stretching.

PUTTING IT INTO PRACTICE 4-5

Performing Flexibility Exercises

- Perform stretching exercises statically. Stretch and hold the position ten to thirty seconds (as long as sixty seconds if your muscles are extremely tight). *Never bounce*.
- For more effectiveness, precede your stretching exercises with an isometric contraction of the muscle to be stretched (a PNF technique).
- To develop more flexibility, practice stretching after exercise because your muscles are warmer then and can be stretched farther.
- You should feel a mild stretch rather than pain while performing these exercises. Stress relaxation.
- Avoid positions that increase the risk of low back injury. For example, if you are performing straight leg toe-touching exercises, bend your knees slightly when returning to a standing position.
- As with other forms of physical conditioning, develop flexibility gradually over time.
- There are large individual differences in joint flexibility. Do not feel you have to compete with other athletes during stretching workouts.
- Practice flexibility exercises at least five days per week. Set aside a special time to develop this type of fitness.

Hamstring Stretches

Statically hold these stretches for ten to thirty seconds.

1. Standing: Bend down slowly from your waist and reach down until you feel stretch in your hamstrings. Bend your knees when returning to the starting position (to place less stress on your back).
2. Sitting: Reach forward toward your feet until you feel stretch in your hamstrings.
3. Supine (assisted): With your hips stabilized, raise your leg until you feel stretch in your hamstrings.

Hamstring stretches

Quadriceps Stretches

Statically hold for ten to thirty seconds.

1. Horizontal half-bow: Lying on your side, grasp the top of your foot and then abduct your thigh and pull your foot medioposteriorly until you feel stretch in your quadriceps.
2. Standing half-bow: Standing, grasp the top of your foot and then abduct your thigh and pull your foot medioposteriorly until you feel stretch in your quadriceps.

Groin Stretches

Statically hold for ten to thirty seconds.

1. Sit with your legs and feet apart; bend forward at your waist until you feel stretch in your groin.
2. Seated, with the soles of your feet apart, push your knees toward the floor and lean forward.

Achilles Stretches

Statically hold for ten to thirty seconds.

1. From a standing position, lean against a wall, post, tree, etc.
2. Place one leg in front of the other (front leg bent and rear leg straight).
3. Push the heel of your straight leg downward until you feel stretch in your calf muscles and Achilles tendon.

Quadriceps stretches: horizontal half-bow and standing half-bow

Groin stretches

Achilles stretches

stretch should produce a mild pulling sensation without pain.

PNF techniques of preceding a stretch with an isometric contraction are particularly helpful for improving flexibility. The isometric contraction is thought to stimulate Golgi tendon organs within the muscle (see Chapter 5), which causes the muscle to relax. This relaxation enables the muscles to be more fully stretched.

Regular flexibility training is probably important in preventing musculoskeletal injury because the increased flexibility allows the muscle-tendon unit to move through its range of motion with less strain. Whether used in injury prevention or treatment, flexibility training must be very gradual because it can cause injury if misapplied.

The athletic conditioning process often places the athlete on the thin edge between improved fitness and injury. The athletic trainer should be involved in planning the conditioning program as part of the injury-prevention process. Knowledge the athletic trainer gains during preseason physical evaluations and through previous injury rehabilitation can be invaluable in helping the coach assess individual tolerances to various types of physical conditioning exercises.

References

Atha, J. Strengthening muscle. *Exercise and Sport Sciences Reviews* 9:1–73, 1981.

Beaulieu, J. E. Developing a stretching program. *The Physician and Sportsmedicine* 9(11):59–69, 1981.

Berger, R. Optimum repetitions for the development of strength. *Research Quarterly for Exercise and Sport* 33:334–338, 1962.

Brooks, G. A., and T. D. Fahey. *Exercise Physiology: Human Bioenergetics and Its Applications.* New York: Wiley, 1984.

Chu, D. A. Plyometrics: the link between strength and speed. *NSCA Journal* April:20–21, 1983.

Chu, D. A. Plyometric exercise. *NSCA Journal* January:56–61, 1984.

Curwin, S., and W. D. Stanish. *Tendinitis: Its Etiology and Treatment.* Lexington, Mass.: D. C. Heath, 1984.

Delorme, T. L. Restoration of muscle power by heavy resistance exercises. *Journal of Bone and Joint Surgery* 27:645–667, 1945.

Edgerton, V. R. Mammalian muscle fiber types and their adaptability. *American Zoologist* 18:113–125, 1976.

Edgerton, V. R. Neuromuscular adaptation to power and endurance work. *Canadian Journal of Applied Sport Science* 1:49–58, 1976.

Fahey, T. D. *Getting into Olympic Form.* New York: Butterick Publishing, 1980.

Fox, E. L. *Sports Physiology.* Philadelphia: W. B. Saunders, 1979.

Gettman, L. R., and M. L. Pollack. Circuit weight training: a critical review of its physiological benefits. *The Physician and Sportsmedicine* 11(9):44–60, 1980.

Gonyea, W. J., and D. Sale. Physiology of weight lifting. *Archives of Physical Medicine and Rehabilitation* 63:235–237, 1982.

Henry, F. M. "The Evolution of the Memory Drum Theory of Neuromotor Reaction," in *Perspectives on the Academic Discipline of Physical Education,* G. A. Brooks, ed. Champaign, Ill.: Human Kinetics Publishers, 1981.

Henry, F. M., and J. D. Whitley. Relationships between individual differences in strength, speed, and mass in an arm movement. *Research Quarterly for Exercise and Sport* 31:24–33, 1961.

O'Shea, P. Effects of selected weight training programs on the development of strength and muscle hypertrophy. *Research Quarterly for Exercise and Sport* 95–102, 1964.

Sady, S. P., M. Wortman, and D. Blanke. Flexibility training: ballistic, static, or proprioceptive neuromuscular facilitation. *Archives of Physical Medicine and Rehabilitation* 63:261–263, 1982.

Salminen, A., and V. Vihko. Susceptibility of mouse skeletal muscles to exercise injuries. *Muscle & Nerve* 6:596–601, 1983.

Selye, H. *The Stress of Life.* New York: McGraw-Hill, 1976.

Sharp, R. L., J. P. Troup, and D. L. Costill. The relationship between power and sprint freestyle swimming. *Medicine and Science in Sports and Exercise* 14:53–56, 1982.

Shyne, K., and R. H. Dominguez. To stretch or not to stretch? *The Physician and Sportsmedicine* 10:137–140, 1982.

Williams, J. G. P., and P. N. Sperryn (eds.). *Sports Medicine.* London: Edward Arnold, 1976.

Wilmore, J. H. *Athletic Training and Physical Fitness.* Boston: Allyn and Bacon, 1977.

5 Soft Tissue

Although they must be able to recognize serious injuries such as fracture, dislocation, and concussion, athletic trainers are primarily involved in evaluating and treating soft tissue injuries. Soft tissues include epithelium, connective tissues, tendons, ligaments, muscles, and nerves. Most soft tissue injuries are minor strains, sprains, contusions, cuts, and abrasions. The causes are often obvious, but soft tissue damage may stem from subtle musculoskeletal abnormalities and improper sports techniques. To recognize and treat soft tissue injury, the athletic trainer must have a knowledge of soft tissue anatomy and an appreciation of the stresses soft tissues experience during physical activity.

This chapter discusses the basic anatomy of soft tissues and the principal injuries that affect them. Chapters 8 and 13 discuss the physiology of trauma and modalities used in the treatment of soft tissue injury.

Epithelial Tissue

Epithelial tissue (epithelium) covers all internal and external body surfaces.

These tissues comprise the outer layer of skin and internal organs and the inner lining of blood vessels. The epithelium is important because it helps protect and structure the other tissues and organs of the body. Skin injuries and diseases are of particular concern to the athletic trainer because they occur so often. (Injuries to and diseases of the skin are thoroughly discussed in Chapter 23.)

Epithelial tissues have no blood supply, so they depend upon the process of diffusion (see Chapter 21) for nutrition, oxygenation, and elimination of waste products. The tissues have a tremendous capacity to reproduce, which is extremely fortunate because most injuries destroy large numbers of epithelial cells.

Epithelial cells are classified according to their structure, function, and arrangement; such cells include *simple squamous*, *simple cuboidal*, *simple columnar*, and *stratified squamous* (see Figure 5-1, p. 80). These cells are sometimes given alternative names when they serve a special function or reside in a specific location. For example, the simple squamous epithelium that forms the inner lining of the blood vessels is called endothelium.

Nucleus

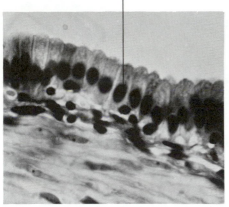

Simple columnar epithelium from gall-bladder. The nucleus contains the cells' genetic material.

Runners quite often suffer soft tissue injuries from overuse.

Simple squamous epithelium

Simple cuboidal epithelium

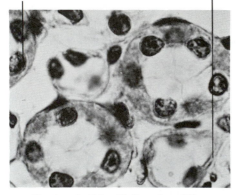

Simple cuboidal epithelium from kidney.

Simple cuboidal epithelium

Simple squamous epithelium

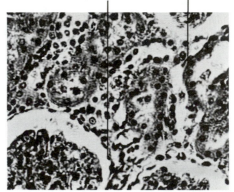

Simple squamous epithelium from kidney.

Squamous cells   Lamina propria

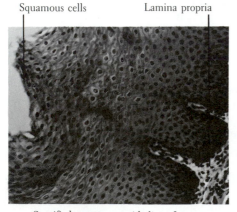

Stratified squamous epithelium from esophagus. The lamina propria is loose connective tissue.

Endothelium

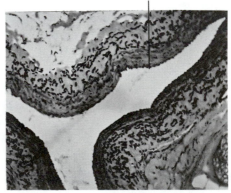

Endothelium lining vein.

Figure 5-1 Photographs of epithelial tissue. (From Crouch, J. E. *Introduction to Human Anatomy*, 6th ed. Palo Alto, Calif.: Mayfield Publishing Co., 1983, pp. 17, 18.)

Connective Tissue

Connective tissue forms a large class of tissues that includes loose connective tissue, dense (fibrous) connective tissue, cartilage, adipose tissue, and bone. (Bone is discussed in Chapter 6.) Connective tissue's main function is to support and protect the body. The **fibroblast** is the principal cell of connective tissue. It produces white fibers called collagen and yellow fibers called elastin. **Collagen** fibers form strong, flexible, and relatively inelastic bundles that comprise the major structural protein of the body (Figure 5-2, p. 82). **Elastin** is a highly elastic tissue that is less strong than collagen.

Loose Connective Tissue

Loose connective tissue is found throughout the body (Figure 5-3, p. 82). This tissue is composed mainly of fibroblasts and lattices of collagen and elastin fibers. It forms the superficial **fascia,** which binds the skin to the underlying surface; forms the deep fascia; fills the spaces between muscles; and composes much of the extracellular space. Fascia is found in the walls of hollow visceral (deep) organs. Loose connective tissue provides support for organs and other structures, eases the movement of adjacent tissues, and helps form and shape the body.

Loose connective tissues are important sites for maintaining fluid equilibrium between the cells and the circulatory and lymphatic systems. Trauma and **inflammation** often cause fluid to accumulate in the spaces composed of loose connective tissue.

Dense (Fibrous) Connective Tissue

Dense (fibrous) connective tissue is composed largely of collagen fibers that are arranged in regular or irregular patterns. Regularly arranged fibrous connective tissue is the principal component of tendons, ligaments, and the cornea of the eye. Irregularly spaced collagenous tissue is found in the dermis, periosteum (outer covering of bone), and capsules of organs.

Tendons connect muscles to bones and isolate the pull of muscles to a small area. The bundles of collagenous fibers that compose the tendon run in regular parallel patterns (Figure 5-4, p. 82). Tendon injuries include strain, tendinitis (inflammation), infection, laceration, and rupture. Ligaments connect bones to bones. Ligaments also include collagenous joint capsules, which run from one bone to another around a joint. Ligaments' structure is similar to that of tendons, but the fibers are more irregularly arranged and their network (matrix) contains more elastin, which makes ligaments more flexible than tendons. Injuries to ligaments are called sprains.

Cartilage

Cartilage is sometimes considered a dense (fibrous) connective tissue. There are three types of cartilage: hyaline, fibrocartilage, and elastic. Hyaline cartilage forms the articular surfaces of bones, the soft portion of the nose, some of the cartilage of the larynx and trachea, and the cartilagenous portion of the rib cage (see Figure 7-2, p. 113). Hyaline cartilage precedes the development of bone during skeletal development. Fibrocartilage comprises the intravertebral disks and forms a protective cushion in the knee and pelvis (see Figure 7-3, p. 114). Damaged hyaline cartilage is sometimes replaced with fibrocartilage. Elastic cartilage, which is much less abundant than the other two types of cartilage, forms the outer portion of the ear and parts of the larynx.

The cells of cartilage are called **chondrocytes;** they secrete a material that gels in the tissue matrix. Cartilage has little or no blood supply, so it depends upon diffusion for its nutrition (see Chapters 7 and 21 for discussions

Connective tissue: Tissue composed mainly of nonliving substances; includes blood, cartilage, bone, fascia, ligaments, and tendons. It supports and protects the body.

Fibroblast: The principal cell of connective tissue; it produces collagen and elastin.

Collagen: A protein component of connective tissue; these white fibers provide structure and support.

Elastin: Yellow fibers that make the collagenous tissue elastic and flexible.

Loose connective tissue: Tissue that helps support organs and other structures; it helps form and shape the body.

Fascia: A layer of loose connective tissue.

Inflammation: Tissue's reaction to trauma, irritation, or infection, characterized by swelling, pain, redness, local temperature increase, and loss of function.

Chondrocyte: A mature cartilage cell.

of synovial fluid and articular cartilage).
Cartilage heals slowly when injured.

Adipose Tissue

Adipose (fat) is a matrix of connective tissue that stores triglycerides (neutral fat) within the cytoplasm (substance of a cell that surrounds the cell nucleus) of its fibroblasts (Figure 5-5). Adipose tissue is found subcutaneously (under the skin) and dispersed around various organs, skeletal muscle, and joints. Adipose tissue is the body's principal reservoir of potential energy, provides insulation against the cold, and protects and pads joint surfaces.

Adipose may help regulate appetite and body weight (through some unknown mechanism). There are two types of adipose tissue: white and brown. White adipose is by far the most abundant. Brown adipose, which is more prevalent in some animal species than humans, has a thermogenic capacity, which allows it to dissipate calories as heat rather than store them as fat. This tissue is thought to be important in acclimatization to cold and may be a vital link in the explanation of the mechanism of some types of obesity.

Skeletal Muscle

The human body contains over 600 muscles, which make up approximately 45 percent of the body mass and are responsible for moving the body and its parts. The athletic trainer should be familiar with the major muscles and their functions in order to properly evaluate, treat, and rehabilitate muscle injuries. There are three types of muscle: smooth, cardiac, and skeletal. Smooth (involuntary) muscle is found around many hollow chambers of the body and performs various movements, such as vasoconstriction of blood vessels, peristalsis, and uterine contractions

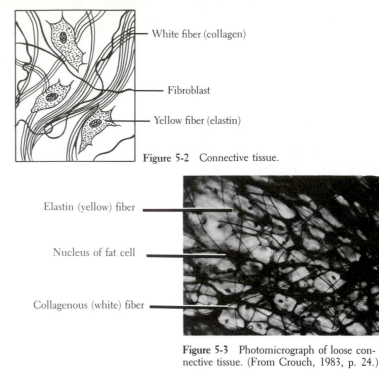

White fiber (collagen)

Fibroblast

Yellow fiber (elastin)

Figure 5-2 Connective tissue.

Elastin (yellow) fiber

Nucleus of fat cell

Collagenous (white) fiber

Figure 5-3 Photomicrograph of loose connective tissue. (From Crouch, 1983, p. 24.)

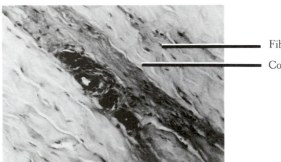

Fibroblast cell nucleus

Collagenous fiber

Figure 5-4 Photomicrograph of a tendon in regularly arranged fibrous connective tissue. (From Crouch, 1983, p. 24.)

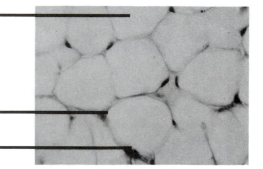

Empty fat cell (fat droplet dissolved out)

Nucleus of fibroblast

Nucleus of adipose cell

Figure 5-5 Photomicrograph of white adipose tissue. (From Crouch, 1983, p. 25.)

during childbirth. Cardiac muscle (my-ocardium) is responsible for contracting the heart and is characterized by an intrinsic rhythmicity. Smooth and cardiac muscles are largely controlled by the autonomic nervous system. **Skeletal muscle,** sometimes called striated or voluntary muscle, is responsible for moving the bony levers of the skeleton. The following discussion is restricted to skeletal muscle because it is the type most often involved in athletic injuries.

The basic muscle cell is multinucleated and is called a muscle fiber. Muscle fibers are arranged in bundles called **fasciculi,** which are bound by connective tissue (Figure 5-6, p. 84). Connective tissue called endomysium runs from one end of the muscle to the other and surrounds each individual fiber within an individual fasciculus. The perimysium surrounds each fasciculus, and the epimysium surrounds the entire muscle. Some muscle fibers run from one end of the muscle to the other, while others extend through only part of the muscle, where they attach to connective tissue.

Muscle fiber can be further subdivided into myofilaments called actin and myosin. Each myosin filament is surrounded by a number of actin myofilaments, which together form a myofibril. Under a microscope, the dark striations, or bands, of muscle appear where these actin and myosin filaments overlap (Figure 5-7, p. 85). Muscle contraction occurs when actin and myosin bind together. These dark (dense) bands are sometimes called anisotropic or A bands. Lighter bands are found in the less dense portions of the fibers. These lighter bands are sometimes called isotropic or I bands.

Muscle Contraction

The basic contractile unit of the muscle fiber is the sarcomere. The sarcomere is bordered on each end by Z membranes or Z lines (Figure 5-6),

which are connected to a series of actin filaments. The myosin filaments are interspersed between these Z line–actin complexes. It is thought that muscles contract by the mechanical movement of myosin cross bridges (cross bridges, which resemble double-ended bottle brushes, project from the myosin filament) pulling against the actin filaments. The breakdown of adenosine triphosphate (ATP) provides the energy for muscle shortening. Huxley originally presented the sliding-filament mechanism of muscle contraction.

Skeletal muscle contraction, which can be consciously controlled, is caused by motor neurons (complexes of muscle fibers with a motor nerve activating the muscle fiber). The contraction process is called **excitation-contraction coupling.** The evaluation of soft tissue muscle injury should always involve a neurological examination because muscles and nerves are so thoroughly integrated in motor function. Refer to basic books in exercise physiology, such as Brooks and Fahey, for a detailed discussion of muscle contraction.

Types of Muscle Fiber

As discussed in Chapter 4, skeletal muscle fibers are classified as types I, IIa, or IIb. Type I fibers are called slow-twitch; type IIa and b fibers are called fast-twitch (type IIa fibers are also sometimes called intermediate fibers). Muscle fibers are differentiated according to their size, biochemistry, preferential substrates (fuels), motor neuron size, strength, fatigability, and blood supply.

Muscle fibers are recruited or used according to the requirements of the muscle contraction and the muscle's basic fiber characteristics. Slow-twitch muscle fibers are recruited when a muscle must perform low-intensity or repeated contractions. For example, slow-twitch muscle fibers are called upon to maintain the body in the up-

Skeletal muscle: Muscle that gives form to the body and moves bones about joints. Also called striated or voluntary muscle.

Fasciculi: Bundles of muscle fibers.

Excitation-contraction coupling: The integration of neural excitation and muscular contraction.

right posture or perform low-intensity exercise such as walking. Fast-twitch muscle fibers are recruited for high-intensity contractions such as heavy weight lifting or sprinting; these fibers fatigue rapidly.

The athletic trainer must consider the characteristics of the different fiber types when rehabilitating injured muscle. The contractile capacities of fast- and slow-twitch fibers will decrease in the athlete who becomes deconditioned from injury or surgery. The rehabilitation program should be constructed to restore the endurance capacity to slow-twitch fibers and the strength capacity to the faster-twitch fibers. Too often, strength is emphasized and muscle endurance neglected.

Fiber Arrangement

The contractile characteristics of the entire muscle are affected by the arrangement of its fibers. Classifications for skeletal muscle fiber arrangements are parallel, unipennate, bipennate, and multipennate. Parallel muscles' fibers run the length of the muscle and end in a terminal tendon. An example is the gracilis muscle in the thigh (Figure 5-8A). Unipennate muscles are attached to one side of a central tendon (e.g., the long extensor of the toes, the extensor digitorum longus (Figure 5-8B); bipennate muscles are attached to both sides of a central tendon (Figure 5-8C, the rectus femoris muscle in the thigh). In multipennate muscles, the fibers attach to the insertional tendon in a variety of directions (e.g., Figure 5-8D, the pectoralis major in the front of the chest). Parallel muscles can react quickly but with little power, whereas pennate muscles are slower but more powerful.

Injury to a multipennate muscle may affect its performance in some motions but not others. For example, strain to the multipennate pectoralis major muscle may affect its capacity to perform horizontal flexion but affect humeral

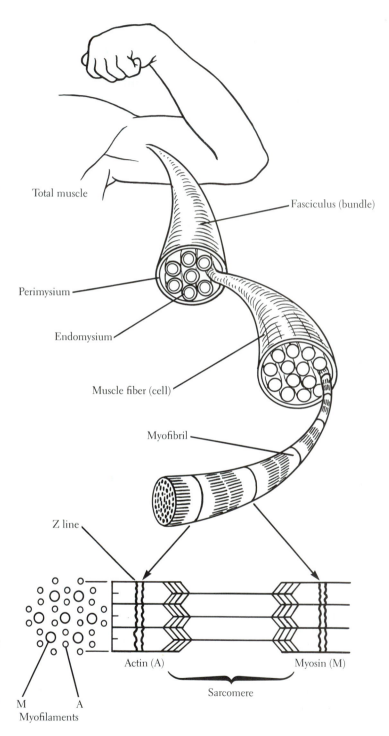

Figure 5-6 Components of skeletal muscle tissue: fasciculi, muscle fiber, myofibrils, and myofilaments.

adduction much less because fibers in one part of the muscle may have been injured while those in another part may be intact.

Skeletal Muscle Blood Supply

Skeletal muscles have prolific blood supply, which is absolutely essential for optimum function. Arterial (from arteries) and venous (from veins) blood flow is necessary for the transport of oxygen, substrates, hormones, and waste products. Blood vessels travel through the perimysium; the thinnest and smallest blood vessels, called **capillaries,** are at the endomysium level. The capillarity around individual muscle fibers is extremely dynamic and can increase or decrease with training and deconditioning.

Trauma and inflammation can profoundly affect the skeletal muscle vasculature (arrangement of the blood vessels). Inflammation can affect the fluid equilibrium among the cells, vasculature, and extracellular space, which in turn can affect the rate that injured tissues heal (see Chapter 8). Compression of the skeletal muscle vasculature can lead to extremely serious conditions, such as anterior compartment syndrome (see Chapter 22).

Capillaries: The thinnest and smallest blood vessels; capillaries connect arteries and veins.

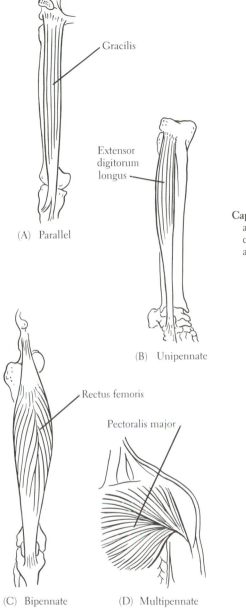

(A) Parallel

(B) Unipennate

(C) Bipennate   (D) Multipennate

Figure 5-8 Muscle fiber arrangements.

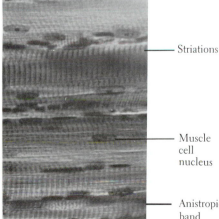

Figure 5-7 Photomicrograph of skeletal muscle. (From Crouch, 1983, p. 78.)

Nerve Tissue

The nervous system is the body's communications network. Nerve tissue gives the body sensitivity and the ability to conduct nerve impulses from one place to another, such as from the spinal cord to muscle. The nervous system receives various sensory signals, such as touch, temperature, and pain, and then sends other signals to muscles or other organs, causing an appropriate action. The system can be subdivided into the central nervous system (CNS), consisting of the brain and spinal cord, the peripheral nervous system (PNS), consisting of the cranial and spinal nerves, and the autonomic nervous system (involuntary nervous system). A thorough discussion of the structure and function of the nervous system is beyond the scope of this book. Refer to basic texts in anatomy and physiology for in-depth discussions of these vital topics.

The **neuron** (nerve cell) is the basic unit of function and structure in the nervous system. Each neuron has at least two fiber appendages extending from its cell body: dendrites and an axon. A neuron has one or numerous **dendrites,** which are fibers that transmit nerve impulses toward the nerve cell body. The neuron's single **axon** is a nerve fiber that transmits nerve impulses away from the cell body. In the CNS and PNS, the axon is covered by a lipid material called **myelin,** which facilitates the conduction of the nerve impulse (see Figure 5-9). Myelin is surrounded by **Schwann cells.** The myelin is regularly interrupted by **nodes of Ranvier,** which act as a branching point for the axon. ATP for the nerves comes principally from mitochondria. (See Figure 5-10.) Neuroglial cells, a type of nervous connective tissue in the CNS, fill spaces and provide support.

Neurons are classified according to their shape (multipolar, bipolar, or unipolar, depending upon the number of

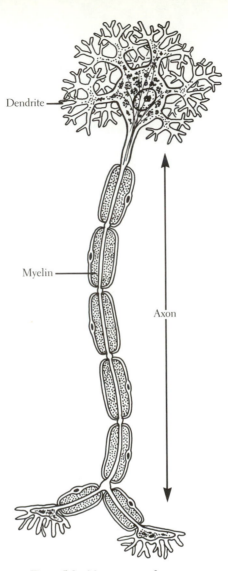

Figure 5-9 Motor neuron from a spinal nerve.

nerve fibers extending from their bodies) and function. Functional classifications are sensory neurons, interneurons, and motor neurons. **Sensory neurons,** sometimes called afferent neurons, carry nerve impulses from receptors in the peripheral parts of the body to the brain and spinal cord. **Interneurons,** which lie totally within the spinal cord and brain, form links with other neurons. **Motor neurons,** sometimes called efferent neurons, carry nerve impulses from the brain or spinal cord to muscles or glands.

Neuron: Nerve cell.
Dendrites: Branches of a nerve cell that conduct impulses toward the nerve cell body.
Axon: Nerve fiber that carries impulses away from the nerve cell.
Myelin: A fatty substance that surrounds the axon of some nerve cells.
Schwann cell: A membrane covering of myelin and nonmyelinated axons.
Nodes of Ranvier: Interruptions in the myelin sheath of nerve axons that serves as a branching point for the neuron.
Sensory neurons: Nerve cells that carry sensory information from the periphery to the CNS. Also called efferent nerves.
Interneurons: Nerves within the brain and spinal cord that form links with other neurons.
Motor neurons: Nerve cells that carry information from the CNS to muscle cells in the periphery. Stimulation of the neurons causes muscle contraction. Also called afferent nerves.

Figure 5-10 Structure of a mixed nerve. (From Crouch, 1983, p. 130.)

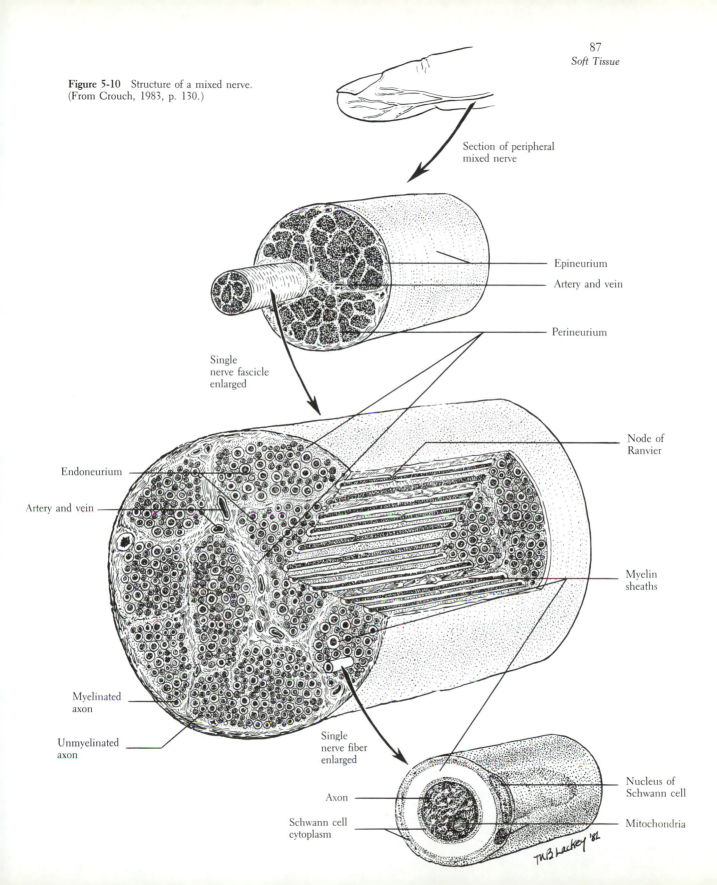

Section of peripheral mixed nerve

Epineurium

Artery and vein

Perineurium

Single nerve fascicle enlarged

Node of Ranvier

Endoneurium

Artery and vein

Myelin sheaths

Myelinated axon

Unmyelinated axon

Single nerve fiber enlarged

Nucleus of Schwann cell

Axon

Mitochondria

Schwann cell cytoplasm

TMB Lackey '82

A **nerve** is a bundle of nerve fibers held together by connective tissue. The **endoneurium** surrounds single neurons, **perineurium** surrounds a single nerve bundle, and **epineurium** surrounds several nerve bundles (Figure 5-10). Nerves are sensory, motor, or mixed, depending upon whether they transmit impulses toward or away from the brain or spinal cord or perform both functions. Most nerves are mixed. Sensory nerves give the central nervous system information from specific receptors located in places such as the eyes, inner ear, muscles, joints, and skin. Motor nerves conduct the nerve impulses that cause muscle contraction.

The Motor Unit

The basic nervous-contractile unit is called the alpha **motor unit,** which consists of a single motor neuron and a number of muscle fibers. Small motor units contain as few as 12 muscle fibers; large motor units may contain as many as 2000 fibers. Movement is accomplished by recruiting (stimulating) one or more of these motor units. Powerful athletic movements require the recruitment of numerous, multifiber motor units, but precise or delicate movements require the recruitment of fewer or smaller motor units. All the muscle fibers within a motor unit have the same biochemical and physiological characteristics; that is, they are all either type I or type II fibers (see Chapter 4).

Afferent Muscle Receptors

Muscles contain a number of afferent (sensory) receptors that are significant in athletic training. These afferent cells include muscle spindles (stretch receptors) and Golgi tendon organs (tension receptors).

Muscle Spindles. Muscle spindles are neural receptor cells that lie parallel to skeletal muscle fibers. The muscle spindles are stimulated when a muscle is stretched suddenly. Muscle spindles also provide **proprioceptive** information about the rate and extent of muscle stretch and limb position.

The gamma loop is a sensory motor reflex that is very valuable in evaluating injury (Figure 5-11). Putting a muscle on a sudden stretch stimulates the stretch receptors. A sensory nerve impulse is sent to the spinal cord to a motor neuron, which sends an impulse back to the muscle, causing a contraction. The knee jerk reflex is probably the most well-known stretch reflex. Sensory-motor reflexes are useful because their execution requires normal neuromuscular function. Specific tests are discussed in Chapters 14 to 23, which cover injuries to specific anatomical areas.

The gamma loop should be considered when performing stretching exercises, either during conditioning or rehabilitation. Static stretching (holding a stretch in a fixed position) should be encouraged because it does not stimulate the muscle spindles to effect a sudden reflex muscle contraction. Bounce stretching, on the other hand, initiates the gamma loop, which could cause injury (particularly during rehabilitation). The sudden stretch the bounce initiates could cause a reflex muscle contraction at the same time the person was preparing to perform another stretch.

Golgi Tendon Organs. Golgi tendon organs are tension receptors that inhibit muscle contraction. Muscle contractile power coupled with external forces is often sufficient to cause serious musculoskeletal injury. These tension receptors inhibit agonists while facilitating the action of antagonists.

It appears that these tension receptors may be inhibited through conditioning and physical training. Golgi tendon inhibition may be essential in sports such as weight lifting and long jumping, where athletes need the ability to lift heavy weights and jump to produce a more forceful muscle contraction.

Nerve: Bundles of fibers connecting the central nervous system and the parts of the body. Nerves transmit sensory stimuli and motor impulses from one part of the body to another.

Proprioception: Spatial awareness caused by sensory input from muscles, tendons, and joints.

Endoneurium: Connective tissue surrounding a single neuron.

Perineurium: Connective tissue surrounding a single nerve bundle.

Epineurium: Connective tissue surrounding a number of nerve bundles.

Motor unit: A structure composed of a motor nerve and many muscle fibers. When the unit is stimulated, all the muscle fibers contract.

Golgi tendon organs: Receptors within skeletal muscle that sense and inhibit tension.

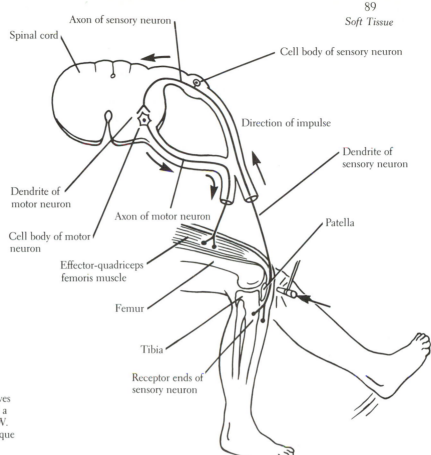

Axon of sensory neuron

Spinal cord

Cell body of sensory neuron

Direction of impulse

Dendrite of
sensory neuron

Dendrite of
motor neuron

Axon of motor neuron

Patella

Cell body of motor
neuron

Effector-quadriceps
femoris muscle

Femur

Tibia

Receptor ends of
sensory neuron

Figure 5-11   The knee jerk reflex involves only two neurons: a sensory neuron and a motor neuron. (Adapted from Hole, J. W. *Human Anatomy and Physiology*. Dubuque Iowa: Wm. C. Brown, 1978, p. 275.)

However, this inhibition may be significant in the development of some types of injuries in accomplished athletes. Inhibited Golgi tendon organs may make it easier to exceed the capacity of soft tissue, resulting in an injury.

Swelling (**edema**) and inflammation following an injury may stimulate Golgi tendon organs, which may speed disuse **atrophy** and dampen the effectiveness of even the most vigorous resistive exercise program. Thus, to maximize the effectiveness of the exercise program, it is essential that swelling be minimized during the early stages of rehabilitation.

Principal Soft Tissue Injuries

In athletes, the principal soft tissue injuries include contusions, strains, ten-

dinitis, bursitis, sprains, and nerve injuries. These injuries often cause inflammation that can intensify the effect of the trauma. See Chapters 14 to 23 for specific injuries and their treatment. Here we describe the principal forms of soft tissue injury.

Contusion

A contusion is a direct blow to the body's outer surface, resulting in soft tissue **hemorrhage** and inflammation. The injury is usually characterized by the appearance of a bruise. The contusion sometimes results in a **hematoma,** which is the collection of blood in a small area. Although contusions are usually trivial, sometimes they can be extremely debilitating and may lead to complications such as **myositis ossificans** (muscular ossification). Common sites of seriously debilitating contusions

Edema: Swelling; a collection of fluid in a tissue space.

Atrophy: Decrease in size and function of a muscle.

Hemorrhage: Bleeding.

Hematoma: A bruise; a mass of partially clotted blood outside the vascular space, typically formed from trauma.

Myositis ossificans: The formation of bone within a muscle, usually caused by trauma; muscular ossification.

include the iliac crest, greater trochanter, and the quadriceps.

Treatment. Contusions rarely require referral to the team physician. Basic treatment includes controlling the bleeding and inflammation by using ice, compression, and elevation (**ICE**). The amount of rest the injured area needs depends upon the extent and site of injury. Vigorous early ambulation, particularly when the contusion occurs around an active joint, may cause further bleeding and inflammation.

With a hematoma, the physician may have to aspirate the blood. Some physicians administer enzymes, such as hyaluronidase, steptokinase, and streptodornase, that speed the absorption of blood. However, this treatment is somewhat controversial and not currently widely practiced.

The contusion must be protected if the athlete is to resume play before the injury has healed. Pads can be made or bought and used to disperse pressures and forces to the tissues around the injured area. However, these pads may aggravate the injury if the contusion is large. As mentioned, repeated trauma (such as a football lineman may incur on his upper arm) may cause myositis ossificans. Never underestimate the possible seriousness of seemingly minor contusions. A small injury that will have minimal effects if treated conservatively can mean the loss of a season if ignored.

Strains

A **strain** is an injury to the musculotendinous unit and one of the most common types of sports injury. A serious strain is known in athletic jargon as a "pulled muscle." A strain tends to occur at the weakest point in the musculotendinous unit, which may be the musculotendinous junction, tendon, or muscle. Strains are graded as first, second, or third degree, according to their severity. Strains can occur suddenly

(acute strain) or chronically (from overuse).

First degree strain is a mild injury characterized by minor disruption of tissue, inflammation, but little or no hemorrhage. The injury is accompanied by local pain, loss of strength, edema, local tenderness, and muscle spasm. This injury may sometimes produce minimal pain and disability, but it can lead to more serious recurrences and complications such as tendinitis or periostitis if not properly treated and rehabilitated.

Second degree strain is more serious and involves some tearing of fibers but not a complete rupture. This injury tends to be acute and occurs from sudden violent trauma. Its signs are similar to those of first degree strain. It tends to be more severe, and is always accompanied by hemorrhage. This more serious strain is particularly susceptible to recurrence.

Third degree strain is a rupture of a muscle or tendon, resulting in a separation of fibers at the site of injury. In addition to the symptoms of the other strains, this injury is often characterized by a palpable or observable defect. Third degree strains may be easily confused with avulsion fractures (the tearing off of a bony prominence), so always refer serious strains to a physician for further evaluation. This injury must be identified and treated by a physician as soon as possible because of the rapid rate of tissue degeneration. Treatment is immobilization or surgery.

Treatment. Initial treatment consists of rest and minimizing inflammation by using ICE. Aspirin or other anti-inflammatory drugs may help. The injured tissue must be protected from further injury; this is accomplished by restricting the athlete from active participation in sports. In severe instances, the injured part may require immobilization. The rest period may last many weeks, depending upon the degree of injury. Heat treatments (or the continu-

ICE: Acronym for ice, compression, and elevation, the basic treatment for contusions and other soft tissue injuries.

Strain: Disruption or injury of a musculotendinous unit. A serious strain is often called a pulled muscle.

ation of cold treatments) can begin after the active inflammatory period has ended.

Mild isometrics, including stretching, can begin after inflammation has begun to subside. If the symptoms begin to flare up again, decrease the intensity of the exercises. Isotonic exercise can be gradually introduced as tolerated, along with specific muscle endurance exercises, complex multiple-joint motions, and exercises to develop fitness for the sport. The athlete should be fully rehabilitated before actively resuming athletics. Most cases of reinjury stem from incomplete rehabilitation. Taping or bracing may help protect the injured part during the more active phases of rehabilitation and early stages of return to competition.

Significant strain (second or third degree) may result in the formation of "stress raisers" and granulation tissue in the area of injury. **Stress raisers** are fibrous or calcified adhesions that bridge from one part of the injured tissue to the other; they can cause irritation or reinjury. **Granulation tissue,** which is formed during the healing process, is weaker than normal tissue. Tissues surrounding the granulation tissue undergo increased stress, subjecting them to an increased risk of injury. Gradual, progressive, and thorough rehabilitation is essential for restoring these tissues to a functional level.

Tendinitis

Tendinitis (tenosynovitis) is inflammation of the tendon sheath (tissue surrounding the tendon). Although it may be initiated by an acute injury, it usually develops gradually through overuse. Tendinitis is extremely common in the tendons that cross the major joints of the body, including the Achilles tendon, patellar ligament, rotator cuff tendons, and wrist extensor tendons.

Tendinitis is often the first step in an ascending series of more serious injuries. For example, in the shoulder-impingement syndrome, tendinitis typically precedes fiber dissociation and progressively more serious rotator cuff tears (see Chapter 17). Likewise, continued overuse of an inflamed Achilles tendon may increase the risk of tendon rupture (see Chapter 22). Complications of this disorder include adhesive and constrictive tendinitis (see Chapter 8). Adhesive tendinitis is the development of **adhesions** (fibrous connective tissue) in the tendon sheath, which impairs the tendon's normal gliding motion. Constrictive tendinitis is the thickening of the tendon sheath, which can also restrict motion. These conditions may require corrective surgery.

Treatment. Treatments for specific types of tendinitis are discussed in the injury chapters (Part Three). Generally, treatment involves rest and anti-inflammatory treatment (ICE and anti-inflammatory drugs). Avoid the injection of corticosteroids because they weaken the tendon. Tendinitis is often caused by subtle factors such as anatomical abnormalities (e.g., pronated feet), overtraining (e.g., running too many miles), poor technique (bending the elbow during the backhand in tennis and not stepping into the ball), and inappropriate equipment (running shoes without a heel lift).

Bursitis

Bursae are flattened sacs of synovial membrane filled with synovial fluid. Bursae reduce friction and facilitate motion. They are located in areas subject to friction, such as between skin and bone or exposed locations where a tendon passes over a bone. Inflammation of a bursa is called **bursitis.**

Bursitis is usually caused by an overuse injury from repeated tissue friction but may be caused by acute trauma. Bursitis is characterized by thickening and inflammation of the synovium. Continued irritation may cause acute calcific bursitis, which is the migration

Adhesion: The binding of adjacent tissue surfaces, caused by the formation of dense (fibrous) connective tissue.

Stress raisers: Fibrous or calcified adhesions that bridge from one part of the injured tissue to the other.
Granulation tissue: Tissue, of mainly collagen, deposited from the process of scar formation following an injury.

Tendinitis: Inflammation of a tendon.
Bursae: Connective tissue sacs over bony prominences and near tendons that facilitate movement by reducing friction.
Bursitis: Inflammation of a bursa.

of calcium salts and water into the bursal space that enlarges the bursa.

Treatment. Treatment involves rest and the standard anti-inflammatory regimen (see Chapters 8 and 13). The most important treatment is preventing the athlete from performing the motion that is causing problems. The underlying cause of the irritation must be determined. This may require an analysis of the athlete's technique, training program, equipment, etc. Chronic problems may require corticosteroid injection or surgical removal of the bursa.

Sprains

Sprains are injuries to ligaments. Like strains, sprains are classified as first, second, or third degree, depending upon their severity. Ligaments stabilize joints, so they must be given enough time to heal and restore joint stability before the athlete resumes normal activity. Refer all serious sprains to the team physician.

First degree sprain is a minor injury consisting of only limited tearing of the ligamentous fibers. The injury is characterized by pain, mild point tenderness, little or no swelling or hemorrhage, and minimal functional loss. There is no decrease in stability during stress testing (see Chapters 9 and 10). This injury may reoccur, so encourage the athlete to strengthen the muscles around the joint as much as possible, and use adhesive taping to aid joint stability (see the appendix).

Second degree sprain is more serious and is partial tearing of the ligament. The injury is characterized by joint instability, marked swelling, localized hemorrhage, point tenderness, and moderate loss of function. These injuries have a high rate of recurrence and often result in a persistently unstable joint. They may eventually lead to **osteoarthritis** because of abnormal friction created on the articular surfaces. These injuries take at least six to ten weeks to heal. One of the biggest causes of rein-

jury is the athlete playing prematurely. The injury appears to be healed, but the ligament has not regained its full functional capacity. Rest is essential, and the joint must be adequately protected when the athlete returns to participation.

Third degree sprain is a complete tearing of the ligament. This injury must be detected and treated early because the ligament rapidly deteriorates once it ruptures. The injury is characterized by loss of joint function, abnormal motion and possible deformity, local tenderness, swelling, and hemorrhage. The athletic trainer's initial evaluation is often invaluable because later evaluations may be hampered by swelling and the athlete's apprehension. Surgery is the preferred treatment for most third degree sprains in athletes.

Treatment. Initial treatment of sprains involves anti-inflammatory use of ICE and immobilization. As discussed, second degree sprain must be protected for an extended period of time. Introduce joint range of motion exercises *very* gradually because they may contribute to joint instability if introduced prematurely. The time of introduction depends upon the severity of injury. Rehabilitation should progress from (1) control of inflammation, (2) rest and protection from injury, (3) range of motion exercises, (4) resistive exercises, (5) introduction of complex motions (e.g., running in straight line, rapidly changing direction while running, (6) specific conditioning for sports, to (7) return to competition.

Nerve Injuries

The three types of nerve injuries are contusion, crush, and complete division. Nerve injuries often occur in conjunction with fractures and dislocations and may be missed during an initial evaluation if not specifically evaluated. Injuries that place pressure on nerves are particularly serious because they tend to interfere with the nerves' blood

Sprain: Disruption or injury of a ligament.

Osteoarthritis: Disease of the joints characterized by degeneration of joint (articular) cartilage and increase in the size (hypertrophy) of local bone.

supply and the transport of their neuroplasm (neural protoplasm). Peripheral nerve fibers can regenerate, although the process is often quite slow. Controlling the swelling should always be a top priority in treating a nerve injury because swelling hampers the healing rate of traumatized nerve tissue.

Nerve contusions are athletes' most common nerve injuries. They are most prevalent in the ulnar, peroneal, and radial nerves and are characterized by numbness and a sudden shocking pain. Usually these injuries are minor, but more serious contusions may cause chronic aching, swelling, and partial paralysis. Treatment for contusion includes protection from further injury, rest, and the use of anti-inflammatory techniques (see Chapters 8 and 13).

Preventing Injury to Soft Tissue

Soft tissue injuries are chronic or acute. Acute injuries are often unpreventable. Some injuries may be essentially unpreventable, such as a knee injury caused by a blindside block to the lateral knee, a head injury caused by a downhill ski racer crashing into an obstacle, or a sprained ankle caused by a basketball player stepping on the edge of another player's shoe. However, many injuries can be prevented by a systematic injury-prevention program (see Chapter 3). Strategies such as identifying and correcting musculoskeletal malalignments and imbalances, physical conditioning, proper selection and use of equipment, and evaluation of training techniques may significantly reduce the incidence of soft tissue injury.

References

Albright, J. A., and R. A. Brand. *The Scientific Basis of Orthopaedics*. New York: Appleton-Century-Crofts, 1979.

Balkfors, B. Course of knee-ligament injuries. *Acta Orthopaedica Scandinavica* supp. 198(53):1–79, 1982.

Brody, D. M. Running injuries. *CIBA Clinical Symposia* 32:1–36, 1980.

Brooks, G. A., and T. D. Fahey. *Exercise Physiology: Human Bioenergetics and Its Applications*. New York: Wiley, 1984.

Cailliet, R. *Soft Tissue Pain and Disability*. Philadelphia: F. A. Davis, 1977.

Harvey, J. S. Overuse syndromes in young athletes. *Pediatric Clinics of North America* 29:1369–1381, 1982.

Hilt, N. E., and S. B. Cogburn. *Manual of Orthopedics*. St. Louis: C. V. Mosby, 1980.

Hole, J. W. *Human Anatomy and Physiology*. Dubuque, Iowa: Wm. C. Brown, 1978.

Huxley, H. E. The mechanism of muscular contraction. *Science* 164:1356–1366, 1969.

Iversen, L. D., and D. K. Clawson. *Manual of Acute Orthopaedic Therapeutics*. Boston: Little, Brown, 1982.

Jobe, F. W., and C. M. Jobe. Painful athletic injuries of the shoulder. *Clinical Orthopaedics and Related Research* 173:117–124, 1983.

Johnson, R. J. The anterior cruciate: a dilemma in sports medicine. *International Journal of Sports Medicine* 3:71–79, 1982.

Johnson, W. R., and E. R. Buskirk (eds.). *Structural and Physiological Aspects of Exercise and Sports*. Princeton, N.J.: Princeton Book Co., 1980.

Martens, M., P. Wouter, A. Burssens, and J. C. Mulier. Patellar tendinitis: pathology and results of treatment. *Acta Orthopaedica Scandinavica* 53:445–450, 1982.

Monaco, B. R., H. B. Noble, and D. C. Bachman. Incomplete tears of the anterior cruciate ligament and knee locking. *Journal of the American Medical Association* 247:1582–1584, 1982.

Moretez, J. A., R. Walters, and L. Smith. Flexibility as predictor of knee injuries in football players. *The Physician and Sportsmedicine* 10:93–97, 1982.

O'Donoghue, D. H. *Treatment of Injuries to Athletes*. Philadelphia: W. B. Saunders, 1985.

Stanish, W. D. Overuse injuries in athletes: a perspective. *Medicine and Science in Sports and Exercise* 16:1–7, 1984.

Vander, A. J., J. H. Sherman, and D. S. Luciano. *Human Physiology: The Mechanisms of Body Function*. New York: McGraw-Hill, 1975.

6 Bone

Bone, a **connective tissue,** is a network (matrix) of **organic** (living) fibers produced by specialized cells and strengthened by the addition of **inorganic** (nonliving) substances, mainly crystallized salts. Most of bone's composition is inorganic. Bone and cartilage are categorized as supporting connective tissues because they are capable of supporting weight. Bone is the primary structural element of the body. Bone thus provides a strong framework for the body, protecting vital organs such as the brain, spinal cord, heart, and lungs. In addition, bones act as levers for skeletal muscles (Figures 6-1 and 6-2, pp. 96, 97).

Bone also plays a significant role in metabolism. Bone contains soft tissue called **bone marrow,** which produces blood cells (erythroctyes, granular leukocytes, and platelets). Bone marrow is particularly productive in the long bones, vertebrae, sternum, and ribs. The marrow of most of the long bones becomes infiltrated with fat and is unproductive after age twenty, but the marrow in the other productive areas continues to produce blood cells throughout life. Bone is also important for storing essential minerals, such as calcium, phosphates, magnesium, and sodium. Bone is affected by nutritional status, hormones, infectious disease,

physical training, and aging. Although bone's metabolic rate is relatively low, it becomes more rapid in certain states, such as during the healing of a fracture.

Organic and Inorganic Components

The organic components of bone are cells, which include a matrix of fibers, blood vessels, and lymphatics. The three types of bone cells are **osteoblasts, osteocytes,** and **osteoclasts.** Osteoblasts build bone tissue by producing the organic matrix where the crystallized salts are deposited. The matrix is called **osteoid;** the process of its formation is called **ossification.** Calcium is deposited in the matrix *after* the matrix has been formed. The terms ossification and calcification are often used synonymously, but this is incorrect.

If an osteoblast has surrounded itself with osteoid, the cell is now called an osteoctye and the space it occupies is called a **lacuna.** It is likely that osteocytes revert to osteoblasts when bone metabolism increases, such as occurs during **bone remodeling,** fracture healing, and **reactive hypertrophy.**

Connective tissue: Tissue composed mainly of nonliving substances; includes blood, cartilage, bone, fascia, ligaments, and tendons. It supports and protects the body.
Organic: Relating to living tissue.
Inorganic: Containing nonliving substances.
Bone marrow: A tissue within the structure of the long and the spongy bones; it is an important site for blood cell production.
Osteoblasts: Bone-forming cells.
Osteocyte: An osteoblast that has become surrounded with osteoid.
Osteoclast: A cell that absorbs bone tissue.
Osteoid: The bony matrix of organic fibers.
Ossification: The process of formation of the organic matrix (osteoid) of bone.

Lacuna: Spaces in which osteocytes reside.
Bone remodeling: Changes in a bone's characteristics from stress or mechanical alignment.
Reactive hypertrophy: Hypertrophy of bone in response to stress.

Epiphyseal injury (injury to the bone-growth centers) is a risk for prepubescent children involved in high-intensity or contact sports.

Osteoclasts exist on the uncovered surfaces of the bone, not in lacunas. These large cells are relatively inactive most of the time, but they respond to the body's need for calcium by initiating a process called **osteoclasis.** Osteoclasis is the simultaneous removal of osteoid and salts (i.e., deossification and decalcification). The osteoclasts' absorption of bone makes minerals, such as calcium, available to other tissues and removes bone during the bone remodeling that occurs in response to injury, mechanical stress, and growth.

The matrix is about 90 percent **collagen** fiber; the remaining 10 percent is a medium called **ground substance,** which is mostly extracellular fluid with dissolved organic compounds called proteoglycans. Ground substances include hyaluronic acid and chondroitin sulfate and provide a chemical environment for the deposit of crystalline salts.

Bone contains blood vessels that arise from one or several nutrient arteries.

These vessels supply the marrow as well as the cortex and cancellous (spongy) bone. In the cortex, vessel passageways are particularly well-developed. Vessels course through the dense bone in **Haversian canals** and form structural units called **osteons** (Figure 6-3, p. 98). Small bones usually have a single nutrient artery, and interruption of blood flow by the vessel's being torn during fracture or dislocation may kill the bone (**avascular necrosis),** a common consequence of fracture of the carpal navicular.

Bone's lymphatics are found primarily in the **periosteum,** the outer covering of bone. Bones are not abundantly supplied with nerves, but some nerves do accompany the vasculature throughout the tissue. The nerve supply consists of **sympathetic fibers,** which provide vascular motor control, and **sensory fibers,** which are primarily pain nerves. Although bone pain from a tumor or surgery is excruciating because the sensory nerve fibers are affected, the pain from a bone fracture is mainly from damage of surrounding soft tissue.

The inorganic components of bone are the crystalline salts. The salts (known as hydroxyapatites) deposited in the osteoid are mainly calcium and phosphorous. Other ions present in the osteoid include sodium, magnesium, carbonate, fluoride, potassium, and hydroxyl. Bone crystals may also combine with ions that are normally foreign to the body, such as strontium, lead, gold, and other heavy metals.

Calcium is the most abundant element in bone. In addition to its structural function in bone, calcium is involved in other vital physiologic functions, such as activating blood-clotting mechanisms, maintaining the normal excitability of nerves, **excitation-contraction coupling** in muscle, acid-base balance, maintenance of adhesiveness between cells and tissues, and regulating the permeability of cell membranes.

Calcium is a very dynamic substance within bone. It is in equilibrium with

Haversian canals: Passages within bone containing blood vessels.
Osteon: A structural unit formed from Haversian canals and blood vessels.

Avascular necrosis: Death of bone from the absence of a blood supply.

Periosteum: The outer covering of a bone.

Sympathetic fibers: Nerve fibers from the autonomic nervous system.
Sensory fibers: Nerve cells that carry sensory information from the periphery to the central nervous system. Also called efferent nerves.

Osteoclasis: The removal of organic bone matrix and inorganic salts from bone; the process is initiated by osteoclasts.

Collagen: A protein component of connective tissue and skin; these white fibers provide structure and support.
Ground substance: A material formed of organic compounds in which certain connective tissues are immersed.
Excitation-contraction coupling: The integration of neural excitation and muscular contraction.

Principles of Injury Prevention and Management

the calcium in the body fluids; both sources comprise a pool of exchangeable calcium that is readily available to supply the body's calcium requirements. The release of calcium from bone is controlled principally by parathyroid hormone. Other hormones that influence the organic as well as inorganic portions of bone include erythropoietin, glucocorticoids, thyrocalcitonin, growth hormone, and the androgens.

Phosphorus is the second most abundant element in bone. It is also vitally important in regulating neuromuscular function and acid-base balance and is extremely important in energy metabolism.

Structure of Bone

Bone's organic and inorganic components combine to form compact (dense) and cancellous (spongy) bone. Bones may be very large, such as the femur, or very small, such as the stapes; they may be flat, such as the scapula and sternum, short, such as the carpus and tarsus, or long, such as the humerus and tibia. Regardless of gross form, most bones have a dense wall called **cortical** bone (compact bone), with an arrangement of "beams" on the inside called trabecular (**cancellous** or spongy bone) (Figure 6-4, p. 99).

In the long bones, the trabeculae are at the ends where complex tensional forces require a strong structural arrangement. The shaft of a long bone is called the **diaphysis** and is composed of cortical bone with a central cavity called the **medullary canal,** which contains bone marrow. The inner surface of the medullary canal is lined with tissue called **endosteum,** which contains cells capable of becoming osteoblasts.

With the exception of **articular surfaces,** the outer surface of bone is lined with tissue called periosteum. The periosteum has a rich vascular and nerve

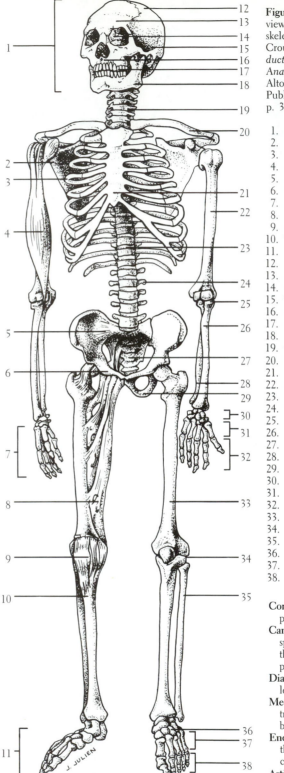

Figure 6-1 Anterior view of the human skeleton. (From Crouch, J. E. *Introduction to Human Anatomy*, 6th ed. Palo Alto, Calif.: Mayfield Publishing Co., 1983, p. 38.)

1. Skull
2. Scapula
3. Rib 4
4. Muscle
5. Ilium
6. Pubis
7. Hand
8. Muscle
9. Patella
10. Tibia
11. Foot
12. Parietal
13. Frontal
14. Orbit
15. Temporal
16. Nasal fossa
17. Maxilla
18. Mandible
19. Cervical vertebra
20. Clavicle
21. Sternum
22. Humerus
23. Thoracic vertebra
24. Lumbar vertebra
25. Elbow joint
26. Radius
27. Sacrum
28. Ulna
29. Ischium
30. Carpals
31. Metacarpals
32. Phalanges of digits
33. Femur
34. Knee joint
35. Fibula
36. Tarsals
37. Metatarsals
38. Phalanges of digits

Cortical bone: The dense portion of bone.
Cancellous bone: The spongy portion of bone that has a latticework appearance.
Diaphysis: The shaft of a long bone.
Medullary canal: The central cavity of compact bone.
Endosteum: Tissue lining the medullary canal; it contains osteoblasts.
Articular surface: The surface of a joint.

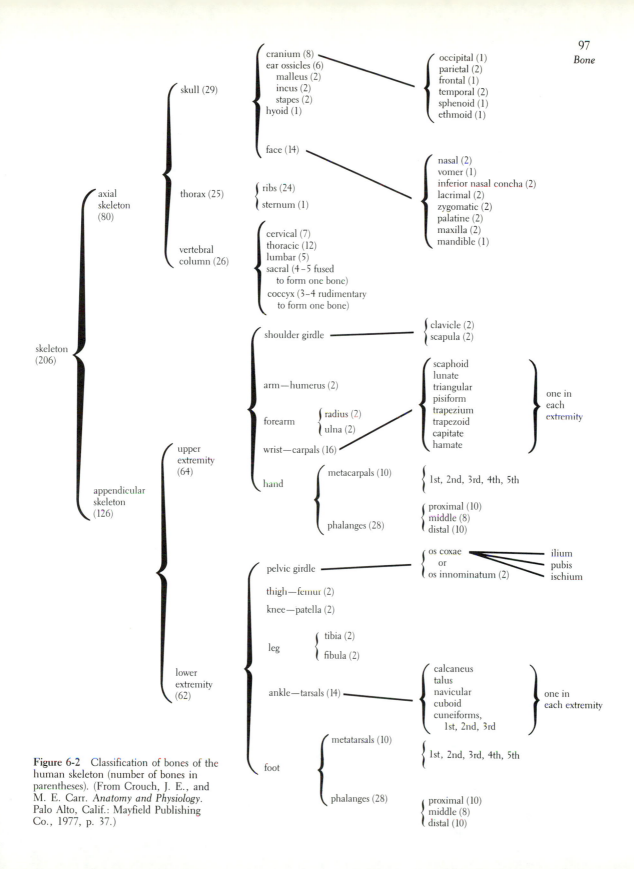

Figure 6-2 Classification of bones of the human skeleton (number of bones in parentheses). (From Crouch, J. E., and M. E. Carr. *Anatomy and Physiology*. Palo Alto, Calif.: Mayfield Publishing Co., 1977, p. 37.)

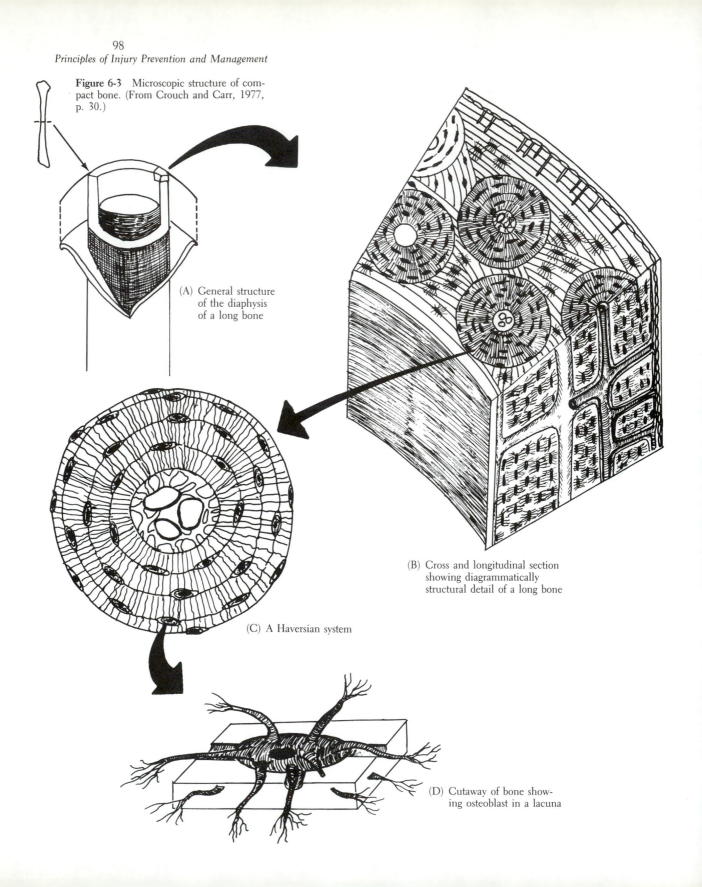

Figure 6-3 Microscopic structure of compact bone. (From Crouch and Carr, 1977, p. 30.)

(A) General structure of the diaphysis of a long bone

(B) Cross and longitudinal section showing diagrammatically structural detail of a long bone

(C) A Haversian system

(D) Cutaway of bone showing osteoblast in a lacuna

Epiphysis (end of bone)   Compact bone (cortical)   Diaphysis (shaft)   Medullary cavity (canal)   Epiphyseal line   Cancellous bone (trabecular)

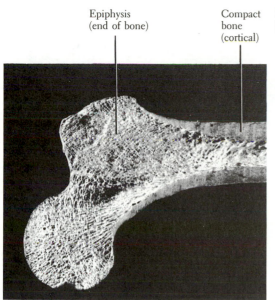
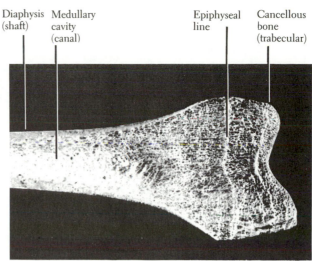

Figure 6-4 Structure of bone. Left is cortical (compact bone); right is cancellous (spongy) bone. (From Crouch, 1983, p. 37.)

supply and contains fibroblasts that can become osteoblasts and participate in the healing of fractures. The articular surfaces of many bones are covered with hyaline cartilage that absorbs shock and protects the underlying subchondral bone from erosion (see Chapter 7).

As a diaphysis flares near the ends of the bone, it gives way to the **epiphysis.** At this point, a cartilage-growth plate, called the **epiphyseal plate,** separates the **metaphysis** from the epiphysis. Some bones, such as the tibia, have an epiphyseal plate and epiphysis at both ends, while shorter bones, such as the phalanges, have only one plate and one epiphysis.

by a process called appositional growth. In endochondral ossification, there is bony encroachment on the epiphyseal cartilage on its proximal side while the cartilage grows outward on the distal side. Appositional growth is a result of osteoblastic activity in the deeper layers of the periosteum.

New bone, such as is formed during fracture reconstruction, is called **immature** or **woven bone.** This type of tissue is composed primarily of collagen fibers and ground substance that has not completely accumulated the inorganic material characteristic of mature bone. Bone is mature when osteoblastic activity ends and the Haversian canals have been constructed.

Bone Formation

Early in life, bone begins as cartilaginous tissue. During growth, cartilage is gradually replaced by bone in a process called **endochondral ossification.** The bone grows by proliferation of cartilage at its growth plates. Bones grow in length by endochondral ossification of the epiphyseal plate; they grow in width

Epiphyseal Growth Centers

The epiphyses of the bone continue to grow until they fuse with the metaphysis (Figure 6-5, p. 100). Epiphyseal fusion appears at different ages in different bones. For example, although the distal femoral epiphysis actually appears before birth, it does not fuse until age nineteen. The earliest epi-

Epiphysis: The end of a long bone. During growth it is separated from the shaft by a cartilagenous growth plate.

Epiphyseal plate: A plate of cartilage growth; it separates the metaphysis from the epiphysis.

Metaphysis: The junction between the diaphysis (shaft of the bone) and the epiphysis (end of the bone).

Immature (woven) bone: New bone formed during fracture reconstruction.

Endochondral ossification: The formation of bone at epiphyseal growth plates.

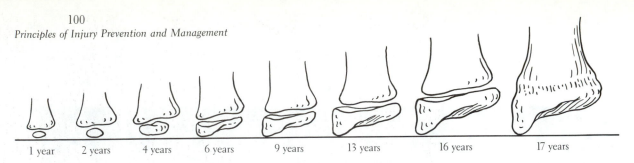

Figure 6-5 Development of the distal radius in males. Bone age, which is determined from a composite of the developmental status of the bones in the hand and wrist, is a measure of a child's maturational level.

physeal fusion usually occurs in the triquetral bone; the latest occurs in the lateral epicondyle of the humerus at ages twenty to twenty-two. Many normative data have been accumulated that clearly establish the ages at which various epiphyses fuse with their adjacent metaphyses. Skeletal age and maturation can be assessed by x-ray examination of a few bones.

Long bones typically have at least two epiphyses; shorter longitudinal bones, such as the phalanges, have only one epiphysis at the distal end. These epiphyses, by virtue of their position between compressive forces, are called **pressure epiphyses.** Some bones develop epiphyses at points where stresses are clearly not compressive but distractive. These epiphyses, called **traction epiphyses,** form bony projections for the attachment of muscles or, in some cases, ligaments. Good examples of traction epiphyses are the greater and lesser trochanters of the femur and the tibial tubercle.

Epiphyseal Injury

Fracture, thermal injury, or infection can cause decreased growth at the epiphyseal plate. It is interesting to note that continuous, excessive pressure may retard epiphyseal plate growth, yet a decrease in normal pressures, which are essentially intermittent, may also retard growth. It is also possible that only part of the plate may be affected by injury, causing nonuniform growth and angular deformities.

Adaptation to Stress

Bone is designed to withstand compressional and tensile stresses. The alignment of collagen fibers provides the tensile strength; the crystalline salts provide the compressional strength. Bone's tensile strength is 12,000 to 17,000 pounds per square inch (psi), which is less than that of copper but greater than that of white oak. Bone's compressive strength is 18,000 to 25,000 pounds per square inch, more than granite (15,000 psi) and white oak (7000 psi). Bone also resists shear forces, largely because of the binding of hydroxyapatites to the collagen fibers.

Bone also responds to stress by its physiologic mechanisms. Normally, osteoblastic activity (bone buildup) and osteoclastic activity (bone breakdown) balance each other, so there are no overt changes in bone. However, if abnormal forces are applied to the bone, bone-building activities can be selectively increased to create new lines of structural strength. Bone responds to stress and disuse by reducing tissue in areas where it is no longer needed and increasing it in areas that are subjected to stress. For example, if a patient's leg is enclosed in a cast and the patient is put on a non-weight-bearing status, the femur may lose up to 30 percent of its mineral content within twenty days. In contrast, healing accelerates if appropriate stresses are applied to the fracture site. As discussed, bone tends to hypertrophy (increase) from heavy exercise

Pressure epiphyses: Growth centers of long bones located in a position where they are subject to compressive forces.

Traction epiphyses: Growth centers of long bones located in a position where they are subject to distractive forces.

and atrophy (decrease) from inactivity. Interestingly, skeletons of inactive males are better developed at muscle attachment sites than skeletons of inactive females. However, there is no such distinction between the bones of active males and females.

Wolff's law describes bone remodeling in response to stress: Bone will be removed from sites where stress is reduced and formed at sites where stress is applied. The mechanism underlying Wolff's law is unclear, but many physiologists believe that bone deposition results from a "piezoelectric effect," the creation of a negative potential at the compression sites and a positive potential at the reduced-compression sites. It is believed that the small electrical current that is created may in some way direct osteoblastic and osteoclastic activities.

The balance between bone growth and degradation is negative or positive. If bone deposition exceeds resorption, as during the growth years, bone balance is positive. In old age, bone deposition falls behind bone resorption, creating negative bone balance.

Bone Abnormalities

Bone responds in several ways to stresses and health threats. It can respond by death (necrosis) of tissue, altering the rate of bone deposition, or altering the rate of bone resorption. Bone density can increase or decrease (density can be detected by x-rays). Increased bone density is called **sclerosis;** decreased bone density is called **rarefaction.** Sclerosis results from increased bone deposition with normal resorption and may occur in work-induced hypertrophy of bone, degenerative **osteoarthritis,** infection, neoplasms, and osteopetrosis.

Rarefaction eventually results in **osteopenia,** in which bone density becomes too low. The best example of osteope-

nia is **osteoporosis,** in which a relative decrease in osteoblastic activity reduces some bone, while the remaining bone is essentially normal in organic and inorganic components. Osteoporosis may be caused by protein malnutrition, vitamin C deficiency, postmenopausal decline in estrogen production, hyperadrenalism (Cushing's disease), excessive exogenous administration of glucocorticoids (see Chapter 27), and disuse of bones. This condition appears in 26 percent of women and 12 percent of men over the age of fifty. Osteoporosis may be seen in masters-level athletes (see Chapter 28).

Osteomalacia is a condition characterized by normal osteoblastic maintenance of the matrix but decreased calcification. The inorganic component of the bone is abnormal. In children, this condition is called rickets and is caused by calcium or phosphate deficiency in the extracellular fluids induced by vitamin D deficiency or parathyroid gland tumor.

Epiphyseal Abnormalities

There are a variety of epiphyseal disorders related to avascular necrosis. Collectively, the disorders form **osteochondroses.** These conditions, which are typically unilateral, are usually clinically apparent before the age of ten and affect boys more than girls. For unknown reasons, osteochondrosis begins with the obliteration of the blood supply to the epiphysis. Bone cells die, but the tissue remains strong for several months because bone resorption cannot occur without a blood supply. Surrounding tissues then begin revascularization of the dead epiphysis, which initiates a period of remodeling (bone proliferation). The new bone is particularly influenced by pressure. Bone is highly plastic and can readily assume abnormal shapes. Fractures may also occur during this period and contribute to deformities that can become permanent. A final phase of bone healing

---

Osteoporosis: Bone disease characterized by loss of bone matrix; most common in postmenopausal women.

Wolff's law: A theory describing how bone remodels in response to stress.

Osteomalacia: Disease characterized by softening and bending of the bones from abnormal bone formation (decreased calcification); most common in adult females.

Osteochondrosis (osteochondritis): Inflammation of bone and its cartilage, typically associated with avascular necrosis.

Sclerosis: A bone abnormality in which the density of the bone increases.
Rarefaction: A bone abnormality in which the density of the bone decreases.
Osteoarthritis: Disease of the joints characterized by degeneration of joint (articular) cartilage and increase in the size (hypertrophy) of local bone.
Osteopenia: A bone abnormality in which the density of the bone becomes low.

leaves the patient with bone of normal strength but abnormal shape and an abnormal articular surface.

Osteochondrosis does not produce symptoms during the initial phase of necrosis. While the bone is undergoing revascularization, fractures of the sub-chondral bone may produce pain, with a synovial effusion (leakage of synovial fluid from the joint) associated with local tenderness and painful range of motion. Signs of disuse atrophy in the muscles are typical. Usually this condition is discovered by accident during examination of some other illness or complaint, such as an athletic injury.

Osteochondroses have specific names in different anatomical locations. Osteochondrosis of the femoral head is called Legg-Perthes disease in children and Chandler's disease in adults. When osteochondrosis occurs in the tarsal navicular, it is called Köhler's disease; when it occurs in a primary center of ossification in the spine, it is called Calvé's disease. Osteochondroses also affect traction epiphyses. When associated with forceful traction through the patellar tendon or specific trauma resulting in an avulsion (detachment) of part of the tibial tubercle, the condition is called Osgood-Schlatter disease (Chapter 21). Similarly, partial avulsion of calcaneal apophysis is known as Sever's disease. It seems apparent that imbalances between skeletal and muscle strength, as might occur in rapidly developing young athletes, are a probable cause of osteochondrosis of traction epiphyses.

Abnormal Bone Deposition

Bone may be deposited in tissues where ossification and calcification normally do not occur; this condition is called traumatic **myositis ossificans** (a form of **heterotopic** ossification or misplaced bone formation). Soft tissue injury, associated with bone fracture or isolated muscle injury, may create physiological conditions under which fibrocytes are transformed into osteoblasts. These new bone cells produce osteoid between the fibers of the injured tissue (i.e., within a **hematoma**) that then becomes calcified. This "misplaced" bone is usually resorbed to a great extent within several months. The condition may be aggravated and more fibers torn if the area is used to any extent during physical activity. Conservative treatment includes rest and splinting. In adults, the hip is a common site of heterotopic ossification, which has a profound effect upon the range of motion. The condition typically does not resolve itself and must be managed surgically.

Do not confuse traumatic myositis ossificans with myositis ossificans progressiva (MOP), which is ossification in the fibrous tissue of muscle, tendons, ligaments, and joint capsules that have no history of local trauma. MOP is a congenital abnormality that may not become clinically apparent until early childhood. Symptoms include episodes of pain and swelling in muscles close to joints. A young athlete who shows signs of heterotopic ossification following a trivial provocation should be examined for this condition. There is no cure for myositis ossificans progressiva.

Aging in Bone

When bone ages, the total amount of bone tissue is reduced as a result of an imbalance between osteoblastic and osteoclastic activities. The result is osteoporosis. Aged bone is weakened and may fail structurally under normally trivial stresses. Osteomalacia (gradual softening and bending of the bone) is also characteristic of aged bone. If this condition develops slowly, as it usually does, bone deformities may become apparent before overt fracture.

Osteoporosis manifests itself in fractures. Men over eighty-five have twice

Hematoma: A bruise; a mass of partially clotted blood outside the vascular space, typically formed from trauma.

Myositis ossificans: Formation of bone within a muscle, usually caused by trauma; muscular ossification.

Heterotopic: Occurring in an abnormal location.

the fracture rate of men under forty, in spite of the younger men indulging in greater activity. Women eighty-five or over have a fracture rate ten times greater than that of younger females. In addition to overt fractures, signs of osteoporosis include compression fractures of the vertebral bodies, loss of height, biconcavity of vertebral bodies, and chronic backache.

Bone loss is difficult to detect. X-rays cannot reveal bone loss until calcium depletion exceeds 30 to 40 percent, but bone scans are usually more effective. When loss is apparent, it is mostly from the endosteal surface. Thus, the medullary cavity expands by osteoclastic resorption of endosteal bone. At the same time, appositional growth of bone on the periosteal surface fails to keep pace, resulting in a net loss of bone.

Since bone loss and fracture rates are greater in postmenopausal women, it is tempting to attribute these problems to the decrease in female steroid hormones. This is an attractive hypothesis because estrogens exert an anabolic influence upon protein metabolism and bone. Estrogens have been used successfully to diminish bone loss in postmenopausal women and to improve "bone health" in patients with senile osteoporosis. In spite of these findings, there is insufficient evidence to positively link osteoporosis in women with cessation of normal ovarian secretion. In men, declining secretion of androgens (male hormones, such as testosterone) may decrease bone growth and lead to osteoporosis.

Other factors that may be involved with bone loss with age include reduced physical activity, deficiency of calcium and protein in the diet, and altered metabolism of bone salts and matrix secretion. In spite of efforts to combat osteoporosis by dietary and estrogen supplements, there is no clearly effective treatment for bone loss with aging. Hip fractures and vertebral compression fractures continue to occur frequently among the elderly.

Fractures

Fracture creates a structural discontinuity in bone, causing it to lose its function as a structural organ. Although there may be no overt alteration in the shape of the limb, impaired function usually becomes glaringly apparent when the limb is tested. In addition, the fracture may place vital internal organs at risk. For example, a fracture of the occipital bone may potentially damage brain tissue, and a fractured rib may damage the lungs, heart, or liver. In other cases, gross deformity may be a strikingly clear sign of fracture.

Most fractures are caused by failure induced by bending or tensile forces. Fractures due to compression and shear forces are uncommon in cortical bone because of its capacity to withstand these types of stresses. Trabecular (cancellous) bone is more susceptible to compression failure, so crush injuries result when the fracture surfaces are impacted.

Fractures in the shaft of a long bone are called **diaphyseal fractures.** Long bones may also experience epiphyseal and metaphyseal fractures. A fracture to the articular (joint) aspect of the bone is called an intraarticular fracture. A fracture is called *simple* if one fracture line is formed but called *comminuted* if there is more than one fracture line and more than two fragments. The term "simple" previously meant that the skin was not broken by the fracture. Currently, the term "closed" means that the skin remains intact, and "open" means that the skin is broken.

The extent of the fracture may be variable: Fragments of fractured bone may be large and palpable, barely visible with the unaided eye at the time of surgery, or unresolved by radiograph. A crack or hairline fracture is called an *incomplete fracture*, such as a greenstick fracture seen in children. The fragments may be pulled apart or distracted, pushed together or impacted,

Fracture: A break in a bone or in cartilage.

Diaphyseal fracture: Fracture to the shaft of a bone.

rotated, angulated, or overriding each other. Finally, the fracture line may be transverse, oblique, or spiral.

The status of the periosteum is an important factor in the management and healing of fractures. An intact periosteum may prevent major displacement of the fracture fragments, protect the surrounding soft tissue, and hasten the healing process. It may also enable the fracture to be treated by **closed reduction** (nonsurgically) and thus prevent overcorrection by the surgeon.

Complications

Surrounding soft tissues are usually injured when a bone is broken. For example, in addition to fracture, bone-crush injuries may affect skin, subcutaneous tissues, muscles, blood vessels, nerves, and connective tissues. These additional injuries are called primary complications of the fracture. Any secondary complications that arise may be iatrogenic (induced by the treatment), including skin, vascular, neurological, joint, and bone problems. Finally, tertiary complications, such as nonunion or myositis ossificans, may arise during the healing period.

Skin problems may include punctures or lacerations sustained during fracture, entrapment of dirt in the dermis as a result of abrasions, and decubitis ulcers from excessive cast pressure or improperly regulated bed rest. In addition, surgical wounds, which are susceptible to infection, may be extensive.

Vascular complications may include arterial rupture, spasm, **thrombosis,** or occlusion by compression. The latter three problems may be side effects of treatment. Stretching an artery by traction can lead to spasm. Occlusion and thrombosis may be caused by a cast that is too tight. If arterial compression is caused by venous engorgement within a fascial compartment with poor expansibility, the resulting vascular insufficiency is called Volkmann's isch-

emia. In this condition, there is severe pain in ischemic muscles (muscles with inadequate blood flow), the skin is cool and pallid, and there is edema with impaired peripheral nerve function, with paresthesia and hypoesthesia. Paralysis is a frequent finding, together with reduced or impalpable peripheral pulses. Sensation, active motion, and peripheral pulses should be checked frequently in the early stages of convalescence. Fat emboli are vascular complications that may be life-threatening. They typically arise from diaphyseal fractures and cause pulmonary vascular insufficiency accompanied by dyspnea and cyanosis. **Petechial hemorrhages** in the skin may be seen, and the patient may develop a fever with headache. In rare cases, cardiac embolization may occur.

Neurological complications of fracture may include contusion, crushing, or complete division of a nerve. Recovery from nerve contusion is generally complete within six weeks; recovery from a nerve-crush injury may take considerably longer. Surgery is usually indicated for nerve-crush injuries that do not heal and injuries involving the complete division of the nerve.

Joint problems almost invariably arise if the fracture is intra-articular. Common problems include fracture of articular cartilage, torn ligaments and capsules, and infection (particularly with open fractures). The latter condition is called septic arthritis and may be potentially more damaging than the fracture.

Bone complications include osteomyelitis and avascular necrosis. Open fractures are especially vulnerable to infection. Osteomyelitis may occur in a closed fracture that was managed by **open reduction.** Moreover, pins inserted to externally fix unstable fragments may provide tracts for infectious organisms. Avascular necrosis results from occlusion, compression, or rupture of the nutrient artery. A particularly good example of a bone complication that may be easily overlooked at

Closed reduction: Nonsurgical reduction of a fracture.

Petechial hemorrhage: Small hemorrhage in the skin, nail beds, or mucous membranes that appears as nonraised, purplish red spots.

Thrombosis: Formation of a blood clot.

Open reduction: Surgical reduction of a fracture.

the time of injury is the carpal navicular fracture, which often fails to achieve union.

Healing

A unique feature of bone is that it is the only tissue in the body capable of healing without a scar. Bone may take several months to heal completely, but fully healed fractures cannot be distinguished from other parts of the bone unless the site is marked by residual deformities.

Cortical bone heals differently from cancellous bone. However, at the time of fracture in either type of bone, blood vessels lying in the Haversian canals are torn and the osteocytes in lacunas die from interruption of their blood supply. (See Figure 6-6.) Thus, the fracture ends become necrotic. The area of necrosis is larger and the healing time increased if the nutrient artery is ruptured by the fracture. In addition, with disruption of larger blood vessels, there is a greater risk of fat emboli. In any event, the bleeding that does occur eventually ends by clotting and the formation of a hematoma. If the periosteum is intact, the hematoma is more localized and more easily resolved with fewer complications. If there has been considerable displacement, because of tearing of the periosteum, the resulting hematoma may spread through adjacent tissues.

Repair cells arise from the undisplaced periosteum and from the endosteum. These are osteogenic cells that are essentially osteoblasts. They form a

Figure 6-6 Phases of bone repair for fractures.
(A) Osteogenic cells migrate to the fracture site and proliferate. These cells begin laying down a collagen matrix.
(B) An external callus and an internal callus begin to form. The fibrous periosteum is not continuous.
(C) There is a bridging between the internal and external calluses, replacement of cartilage with new bone, calcification of new bone, and the development of Haversian canals in the new tissue.

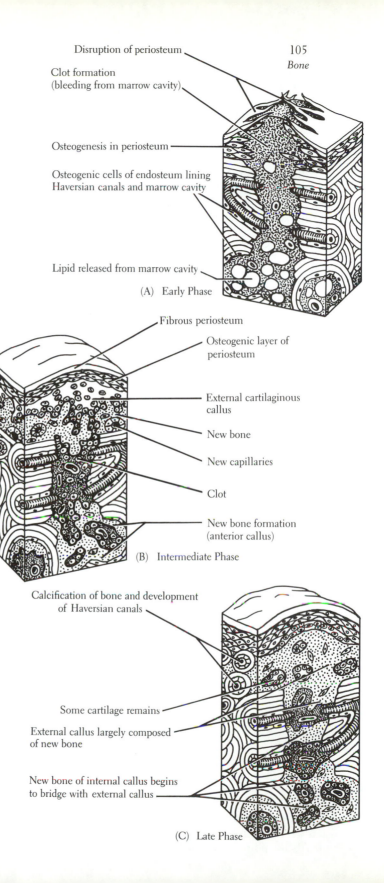

Disruption of periosteum

Clot formation
(bleeding from marrow cavity)

Osteogenesis in periosteum

Osteogenic cells of endosteum lining
Haversian canals and marrow cavity

Lipid released from marrow cavity

(A) Early Phase

Fibrous periosteum

Osteogenic layer of periosteum

External cartilaginous callus

New bone

New capillaries

Clot

New bone formation
(anterior callus)

(B) Intermediate Phase

Calcification of bone and development of Haversian canals

Some cartilage remains

External callus largely composed of new bone

New bone of internal callus begins to bridge with external callus

(C) Late Phase

soft tissue bridge called a **callus,** which connects the fracture fragments. If the periosteum is displaced, the surrounding soft tissues give rise to undifferentiated mesenchymal cells that grow into the hematoma and necrotic tissue forming the callus. The growth rate of a callus is remarkable. By the end of the second week following fracture, the ends of the bone may be completely united by soft osteogenic tissue. Few bone tumors have comparable growth rates.

A callus cannot be visualized on a radiograph until bone is deposited within it. For example, stress fractures, which are common in portions of the skeleton subject to overuse, cannot be seen on x-ray until the callus has formed and the injury has essentially healed (see Figures 6-7, p. 107, and 6-8, p. 108). As healing proceeds from the initial stage, the callus loses its soft, fluidlike character and becomes tighter, with a gluelike consistency. An osteogenic callus then appears, initially at some distance from the fracture line in an area of good blood supply. Osteogenic cells begin laying down a dense network of collagen and they deposit bone salts. As the callus alteration proceeds, immature or woven bone appears. At the fracture line, where blood supply remains poor or nonexistent, chondroblasts (cells that form cartilage) appear and form a cartilage bridge. After several weeks, the fracture is bridged by woven bone at the periphery and cartilage at the center. Final consolidation occurs through endochondral ossification. The time it takes this process varies; it depends upon such factors as the cross-sectional area of the fracture, degree of displacement or gaps between fragments, nutritional status, endocrinological status, local blood supply, site and configuration of the fracture, presence of infection, and age of the patient.

Clinical union is achieved when bending and twisting forces on the fractured bone do not produce movement or pain. At this point, x-rays will reveal a bony callus, with some signs of the fracture line. Immobilization is no longer required when clinical union has occurred, but the injured part must be protected until consolidation has obliterated the fracture line. **Radiographic union** occurs when the fracture is replaced by complete bony union. The bony callus is replaced by mature bone showing Haversian canals with no signs of temporary cartilaginous callus. X-rays may show some angulation and even "sharp corners," but these will disappear in ensuing months as the bone remodels according to the principles of Wolff's law.

Cancellous bone has a greater blood supply than cortical bone. Thus, when cancellous bone is fractured, there tends to be better nutrition and less necrosis of tissue. In addition, the area of bony contact is usually much larger than in a cortical bone fracture, and there is less displacement. Healing in cancellous bone occurs through the formation of an endosteal callus. This process is primarily "internal" and spreads from points of bony contact between fragments. Clinical union proceeds from the point of fracture outward. Initially, woven bone appears, followed by consolidation with a lamellar pattern similar to that of cortical bone. The structure of cancellous bone then reappears, across the fracture zone, with the restoration of trabeculae.

Crush injuries (they produce fracture fragments) occur more frequently in cancellous than cortical bone because cancellous bone more readily fails under compressive forces. The only beneficial aspect of a cancellous bone-crush injury is that the impaction promotes good surface contact between the fragments, which promotes better healing. Healing may be delayed if the fragments are pulled apart during reduction of the fracture.

Abnormal Healing

Problems in fracture healing arise when the fragments are improperly set

Callus: A bonelike mass formed in the process of fracture repair.

Radiographic union: During fracture healing, the period when the bony union is complete and there is no sign of the cartilaginous callus.

Clinical union: During fracture repair, the period when pain is gone and the bone has assumed structural integrity. Healing is not yet complete, but immobilization is no longer required.

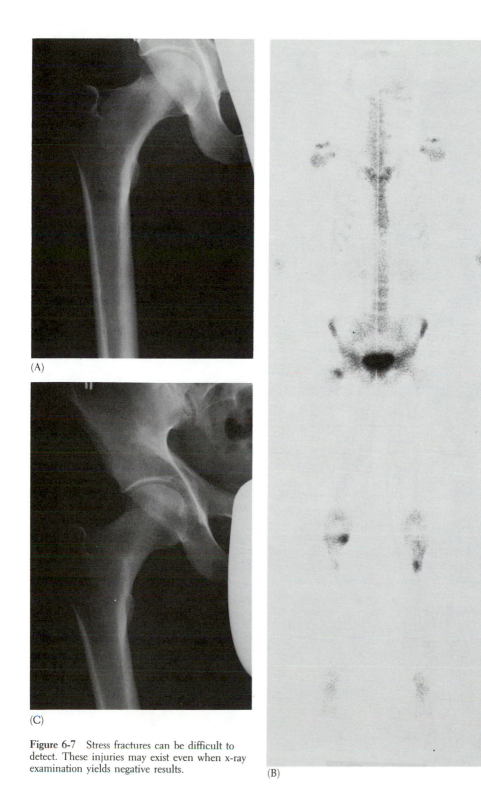

(A)

(C)

(B)

Figure 6-7 Stress fractures can be difficult to detect. These injuries may exist even when x-ray examination yields negative results.

(A) X-ray of pelvic stress fracture during early symptomatic period (three weeks after onset of symptoms). At this point, the x-ray appears normal. Subject is a marathon runner.

(B) Bone scan showing increased biological activity in pelvis (hot spot), possibly indicating a stress fracture (six weeks after onset of symptoms). Notice the hot spot around the knee joint.

C) X-ray eleven weeks after onset of symptoms showing callus formation at stress fracture. Stress fractures are typically not evident on an x-ray until the fracture is almost healed.

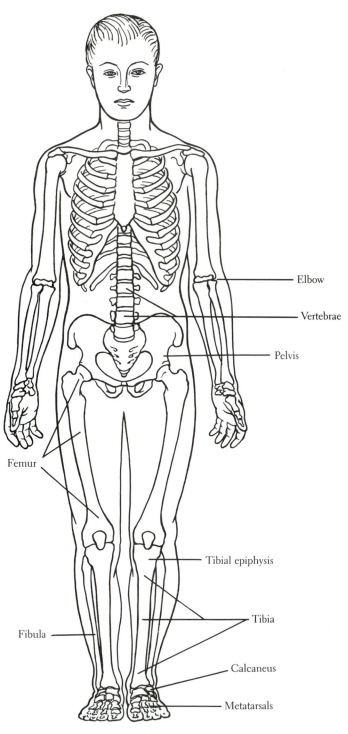

Figure 6-8 Stress fractures can occur in any bone, but the sites shown here are the most common ones in athletes.

Elbow

Vertebrae

Pelvis

Femur

Tibial epiphysis

Tibia

Fibula

Calcaneus

Metatarsals

or carelessly moved during the early stages of convalescence. Other problems may be related to the age of the patient, infection, coexisting endocrinological disorders such as **hyperthyroidism,** and site and configuration of the fracture. In some bones, an oblique fracture may heal faster because of greater surface contact. Bones surrounded by muscle tend to heal faster than superficial bones.

Malunion occurs if the fracture fragments heal with residual deformity. The unsightly lump seen in many "healed" clavicular fractures is an example of malunion. Delayed union occurs if bony consolidation takes longer than expected. In some cases, fracture fragments fail to unite, resulting in nonunion. Nonunion may not occur totally if a fibrous connection is established that prevents full displacement of the fragments. A false joint or pseudoarthrosis may be created if the fragment allows some bending. These conditions are not permanent in every case. Bone grafts and extensive internal or external fixation may correct malunion or nonunion and promote normal union.

Fractures in Children

Although fractures are more common in children, they generally respond to the injury more effectively than adults' fractures (see Chapter 28). Children tend to have a stronger and more active periosteum, which prevents bone displacement and fosters intensive osteogenic activity during healing. Thus fractures tend to heal much faster in children. For example, a diaphyseal femur fracture in a twelve-year-old child will be united in twelve weeks; in a twenty-year-old, this process will require twenty weeks. Moreover, after

healing, residual deformities tend to be spontaneously corrected in children, whereas they tend to be permanent in adults.

Children do have unique problems when sustaining fractures. Diagnosis problems may arise when epiphyseal lines are confused with fractures. A fracture that includes an epiphyseal plate may lead to growth disturbances that of course would not be of concern in an adult with an identical fracture. Osteomyelitis also tends to run a more serious and damaging course in children, and Volkmann's ischemia, traumatic myositis ossificans, and refracture all occur more often. Finally, children are less tolerant of blood loss.

Hyperthyroidism: Excessive production of thyroid hormone, characterized by weight loss, increased appetite, tachycardia, tremor, and fatigue.

Malunion: Healing of fracture fragments but with residual deformity.

References

Aegerter, E., and J. A. Kirkpatrick. *Orthopaedic Diseases.* Philadelphia: W. B. Saunders, 1968.

American College of Surgeons, Committee on Trauma. *The Management of Fractures and Soft Tissue Injuries.* Philadelphia: W. B. Saunders, 1965.

Apley, A. G. *A System of Orthopaedics and Fractures.* London: Butterworth, 1968.

Bryant, W. M. Wound healing. *CIBA Clinical Symposia* 29:1–36, 1977.

Guyton, A. C. *Textbook of Medical Physiology.* Philadelphia: W. B. Saunders, 1981.

Ham, A. *Histology.* New York: Lippincott, 1965.

Hollinshead, W. H. *Textbook of Anatomy.* New York: Harper & Row, 1974.

Rang, M. (ed.). *The Growth Plate and Its Disorders.* Edinburgh: Livingstone, 1968.

Salter, B. *Textbook of Disorders and Injuries of the Musculoskeletal System.* Baltimore: Williams & Wilkins, 1970.

Tanner, J. M., R. H. Whitehouse, W. A. Marshall, M. J. R. Healy, and H. Goldstein. *Assessment of Skeletal Maturity and Prediction of Adult Height.* New York: Academic Press, 1975.

Synovial Joints and Range of Motion

JOINTS (articulations) are skeletal structures that serve as interfaces between bones. They are constructed to facilitate motion yet protect the articular surfaces of connecting bones and their adjoining soft tissues. Joints play a critical role in the synchronized motions that are the essence of athletics. A primary goal of sports medicine practitioners, including athletic trainers, is to preserve normal joint function by preventing injury and to properly treat and rehabilitate joint injuries when they do occur.

The three types of joints are **fibrous, cartilaginous,** and **synovial** (Table 7-1, p. 111, and Figure 7-1, p. 118). Fibrous and cartilaginous joints are not discussed in detail here because they have little functional significance in sports medicine. Fibrous joints are fixed joints, such as the syndesmoses (bones united by fibrous connective tissue) formed by the inferior tibiofibular joint. Cartilaginous joints are characterized by articulated bones separated by a cartilaginous junction or fibrocartilage disk. The symphysis pubis is a cartilaginous joint formed by the articulation of the pubis bones with fibrocartilage that lacks a **synovial surface.** Synchondroses are temporary cartilaginous junctions between the metaphysis and epiphysis

that disappear after growth has ceased.

Synovial joints differ from fibrous and cartilaginous joints in that the bones of the joint are not continuous with each other but in extremely close proximity. The **osseous surfaces** are covered by a thin layer of specialized **hyaline cartilage** (and, occasionally, fibrocartilage) that is bathed in synovial fluid. This joint structure allows a very low **coefficient of friction** and facilitates sliding between the articular surfaces.

Characteristics of Synovial Joints

The synovial joints can be classified by complexity of organization, movement capability, and gross **morphology.** Synovial joints are organized as simple, compound, or complex. A *simple* joint has two articulating surfaces. A *compound* joint has more than one pair of articulating surfaces. A *complex* synovial joint has an intracapsular disk or **meniscus** composed of fibrocartilage.

The movements of synovial joints are uniaxial, biaxial, or triaxial. A *uniaxial* (single axis) joint can only rotate. A *biaxial* joint can perform completely independent movements around two axes.

Osseous surface: Bone surface.

Hyaline cartilage: A translucent, elastic, bluish white cartilage that covers the articular surface of bones.

Coefficient of friction: The tendency of one surface to rub against another.

Fibrous joint: A fixed joint.

Cartilaginous: Composed of cartilage.

Synovial joint: A joint with a capsule lined with synovial membrane.

Morphology: The form or structure of an organism or body segment.

Menisci: Interarticular fibrocartilages.

Synovial surface: A surface composed of synovial membrane.

Success in sports like gymnastics partly depends upon maximizing the joints' ranges of motion.

Table 7-1 *Joint Classification*

Fibrous joints

Synarthrosis: Minimum fibrous tissue between bones. No movement. Adjacent bones overlap or form interlocking edges.
    Example: Sutures of the skull

Syndesmosis: More fiber between bones than in synarthrosis, so some movement is possible.
    Example: Distal tibiofibular joint

Cartilaginous joints

Synchondroses: Temporary cartilaginous junctions between the diaphysis (metaphysis) and epiphysis that disappear when the skeleton is mature.
    Example: Growth plates of the long bones

Fibrocartilaginous joints: Composed of a slightly movable fibrocartilage disk that separates bones covered with hyaline cartilage.
    Example: Symphysis pubis and vertebral joints

Synovial joints

Freely movable joints surrounded by a joint capsule and lined (except on the articular surfaces) by synovium that secretes synovial fluid.
    Example: Most joints of the body, including the knee, hip, and elbow (see Table 7-2, p. 113)

A *triaxial* joint can move about three axes and thus has the maximum degree of freedom of motion (e.g., glenohumeral joint).

There are seven gross morphological classifications of synovial joints (Table 7-2, p. 113). *Plain joints* are formed by the apposition of flat articular surfaces. *Hinge joints* (ginglymi) look like the hinges of a door and their movement is uniaxial. *Pivot (trochoid) joints* are formed by a cylindrical surface of one bone and a ringed surface of another bone and their movement is uniaxial. *Bicondylar joints* have surfaces formed by two distinct, convex, knuckle-shaped condyles that articulate with two concave surfaces. *Ellipsoid joints* are biaxial. *Sellar (saddle) joints* are characterized by the concave surface of one bone fitting complementarily into the convex surface of another. *Spheroidal (ball-and-socket) joints* involve the ball-shaped head of one bone fitting into the concave socket of another bone.

Articular Surface of Synovial Joints

The articular surface of most bones is formed of a special variety of hyaline cartilage (see Chapter 5) that facilitates movement, absorbs shock, and protects the **subchondral bone** (Figure 7-2, p. 113). Articular cartilage is typically

Subchondral bone: The bone immediately below the articular cartilage.

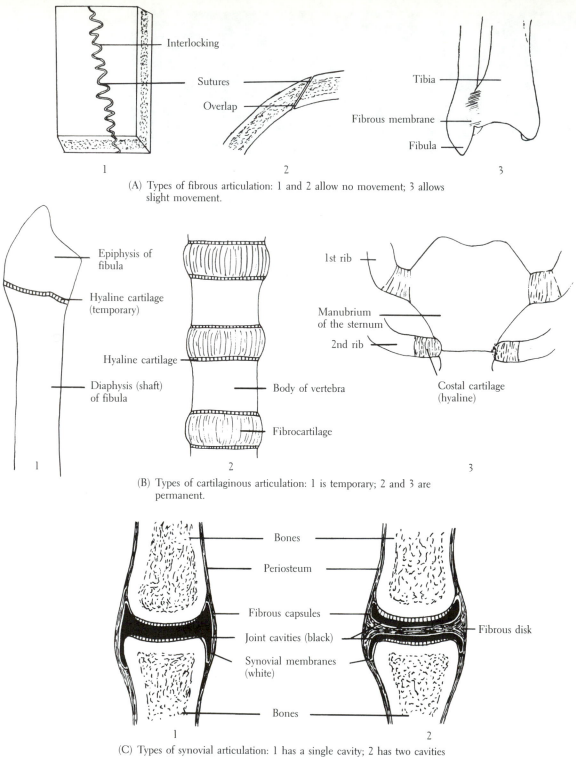

(A) Types of fibrous articulation: 1 and 2 allow no movement; 3 allows slight movement.

(B) Types of cartilaginous articulation: 1 is temporary; 2 and 3 are permanent.

(C) Types of synovial articulation: 1 has a single cavity; 2 has two cavities and a fibrous disk.

Figure 7-1 Fibrous, cartilaginous, and synovial joints. (From Crouch, J. E. *Introduction to Human Anatomy*, 6th ed. Palo Alto, Calif.: Mayfield Publishing Co., 1983, p. 42.)

Table 7-2 *The Seven Morphological Classifications of Synovial Joints*

1. *Plain joints:* Formed by the opposition of flat articular surfaces.
   Example: Intercarpal joints
2. *Hinge joints (ginglymi):* Uniaxial joints that resemble door hinges.
   Example: Interphalangeal joints
3. *Pivot (trochoid) joints:* An articulation formed by a cylindrical surface of one bone and a ringed surface of another bone.
   Example: Articulation of proximal radius and ulna
4. *Bicondylar joints:* Two distinct, convex, knuckle-shaped condyles of one bone articulate with two concave surfaces of another.
   Example: Knee joint
5. *Ellipsoid (condyloid) joints:* Biaxial joints that allow movements about two axes at right angles.
   Example: Metacarpophalangeal joints
6. *Sellar (saddle) joints:* Concave surface of one bone fits complementarily into the convex surface of another.
   Example: Articulation of the first metacarpal with the trapezium
7. *Spheroidal (ball-and-socket) joints:* Ball-shaped head of one bone fits into a concave socket.
   Example: Hip

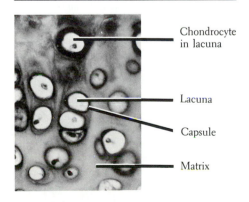

Chondrocyte in lacuna

Lacuna

Capsule

Matrix

Figure 7-2 Photomicrograph of hyaline cartilage. (From Crouch, 1983, p. 26.)

from one to two millimeters thick but may be as thick as five to seven millimeters in the larger joints. Young cartilage is typically white, smooth, and to the naked eye it glistens; aging cartilage is thinner, less cellular, more brittle, and has a yellowish opacity and irregular surfaces. Articular cartilage is porous, which enhances this tissue's shock-absorbing capability. Microscopically, **chondrocytes** (mature cartilage cells) are embedded in a matrix of water, proteoglycans, lipid, collagen, noncollagenous protein, and electrolytes.

Articular cartilage's potential for healing depends upon the chondrocytes' ability to form new cells. The articular cartilage chondrocytes of adults and adolescents have the capacity to substantially increase their rate of matrix synthesis, thereby contributing to the repair of articular cartilage. The ability of these chondrocytes to respond to injury depends upon the acuteness of the injury, the general health of the articular cartilage, and the possibility of repetitive injury to the cartilage base.

Until recently, articular cartilage was considered metabolically inert. However, research conducted over the last twenty-five years has shown that this tissue has a surprisingly active metabolism. The processes involved in replacement and repair of cartilage take place under avascular condition (no blood supply) and are extremely complex. **Anaerobic glycolysis** is the major metabolic pathway articular cartilage uses.

As discussed in Chapter 5, the other types of cartilage are white and yellow. White fibrocartilage, consisting of dense white fibrous tissue arranged in bundles, is the major constituent of intervertebral disks and the knee menisci. (See Figure 7-3, p. 114). Yellow fibrocartilage is found in the corniculate cartilages of the larynx and epiglottis.

Chondrocyte: A mature cartilage cell.

Anaerobic glycolysis: Breakdown of glucose (sugar) into pyruvic or lactic acid without oxygen (anaerobic).

Synovial Fluid

Synovial fluid is a clear, viscous fluid of slightly alkaline **pH** located within the cavities of synovial joints, bursa, and tendon sheaths. It provides a liquid environment with a narrow pH range for the joint surfaces; is a source of nutrition for the articular cartilages, disks, and menisci; and is a lubricant, which increases joint efficiency and reduces erosion of surfaces. In addition to producing synovial fluid, the synovial membrane is involved in the removal of materials from the joint cavity. Synovial inflammation, called **synovitis**, may occur if this removal function is upset by joint injury.

Joint Capsule

Synovial joints possess a fibrous capsule that consists of parallel and interlacing bundles of white connective tissue fibers. The capsule is perforated by the articular blood vessels and nerves and may contain one or more openings through which the synovial membrane protrudes to form a pouch or sac. Capsular ligaments are often formed by two or more localized thickenings that contain parallel fiber bundles. Fibrous **joint capsules** are often reinforced or replaced by tendons or expansions of tendons from neighboring muscles.

Some joints also contain extracapsular or intracapsular accessory ligaments that are independent of the fibrous capsule. Ligamentous tissue is tough and unyielding but flexible enough to offer no resistance to normal movement. Such tissue is designed to prevent excessive or abnormal movements and become tight at the normal limit of the joint's range of motion.

The synovial membrane, which lines the nonarticular parts of synovial joints, synovial bursae, and synovial tendon sheath, is derived from embryonic

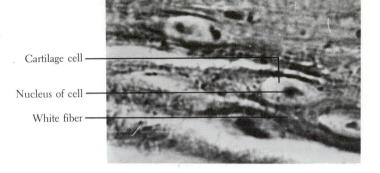

Cartilage cell —
Nucleus of cell —
White fiber —

Figure 7-3 Photomicrograph of white fibrocartilage. (From Crouch, 1983, p. 27.)

mesenchyme (an embryonic tissue). In joints, the membrane lines the fibrous capsule and blankets any bony surfaces, ligaments, and tendons contained within the capsule. The surfaces of intra-articular disks or menisci are not clothed in synovial membrane, and the synovial membrane ends at the margin of the articular cartilages. Most of the inner surface of the synovial membrane is pink, smooth, and shiny and contains occasional **synovial villae**, which are fingerlike projections that produce as well as filter the synovial fluid. Accumulations of adipose tissue are characteristic of the synovial membrane of many joints, and these articular fat pads may be sources of secondary pain from single or repetitive trauma. Plicae (synovial membrane folds), which represent a persistence of embryonic septa in the synovial membrane, may also become symptomatic and limit joint function.

Bursae

Bursae are flattened sacs of synovial membrane supported by dense irregular connective tissue and interposed in the loose areolar tissue (connective tissue formed of cells and interlacing collagenous and elastic fibers) between skin and bone (Figure 7-4). They reduce friction and facilitate movement over a limited range of motion. Each bursa contains a capillary film of synovial fluid that acts as a lubricant and pro-

Synovial fluid: Fluid secreted by the joint synovium; it lubricates and nurtures the joint.

pH: The relative alkalinity or acidity of a solution.

Synovitis: Inflammation of a synovial membrane.

Mesenchyme: Portion of the mesoderm that produces all the connective tissues of the body, blood, blood vessels, lymphatic system, and heart.

Synovial villae: Fingerlike projections of the synovium.

Joint (articular) capsule: A structure composed principally of connective tissue and synovial membrane and that surrounds diarthroidal joints.

Bursae: Connective tissue sacs over bony prominences and near tendons that facilitate movement by reducing friction.

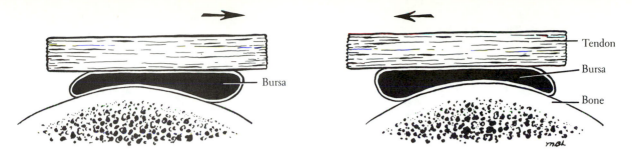

Figure 7-4 A bursa in relation to tendon and bone. Arrows show direction of movement. (From Crouch, J. E., and M. E. Carr. *Anatomy and Physiology*. Palo Alto, Calif.: Mayfield Publishing Co., 1977, p. 122.)

vides a moist environment for the cells of the synovial membrane. Most synovial bursae lie between tendons and bone or tendons and ligaments. Bursae that lie between one tendon and another tendon are called subtendinous bursae. Bursae may also separate nerves or muscle from bone.

Joint Injuries

Joint injuries occur frequently in sports and may affect the bony or soft tissues. An understanding of the individual arthrokinematics (joint biomechanics) and anatomy of a joint will help the athletic trainer determine the nature and scope of an injury.

Joint motion is dictated by the shape of the joint's surface. For example, the shoulder is a ball-and-socket (spheroidal) joint, and its movement is not restricted to any particular plane (i.e., it is a universal joint). In contrast, the knee is a hinge joint, and its movement is restricted primarily to one plane (the knee does allow for a small amount of rotation in addition to its primary flexion and extension motions; see Chapter 21). Joint stability is influenced by the shape and congruity of the weight-bearing surfaces; the integrity of the fibrous capsule, tendons, and ligaments that support the joint; neuromuscular control; joint mechanics (kinematics); and past injury. In addition, strong and coordinated muscles also serve a protective function (Figure 7-5, p. 116).

Abnormalities in articular cartilage are often secondary to the original injury (Figure 7-6, p. 116). (See Chapter 8 for the mechanism of the **pathophysiology** of inflammation.) Briefly, cellular necrosis (death) begins immediately after injury. The extent of cell death varies and depends largely upon the extent of the injury. Inflammation is the second phase, in which disturbances upset the balance among the vascular, intracellular, and extracellular compartments. Vascular channels dilate, the permeability of vessel walls increases, and cellular and protein material moves into the extracellular spaces of the traumatized area, forming a fibrinous mass (ulcer). Repair is the third and final phase. Repair occurs when the fibrinous mass is invaded by the newly formed blood vessels. This final phase may be associated with replication of the damaged tissue by the same tissue that was originally injured or with a fibrous scar. The replacement of damaged tissue with identical material is a prolonged remodeling process to restore and approximate normal anatomy.

Inflammation cannot occur in cartilage because it is an **avascular** structure. However, if the damage extends from the basal layer of the cartilage to the vascular subchondral cortex, all three phases of inflammation may occur. Superficial **lacerations** of articular cartilage have been known to remain unchanged for at least two years and not progress to **chondromalacia** or degenerative **osteoarthritis** (see Chapter 21). In

Pathophysiology: The physiological basis of a disease or disorder.

Avascular: Without blood supply.
Laceration: A wound caused by the tearing of skin tissue.
Chondromalacia: Softening of the patella's (kneecap) cartilage. Not necessarily painful.
Osteoarthritis: Disease of the joints characterized by degeneration of joint (articular) cartilage and increase in the size (hypertrophy) of local bone.

Principles of Injury Prevention and Management

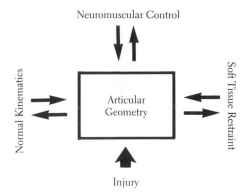

Figure 7-5 Factors affecting the articular geometry.

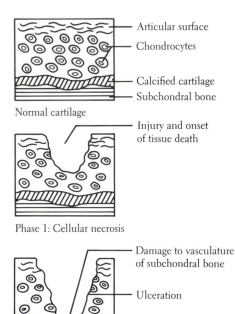

Normal cartilage

Phase 1: Cellular necrosis

Phase 2: Inflammation and superficial ulceration (if injury extends to subchondral bone)

Phase 3: Repair of damaged tissue

Figure 7-6 Process of articular cartilage injury and degeneration.

contrast, and of somewhat greater clinical importance, is cartilage's response to a deep **lesion,** in which the defect violates the underlying bone-cartilage interface, damaging the vasculature of the subchondral bone. This initiates a repair response much more characteristic of that which occurs in tissues that do have a blood supply.

The site of old deep lacerations or damage to the articular cartilage may be clearly visible years after the injury and look like (during surgical examination) a slightly discolored, roughened pit or linear groove occurring within otherwise smooth and normal hyaline cartilage. Armstrong and Mao demonstrated that articular cartilage defects with a diameter of less than three millimeters exhibit complete repair after three months and are difficult to locate after nine months. However, defects nine millimeters or larger in diameter do not repair completely. Loading or impact injuries to the cartilaginous surface, whether single or repetitive, that exceed a critical threshold can injure not only mature cartilage cells but also the underlying bone and progress rapidly to an osteoarthritic degenerative lesion. This degenerative lesion then significantly alters the individual joint's load-bearing characteristics and mechanics.

Joint injuries often involve ligament and capsular tears (e.g., medial collateral ligament tear of the knee). There may also be dislocations and subluxations, such as occur at the glenohumeral joints, and fractures involving the articular surfaces, which commonly occur at the ankle joint. Isolated injury to the fibrocartilage, as in a knee meniscus injury, is also within the scope of joint trauma. Isolated articular cartilage injuries from single or repetitive joint impact are one of the more severe varieties of joint injury. The severity of a joint injury depends upon the stress and stress concentration applied to the joint, the direction of force, and the repetitiveness of the insult (Figure 7-5).

Lesion: Any pathological change in tissue structure due to injury or disease.

Subsequent chapters discuss the nature of injuries involved in specific joints.

The fibrous capsule and ligaments have at their attachments numerous free nerve endings that mediate pain sensations. The quantity of pain is not a good parameter to use when judging the severity of joint injury. Partial fibrous capsular and ligament injuries cause more pain than complete fibrous capsule and ligament injuries. The total disruption of the fibrous capsule severs the connections of these free nerve endings. Complete disruption of the fibrous capsule causes fluid to leave the interior of the joint, thereby reducing pressure and lessening stretching of the joint capsule (increased capsular stretching and pressure are painful). The synovial membrane contains no special pain sensors, but pain may arise from continuous reflex contraction of muscles surrounding the joint in reaction to the joint injury.

Range of Motion

An understanding of the normal and **pathological** motion of joints is the key to comprehending functional anatomy (see Box 7-1, p. 118). It is also the foundation for evaluating injured joints, prescribing meaningful therapeutic exercises, and knowing when to modify or terminate the program.

The best system of numerically describing joint motion is the one proposed by the American Academy of Orthopedic Surgeons. The system is based upon 0 to 180 degrees of measurement. The values can then be compared with a normative-value table of full ranges of motion (see Table 9-2, p. 144). The comparison enables the examiner to differentiate normal from restricted motion and to facilitate the organization of a treatment and rehabilitation program. It is important that practitioners standardize their techniques of determining range of motion.

Obviously, trauma to a joint and its surrounding tissue will affect the joint's normal range of motion. Comparing ranges of motion of the traumatized joint to tables of normalized data and to the contralateral, uninvolved joint helps individuals understand the nature of the joint injury.

Serial evaluations of joint motion should be recorded, to monitor progress during the rehabilitation and restorative phases of treatment. These measurements are a concrete and objective form of evaluation that should be reproducible when performed by the same examiner. Problems frequently arise when the serial evaluations are performed by different examiners, which may lead to uninterpretable data that can confuse the true clinical picture.

Prevention of Joint Injury

As discussed in Chapter 3, conditioning is one of the most important injury-prevention measures, and it is particularly important in preventing joint injuries. The muscular system is an important stabilizer and shock absorber for the articular components of the skeletal system. Weakness or early fatigue of the muscles during a sporting contest makes the joints more vulnerable to injury.

The maintenance of normal range of motion is imperative for efficient articular biomechanics. The mechanical efficiency of the joint structure dramatically changes with alteration of its range of motion. For example, the loss of normal range of motion in the ankle joint leads to increased stress on the articular surfaces, poor efficiency and early fatigue of the associated muscles, and diminished capacity to fully perform gross motor movements (e.g., jumping). Following an injury, the normal joint motion must be reattained

Pathological: Pertaining to the nature, cause, development, and consequences of disease or injury.

BOX 7-1	Movement at Joints

The athletic trainer should use precise terms when describing joint motions.

Flexion: Movement of a joint that results in a decreased angle between two adjacent segments (bones)

Dorsiflexion: Movement of the foot toward its dorsal (upper) surface

Plantar flexion: Movement of the foot toward its plantar (lower) surface

Extension: Return from flexion; movement of a joint that results in an increased angle between two adjacent segments

Abduction: Lateral movement of a body segment away from the midline of the body

Adduction: Lateral movement of a body segment toward the midline of the body

Rotation: Movement of a body segment around its longitudinal axis

Pronation: Inward rotation of the forearm

Supination: Outward rotation of the forearm

Inversion: Rotation of the foot that lifts the medial border of the foot upward

Eversion: Rotation of the foot that lifts the lateral border of the foot upward

Circumduction: Movement of a body segment around a point so that the free end traces a circle and the segment traces a cone

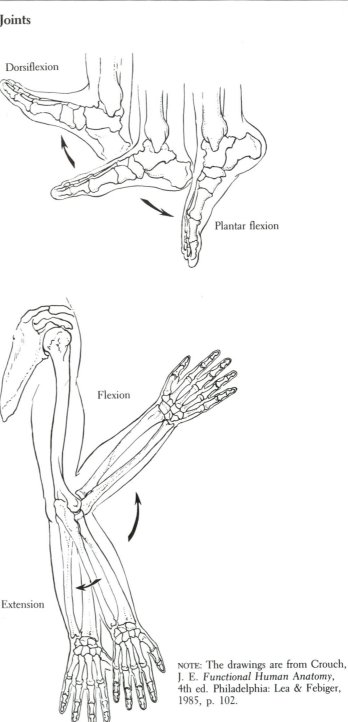

Dorsiflexion

Plantar flexion

Flexion

Extension

NOTE: The drawings are from Crouch, J. E. *Functional Human Anatomy,* 4th ed. Philadelphia: Lea & Febiger, 1985, p. 102.

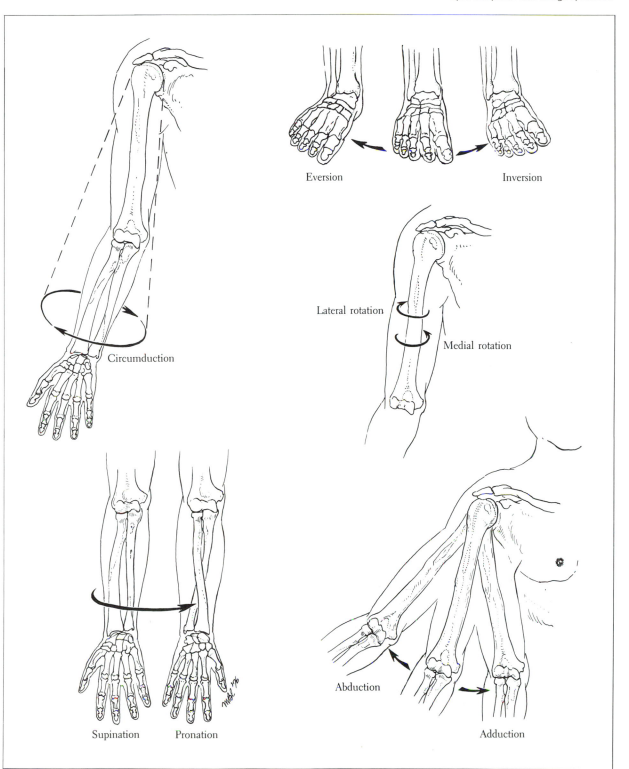

Eversion

Inversion

Lateral rotation

Medial rotation

Circumduction

Abduction

Supination   Pronation

Adduction

before the athlete can resume full participation in sports.

Joint laxity secondary to the original injury also predisposes the articular surfaces to increased stress and leads to early degenerative disease in the articular cartilage. Loss of joint integrity may also predispose the individual to injury of uninvolved joints that are attempting to compensate for this unstable joint's mechanical insufficiency. For example, improving strength may compensate for lack of joint integrity that may occur in the anterior cruciate-deficient knee (see Chapter 21). The use of protective equipment, such as bracing or taping (see Chapter 13 and the appendix), may also be necessary in the unstable joint to allow athletic participation. For example, a shoulder harness may be useful for restricting shoulder abduction in external rotation and eliminate recurrent anterior glenohumeral dislocations. Congenital or acquired excessive ligamentous laxity may predispose an athlete to contact- and noncontact-induced joint injuries. Preparticipation screening can identify these individuals so that appropriate action, such as exclusion from participation, bracing, or rehabilitation, can be initiated.

The athletic trainer plays a key role in initiating therapeutic exercise to rehabilitate previously injured articular structures and in instituting specific conditioning programs to reduce the incidence of joint injuries.

References

The American Academy of Orthopedic Surgeons. *Joint Motion: Methods of Measuring and Recording.* Chicago, 1965.

Armstrong, C. G., and B. C. Mao. Variations in the intrinsic mechanical properties of human articular cartilage with age, degeneration, and water content. *Journal of Bone and Joint Surgery* 64:88–94, 1983.

Ashurst, A. P. C. The motion of larger joints. *Internal Clinics* 1:74, 1926.

Basmajian, J. V. *Therapeutic Exercise.* Baltimore: Williams & Wilkins, 1976.

Brodie, D. A., H. A. Bird, and V. Wright. Joint laxity in selected athletic populations. *Medicine and Science in Sports and Exercise* 14:190–193, 1983.

Cave, E. F., and S. N. Roberts. A method for measuring and recording joint function. *Journal of Bone and Joint Surgery* 18:455, 1936.

Clark, W. A. A system of joint measurement. *Journal of Orthopedic Surgery* 2:687, 1920.

Clark, W. A. A protractor for measuring rotation of joints. *Journal of Orthopedic Surgery* 1:154, 1921.

Conwell, H. E. Flexo-extensometer. *Surgery Gynecology & Obstetrics* 40:710, 1925.

Dorinson, S. M., and M. L. Wagner. An exact technique for clinically measuring and recording joint motion. *Archives of Physical Medicine and Rehabilitation* 29:468, 1948.

Ekstrand, J., and J. Gillquist. The frequency of muscle tightness and injuries in soccer. *American Journal of Sports Medicine* 10:75–78, 1982.

Ekstrand, J., J. Gillquist, M. Moller, B. Ogberg, and S. Liljedahl. The incidence of soccer injuries and their relation to training and team success. *American Journal of Sports Medicine* 11:63–67, 1983.

Gonzna, E. R., I. J. Harrington, and D. C. Evans. *Biomechanics of Musculoskeletal Injury.* Baltimore: Williams & Wilkins, 1982.

Jobe, F. W., and R. D. Moynes. Delineation of diagnostic criteria in a rehabilitation program for rotator cuff injuries. *American Journal of Sports Medicine* 10:336–339, 1982.

Jobe, F. W., J. E. Tibone, J. Perry, and D. Moynes. EMG analysis of the shoulder in throwing and pitching. *American Journal of Sports Medicine* 11:3–5, 1983.

Lieb, F. J., and J. Perry. Quadriceps function in anatomical and mechanical study using amputated limbs. *Journal of Bone and Joint Surgery* 50a:1535–1547, 1968.

Mankin, H. J. Current concepts review of the response of articular cartilage to mechanical injury. *Journal of Bone and Joint Surgery* 64a:460–466, 1982.

Moore, M. L. The measurement of joint motion, part 1: introductory review of literature. *Physical Therapy Review* 29:195, 1949.

Moore, M. L. The measurement of joint motion, part 2: the technique of goniometry. *Physical Therapy Review* 29:256–264, 1949.

Mundale, M. O., R. J. Rabideau, and F. J. Kottke. Evaluation of the extension of the hip. *Archives of Physical Medicine and Rehabilitation* 37:75, 1956.

Nicholas, J. A. Injuries to the knee ligaments. *Journal of the American Medical Association* 212:2236–2239, 1970.

Nygaard, E., P. Andersen, P. Nilsson, E. Eriksson, T. Kjessel, and B. Saltin. Glycogen depletion pattern and lactate accumulation in leg muscles during recreational downhill skiing. *European Journal of Applied Physiology* 38:261–269, 1978.

Richmond, J. C., and J. B. McGinty. Segmental arthroscopic examination of the hypertrophic medio-patellar plica. *Clinical Orthopaedics and Related Research* 178:185–189, 1983.

Silver, D. The measurement of the range of motion in joints. *Journal of Bone and Joint Surgery* 21:569, 1923.

Simon, W. H. *The Human Joint in Health and Disease.* Philadelphia: University of Pennsylvania Press, 1978.

Thompson, R. C., and H. J. Robinson. Current concepts review of the articular cartilage matrix metabolism. *Archives of Physical Medicine and Rehabilitation* 26:414, 1952.

West, C. C. Measurement of joint motion. *Archives of Physical Medicine and Rehabilitation* 26:414, 1952.

8 Inflammation

Participation in sports exposes athletes to numerous traumatic events and infectious material that can severely impair functional ability. Injury to tissue initiates a series of physiological events that must be properly managed, including swelling, irritation, pain, muscle spasm, and loss of function. The athletic trainer must recognize the physiological processes associated with the different types of injuries and use the processes as a basis for a program of rehabilitation that will ensure proper healing and early return to full function.

Pathophysiology

Figure 8-1 (p. 124) illustrates the trauma-inflammation-disability process. Internal and external agents (see below) cause local tissue injury, which disrupts cellular balance. This disruption initiates **inflammation,** which is a vascular and cellular response to **trauma.** The body tries to dispose of microorganisms, foreign material, and dying tissue so that subsequent tissue repair can occur.

The classic effects of inflammation are redness, swelling, increased temperature, pain, muscle spasm, and loss of

function. Secondary effects are **edema, pus, cellular necrosis,** and formation of **adhesion.** Blood vessel dilation and congestion produce the redness; the **exudate** and congestion cause the swelling. As the dilated blood vessels bring warm blood to the injured area, temperature increases.

Edema causes pain by producing tension on the adjacent tissues and nerves. Chemicals such as **histamine,** kinins, and **prostaglandins** also irritate the free nerve endings in the area. Pain causes a reflex splinting or guarding reaction within the muscle in an attempt to prevent further injury. This muscle spasm can increase the pain by exerting tension on the injury site. In addition, there is an initial decrease of blood flow in the muscle because the muscle spasm causes constriction. This **ischemia** (lack of blood flow) causes metabolic waste products to collect and the delivery of nutrients to the tissues to decrease. The spasm also compromises lymph flow, tending to contribute to the buildup of fluid at the injury site.

External and Internal Agents

Inflammation is initiated by external and internal agents that disrupt tissue.

Edema: Swelling; a collection of fluid in a tissue space.

Cellular necrosis: Death of a cell.

Adhesion: The binding of adjacent tissue surfaces, caused by the formation of fibrous (dense) connective tissue.

Exudate: Material tissue discharges as a result of inflammation.

Histamine: A chemical formed during inflammation and immune response. Among other things, it causes arteriolar vasodilation and increased membrane permeability.

Prostaglandins: Hormone-like substances that produce physiological effects. They cause vasodilation during the inflammation process. Their synthesis is blocked by certain drugs such as aspirin.

Ischemia: Inadequate blood flow.

Inflammation: Tissue's reaction to trauma, irritation, or infection, characterized by swelling, pain, redness, local temperature increase, and loss of function.

Trauma: Injury or damage.

External agents are peripheral physical trauma that disrupt **cellular homeostasis** (cellular balance) and include blows, torsional stresses, bacteria, viruses, and chemicals. Internal agents are stressors that disrupt cells from within and include immobilization, infection, and emotional tension and internally produced chemicals like histamine.

Physical Trauma. Physical trauma causes most of the injuries in athletics. Trauma may be in the form of direct contact, as in a **contusion**; extreme forces placed on tissue, as in **sprains** and **strains**; or penetrating wounds, such as **lacerations, abrasions, incisions,** and **punctures.** All these occurrences disrupt the tissue, which inevitably leads to inflammation.

Immobilization. As part of the treatment of an athletic injury, immobilization may irritate the tissues and delay healing. **Hypertrophic scarring** and formation of adhesion (fibrous connective tissue formed during the healing process) occur when ordinarily mobile structures are immobilized for long periods of time. The formation of weak, inelastic **scar tissue** is perhaps the single most debilitating effect of immobilization (see Figure 8-2, p. 125). Additionally, the circulation and metabolism of the injured cells are altered, which leads to a buildup of metabolites such as leukotoxins and histamines. These effects cause pain and increase the permeability of tissue membranes, which produces edema and tension on the adjacent tissue (causing secondary damage). If not properly managed, the vascular and cellular events of inflammation may cause a vicious cycle of tissue damage and edema.

Infection. Infection is the toxic effect of pathogenic microorganisms invading parts of the body. It may result from insect bites, communicable diseases, and contaminated wounds. Usually,

Cellular homeostasis: The balance or physiological equilibrium of a cell.

Contusion: A bruise.
Sprain: Disruption or injury of a ligament.
Strain: Disruption or injury of a musculotendinous unit. A severe strain is often called a pulled muscle.
Laceration: A wound caused by the skin tissue being torn.
Abrasion: A wound caused by a portion of the skin being scraped away.
Incision: A wound caused by the skin tissue being cut.
Puncture: A wound caused by the skin tissue being pierced with a pointed instrument.
Hypertrophic scarring: Excessive scarring that may limit range of motion.
Scar tissue: Fibrous tissue formed in response to trauma.

Freedom from injury is critical if athletes are to play at their peak levels. By intervening in the trauma-inflammation-disability process, the athletic trainer plays a vital role in ensuring this freedom.

Principles of Injury Prevention and Management

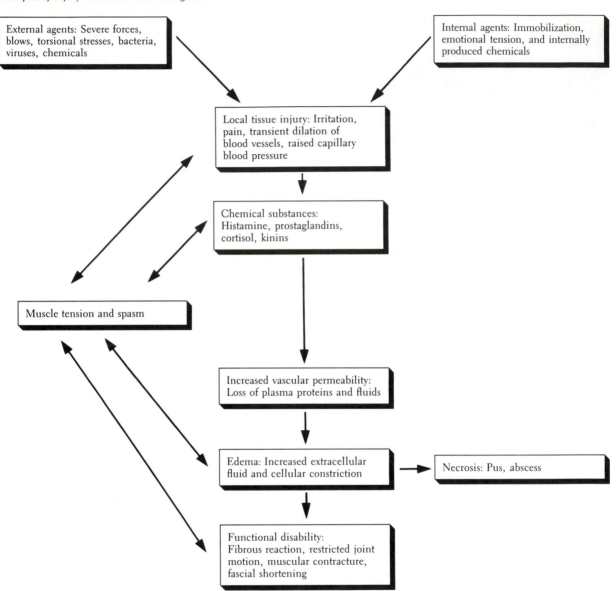

Figure 8-1 The trauma-inflammation-disability process.

infection creates an inflammatory response characterized by increased local temperature, rubor (redness), swelling, pain, and dysfunction (see Putting It into Practice 8-1, p. 126).

Emotional Tension. Emotional tension (emotional stress) adversely affects the body's chemical balance by stimulating the secretion of **cortisol** from the adrenal cortex. Cortisol has a catabolic (breakdown) effect on cells. During emotional stress, the body is less able to combat the effects of other stressors, such as bacteria and viruses. In addition, emotional tension may intensify the effects of muscle spasm, which contributes to the process of trauma-inflammation-disability. Fine motor movements and coordination may be impaired by muscle spasm, which could predispose an athlete to further injury.

Vascular Changes

Trauma walls off an injury by initiating a reflex contraction of arterial smooth muscle and the formation of blood clot. Chemicals (histamine, kinins, prostaglandins) are then released (Figure 8-3, p. 126), which increase vascular permeability and blood flow, causing the circulatory system to lose plasma protein and fluid into the extracellular spaces (the area around the cells). Plasma protein has the ability to draw fluid toward itself (i.e., it exerts an **osmotic pressure**), causing fluid to move from the **capillaries** to the injury site, leading to extracellular edema. In addition, local lymphatic channels are blocked, which localizes the inflammation by preventing fluid from draining from the injured area. These vascular changes can cause swelling (edema), muscle spasm, and cellular constriction.

As part of the inflammatory process, white blood cells concentrate at the injury site and attempt to rid the body of foreign substances and dead tissue. At

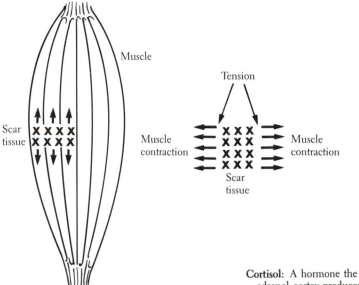

Figure 8-2 Schematic representation of the effects of scar tissue upon muscle contraction. Contraction of muscle fiber causes tension on borders of scar tissue, which can lead to chronic inflammation.

the first line of defense, **neutrophils** adhere to the walls within the capillaries (**margination**) and through the process of **phagocytosis** (cell ingestion) cleanse the area of bacteria and tissue fragments. Neutrophils' activity reaches its maximum effectiveness about seven to twelve hours following injury.

At the second line of defense, **monocytes** form great amounts of cytoplasmic **lysosomes** that begin to migrate toward the damaged tissue. These cells, called macrophages, also begin phagocytosis, which cleanses the area of dead tissue. The macrophages and neutrophils die after they have engulfed large amounts of necrotic (dead) tissue. The combination of all this dead material forms the substance called **pus.**

Soft Tissue Repair

After trauma has caused inflammation, the body has to repair the injured tissues. Three processes restore normality to the soft tissues: resolution, granu-

Cortisol: A hormone the adrenal cortex produces and releases in response to stress.

Neutrophils: Mature white blood cells that ingest and digest material such as bacteria. Also called polymorphonuclear leukocytes.

Margination: The adherence of neutrophils to the capillary walls during the early stage of inflammation.

Phagocytosis: A process cells such as leukocytes perform; they capture and digest materials, such as foreign organisms.

Monocytes: Large white blood cells with one nucleus.

Lysosomes: Cytoplasmic particles that can break down organic material.

Osmotic pressure: Pressure a substance exerts on a semipermeable membrane (a membrane some substances may pass through).

Capillaries: The thinnest and smallest blood vessels; capillaries connect arteries and veins.

Pus: A thick, yellowish fluid composed of white cells, dead tissue, and pathogenic material and formed during inflammation.

Preventing Infection

Infections can occur when a portion of the body's tissue is invaded by microorganisms like bacteria, virus, parasites, and fungi. The symptoms of infection include local edema, pain, redness, increased skin temperature, and tenderness. Lymph nodes may swell if the infection spreads, and become generalized.

The athletic trainer should be particularly careful not to contaminate open wounds. Seemingly trivial injuries may result in chronic infections that can be serious. Athletic training rooms, locker rooms, and sports facilities are potential breeding grounds for infectious organisms if proper sanitary precautions are not taken. For example, unclean whirlpool baths can easily transmit pathogens into open wounds.

The proper sequence for treating wounds and preventing infection is controlling bleeding, cleaning the wound, closing the skin, and protecting the area. The risk of infection and accompanying inflammation can be minimized by meticulously cleaning and removing dead tissue and foreign material. (These procedures are discussed in Chapters 10 and 23.)

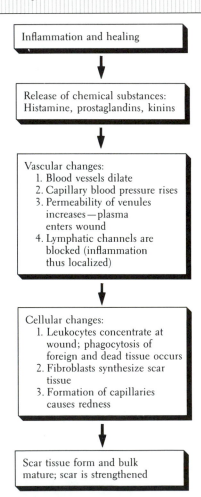
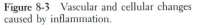

Figure 8-3 Vascular and cellular changes caused by inflammation.

lation, and regeneration. **Resolution** occurs when the injury is very slight and there is no local cellular necrosis (death). The cells grow and return to normal after the inflammatory response has subsided.

Granulation is the formation of scar tissue in response to an injury severe enough to degenerate and/or kill tissue. This process follows the vascular changes that inflammation induces. **Fibroblasts** and **endothelial tissue** develop within the exudate and produce granulation tissue. This tissue replaces the exudate and reconnects the disrupted tissue. The fibroblasts eventually form a fibrous scar that is composed principally of collagen and protein polysaccharide. Initially, this scar tissue is inelastic and structurally weak, but with time its form and bulk mature into elastic, strong tissue.

Regeneration is the replacement of destroyed cells by the proliferation of healthy cells adjacent to the wound. Human capacity for regeneration decreases with age and is affected by nutritional status. Some tissues, such as nerve cells, are incapable of regenerating, although peripheral nerve fibers can regenerate.

Resolution: Return of a cell to its normal condition following inflammation.

Granulation: Formation of scar tissue.

Fibroblast: The principal cell of connective tissue; it produces collagen and elastin.
Endothelial tissue: Squamous epithelial cells that form the lining of blood vessels and the cavities of organs.

Regeneration: Replacement of dead cells with healthy ones.

Management

In a majority of cases, the immediate control of soft tissue trauma is the athletic trainer's most important responsibility. The athletic trainer is in an excellent position to minimize the cellular and vascular disruption and the other effects of inflammation. Edema, wounds (cellular necrosis or loss of tissue), scars, and pain often harm the athlete more than the original physical trauma. Early rehabilitation for most injuries is important for preventing atrophy and impaired circulation. **Atrophy** can be prevented to a certain extent through isometric exercise and electrical stimulation, even when a joint is immobilized. The athletic trainer should also attempt to minimize pain by applying the appropriate modalities and monitoring medications the physician prescribed.

Caring for the athlete after surgery can be one of the athletic trainer's most gratifying experiences. Restoration of full function more often depends upon the rehabilitation program than upon the surgeon's skill. The rehabilitation process includes not only specific care for the injured area but maintenance of the athlete's general condition. (Chapter 4 covers general conditioning principles.)

The application of ice, compression, and elevation (**ICE**) (and sometimes immobilization) can help prevent certain effects of inflammation. Aspirin may also be useful because it decreases the production of prostaglandins, which have been implicated in the inflammation process. (*Note:* The use of aspirin or other nonsteroidal anti-inflammatory drugs presents a dilemma. Although these drugs decrease inflammation, they also increase the tendency to bleed.) These procedures enable the athlete to return to participation earlier because they tend to minimize the inflammatory response. Full function is not possible as long as the inflammation symptoms persist (see Chapter 5).

Edema

A suggested ICE procedure is to dampen an elastic bandage and wrap it around the injured body part. Then an ice bag is applied and secured with another bandage. The athlete then elevates the injured part above the heart to prevent local edema.

Many practitioners advocate early administration of electrical stimulation with positive polarity (see Chapter 13), believing that positively charged ions are primarily responsible for swelling. A positively charged electrical flow elicited by electrical stimulation may effect a return to normality within the capillaries by repelling the positive ions away from the injury site. This effect remains highly speculative. It is possible that the muscle's pumping action induced by the electrical impulse removes the extracellular exudate and edema from the area, which diminishes the secondary effect of increased tension on the adjacent tissues. The electrode pads should be placed proximally and distally to the injury site to maximize the effects of the muscle pump on blood and lymphatic circulation.

Wounds

Open wounds may also cause prolonged inflammation, and they must be properly cared for to prevent contamination, which can infect the wound and complicate and prolong the healing process. (See Putting It into Practice 8-1.) Immediate care of penetrating wounds consists of cleansing the area of debris and applying appropriate protection. It is very important that the athlete have a current tetanus innoculation to preclude the development of severe blood poisoning and tetanus.

Staphylococcus (staph) infection is of particular concern. This infection may stem from a seemingly trivial source such as dirty athletic equipment (e.g., wrestling mats). Staph infection is typically initiated through an open passageway, like a wound. This infection may

Atrophy: Decrease in size and function of a muscle.

ICE: Acronym for ice, compression, and elevation, the basic treatment for contusions and other soft tissue injuries.

Staphylococcus: A pathogenic bacterium.

also be intensified by squeezing pus-filled boils, which may force the pus inward into the bloodstream. Appropriate antibiotics must be administered once the athlete has been infected. In addition, any contaminated equipment must be thoroughly cleaned with antiseptic solution. Staphylococcus and many other types of infectious bacteria thrive in areas of warmth, moisture, and darkness. It is better to prevent staph infections through cleanliness and equipment maintenance than to have to seek medical treatment.

Scar Tissue and Loss of Function

Historically, immobilization has been the principal treatment for damaged tissues. Rest and immobilization are indeed necessary to facilitate healing of skeletal fracture, third degree sprains and strains, and joint dislocations. However, this strategy is counterproductive in treating joint injuries such as first and second degree sprains because immobilization impairs the range of motion of these highly mobile structures. Immobilized joints form weak, inelastic scar tissue rather than the strong mobile scar tissue that allows normal restoration of function. Pain and chronic inflammation often occur when activity is resumed because the tendons, ligaments, and muscle create tension on this inelastic scar tissue.

Scars can cause **contractures** or chronic irritation if they are formed within joints or muscles' contractile mechanisms. Also, when movement is resumed after an injury, tension is produced on the scar tissue; this tension continues to irritate the local tissues. The irritation further stimulates the release of prostaglandins, and so the inflammation process tends to perpetuate itself. Proper rehabilitation is necessary to ensure that the scar tissue does not interfere with normal joint motions.

The collagenous formation of scar tissue tends to be in the direction of applied stress. Early and *gentle* massage of the scar tissue should be instituted to begin stretching the fibers, to make the scar more elastic and prevent significant development of disabilities related to overly static scar tissue. Initially, the athlete will not be able to tolerate vigorous massage because the injured area is so sensitive, as a result of the trauma of surgery. This sensitivity decreases as the tissues heal, which allows more vigorous massaging. The **mobilization** of scar tissue should be gradually introduced and begun in a direction transverse to the surgical incision or injured fibers. Athletes should be instructed in how to care for the scar on their own because these tissues have to be frequently mobilized throughout the day.

Pain

Pain has long been an enigma to researchers and clinicians. There are many theories about its cause and cure. Melzak and Wall suggested a gate theory of pain; Figure 8-4 summarizes the theory, which is that smaller nerve fibers transmit pain while large-diameter fibers tend to carry sensations like touch and proprioception (feelings of location in space). Large and small nerve fibers project into the **substantia gelatinosis (SG)** of the dorsal horn in the spinal cord and continue on to specialized T cells. T cells are connected to higher neural centers that facilitate the integration of these peripheral neural signals. Pain may be blocked by stimulating impulses in the large fibers, which travel faster than the pain impulses the smaller fibers carry. This in effect closes the gate to pain sensations. The exact mechanism of pain transmission is unknown. Other researchers have postulated that pain is caused by neural stimulation emanating from specific sources, such as chemicals, mechanical displacement, or electromagnetic forces.

The reason for individual differences in the perception of pain is not known.

Mobilization: Manual manipulation of a joint or soft tissue.

Substantia gelatinosis (SG): Gelatinous tissue containing small nerve cells and located on the posterior gray column of the spinal cord.

Contracture: Shortening of a musculotendinous unit due to scar tissue, atrophy, or muscle spasm.

Recently it was hypothesized that internally produced substances such as **endorphins** may dampen pain by producing an opiatelike effect. Thus, physiological factors such as differences in specific hormone-secretion rates may account for variations in pain tolerance rather than psychological factors. Researchers are currently seeking explanations of the mechanism of pain that may help in the ultimate management of pain.

Mechanical problems such as **spinal malalignment** can cause pain. These aberrations may often be extremely subtle and difficult to detect. The athlete who claims to be suffering pain but manifests no obvious symptoms is often considered a malingerer. However, the pain may be caused by barely perceptible chronic mechanical problems such as poor posture (e.g., sleeping on the stomach) or improper sports techniques (e.g., lifting with straight legs).

Chronic pain can also be induced by overuse injuries. Often, there are no readily observable physical or clinical signs to help in the evaluation of the injury. As discussed in Chapters 9 and 11, a thorough history of injury considering time of onset, intensity of workouts, and playing surface can often reveal the cause of the injury and the source of pain. When investigating pain of unknown origin, it is important to note postural deviation, recent changes in footwear, possible spinal dysfunction, changes in activities or emotional state, and the biomechanics of the athlete's sports techniques. See Putting It into Practice 8-2, p. 130.

The many attempts at pain control throughout history have included drugs, spinal manipulation, acupuncture, thermal (heat) **modalities,** and psychological counseling. Drugs such as aspirin or **nonsteroidal anti-inflammatants** can play an important part in pain control. Modalities such as ice (cryotherapy), moist heat, or **transcutaneous neural stimulation** (see Box 8-1, p. 131) also

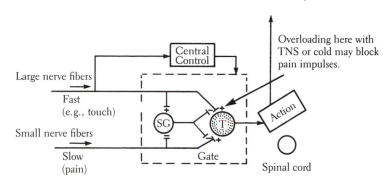

Figure 8-4 The gate theory of pain transmission. Pain may be blocked with devices such as transcutaneous nerve stimulators by loading the fast pathways; this blocks the slower pain pathways. SG = substantia gelatinosa, T = T cells. (Adapted from Melzack, R., and P. D. Wall. Pain mechanisms: a new theory. *Science* 150: 971–979, 1965.)

often effectively reduce pain during various phases of the healing process (see Chapter 13). The athletic trainer should not view these modalities as curative in themselves; their application must be accompanied by movement and muscle contraction. Appropriate modalities can be very useful in reducing an athlete's hesitancy to move because of pain, but the simple decrease of pain is not sufficient to allow the athlete to return to participation. It is imperative that the basic cause of pain be uncovered to ensure appropriate treatment. Medication or treatment that simply masks the pain while allowing the mechanical dysfunction that is causing the pain to continue is of little benefit to the athlete.

The etiology (cause) of pain has not been determined if pain persists after many weeks of treatment (the exact time depends upon the nature and severity of injury). The athletic trainer should further evaluate chronic inflammation that does not respond to drug therapy to determine if a mechanical factor is causing the pain. For example, pain may be caused by movement restriction at a spinal segment or a lateral

Endorphins: Substances produced in the brain and thought to decrease pain by acting like "natural" opiates.

Spinal malalignment: Abnormal spinal curve or pelvic tilt.

Modality: A physical technique or substance administered to produce a therapeutic effect.

Nonsteroidal anti-inflammatory drugs: Drugs that decrease inflammation by blocking prostaglandins.

Transcutaneous neural stimulation (TNS): Therapeutic modality involving the application of electrical nerve impulses to decrease pain.

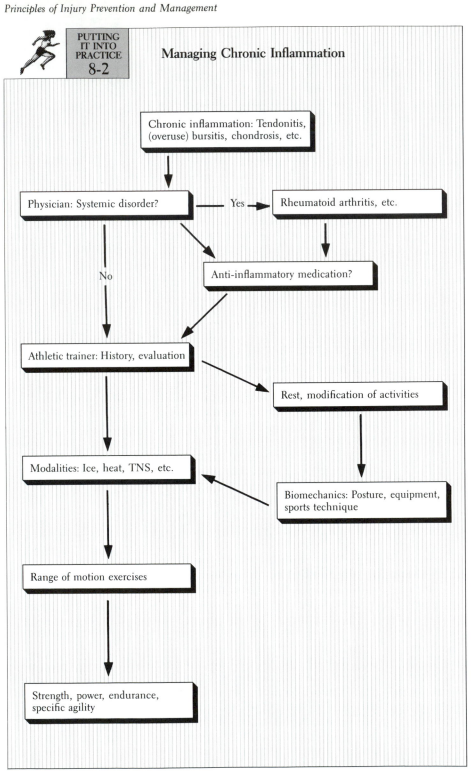

PUTTING
IT INTO
PRACTICE
8-2

Managing Chronic Inflammation

Chronic inflammation: Tendonitis, (overuse) bursitis, chondrosis, etc.

Physician: Systemic disorder? — Yes → Rheumatoid arthritis, etc.

No

Anti-inflammatory medication?

Athletic trainer: History, evaluation

Rest, modification of activities

Modalities: Ice, heat, TNS, etc.

Biomechanics: Posture, equipment, sports technique

Range of motion exercises

Strength, power, endurance, specific agility

| BOX 8-1 | Transcutaneous Neural Stimulation |

Transcutaneous neural stimulation (TNS), used extensively in pain management (see Chapter 13), is thought to overload the proprioceptive nerve fibers that, according to the gate theory of pain, block pain impulses. TNS may also stimulate the production of pain-reducing hormones like endorphins and enkephalins.

TNS appears to be particularly beneficial during the early phases of rehabilitation. Smith found that patients who were recovering from meniscectomies and total knee arthroplasty and treated with TNS spent fewer days in the hospital, began their rehabilitation programs earlier, took less pain medication, and became ambulatory earlier than patients who did not use TNS.

TNS may offer the athlete a method of pain relief that does not require medication or frequent visits to the training room or physician. The TNS unit is usually worn continuously and turned on and off during the day. Like other modalities, it should not be used as a substitute for proper rehabilitation. TNS is a useful tool that enables athletes to reduce pain and thus begin appropriate exercises. Although the use of this device is still in its infancy, the TNS unit appears to be a useful pain-management tool.

tracking of the patella within the intercondylar groove because of a pathological Q angle (see Chapter 21).

Frequently, pain is referred from one area of the body to another. The shoulder is perhaps the most common site of **referred pain;** shoulder pain may be referred from the heart, esophagus, and other musculoskeletal areas. The athletic trainer can determine if a local lesion is causing pain by noting whether pain increases or decreases during active or passive movement of the joint. If motion has no effect upon pain, then chances are pain is being referred from another location.

Many rehabilitation techniques hurt the athlete, but this does not necessarily indicate that harm is being committed. Benign pain often accompanies such procedures as mobilizing scar tissue or exercising a muscle. Pain can be very helpful in determining the direction of treatment and the location of injury. It is nevertheless important to listen to the athlete's complaints to ensure that the injured site is not suffering further damage. It is the athletic trainer's responsibility to determine whether the amount of pain the athlete experiences during the treatment is normal. The trainer should ask about the type, duration, persistence, and location of pain, as well as whether the pain is being experienced at rest and whether it increases during treatment. Although an accurate determination of significant and incidental pain is gained only by experience, generally, pain is bad if it results from the rehabilitation exercises and persists after treatment.

Finally, the athletic trainer must always consider the psychological and perceptive aspects of pain when treating athletes. Pain may give the athlete a way to gain attention and sympathy. The athletic trainer must keep the athlete from dwelling upon pain and instead present an attractive alternative to being injured. For example, try to help the athlete formulate and achieve short-term goals in the rehabilitation. Successful experiences will take the athlete's mind off pain.

Referred pain: Pain experienced at one location but caused by injury in another location.

References

Anderson, W. A. D., and T. M. Scotti. *Synopsis of Pathology.* St. Louis: C. V. Mosby, 1976.

Bryant, W. M. Wound healing. *Clinical Symposia* 29:1–36, 1977.

Caillet, R. *Soft Tissue Pain and Disability.* Philadelphia: F. A. Davis, 1980.

Cyriax, J. *Textbook of Orthopaedic Medicine*, vol. 1. Baltimore: Williams & Wilkins, 1975.

Depalma, A. *The Management of Fractures and Dislocations*. Philadelphia: W. B. Saunders, 1970.

Eriksson, E. Rehabilitation of muscle function after sport injury: major problem in sports medicine. *International Journal of Sports Medicine* 2:1–6, 1981.

Ersek, R. A. Transcutaneous electrical neurostimulation: a new therapeutic modality for controlling pain. *Clinical Orthopaedics and Related Research* 128:314–324, 1977.

Goldstein, A. Opioid peptides (endorphins) in pituitary and brain. *Science* 193:1081–1086, 1976.

Grant, M. E., D. Phil, and D. J. Prockop. The biosynthesis of collagen. *New England Journal of Medicine* 286:194–198, 242–248, 291–299, 1972.

Guyton, A. *Textbook of Medical Physiology*. Philadelphia: W. B. Saunders, 1970.

Melzack, R., and P. D. Wall. Pain mechanisms: a new theory. *Science* 150:971–979, 1965.

Peacock, E. E., and W. Van Winkle. *Surgery and Biology of Wound Repair*. Philadelphia: W. B. Saunders, 1970.

Roesch, R., and D. E. Ulrich. Physical therapy management in the treatment of chronic pain. *Physical Therapy* 60:53–57, 1980.

Smith, M. J. Electrical stimulation for relief of musculoskeletal pain. *The Physician and Sportsmedicine* 11(5):47–55, 1983.

Steadman, J. R. Nonoperative measures for patellofemoral problems. *American Journal of Sports Medicine* 7:374–375, 1979.

9 Injury Evaluation

When evaluating injuries, the athletic trainer must consider both the established norms and the individual athlete's levels of strength and ranges of motion. A world-class athlete such as Nadia Comaneci may demonstrate a "normal" range of motion, for example, even when she is injured.

AMONG an athletic trainer's most important responsibilities are emergency care and medical referral of athletic injuries. To properly execute these responsibilities, the athletic trainer must be able to recognize the nature and severity of injury.

The basis for sound injury management is thorough evaluation of acute injuries during field emergencies and training room examinations. Almost daily, the athletic trainer has to provide field care for mild or moderately severe injuries. Occasionally, more serious situations demand immediate recognition of life-threatening signs and implementation of lifesaving procedures. In the absence of a physician, in the training room the athletic trainer must conduct a thorough evaluation of the injury to determine the need for medical referral.

Documentation of the clinical signs and symptoms the athletic trainer identified during the initial examination are of significant value to the attending physician. Critical signs that are readily observed immediately after an injury may be less evident later during the physical examination. For example, ligament instability detected during initial stress testing is frequently more obvious than after the swelling, pain, and muscle spasm intensify.

Recognition and Diagnosis

From a medicolegal viewpoint, there must be a clear distinction between recognition of an injury and a diagnosis. Recognition is "the perception of something" and has no medical connotation. A **diagnosis** is determining by examination the nature of a diseased condition and also involves the decision reached from such an examination. The athletic trainer develops certain "perceptions" based upon a clinical evaluation of an injury and acts accordingly with respect to initial management and medical referral, but the diagnosis of the injury remains solely within the physician's domain. For example, the chest pain a middle-aged runner experiences may be from **angina pectoris** (pain caused by inadequate blood flow to the heart muscle), musculoskeletal injury, or other factors. The athletic trainer should be able to recognize the possible causes of chest pain and take appropriate action but not make a diagnosis that would require medical treatment. The athletic trainer must be acutely aware of the distinction between recognition and diagnosis and refrain from actions or words that in any way imply that he or she has made a diagnosis.

Knowledge Required

Technical knowledge is a necessary prerequisite for effective field and training room **evaluations.** The athletic trainer must have a sound knowledge of anatomy and **biomechanics.** Most evaluation procedures are based upon the ability to distinguish among normal and abnormal anatomical and biomechanical characteristics. The athletic trainer should consider anatomical variations among individual athletes due to age, sex, or congenital factors. As a basis for effective palpation and functional testing, the examiner must understand the anatomical relationships among bony landmarks, joint structures, and muscle groups. Knowledge of the normal range of joint motion provides an essential baseline for recognizing pathologically significant restrictions in joint mobility. To conduct appropriate neurological tests, the examiner must understand sensory and motor nerve innervations.

Knowledge of injury pathology and an awareness of the **etiology** of common injuries are also important in clinical evaluation. Understanding these factors enables the athletic trainer to make a preliminary association between the mechanism of injury and the resulting **pathology.** For example, the college football player who reports that he was "hit on the outside of the knee" by an opposing player might reasonably be expected to have sustained, at least, a sprain of the medial collateral ligament. On the other hand, this scenario, when reported by an adolescent athlete, might lead the athletic trainer to suspect an injury to the **distal** femoral or **proximal** tibial epiphyseal plate as well as trauma to the medial joint structures. A Colles' fracture, a dislocated lunate, or an injury to the distal radial epiphyseal plate in the adolescent are possible results of forceful **hyperextension** of the wrist. Further clinical evaluation will be necessary to substantiate the athletic trainer's initial suspicions.

Determination of the athlete's chief complaint or major **symptom** (unusual or unpleasant sensation) is an initial step in the injury-evaluation process. Typically, the chief complaint includes pain, unusual sensations such as numbness or tingling, or vague feelings articulated as "my knee gave out" or "my shoulder slips out." The athletic trainer's ability to associate common symp-

Diagnosis: Medical determination of the cause and symptoms, and subsequent identification of a disease or injury. Athletic trainers may not legally diagnose.
Etiology: Cause.

Angina pectoris: Deep, visceral pressure or discomfort, typically substernally in the chest, that may radiate to the neck and left arm. Caused by lack of blood flow to the heart muscle, possibly from atherosclerosis or coronary artery vasospasm.
Pathology: The nature, cause, development, and consequences of disease or injury.
Distal: Farthest away from the point of reference.
Proximal: Near the point of reference.
Hyperextension: Extension beyond the normal limit or beyond 180 degrees.

Symptoms: The manifestations of an injury or disease.
Evaluation: Assessment of an injury; the process typically includes past and present history, inspection, and testing.
Biomechanics: Study of the physics of motion in humans and animals.

toms with specific injury pathology is of vital importance.

Once the athlete's chief complaint has been established, the athletic trainer should systematically proceed to identify any alterations in anatomical structure or biomechanical, neurological, or physiological function that injury may have produced. Clinical signs are objective evidence of these alterations; they include what the athletic trainer may see, hear, or feel (Prior and Silberstein).

The Clinical Evaluation

The clinical evaluation of an acute athletic injury is a systematic procedure of specific methods and techniques. The examination must be thorough and should be conducted in a logical, sequential manner. An effective format includes (1) history, (2) inspection, (3) palpation, and (4) functional testing. Putting It into Practice 9-1 summarizes the recommended clinical evaluation format; this system is readily adaptable to a clinical evaluation of most types of athletic injuries.

Clinical signs and the severity of injury determine the extent of the clinical evaluation. The athletic trainer may have to exhaust all basic evaluation procedures when faced with conditions presenting ambiguous symptoms. For example, an athlete who "twists her knee" may require extensive tests to determine the effect of the injury upon the stability of the joint. But in other instances, only a few selected procedures may be necessary. An athlete struck on the front of the thigh with a softball may not require a thorough examination because the extent of the injury is obvious. Certain functional tests are not necessary and in fact are

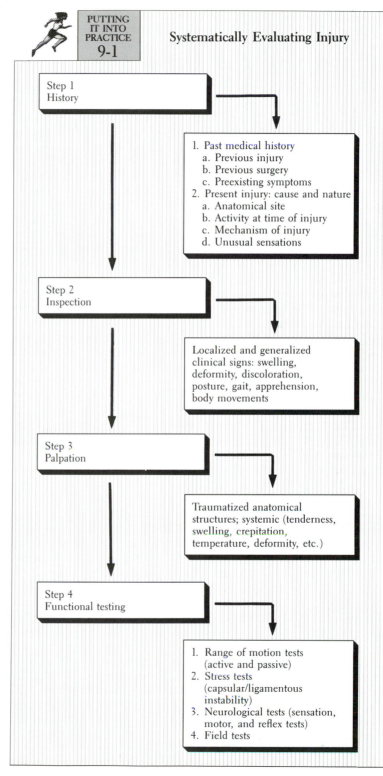

PUTTING IT INTO PRACTICE 9-1

Systematically Evaluating Injury

**Step 1
History**

1. Past medical history
   a. Previous injury
   b. Previous surgery
   c. Preexisting symptoms
2. Present injury: cause and nature
   a. Anatomical site
   b. Activity at time of injury
   c. Mechanism of injury
   d. Unusual sensations

**Step 2
Inspection**

Localized and generalized clinical signs: swelling, deformity, discoloration, posture, gait, apprehension, body movements

**Step 3
Palpation**

Traumatized anatomical structures; systemic (tenderness, swelling, crepitation, temperature, deformity, etc.)

**Step 4
Functional testing**

1. Range of motion tests (active and passive)
2. Stress tests (capsular/ligamentous instability)
3. Neurological tests (sensation, motor, and reflex tests)
4. Field tests

inappropriate if there is observable deformity associated with a fracture or dislocation. For example, range of motion tests are **contraindicated** if a dislocated cervical vertebra is suspected.

History

A complete and accurate medical history is one of the most important and useful parts of the clinical examination. The history should be a chronological record of all factors contributing to the nature and severity of the athlete's present injury. A complete medical history consists of (1) past history (see Chapter 11) and (2) history of the present injury.

Past History. Obtaining a past history is the athletic trainer's initial attempt at identifying the cause of the athlete's chief complaint. The past history should include information regarding (1) previous injury to the body part or related structures, (2) previous surgery, and (3) preexisting symptoms, including specific characteristics, anatomical location, date of onset, and duration. In addition to information obtained from the athlete, the athletic trainer may have firsthand knowledge of various aspects of the athlete's medical history. Accident reports, treatment and rehabilitation records, medical and surgical reports, and personal communication with attending physicians are additional sources of valuable information.

All information collected should be synthesized, in an attempt to identify the factors that contributed to the present injury. Careful consideration of past history is often critical in assessing the status of a present injury. As examples, documentation of the nature and severity of previous joint injuries may help the athletic trainer distinguish between chronic ligamentous laxity (preexisting loose ligaments) and newly acquired instability (recent ligament injury). Chronic inflammation or muscular-strength imbalances (disproportionate strengths between muscle groups) may help explain the cause of acute muscle or tendon injuries.

History of Present Injury. To obtain a history of the present injury, the athletic trainer gathers facts surrounding the circumstances of the injury from such sources as (1) personal observation of the trauma-producing incident, (2) the injured athlete, and (3) other players or coaches who witnessed the incident. It may be necessary to consult the third source if the athletic trainer did not observe the incident or if the athlete is unconscious and unable to communicate. A history of the present injury should include (1) exact anatomical site of injury, (2) activity engaged in at the time of injury, (3) mechanism of injury (how the injury occurred), (4) evidence of unusual sensations the athlete experienced, and (5) type of pain (see also Putting It into Practice 9-1).

Establishing the exact anatomical site of injury is part of determining the cause of the chief complaint. It is not sufficient to accept an athlete's superficial explanation of an injury, such as "My thigh hurts." The athlete should be asked to pinpoint specific areas of maximum tenderness. Asking the athlete to palpate for painful areas is often helpful (Figure 9-1). Additional evaluation procedures may be necessary to determine the involvement of specific structures (specific ligaments, bursae, etc.).

Knowledge of the type of activity at the time of injury (e.g., blocking, sliding into a base) and the exact mechanism of injury often provides valuable clues to the underlying pathology. The athlete should be asked to describe the activity as explicitly as possible. Open-ended questions such as "How did you get hurt?" elicit more information than questions that require only "yes" or "no" answers, such as "Did you fall on your shoulder?"

Identification of unusual sensations

Contraindicated: Not appropriate or recommended.

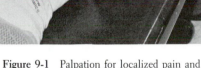

Figure 9-1 Palpation for localized pain and tenderness. It helps to have the athlete point to painful areas.

can frequently suggest specific pathologies. For example, an exclamation that "It felt like I got kicked in the calf" is often associated with a rupture of the Achilles tendon. Numbness (**anesthesia**) or tingling (**paresthesia**) in the little finger and the ulnar half of the ring finger indicates ulnar nerve involvement. "Popping" or "snapping" sensations are sometimes associated with tendon ruptures or fractures.

The sensation of pain should be evaluated in some detail. Barber and Budassi recommend various questions to evaluate pain. The athletic trainer can determine what *provokes* the pain by asking questions such as "What makes the pain worse?" and "What makes it better?" A question such as

"What does it feel like?" can help define the *quality* of the pain. The question "On a scale of one to five, how bad is it?" can help determine the *severity* of pain. A question such as "Does it hurt any place else?" assesses the *radiation* of pain. Finally, questions such as "When did it start?" or "How long has it lasted?" can help determine the *duration* of pain.

Inspection

Inspection is observation for local and generalized clinical signs. Swelling, deformity, and discoloration (redness, **ecchymosis**, etc.) are observable localized signs. General conditions that should be observed during a clinical evaluation of musculoskeletal injuries include the athlete's posture, **gait,** and body movements. Facial expressions are often clues to the severity of pain, or anxiety, as in the case of the patellar and glenohumeral "apprehension" tests (a positive **apprehension test** involves a sensation of joint instability elicited during passive movement) (Hoppenfeld).

The athletic trainer should bilaterally (right and left sides of the body) observe specific anatomical areas whenever possible. For example, while examining the shoulder girdle, the athletic trainer should visually compare the involved sternoclavicular joint with the uninvolved sternoclavicular joint. The athletic trainer can then compare the clavicles, acromioclavicular joints, and the glenohumeral joints to identify differences in anatomical contours that may be from injury (Figure 9-2, p. 138).

Palpation

Palpation is a valuable supplement to visual inspection for swelling, deformity, or other anatomical irregularities. It is often helpful to palpate the opposite, uninvolved body part (e.g., check left elbow when right elbow is injured) to identify pathologically significant dif-

Ecchymosis: Black and blue coloring under the skin, caused by blood escaping from the vasculature as a result of injury.
Gait: Walking characteristics.

Apprehension test: A test that assesses fear of a particular movement. Often helpful in determining the nature of the injury.

Anesthesia: Lack of feeling; numbness.
Paresthesia: Abnormal sensation or feeling, such as tingling or burning.

Palpation: Touching an area with the hands.

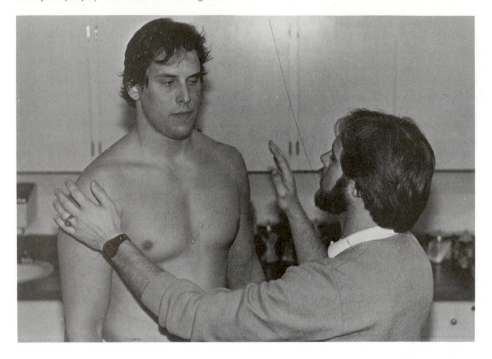

Figure 9-2 Bilateral visual comparison of the clavicles and their articulations. In this case, the clavicles appear normal.

ferences. One of the most valuable uses of palpation is the identification of localized pain and **point tenderness** (pain that manifests itself at a specific point during palpation). The athlete's reaction to a progressive increase in digital pressure may define the quality of pain and help identify lesions of specific ligaments, muscles, tendons, or bony structures. In addition, certain classical signs like "snowball" **crepitation** can be identified by palpation. Circulatory disturbances, which may occur during **heat stress** or **cardiac arrest,** can be evaluated by palpating the pulse for rate, strength, and rhythm.

Palpation should be performed thoroughly and systematically. The examination's thoroughness is enhanced by a sound knowledge of anatomy, which lets the athletic trainer "visualize" the structures to be palpated. Evaluation of joint injuries, for example, requires a precise knowledge of the proximal and distal attachments of ligaments so that they may be palpated in their entirety.

The sequence of palpation may vary as long as the procedure is thorough. Identify and palpate all "key" anatomical areas that conceivably may be involved in injury. The athletic trainer may first palpate bony structures and proceed to soft tissues, such as ligaments, capsular structures, muscles, and tendons. In other instances, palpation may proceed from medial to lateral or from proximal to distal aspects of the anatomy. For example, during a shoulder examination, palpation may begin with the sternoclavicular joint and progress laterally to the clavicle and acromioclavicular joint (Figure 9-3). The sequence of ligamentous palpation in a suspected inversion ankle sprain may begin with the commonly involved anterior talofibular ligament and progress posteriorly to the calcaneofibular and posterior talofibular ligament. Certain types of fractures are classically associated with the inversion mechanism. The athletic trainer should palpate the tip of the lateral malleolus for point

Point tenderness: Pain elicited at a specific anatomical location.

Crepitation (crepitus): A grinding, crackling sound produced by friction of adjacent tissues.
Heat stress: The body's inability to control its temperature because of decrease in central blood volume or failure of the hypothalamus' temperature regulatory center.
Cardiac arrest: Cessation of the normal cardiac cycle and blood pressure.

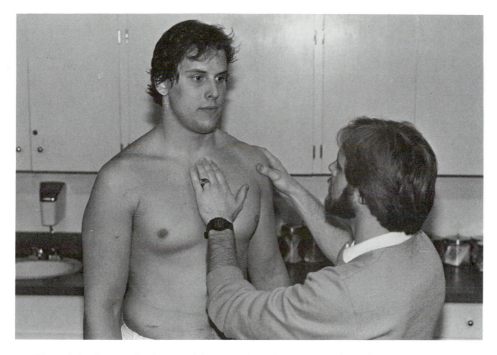

Figure 9-3 Sequential palpation of the sternoclavicular joint, clavicle, and acromioclavicular joint. The palpation sequence should proceed systematically, to detect any abnormalities.

tenderness associated with a possible **avulsion fracture** and the medial malleolus for evidence of a "push-off" fracture (O'Donoghue).

In some instances it is advisable to begin palpation in an uninvolved, pain-free area, to alleviate the anxiety of a particularly apprehensive athlete.

Functional Testing

Functional testing is assessing the degree of impairment of an injured body part by performing (1) range of motion, (2) stress, and (3) neurological tests. Functional tests should be conducted after the medical history, inspection, and palpation have been completed.

Range of Motion Tests. Range of motion tests are used to evaluate joint function. Both the degree and possible cause(s) of the restriction in joint motion should be determined. Measurement of the degree of restriction is determined from comparison with

established normal values (Table 9-1, p. 140). When using these norms, it is important to recognize the effects of specific sports activities and individual differences due to sex or **congenital** factors. Joint mobility in an uninvolved counterpart can also be a baseline for comparison. **Goniometric measurements** may be taken, but the athletic trainer can often conduct a meaningful assessment through a bilateral visual comparison of joint movements (Figure 9-4, p. 141). All motions that are normally possible in a particular joint should be measured unless contraindicated, such as when gross deformities are present.

Impairment of joint motion may be caused by either **intra-articular** abnormalities within the joint capsule or **periarticular** conditions involving the soft tissue around the joint. Both active and passive range of motion (ROM) tests are necessary to assess the pathological factors contributing to decreased joint mobility.

Avulsion fracture: A fracture caused by a small fragment of bone breaking away at the site of attachment of a ligament or tendon.

Congenital: Present at birth.

Goniometric measurements: Measurements of a joint's range of motion with a goniometer (a device that measures joint angles).

Functional testing: Performance testing to assess the degree to which an injured body part is impaired.

Intra-articular: Within a joint.

Periarticular: Near the joint.

Active Range of Motion Tests. These tests are used to evaluate contractile tissues (muscles and tendons) and the athlete's willingness to perform certain movements (Davies and Larson). The athletic trainer should realize that in the absence of contractile tissue injury, active motion may be limited by pathological conditions involving noncontractile tissues (bones, joint capsules, ligaments). While the active ROM tests are being executed, the athletic trainer should be aware of pain and decrements in muscular strength, which may cause the athlete to use substitute muscle actions. The athletic trainer should assess active ROM before passive motion because active ROM lets the athlete remain in control and thus stop or restrict a movement should pain be experienced at any particular point.

Passive Range of Motion Tests. Passive ROM tests are used to evaluate noncontractile structures such as joint capsules and ligaments (Davies and Larson). The subjective "end feel" at the extremes of a range of motion provides useful information about the nature of the articulation. For example, an athlete with an acute knee injury may be unable or unwilling to fully extend the knee actively because of a **hemarthrosis,** pain, muscle spasm, or a number of other reasons. A "springy block" during passive extension, however, indicates a mechanical block caused by a torn and displaced meniscus (Davies and Larson).

Stress Tests. ROM tests measure restrictions in joint mobility; **stress tests** check for joint instability from ligamentous or capsular trauma. During stress testing, the joint should be positioned so that the particular structures being tested are taut. Positioning should also allow for maximum relaxation of those joint structures not being tested. Basically, stabilize the body segment immediately proximal to the joint being tested. Then apply force by manually exerting pressure on the bony segment distal to the joint and in a line parallel to the length of the taut ligament. These procedures allow maximum "isolation" of joint structures, consequently greatly enhancing the validity of the stress testing.

An "empty" end point implies a posi-

Table 9-1 *Normal Range of Joint Motion*

Joint	Motion	Range of Motion(°)
Cervical spine	Flexion	65
	Extension[a]	50
	Lateral flexion	40
	Rotation	55
Lumbar spine	Flexion	95
	Extension[a]	35
	Lateral flexion	40
	Rotation	35
Shoulder	Flexion	180
	Extension[a]	45
	Abduction	180
	Adduction[a]	40
	Medial rotation	80
	Lateral rotation	90
Elbow	Flexion	145
Forearm	Supination	90
	Pronation	90
Wrist	Extension	70
	Flexion	80
	Abduction	20
	Adduction	35
Hip	Flexion	125
	Extension[a]	10
	Abduction	45
	Adduction[a]	15
	Medial rotation	45
	Lateral rotation	45
Knee	Flexion	140
Ankle	Plantar-flexion	45
	Dorsiflexion	20
Foot	Inversion	40
	Eversion	20

[a]Past 180° (e.g., hyperextension, etc.)

Hemarthrosis: Blood within a joint.

Stress test: Mechanical manipulation of a joint to test its stability.

tive stress test and a third degree injury, or complete ligament tear. A "soft" or "mushy" end point indicates a partial tear, or a second degree injury. Pain during stress testing, with a "hard" end point, may indicate a first degree, or mild, ligamentous involvement.

Figure 9-5 (p. 142) illustrates the basic principles of stress testing. The anterior talofibular ligament is positioned for maximum tension by plantar flexing the foot. In this position, the anterior talofibular ligament is taut while the calcaneofibular ligament is comparatively relaxed (Inman). The distal tibia and fibula are stabilized while force is applied to the dorsal aspect of the foot below the joint line in the direction of inversion and plantar flexion. As is the case in most stress testing, these procedures are an attempt to recreate the motions most commonly associated with the suspected injury.

Neurological Tests. Spinal cord injuries caused by unstable fractures or dislocations of the vertebrae may involve serious neurological complications. In the extremities, peripheral nerve injuries involving sensory or motor loss are often associated with specific types of soft tissue or bony trauma. For example, involvement of the median nerve should be suspected in wrist injuries associated with the carpal tunnel or an elbow injury involving a supracondylar fracture of the humerus. Contusions to the medial aspect of the elbow may involve the ulnar nerve. Radial nerve involvement may be associated with a fracture of the shaft of the humerus. The athletic trainer should know how to conduct a basic neurological examination to recognize the presence of neurological complications. The clinical neurological examination includes (1) sensation, (2) motor, and (3) reflex tests.

Sensation testing is the application of various stimuli (light touch, scratch, etc.) to specific areas of the skin that

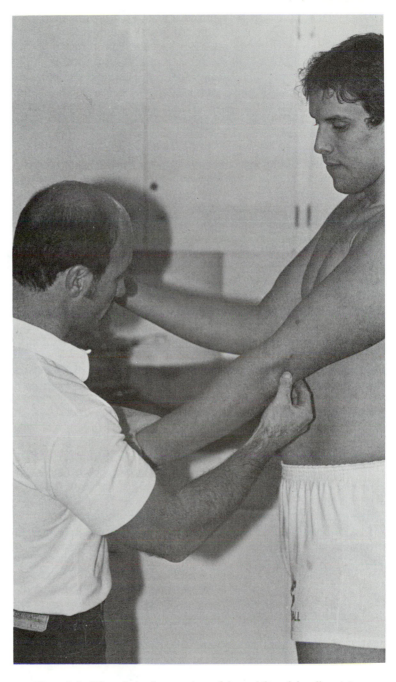

Figure 9-4 Bilateral visual comparison of the mobility of the elbow joint. Often, the uninjured limb can be a point of comparison for the extent of damage to the injured side.

are innervated by particular sensory nerves. Figure 9-6 illustrates the cutaneous distribution of sensory nerves, which are sometimes called **dermatomes.** The athletic trainer should be familiar with the most likely areas of sensory loss associated with specific peripheral nerve and nerve root trauma.

Appropriate cutaneous areas should be tested for sensitivity to light touch and pain sensation (Prior and Silberstein). Because loss of sensation is usually relative, the degree to which the athlete perceives a stimulus should be determined by noting the reaction to a stimulus of gradually increasing intensity.

To assess sensitivity to touch, the athletic trainer can use a cotton ball to monitor the athlete's verbal response as the stimulus is perceived. To test for pain sensation, apply the head (dull) and sharp end of a pin and note whether the athlete correctly perceives the dull or sharp stimulus (Figure 9-7). Abnormal responses to sensory testing include **hypoesthesia** (decreased tactile sensation), **hyperesthesia** (excessive tactile sensitivity), and anesthesia (complete loss of sensation). Paresthesia, another unusual neurological sensation, is characterized by numbness, tingling, burning, or **formication** (sensation of insects crawling on the skin). If percussion (tapping) of a peripheral nerve (e.g., the ulnar nerve at the medial elbow) produces a tingling sensation in the distal end of the limb, a positive Tinel's sign and a possible nerve lesion are indicated.

Testing for the integrity of motor nerves involves active or resisted muscle tests. **Paralysis** (complete loss of motor function) or **paresis** (partial paralysis or weakness) may be found (Prior and Silberstein). Complete loss of motor function rarely occurs in athletic injuries. For example, a peroneal nerve lesion with resulting "foot drop" illustrates complete paralysis only if the dorsiflexors of the ankle are unable to demonstrate any degree of muscular contrac-

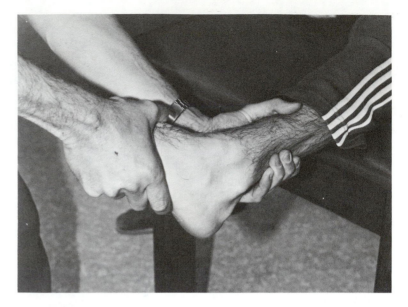

Figure 9-5 Stress testing the instability of the anterior talofibular ligament of the ankle.

tion. Inability to dorsiflex the ankle against gravity but retention of the ability to dorsiflex with gravity eliminated indicates partial rather than complete paralysis.

Muscle testing is based upon a subjective grading of strength. Table 9-2 (p. 144) is a commonly used muscle-testing grading scale. Preliminary testing of an opposite, uninvolved extremity is helpful for establishing a baseline for comparison. To assess strength, a muscle or muscle group is subjected to varying degrees of resistance from gravity and/or manual pressure. A muscle capable of moving a body segment through a full range of joint motion against maximum or full resistance is graded "normal." A "good" grade indicates movement through a full range of motion with moderate resistance. Movement through a full range against gravity is graded "fair"; joint movement with gravity eliminated is "poor." Muscles that demonstrate slight contraction without joint motion are graded "trace." A "zero" grade indicates no evidence of muscle contractility (Daniels and Worthingham).

Dermatomes: Areas of the skin supplied by sensory nerves of a single spinal nerve. Dermatomes help identify the location of spinal lesions.

Hypoesthesia: Lack of sensitivity to pain, touch, or other sensory stimuli.

Hyperesthesia: Abnormal sensitivity to pain, touch, or other sensory stimuli.

Formication: An abnormal sensation characterized by the feeling of insects crawling on the skin.

Paralysis: Partial or complete loss of capability to move.

Paresis: Partial paralysis.

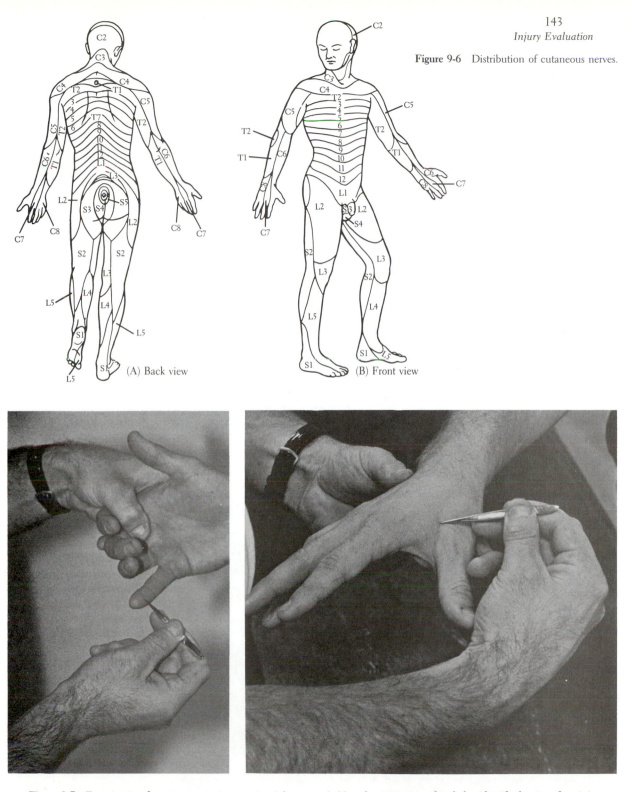

Figure 9-6 Distribution of cutaneous nerves.

(A) Back view

(B) Front view

Figure 9-7 Examination for cutaneous pain sensation (ulnar nerve). Neural examination often helps identify the site of an injury far from the site where the athlete feels pain.

Principles of Injury Prevention and Management

Table 9-2 *Muscle-Testing Grading Scale*

Grades	Interpretation
5 (normal)	Complete range of motion against gravity with maximum or full resistance
4 (good)	Complete range of motion against gravity with moderate resistance
3 (fair)	Complete range of motion against gravity
2 (poor)	Complete range of motion with gravity eliminated
1 (trace)	Evidence of slight contractility/no joint motion
0 (zero)	No evidence of contractility

SOURCE: Adapted from Daniels, L., and C. Worthingham. *Muscle Testing*. Philadelphia: W. B. Saunders, 1980.

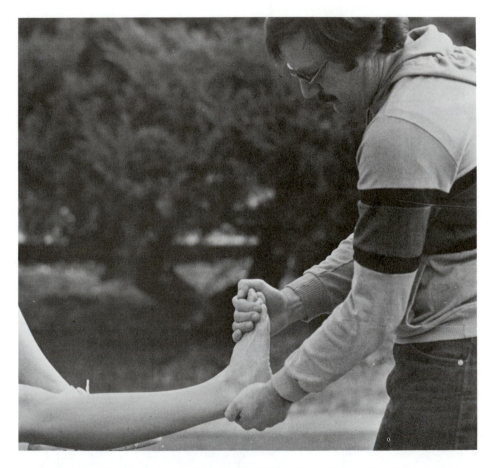

Figure 9-8 Manual muscle test of the strength of the ankle dorsiflexors. The athletic trainer is resisting the athlete's effort to dorsiflex the ankle.

To determine the muscle testing's **validity** and **reliability,** the athletic trainer must have working knowledge of muscle innervation and the principles of segmental fixation, muscle isolation, and manual resistance (Figure 9-8). The athletic trainer must also consider the relationship of strength to age and sex (females and young and old persons of both sexes tend to be weaker than young adult males). (See Kendall et al. and Daniels and Worthingham for a more detailed discussion of the principles and techniques of muscle testing.)

The integrity of sensory and motor nerve fibers can be evaluated by testing muscles' **stretch reflexes.** Assuming spinal reflex integrity, a brief muscle stretch provides a stimulus to stretch receptors in the muscle that, in turn, transmit afferent impulses to the spinal cord via sensory fibers. Efferent impulses transmitted from the spinal cord to the muscle via motor fibers produce a brief contraction called a stretch reflex (Prior and Silberstein).

Clinically, to initiate a stretch reflex in the muscle, tap on the muscle's tendon with a reflex hammer. Place the extremity in a relaxed position, with slight tension in the muscle. Prior and Silberstein suggest that the examiner place his finger on the tendon and tap the finger, thus permitting better assessment of muscular tension, the strength of the tap, and the quality of the reflex. The reflex is graded as normal, increased, decreased, or absent. Abnormal responses include **hyporeflexia** (diminished reflex), which may be associated with lower motor neuron lesions, and **hyperreflexia** (exaggerated reflex), indicating an upper motor neuron involvement (Barber and Budassi, Davies and Larson). Most commonly tested muscles include the biceps, brachioradialis, triceps, quadriceps, and gastrocnemius-soleus.

References

The American College Dictionary. New York: Random House, 1962.

Barber, J. M., and S. A. Budassi. *Manual of Emergency Care.* St. Louis: C. V. Mosby, 1979.

Basmajian, J. V. (ed.). *Therapeutic Exercise.* Baltimore: Williams & Wilkins, 1978.

Daniels, L., and C. Worthingham. *Muscle Testing.* Philadelphia: W. B. Saunders, 1980.

Davies, G. J., and R. Larson. Examining the knee. *The Physician and Sportsmedicine* 6:49–67, 1978.

Goss, C. M. (ed.). *Gray's Anatomy.* Philadelphia: Lea & Febiger, 1973.

Hoppenfeld, S. *Physical Examination of the Spine and Extremities.* New York: Appleton-Century-Crofts, 1976.

Inman, V. T. (ed.). *DuVries' Surgery of the Foot.* St. Louis: C. V. Mosby, 1973.

Kendall, H. O., F. P. Kendall, and G. E. Wadsworth. *Muscles: Testing and Function.* Baltimore: Williams & Wilkins, 1971.

Kuprian, W. (ed.). *Physical Therapy for Sports.* Philadelphia: W. B. Saunders, 1982.

O'Donoghue, D. H. *Treatment of Injuries to Athletes.* Philadelphia: W. B. Saunders, 1984.

Prior, J. A., and J. S. Silberstein. *Physical Diagnosis: The History and Examination of the Patient.* St. Louis: C. V. Mosby, 1973.

Validity: The degree to which a test measures what it is supposed to measure.
Reliability: The degree to which results of a test are reproducible.

Stretch reflex: A muscle contraction initiated by sudden stretch of muscle spindles.

Hyporeflexia: Diminished reflexes.

Hyperreflexia: Exaggerated reflexes.

10 Emergency Care

T HE purpose of the athletic emergency plan is to render first aid and obtain medical assistance as quickly as possible. If, after careful evaluation, an injury is judged serious, the athlete should be moved in a manner that does not compound the problem. Safe, efficient emergency care of an injured athlete is facilitated by consistently assessing the injury and then rendering care (Putting It into Practice 10-1). The athletic trainer, coach, or physician should always approach the injured athlete anticipating the most serious problems, such as cardiac arrest or cervical injury. (However, most sports injuries occur in musculoskeletal tissue and are not life-threatening.) The athlete's level of consciousness should be determined first and then vital signs taken. Then CPR or other first aid should be applied. This emergency care has to cover respiratory or cardiac arrest, external and internal bleeding, and central nervous system and musculoskeletal injuries.

Proper emergency planning is important for sports at all levels. Serious injuries sometimes occur in youth football and should be anticipated.

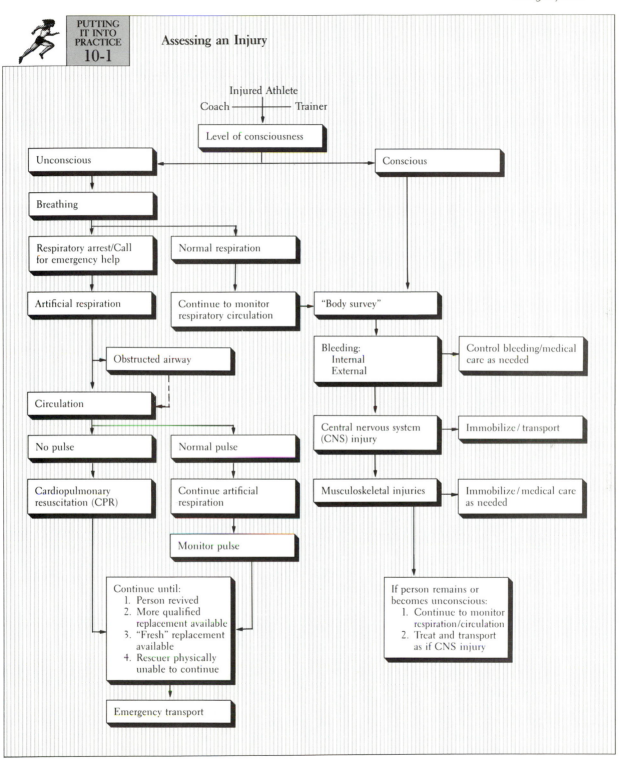

Assessing an Injury

PUTTING IT INTO PRACTICE 10-1

Determining Level of Consciousness

The primary concern is to determine the injured athlete's level of **consciousness.** Obviously, an ambulatory athlete is conscious; however, consciousness may not be obvious if the athlete is lying on the field or floor. Unconsciousness is the inability to respond to external stimuli. To establish consciousness, get as close as possible to the athlete's head without moving the person. Talk to the athlete, thereby providing external stimuli. Ask "Are you OK? What happened?" In certain instances, shaking the athlete may provide further stimuli. However, if you suspect head or cervical injury, shaking is **contraindicated.** The athlete's failure to respond to external stimuli establishes unconsciousness.

The next step is to determine if the athlete is breathing. Without moving the injured person, get as close to the head as possible and (1) look for respiratory movements (chest rising and lowering), (2) listen for breathing sounds from the nose and mouth, and (3) feel for moving air from the nose and mouth (Figure 10-1). When checking for breathing, determine the rate (normal resting adult rate is twelve to fifteen breaths per minute) and quantify the volume (deep, shallow, labored). Respiratory arrest is indicated when the breathing rate and volume are inadequate to sustain life. Normal rate and volume suggest that the unconsciousness is not caused by direct respiratory problems.

Respiratory Arrest

Although respiratory arrest is rare in athletics, it may occur. When it does, breathing must be reestablished immediately. Emergency transportation must be called and steps taken to artificially

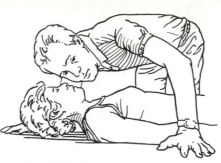

Figure 10-1 Determining whether an athlete is breathing. Look, listen, and feel for air moving from the nose and mouth. Tilt the athlete's head back to clear the airway *only* if you do *not* suspect head or neck injuries.

ventilate the lungs. The most effective ventilation method is mouth-to-mouth resuscitation. Anyone working with athletes (including the athletes themselves) should be trained and currently certified in **cardiopulmonary resuscitation (CPR)** through the American Red Cross or the American Heart Association. The descriptions and sequences in this chapter are overviews only; they will *not* make the reader skilled in life-support techniques.

The inability to ventilate the lungs suggests an obstructed airway (e.g., gum, chewing tobacco, food). You *must* manually clear the obstructed airway before initiating artificial ventilation. When the athlete is lying down, do the following:

1. Roll the athlete on his or her side.
2. With the heel of your hand, deliver four back blows between the athlete's shoulder blades.
3. Roll the athlete onto his or her back and perform four inward and upward abdominal thrusts (Heimlich maneuver).
4. Sweep the athlete's mouth with one or two of your fingers to remove any dislodged object. Repeat the sequence until the airway is cleared.

When the athlete is seated or erect, again, use the Heimlich maneuver:

1. Standing behind and to the side of the athlete, deliver four back blows (you can use your other

Consciousness: Responsiveness to sensory input.

Cardiopulmonary resuscitation (CPR): Mechanically compressing the heart of a pulseless, nonbreathing person to increase cardiac output and blowing air into the mouth to increase lungs' oxygen content.
Contraindicated: Not appropriate or recommended.

hand to support the athlete) and then prepare to initiate abdominal thrusts.

2. Stand behind the athlete with your arms wrapped around her or his waist.

3. Make a fist with your right hand; place the thumb side of your fist on the athlete's abdomen between the xyphoid process of the sternum and the umbilicus.

4. Grasp your fist with your left hand.

5. Press your fist into the athlete's abdomen with a quick upward thrust.

6. Manually remove the foreign body (Figure 10-2).

The spontaneous return of respiration or successful artificial ventilation of the lungs indicates an open airway. After the airway has been successfully cleared, give four quick ventilations. Now check the athlete's pulse by palpating the **carotid artery.** Using two or three fingers, locate the carotid pulse by palpating the side of the Adam's apple in the midthroat area. Determine whether the pulse's rate and amplitude are weak, strong, or irregular (normal resting adult heart rate is sixty to eighty beats per minute). If the pulse rate and strength are normal, continue to ventilate the lungs once every five seconds (twelve per minute), periodically rechecking the status of the pulse and respiration. If the rate and intensity of the pulse are both inadequate to sustain life, the athlete is in cardiac arrest.

Cardiac Arrest

Once it has been established that the athlete is in **cardiac arrest,** steps must be taken to both artificially ventilate the lungs and artificially compress the heart to circulate blood (i.e., CPR). To artificially circulate the blood, rhythmically compress the chest, thereby squeezing the heart between the sternum and spi-

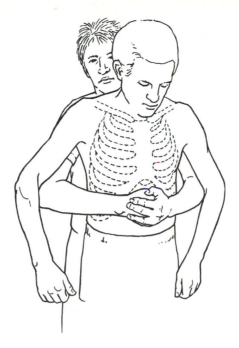
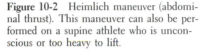

Figure 10-2 Heimlich maneuver (abdominal thrust). This maneuver can also be performed on a supine athlete who is unconscious or too heavy to lift.

nal column. The squeezing artificially pumps the blood from the heart chambers through the peripheral vessels to the tissues. The American Red Cross sequence when a single rescuer is present calls for fifteen compressions of the chest followed by two lung inflations, or when two rescuers are present, five compressions followed by one lung inflation. Whether one or two rescuers are in attendance, a check for spontaneous return of breathing and circulation must be made every one to two minutes (Figure 10-3, p. 150).

Continue cardiopulmonary resuscitation until the

1. Athlete is revived (at which time the athlete must be periodically monitored for relapse)

2. Rescuer is replaced by someone more qualified (emergency care or hospital personnel)

3. Tired rescuer is replaced by someone equally qualified

4. Rescuer is unable to continue because of extreme fatigue

Carotid artery: An important artery that supplies blood to the brain; often used to measure pulse rate. To palpate, place hands on the anterolateral aspect of the athlete's neck.

Cardiac arrest: Cessation of cardiac output and blood pressure.

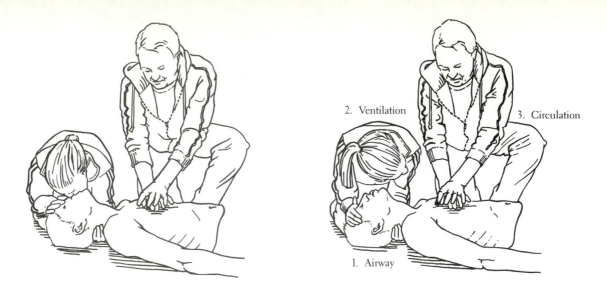

2. Ventilation

3. Circulation

1. Airway

Figure 10-3 Principles of one- and two-rescuer cardiopulmonary resuscitation (CPR). For one-rescuer CPR, perform fifteen chest compressions; use two quick lung inflations. For two-rescuer CPR, perform five chest compressions with no pause for ventilation. After each five compressions, perform one lung inflation. In actual practice, the rescuer doing lung inflation would be on the other side of the victim's body.

Unconscious with Normal Respiration

When the athlete is unconscious with normal breathing and circulatory rates, the body should be surveyed to determine the cause of unconsciousness and any other problems. This is most difficult when the athlete is unconscious because the athletic trainer must rely upon visible physical evidence only, without the benefit of the athlete verbalizing the symptoms. (The body survey can also be performed when the athlete is conscious, which will confirm the findings more readily.)

Body Survey. The athletic trainer begins at the athlete's head and works down one side of the body and then the other. Factors to be evaluated during the examination are bleeding, skin color, temperature, **pupil reflex,** body position, deformity, pain, sensation, and the ability to move (when not contraindicated). Combining these findings with the previously established evaluation of breathing and circulation helps determine the nature and extent of the injuries and decide the appropriate course of emergency care.

External Bleeding

Bleeding is either external or internal. External bleeding is the result of an open wound, such as an **abrasion, incision, laceration, puncture,** or **avulsion.** After cardiorespiratory distress, severe external bleeding is the second emergency priority. Emergency care procedures for severe bleeding are (1) control the bleeding, (2) prevent contamination, (3) immobilize the part, and (4) transport the athlete to a physician.

Control Methods

The four methods for controlling external bleeding are direct pressure, elevation, indirect digital pressure, and tourniquet. Direct pressure and elevation are the methods of choice and thus used most often. (See Putting It into Practice 10-2.)

Direct Pressure. To apply direct pressure at the wound site, place a sterile gauze dressing over the wound and compress the tissue against the underly-

Abrasion: A wound caused by a portion of the skin being scraped away.

Incision: A wound caused by the skin tissue being cut.

Laceration: A wound caused by the skin tissue being torn.

Puncture: A wound caused by the skin tissue being pierced with a pointed instrument.

Avulsion: An injury in which tissue (e.g., skin, muscle, bone) is torn away.

Pupil reflex: Contraction of the pupil in reaction to a bright light.

Figure 10-4 Elevation and direct pressure are the two most important methods for stopping external bleeding.

> **PUTTING IT INTO PRACTICE 10-2**
>
> **Controlling External Bleeding**
>
> I. Control bleeding
>   A. Direct pressure
>   B. Elevation
>   C. Indirect digital pressure
>   1. Brachial
>   2. Femoral
>   D. Tourniquet (life versus limb decision)
> II. Prevent contamination
>   A. Cleanse wound site
>   B. Cover with sterile dressing
> III. Immobilize involved extremity
> IV. Transport athlete to physician

ing bone. When done properly, the pressure compresses the blood vessels and assists the body's clotting process. If the wound has an object in it, such as wood or metal, direct pressure is inappropriate and may cause further damage. In this instance, indirect digital pressure is usually preferable (see below).

Elevation. Elevation is an appropriate supplement to direct pressure (Figure 10-4). Gravity assists in clot formation when the wound site is above the level of the heart. However, elevation is contraindicated in cervical injury, internal injury, or fracture of the involved limb because in these cases the movement may cause additional problems or intensify the bleeding.

Indirect Digital Pressure. Indirect digital pressure is the application of

pressure with your hands or fingers over a major artery against the underlying bone. It should be applied when direct pressure is inappropriate (e.g., the site of bleeding is a major artery) or ineffective (wound is still bleeding after one to two minutes). The digital pressure compresses the artery, which slows the delivery of blood to points **distal** to the site. For upper extremity bleeding distal to the midarm, locate the brachial digital pressure point, which is on the medial surface of the midbiceps. Using your fingers or the heel of your hand, compress the tissue inward against the humerus. This process will facilitate clot formation by slowing the blood flow to the wound site (Figure 10-5, p. 152). If not contraindicated, elevation can also be used with indirect digital pressure.

For lower extremity bleeding distal to the midthigh, locate the femoral digital pressure point, which is in the midgroin. Using your fingers, push inward at the site of the femoral pulse. This action compresses the femoral artery against the pelvis, thus slowing the circulation distally and assisting the natural clotting process. Again, elevation is an effective supplement if not contraindicated.

Most wounds sustained in athletics do *not* require a **tourniquet.** Although a tourniquet is the most effective method for controlling bleeding, it also greatly increases the chance of a limb being lost from necrosis of tissue. In

Distal: Farthest away from the point of reference.

Tourniquet: A constrictive band tied tightly around an extremity to stop bleeding. Use only as a last resort.

cases of a partial or complete avulsion of an extremity when the other pressure methods are ineffective, use the tourniquet as a last resort. Apply a thick material (four inches) two inches above the wound and with a pen or stick tighten the material enough to stop the bleeding.

Preventing Contamination

Preventing contamination and **infection** involves cleaning the wound, but there is little need for this when the injury requires immediate hospital care. Simply secure the dressing with a bandage, immobilize the extremity, and transport the athlete to the hospital. When hospitalization is not immediately needed and the bleeding is superficial, clean the area with soap and water, making sure to thoroughly rinse the area. Cover the area with a sterile dressing and secure the dressing with a bandage. At this point, refer the athlete to a physician as needed. Referral for possible **suture** is appropriate for facial wounds or when the wound is deeper than the superficial skin layers. Following initial treatment, daily examine the wound for signs of infection and change the dressing.

Immobilizing the Involved Extremity

Immobilizing the involved extremity prevents any unnecessary movement that could cause bleeding to resume. To immobilize the part, secure it to an adjacent body part by bringing the individual's arm against the body (the adjacent body part is used to prevent motion) or by bringing the two legs together, or apply an appropriate splint.

Transporting the Injured

The final priority in an external bleeding emergency is to quickly and efficiently transport the injured athlete to a medical facility. Rapid transportation is particularly important following

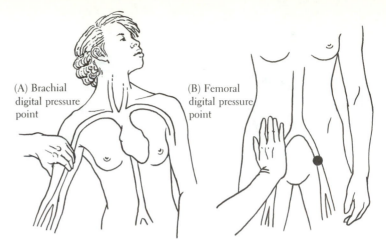

(A) Brachial digital pressure point

(B) Femoral digital pressure point

Figure 10-5 Indirect digital pressure over arterial pressure points often helps stop serious arterial bleeding.

profuse bleeding, facial wounds, or wounds that present a high risk of infection. The athlete should be transported supine, with the feet elevated and the injured parts immobilized, to prevent the resumption of bleeding and avert complications, such as shock (collapse of the cardiovascular system).

Infection: An inflammatory condition caused by the body being invaded by pathogenic organisms.

Suture: Stitches that unite two tissue surfaces.

Internal Bleeding

Internal bleeding is difficult to establish and control (Putting It into Practice 10-3) because it occurs as a result of closed wounds—the external evidence is not as obvious as with an open wound. Accordingly, the athletic trainer should be extremely suspicious when completing the body survey and evaluating an athlete who has sustained some form of direct trauma.

Internal bleeding manifests itself in several ways. The athlete's pulse will be weak and rapid, and blood pressure will drop. This is the body's compensatory response in an attempt to maintain tissue **perfusion.** The skin will be cool; this is another compensatory response, whereby the body directs the available blood to the major organs at the expense of the periphery (skin) by constricting the peripheral blood vessels.

Perfusion: Movement of blood (or other fluid) through a tissue.

The athlete's mental responsiveness may be diminished from cerebral **hypoxia** caused by decreased blood flow. The existence of abdominal rigidity suggests internal abdominal bleeding, although this point is controversial (Chapter 19). Blood in the urine (**hematuria**), stool, or vomitus are further indications of internal injury and bleeding. Bleeding from the ears suggests possible **intracranial** injury.

Given the insidious nature of internal bleeding, it is a very difficult problem to evaluate and treat. Thus the emergency care for internal bleeding is much more general than that for external bleeding. A general strategy for dealing with internal bleeding is to treat the athlete for shock and transport the individual to a medical facility. Specific procedures include (1) positioning the athlete to maximize the effect of gravity in slowing bleeding, (2) maintaining the body temperature as close to normal (98.6°F, 37°C) as possible by covering the body with blankets or removing extra clothing or equipment, and (3) transporting the athlete to the hospital as quickly and as gently as possible to minimize aggravation of the bleeding.

Shock

Shock is inadequate perfusion of blood to the tissues and organs caused by collapse of the cardiovascular system. It is characterized by inadequate cardiac output (blood flow from the heart) in relation to tissue metabolism. The major causes of shock are damage to the heart, which results in a decreased ability to pump blood, and a decreased venous return of blood to the heart, which is caused by blood loss or loss of circulatory resistance. Shock often occurs after serious injury, but it may occur following seemingly trivial emotional upset, bee sting, or allergic reaction to a food. Therefore, suspect shock whenever its symptoms appear in an athlete.

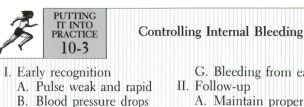

Putting It Into Practice 10-3 — Controlling Internal Bleeding

I. Early recognition
   A. Pulse weak and rapid
   B. Blood pressure drops
   C. Skin is cool
   D. Mental disorientation
   E. Abdominal rigidity
   F. Blood in urine (hematuria), stool, or vomitus
   G. Bleeding from ears
II. Follow-up
   A. Maintain proper body position to maximize gravity
   B. Maintain normal body temperature
   C. Early transport to medical facility

General symptoms of most types of shock include weak, rapid pulse, falling blood pressure, cold, clammy skin, **dyspnea,** psychological upset, and a pale, ashen complexion. Shock decreases metabolism, causes muscular weakness, depresses body temperature, decreases mental function, and reduces renal function. Shock may lead to decreased cardiac nutrition, decreased tissue nutrition, and blood clotting.

Severe shock can lead to a vicious cycle of progressively more severe shock. Shock is a major medical emergency: Medical assistance must be obtained and first aid administered immediately.

Types

The types of shock are hemorrhagic (hypovolemic), respiratory, neurogenic, psychogenic, cardiogenic, septic, anaphylactic, and metabolic. The athletic trainer may encounter any of the types when working with athletes.

Hemorrhagic or hypovolemic **shock** results from blood loss or blood being prevented from returning to the heart (severe dehydration and heat exhaustion). This type of shock is common following fractures, internal injuries, and severe contusions. Hemorrhagic shock may also result from a severe contusion that causes capillary damage and plasma to leak into the tissues.

Hypoxia: Low level of oxygen.

Hematuria: Blood in the urine.

Intracranial: Within the skull.

Dyspnea: Labored or uncomfortable breathing.

Shock: Blood not being delivered to the tissues and organs, caused by failure of the cardiovascular system.

Hemorrhagic shock: Shock caused by blood loss or circulation's inability to return blood to the heart (as in heat exhaustion).

Respiratory shock may result from a **pneumothorax** or obstructed airway, which causes hypoxemia (low oxygen content in the blood). Respiratory shock may occur following a neck injury that causes paralysis of the thorax muscles.

Neurogenic shock is caused by a loss of circulatory tone (vasomotor tone), which effectively increases the body's vascular capacity, making it more difficult for blood to return to the heart. Brain damage is the most common cause of neurogenic shock in athletics. The pain associated with serious injury can also inhibit the **vasomotor center** (the center in the brain that controls circulatory vasoconstriction) and exacerbate or initiate shock.

Psychogenic shock (also called vasovagal syncope or emotional fainting) appears similar to neurogenic shock except that the physiological mechanism is different. Neurogenic shock is caused by failure of the vasomotor center; psychogenic shock is induced by a strong stimulation of the **parasympathetic nervous system,** which suppresses heart rate and vasodilates blood vessels in the tissues. Psychogenic shock is usually self-limiting because the fainting person generally falls to a horizontal position, which facilitates the resumption of normal cardiac output.

Cardiogenic shock may result when the heart's function is impaired by myocardial infarction (heart attack), heart failure, or inflammatory conditions. **Septic shock,** also known as blood poisoning, is caused by infection. In athletics, septic shock often results from peritonitis, which is infection or rupture of the gut. Initial stages of septic shock are high fever, marked circulatory vasodilation, high cardiac output, and thickening of the blood.

Anaphylactic shock is a severe allergic reaction caused by oversensitivity of the body's immune system to a particular substance. This type of shock may be caused by reactions to drugs such as penicillin, ingestion of certain foods, bee stings, and inhalation of pollens or dust to which the athlete is sensitive. Anaphylactic shock is characterized by a drastic fall in cardiac output and blood pressure. The physiological mechanism is exaggerated vasodilation caused by the release of histamine and prostaglandins and destruction of blood vessels caused by the immune reactions.

Metabolic shock is caused by excessive fluid loss from vomiting, diarrhea, or electrolyte disturbances. This type of shock may occur as a result of heat illnesses and in diabetics experiencing diabetic coma.

Treatment

Figure 10-6 describes general first-aid treatment of shock. Procedures include clearing the airway and performing CPR (if necessary), obtaining medical assistance, controlling bleeding (includes fracture splinting), placing the athlete in a comfortable, supine position and elevating the legs (if possible), placing blankets under and over the athlete, and monitoring the vital signs. Do not give the athlete any food or fluids. The use of pneumatic splints may help prevent fluid from accumulating in the legs and facilitate the return of blood to the heart. The athlete must be treated gently, and onlookers must be cleared from the area.

Medical treatment for shock includes blood or plasma transfusion (for hemorrhagic shock) to increase circulation volume and administration of sympathomimetic drugs (drugs that mimic the action of the sympathetic nervous system) to increase cardiac output and circulatory resistance. Pain-relieving drugs are helpful when pain is contributing to the development of shock.

Respiratory shock: Shock caused by an inadequate oxygen supply.
Pneumothorax: Presence of air within the chest cavity (outside the lungs).
Neurogenic shock: Shock caused by the nervous system's loss of vascular control (as in heatstroke).
Metabolic shock: Shock induced by loss of body fluid through vomiting, diarrhea, or excess urination.
Vasomotor center: A portion of the brain that controls vasoconstriction (narrowing) of blood vessels. Inhibition of the center causes vasodilation (opening of blood vessels).
Psychogenic shock: Shock caused by a psychologically induced vasodilation (opening) of blood vessels that results in an inadequate amount of blood returning to the heart.
Parasympathetic nervous system: One of the two major subdivisions of the autonomic nervous system. Effects include decreased heart rate, constriction of the coronary arteries, dilation of skin blood vessels, and contraction of the pupils.
Cardiogenic shock: Shock caused by heart failure.
Septic shock: Shock caused by injury to blood vessels or severe infection.
Anaphylactic shock: Shock induced by an allergic reaction, e.g., to a bee sting.

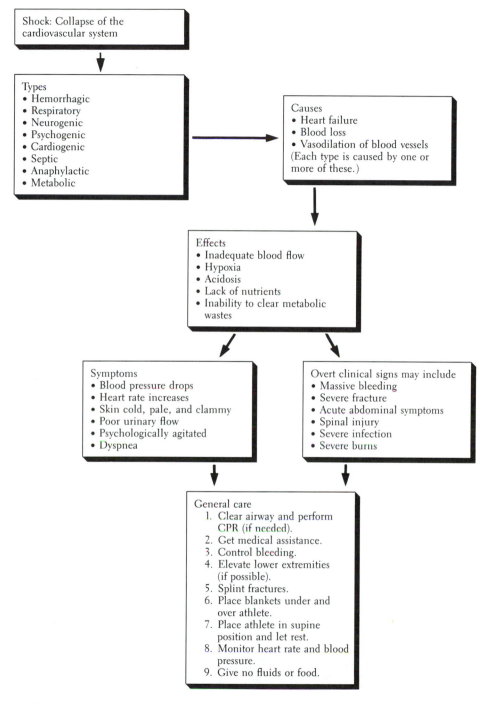

Figure 10-6 Shock cycle flowchart.

Central Nervous System Injuries

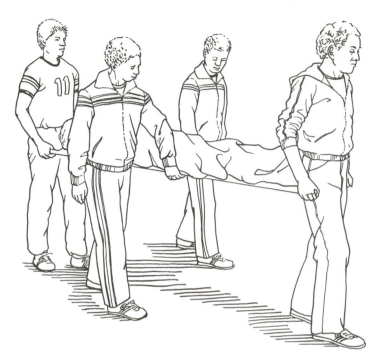

The next most important injury area is the central nervous system (CNS). Injuries to the brain and spinal cord leave little margin for error on the part of those caring for the athlete. One basic rule for the coach or athletic trainer is to assume that any *unconscious* athlete with stable breathing and circulation has a head and/or cervical injury. *Never* move a victim with head, neck, or back injury unless qualified medical personnel is present. With the conscious athlete, the body survey and evaluation will provide more specifics to help determine the existence of a head or neck injury.

Head Injury

Concussions, intracranial **hemorrhage,** and skull fracture are the most common serious head injuries in athletics. Take the following steps when you suspect significant concussion and/or hemorrhage (Chapter 14):

1. Immediately transport the athlete to a medical facility. Move the athlete on a litter, scoop, or spine board to minimize movement (Figure 10-7). Move the injured athlete only in the presence of qualified medical personnel.
2. Elevate the head and shoulders if the athlete is conscious and has no suspected neck injury.
3. If the athlete with no suspected neck injury loses consciousness, roll him or her on his or her side to prevent the aspiration of any vomitus.
4. Maintain body temperature.
5. Give no liquids.
6. Monitor athlete's vital signs.
7. Implement resuscitation techniques as needed.

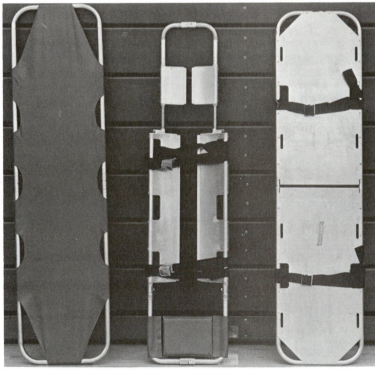

Figure 10-7 Transporting the injured athlete. Stretchers commonly used in sports medicine are (from left) the army-type stretcher, scoop stretcher, and spine board.

8. Contact the receiving medical facility and inform them of the arrival of a head-injury victim. This will give the facility time to mobilize the necessary personnel, including a neurosurgeon. Time is critical.

Cervical Cord Injury

The athlete with a head or neck injury (or unknown trauma) who is unconscious or exhibits motor weakness, paralysis, or decreased sensory function in one or more extremities should be handled definitively and carefully. These symptoms suggest a strong probability of cervical cord injury associated with cervical fracture and/or dislocation. Emergency care for a suspected cervical injury involves the following steps:

1. Monitor the athlete's **vital signs;** attempt artificial ventilation or CPR if necessary. In sports like football, where a helmet and face mask may impair access to the airway, cut off the mask with bolt cutters, or cut the snaps with a knife and flip up the mask. The athletic trainer should *never* remove the helmet when a cervical injury is suspected.
2. When maintaining the airway, move the head and neck as little as possible. Do not extend the head beyond the neutral position. When ventilating is difficult, use the jaw thrust method suggested by the American Red Cross (place your fingers behind the athlete's mandible and exert traction in an anterior direction; this forced motion pulls the tongue anteriorly, which opens the airway because the tongue is attached to the mandible).
3. Move the athlete onto a rigid spine board (litter/scoop) only in the presence of qualified medical personnel.

4. One person should hold the athlete's head in a slight **axial traction** (pull) to prevent neck movements.
5. Two or three other people should lift or roll the body as a unit onto the board (Figure 10-8, p. 158). One rescuer, preferably the one at the athlete's head, gives the commands and directs the transfer.
6. Transport the injured individual to a medical facility that has been alerted to the athlete's impending arrival.
7. Constantly monitor the athlete's cardiorespiratory status during transport.

As with head injuries, time is of the essence in seeking medical care (but not to the point of potentially injuring the athlete by rushing or moving the body carelessly).

Musculoskeletal Injuries

Most athletic injuries are to musculoskeletal structures such as soft tissues (**contusions**), muscles (**strains**), bones (**fractures**), and joints (**sprains, subluxations,** and **dislocations**). The nature of these injuries is the same, whether they are the result of direct trauma, indirect trauma, or overuse. However, the degree or severity of injury is often difficult to determine, so the athletic trainer must systematically evaluate the injury (Chapter 9) and be prepared to render emergency care.

Contusions

Contusions are soft tissue injuries from a direct blow to the body. The trauma damages blood vessels, which in turn produces localized bleeding that is proportional to the amount of damaged tissue. Although this is not the most

Concussion: Brain injury caused by the skull being jarred or shaken; characterized by unconsciousness, dizziness, cold sweat, and visual disturbance.
Hemorrhage: Bleeding.
Axial traction: Slight pulling of the head along the longitudinal axis of the spine.

Vital signs: Heart rate, ventilatory rate, level of consciousness, blood pressure, and body temperature.

Contusion: A bruise.
Strain: Disruption or injury of a musculotendinous unit. A severe strain is often called a pulled muscle.
Fracture: A break in a bone or in cartilage.
Sprain: Disruption or injury of a ligament.
Subluxation: Partial dislocation.
Dislocation: Displacement of a bone from a joint.

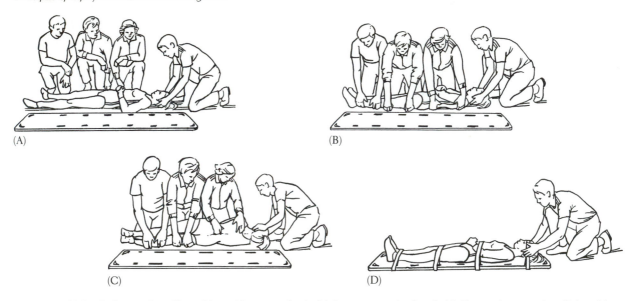

Figure 10-8 Technique for rolling athlete with suspected spinal injury onto a spine board. (A) Two or three people roll the athlete onto his side while the leader stabilizes his head. (B) The athlete is rolled as a unit. (C and D) The athlete is placed on the spine board.

serious type of athletic injury, additional injury may have occurred and should be suspected (fracture, nerve injury, etc.). The code word for the emergency treatment of contusions and other soft tissue injuries is ICE: Ice, Compression, and Elevation (Putting It into Practice 10-4).

Ice (I): Application of cold decreases the amount of bleeding and swelling following a contusion and other musculoskeletal injuries by vasoconstricting local blood vessels. In addition, ice significantly decreases pain and muscle spasm resulting from the injury. Proper application of cold also depresses local metabolism so that the injured tissue may be able to withstand the hypoxia the trauma and contusion cause. The use of ice is discussed in Chapter 13.

Methods of applying cold include immersion, commercial ice packs, ice bags, and ice massage. McMaster suggests applying twenty to thirty minutes of cold to cool deeper tissue. This concept is controversial because there is little evidence of deep tissue cooling occurring in areas other than the feet and hands (Chapter 13).

Compression (C): An elastic compression bandage effectively controls edema. The elasticity allows some expansion in the event of extreme swelling. On an extremity, apply the wrap in a distal to **proximal** direction, which will prevent the distal collection of extracellular fluid. A properly applied elastic wrap protects and reduces pain caused by the compression. Be careful to not wrap the bandage too tightly or circulation may be impaired.

Elevation (E): Elevation uses gravity to minimize swelling and support venous and lymphatic circulation. This process facilitates removal of waste and the restoration of normal circulation.

Fractures and Dislocations

The goal of soft tissue injury management is to minimize inflammation. However, the primary emphasis of acute fracture and dislocation management is protecting the integrity of bones and joints.

Proximal: Near the point of reference.

PUTTING IT INTO PRACTICE 10-4

Caring for Musculoskeletal Injuries: ICE

Ice (cold application)
1. Decreases bleeding
2. Decreases swelling (vaso-constriction)
3. Decreases pain
4. Decreases metabolism
5. Decreases muscle spasm

Compression (elastic bandage)
1. Decreases swelling (mechanical deterrent)
2. Immobilizes part (more specific splinting required with fractures and dislocations)
3. "Feels good" (proprioceptive)

Elevation
1. Decreases swelling
2. Increases venous and lymphatic circulation
3. Facilitates waste removal
4. Facilitates return of circulation

Reduction. Fractures and dislocations are caused by direct or indirect trauma and are treated essentially the same. The first principle of emergency care of these injuries is that a **displaced fracture** or dislocation not be intentionally reduced (realigned) by a nonphysician. Reduction is a medical procedure that could cause further injury and, if practiced by an untrained and unauthorized person, become a legal liability (Box 10-1, p. 160).

Splinting. Immobilization is the principal emergency procedure for fractures and dislocations. Proper immobilization prevents movement at the site and of adjacent joints. The three major types of splints are (1) fixation splints (boards, wire, ladder, pillows, and blankets), which are the most common and are adaptable to most fractures and dislocations; (2) pneumatic (air) splints, which are easy to apply and best suited for nondisplaced fractures but not appropriate for dislocations; and (3) traction splints, used for long-bone fractures, such as the femur, and to prevent overriding of the bones and protect the fracture site (Figure 10-9). The choice of splint depends upon the available equipment and the nature of the fracture or dislocation. Figure 10-10 (p. 161) illustrates emergency splinting procedures.

Figure 10-9 Fracture splints are used to prevent the bones from overriding and to protect the fracture site.

Complications. Fractures and dislocations are sometimes complicated by neurovascular impairment, which results from the **impingement** of nerves and/or blood vessels. Impingement can impair neural innervation and circulation distal to the injury site. When there is nerve involvement, any impairment is manifested by decreased sensation or movement. When there is vascular impairment, the impairment is manifested by weak peripheral pulse and coldness. No attempt should be made to relieve any suspected neurovascular impairment. The athlete should

Displaced fracture: A bone break causing deformity of the limb.

Impingement: Entrapment of tissue.

BOX
10-1

Dislocation?!?

On the same play both cornerbacks were hurt, one with a serious knee sprain and the second with a dislocated ring finger. The player wanted the trainer to put the finger back in place. The trainer hesitated. Despite the coaches' anger, both players were taken to the hospital. After x-raying the hand and finger, the physician came out to the trainer and said, "It's a good thing someone didn't think this was a dislocation and try to reduce it. It is not dislocated but broken in four places."

be immediately transported to a medical facility for appropriate medical care.

Strains and Sprains. Strains and sprains are two of the most common musculoskeletal injuries. Mild sprains and strains are best treated with the ICE procedure. Proper medical **diagnosis** and care (immobilization, surgery) is essential in moderate to severe injury.

Emergency Transport Plans; Supplies and Equipment

The quality of emergency care is only as good as the emergency transport plan. Many athletic programs have top facilities, equipment, and highly trained staff but do not fully prepare for the possible serious injury. What is needed is an established, carefully planned, well-organized, practical emergency transport plan. This plan should include whom to call for transport, where to call from, where to take the athlete, and phone numbers of doctors to contact. All members of the athletic and physical education programs should have written copies of emergency procedures; the procedures should be reviewed and updated regularly by a safety committee.

Specific supplies and equipment are required as part of the athletic emergency plan. The components of the emergency field kit include

- Antiseptic solution
- Sterile gauze, including eye pads
- Band-aids (several sizes)
- Roll gauze (several sizes)
- Adhesive tape ($1\frac{1}{2}$ and 1 in, elastic)
- Butterfly bandages or sterile strips
- Bandage scissors
- Tweezers
- Fingernail clippers
- Ring cutter
- Mirror
- Eye cup
- Sharp knife or scalpel blades
- Elastic wraps (several sizes)
- Cervical collar
- Triangular bandage
- Flashlight
- Coins for pay phone
- List of emergency phone numbers
- Plastic bags
- Paper bags
- Rectal thermometer

Additional field and court equipment includes

- Ice
- Water
- Splints (pneumatic, traction)
- Blanket
- Bolt cutters (football games)
- Litters (spine board, scoop, or stretcher)
- Immediate access to phone

Diagnosis: Medical determination of the cause and symptoms and subsequent identification of a disease or injury. Athletic trainers may not legally diagnose.

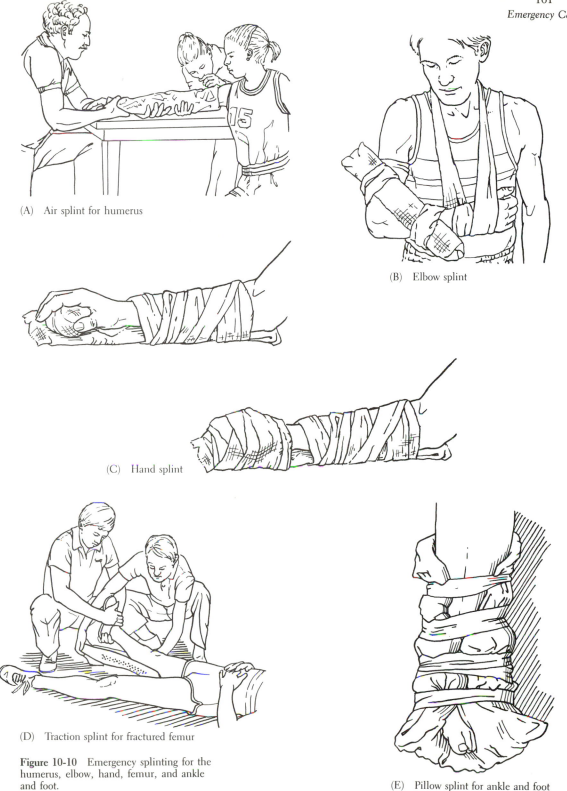

(A)   Air splint for humerus

(B)   Elbow splint

(C)   Hand splint

(D)   Traction splint for fractured femur

Figure 10-10   Emergency splinting for the humerus, elbow, hand, femur, and ankle and foot.

(E)   Pillow splint for ankle and foot

- Cups
- Towels
- Blood pressure cuff and stethoscope
- Physician's crash kit (emergency drugs)

The athletic trainer is often the key person when a serious or catastrophic athletic injury occurs. A satisfactory outcome depends upon an efficient and well-planned emergency procedure.

References

American Academy of Orthopedic Surgeons. *Emergency Care and Transportation of the Sick and Injured.* Chicago, 1981.

American Red Cross. *Advanced First Aid and Emergency Care.* Garden City, N.Y.: Doubleday, 1979.

American Red Cross. *Cardiopulmonary Resuscitation.* American National Red Cross, 1981.

Hafen, B. Q., and K. J. Karren. *Prehospital Emergency Care and Crisis Intervention.* Denver: Morton Publishing Co., 1981.

Knight, K. L. ICE for immediate care of injuries. *The Physician and Sportsmedicine* 10:137, 1982.

McMaster, W. C. A literary review on ice therapy in injuries. *American Journal of Sports Medicine* 5:124–126, 1977.

Paul, G. S. *Basic Emergency Care of the Sick and Injured.* St. Louis: C. V. Mosby, 1982.

Ryan, A. Guidelines to help you in giving on-field care. *The Physician and Sportsmedicine* 3:50–63, 1979.

Schneider, R. C. *Head and Neck Injuries in Football: Mechanisms, Treatment, and Prevention.* Baltimore: Williams & Wilkins, 1973.

The Preparticipation Medical Examination

Sports such as basketball may present an unacceptable health risk for some people. The preparticipation medical examination helps screen people with preexisting problems.

MANY sports authorities maintain that a thorough, carefully planned preparticipation medical examination will diminish the injury rate. These examinations are most useful for preventing injuries by identifying dangerous preexisting conditions. For example, the physician may discover that the athlete has a disease, such as mononucleosis, which means temporary disqualification from play. Other athletes may exhibit joint laxity, excess body fat, or minimal muscle mass, all of which increase the risk of injury in contact sports. All athletes should undergo a thorough medical examination that considers their medical well-being and the stresses of their sports.

Unfortunately, negative perceptions are prevalent among those involved in preparticipation medical examinations. Parents and athletes often complain that the examinations are hurried and haphazard and seem to bear little relationship to subsequent participation in vigorous physical activity. Coaches complain about the time requirements of such a seemingly esoteric ritual. Administrators often worry about cost factors and legal implications. Sports-oriented physicians criticize using methodologies intended for a nonathletic population (see Box 11-1, p. 164).

BOX
11-1

The Preparticipation Examination: What Is It?

The preparticipation examination is much like the elephant being examined by blind men: It appears differently, depending upon how it is approached. To the school administrator, it fulfills the school's legal and insurance requirements. To the coach, it is theoretically a means of starting the season with athletes who have some common level of health and fitness. To the idealist, it may be a means of attempting to prevent injuries. To the physician, it may be an opportunity to discover "treatable" conditions or conditions that will interfere with or be worsened by athletic participation. In reality it is probably an annual period of frustration. . . . .

SOURCE: Garrick, J. G. Sports medicine. *Pediatric Clinics of North America* 24(4), November 1977.

An acceptable sports-oriented medical examination should determine contraindications of sports participation. It should identify correctable musculoskeletal conditions that predispose athletes to reinjury. Finally, the examination should be an opportunity for medical personnel to evaluate the status of previous injuries. No potential athlete should be allowed to participate in strenuous exercise until he or she has completed the preparticipation medical examination.

The medical examination can be a valuable counseling tool for the physician, athletic trainer, and coach. It can be used to guide the medically disqualified athlete into acceptable types of physical activity or physical education classes and assist in additional medical follow-up (Table 11-1). Appropriate sports or exercises can be suggested to athletes predisposed to injury. For example, swimming may be more appropriate than football for an obese, immature child. The examination can be extremely useful for assessing the status of an injury and planning strategies for further rehabilitation.

The information gathered during the examination is valuable only if used to improve the quality of the athletes' health care. Far too often the data are neither recorded nor disseminated usefully. Carefully planned, properly completed, and readily retrievable forms are essential if the preparticipation medical examination is to play a meaningful role in sports medicine throughout a season of participation.

Table 11-1 *Results of a Preparticipation Medical Examination*

	Henderson High School	East High School	Fugett Middle School	Pierce Middle School	Stetson Middle School	Other	Total
No problems	28	17	6	6	10	1	68
Exercise program	47	79	26	22	36	2	212[a]
Recommend further follow-up	2 ortho 2 medical 1 both	7 ortho 5 medical	1 ortho	1 ortho 1 medical	1 medical		21
	5	12		2			
Total	80	108	33	30	47	3	301

[a]Of 301 potential athletes who participated in the examination, 212 or 68 percent were given exercise programs designed to correct musculoskeletal imbalances that were discovered during the examination.
SOURCE: West Chester Area School District, West Chester, Pa.

The logistics of a suitable preparticipation medical examination vary according to circumstance. The best exam is individually conducted in a medical environment by a physician who has a background in sports medicine. Unfortunately, this rarely happens. Most family physicians do not have the time to conduct acceptable individualized exams, and many are not aware of the special factors that should be considered when examining potential athletes.

Successful group examinations, in which the physician plays a relatively limited role, are both feasible and successful if properly planned and adequately staffed with professional assistance. These examinations facilitate the use of the "sports medicine team" (the athletic trainer, coach, physician, school nurse, etc.), particularly when the examining physician has a limited background in sports medicine. The athletic trainer can assist the physician in evaluation procedures, making the preparticipation medical examination more useful.

The preparticipation medical examination described in this chapter is applicable to both individual and group evaluations. The various components are essential in any medical examination conducted to determine medical clearance for participation in athletics. See Putting It into Practice 11-1, p. 166.

Medical History

One of the most important components of any medical examination and evaluation is an accurate, thorough medical history (see Figure 11-1, p. 167). Knowledge of past illness, injury, and other medical conditions aids in correctly assessing health status. The information contained in a good medical history is significant in subsequent evaluation of injury. Just as the study of history enables us to prepare strategies for the future, the medical history helps us to predict the risk of injury and safeguard the health of an athlete while he or she is participating in sports. The knowledge of past diseases or injuries can help explain current findings, thus enhancing the decision-making process.

Pertinent Information

The medical history should include information about past diseases and illness and impairments in the visual, auditory, cardiovascular, respiratory, neurological, and urogenital systems. A thorough history of musculoskeletal injuries is particularly important since most athletic medical problems involve the muscles, bones, and joints. There should be a separate section for head and neck problems because they are

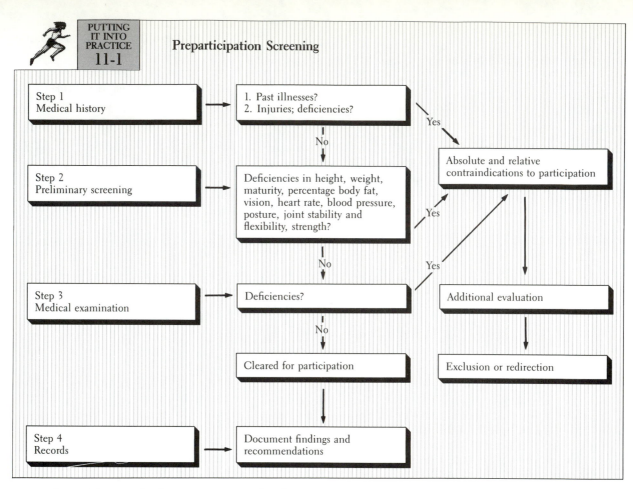

Preparticipation Screening

Step 1
Medical history

1. Past illnesses?
2. Injuries; deficiencies?

Yes

No

Step 2
Preliminary screening

Deficiencies in height, weight, maturity, percentage body fat, vision, heart rate, blood pressure, posture, joint stability and flexibility, strength?

Absolute and relative contraindications to participation

Yes

No

Yes

Step 3
Medical examination

Deficiencies?

Additional evaluation

No

Cleared for participation

Exclusion or redirection

Step 4
Records

Document findings and recommendations

extremely significant. The history for female athletes should include any menstrual-cycle irregularities, including **amenorrhea, oligomenorrhea,** and **dysmenorrhea.**

The special requirements of the particular sport should be considered. For example, the examination of the potential football or ice hockey player should emphasize the head, neck, and knees, whereas critical areas for the swimmer are the nose, ears, throat, and shoulders. Also, remember that an athlete who is approved for participation in one sport, such as tennis or track, may not necessarily be qualified for another sport, such as football or wrestling (see Box 11-2, p. 168).

Frequently, parents and athletes do not fully understand many items on the medical history. They should have an opportunity to discuss their health-related concerns with the physician and athletic trainer, to facilitate meaningful communication among athlete, family, and health professionals.

Forms

Concise and easily understood forms facilitate an accurate and complete medical history. Experience has shown that people tend to complete lengthy forms hastily and thoughtlessly. Also, unclear or technical forms can confuse and frustrate athletes and parents who do not have sufficient medical background.

Parents and athletes should complete the medical history form in a relaxed, private setting, one conducive to purposeful thought. The athlete and family should be given medical history forms with a letter of explanation several days

Amenorrhea: Absence of menstruation.
Oligomenorrhea: Irregular menstruation.
Dysmenorrhea: Painful menstruation.

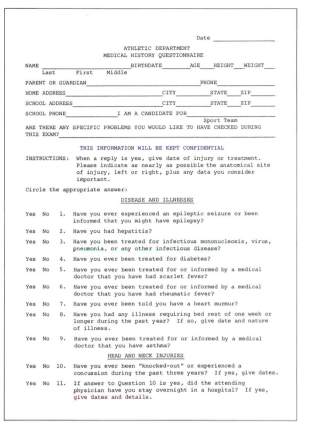

Date _____

ATHLETIC DEPARTMENT
MEDICAL HISTORY QUESTIONNAIRE

NAME _____BIRTHDATE_____AGE___HEIGHT___WEIGHT___
   Last   First   Middle

PARENT OR GUARDIAN_____PHONE _____

HOME ADDRESS_____CITY_____STATE___ZIP_____

SCHOOL ADDRESS_____CITY_____STATE___ZIP_____

SCHOOL PHONE_____I AM A CANDIDATE FOR_____
                                         Sport Team

ARE THERE ANY SPECIFIC PROBLEMS YOU WOULD LIKE TO HAVE CHECKED DURING
THIS EXAM?_____

THIS INFORMATION WILL BE KEPT CONFIDENTIAL

INSTRUCTIONS: When a reply is yes, give date of injury or treatment.
              Please indicate as nearly as possible the anatomical site
              of injury, left or right, plus any data you consider
              important.

Circle the appropriate answer:

DISEASE AND ILLNESSES

Yes No   1. Have you ever experienced an epileptic seizure or been
              informed that you might have epilepsy?

Yes No   2. Have you had hepatitis?

Yes No   3. Have you been treated for infectious mononucleosis, virus,
              pneumonia, or any other infectious disease?

Yes No   4. Have you ever been treated for diabetes?

Yes No   5. Have you ever been treated for or informed by a medical
              doctor that you have had scarlet fever?

Yes No   6. Have you ever been treated for or informed by a medical
              doctor that you have had rheumatic fever?

Yes No   7. Have you ever been told you have a heart murmur?

Yes No   8. Have you had any illness requiring bed rest of one week or
              longer during the past year? If so, give date and nature
              of illness.

Yes No   9. Have you ever been treated for or informed by a medical
              doctor that you have asthma?

HEAD AND NECK INJURIES

Yes No 10. Have you ever been "knocked-out" or experienced a
              concussion during the past three years? If yes, give dates.

Yes No 11. If answer to Question 10 is yes, did the attending
              physician have you stay overnight in a hospital? If yes,
              give dates and details.

- 2 -

Yes No 12. Have you ever had any injury to the neck involving nerves,
              vertebrae (bones), or vertebrae disks that incapacitated
              you for a week or longer? If answer is yes, give dates.

EYES AND DENTAL

Yes No 13. Do you wear eyeglasses or contact lenses?

Yes No 14. If answer to Question 13 is yes, do you wear them during
              athletic participation?

Yes No 15. Do you wear any dental appliance? If answer is yes,
              underscore appropriate appliance: permanent bridge,
              permanent crown or jacket, removable partial or full plate.

BONE AND JOINT

INSTRUCTIONS: Please give dates and indicate left or right for any
              injuries listed below that you received during the past
              three years.

Yes No 16. Have you ever been treated for Osgood-Schlatter disease?

Yes No 17. Have you ever been treated for osteomyelitis?

Yes No 18. Have you had a fracture? If answer is yes, indicate site
              of fracture and date.

Yes No 19. Have you had a shoulder dislocation, separation, or other
              shoulder injury?

Yes No 20. Have you ever been advised to have surgery to correct a
              shoulder condition?

Yes No 21. If answer to Question 20 is yes, has the surgery been
              completed? Give date.

Yes No 22. Have you experienced a severe sprain, dislocation, or
              fracture to either elbow? If answer is yes, give date.

Yes No 23. Have you ever had an injury to your back?

Yes No 24. If answer to Question 23 is yes, did you seek the advice
              or care of a medical doctor?

Yes No 25. Do you experience pain in the back? If answer is yes,
              indicate frequency with which you experience pain by
              underscoring answer: very seldom, occasionally, frequently,
              only with vigorous exercise or heavy lifting.

Yes No 26. Have you experienced a sprain of either knee with severe
              swelling accompanying the injury?

Yes No 27. Have you ever been told that you injured the ligaments of
              either knee joint?

Yes No 28. Have you ever been told that you injured the cartilage of
              either knee joint?

Yes No 29. Have you ever been advised to have surgery on a knee to
              correct a condition?

prior to the examination. On the date of the examination, qualified medical personnel should be available to provide any assistance necessary for accurate completion of the medical history.

Forms should be constructed so that significant facts are readily visible. For example, questions should be worded so that any "yes" answer indicates a situation that might require further investigation. The form should be arranged with all "yes" answers in one column and all "no" answers in another, thus allowing for easy identification of potentially significant medical information. Consideration should be given to structuring forms so they readily lend themselves to computer data storage. Figure 11-1 is a form that several institutions have successfully used.

Figure 11-1 Medical history questionnaire.

- 3 -

Yes No 30. If answer to Question 29 is yes, has the surgery been
              completed? Give date.

Yes No 31. Have you ever experienced a severe sprain of either ankle?

Yes No 32. Do you have a pin, screw, or plate somewhere in your body
              as a result of bone or joint surgery? If answer is yes,
              indicate anatomical site and date of surgery.

Yes No 33. Have you ever had a bone graft or spinal fusion? If
              answer is yes, indicate anatomical site and date of surgery.

GENERAL

Yes No 34. Have you ever been told that you have a hernia? If yes,
              has the hernia been surgically repaired? When?

Yes No 35. Have you had any operations? If answer is yes, indicate
              anatomical site of operation and date.

Yes No 36. Have you ever been inoculated for tetanus? Give date.

Yes No 37. Are you currently on prescribed medications or drugs on a
              permanent or semi-permanent basis? If so, indicate name of
              drug and indicate why it was prescribed. (Ex.: birth
              control, epilepsy, high blood pressure, etc.)

Yes No 38. Are you allergic to any medication? (Ex.: aspirin,
              penicillin, etc.)

Give full name and address of your family physician.

Doctor_____

Address_____

All the above questions have been answered completely and truthfully to
the best of my knowledge.

                              Signature_____

The Examination

Figure 11-2 (p. 170) is a flowchart for a typical preparticipation medical examination. Decision-making steps and their consequences must be clear and follow a natural progression. Everyone must know their responsibilities if the process is to run smoothly and the information is to be put to good use.

Preliminary Screening Procedures

Prior to the physician's evaluation, paramedical personnel can complete several very important components of the examination. These components are screening mechanisms that will give the physician specific data and indicate possible areas of concern.

Height, Weight, and Body Composition. Anthropometric measurements are invaluable aids for assessing growth, development, maturity, nutritional status, and physical fitness. Body weight is a product of several factors, including the skeleton, muscle, water in the body, and fat. Excess fat is detrimental to performance and may increase the risk of injury in some sports. Since height and weight measurements give

Anthropometric: Structural measurement of the human body.

BOX 11-2	Disqualifying Conditions for Sports Participation			
Conditions	**Collision**[a]	**Contact**[b]	**Noncontact**[c]	**Other**[d]
General				
Acute infections:				
Respiratory, genito-urinary, infectious mononucleosis, hepatitis, active rheumatic fever, active tuberculosis	X	X	X	X
Obvious physical immaturity in comparison with other competitors	X	X		
Hemorrhagic disease:				
Hemophilia, purpura, and other serious bleeding tendencies	X	X	X	
Diabetes, inadequately controlled	X	X	X	X
Diabetes, controlled	[e]	[e]	[e]	[e]
Jaundice	X	X	X	X
Eyes				
Absence or loss of function of one eye	X	X		
Respiratory				
Tuberculosis (active or symptomatic)	X	X	X	X
Severe pulmonary insufficiency	X	X	X	X
Cardiovascular				
Mitral stenosis, aortic stenosis, aortic insufficiency, coarctation of aorta, cyanotic heart disease, recent carditis of any etiology	X	X	X	X

Conditions	Collision[a]	Contact[b]	Noncontact[c]	Other[d]
Hypertension on organic basis	X	X	X	X
Previous heart surgery for congenital or acquired heart disease	f	f	f	f
Liver, enlarged	X	X		
Skin				
Boils, impetigo, and herpes simplex gladiatorum	X	X		
Spleen, enlarged	X	X		
Hernia				
Inguinal or femoral hernia	X	X	X	
Musculoskeletal				
Symptomatic abnormalities or inflammations	X	X	X	X
Functional inadequacy of the musculoskeletal system, congenital or acquired, incompatible with the contact or skill demands of the sport	X	X	X	
Neurologic				
History or symptoms of previous serious head trauma or repeated concussions	X			
Controlled convulsive disorder	g	g	g	g
Convulsive disorder not moderately well controlled by medication	X			
Previous surgery on head	X	X		
Renal				
Absence of one kidney	X	X		
Renal disease	X	X	X	X
Genitalia				
Absence of one testicle	h	h	h	h
Undescended testicle	h	h	h	h

[a]Football, rugby, hockey, lacrosse, etc.
[b]Baseball, soccer, basketball, wrestling, etc.
[c]Cross-country, track, tennis, crew, swimming, etc.
[d]Bowling, golf, archery, field events, etc.
[e]No exclusions.
[f]Each patient should be judged individually in conjunction with the patient's cardiologist and surgeon.
[g]Each patient should be judged individually. All things being equal, it is probably better to encourage a young boy or girl to participate in a noncontact sport rather than a contact sport. However, if a patient wants to play a contact sport and this is deemed a major ameliorating factor in his or her adjustment to school, associates, and the seizure disorder, serious consideration should be given to letting the patient participate if the seizures are moderately well controlled or the patient is under good medical management.
[h]The Committee approves the concept of contact sports participation for youths with only one testicle or with an undescended testicle(s), except in specific instances such as an inguinal canal undescended testicle(s), following appropriate medical evaluation to rule out unusual injury risk. However, the athlete, parents, and school authorities should be fully informed that participation in contact sports for youths with only one testicle carries a slight injury risk to the remaining healthy testicle. Fertility may be adversely affected following an injury. But the chances of an injury to a descended testicle are rare, and the injury risk can be further substantially minimized with an athletic supporter and protective device.

SOURCE: Adapted from American Academy of Pediatrics. Committee on Sports Medicine. *Sports Medicine: Health Care for Young Athletes*, Nathan Smith, ed. Evanston, Ill., 1983, pp. 77–79.

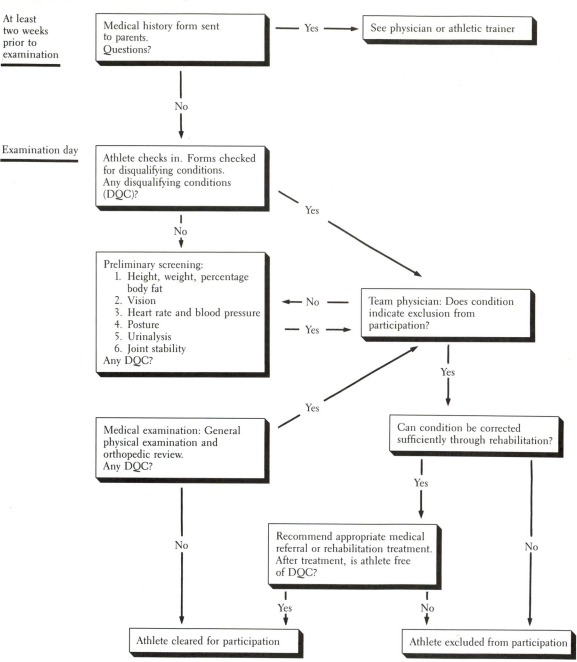

Figure 11-2 Flowchart for preparticipation medical examination.

only a rough estimate of body composition, it is now common procedure to measure body fat because it provides an estimate of the "quality" of body mass and stature.

Although the precise calculation of body fat requires rather intricate procedures, such as underwater weighing, anthropometric and **skinfold techniques** provide a valid approximation. A variety of population-specific skinfold regression equations have been developed to estimate body composition. However, it is proposed that the standards and techniques suggested by the American Alliance of Health, Physical Education, Recreation, and Dance be adopted since their widespread use will facilitate standardization and interpretation.

Here is the correct technique for obtaining **subcutaneous** skinfolds:

1. Firmly grasp the skinfold between your thumb and index finger.
2. Place the contact surfaces of the skinfold calipers one-half inch above or below your index finger.
3. Slowly release the grip of the calipers, developing full tension on the skinfold.
4. Read the indicator to the nearest 0.5 millimeter.
5. Take several measurements, to get an average reading.

Vision. Athletes should be tested for visual acuity. Although some authorities recommend the use of special apparatus such as the Titmus machine, the Snellen eye charts are acceptable and practical. Refer any athlete with less than 20/40 vision to the physician for further evaluation. Examine athletes who wear corrective lenses with and without lenses. Suggest contact lenses for use in collision sports, such as rugby, where glasses are not practical. In most cases, soft contact lenses are preferable to hard lenses or eyeglasses during athletic competition.

Pulse and Blood Pressure. Resting pulse and blood pressure measurements are important in assessing cardiovascular status. Blood pressure greater than 140/90 may indicate **hypertension,** and a resting pulse rate greater than 100 beats per minute may be a result of anxiety, overtraining, or disease. A resting pulse rate less than forty to fifty beats per minute may be normal in a trained athlete but may indicate an aberration in cardiac pacing or conduction in an untrained individual. If cardiovascular disease is suspected, a more extensive evaluation, such as exercise blood pressure and electrocardiogram, can be conducted.

Use a large adult-sized blood pressure cuff if an athlete has an unusually muscular arm. A standard-sized cuff on a muscular individual gives a spuriously high reading because more pressure is required to collapse the artery.

Urinalysis. The presence of significant amounts of sugar, blood, and protein in the urine warrants further medical investigation before unqualified clearance can be granted for athletic participation. Simple, inexpensive, and rapid dip-stick procedures are available for testing.

Posture Screening. Postural malalignments are related to soft tissue imbalances and injury. The postural examination should include a visual inspection from the anterior, lateral, and posterior views and Adam's position to check for deviations such as rotation of the spine or scoliosis (curvature of the spine) (Figure 11-3, p. 172). Orthopedic evaluation and corrective exercises should be suggested for significant postural aberrations. Figure 11-4 (p. 173) is a recording form that has been successfully used for athletic musculoskeletal evaluation, including posture assessment.

Joint Stability. Assessment of joint stability is absolutely essential because of the prevalence of joint injuries in athletics. Although the joints tested will vary with the sport, several studies indi-

Hypertension: High blood pressure; generally considered above 140/90.

Skinfold technique: Predicting body fat and fat-free weight from subcutaneous skinfold thicknesses. Skinfold equations are typically validated by comparison with the results from underwater weighing of the body.

Subcutaneous: Underneath the skin.

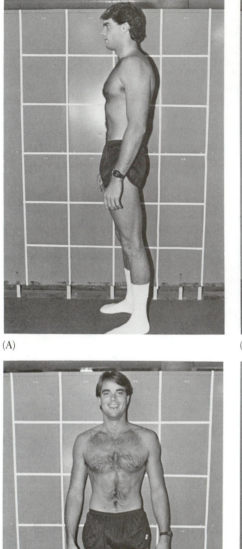

(A)

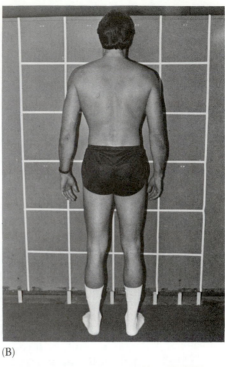

(B)

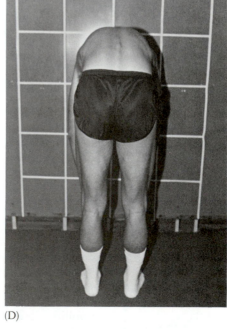

(C)

(D)

(A) Lateral view: Look for excessive kyphosis (angular curvature of the spine) and cervical lordosis. Observe sloping shoulders and forward head.

(B) Posterior view: Look for symmetry between shoulders and hips and for lower extremity malalignment. If symptoms of low back pain are present, look for lateral pelvic shifting.

(C) Anterior view: Check for symmetry between shoulders and hips and for lower extremity malalignment.

(D) Trunk flexed: Look for any abnormal lateral curvature or rotation of the spine.

Figure 11-3 Postural deviations often indicate an increased risk of neck and back injuries. Posture should be examined laterally, posteriorly, anteriorly, and with trunk flexed.

cate that the lower extremities account for most sports injuries. Therefore, tests for ankle and knee stability should be included in all athletic physical examinations. These tests should include assessment of excessive eversion or inversion and anterior-posterior stability (Drawer test) of the ankle, and medial, lateral, and cruciate (Lachman test) ligament stability of the knee (see Chapters 21 and 22).

Since injuries to the shoulder joints are also relatively common, glenohumeral, acromioclavicular, and sternoclavicular stability should also be tested. Figure 11-5 (p. 174) illustrates the acceptable techniques for performing these tests.

Joint stability tests can be performed by athletic trainers during group examinations, but any suspected joint laxity must be documented and further examined by a qualified physician. Orthopedic referral is indicated for all cases of joint instability, particularly if associated with injury or disability. The minimal exercise prescription should strengthen the muscles surrounding the unstable joint. In some cases, joint instability indicates a need for surgical intervention and/or exclusion from some sports.

Joint Flexibility. The athlete who lacks sufficient flexibility may be more prone to muscle strains and tendon irritations. Conversely, excessive joint flexibility, required in some athletic endeavors such as gymnastics, may increase the risk of injury in contact sports. Marked joint flexibility without adequate strength in supporting muscles increases the potential for injury in sports requiring powerful movements, generation of significant torque, or collisions with opponents and teammates. Figure 11-6 (p. 174) is an appropriate form for common range of motion tests.

Strength. Strength, a critical fitness component, is the ability to exert force. Weak muscles and **strength imbalances**

```
POSTURE EVALUATION:_____    OK   NOT OK (w/remarks if necessary)
   I. FRONT VIEW:
      1. NIPPLE LEVELS_____
      2. MUSCLE SYMMETRY_____
      3. LEVEL OF HIPS_____
      4. LEVEL OF PATELLAE_____
      5. GENU VARUS OR VALGUS_____
      6. PES CAVUS/PES PLANUS_____
      7. Q ANGLE_____
  II. BACK VIEW:
      1. SCOLIOSIS (ADAMS POSITION)
      2. SHOULDER LEVELS_____
      3. SCAPULAE_____
      4. LEVEL OF HIPS_____
      5. ANKLE ALIGNMENT_____
 III. SIDE VIEW:
      1. SPINAL CURVES
         (LORDOSIS/KYPHOSIS)_____
      2. GENU RECURVATUM
         (OK IF ABSENT)_____
      3. HEAD ALIGNMENT_____
  IV. GAIT EVALUATION:_____

ORTHOPEDIC STABILITY:_____    OK   NOT OK (w/remarks if necessary)
    I. KNEE_____
   II. ANKLE_____
  III. SHOULDER_____
```

Figure 11-4 Musculoskeletal evaluation form.

between muscle groups can increase the risk of injury. Therefore, the strength of major muscle groups should be evaluated. The most important muscles to test are those responsible for the movements of the knee, shoulder, trunk, and neck. Any significant weakness or strength imbalance in these muscles may indicate exclusion from participation or necessitate remedial exercises.

Ideally, strength tests should be performed with sophisticated devices like the Cybex isokinetic dynamometer (Figure 3-6). However, many institutions cannot afford such costly instruments, and the use of the machines is impractical for large group medical examinations. Manual testing by experienced, qualified personnel is practical and valid for gross evaluation of specific muscle groups and for comparisons of **bilateral** and **antagonistic muscles.**

Strength imbalance:
  Abnormal strength differences between antagonistic or contralateral muscles.
Bilateral muscle: The same muscle on the opposite side of the body.
Antagonistic muscle: A muscle that directly opposes the action of another muscle; e.g., the biceps brachius, an elbow flexor, is antagonistic to the triceps, an elbow extensor.

Figure 11-7 is an example of manual muscle testing; Figure 11-8 illustrates an appropriate form for recording data.

Medical Examination

The medical examination is conducted by the physician, who may be aided by a qualified physician's assistant. The examination of the head includes inspection of the pupils of the eye for size and reflexes and the ears, nose, throat, scalp, thyroid, and lymph nodes for aberrations such as swelling, infection, and past injury. Chest structure and heart-lung sounds are evaluated for cardiopulmonary disorders. The female breasts and male rectum and genitals should be examined. The abdomen and inguinal nodes of all athletes should be palpated. The skin should be examined for conditions such as severe acne, herpes, fungal infections, and surgical scars. Figure 11-9 (p. 176) is a summary of items that should be included in the general physical examination.

Orthopedic Review. The musculoskeletal system should be carefully examined by a physician well versed in sports medicine. All previous injuries to the musculoskeletal system should be evaluated. Ideally, this review is best conducted by a board-certified orthopedic surgeon. (This is not a legal requirement in any state. In fact, only thirty-five states currently require a physician to administer the preparticipation medical examination.) Any significant finding a nonspecialist detects during the musculoskeletal evaluation should be referred to an orthopedic specialist.

The examining physician is responsible for initiating proper management following the discovery of any significant condition. This responsibility includes medical referral, recommendation of surgical intervention, and prescription of corrective exercises, orthotic appliances, immobilization devices, and braces. For the orthopedic review to be beneficial, the athletic

Figure 11-5 Test of shoulder stability. Joint instability exhibited during the preparticipation medical examination may indicate an increased risk of injury in the future.

RANGE OF MOTION (FLEXIBILITY) EVALUATION:	OK	TIGHT	LOOSE	REMARKS
I. NECK:				
II. TRUNK (PAIN, DIFFICULTY MOVING, ETC.)				
III. SHOULDERS:				
1. ARMS OVER HEAD				
2. HANDS BEHIND BACK				
3. HANDS CLASPED BEHIND NECK				
IV. ELBOWS:				
1. FLEXION				
2. HYPEREXTENSION (10° OK IN GIRLS)				
3. CARRYING ANGLE (GIRLS MORE THAN BOYS)				
V. FOREARMS: (PRONATION/SUPINATION)				
VI. WRISTS AND HANDS: (FLEXION/EXTENSION)				
VII. LOWER EXTREMITIES:				
1. HAMSTRING (SUPINE)				
2. HEEL CORDS (SUPINE OR STANDING)				
3. QUADRICEPS (PRONE)				
4. HIP FLEXORS				

Figure 11-6 Joint-flexibility evaluation form.

trainer must be responsible for implementing the prescribed program with the athletes' cooperation. The preparticipation examination must be augmented with adequate and systematic follow-up procedures.

Medical Review. At the conclusion of the examination, the physician must evaluate the athlete's medical eligibility for sports participation. The physician should not hesitate to recheck any significant or questionable findings before rendering a decision. After evaluating the data, the physician should make one of the following determinations:

- No athletic participation allowed
- Approval for participation denied until specific conditions are met (i.e., adequate rehabilitation, completion of specific tests, or further examinations)
- Limited approval, with exclusion from participation in specific sports
- Participation permitted but specific therapeutic exercises prescribed
- Unlimited participation allowed

The basis for all decisions should be documented and properly recorded, and the form signed and dated.

Physical Fitness Testing. Physical fitness testing should be considered part of the preparticipation examination and conducted after the other procedures have been completed. The fitness evaluation should reflect the physical demands of the sport as well as the preseason conditioning program the coach has assigned. For example, football fitness requirements include cardiovascular and muscular endurance, power, speed, agility, and flexibility. Additionally, the coach may have assigned an off-season conditioning program consisting of running, sprinting, calisthenics, and weight lifting. Therefore, the fitness test might include a test of cardiovascular endurance, such as a Cooper twelve-minute run; a test of sprinting speed, such as the forty-yard dash; a

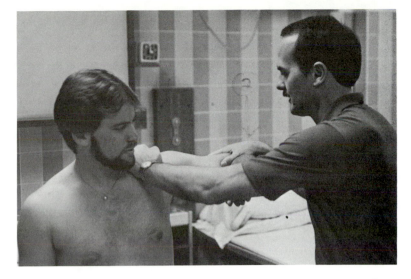

Figure 11-7 Manual muscle testing for shoulder flexion. The examiner stabilizes the shoulder by placing his left hand on the athlete's clavicle. With his right hand he applies a breaking force to the distal end of the humerus while the shoulder is abducted to 90 degrees. Obvious muscle weakness exhibited during the examination should be corrected before allowing the athlete to participate.

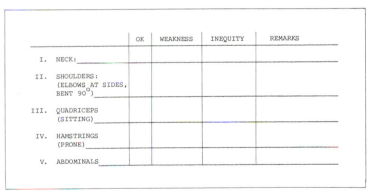

		OK	WEAKNESS	INEQUITY	REMARKS
I.	NECK:				
II.	SHOULDERS: (ELBOWS AT SIDES, BENT 90°)				
III.	QUADRICEPS (SITTING)				
IV.	HAMSTRINGS (PRONE)				
V.	ABDOMINALS				

Figure 11-8 Gross-strength evaluation form.

test of specific agility, such as a run and cut test; weight lifting tests, such as the power clean, bench press, or squat; and a test of muscle endurance, such as timed, bent knee sit-ups.

Fitness is task-specific, so a category of fitness, such as cardiovascular capacity, should be tested in a manner that reflects the sport. The twelve-minute run, a good test for the football or basketball player, is much less useful for the swimmer or water polo player, whose endurance and capacity for high-intensity exercise is better tested with a 400-yard swim and sprinting in a pool, respectively.

Physical fitness is among the most important factors that determine **heat tolerance.** Fitness testing prior to active practice objectively measures an athlete's probable tolerance to heat stress. Unfit athletes must be watched more closely and restricted more quickly in hot weather than fit athletes. If an athlete experiences a thermal emergency and the coach failed to conduct a fitness evaluation, the coach is in legal jeopardy.

SPORTS MEDICINE PHYSICAL EVALUATION FORM

NAME:__________ DATE:_____ SEX__F__M AGE:_____

SCHOOL:__________

STATION #2 Height_____Weight_____ STATION #3 Vision R / L /

STATION #4 Percent Body Fat_____ STATION #5 Blood Pressure_____ Sitting-Right Arm

Radial Pulse_____

STATION #6 Urinalysis	-	+
Protein		
Sugar		
Blood		

STATION #7 General Physical	NORMAL	ABNORMAL	COMMENTS
EYES: ACUITY			
EOM'S			
CORRECTIVE LENS OR CONTACTS			
EARS: PINNA			
CANAL			
TM			
HEARING			
NOSE, THROAT, SINUSES			
TEETH, GUMS			
NECK, THYROID, NODES			
CHEST, BACK (CONFIG & INSPECT)			
HEART			
LUNGS			
BREASTS (FEMALES)			
NODES (AXILLARY)			
ABDOMEN (MASSES, ORGANOMEG)			
HERNIAS (DIR. INDIR. CENTRAL)			
SURGI SCARS			
ING NODES			
SKIN			
GENITALIA (MALES)			
RECTAL INSPEC (MALES)			

EXAMINER__________

Figure 11-9 Sports medicine physical evaluation form.

Logistics of the Group Examination

The logistics of the group evaluation will vary with personnel, facilities, and equipment. However, certain factors should be considered in all situations.

Timing of Evaluation

There should be particular emphasis upon evaluating younger athletes in middle school and junior high school; potentially serious problems may be effectively controlled if detected early. The evaluation of these children should be as thorough as that of the high school and college athletes.

Opinion about the required frequency of athletic medical examination varies from annual to periodic (that is, eleven, fourteen, and sixteen years). The yearly repetition of such an expensive, time-consuming procedure on seemingly healthy athletes who have experienced no intervening trauma, illness, or symptoms is probably inordinate. Most sports medicine authorities agree that it is not necessary to repeat medical examinations for athletes competing in several sports during a given year unless indicated by an intervening medical problem.

The preparticipation examination should be conducted at least one month but preferably six weeks before the first day of practice, to provide adequate time to correct remedial conditions. Such scheduling avoids hurried, ineffective, last-minute examinations. Similarly, the examination should not be scheduled too far in advance of the first day of participation, to avoid the occurrence of a significant number of medical problems in the interim.

Heat tolerance: The body's ability to maintain body temperature when exposed to a hot environment. Usually called heat acclimatization.

Personnel and Equipment

Physicians administer only a small part of the examination; **paramedical** and nonprofessional **personnel** conduct most of the examination. Personnel for group athletic examinations can be drawn from the ranks of physicians, coaches, athletic trainers, parents, teachers, nurses, and physician's assistants. Table 11-2 itemizes required personnel and equipment.

Facilities

The typical school building can be used for the group evaluation. Specific requirements include (1) large open area, such as a gymnasium or cafeteria; (2) separate room for each professional conducting medical examinations; (3) easily accessible lavatories for urinalysis; (4) dressing or locker room facilities; (5) adequate assembly area, with an adjacent room for checking the medical history; (6) appropriate private examination area close to the orthopedic medical review stations. The professional personnel should thoughtfully plan, to permit the sensible, orderly use of typical school facilities.

General Procedures

All athletes should report to the staging area in proper dress: shorts for boys,

Paramedical personnel: Nonphysician medical professionals, e.g., nurses, physician's assistants, paramedics.

Table 11-2 *Personnel and Equipment Requirements for Group Evaluation of Thirty Athletes per Hour*

Stations	Equipment	Personnel
1. Medical history	3 tables, 3 chairs, map, blackboard	1 Supervisor—Nurse or other qualified professional 3 Recorders—Nonprofessional
2. Height/weight	2 scales, 2 wall measurers	2 Evaluators—2 Student Managers
3. Vision	2 Snellen charts	2 Evaluators—Nurses
4. Percentage body fat	2 skinfold calipers	2 Evaluators—Physical Educators or Athletic Trainers
5. Blood pressure/pulse	3 BP cuffs, 3 stethoscopes, 3 tables, 6 chairs	3 Evaluators—Nurses
6. Urinalysis	Test sticks	1 Evaluator—Nurse 1 Recorder—Nonprofessional
7. General physical a. ENT exam b. Chest, heart, lungs, etc. c. Abdomen, hernias, genitalia	Supplied by physicians	4 Evaluators—1 Physician and 3 Physician's Assistants 4 Recorders—Nonprofessional
8. Musculoskeletal evaluation Posture and joint stability	3 treatment tables	3 Evaluators—Certified Athletic Trainers 3 Recorders—Nonprofessional
9. Musculoskeletal evaluation (range of motion/strength)	4 treatment tables, 4 tables, 4 chairs	3 Evaluators—Certified Athletic Trainers or Licensed Physical Therapists 4 Recorders—Nonprofessional
10. Orthopedic review	2 treatment tables, 1 table, 1 chair	2 Evaluators—Orthopedists 2 Recorders—Nonprofessional
11. General physical review	1 table, 2 chairs	1 Evaluator—Family Practice Physician 1 Recorder—Nurse or qualified clerical

NOTE: The addition of personnel for items 7, 9, and 11 will increase the number of athletes examined per hour.

and a two-piece bathing suit or similar attire for girls. Groups of fifteen to twenty athletes should begin the examination cycle every fifteen minutes. Each group begins at the medical history review station. Participants then proceed to the open area (gymnasium or cafeteria) so their height, weight, vision, body composition, pulse, and blood pressure can be measured. Next, each athlete proceeds to the urinalysis station and then to one of the physician's rooms for the general physical examination. Then the athlete goes to the musculoskeletal and orthopedic review stations and finally to the medical review area for final checkout and disposition. Immediately following the musculoskeletal evaluation, a certified athletic trainer can review each form so those athletes who do not need orthopedic examination can be routed directly to the medical review and checkout area.

Records

Well-kept records are absolutely essential. They demonstrate a well-organized, systematic injury-management program that reflects careful consideration and follow-up of each athletic condition. Obviously, records are critical in the event of litigation.

Forms

The examination forms should be clear and easily understood so that data that help the physician determine if an athlete is qualified for athletic participation can be recorded. Their design is difficult, but the forms suggested in this chapter can be a basis for those used in other circumstances. The forms should be structured to fit methodology; they should not dictate methodology. Finally, they should facilitate **computer storage and retrieval.**

Use of Information

The examination serves a purpose only if the information is used. Proper use of the results includes (1) prediction of injury predisposition, (2) medical referral to deal with aberrant medical conditions, (3) education of athletes, parents, and coaches, and (4) implementation of injury-control programs. In other words, the information is properly used only if it improves athletic health care.

Dissemination

The school should retain a signed copy of the examination and forward duplicate copies to the family physician and parents. Within the school, the athletic trainer and/or adaptive physical education instructor (an instructor who works with handicapped students) should be given pertinent information from the examination so that any remedial exercise programs can be implemented.

Storage

The athletic trainer should maintain a file of all pertinent medical information for each athlete in the school as long as the athlete is attending the institution. After the athlete has graduated or left, the file should be stored for a period determined by the administration and legal counsel. Security should be an important consideration, to ensure that the records remain confidential.

Computerization

Low-cost and **user-friendly** computers have made computer technology accessible and practical for the athletic trainer. Record-keeping programs for the preparticipation examination are available and facilitate the use of the data. Computerization enables personnel to regularly update records, to provide a more current analysis of athletes' health status.

User-friendly: The ease with which a computer or computer program may be used by a person relatively inexperienced in the use of computers.

Computer storage and retrieval: The capacity of computers to store and retrieve information.

There is a vast potential for computers in sports medicine. Available hardware and software allow instruments to be computer interfaced and operated **on-line.** The athletic trainer must be able to understand and utilize computers for maintaining records, gathering data, and retrieving information because computer use will become increasingly common in the health professions.

On-line: Computer control of a device; a direct interface between instruments in the athletic training room, e.g., an isokinetic dynamometer and a computer.

References

American Academy of Pediatrics. Cardiac evaluation for participation in sports. *The Physician and Sportsmedicine* 6:102–108, 1978.

American Alliance for Health, Physical Education, Recreation, and Dance. *Health Related Physical Fitness Manual.* Reston, Va., 1981.

American Medical Association. A *Guide for Medical Evaluation of Candidates for School Sports.* Chicago, 1972.

Goldberg, B., P. Whitman, G. Gleim, and J. A. Nicholas. Children's sports injuries: are they avoidable? *The Physician and Sportsmedicine* 7:93–101, 1979.

Jensen, C. R., and G. W. Schultz. *Applied Kinesiology: The Scientific Study of Human Performance.* New York: McGraw-Hill, 1977.

Kulund, D. N. *The Injured Athlete.* New York: Lippincott, 1982.

Smilkstein, G. Health evaluation of high school athletes. *The Physician and Sportsmedicine* 9:73–80, 1981.

Wilmore, J. H. *Training for Sport and Activity.* Boston: Allyn and Bacon, 1982.

Philosophy of Rehabilitation

REHABILITATION is the process of restoring fitness and ability. The word stems from the Latin *rehabilitare*—to make fit—and *habilitas*—ability. The Latin highlights an important dictum that should be followed after an athletic injury has occurred: It is not enough to make the athlete physically fit, it is also necessary to restore ability (which is often much more difficult to do).

Athletic rehabilitation requires that the athletic trainer be as much an artist as a scientist. The rehabilitation "artist" must seek a variety of creative means of restoring the athlete to normal function. This process often involves assessing individual differences in personality, motivation, type of injury, and physiological characteristics. For example, some athletes require a "pushy, authoritarian" approach to rehabilitation. The athlete is given specific instructions and constantly prodded to carry them out. Other athletes do not respond to this type of program and perform better with less precise guidelines and more gentle treatment. The choice of approach is based upon such factors as intuition and experience and cannot be learned readily from a textbook.

The athletic trainer must also be a

The difference between winning and losing can be less than a stride. The rehabilitation program the athletic trainer conducts is an important factor in determining victory or defeat.

180

scientist. All injuries result from specific causes and respond to some treatments better than others. Injuries must be systematically evaluated and treated for the best results. This scientific process is based upon knowledge of basic principles from various disciplines (anatomy, physiology, biomechanics, modalities, etc.) and the systematic application of these principles. The scientist-athletic trainer uses the **stimulus-response method,** whereby specific rehabilitation methods are methodically applied and the responses noted. A basic axiom of rehabilitation and physical conditioning is progressive overload: The body is systematically and progressively overloaded in an attempt to produce a desirable adaptation (e.g., increased strength, endurance, etc.). But this process works only when the stimulus is applied one step at a time.

Rehabilitation can be divided into two phases. The first phase is preparation, including injury assessment and program strategy. The second phase is program implementation, including reevaluation, return to competition, and counseling.

Preparation

All aspects of sports involve some type of preparation. Coaches must have game plans, and athletes must be conditioned and skilled before beginning competition. Likewise, the athletic trainer must have specific procedures for dealing with various problems. Starting a rehabilitation program without adequate preparation may lead to inappropriate treatment and cause an athlete to lose additional time from practice and competition.

The basic philosophy of all sports medicine professionals should be to quickly restore or increase normal function and conditioning so that the athlete can safely and competitively return

to play and avoid reinjury. Saving a day or a week may be insignificant to the recreational sportsperson or casually active individual, but it may be critically important to the professional or team athlete.

The Interface Between the Athletic Trainer and Physician

The team or family physician begins the rehabilitation process with the **diagnosis** of the injury. Then health professionals should be coordinated to begin rehabilitation. Depending upon individual state laws, the physician will convey information in the form of a diagnosis or specific orders.

Optimum rehabilitation depends upon open communication between the physician and athletic trainer or physical therapist. The physician's diagnosis should be informative, describing the extent and type of injury and specific directions for rehabilitation. These directives should clearly describe both approved and contraindicated procedures. For example, knee surgery that involved patellar shaving may require that the patellar surface be extra carefully protected, but this may not be quite as important following other procedures.

Open communication and trust help ensure that the physician does not give the athletic trainer a vague and imprecise description of the diagnosis and medical intervention procedure. Too often the physician provides minimal information, such as "knee ligament reconstruction," which does not identify a specific ligament, how it was reconstructed, what was done to augment the reconstruction, and what other tissues were also injured.

Often only the major injury receives a diagnosis, even though athletes frequently sustain multiple injuries. Minor injuries can be masked by the major injury or assumed to be included in the diagnosis. For example, a diagnosis of

Stimulus-response method: Basis of scientific method. A specific and reproducible stimulus is introduced and the response measured.

Diagnosis: Medical determination of the cause and symptoms and subsequent identification of a disease or injury. Athletic trainers may not legally diagnose.

"chondromalacia patella" may refer as much to a **syndrome** or collection of symptoms as to the condition of the kneecap (see Box 12-1 and Chapter 21). Another common diagnosis that does not convey accurate information is "low back strain." Even though **strain** refers to muscles, to a lesser degree ligaments and nerve tissue may also be involved in the injury.

Relying upon the athlete for medical information is unreliable and risky because athletes are untrained and emotionally involved with their own injury. Although the symptoms that athletes report are helpful, do not rely on their secondhand reports of the physician's diagnosis.

The athletic trainer's good relations with the physician and perhaps access to medical records help ensure that the athlete receives the appropriate rehabilitation program. The athletic trainer and the physician can communicate via phone conversations, informal lunches, written progress reports, and professional involvement. All this fosters an environment of trust between the athletic trainer and physician. Such a relationship is critical because accurate information must be obtained before the athlete can be evaluated and begin an effective rehabilitation program.

Evaluation

In the rehabilitation scheme, the athletic trainer's evaluation follows the physician's diagnosis. As discussed in Chapter 9, this process begins with a history that details the mechanism of injury, previous injuries, and symptoms. Included are the athlete's goals, attitude, and expectations. The objective examination follows and focuses upon static and dynamic function. Because much time may pass between the initial diagnosis and the beginning of the rehabilitation program, the evaluation should confirm the diagnosis and help determine the extent and rate of healing.

Objective and subjective examinations provide a sense of the nature of injury and the biomechanical, psychological, and physiological characteristics of the athlete. Objective measurements include strength, range of motion, and dynamic testing techniques. These tests can be a baseline for later comparison and even determine the nature of the rehabilitation.

Body language, facial expressions, attitude, and personality sometimes offer as much information as objective tests and measurements. A stoic or overmotivated athlete can disrupt even the best-designed treatment program by hampering the open communication that is necessary for periodic adjustments to the program. For example, pain is often a good indication that the intensity of the rehabilitation program is too vigorous. The athlete who is in pain as a result of the program but withholds this information may be delaying recovery. Such athletes need to be protected from doing too much; they need to be protected from themselves.

The athletic trainer must be astute and observant in determining the direction and intensity of the rehabilitation program. Rehabilitation must be individualized. Cookbook remedies have to be avoided because every athlete has a different body type, body chemistry, and biomechanical characteristic.

Holistic Athletic Training

The current attitude in sports medicine rehabilitation is to treat the whole person rather than just the injured area. Numerous studies have shown that injuries have effects beyond the injured site. The inactivity and deconditioning that result from specific athletic injuries can have profound physiological effects. The rehabilitation program should deal not only with the injury but attempt to minimize general **deconditioning** and **atrophy.**

The **holistic** program should pay particular attention to the cardiovascular

Syndrome: A group of signs and symptoms that appear together in a predictable manner.

Strain: Disruption or injury of a musculotendinous unit. A serious strain is often called a pulled muscle.
Body language: Nonverbal communication through the use of body posture and facial expression.

Deconditioning: Loss of fitness from inactivity or immobilization.
Atrophy: Decrease in size and function of a muscle.
Holistic: Dealing with the entire athlete rather than with the specific injury.

BOX 12-1

General Versus Specific Diagnoses

Diagnosis is specific or general and so may offer little or much information about which tissues are involved in an injury and to what extent. For instance, the diagnosis "chondromalacia patella" specifically refers to inflammation under the kneecap caused by chronic degeneration, excessive friction, or contusion (see Chapter 21). But it can also describe a general condition of poor alignment of the lower limbs, such as "the miserable malalignment syndrome," illustrated by the individual with a wide pelvis, knocked knees, and flat feet that toe out (Brody). Because of the poor alignment, other tissues besides the undersurface of the kneecap may be irritated, such as tendons, ligaments, and muscles. Therefore, the diagnosis in the second case provides little information about the secondary injuries that, together with the kneecap problem, constitute a syndrome. It is best to assume that other minor injuries exist and screen them during the evaluation procedures. Once a clear picture of the injury has been obtained, rehabilitation can proceed.

system, local tissue metabolism, joints above and below the injury, and the uninvolved side of the body. Care must be taken to assess deficiencies and return all aspects of the system to normal (if possible). The athlete's psychological state should also be considered. Strength, flexibility, muscular and cardiovascular endurance, agility, coordination, skill, and confidence must be restored.

Implementation of the Rehabilitation Program

A basic principle of all the health care professions is "Do no harm." As discussed in Chapter 4, the purpose of rehabilitation exercises is to systematically introduce stimuli that cause the body to adapt and improve its function. However, very often specific structures are not capable of sustaining additional stresses following an injury. Sometimes the athlete is best served by being given no treatment—rest is sometimes the best healer.

The rehabilitation program should be implemented only after careful planning for each individual athlete has been done. The planning process involves (1) assessment of physical status, (2) determination of the goals and objectives of the rehabilitation program (systematic program, with objectives and criteria for progression), and (3) selection of safe and effective therapeutic techniques. When treatments are presented, they should be applied systematically and rationally. Each procedure should be based upon sound theoretical principles and instituted in an order that results in the fastest rate of recovery.

Triage is the determination of the priority for treatment based upon the nature of the injury. Abnormalities noted upon examination must be triaged to determine which ones to correct first, which ones to emphasize later, and which ones will resolve on their own. In general, rehabilitation priorities include dealing with the athlete's chief complaint (which usually means diminishing the acute effects of injury, such as inflammation, edema, pain, etc.), general conditioning, range of motion, strength, power, muscle endurance, functional stability, and coordinated motion.

The athlete's chief complaint or principal symptoms must always be among the top priorities for rehabilitation. Failure to resolve the principal source of

Triage: Sorting athletes (or injuries within the same athlete) by severity of injury to determine treatment priority.

pain may disillusion the athlete and lead to a loss of trust in the athletic trainer. Achieving this priority may be a formidable task since the primary treatment may be rest, something that most athletes do not like to do.

Phases of Rehabilitation

The first priority of the rehabilitation program should be to reduce pain and swelling. Although this objective may be considered as falling under the category of initial treatment, pain and swelling may persist during the early stages of rehabilitation. Joint surfaces need motion for proper nutrition because the synovial fluid carries up to 80 percent of the oxygen and nutrients. Movement pumps this fluid through the thin cartilage covering of the joint surfaces, which increases nutrition and flushes out waste products. Swelling hampers joint lubrication, **chondrocyte** nutrition, and removal of waste products.

Symptoms such as pain, swelling, edema, and **effusion** must be eradicated to effectively advance rehabilitation and prevent reinjury. Recent studies have shown that these factors can cause weakness from reflex inhibition of the musculature. Increased pressure on damaged or normal nerve endings sends an inhibitory signal to muscles, which leads to atrophy, even though the muscle may be exercised regularly. Likewise, immobilization or inactivity can decrease the tensile strength of tendons and ligaments and reduce the tolerance of joint surfaces to friction. Therefore, one of the first priorities is to treat these acute symptoms because they hamper the rehabilitation process and enhance the effects of disuse and deconditioning.

In addition to reducing pain and swelling, an early goal of the rehabilitation program is to make the athlete ambulatory and functional for daily activities (see Putting It into Practice 12-1). When appropriate, early mobility (e.g., walking, climbing stairs, sitting,

kneeling) provides essential conditioning for the strength training and more vigorous exercises that follow. Overloading tendons and joint surfaces, a common problem in rehabilitation, can usually be avoided by taking time to precondition the athlete before applying aggressive resistive exercises. The initial program should be endurance-oriented because endurance exercise places less stress on the tissues.

The second area of emphasis is physical conditioning. Initially, this phase is designed to prevent the deconditioning that invariably results from forced inactivity. Conditioning progresses from range of motion and static exercises to resistive exercises that progressively increase in intensity. The conditioning phase should include specific exercises to develop cardiovascular and muscular endurance. Studies have shown marked decreases in **oxidative enzymes** from deconditioning and surgery. Muscular enzyme systems are not developed to any great extent with strength and power exercises. Endurance training is also helpful for preparing athletes for the high-intensity conditioning that occurs during the later stages of rehabilitation.

The timing of exercises can make a difference in the smoothness and speed of recovery. For example, premature heavy resistance training of the quadriceps after a knee injury can lead to patellofemoral dysfunction and tendinitis. Excessive passive stretching of a repaired or reconstructed ligament during the early stages of recovery, especially in the knee, can lead to structural weakness and permanent instability. Shoulders are particularly susceptible to irritation caused by prematurely vigorous rehabilitation programs.

The last phase of rehabilitation should include exercises and drills that restore smooth, coordinated movement patterns. Specificity of training must be rigidly observed to achieve full recovery (see Box 12-2 and Chapter 4). For example, a soccer player must be able to

Oxidative enzymes: Enzymes that participate in aerobic metabolic pathways; found in cells' mitochondria.
Chondrocyte: A mature cartilage cell.
Effusion: The movement of fluid into a body cavity.

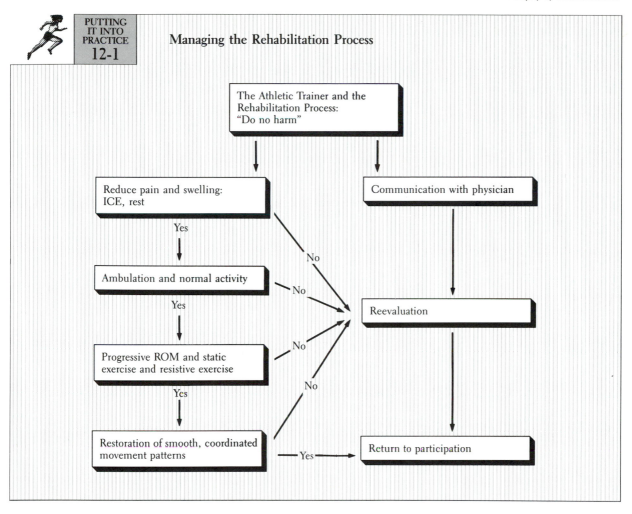

PUTTING IT INTO PRACTICE 12-1

Managing the Rehabilitation Process

The Athletic Trainer and the Rehabilitation Process: "Do no harm"

Reduce pain and swelling: ICE, rest

Communication with physician

Yes

Ambulation and normal activity

Yes

Progressive ROM and static exercise and resistive exercise

Yes

Restoration of smooth, coordinated movement patterns

No

No

No

No

Reevaluation

Return to participation

Yes

BOX 12-2

Rehabilitation and Specificity

Specificity of exercise means that the body adapts to the specific stress to which it is subjected (see Chapter 4). To provide optimal benefit, exercises to improve or restore fitness should be similar in intensity, speed of motion, and movement pattern. For example, it makes no sense to train a baseball pitcher with an activity like bowling. The rehabilitation program must be designed to closely mimic or duplicate the activities of the sport. The current use of high-speed exercise on isokinetic devices is a step in the right direction. However, the maximum speed of these instruments (300 degrees of arc per second) is slower than the motion of throwing a baseball (600 to 700 degrees of arc per second), and the motions do not involve eccentric muscle contractions, which are common in most movements. Ideally, rehabilitation exercises should be designed to have the maximum carryover effect.

rapidly change directions; doing so often places tremendous lateral pressure upon the joints of the lower extremity. This lateral pressure is difficult to apply in the training room, even with weight machines or manual resistance exercises. There is no substitute for the rigors of the playing field.

Home programs often can be used to supplement and speed rehabilitation. These programs must be specific and designed so that the athletes do not do too much. Home programs may include the application of ice or heat and various exercises.

Modalities

Modalities are therapies applied to accelerate the healing process (see Chapter 13); they include exercise, ice, heat, electrical stimulation, massage, and ultrasound. Selecting an appropriate modality depends upon what is available, which is most useful in accelerating healing for a specific injury, the athlete's previous response, available time, and how one modality combines with others.

The "shotgun" approach (using every available modality) is not recommended because the effects of individual modalities cannot be determined. Proper knowledge of each modality's properties can make the use of several of these aids an effective procedure. For example, knowing that both ultrasound and galvanic electrical stimulation reduce swelling, using them in combination may speed healing time. Procedures such as massage, joint mobilization, and passive stretching are usually more effective when preceded by modalities such as heat or traction. Sports medicine is becoming increasingly machine-oriented. However, there is no substitute for the "laying on of the hands"— the application of modalities—for gaining the trust of athletes.

Returning to Competition

Many athletes have unrealistic expectations about their injury, often from self-imposed pressure or influence from coaches, parents, or peers. Physicians sometimes add to the confusion by failing to provide a realistic time frame for recovery. The athletic trainer can help establish a rational program for rehabilitation based upon personal knowledge and consultation with the physician. After the nature of the injury and other pertinent factors have been carefully analyzed, the athlete should be consulted to plan short- and long-term goals. Goals help instill a feeling of progress and achievement and can reduce the anxiety of being injured.

Minimum standards of flexibility, strength, power, endurance, agility, and coordination should be established so that the athlete has a clear idea of when she or he can safely return to participation. The sport, level of competition, and position on the team must be considered to accurately set these performance standards. Basic guidelines for returning to full participation include

- Full range of motion, both actively and passively
- Normal strength and power
- Normal, coordinated patterns of movement, with all injury-compensated movement patterns, such as limping, eliminated
- Relatively pain-free

Return to practice is usually the joint decision of the athletic trainer, coach, athlete, and physician (see Putting It into Practice 12-2), although the determination of *medical* readiness lies strictly with the physician, who may be advised by the athletic trainer. Full competition is usually permitted when the athlete is at least 90 percent recovered. But even athletes who are fully physically recovered may not be emotionally prepared to resume competi-

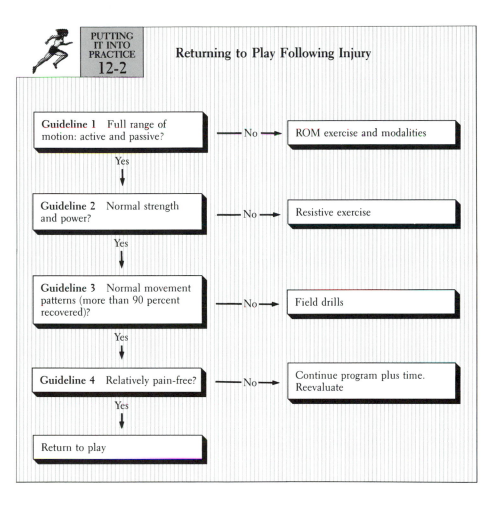

PUTTING
IT INTO
PRACTICE
12-2

Returning to Play Following Injury

Guideline 1 Full range of motion: active and passive? —No→ ROM exercise and modalities

Yes

Guideline 2 Normal strength and power? —No→ Resistive exercise

Yes

Guideline 3 Normal movement patterns (more than 90 percent recovered)? —No→ Field drills

Yes

Guideline 4 Relatively pain-free? —No→ Continue program plus time. Reevaluate

Yes

Return to play

tion. Anxiety and apprehension may affect the level of play and the predisposition to reinjury. Little is known about the emotional aspects of injury rehabilitation in athletics; currently sports psychologists are studying the subject.

Bracing and taping are physically and psychologically valuable to the athlete returning to competition following an injury, but the practices should not be substituted for proper conditioning and rehabilitation. Neither the athlete nor coach should put full faith in an injured area that is heavily taped or braced.

Many athletes return to competition before meeting the optimal standards of

rehabilitation. This is an unfortunate reality of athletics. However, proper communication among the athlete, coach, and team physician can minimize the potential for premature discharge from the rehabilitation program.

Because athletes and coaches are actively involved in competition, they sometimes lose sight of the possible negative long-term effects of playing on an inadequately rehabilitated knee or ankle. For example, ligament injuries in the knee often take eight to twenty-four months to reach full tensile strength. Likewise, inadequately rehabilitated ankle sprains have a very high rate of reinjury. Strength and flexibility must be restored without the risk of trauma that caused the injury in the first place. The athlete's flexibility and strength may be recovered well before the ligament is ready for full participation. The athlete may desperately want to return to play before being ready. But the athletic trainer is doing the athlete an extreme disservice if he or she does not render sound professional judgment.

Reevaluation

Reevaluation is the key to a successful rehabilitation program. Signs and symptoms, improvement or lack of progress should be continuously assessed. The athletic trainer should judge progress both subjectively and objectively. As discussed, body language and facial expressions can reveal a great deal about an athlete's status. These observations can be reinforced by noting such physical signs as pain and swelling.

"No pain—no gain" may have been the battle cry of the past, but "Ignore pain—no brain" is more applicable today. There are few if any painful conditions which can be "worked through." Some problems, such as subpatellar chondrosis (Chapter 21) and epicondylitis (Chapter 18), may give a false sense of being able to work it through because discomfort is often minimal during activity, but usually there will be increased pain two or three hours later. This "rebound effect" must be used as the indicator of the appropriateness of an exercise, not just the pain experienced during the performance of the exercise. Wait twenty-four hours before making important decisions about therapeutic exercises. Rehabilitation does not have to be painful, except for passive stretching under some circumstances. A dull ache may have to be tolerated, but sharp or intense pain should be respected and the activity stopped or modified.

A good rule is to note the progression of pain and swelling during a twenty-four hour period. The quality and intensity of symptoms at various times of the day help indicate which tissues are affected and the appropriateness of the treatment program. Musculotendinous injuries tend to ache early in the day but often feel better as the day progresses. Nerve irritation and joint trauma usually worsen as the day progresses. The time of onset of swelling and the time interval between the rehabilitation session and the onset of symptoms indicate exercise tolerance and speed of recovery.

In sports rehabilitation, the athlete is often pushed almost to the point of overexercising, to accelerate the return to participation. Proper attention to the pain and swelling cycles can guide the exercise program to the point of maximum efficiency. The athlete must be educated about the importance of accurately reporting personal symptoms. Fine-tuning the program will become easier as the athlete and health professional become better acquainted.

Measurement instruments such as the isokinetic dynamometer provide objective indices of strength and power, indicating maximum strength and endurance at different speeds of motion and allowing comparison between **contralateral** limbs and **antagonistic muscle** groups. These devices are also valuable modes of exercise. Manual muscle testing, although valuable during the early stages of recovery, does not provide accurate information during the later stages. Weight lifting comparisons of right and left sides may also be inaccurate because although the athlete may sense equal effort and lift equal weight, there can still be 15 to 20 percent imbalance that may affect performance.

Isokinetic testing is the preferred state of the art technique, but most institutions cannot afford the luxury of these expensive dynamometers. The athletic trainer should become skilled at manual muscle testing to assess muscle weakness as accurately and objectively as possible.

Contralateral: The same part on the other side of the body.
Antagonistic muscle: A muscle that directly opposes the action of another muscle; e.g., the biceps brachius, an elbow flexor, is antagonistic to the triceps, an elbow extensor.

The conditioning program must also be integrated with the athlete's other activities. The combined load of daily activities and the rehabilitation program must be assessed to determine if the total exertion is excessive. The athlete must be instructed to avoid irritating the injury during nonessential activities. For example, avoiding using the arms above shoulder height can help accelerate the healing of tendinitis of the shoulder as much as formal treatment. Sometimes something as simple as sleeping with the arm above the head is the main reason someone with shoulder tendinitis does not respond to treatment. Likewise, poor posture while sitting, sleeping, and driving may negate the beneficial effects of a low back rehabilitation program.

In summary, the rehabilitation process is a series of evaluations based upon an initial diagnosis. These appraisals result in a fine-tuning of the program so that the athlete can eventually achieve optimal conditioning and safely return to participation.

References

Basmajian, J. *Therapeutic Exercise.* Baltimore: Williams & Wilkins, 1978.

Brody, D. M. Running injuries. *CIBA Clinical Symposia* 32:1–36, 1980.

DeAndrade, J. R., C. Grant, and A. S. Dixon. Joint distension and reflex muscle inhibition in the knee. *Journal of Bone and Joint Surgery* 47:313–322, 1965.

Donatelli, R., and H. Owen-Burkhart. Effects of immobilization on the extensibility of periarticular connective tissue. *Journal of Orthopedic Sports and Physical Therapy* 3:61–72, 1981.

Gleim, G. W., J. A. Nicholas, and J. N. Webb. Isokinetic evaluation following leg injuries. *The Physician and Sportsmedicine* 5:75–82, 1978.

Hettinga, D. L. Normal joint structures and their reactions to injury. *Journal of Orthopedic Sports and Physical Therapy* 1:16–21, 1980.

Sherman, W. M., M. J. Plyley, D. R. Pearson, A. J. Habansky, D. A. Vogelgesang, and D. L. Costill. Isokinetic rehabilitation after meniscectomy: a comparison of two methods of training. *The Physician and Sportsmedicine* 11:121–133, 1983.

Sprague, R. B. Factors related to extension lag at the knee joint. *Journal of Orthopedic Sports and Physical Therapy* 3:178–182, 1982.

Watkins, M. P., and B. A. Harris. Evaluation of isokinetic muscle performance. *Clinics in Sports Medicine* 2:45–50, 1983.

13 Modalities

A N athletic trainer's most important tools are a keen mind, highly skilled hands, and a thorough professional background. These formidable tools must be used to facilitate the prevention, immediate treatment, and rehabilitation of athletic injuries. **Modalities** are also available to help fulfill these critically important responsibilities. A modality is any physical agent, such as light, electricity, heat, or cold, applied for a therapeutic effect.

Numerous modalities have been used in athletic medicine, many of dubious value. The athletic trainer must not be a mere technician, mechanically applying tape, exercising athletes on machines, or rubbing **analgesic** balm on sore muscles. The athletic trainer should be a professional who is capable of using appropriate modalities as part of a systematic and well-planned rehabilitation program. This chapter discusses the principal modalities used in sports medicine and their physiological effects. In addition, we describe three other tools the athletic trainer uses: taping, padding, and bracing.

Legal Considerations

Presently, most states do not require that athletic trainers be licensed (certification by the National Athletic Trainers Association does not constitute licensure). This means that the law does not specifically allow athletic trainers to use modalities, which are generally considered as falling within the domain of physicians and physical therapists. In most cases, athletic trainers use modalities under the prescription and direction of a team physician. Unfortunately, the law in most states is unclear about whether the physician must be physically present while the athletic trainer applies these treatments.

Athletic trainers may be held legally accountable if they are found negligent, even though they are not licensed. **Negligence** is conduct falling below that of a reasonably prudent athletic trainer acting in a similar situation. This definition allows the court to weigh a person's conduct in a specific situation against accepted professional standards. Since athletic trainers use modalities, it is their responsibility to be knowledgeable about them. Modalities should not

Modality: A physical technique or substance administered to produce a therapeutic effect.

Analgesic: A substance that reduces pain.

Negligence: Acting imprudently. Regarding athletic trainers, actions not typical of the average qualified athletic trainer.

Following a rotator cuff injury, Soviet gymnast Nikolai Adrianov performs on the rings. Modalities are useful for returning an athlete to peak form, but for maximum effect they must be integrated with a well-planned treatment and rehabilitation program.

be used unless the athletic trainer thoroughly understands their indications, contraindications, and use. It may be argued that since there is no clear-cut legal mandate, an athletic trainer has an even greater responsibility than the physical therapist to be completely informed about the theory and practice of therapeutic procedures. When in doubt about the use of a modality, seek advice from the team physician.

Thermal Modalities

Thermal modalities, such as heat and ice, are popular and readily available for athletic trainers and the general public. Unfortunately, there is considerable confusion about when to apply them and under what circumstance.

Physiological Effects

Humans are able to maintain a relatively constant central body temperature (core temperature) even in the face of widely varying environmental temperatures (see Chapter 25) because complicated regulatory mechanisms let the body increase heat production as the core cools and increase heat loss when the core is heated. Core temperature is usually considered the temperature of

Thermal: Pertaining to heat.

the hypothalamus, the body's temperature regulatory center, but it can be considered as that of all the critical "central organs," such as the heart and brain.

An important temperature regulatory mechanism is controlling the relative size of the core and shell (tissues other than the core) by dilating or constricting peripheral blood vessels. This process forms a temperature gradient that can be used to either conserve or dissipate heat. The circulation helps control the gradient between the core and the shell by vasoconstricting peripheral blood vessels when core heat must be either conserved or dissipated.

Therapeutic use of external heat increases the blood flow through the skin in the area being treated. If the skin is heated above the core temperature, the gradient is reversed and the blood flow helps distribute heat throughout the body. During this process, blood vessels open up in the tissues that are close to the heat source.

External application of cold (cryotherapy) cools tissue in three ways: (1) cooling decreases blood flow through the skin, (2) this decreased blood flow in the skin diminishes heat transport from the core to the skin and reinforces the cooling effect of the cold application, and (3) the hypothalamus also stimulates further peripheral vasoconstriction when it is stimulated by cooled blood from the skin that has returned to the circulation. After the initial vasoconstriction, there is alternate vasodilation and vasoconstriction known as the **hunting reaction** (see Chapter 25 and Box 13-1).

Depth of Penetration. Prolonged externally applied cold is more penetrating and long-lasting than externally applied heat. The circulation vasodilates in response to heat. Externally applied heat increases blood flow to an area, but the heat is absorbed by the circulation and carried away, which results in minimal penetration. On the other hand, the application of cold causes vasoconstriction, so the circulation is less able to carry away the cold, which results in deeper penetration.

Subcutaneous fat is a barrier against heat exchange because it has low **thermal conductivity.** If cold is applied for a short time over an area containing significant amounts of fat, there will be little decrease in muscle temperature. However, if the cold has been applied for a longer period (thirty minutes or more), fat will help depress muscle temperature for a longer period because the fat acts as a gradient that "holds the cold in."

Cold, Heat, and Trauma. Traumatic injury produces an inflammatory response characterized by hemorrhage and the release of **histamine,** which increases the permeability of blood vessels and cell walls (see Chapter 8). This results in **edema** (swelling). The disrupted circulation causes **ischemia** (lack of blood flow) and **hypoxia** (inadequate oxygen).

Muscle spasm often accompanies trauma-induced pain and is the body's attempt to immobilize and protect an injured area. **Muscle spasm** is an involuntary, sustained contraction that causes consumption of large amounts of nutrients (because of the high metabolic rate of sustained contraction) and ischemia (due to compression of blood vessels). The side effects of spasm cause more spasm, resulting in a **vicious cycle.**

The application of cold following acute trauma may be very beneficial. Knight's data suggest that cold limits the formation of **hematoma** and the amount of bleeding into an area by inducing vasoconstriction and increasing blood viscosity (thickness) (both processes slow the blood flow). Healing is facilitated because the hematoma is minimized. In addition, there is less hypoxic injury because of lower cellular metabolism and reduced need for oxygen in tissues that survive the initial

Thermal conductivity: The ability to conduct heat.

Histamine: A chemical formed during inflammation and immune responses. Among other things, it causes arteriolar vasodilation and increased membrane permeability.

Edema: Swelling; a collection of fluid in a tissue space.

Ischemia: Inadequate blood flow.

Hypoxia: Low level of oxygen.

Cryotherapy: Use of cold as therapy.

Muscle spasm: An involuntary convulsive muscle contraction or cramp. Spasms can occur in both skeletal and smooth muscle.

Vicious cycle: A results in B, and B causes a further increase in A.

Hunting reaction: Alternating vascular vasoconstriction and vasodilation in an extremity (e.g., the hands and feet).

Hematoma: A bruise; a mass of partially clotted blood outside the vascular space, typically formed from trauma.

Temperature Sensation

Temperature sensation is influenced more by the rate of change of skin temperature than by skin's actual temperature. The danger in prolonged heat or cold treatment is that the athlete may be unaware that the skin is being burned or frostbitten because the rate of temperature change is very slow. The therapeutic benefit of most treatments is achieved in a relatively short time; no greater benefit is realized if treatment is continued longer. Following an acute injury when ice packs may be continuously applied, remove the packs at half-hour intervals to let the skin return to normal temperature. This helps prevent frostbite and the development of reflex vasodilation that occurs with prolonged exposure to cold (the so-called hunting reaction).

trauma. Thus, the total amount of tissue damage is less.

Cold may relieve pain by **anesthetizing** local pain fibers. Cold decreases nerve-conduction velocity, completely abolishing conduction when tissue temperature is decreased to 10 to 15°C. Cold application may "overload" central pain receptors by bombarding them with intense cold impulses (a process called competitive inhibition; see Chapter 8 for a discussion of the gate theory of pain). Muscle spasms stop when pain sensations are overcome.

Heat is effective in reducing muscle spasm but should not be used following acute tissue damage (see Putting It into Practice 13-1, p. 194). Heat decreases muscle spasm by reducing **muscle spindles'** activity and sensitivity to stretch. Muscle spindles, sometimes called stretch receptors, cause muscles to contract when they are stimulated and to relax when they are inhibited. Heat also decreases muscle spasm by initiating reflexes mediated through thermal receptors. However, because heat enhances blood flow, it tends to intensify local edema and hemorrhage following trauma. It is generally considered safe to use heat when swelling has subsided, the athlete has complete, pain-free range of motion, and the temperature of the injured part is normal (no signs of acute inflammation).

Heat and cold modalities are most effective when used with resistive and range of motion exercises. This treatment strategy helps remove **exudates,** improves the nutritional status of tissues, and prevents tightness and adhesions in soft tissue. Heat has been shown to produce a residual elongation of collagen tissue after stretching exercises. This beneficial effect does not occur if stretching and heat are not applied together.

Selecting the Proper Thermal Modality

Criteria for selection of a thermal modality include the

- Nature, location, and extent of the injury
- Desired effects of treatment
- Availability of various modalities

The appropriate modality must produce the desired temperature at the proper location. If vigorous deep heating is indicated (e.g., muscle spasm of a deep muscle, such as the pectoralis minor) and a modality with an inappropriate distribution is selected, the result may be inadequate treatment at the site of pathology and damage to the tissues in the area of peak temperature. Deep-heating modalities include ultrasound and shortwave diathermy; superficial heating modalities include hot packs and whirlpool. As discussed, cold tends

Exudate: Material tissue discharges as a result of inflammation.
Anesthetize: To decrease or eliminate sensitivity.

Muscle spindles: Receptors within muscles sensitive to stretch.

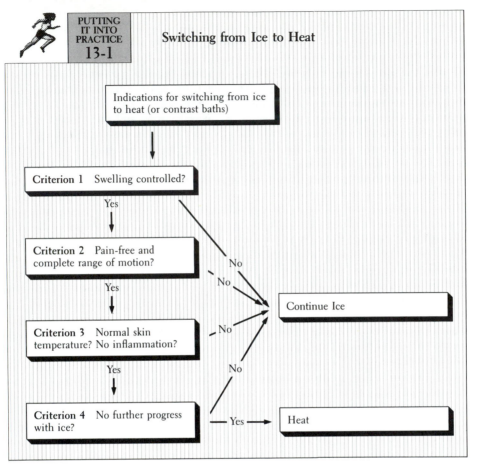

PUTTING IT INTO PRACTICE 13-1

Switching from Ice to Heat

Indications for switching from ice to heat (or contrast baths)

Criterion 1 Swelling controlled?

Yes

Criterion 2 Pain-free and complete range of motion?

Yes

Criterion 3 Normal skin temperature? No inflammation?

Yes

Criterion 4 No further progress with ice?

No → No → No → No → Continue Ice

Yes → Heat

to be more penetrating than heat. However, specific modes of cold application (i.e., ice packs, ice massage, ice bath) vary in their penetration. Cold applied directly to soft tissue, such as with ice massage and ice bath, tends to be more penetrating than ice applied as a pack.

Deep-Heating Modalities

Modalities such as ultrasound and shortwave diathermy let heat penetrate to deep tissues while minimizing the heating of superficial tissues.

Ultrasound

Ultrasound is acoustical vibration that occurs at frequencies too high for humans to hear (Figure 13-1). This modality causes molecular movement (heat) in target tissues. Ultrasound is a useful therapeutic tool because it is selectively absorbed by tissues such as superficial bone and its immediate covering (cartilage, synovium, and capsular tissue), ligaments, scar tissue within soft tissue, myofascial interfaces, nerve trunks, tendons, and tendon sheaths. Thus, it may be applied to a ligament or tendon injury; if applied correctly, it will minimally heat the surrounding soft tissue.

Ultrasound: Use of high-frequency sound waves (greater than 20,000 hertz) as deep-heating therapy.

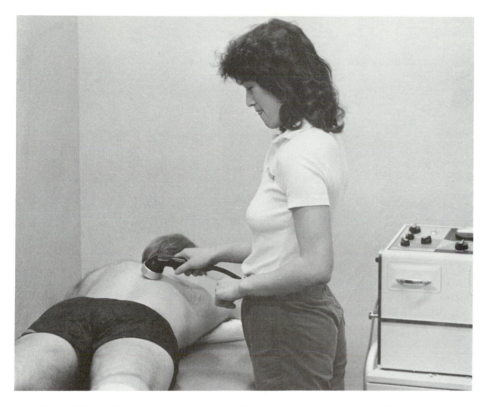

Figure 13-1 Athlete receiving ultrasound, a thermal modality often used to relax muscle tissue.

Indications. Ultrasound is used during rehabilitation of soft tissue injuries like sprains, strains, and contusions. In addition to heating, many therapeutic effects have been attributed to ultrasound, including **cavitation,** which destroys tissues (such as adhesions), acceleration of enzyme activity (increased metabolic rate), increased cell permeability (an aid to tissue nutrition in areas with minimal blood supply, such as cartilage, tendons, and ligaments), and increased tendon extensibility from thermal **denaturing** of proteins. These effects may be beneficial in facilitating bone healing and producing a mechanical effect on scar tissue. Unfortunately, research results are equivocal regarding the therapeutic effectiveness of ultrasound's nonthermal properties.

Application and Dosage. Apply ultrasound in fields of four to twenty-five square inches (two to five inches from side to side and up and down). You can use multiple fields if the area to be treated is larger. Perform the treatment under water if the area is small or extremely tender to touch. Ultrasound is not effective if the waves must travel through the air. Use a **coupling agent** such as mineral oil, a water-base gel, or water to facilitate penetration. There is better penetration if the surface is cold. Pretreatment with ice massage can effectively lower skin temperature.

Apply ultrasound by stroking the transducer on the skin at a rate of about four inches per second. Use a relatively firm, steady, overlapping motion. With underwater treatment, use the same stroking pattern, but immerse the transducer and hold it parallel at about one-half inch from the part to be treated. With your finger, periodically wipe away gas bubbles, which collect

Cavitation: Formation of a cavity. As a property of ultrasound, the capacity to break up tissue structure.
Coupling agent: A chemical agent, e.g., mineral oil, electrode gel, or water, that facilitates the interface between an instrument (i.e., ultrasound transducer or electrode) and the skin.
Denature: To break down the basic structure.

on the skin and transducer head. Do not let the transducer head operate without contact with tissue, water, or in its cradle on the machine or the ultrasonic crystal may become damaged.

Ultrasound can drive surface contaminants through the skin, so it is important to thoroughly clean the area. The thermal nature of this modality increases the skin's permeability. This effect can be used to move drugs through the skin into local soft tissues (a process called **phonophoresis**). Ultrasound provides better depth penetration of a drug than simple surface application, but there is no reliable documentation regarding the depth of penetration of various drugs.

The accurate determination of the dosage of ultrasound (**dosimetry**) depends upon such factors as the desired depth and intensity of heating and existing bony prominences in the beam field. A rough guide for setting intensity is 0.1 to 0.8 watts per centimeter squared for low intensity, 0.8 to 1.5 watts per centimeter squared for medium intensity, and 1.5 to 3.0 watts per centimeter squared for high intensity. The intensity is too great if the athlete suddenly feels deep pain in the area being treated.

Contraindications. Contraindications to ultrasound are tissue with impaired sensation or circulation (e.g., limbs of a circulatory impaired diabetic or a patient suffering from severe claudication—lameness or limping), **malignancies,** or over eyes, a pregnant uterus, or gonads. Use it for only *short* periods of time over the spinal column and the epiphyses of growing children. You can use ultrasound in areas of metal implants with little danger of burning surrounding tissues because the sound waves reflect off metal (this is not true of shortwave diathermy).

Some experts advocate pulsed ultrasound because it appears to be effective while presenting less danger of burning tissues. However, the pulsed technique is probably less effective than the continuous method for applying heat because the temperature elevation of ultrasound depends upon the average output of the machine. In addition, the energy peaks necessary to achieve temperature elevation during the pulses may be destructive.

Shortwave Diathermy

Shortwave diathermy is the therapeutic application of high-frequency current; the greatest amount of heat is delivered to the area of greatest current density (Figure 13-2).

Indications. This modality is used during the rehabilitation of strains, but the technique has become less common in athletic medicine.

Application and Dosage. Shortwave diathermy is administered through devices such as condenser plates, condenser pads, an induction coil, and a monode applicator. The mode of administration determines the depth of heat penetration. Heating tends to occur in subcutaneous tissues and superficial muscles when condenser plates or pads are used. If the modality is used with an induction coil, the highest temperature will be in the superficial and moderately deep muscles. The monode applicator achieves the greatest penetration but is able to heat only a small field.

Dosage depends upon the athlete's heat tolerance. Always tune the instrument to its lowest setting to prevent excessive surges of current, which may occur when an instrument is suddenly turned on and adjusted to a high setting. The correct setting should give the athlete a comfortable sensation of heat.

Contraindications. The treatment field should be free of metal, including metal implants, metal jewelry, and patient contact with metal furniture. Since fluid is preferentially heated, do

Shortwave diathermy: Therapeutic application of high-frequency current to deliver deep heat.
Phonophoresis: The process of driving drugs through the skin with ultrasound.

Dosimetry: Dosage.

Malignancy: A process resistant to treatment and characterized by uncontrollable growth.

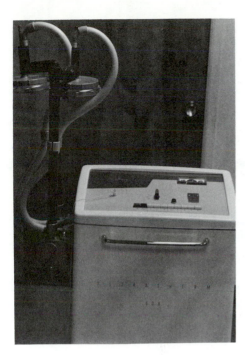

Figure 13-2 Diathermy was once popular as a thermal modality, but today it is only occasionally used in athletic training rooms. The condenser plates, used to deliver the diathermy, are in the upper left-hand corner.

not treat any fluid-filled cavities with shortwave diathermy, especially edematous joints. Do not let perspiration accumulate because it can burn skin. Place a towel between the electrode and the skin to absorb perspiration and facilitate sanitation. Shortwave diathermy is contraindicated with pacemakers and pregnancy. In addition, all contraindications listed for heat apply to this modality. Older machines often have several leads or cords; they must not touch or cross each other, must not touch metal, and must not touch the athlete.

Microwave Diathermy

Microwave diathermy delivers deep heat in the form of electromagnetic radiation. This technique is used to facilitate deep vasodilation of blood vessels (stimulating muscle blood flow) and lymph flow.

Indications. This modality is used during the rehabilitation of strains. The indications are the same as for shortwave diathermy. Like shortwave diathermy, microwave diathermy is not widely used in sports medicine.

Application and Dosage. The depth of heating depends upon the frequency of the microwave beam. The optimum frequency for muscle heating occurs at approximately 900 megacycles; a frequency of slightly higher than 2400 megacycles is best for heating subcutaneous tissues.

Contraindications. This technique may cause burns (called hot spots) in tissues directly over bone, which result from heat radiating from the bones' surface. Hot spots are less of a problem if a frequency of less than 900 megacycles is used.

Superficial Heating Modalities

Superficial heating modalities, such as hot packs and whirlpools, are extremely popular because they are readily available to athletic trainers and the public.

Hot Packs

Hot packs (**hydrocollator packs**) provide superficial moist heat. These canvas packs are filled with silica gel and stored in a thermostatically controlled water bath maintained at 170°F (Figure 13-3, p. 198). When the packs are applied, the skin temperature rises and then drops after about eight minutes, but not to its previous level. The skin temperature drops because the blood flow in the skin and subcutaneous tissue is markedly increased and the blood from the circulation is cooler than the heated tissues. Deeper tissues are barely affected by this treatment.

Hydrocollator pack: Canvas pack filled with silica gel, used to apply superficial moist heat.

Microwave diathermy: Therapeutic use of electromagnetic radiation to deliver deep heat.

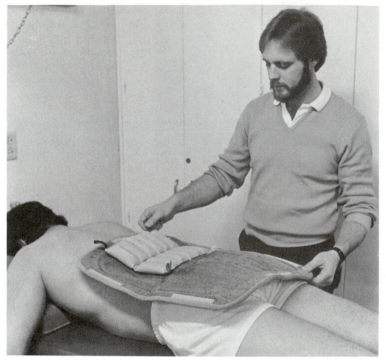

Figure 13-3 Hot packs are typically stored in a hot water bath, with the temperature set at 175°F.

Figure 13-4 When hot packs are being applied, insulation should be placed directly on the athlete's skin to protect it from burning.

Indications. Hot packs are used to induce relaxation in superficial muscles. They are indicated in nonacute, postinflammatory conditions involving superficial soft tissue.

Application and Dosage. Wrap the pack in about six layers of towels or a commercial terry cover and one towel layer (Figure 13-4). Since the terry cover is reused many times between launderings, the additional layer facilitates sanitation. The athlete should feel a comfortable sense of warmth. Add or remove towel layers if the pack is too hot or cold.

Apply the pack for approximately eight to ten minutes. Repeated application of freshly heated packs does not significantly reheat the area to the same extent as during the first eight minutes of treatment.

Contraindications. Never apply the pack directly to the skin because of the danger of skin burns and poor sanitation. Do not use hot packs on athletes with impaired sensitivity to temperature.

Hydrotherapy:
Whirlpools and Hot Tubs

Hydrotherapy is a good method of superficial heating because moving water has a massaging, sedative, and cleansing action (Figure 13-5). This method permits all surfaces of the affected part to be simultaneously treated at a constant temperature. In addition, it is generally popular with the athletes.

Indications. The **whirlpool** or hot tub is an excellent location for therapeutic exercise designed to develop

Hydrotherapy: Use of water as therapy.

Whirlpool: Hydrotherapy tub or pool of cold to hot aerated water used to supply a therapeutic effect.

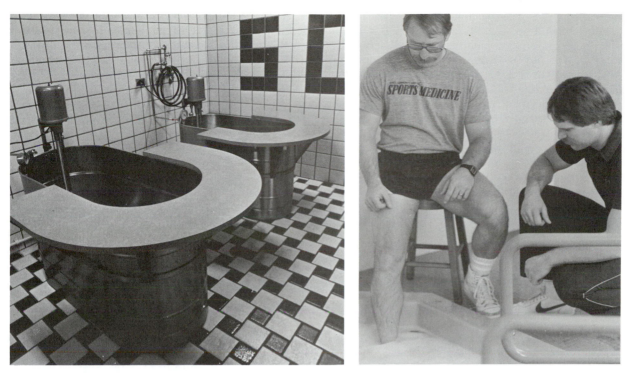

Figure 13-5 Hydrotherapy effectively applies heat and cold. The whirlpool bath (*left*) is the most common hydrotherapy device in the athletic training room. Full immersion is not always needed to receive the full benefits of hydrotherapy, however. The athlete may immerse only the injured part in a therapy pool (*right*).

range of motion and strength (early rehabilitation phase). The human body is extremely buoyant in water (most totally submerged humans weigh less than six kilograms), which facilitates exercising weak limbs that could be overwhelmed if subjected to the effects of gravity. Water can also be used to provide resistance for the exercises (water is more viscous than air, so moving through it is more difficult). In fact, edema may result if the athlete does not exercise during the treatment (see Putting It into Practice 13-2).

Application and Dosage. Administer hydrotherapy treatments for approximately ten minutes, less if the athlete is not used to the treatment. Carefully monitor the temperature of the whirlpool. In general, the greater the percentage of body immersion, the lower

PUTTING IT INTO PRACTICE 13-2   **Whirlpool Precautions**

- *Uses of whirlpool baths*: Cold water, hot water, and hot-cold contrast immersions.
- *Location*: Should be easily supervised but separated from main training room to reduce humidity and noise.
- *Dangers*: Electrocution, fainting, heat stress, burns, drowning.
- *Precautions*:
  1. Supervise whirlpool at all times.
  2. Post warnings of dangers and rules.
  3. Install ground fault interrupter and rubber-insulated wall switch to prevent electrical shock.
  4. Have someone outside the whirlpool turn the motor on and off.
  5. Maximum water temperature 104°F (100°F for total body immersion).
  6. After vigorous exercise, cool down before entering whirlpool.

the temperature. The maximum temperature for full body immersion is 104°F. Maximum appropriate temperatures are 106° for the ankle and elbow, 104° for the knee, hips, and back (acute: 100 to 104°F; acute, chronic: 104 to 105°F), and as much as 106° for the hand. Never set the whirlpool for higher than 106°F.

Always clean the whirlpool at the end of each day and, if appropriate, between treatments if athletes with skin infections have used it or if the water gets particularly dirty. Diseases such as Pseudomonas folliculitis can be a problem if high standards of sanitation are not maintained in whirlpools and hot tubs (Putting It into Practice 13-3). Normally, whirlpool treatment for large open wounds or burns is beyond the scope of treatment of the athletic training room; this treatment is best left to a hospital physical therapy department.

Contraindications. Contraindications to superficial heating modalities are

---

PUTTING IT INTO PRACTICE 13-3

Maintaining Sanitation and Safety Standards for Hot Tubs and Whirlpools

Measures to Reduce the Growth of Pseudomonas *in Hot Tubs and Whirlpools*

1. Have a good filtration and recirculation system and make sure it is operating properly, with well-functioning valves and clear lines. A dirty filtration system impairs function and may accelerate free chlorine inactivation and serve as a breeding ground for bacteria.

2. Monitor residual free chlorine levels frequently, using the DPD test kit method. Monitoring should be performed hourly to daily at predetermined times, depending on how much the tub is used.

3. Maintain chlorine levels by adding liquid, granular, or tablet chlorine as needed to keep the free residual chlorine between 1 and 3 ppm (ideal range 1.0 to 1.5 ppm). Use of a timed pumping device that continuously and automatically delivers

chlorine is suggested.

4. Monitor the pH at the same time as the residual chlorine and keep it between 7.2 and 7.8 (ideal 7.5) by adding appropriate amounts of alkali or acid. When the pH is above 8.0, 20% or less of the free chlorine is active against bacteria.

5. Check total alkalinity weekly and adjust to between 60 and 200 ppm (ideal 100 ppm) to help ensure pH stability.

6. Check calcium hardness weekly and adjust to between 50 and 500 ppm (ideal 125 ppm) to avoid tub etching, corrosion, scale, and reduced filter life.

7. Superchlorinate after each cleaning and refilling to raise the initial level of chlorine. After superchlorination, the spa or hot tub should not be used until the level of re-

sidual chlorine has dropped to less than 3 ppm.

8. Drain, clean, and refill with fresh water at least every three months for private spas or hot tubs and after every 250 uses for commercial units. Scum formation on the sides can be reduced by maintaining proper pH and alkalinity and by using silicone antifoaming agents. Cleaning and scrubbing should be done using acidic cleaning solutions. Proper water levels must be maintained to ensure adequate circulation. Evaporation can be reduced by having a cover for the pool and an automatic timer for activating the hydrojets.

9. Keep pool temperature in the recommended range of 102 to 104°F. The temperature should never exceed 104°F.

Maintaining Sanitation and Safety Standards for Hot Tubs and Whirlpools (*continued*)

Hot Tub Maintenance Form

Date _____

Day of the week _____

	6 AM	7 AM	8 AM	9 AM	10 AM	11 AM	Noon	1 PM	2 PM	3 PM	4 PM	5 PM	6 PM	7 PM	8 PM	9 PM	10 PM
Initial																	
DPD																	
Sodium hypochlorite added (oz)																	
pH																	
Plus add (oz)																	
Minus add (oz)																	
Temperature F																	
Superchlorinate sodium hypochlorite (oz)																	
DPD check																	
Auto chlorinate (sec/min)																	
Defoam added																	

Total alkalinity	_____	Filter check	_____	Tub drained	_____
Alkali added	_____	Filter backwash	_____	Tub cleaned	_____
Water hardness	_____	Auto chlorine		Tub refilled	_____
Pump pressure	_____	pump check	_____	Tub cultured	_____
Pump check	_____	Filter change	_____	Other	_____

Safety Precautions for Posting Near Hot Tubs

1. Showers are *required* before entering the hot tub. The use of oils, body lotion, soap, shampoo, or minerals in the hot tub is prohibited.
2. Elderly persons and those suffering from heart disease, diabetes, and high or low blood pressure should not use the hot tub.
3. Do not use hot tub while under the influence of alcohol, anticoagulants, antihistamines, vasoconstrictors, vasodilators, stimulants, hypnotics, narcotics, or tranquilizers.
4. Unsupervised use by children is prohibited, and children under 6 years of age are not permitted in the hot tub.
5. Do not operate at water temperature higher than 104°F (40°C).
6. Observe a reasonable time limit (ten minutes), then shower, cool down, and, if you wish, return for another brief stay. Long exposure may result in nausea, dizziness, or fainting. During pregnancy, a shorter time limit is recommended.
7. Always exit and enter slowly and cautiously and avoid using the tub when alone.

SOURCE: Randt, G. A. Hot tub folliculitis. *The Physician and Sportsmedicine* 11:74–83, 1983.

diminished sensation, vascular insufficiency, large open wounds, malignancy, bleeding diseases, or ischemic tissues that are unable to handle increased metabolism.

Great care must be taken to ensure that the whirlpool has been correctly wired and grounded and that it is periodically checked by an electrician. Do not have any electrical switches within reach of the athlete who is immersed because this could be a severe shock hazard.

Hydrotherapy may induce heat stress and heat injury in anyone. Athletes should be warned about excessive exposure to this modality and using inappropriately high water temperatures. Be sure that the whirlpool is located in a place that can be easily supervised rather than in an obscure corner of the facility.

Paraffin Bath

A paraffin bath is a means of superficially heating the hands, wrists, and feet. The bath contains a mixture of paraffin and mineral oil that is heated to a temperature of approximately 125.6°F. This modality is seldom used in athletic medicine.

Indications. This modality is used during the rehabilitation of soft tissue injuries of the hands, wrists, and feet.

Application and Dosage. Generally, administer treatments for approximately fifteen minutes. The wax may be painted on in layers or the body part submerged directly into the bath.

Contraindications. This modality is contraindicated in athletes with diminished peripheral temperature sensitivity.

Heat Lamps

Heat lamps generally use infrared rays, rays that are at the long end of the spectrum. Infrared radiation is also called **radiant heat** because of its capacity to induce random motion of molecules (heat). Although infrared heating is essentially a superficial heating modality, some deep heating occurs by conduction (see Chapter 25). Heat lamps are not widely used in athletic medicine.

Athletes sometimes use ultraviolet lamps to improve their suntan. The lamps are sometimes used in the treatment of some types of skin lesions, but they are of limited use in the athletic training room. Ultraviolet sun lamps can cause burns and may predispose athletes to skin cancer.

Indications. Radiant heat lamps are used during the postacute phase of treatment of soft tissue injury.

Application and Dosage. The power output of radiant heat lamps is from 250 to 1200 watts. The distance between the bulb and the athlete should be fifteen to twenty-four inches, depending upon the bulb's power output and the athlete's tolerance. Apply the heat treatment for approximately twenty to thirty minutes (as tolerated).

Contraindications. Do not use radiant heat lamps on athletes who have problems with peripheral temperature sensitivity. If possible, do not directly suspend the heat lamps over the athlete because the bulb may break and hot glass may fall on the athlete.

Cryotherapy

Cold has replaced heat as the principal athletic training modality, mainly because of its effect upon inflammation. Cold is particularly valuable to the athletic trainer because it allows early ambulation of the injured body part. Present evidence suggests that for most injuries, healing is facilitated by early rehabilitation. Cryotherapy seems to speed the transition from the acute

Radiant heat: Heat emitted in waves.

phase to the rehabilitation phase of injury treatment.

Indications

Cryotherapy is used as an anti-inflammatory technique in the treatment of soft tissue injury (see Chapter 8 and the discussion of hot and cold modalities in this chapter). During rehabilitation, it can be used to facilitate the development of range of motion (a technique called **cryokinetics**). Some athletic trainers use ice during all phases of treatment and rehabilitation of soft tissue injury, never using heat.

Application and Dosage

Application techniques include ice packs, ice massage, and ice baths. Criteria for selecting a technique include the user's experience, available supplies, and the target area (see Putting It into Practice 13-4, p. 204).

Ice Packs. Ice packs are the preferred method of cold application following an acute injury because cold, compression, and elevation can be used simultaneously (Figure 13-6). Crushed or flaked ice in a plastic bag conforms to the body better than cubed ice. Place the bag directly on the skin. Alternatively, place one layer of a cold, wet elastic wrap around the part, followed by an ice pack; secure both in place with the remainder of the wrap (this method provides both compression and cold). Elevate the body part and keep the ice in place for twenty to thirty minutes. Then remove the ice and inspect the skin for frostbite. Reapply the ice pack (if desired) when the skin has returned to normal temperature.

Ice Massage. Ice massage is accomplished with an ice cube that has been frozen in a paper or insulated cup (Figure 13-7). The ice is vigorously massaged over the area for five to ten minutes or until the athlete has experienced

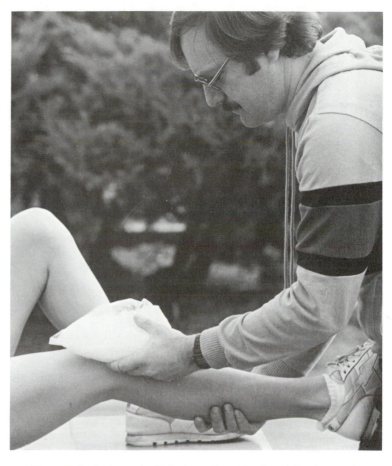

Figure 13-6 An ice pack effectively applies cold to large joints because it readily molds itself to a joint's shape.

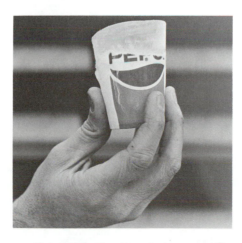

Figure 13-7 Freezing water in paper or Styrofoam cups provides the ice cups used in ice massage.

Cryokinetics: The concurrent and therapeutic use of ice and range of motion exercises.

PUTTING
IT INTO
PRACTICE
13-4

Guidelines and Contraindications for Cold Therapy

The following points should be kept in mind when considering using cold therapy on a patient.

When to Apply Cold

Cold therapy is used primarily in the first 36 hours after an injury. Use ice, compression, and elevation for managing acute injuries. Cold should be applied intermittently and under moderated circumstances. The earlier ice is applied, the more it will help.

Icing is very helpful in acute inflammatory conditions such as bursitis, tendinitis, and tenosynovitis. Contrast treatments are helpful in chronic conditions.

About 20 minutes of ice massage after activity helps rehabilitate chronic injuries. It reduces inflammation and has a local anesthetizing effect on the pain caused by therapeutic exercises. Freezing ice in a

Styrofoam cup that can be peeled back provides an insulated handle for athletes to do their own ice massage. Most athletes like to be actively involved in the rehabilitation process.

Of all the methods of applying cold, ice works the best. It is also the cheapest and simplest to make.

Due to the insulating effects of the subcutaneous fat and the circulation to the skin, it takes 20 to 30 minutes to cool deep tissues. It takes only ten minutes for a topical effect on the skin.

Risks

The skin is a potential victim of cold therapy. Frostbite can occur, although ice massage rarely causes it. Ethyl chloride, however, can reduce skin temperatures to as low as 4°C and can produce second- and third-degree damage.

Great care should be used in using cold therapy on patients who are comatose, unable to respond, or who lack sensation.

There are some general contraindications to the use of cold therapy. Patients who have collagen diseases such as lupus erythematosis and rheumatoid arthritis often manifest Raynaud's phenomenon when exposed to cold. Some patients have a cold allergy that produces hives and joint pain. Some develop cryoglobinemia. Paroxysmal cold hemoglobinuria is also well known, producing a flood of free hemoglobin that can result in renal damage and shutdown. Patients with pheochromocytoma may have a blood pressure rise in response to cold exposure.

SOURCE: McMaster, W. C. Cryotherapy. *The Physician and Sportsmedicine* 11:112–119, 1982.

each of the following stages: (1) cold, (2) burning, (3) aching, and (4) numbness. Note that these sensations are characteristic of *all* forms of ice therapy. Ice massage causes a higher skin temperature (about 18°F) than the other types of cold application. Pain relief (numbness) and decreased muscle spasm are its primary effects. Its primary application is use before and after practice, during competition, or as therapeutic exercise to prevent pain and muscle spasm (which can greatly facilitate range of motion exercises). Ice massage is not the technique of choice for an acute injury because it does not cool as effectively as other methods,

and it does not allow simultaneous compression and elevation.

Ice Bath. An ice bath is a water and ice mixture that can be administered in a tub or whirlpool and allows all surfaces of the injured area to be treated at once. A disadvantage of this treatment is that the limb is placed in a dependent position, one that does not allow the limb to be elevated. Ice baths can be given in a whirlpool with a water temperature of 50 to 60°F for approximately ten to fifteen minutes.

Contrast Bath. A **contrast bath** is an alternation between a hot and cold

Contrast bath: Use of alternating hot and cold baths as therapy.

bath. Empirically, contrast baths have been found extremely helpful with edematous parts, such as a subacute sprained ankle. The alternate contraction and dilation of the blood vessels encourages a maximum increase in local blood flow.

Contrast baths are typically administered for twenty to thirty minutes, with treatment time consisting of a series of five-minute alternating hot and cold cycles. For a relaxing effect, the treatment ends in the hot bath. For a stimulating effect, the treatment ends with the cold bath. As with the whirlpool, the temperature of the hot bath should be appropriate for the body part.

Fluorimethane Spray. Sprays consisting of **fluorimethane** or ethyl chloride cause the greatest decrease in skin temperature. Rapid evaporation causes a decrease of up to twenty-eight degrees in a matter of seconds. This treatment is used primarily for its anesthetic effect and can potentially cause tissue damage (frostbite). Its use could be especially dangerous in the hands of an untrained person, such as an athlete. This modality should be used very judiciously, if at all.

Contraindications

Cold hypersensitivity is the principal contraindication of cryotherapy. In this condition, histamine or histaminelike substances are released in response to cold, causing a local or **systemic** reaction. Symptoms of this allergic response include **urticaria** (itching and elevated patches of skin that are either redder or paler than surrounding skin); sweating; facial flushing; puffy, itchy eyelids; and laryngeal edema. The signs usually disappear when the cold is removed. Severe reactions can cause **anaphylactic shock,** and **adrenalin** must be administered. Raynaud's disease, characterized by capillary spasm in the fingers and toes, is another contraindication of cryotherapy. Use ice with caution in the

area of superficial nerves because they are more susceptible to damage from the cold than musculoskeletal tissues. Do not use ice to treat a nosebleed.

Massage

Massage is one of the oldest forms of treatment for human ills but is used less in the United States for athletic injuries than in most other countries. In fact, the rule in many training rooms is "No massages or rubdowns given on a routine basis," the rationale being that if one athlete has a massage, everyone wants a massage. Many athletic trainers feel that massages are an inefficient use of time. This is a valid argument, despite the fact that massage is an effective modality.

Indications

Massage can break the vicious cycle between pain and muscle spasm by inducing relaxation. It indirectly improves circulation by increasing lymph flow and venous return and can soften scar tissue. The skilled use of hands required in massage can give an athlete encouragement and confidence. The laying on of the hands is an important psychological component that goes along with any form of medical treatment. An athlete may receive a rubdown (vigorous massage) to help prepare for optimum performance in competition, especially in swimming and track and field.

Massage Technique (Application)

The athlete must be relaxed and preferably reclining. If the athlete is supine, position a small pillow under the head and a smaller one under the knees. If the athlete is prone, place a pillow under the stomach, letting the toes extend over the bottom edge of the table (the head is given no support).

Massage: Manipulation of soft body tissue by rubbing, kneading, and tapping to induce therapeutic relaxation.

Fluorimethane spray: A spray of fluorimethane, used to cause rapid cooling. Use with great caution, if at all.

Systemic: Relating to the entire body.
Urticaria: A skin condition characterized by itching and elevated patches of skin that are either redder or paler than the surrounding skin.
Anaphylactic shock: Shock induced by an allergic reaction, e.g., bee sting.
Adrenalin (epinephrine): A hormone secreted by the adrenal medulla; it causes increased heart rate, increased contractility of the heart, vasodilation of blood vessels, and bronchiolar relaxation.

Apply a friction-reducing medium, such as oil or powder, with the first few strokes. Exert pressure *toward* the heart, to encourage lymph flow to go in a central direction. Massage the proximal areas before distal areas, to encourage lymph flow in a central direction.

The two most common massage strokes are effleurage and petrissage (Figures 13-8 and 13-9). **Effleurage,** which begins and ends a massage, is stroking with the palms of the hands and fingers. Pressure can vary from a light touch to one of considerable force. **Petrissage** is kneading or picking up of tissue. It is done in the areas of the body where the muscle can actually be picked up and wrung out.

Friction massage is moving superficial tissues over deeper tissues and is usually performed with the thumbs or heel of the hand. This technique is used to help break up adhesions, stretch connective tissue, and increase skin elasticity. Friction is applied perpendicular to the direction of the muscle fiber or scar tissue (see Chapter 8).

Contraindications

Although massage is thought to help relax tight muscles, it should never be used as a substitute for warm-up. Never use massage in the presence of **thrombophlebitis,** inflammation due to infection, or malignancy. Massage does not remove fat, increase muscle strength, or hasten nerve growth.

Manipulation

Manipulation is the passive movement of joints in an effort to improve range of motion, break up adhesions, and facilitate skeletal alignment. This technique is particularly useful for helping athletes with relatively poor flexibility from exercising muscles in restricted ranges of motion (runners, gymnasts, etc.) develop full ranges of motion in

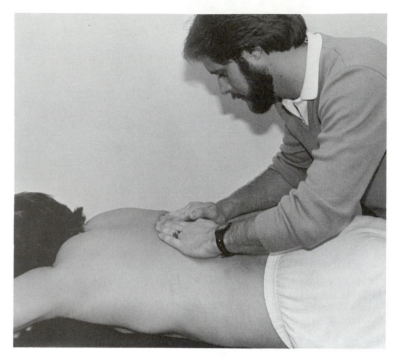

Figure 13-8 Effleurage is a massage technique involving deep stroking motions.

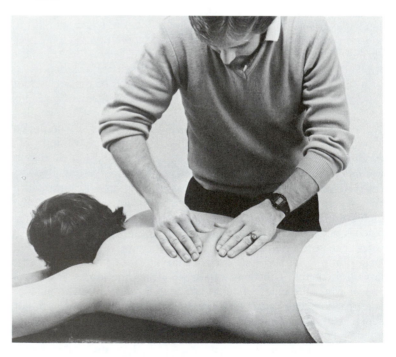

Figure 13-9 Petrissage is a massage technique involving kneading or picking up the muscles and other soft tissues.

their joints. Some states have specific licensing requirements for the application of certain manipulative techniques. The athletic trainer must be thoroughly trained in manipulative techniques before applying them. The use of joint manipulation carries with it the possibility of creating serious injury (particularly spinal manipulation). A description of manipulation techniques is beyond the scope of this book.

Indications

Joint manipulation is useful in athletes who have limited passive range of motion of a joint.

Contraindications

Joint mobilization should not be used in persons with inflamed joints, muscle spasms, or recent sprains (acute and early rehabilitation phases). This procedure is also contrainidicated during the acute phase of any soft tissue injury when significant inflammation is present.

Electrical Stimulation

Electrical stimulation has been used as a diagnostic procedure and as a treatment modality to stimulate denervated muscles and maintain metabolic activity. Recently, electrical stimulation has been extensively used in sports medicine to relieve pain, maintain or increase range of motion, strengthen muscle, prevent atrophy, and reduce edema. Advances in electronic technology have made electrical stimulation instruments more portable, precise, safe, and convenient (Figure 13-10).

Types

Various types of electric current are used for electrical stimulation, including galvanic, faradic, pulsatile, and al-

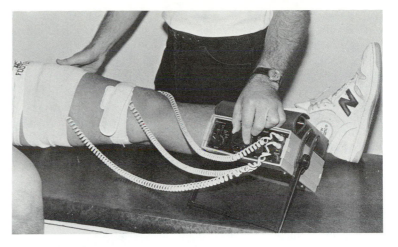

Figure 13-10 Electrical muscle stimulation of the quadriceps. Stimulation has been shown effective in increasing strength, particularly when normal movement is not possible.

ternating. Galvanic and faradic stimulators have been prevalent in physical therapy, but the use of assorted pulsatile currents is becoming more common with the advent of small, portable electrical muscle stimulators (EMS). Alternating (common household) current is seldom used in the United States for neuromuscular stimulation.

Galvanic or direct **current** is a flow of electrons in only one direction. The electron flow is changed to ion flow at the electrode-tissue interface. Clinically, galvanic current has been used for applications such as pain relief, edema reduction, and stimulation of denervated muscle and as a tool for iontophoresis (the transfer of ions from a medium through the skin into the body). Galvanic current is not used to strengthen innervated muscle because a response occurs only when the current is turned on or off. Recently, pulsed galvanic current modalities have become popular, but the pulses are too short to allow adequate stimulus for muscle contraction. These pulsed galvanic current machines do appear effective for reducing pain and edema.

Faradic or alternating **current** is electrons moving in either a positive or negative direction and then reversing

Effleurage: A massage stroke that involves stroking with the palms of the hands and fingers.
Petrissage: A massage stroke that involves kneading and picking up of tissue.
Thrombophlebitis: Inflammation of a vein.

Galvanic current: Direct current; a flow of electrons traveling in only one direction.

Faradic current: Alternating current; a flow of electrons traveling in either a positive or negative direction.

Principles of Injury Prevention and Management

themselves. This current has been effectively used for both pain relief and the contraction of innervated muscles. Table 13-1 describes general characteristics of faradic and galvanic current.

Pulsatile current follows a rectangular pattern, during which the current rises rapidly to a given amplitude, levels off, and then falls rapidly. The ion flow may be uni- or bidirectional.

High-voltage, high-frequency stimulators are receiving increasing notice here and are widely used in the Soviet Union. They have been used to strengthen the muscles of healthy athletes. Unfortunately, the effectiveness of this type of electrical stimulation has not been adequately documented experimentally.

There are several differences between muscle contractions initiated within the central nervous system and those initiated by electrical stimulation. **Motor neurons** excite motor units **asynchronously** (firing at different times and rates), which allows for smooth contraction of muscle, requires less energy, and prolongs the onset of fatigue. With electrical stimulation, the motor nerves fire synchronously. This is metabolically expensive and fatiguing because the same nerves and muscle fibers are repeatedly stimulated. The higher the stimulation frequency, the quicker the muscle fatigues. When innervated muscle is electrically stimulated, the muscle fiber's motor nerve is the chosen site for stimulation because it has a lower threshold than the muscle tissue itself.

The pattern of excitability also differs in the physiological and artificial electrical modes of stimulation. In physiologically stimulated muscle, the small, slow motor units are usually excited first, followed by the larger, faster motor units. When muscles are stimulated to contract by electrical stimulation, the pattern is reversed: The large, fast units are excited before the smaller, slower units. In addition, the fast fibers are more superficial to the smaller fibers. Surface stimulation is more effective in stimulating large fibers. Thus, muscle contractions initiated by electrical stimulation cause fatigue much faster than those elicited by voluntary control.

Table 13-1 *Characteristics of Faradic and Galvanic Current*

Faradic or Alternating Current

EMS or FES

- 25–30 pulses/s
- 500 μs-pulse width (approx.)
- Increases strength
- Retards biochemical deconditioning in muscle caused by immobilization (decreased oxidative enzymes, etc.)

TNS

- 70–150 pulses/s
- Less than 130 μs-pulse width
- Relieves pain
- Induces muscle relaxation

Galvanic or Direct Current

Pulses Galvanic Stimulation

- 2–20 μs-pulse width
- 0–500 v (high voltage)
- Reduces pain, edema, and muscle spasm

Motor neurons: Nerve cells that carry information from the CNS to muscle cells in the periphery. Stimulation of the neurons causes muscle contraction. Also called efferent nerves.

Asynchronous: Out of synchrony; not coordinated.

Application

Although the manufacturer's instructions should be studied, there are general considerations when using any form of electrical stimulation. The skin must be clean to get good contact with the **electrode**. Conductivity is enhanced with an electrode gel or water. Electrodes are generally placed on the same side of the body because of the possible danger of the current crossing the heart or reproductive organs.

The characteristics of the electrodes are critical to the delivery of electrical

Electrode: One of two ends of an electric circuit. Clinically, electrodes are used in electrocardiography, TNS, and electrical muscle stimulation.

stimulation. The electrode size is important in regulating current density because the current density increases as the electrode becomes smaller. The depth of stimulation can be controlled by the distance between the electrodes: The stimulation will be superficial if the electrodes are placed close together, deeper if they are placed farther apart. Conduction can be facilitated by reducing the skin's impedance by using an electrode gel and cleaning the skin before applying the electrode.

The literature is ambivalent about the effectiveness of this modality. Important factors such as the ideal voltage, frequency, and waveform for increasing muscle strength have not been agreed upon. Factors such as joint position during the treatment may also be important.

Contraindications

General contraindications include use with pacemakers or stimulation over the carotid sinus or a pregnant uterus.

Transcutaneous Neural Stimulation

Transcutaneous neural stimulation (TNS) was discussed in Chapter 8 (see Box 8-1, p. 131) in conjunction with the gate theory of pain. It has gained popularity among some physical therapists as a technique for reducing acute and chronic musculoskeletal pain, but it is not widely used by athletic trainers. TNS is thought to work by blocking sensory pain pathways and stimulating the production of pain-reducing hormones such as endorphins and enkephalins. The stimulator (Figure 13-1) can be used during treatment sessions or worn continuously by the athlete. More research is needed to establish the effectiveness and practicality of this and similar devices, such as the neuroprobe, before their use becomes a mainstay technique in athletic training.

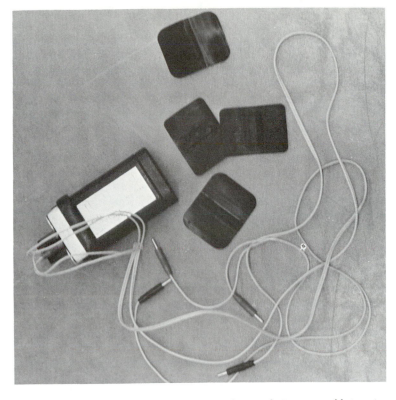

Figure 13-11 A transcutaneous nerve stimulator, a device many athletic trainers use to control pain. This TNS unit is composed of impulse generator, lead wires, and electrodes (black squares).

Taping

Taping is a skill that requires many hours to master. Neatness and speed of application are the trademarks of the expert. Taping serves many important functions, including limiting motion, compressing injured parts, increasing stability, and improving kinesthetic sense. Specific taping techniques are extensively detailed in the appendix.

Proper positioning of the part to be taped is the most important consideration. For example, taping an ankle in a down or relaxed position may increase the chance of reinjury. At the very least, improper positioning makes the taping procedure a waste of time.

Make sure the skin is clean and dry before applying tape. Tape will not stick to oily, wet, powdered, or greasy surfaces. Before applying tape, let the skin temperature return to normal if the athlete has just received thermal therapy. Applying an adherent to the skin before taping can help set the tape, protect the skin (although some individuals are allergic to adherent), and facilitate removal of the strapping. Protect prominent bony ridges and tendons with a lubricant and gauze or foam pads.

Have the athlete shave the area if the tape will be applied directly to the skin, a practice that minimizes slipping. An **underwrap** is generally used when the body part is taped daily because skin can become irritated from frequent applications.

The proper tape width is important. Use narrow strips for small curved surfaces, wider tape for larger areas. Generally, each strip should overlap the previously applied strip by one-half its width. Unless the tape stretches, never wind it continuously around a limb or it may cut off circulation. The tape application must be smooth and wrinkle-free to prevent blisters and present a professional looking "tape job." There should be a purpose for applying each strip of tape.

Do not pull up the tape quickly when removing it. Pull it back over itself while holding down the skin as the tape is removed. This method allows the application of force in both directions with a minimum of pulling on the skin. Check the skin for irritation. If skin is irritated, treat it with a recommended antiseptic (Chapter 23). Protect the irritated areas with a dressing if the skin is irritated and the strapping must be repeated.

Protective Padding

Protective padding is used mainly to prevent injury and is part of the uniform for contact sports like football, hockey, and lacrosse. For other sports,

protective pads may be worn to protect a previous injury. In some cases, padding is worn in noncontact sports to protect body parts that are subject to repeated blows or falls (e.g., a volleyball player wears knee pads to protect against repeated **abrasions** and **contusions** to the knee). An athletic trainer must be skilled at recognizing the indications for protective padding, fitting the pads, fabricating pads for unique situations, and inspecting pads for breakdown and wearing.

Padding disperses and absorbs forces. Pads disperse the forces of a blow by spreading them over a larger area than the blow's initial point of contact. Harder materials are better able to disperse forces. Pads are typically constructed of fiberboard covered with vinyl or molded polyethylene, but the type of material used in a pad depends upon the part to be protected.

The **donut pad** lets the force be dispersed to a specific area surrounding the affected part and is commonly used to protect blisters (Figure 13-12). For example, a hole is cut in one-eighth-inch adhesive foam or felt and the pad

Abrasion: A wound caused by a portion of the skin being scraped away.
Contusion: A bruise.

Underwrap: Used in taping to protect the skin from the adhesive tape. Usually composed of a thin layer of foam rubber.

Donut pad: A pad, usually of felt or foam rubber, with a hole in its middle. The pad protects the injury and takes pressure off the traumatized part.

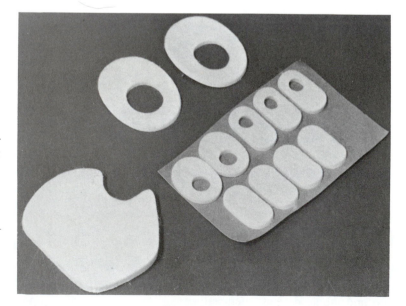

Figure 13-12 Donut blister pads. These pads, which come in all sizes, protect the injury and prevent further irritation.

is applied to the area, with the blister occupying the donut hole. Pads can also be constructed with the center raised from the body, a technique used for thigh pads. The force is dispersed to the area of the pad that makes contact with the body.

Pads can be designed to absorb blows by constructing them with closed-cell foam, air or water cells, or a semiliquid, highly viscous material. These pads are designed to absorb a blow and then quickly rebound to their normal size.

Most protective pads incorporate dispersive and absorptive characteristics into their design. For example, many pads are constructed so that a hard outer layer disperses the force of a blow over a larger area while a softer, inner material absorbs the remainder of the force into the body.

All protective equipment, including padding, must be regularly checked. Signs of wear include split or cracked outer shell, flattened contour, and loss of resiliency. An overly hard or soft pad will transfer the force directly to the body rather than dispersing or absorbing it. Protective pads must not be excessively heavy and must stay in place without interfering with normal range of motion.

Athletic trainers must often fabricate pads that are not commercially available to satisfy an athlete's individual requirements. The artistic athletic trainer can make highly satisfactory pads with available materials. For example, a removable cast or splint can be fashioned for a thumb or finger using materials such as Orthoplast, fiberglass casting material, or even collodion and gauze. Appropriate padding is added after the cast has formed and dried. The athlete can have the splint or cast taped to the affected part for sports activity (hard pads worn at or below the elbow are usually prohibited in most contact sports). Never construct pads in such a way that they can be used as weapons against opponents.

Braces

Bracing is a controversial subject. Some sports medicine physicians and athletic trainers believe that if an athlete has to rely on a brace, the athlete should not participate. Others believe that even if the athlete is fully rehabilitated from an injury, there may be laxity, which is justification for protection.

A variety of braces are commercially available to support various joints. The **derotation brace** (Lennox-Hill) has become very popular for athletes with an anterior cruciate-deficient knee (Figure 13-13). Myriad other braces are available, such as the McDavid Knee Guards, the Anderson knee stabilizer, Boston brace (low back), ankle joint T brace (ankle), and the cervical collar (neck). These braces provide various degrees of protection and support.

Derotation brace: A brace used in anterior cruciate-deficient knees; principally protects against knee hyperextension.

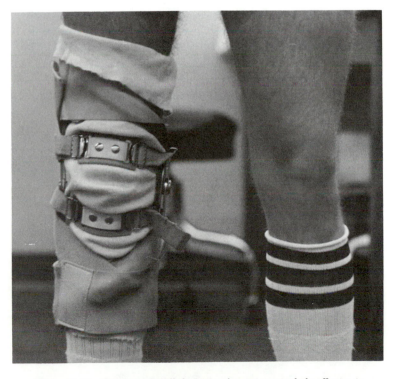

Figure 13-13 The Lennox-Hill derotation brace is particularly effective in preventing hyperextension of the knee.

References

Andreasson, G., and B. Edberg. Rheological properties of medical tapes used to prevent athletic injuries. *Textile Research Journal* 53:225–230, 1983.

Beard, G. A history of massage technic. *Physical Therapy Review* 32:613–614, 1952.

Benton, L. A., L. L. Baker, B. R. Bowman, and R. L. Waters. *Functional Electrical Stimulation: A Practical Clinical Guide.* Downey, Calif.: Rancho Los Amigos, 1981.

Cyriax, J. *Treatment by Manipulation and Deep Massage.* New York: Paul B. Hoeber, 1959.

Ersek, R. A. Transcutaneous electrical neurostimulation: a new therapeutic modality for controlling pain. *Clinical Orthopaedics and Related Research* 128:314–324, 1977.

Fahey, T. D., M. Harvey, R. Schroeder, and F. Fergeson. The effects of sex differences and joint position on electrical stimulation modulated strength increases. *Medicine and Science in Sports and Exercise* 17:144–147, 1985.

Hughes, L. Y., and D. M. Stetts. A comparison of ankle taping and a semirigid support. *The Physician and Sportsmedicine* 11:99–103, 1983.

Kaufman, W. C. The hand and foot in the cold. *The Physician and Sportsmedicine* 11:156–168, 1983.

Knight, K. The effects of hypothermia on inflammation and swelling. *Athletic Training* 11:1–8, 1976.

Krusen, F. H. (ed.). *Handbook of Physical Medicine and Rehabilitation.* Philadelphia: W. B. Saunders, 1972.

Malina, R. M., L. B. Plagenz, and G. L. Rarick. Effect of exercise upon the measurable supporting strength of cloth and tape wraps. *Research Quarterly for Exercise and Sport* 34:158–165, 1963.

McMaster, W. C. Cryotherapy. *The Physician and Sportsmedicine* 10:112–119, 1982.

Rarick, G. L., G. Bigley, R. Karst, et al. The measurable support of the ankle joint by conventional methods of taping. *Journal of Bone and Joint Surgery* 44:1183–1190, 1962.

Romero, J. A., T. L. Sanford, R. V. Schroeder, and T. D. Fahey. The effects of electrical stimulation of normal quadriceps on strength and girth. *Medicine and Science in Sports and Exercise* 14:194–197, 1982.

Scull, C. W. Massage—physiological basis. *Archives of Physical Medicine and Rehabilitation* 26:159–167, 1945.

Smith, M. J. Electrical stimulation for relief of musculoskeletal pain. *The Physician and Sportsmedicine* 11:47–55, 1983.

Smith, M. J. Muscle fiber types: their relationship to athletic training and rehabilitation. *Orthopedic Clinics of North America* 14:403–411, 1983.

Tappan, F. M. *Massage Technique: A Case Method Approach.* New York: Macmillan, 1961.

Tappan, F. M. "Massage," in *Encyclopedia of Sports Sciences and Medicine,* L. A. Larson, ed., New York: Macmillan, 1971, pp. 1594–1596.

PART THREE

Prevention, Treatment, and Rehabilitation of Specific Injuries

Head Injuries

14

H EAD injuries warrant critical concern because they can have catastrophic consequences. These injuries are relatively common in contact sports like football, rugby, boxing, and hockey, but they also occur in other sports. Accurately assessing head injuries requires knowledge of **neuroanatomy** and physiology and a pervasive awareness of neural abnormalities. Never underestimate any head injury because even apparently minor trauma can cause more serious injury or death. This chapter discusses the nature and management of head injuries, including concussions, ear, eye, nose and maxillofacial, soft tissue, and dental injuries.

Anatomy

The scalp is the outermost anatomical structure of the head and the first part to receive trauma from external forces. The scalp is the skull's protective covering; when the head is traumatized, the scalp absorbs some shock, lessening the impact to deeper structures.

The skull is located at the superior (upper) end of the vertebral column and is divided into the cranium and the face. Within the cranium is the brain,

a large soft mass of nerve tissue. The brain's blood supply comes from two carotid and two vertebral arteries. The internal and external jugular veins drain the venous blood.

The cranium is composed of eight bones (Figure 14-1, pp. 217–218): frontal, occipital, ethmoid, sphenoid, parietal (two), and temporal (two). The structures of the face are the eyes, eyeballs, eyebrows, ears, nose, mouth, cheeks, and chin. (Figures 14-3, 14-4, and 14-6 illustrate the surface anatomy of the ear, eye, and nose and lips, respectively; see pp. 224, 225, 227.)

Three fibrous membranes, the dura mater, arachnoid, and pia mater, lie directly beneath the skull. The **dura mater** is a dense, fibrous, inelastic sheath that encloses and protects the brain and provides a firm structure for venous sinuses, which return blood from the brain to the heart. The **arachnoid** is an extremely delicate, paperthin membrane lying directly under the dura mater. It produces cerebrospinal fluid (CSF). The **pia mater** is a very fine, transparent, fairly strong structure intimately associated with the surface of the brain. The subarachnoid space, the void between the arachnoid and pia mater, contains the **cerebrospinal fluid**, which acts as a cushion, thus diminishing shock to the brain.

Neuroanatomy: The study of the structure of the nervous system.

Dura mater: A white, fibrous membrane that serves as the outermost covering of the brain and spinal cord.

Arachnoid: A membrane covering the brain; it lies between the dura mater and the subarachnoid space and pia mater.

Pia mater: A delicate membrane that serves as the innermost covering of the brain and spinal cord.

Cerebrospinal fluid (CSF): A clear, watery fluid produced by the arachnoid membrane; CSF fills the ventricles of the brain and subarachnoid spaces of the brain and spinal cord.

Injuries to the Head

Head injuries in sports are the most serious and perhaps most commonly misevaluated. Direct or indirect blows to the head can injure the skull, the brain, or the blood vessels between the brain and the skull. Cerebral concussions are by far the most common head injuries athletes sustain. An examination of head injuries should include evaluation of **vital signs, neurological** status, and motor function. Specific techniques are discussed throughout the chapter.

Concussions

Head injuries result from static or dynamic mechanical forces. Static forces are applied slowly and occur in crushing-type injuries. Dynamic forces are implicated in most athletic head injuries and are involved in both direct and indirect blows. Direct blows include the jab to the face in boxing, the stick to the head in hockey, and the helmeted head to the body in football. Indirect blows stem from whiplash motions caused by sudden accelerations or decelerations. For example, when a hockey player falls on the base of his spine, the force may be transmitted to the skull and cause a concussion. The extent of injury depends upon the amount and duration of forces applied to the head. Because of their insidious nature, refer all concussions to a physician.

Concussion is caused by physical trauma to the brain and is characterized by neural aberrations such as unconsciousness, disturbed vision, and upset equilibrium. Concussions are mild, moderate, or severe.

The mild concussion is transient and the most common and is sometimes described in athletic jargon as "having your bell rung." Athletes who sustain more serious concussion may exhibit

Athletes participating in contact sports like ice hockey face increased risk of sustaining head injury.

postconcussion syndrome: headache, inability to concentrate, irritability, and loss of certain cognitive functions. Severe concussions may be life-threatening. The severity of concussion can be partially determined by a brief neurological examination.

Mild Concussion (First Degree). A mild concussion is usually caused by moderate forces. Neurological function is very briefly disturbed, and there is either transient or no loss of consciousness. The athlete may experience impaired performance, mental confusion, memory loss, dizziness, light-headedness, blurred vision, and mild **tinnitus.**

Any athlete who sustains a mild concussion should be removed from the game or practice for several minutes and carefully watched for symptoms of fatigue, disorientation, and abnormal behavior. Under no circumstances let the athlete resume play until he or she is perfectly oriented, moves with normal dexterity, and appropriately answers all questions. (Note that the physician

Vital signs: Heart rate, ventilatory rate, level of consciousness, blood pressure, and body temperature.

Neurological: Pertaining to the nervous system.

Tinnitus: Unusual sound sensations in the ear, e.g., ringing or buzzing.

Concussion: Brain injury caused by the skull being jarred or shaken; characterized by unconsciousness, dizziness, cold sweat, and visual disturbance.

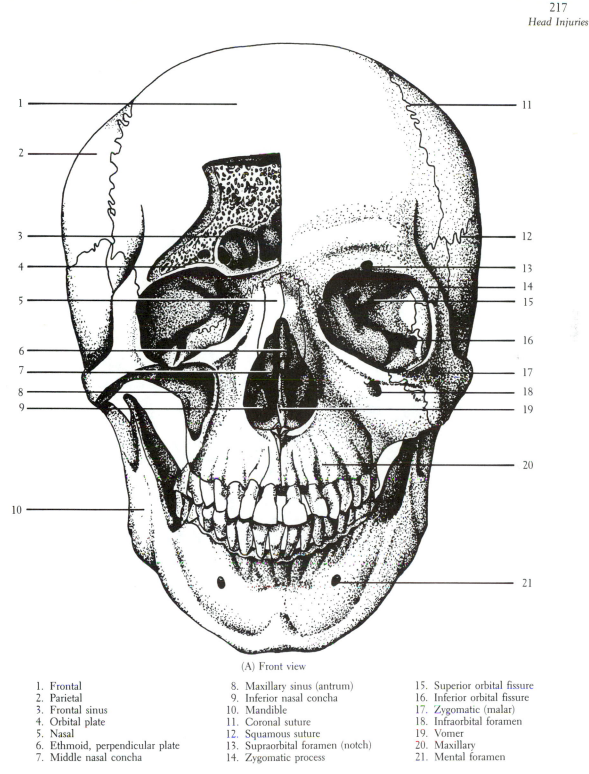

(A) Front view

1. Frontal	8. Maxillary sinus (antrum)	15. Superior orbital fissure
2. Parietal	9. Inferior nasal concha	16. Inferior orbital fissure
3. Frontal sinus	10. Mandible	17. Zygomatic (malar)
4. Orbital plate	11. Coronal suture	18. Infraorbital foramen
5. Nasal	12. Squamous suture	19. Vomer
6. Ethmoid, perpendicular plate	13. Supraorbital foramen (notch)	20. Maxillary
7. Middle nasal concha	14. Zygomatic process	21. Mental foramen

Figure 14-1 The human skull. (From Crouch, J. E. *Introduction to Human Anatomy*, 6th ed. Palo Alto, Calif.: Mayfield Publishing Co., 1983, pp. 45, 48.)

(continued on next page)

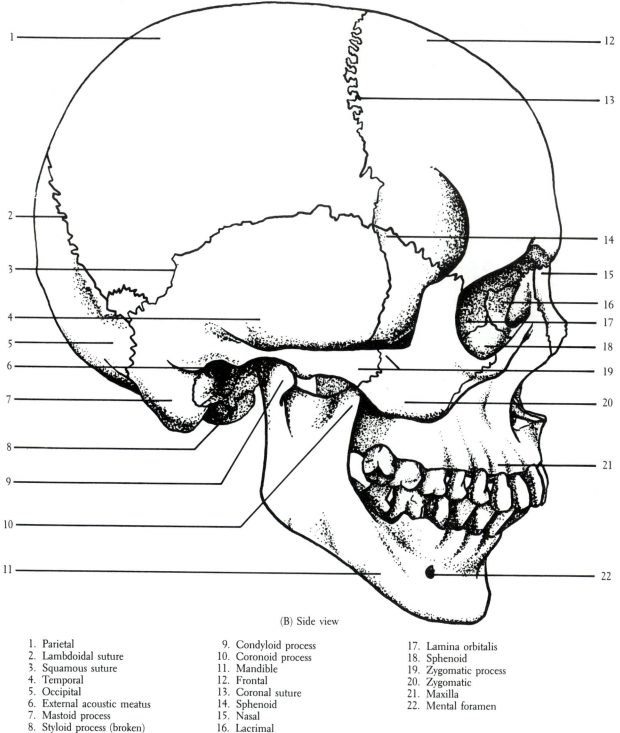

(B) Side view

1. Parietal
2. Lambdoidal suture
3. Squamous suture
4. Temporal
5. Occipital
6. External acoustic meatus
7. Mastoid process
8. Styloid process (broken)

9. Condyloid process
10. Coronoid process
11. Mandible
12. Frontal
13. Coronal suture
14. Sphenoid
15. Nasal
16. Lacrimal

17. Lamina orbitalis
18. Sphenoid
19. Zygomatic process
20. Zygomatic
21. Maxilla
22. Mental foramen

Figure 14-1 *(continued)*

makes this decision.) Verbal examination of the concussion victim should stress information-processing skills, such as assignments in specific plays, rather than static memory abilities, such as recognition of names and dates. Injured athletes may appear normal, but they should be watched closely because the severity of symptoms varies from one time to another.

Moderate Concussion (Second Degree). With a moderate concussion there is loss of consciousness for up to three to four minutes, followed by transient mental confusion, retrograde amnesia (loss of memory for events leading up to the injury), headache, moderate tinnitus, dizziness, and **ataxia.** Recovery is usually complete within five minutes, but some individuals may continue to have symptoms for several weeks. The athlete who sustains a moderate concussion should be removed from the game or practice and not permitted to reenter. This athlete should be prohibited from practice and game participation for several days or longer if headache, visual disturbances, or any neurological abnormality persists. (The physician makes these decisions.)

Severe Concussion (Third Degree). With a severe concussion there is unconsciousness lasting longer than five minutes, followed by mental confusion, prolonged retrograde amnesia, severe tinnitus, dizziness, abnormal eye signs, and marked ataxia. Aberrant neurological eye signs include dilated or irregular pupils, poor light accommodation by the pupils, blurred vision, and **nystagmus.** Recovery is slow (longer than five minutes) and usually accompanied by postconcussion syndrome. An athlete with a severe concussion should be sent directly to the hospital for evaluation and observation because of the possibility of expanding intracranial injury. Most experts recommend that the physician not let the athlete return to play for a full season.

Putting It into Practice 14-1 summarizes the signs and symptoms of the three degrees of concussion and includes a checklist for initial and follow-up examination (see p. 220). A copy of the list, which identifies procedures for monitoring the person's condition, should be sent home with the athlete to roommates or to the parents. If any of these conditions appears, the athlete may have a serious head injury and should be taken to a hospital for further examination.

Concussion Evaluation. The first step in evaluating the concussion is determining the athlete's state of consciousness. The athlete may appear alert for a short time but then lapse into unconsciousness. This event is known as the "lucid interval," which may last from a few minutes to an hour or two. The presence of the lucid interval suggests an expanding **intracranial hemorrhage.** When the athlete is conscious, assess his or her mental status by asking questions that determine orientation: "What is your name?" "What day is today?" "What are you playing?"

During the questioning, check the equality (equal opening) of the pupils, observe eye movements for coordination and tracking, and check for nystagmus. Measure the pulse rate and monitor any change. Next, have the athlete stand with arms outstretched to the side, fingers spread, and eyes closed. If one arm tends to drift downward and outward, a brain contusion or formation of a blood clot on the side of the head opposite the drifting arm is indicated. The **Romberg test,** in which the athlete stands with feet together, arms held at sides, and then closes his or her eyes, is another test for an expanding clot. Closing the eyes should not cause any loss of posture or swaying or falling toward one side. For even further assessment, ask the athlete to repeat a number sequence.

As discussed, do not let athletes

Ataxia: Loss of muscular coordination.

Intracranial hemorrhage: Bleeding within the skull.

Nystagmus: Involuntary movement of the eyes in a vertical, horizontal, or rotary direction.

Romberg test: A test to detect loss of awareness of body position. Test is positive if the athlete sways or loses balance when standing with feet together and eyes closed.

PUTTING IT INTO PRACTICE 14-1

Signs and Symptoms of the Three Degrees of Concussion

Signs	Mild	Moderate	Severe
Consciousness	No loss	Transistory loss (up to 4 min)	Prolonged loss (over 5 min)
Mental confusion	Slight	Momentary	Lasting 5 or more min
Memory loss	None or very transient	Definite mild retrograde amnesia	Prolonged retrograde amnesia
Tinnitus (ringing in ears)	Mild	Moderate	Severe
Dizziness	Mild	Moderate	Severe
Unsteadiness	Usually none	Moderate	Marked
General recovery	Very rapid	Complete in 5 min	Slow, longer than 5 min

Signs and Symptoms of Concussion: Checklist

Signs	Present	Absent
1. Increasing headache	( )	( )
2. Nausea and vomiting	( )	( )
3. Inequality of pupils	( )	( )
4. Disorientation	( )	( )
5. Progressive impairment of consciousness	( )	( )
6. Gradual rise in blood pressure	( )	( )
7. Decrease in pulse rate	( )	( )

reenter practice or competition until they can demonstrate adequate information-processing skills. It cannot be over-emphasized that this decision should be made only after a physician has made a thorough evaluation. See Putting It into Practice 14-2.

Epidural Hematoma

Epidural hematoma is a rapid accumulation of blood between the skull and the dura mater (Figure 14-2, p. 222). It usually follows a skull fracture, which damages the middle meningeal artery. Typically, the patient is uncon-

scious for a short time and then returns to normal. An hour or more later, the person may experience drowsiness and headache, followed by vomiting, dilation of the pupil on the same side of the hematoma, and weakness on the opposite side of the hematoma. The formation of the hematoma leads to rapid compression of the brain stem, causing death unless the pressure is released and the bleeding controlled.

Subdural Hematoma

A **subdural hematoma** is hemorrhage in the subdural space, the area between

Epidural hematoma: Bleeding between the skull and dura mater.

Subdural hematoma: Bleeding in the subdural space, the area between the dura mater and the arachnoid.

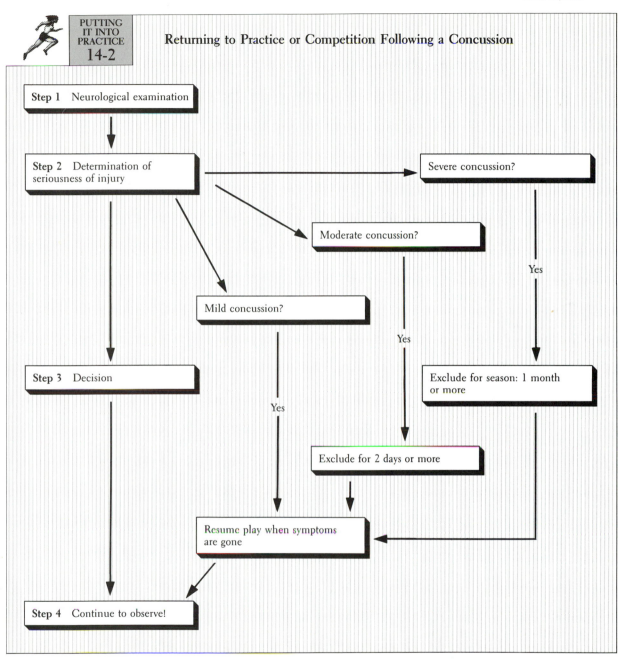

PUTTING IT INTO PRACTICE 14-2

Returning to Practice or Competition Following a Concussion

Step 1   Neurological examination

Step 2   Determination of seriousness of injury

Severe concussion?

Moderate concussion?

Mild concussion?

Step 3   Decision

Yes

Exclude for season: 1 month or more

Yes

Yes

Exclude for 2 days or more

Resume play when symptoms are gone

Step 4   Continue to observe!

the dura mater and the arachnoid. Cerebral veins that extend from the brain to the dura transverse this space. A blow to one side of the head can contuse or lacerate the brain and tear the vessels on the opposite side of the head as the brain is moved away from the skull. This tearing of the cerebral veins causes subdural hematoma.

Acute. Acute subdural hematoma is the most frequent cause of death from trauma in contact sports. Following the injury, which is caused by a direct blow, the athlete usually remains unconscious and shows signs of rapidly increasing intracranial pressure, such as dilated pupils on the affected side, diminished pulse rate, vomiting, and **dyspnea.** Even if the injury is treated early, the mortality rate among affected athletes is extremely high, and many athletes succumb without the benefit of neurosurgical consultation.

Chronic. Chronic subdural hematoma is always caused by a direct blow to the head. Following the blow, there is a relatively small amount of bleeding in the subdural space. After about a week, a neomembrane (a false or new membrane) surrounds the hematoma, gradually increasing its size by the process of osmosis. Initial symptoms are mild to nonexistent but may include persistent headache, vomiting, or changed behavior. With time, the headache may become more severe. Other symptoms may include loss of appetite, vomiting, personality change, drowsiness, blurred vision, and gait disturbance. Surgery is required to remove the hematoma. The symptoms quickly disappear following surgery, and recovery is usually complete.

Intracerebral Hematoma

An intracerebral hematoma is hemorrhage within the cerebrum (brain substance), typically resulting from the athlete's head striking an immovable playing surface, such as a basketball court, boxing ring, ice, or ski slope. The injury usually occurs on the side of the brain opposite the point of contact between the playing surface and skull.

Athletes with this injury will not necessarily lose consciousness or suffer significant neurological impairment. The injury is characterized by persistent headache, periods of confusion, and amnesia. The symptoms are caused by increased intracranial pressure that results in cerebral ischemia and hypoxia.

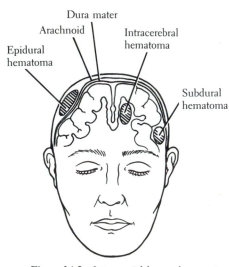

Figure 14-2 Intracranial hemorrhage: epidural, subdural, and intracerebral.

Dyspnea: Labored or uncomfortable breathing.

As with other intracranial injuries, intracerebral hematoma is a medical emergency. If the athlete does not lose consciousness, personnel may treat the injury too casually. Failure to obtain adequate medical treatment may permanently impair an injured athlete's neurological, intellectual, and psychological functions.

The medical-treatment goal of intracerebral hematoma (and any intracranial hematoma) is to reduce intracranial pressure. Initial management procedures (performed by a physician) include (1) establishing a viable airway and inducing hyperventilation (with a manual airbag or increasing the carbon dioxide content of the inspired air), (2) administering drugs such as corticosteroids, mannitol, and barbiturates to control inflammation and lower the brain's metabolism, and (3) performing a CT scan to assess the nature and severity of the head injury. Surgical removal of the hematoma may be indicated if the injury is large.

Skull Fractures

A severe blow to the unprotected head may cause skull fractures. Such fractures are most common in sports played on hard surfaces and in those in which a ball and club are used. Skull fractures are classified as (1) **closed** (simple), which do not involve a break in the overlying skin or membrane; and (2) **open** (compound), which do involve a tear in the covering adjacent to the fracture.

Fractures in the bones at the base of the skull may cause discoloration around the eyes and nose, bleeding from the ears, and dripping of clear cerebrospinal fluid from the nose. These injuries are sometimes accompanied by **Battle's sign,** which is **ecchymosis** just behind the ear caused by the involvement of the basilar artery. A fracture on either side of the temple may damage the middle meningeal artery, causing an epidural hematoma. Fracture of one of the frontal sinuses is the most common cause of cerebrospinal fluid's leaking from the nose. When CSF is leaking from the nose, do not tightly bandage or pack the nose, ears, or the wound because preventing CSF from escaping may increase intracranial pressure, which could worsen a brain injury.

Emergency treatment for a skull fracture includes (1) monitoring vital signs, (2) initiating emergency ventilation and circulation procedures (CPR or artificial ventilation) if necessary, (3) obtaining medical assistance, (4) treating any bleeding by dressing the wound from its edges (the goal is to minimize any increase in intracranial pressure), (4) covering open wounds with a sterile dressing, (5) splinting the cervical spine (the neck may also be injured—see Chapter 15), and (6) continuing to periodically evaluate vital signs until medical help arrives.

Prevention of Head Injuries

The incidence and risk of head injuries vary with the sport. Head injuries

can be prevented by having athletes wear well-maintained, high-quality equipment and observing injury-prevention rules. For example, in football the number of head injuries has been reduced because of improved helmets and the banning of **spearing.** In diving, head injuries can be prevented by ensuring that athletes not attempt dives that are beyond their ability.

After a head injury occurs, complications can be minimized by careful observation and proper medical referral. Continue to closely observe the athlete for signs of secondary brain damage, even after an apparently mild injury. Refer athletes who have been unconscious or who have experienced more than a few minutes of retrograde amnesia to a neurologist for further examination. Do not let an athlete who is suffering from postconcussion syndrome return to play until all symptoms have been resolved and a physician has cleared the person. The effects of repeated mild head injuries are cumulative and can lead to more serious injury. The physician and athletic trainer should not let coaches, players, and fans pressure them into prematurely returning an athlete to play.

Ear Injuries

External

External ear injuries are common occurrences in athletics and typically include **contusions, abrasions,** and **lacerations.** In a simple ear contusion, the ear is compressed against the **mastoid;** proper care may prevent a more serious injury. Carefully examine the ear for hemorrhage between the cartilage and its covering, the **perichondrium** (Figure 4-3). Apply an ice pack to minimize local **edema,** even in the absence of early hemorrhage.

A hematoma that forms between the perichondrium and the cartilage of the

Closed fracture: A broken bone in which the skin is not broken; also called simple fracture.

Open fracture: A broken bone in which the skin is broken; also called compound fracture.

Spearing: In football, an illegal blocking and tackling technique in which the tackler's head is the first point of contact with an opponent. This technique has caused many serious head and neck injuries.

Battle's sign: Discoloration behind the ear that often accompanies a fracture at the base of the skull.

Ecchymosis: Black and blue coloring under the skin, caused by blood escaping from the vasculature as a result of injury.

Contusion: A bruise.

Abrasion: A wound caused by a portion of the skin being scraped away.

Laceration: A wound caused by the skin tissue being torn.

Mastoid: A portion of the temporal bone that projects downward behind the ear.

Perichondrium: A fibrous membrane that covers nonarticular cartilage, e.g., the cartilage of the external ear.

Edema: Swelling; a collection of fluid in a tissue space.

ear should be aspirated (drained) by a physician as soon as possible to prevent cosmetic deformity (i.e., "cauliflower ear"). Following **aspiration,** apply a contoured pressure bandage (an Ace bandage) to force the perichondrium against the underlying cartilage and prevent reaccumulation of the hematoma. If the hematoma is not evacuated, the blood filters through the soft tissues and thickens the **subcutaneous** and perichondrium tissues. The end result is cauliflower ear, in which the delicate cartilaginous contours of the external ear are lost.

Internal

Internal ear injuries are rare in athletics, but of those that do occur, **tympanic membrane** rupture is most common. This injury is caused by a blow to the side of the head and results in pain, slight bleeding from the ear, and a feeling of fullness in the ear. This injury may also occur in scuba diving from pressure changes and may cause **vertigo** and nausea, tinnitus, and hearing loss. The injury usually heals itself spontaneously. If the extent of the damage is questionable, refer the athlete to a physician.

Swimmer's Ear

Swimmer's ear (otitis externa) is a common superficial skin infection that afflicts swimmers and people who inadequately dry their ears after showering. It is caused by bacteria that develop from a change in the **pH** of the ear canal's skin. Symptoms include itching and pain. A gentle tug on the ear lobe (helix) will cause increased pain and fluid to drain from the ear.

The infection can be prevented by using ear drops that dry the canal. After swimming, the athlete should first gently wash the ear. Then, using a dropper, the athlete should fill the ear

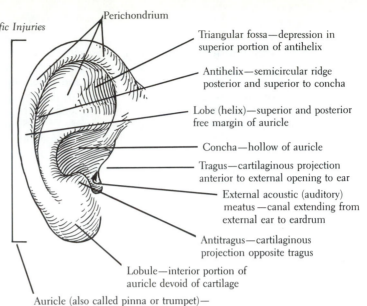

Perichondrium

Triangular fossa—depression in superior portion of antihelix

Antihelix—semicircular ridge posterior and superior to concha

Lobe (helix)—superior and posterior free margin of auricle

Concha—hollow of auricle

Tragus—cartilaginous projection anterior to external opening to ear

External acoustic (auditory) meatus—canal extending from external ear to eardrum

Antitragus—cartilaginous projection opposite tragus

Lobule—interior portion of auricle devoid of cartilage

Auricle (also called pinna or trumpet)—portion of external ear not contained in head

Figure 14-3 Lateral view of the right ear.

with a mild boric acid solution (the boric acid reestablishes the proper pH). The athlete should turn his or her head to let the solution and water drain. If the athlete cannot tolerate the boric acid solution or the solution is not effective, alternative solutions containing antibiotics are available by prescription. Refer the person to a physician if pain or itching persists.

Eye Injuries

Eye injuries must be evaluated *very* carefully because they may cause permanent damage. Accurate assessment of the severity of injury and rapid application of first aid are essential. Eye injuries occur most often in baseball, basketball, and racquetball but occur to a certain extent in all sports. Eye injuries result from low-impact, high-velocity forces stemming from an object like a ball, stick, racket, or bat. Assessment of eye injuries involves general examination for intracranial injury followed by specific examination of the ocular area (Figure 14-4).

Aspiration: Removal of fluid from a cavity by use of a suction device.
Subcutaneous: Underneath the skin.
Tympanic membrane: The eardrum; the membrane separating the middle ear chamber from the external acoustical meatus.
Vertigo: Dizziness characterized by the sensation that you or your surroundings are moving.

Swimmer's ear: Infection of the outer ear canal (external auditory canal) that occurs in some athletes who do not let their ear canals dry after swimming; also called otitis externa.
pH: The relative alkalinity or acidity of a solution.

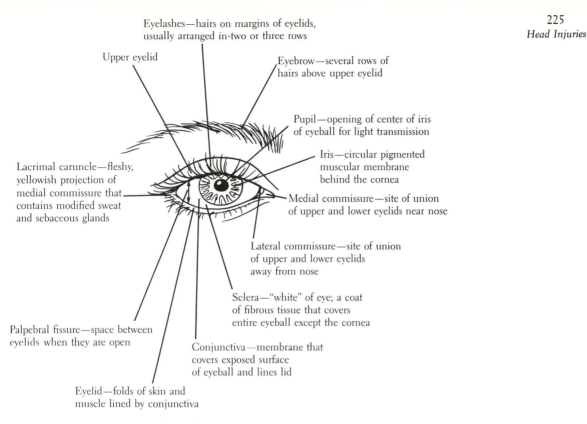

Eyelashes—hairs on margins of eyelids, usually arranged in two or three rows

Upper eyelid

Eyebrow—several rows of hairs above upper eyelid

Pupil—opening of center of iris of eyeball for light transmission

Iris—circular pigmented muscular membrane behind the cornea

Lacrimal caruncle—fleshy, yellowish projection of medial commissure that contains modified sweat and sebaceous glands

Medial commissure—site of union of upper and lower eyelids near nose

Lateral commissure—site of union of upper and lower eyelids away from nose

Sclera—"white" of eye; a coat of fibrous tissue that covers entire eyeball except the cornea

Palpebral fissure—space between eyelids when they are open

Conjunctiva—membrane that covers exposed surface of eyeball and lines lid

Eyelid—folds of skin and muscle lined by conjunctiva

Figure 14-4 Anterior view of the right eye.

Lacerations

During the evaluation, note gross deformities of the face, eyelids, and orbital area. External trauma, which results in penetration of the eyelids, orbital areas, or **conjunctiva** of the eye area, may affect the movement of the extraocular muscles and eyelid function.

Lacerations of the eyelids can lead to special problems because the lids are highly vascular and susceptible to the rapid onset of edema and ecchymosis. This type of injury leads to periorbital and subconjunctival hemorrhage, with **exophthalmos** (protrusion of the globe). Other similar injuries include corneal abrasions, laceration of the **sclera,** and **hyphema.** Refer all these injuries to a physician.

Orbital Fractures

Orbital ("blow out") fractures result from the bony rim of the orbit being struck by a round object greater in circumference than the orbit itself (see Putting It into Practice 14-3, p. 226, for symptoms). To assess this injury, palpate the orbital rim *carefully* and *gently* while looking for the symptoms. Without manipulating the injured structure, place a nonpressure oval bandage over the eye. Secure the pad with diagonally placed strips of tape. Also bandage the uninjured eye to minimize eye movement. Seek medical attention as quickly as possible.

Foreign Bodies

Superficial foreign bodies may lodge in the eye from windborne grit, insects,

Conjunctiva: The mucous membrane lining the inner surface of the eyelids and anterior sclera. Inflammation of the conjunctiva is conjunctivitis.

Exophthalmos: Abnormal bulging or protrusion of the eyeballs.
Sclera: The tough, outer white membrane that covers most of the eyeball.
Hyphema: Bleeding in the anterior chamber of the eye.

Signs and Symptoms of Orbital Fractures

Orbital hematoma (black eye) occurs often in sports but should not be automatically dismissed as trivial because it may be symptomatic of a fracture of the orbit, zygomatic arch, or maxilla. Look for the following symptoms:

1. Pain at point of impact
2. Pain and impaired movement of eye
3. Transient blurring
4. Double vision (diplopia)
5. Loss of sensation on facial area
6. Nausea and vomiting
7. Bulging of eye from the orbit (exophthalmos)
8. Recession of eye from the orbit (enophthalmos)
9. Crepitus in orbital area
10. Subconjunctival and conjunctival hemorrhage
11. Lid edema, with possible ecchymosis

Be aware of disturbances in vision and changes in the appearance of the eyes. Compare one eye with the other. Are the pupils the same size? Are the irises symmetrical? Thorough evaluation pays off, even in the face of seemingly trivial injuries.

concussive forces, or a misdirected fingertip from an opposing player. These bodies, along with corneal abrasions, are the most commonly reported eye injuries. Pain and tearing are the primary signs and symptoms of foreign bodies in the eye. Excessive eye motion and spasm in the muscles about the eye may follow and complicate the situation.

To examine an athlete's conjunctiva, have the person sit in an upright position and attempt to open her or his eye as wide as possible. Examine the lower lid first; gently pull down on the skin below the eye, which exposes the conjunctiva to visual inspection. To examine the upper lid, have the athlete gaze downward; gently grasp the upper eyelid by the eyelashes and secure the lid with a cotton-tipped applicator (Figure 14-5).

Be extremely careful when removing a foreign body from an eye. Safe and effective methods of removal include using the tip of a sterile gauze pad or irrigating the area with a sterile saline solution to wash the debris from the surface. If the foreign body remains embedded, cover the eye with a nonpressure oval pad and refer the athlete to a physician.

The athletic trainer should know which team members wear contact lenses. Particles of debris lodged be-

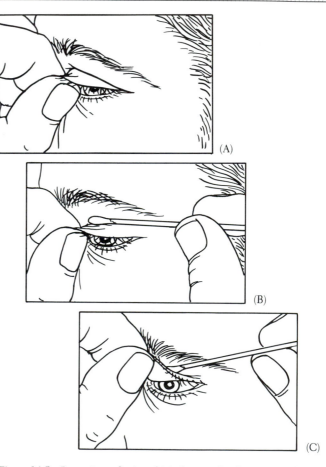

Figure 14-5 Removing a foreign object from under the upper eyelid.
(A) Gently pull the eyelid away from the eyeball.
(B) Place a cotton-tipped applicator on the outside portion of the eyelid.
(C) Roll the eyelid over the applicator and have the assistant remove the foreign object with a moist, sterile applicator.

Controlling Nose Bleeding

Epistaxis (nose bleeding) is often encountered in athletes and may be caused by injury, low humidity, exposure to altitude, allergies, and the common cold. It is seldom serious and is generally self-limiting. However, improper treatment, such as stuffing cotton into the nose, may break up the clot and delay or disrupt healing.

The best treatment is to apply direct pressure by grasping the nose between the thumb and forefinger. Bleeding should stop within five minutes. If it does not, the hemorrhage can usually be stopped by packing the nostril with Vaseline gauze on a tampon soaked in **thrombin** and applying ice. Instruct the athlete to

stand upright with head bowed.

Following treatment, tell the athlete to avoid vigorous activity for an hour or so, to avoid dislodging the clot. Uncontrolled bleeding may indicate a nasal fracture (or, in rare instances, a bleeding disorder) that requires medical referral.

---

tween the lens and cornea can be very irritating to the corneal surface. In the event of an eye irritation, ask the athlete to remove the lens. (Remove the lens with a rubber suction-tipped lens remover if the athlete is unable to do so personally.)

Nose and Maxillofacial Injuries

Bleeding from the nose often accompanies a blow to the external nasal area (Figure 14-6). It is usually controlled by squeezing the nostrils together. See Putting It into Practice 14-4.

Always suspect more complicated injuries, such as fracture. Careful observation may reveal a facial deformity, particularly a lateral deviation of the nose and sinus area. The athlete is usually the best judge of whether the nose has been displaced. Palpation of the two nasal bones between the fingers may initiate pain or **crepitus** and may determine a deviation in the angle of the ridge of the nose. If there are any abnormalities, refer the athlete to a physician to rule out the possibility of a fracture to facial bones.

Evaluation of facial injuries should include a total examination of the head and neck because these areas often suffer concomitant trauma. Putting It into

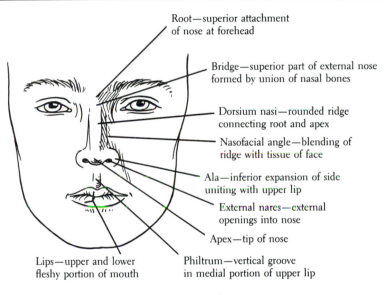

Root—superior attachment of nose at forehead

Bridge—superior part of external nose formed by union of nasal bones

Dorsium nasi—rounded ridge connecting root and apex

Nasofacial angle—blending of ridge with tissue of face

Ala—inferior expansion of side uniting with upper lip

External nares—external openings into nose

Apex—tip of nose

Lips—upper and lower fleshy portion of mouth

Philtrum—vertical groove in medial portion of upper lip

Figure 14-6 Anterior view of the nose and lips.

Practice 14-5 (p. 228) is a checklist for signs and symptoms.

Following a collision, asymmetry of the facial bones may indicate a displacement fracture of the **zygomatic arch** and look like a cheek is missing. Always consider dental injuries after this type of injury has occurred.

To evaluate for fracture of the **maxilla**, (1) stabilize the bridge of the nose with one hand, (2) grasp the anterior portion of the maxilla with the other hand, (3) try to move the maxilla from side to side. If there is motion in the

Thrombin: An enzyme involved in the formation of blood clots.
Crepitation (crepitus): A grinding, crackling sound produced by friction of adjacent tissues.
Zygomatic arch: A bony arch that joins the temporal and zygomatic bones.
Maxilla: A bone (one on each side) that forms the upper part of the jaw and is the base for the upper teeth.

bridge of the nose or the maxilla, suspect a fracture. Support the jaw and refer the athlete to a physician as soon as possible.

To evaluate for fracture of the **mandible,** (1) have the athlete open his or her jaw slightly. (2) Apply moderate, bilateral pressure at the angle of the mandible. A fracture will elicit pain in the area. Dental **malocclusion** and abnormal speech pattern are other common indicators of mandibular fracture.

Soft Tissue Injuries

Contusions and lacerations are the most common soft tissue injuries to the face and usually stem from collisions with objects or other athletes. Lacerations are obvious and sensational because when injured, the face's extensive capillary network bleeds considerably.

The athletic trainer must differentiate between injuries that are "playable" and those that are not. Generally, let athletes with smaller (less than one inch long), superficial (outer layer of epidermis and less than one-eighth inch deep), and uncomplicated lacerations continue play after they have received **prophylactic** treatment. Even borderline lacerations that appear to require sutures may be sufficiently treated to allow the athlete to complete a game. When the game is over, refer the injured person to medical care. See Putting It into Practice 14-6.

The treatment goals for head lacerations are to stop bleeding, prevent infection, and minimize formation of scar tissue. Clean the wound with surgical soap and irrigate with a sterile saline solution (Figure 14-7, p. 230). With a cotton-tipped applicator, apply a tape adherent to the sides of the laceration, in preparation for adhesive skin closures (e.g., butterfly bandages). Avoid contaminating the open wound with the tape adherent because the material is particularly irritating. Allow enough

PUTTING IT INTO PRACTICE 14-5

Signs and Symptoms of Maxillofacial Injuries: Checklist

Signs	Normal	Abnormal
1. Posture	( )	( )
2. Speech	( )	( )
3. Swallowing	( )	( )
4. Symmetry of face	( )	( )
5. Visual acuity	( )	( )
6. Eye movements	( )	( )
7. Deformities	( )	( )

time for the adherent to become tacky (partially dry). Place one end of a skin closure on one side of the wound, and use a clean cotton-tipped applicator to fold down the edges of the skin. Then place enough tension on the skin closure to tightly bind the two edges of the laceration. Letting skin flaps stick makes it difficult for the skin closure to adhere with the proper tension and may cause excessive scar tissue to form if the wound heals in this position.

Refer larger or complicated injuries, such as those with jagged edges or accompanied by possible damage to blood vessels, nerves, or bony structures, to a physician for surgical repair. Preserve any flaps or loose tissue for possible replacement and inclusion during the repair. Use a sterile compression bandage and **cryotherapy** to limit bleeding. Seek medical assistance as soon as possible.

Lacerations of the Tongue

Lacerations of the tongue usually cause profuse bleeding, which may obstruct the airway, impair swallowing, and bring on nausea. Apply direct pressure over the wound to control bleed-

Mandible: The bone that forms the lower jaw and chin.

Malocclusion: Abnormal alignment of maxillary (top) and mandibular (bottom) teeth.

Prophylactic: An agent or technique that prevents disease or injury.

Cryotherapy: Use of cold as therapy.

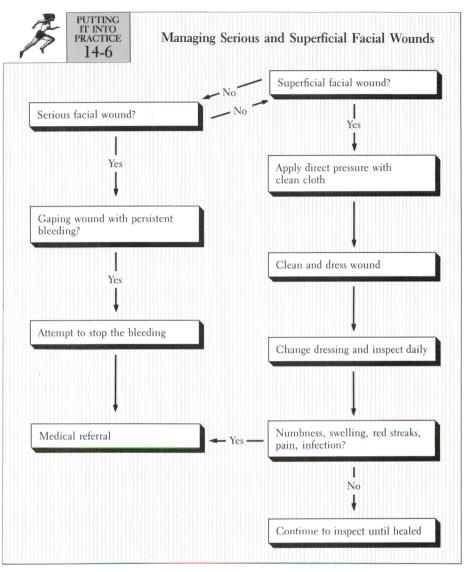

Managing Serious and Superficial Facial Wounds

Superficial facial wound?

Serious facial wound?

No ← No →

Yes

Gaping wound with persistent bleeding?

Apply direct pressure with clean cloth

Yes

Attempt to stop the bleeding

Clean and dress wound

Change dressing and inspect daily

Medical referral ← Yes ── Numbness, swelling, red streaks, pain, infection?

No

Continue to inspect until healed

ing; it may be necessary to grasp the tongue and pull it out with your fingers or by mechanical means. Medical referral is essential because of the high risk of infection and the possible need for sutures.

Contusions

Always suspect possible injury to underlying bony structures when evaluating contusions to facial tissue. Most uncomplicated facial contusions respond to cryotherapy and heal quickly (see Chapter 5).

Dental Injuries

Dental injuries are complicated because the mouth is a highly sensitive area, with many fragile parts. If a dental problem arises, the athlete should see a dentist or **orthodontist** as soon as

Orthodontist: A dentist who specializes in preventing and treating alignment abnormalities of the teeth.

possible. Dental injuries can be minimized by having athletes wear properly fitted protective mouthpieces. Mouthpieces are commonly used in football and hockey, but they are available for all sports.

The loose tooth, the most common dental injury, is usually caused by blows to the jaw and mouth. Instruct the athlete to avoid chewing or biting on the tooth and avoid any situation that might aggravate the condition. If a tooth is obviously displaced, push it back into its proper position and refer the athlete to a dentist or oral surgeon for **splinting**. Splinting may last one to two weeks.

The complete **avulsion** of one or more teeth is a fairly common occurrence in sports. Teeth that have been completely knocked out should be reimplanted as soon as possible; a tooth reimplanted within thirty minutes has a 90 percent chance of surviving. Make no attempt to scrub or abrasively clean an avulsed tooth. Rinse the tooth with saline solution to remove any debris; then store the tooth in saline solution or milk until the athlete gets to the dentist or oral surgeon.

Fractures of the teeth range from simple chipping of the enamel to exposure of the dentin and pulp. Fractures of the enamel are of little consequence, other than being a cosmetic concern. Exposure of the dentin or pulp can cause **cellular necrosis** and possible internal and external root absorption. Athletes with serious dental fractures must seek proper dental care to avoid permanent damage or loss of injured teeth.

Athletes should take out any artificial dental plates or removable appliances before participating in a practice or game, to lessen the chance of the dental fixture breaking or the appliance lacerating, contusing, or becoming lodged in the mouth. Encourage athletes who wear braces to wear mouthpieces or cover the braces with soft wax to avoid lacerating the gums or the mouth's

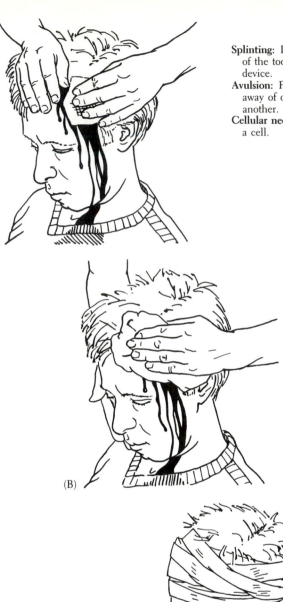

Splinting: Immobilization of the tooth with a rigid device.
Avulsion: Pulling or tearing away of one tissue from another.
Cellular necrosis: Death of a cell.

Figure 14-7 Closing a head wound. (See the text regarding precautions when skull is fractured.)
(A) Clean the wound and replace any skin flaps.
(B) Apply a sterile dressing.
(C) Bandage the wound.

inner mucosal lining. It is not uncommon for wires to come loose or break during athletic participation. Refer problems to an orthodontist.

References

Lindsay, K., et al. Serious head injury in sport. *British Medical Journal* 281:789–791, 1980.

O'Donoghue, D. *Treatment of Injuries to Athletes*. Philadelphia: W. B. Saunders, 1976.

Ommaya, A. K., and T. Gennarell. Cerebral concussion and traumatic unconsciousness. *Brain* 97:633–654, 1974.

Ryan, A. Concussion in athletes. *The Physician and Sportsmedicine* 10:95–108, 1982.

Sandusky, J. Field evaluation of eye injuries. *Athletic Training* Winter, 253–258, 1981.

Schneider, R. *Head and Neck Injuries in Football*. Baltimore: Williams & Wilkins, 1973.

Schneider, R., and F. Kriss. Decisions concerning cerebral concussions in football players. *Medicine and Science in Sports and Exercise* 1:112–115, 1969.

Strauss, R. H. *Sports Medicine and Physiology*. Philadelphia: W. B. Saunders, 1979.

Torg, J. *Athletic Injuries to the Head, Neck, and Face*. Philadelphia: Lea & Febiger, 1982.

Tortora, G. *Principles of Human Anatomy*. San Francisco: Harper & Row, 1977.

15 Neck Injuries

ECK injuries are among the most serious in athletics, accounting for a disproportionate number of sports-related deaths and **paralysis**. The **etiology** of neck injuries is complex, but contributing factors include poor muscular strength, flexibility, and endurance; unsafe sports techniques; the vulnerability of the neck in contact sports; and ill-fitting equipment. To effectively deal with neck injuries, the athletic trainer should have a thorough knowledge of the anatomy and **kinesiology** of the neck and an appreciation of the potential seriousness of any neck injury. This chapter covers all aspects of neck injuries, including soft tissue injuries, evaluation, and treatment.

Anatomy

The neck is composed of seven cervical vertebrae that form the cervical spine. As with other joints that have considerable mobility (e.g., the shoulder), the neck is vulnerable to injury, especially in contact sports, because its soft tissue support is relatively fragile. Between each vertebra are **intervertebral disks** that help form strong joints and permit various movements. (Chap-

ter 16 discusses the function and structure of the disks in more detail.) Among its functions, the cervical spine

- Provides musculoskeletal support and stability for the head
- Provides sufficient flexibility to permit **flexion, extension,** rotation, and **lateral flexion** because of the structure of its articulating (jointed) vertebral facets
- Provides for the transport of the spinal cord and **motor neurons** from the brain to the rest of the body and gives these structures adequate protection

The first (1st) vertebra is the atlas, named because it supports the head; the second (2nd) vertebra is the axis, which houses a peglike structure called the **dens** that allows the atlas to pivot. This arrangement permits side-to-side movement, such as when the head is moved from side to side to signify "no." Figure 15-1 shows the structure of the atlas and axis.

Eight pairs of cervical nerves exit through the cervical spine. The first seven pairs exit above the cervical vertebrae (CV); the eighth pair exits through the **foramen** between the seventh CV and the first thoracic (T1) vertebra.

Paralysis: Partial or complete loss of capability to move.

Etiology: Cause.

Kinesiology: The study of muscular movement.

Flexion: Bending of a joint, resulting in a decrease in the joint angle.

Extension: Straightening of a joint, thus increasing the joint angle. The opposite of flexion.

Lateral flexion: Sideward bending of a joint; possible in the neck and trunk.

Motor neurons: Nerve cells that carry information from the CNS to skeletal muscle cells in the periphery. Stimulation of the neurons causes muscle contraction. Also called efferent nerves.

Dens: A peg- or toothlike component of the second cervical vertebra that facilitates rotation of the neck.

Foramen (foramina): A natural opening in a bone or tissue.

Intervertebral disk: A fibrocartilage structure with a jell-like center that separates the bodies of adjacent vertebrae.

Wrestlers run a higher risk of sustaining neck injuries than most other athletes. Neck exercises are important for preventing neck injuries.

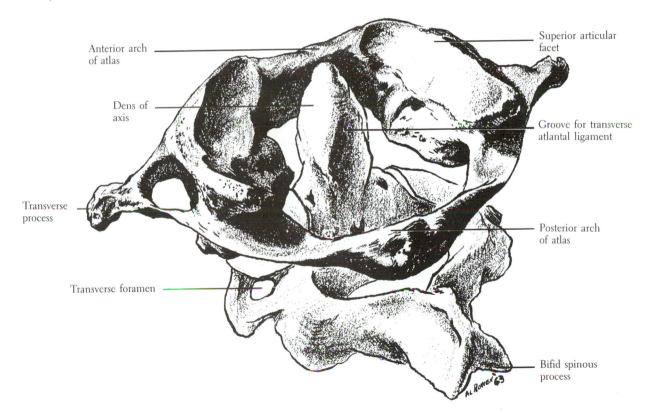

Anterior arch of atlas

Dens of axis

Transverse process

Transverse foramen

Superior articular facet

Groove for transverse atlantal ligament

Posterior arch of atlas

Bifid spinous process

AL ROWE 63

Figure 15-1 The first (atlas) and second (axis) cervical vertebrae. (From Crouch, J. E. *Introduction to Human Anatomy*, 6th ed. Palo Alto, Calif.: Mayfield Publishing Co., 1983, p. 58.)

Two networks of nerves—the cervical and brachial plexi—emerge from the cervical region. The uppermost **plexus,** the cervical plexus, is located along both sides of C1 to C4. The cervical plexus supplies the skin and muscles of the head, neck, and upper shoulders. The phrenic nerve, which arises from the cervical plexus, supplies motor fibers to the diaphragm. Damage to the phrenic nerve or to the spinal cord above this nerve could paralyze the diaphragm, which could cause death since contractions of this muscle are essential for breathing.

The brachial plexus, the second or lower plexus, is formed by nerves emerging from the four lower cervical levels (C5 to C8) and T1. The brachial plexus supplies nerves to the upper extremity and to certain neck and shoulder muscles. Table 15-1 summarizes neuromuscular characteristics of the brachial plexus.

Numerous small muscles move the head and neck. Their kinesiology is complex and beyond the scope of this text; briefly, here are the major muscles, listed according to function (see also Figure 15-2 and Chapter 16):

Flexors: Sternocleidomastoid, capitis (splenius, longissimus); scaleni hyoids

Extensors: Splenius cervicis; capitis (splenius, semispinalis, longissimus); trapezius

Rotators: Splenius cervicis; capitis (semispinalis, splenius); erector spinae, sternocleidomastoid

Lateral bending: Scalenus anticus, scalenus medius

Plexus: A network of nerves, blood vessels, or lymphatics.

Soft Tissue Injuries

Soft tissue injuries to the neck can be extremely debilitating and take considerable time to recover. Contusions, strains, and sprains are the most common soft tissue neck injuries in athletics.

Contusions

A blow to the anterior area of the neck may cause a **contusion** to the larynx and trachea (see Putting It into Practice 15-1, p. 236). During the acute injury phase, the individual may become stressful and apprehensive and develop **systemic** shock. The athlete may be speechless and have trouble

Contusion: A bruise.

Systemic: Relating to the entire body.

Table 15-1 *Neurology of the Upper Extremity*

Disk	Root	Muscle(s)	Motor Activity	Sensation	Reflex	Nerve(s)
C4–C5	C5	Deltoid Biceps	Shoulder abduction Elbow flexion	Lateral upper arm	Biceps	Axillary, Musculocutaneous
C5–C6	C6	Biceps Wrist extensors	Elbow flexion Wrist extension	Lateral forearm	Brachio-radialis	Musculocutaneous Radial
C6–C7	C7	Wrist flexors Finger extensors Triceps	Wrist flexion Finger extension Elbow extension	Middle finger	Triceps	Radial Median Ulnar
C7–T1	C8	Hand interossei Finger flexors	Finger flexion	Medial forearm	None	Median Ulnar
T1–T2	T1	Hand intrinsics	Finger abduction	Medial arm	None	Ulnar Cutaneous

NOTE: C = cervical; C4 = fourth cervical disk; T = thoracic; T1 = first thoracic disk.

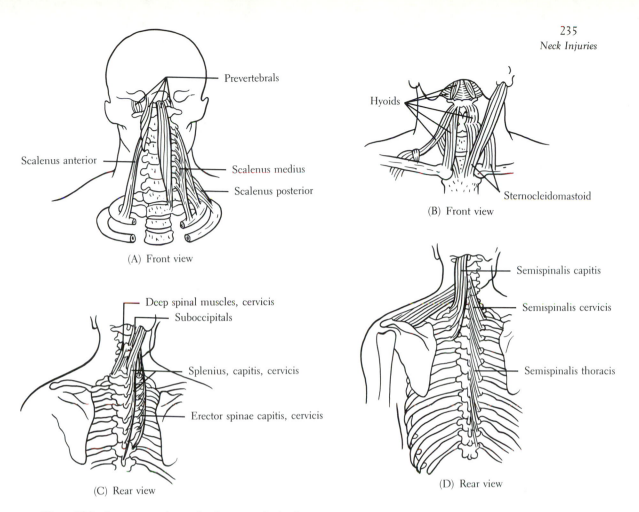

Prevertebrals

Scalenus anterior

Scalenus medius

Scalenus posterior

(A) Front view

Hyoids

Sternocleidomastoid

(B) Front view

Deep spinal muscles, cervicis

Suboccipitals

Splenius, capitis, cervicis

Erector spinae capitis, cervicis

(C) Rear view

Semispinalis capitis

Semispinalis cervicis

Semispinalis thoracis

(D) Rear view

Figure 15-2 Important neck muscles that move the head.

breathing. Under normal circumstances, complete recovery from these symptoms takes only a few minutes. Have the athlete lie down on his or her back and elevate the feet. Persistent symptoms indicate possible severe injury to the larynx or trachea or a fractured thyroid cartilage; in such cases, refer the athlete to a physician.

A blow to the back of the neck can affect vital underlying structures (cervical vertebrae and spinal cord), causing serious complications. A severe enough blow may fracture one of the vertebral **spinous processes** (portion of a vertebra that projects dorsally) or stretch the supporting ligaments and muscles. The blow may cause **hematoma,** muscle

spasm, and pain. Occasionally, severe trauma to the spinal cord causes transitory paralysis. The athlete may complain of a generalized feeling of numbness and **paresthesia** that usually disappears within a few minutes after the initial blow. If these symptoms continue, a more thorough examination is necessary.

Strains

The cervical area is particularly subject to muscular **strain** because its muscles are small. Typically, neck muscle injuries are caused by unanticipated, rapid head movements. When an athlete receives an unsuspected force from

Paresthesia: Abnormal sensation or feeling, such as tingling or burning.

Spinous process: Portion of a vertebra that projects rearward (dorsally); acts as attachments for spinal muscles and ligaments.

Strain: Disruption or injury of a musculotendinous unit. A serious strain is often called a pulled muscle.

Hematoma: A bruise; a mass of partially clotted blood outside the vascular space, typically formed from trauma.

PUTTING IT INTO PRACTICE 15-1

Managing Neck Sprains and Strains

It is extremely difficult to differentiate between sprains and strains in the cervical area because this area's anatomy is so complex. In fact, an athlete with a neck injury may have both a sprain and a strain. A physician should always evaluate these injuries, unless they are extremely mild. Injury may include axial loading of the spine and acute or chronic muscle overloading.

- *Signs and symptoms*: Spasm may become worse twenty-four to forty-eight hours after injury; pain when moving the neck through its ranges of motion; abnormal cervical posture; and point tenderness. Other symptoms are radiating pain and paresthesia (feeling of tingling, crawling, or burning of the skin).
- *Evaluation*: Neck sprains and strains may injure muscles, ligaments, intervertebral disks, nerves, and skeletal structures. Again, because of their complexity, refer all injuries (except those that are obviously mild and self-limiting) to a physician. Evaluation should include a thorough history; palpation of muscles, skeletal structures, and brachial plexus; range of motion, neurological function, and muscle strength tests (see text).
- *Treatment and rehabilitation*: Initially, minimize the inflammation with ice, immobilize the neck with a cervical collar, apply anti-inflammatory medication, and have the athlete rest. The physician may order cervical traction and additional modalities, such as electrical muscle stimulation. Range of motion exercises may be initiated when muscle spasms have largely subsided. Range of motion exercise should not cross the midline of the body (i.e., circumduction) during early stages of rehabilitation, to avoid reinjury. Strength exercise may be initiated when movements through the normal range of motion (including those that cross the body's midline) are pain-free (see Box 15-1, p. 245).
- *Returning to practice*: As discussed in Chapter 12, an athlete may return to practice when pain is gone, normal (or appropriate for the activity) strength and range of motion are restored, and all abnormal neurological symptoms have disappeared. Periodically reevaluate the athlete after he or she returns to active participation.

behind, the head and neck are abruptly propelled backward into a hyperextension. This violent **hyperextension** of the cervical spine is the same type of movement that causes the whiplash injury in a rear-end auto collision. The marked hyperextension causes an acute stretch of the neck flexor muscles. If an athlete receives a blow head-on, the head and neck are propelled forward into **hyperflexion,** causing an acute stretch of the neck extensor muscles.

The sternocleidomastoid and scalenus muscles are the most commonly strained neck muscles. The amount of damage depends upon the strength of the forces causing the injury. Injury occurs at the weakest link of a musculotendinous unit and may include rupture of the tendon, damage to the musculotendinous unit, or damage to muscle itself. A strain is classified by degrees. In first degree strain, fibers are stretched but the **fascia** remains intact. In second degree strain, a number of fibers are torn, but the fascia remains intact (localized hematoma). In third degree strain, the muscle and fascia are completely torn.

Sprains

An athlete with a cervical **sprain** may complain of pain, muscle spasm, and

Hyperextension: Extension beyond the normal limit or beyond 180 degrees.

Fascia: A layer of loose connective tissue.

Hyperflexion: Flexion of a joint beyond its normal maximally flexed position.

Sprain: Disruption or injury of a ligament.

restricted range of motion (ROM). The signs and symptoms vary, depending upon the type of injury. With moderate to severe sprains there is some loss of ligament function and local tenderness over some portion of the ligament. Typically, the injured athlete will carry her or his head in an extended position and resist any attempt to flex it forward. However, an athlete with a sprain that occurs in extension will typically carry her or his head in flexion.

If there is a dislocation, palpation will reveal a prominent spinous process directly below the site of dislocation, with a corresponding deficit (displacement) or "shelf" above. The athlete will be extremely apprehensive and resist any attempt to move the head. Neurological damage may be present. In a unilateral dislocation, the neck will be tilted toward the dislocated side, with muscle spasm and tightness on the opposite side and relaxed muscles on the same side. With a bilateral dislocation, the head will be characteristically held forward in a hyperextended position.

Figure 15-3 Mechanism of axial compression injury. Improper use of the head while tackling may cause cervical axial compression.

Mechanism of Neck Injuries

Serious neck injuries can be caused by direct trauma delivered by an opponent, as might occur in basketball, hockey, football, wrestling; trauma from collisions with objects, as might occur in diving, skiing, or gymnastics; or trauma induced by muscular overload, as might occur in discus throwing, volleyball, or baseball. Because of the neck's great mobility, there are many possible mechanisms of injury; these injuries may damage a variety of tissues.

Axial Compression

Axial compression injuries usually occur when the cervical spine is in forward flexion, but they can occur in any position when a blow is delivered to the crown of the skull (Figure 15-3). These injuries occur in sports like football (spear blocking or landing on the head), diving (shallow water), trampoline, and free-style skiing. In the flexed position, the vertebrae have lost their normal cervical **lordosis** (concave curve), resulting in a straight spine, which greatly reduces or eliminates the soft tissue's and skeletal structure's ability to absorb shock. Impact forces are now transmitted along the spine's **vertical axis** and can injure the intervertebral disks, vertebral body, spinous processes, **transverse processes** (lateral vertebral projection), and ligamentous structures.

If compression forces are great enough, the excessive force may cause flexion and/or rotation of the cervical spine, possibly leading to **subluxation**, fracture, and cervical facet dislocation (dislocation of either the superior or inferior articular process). Exceeding

Lordosis: The concavities of the cervical (neck) and lumbar (low back) spine. Often used to refer to an abnormal forward curvature of the low back.

Vertical axis: An imaginary line passing through the body vertically.

Transverse process: Portion of a vertebra that projects laterally (each side) from the point where the lamina joins the pedicle.

Subluxation: Partial joint dislocation.

Axial compression: Compression to the long or longitudinal axis.

the cervical spine's load limits (estimated as 750 to 1000 pounds) may cause a compression fracture to the vertebral bodies, which may lead to buckling, excessive flexion, and dislocation.

Flexion Injuries

The most serious athletic neck injuries are caused by excessive flexion of the cervical spine. This flexion may result from a blow on the head, as when a diver's head hits the bottom of a swimming pool (Figure 15-4) or a football player attempts to tackle with his head down. As the neck flexes, the cervical vertebrae are forced together anteriorly and apart posteriorly.

The **supraspinous** and **interspinous ligaments** that attach along the spinous processes prevent excessive flexion. When the neck is forced into hyperflexion, these ligaments may be stretched or torn and, if the force persists, progress into subluxation or complete dislocation, with possible damage to the spinal cord. If the ligaments tear completely, one of the vertebra may be displaced forward over the vertebra below it. If the vertebra is displaced too far forward, the nerve roots, the spinal cord, or both may be damaged. There may be pain and paralysis with possible **quadriplegia**. If the spinal cord is completely crushed at the time of injury, damage is usually irreversible. Aside from a fracture that may occur concurrently with a subluxation or dislocation, hyperflexion may cause other portions of the vertebrae to be fractured. True fractures of the cervical spine involve the vertebrae bodies. The extent of the fracture will depend upon the amount of force and the degree of flexion applied to the neck.

Lateral Flexion Injuries

Lateral flexion injuries occur from impact forces that suddenly increase the normal angular relationship of the head and neck to the shoulder (Figure 15-5).

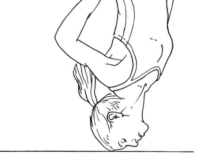

Figure 15-4 Mechanism of a cervical injury in a diver.

In football, four typical circumstances surround this type of injury:

1. The involved player is tackling from the side and his head strikes the opposing player's thigh, knee, or hip. This situation lends itself to lateral flexion injuries because football players generally are taught to keep the head between the runner and his forward progress.
2. To intercept an opposing player, the player dives in a layout position and is struck on the side of his head.
3. The opposing player turns back toward the involved player, who is positioning himself for an attempted tackle. Impact is thus

Supraspinous ligaments: Ligaments that extend between the ends of the vertebral spinous processes; they restrict flexion of the vertebral column.

Interspinous ligaments: Ligaments that extend between the vertebral spinous processes; they restrict flexion of the vertebral column.

Quadriplegia: Paralysis of the arms and legs.

going to be on the tackler's shoulder before he has had a chance to "set" himself. The impact forces are in favor of the opposing runner, and he actually drives the involved player's shoulder away from his head and neck.

4. The player's shoulder receives a direct blow, which causes sudden, violent lateral flexion and injury (similar to whiplash).

Lateral flexion injuries are sometimes called "cervical nerve pinch syndrome" or cervical neuropathy, in athletic jargon "burners" or **stingers** (which aptly describes the athlete's subjective symptoms). The athlete may assume various postures, but the classic sign of lateral flexion injury is the "injury posture": The head is flexed laterally in the direction of injury supported by the athlete's arm (Table 15-2, p. 240). This stance enables the athletic trainer to make a rapid on-field estimate of the problem.

Extension Injuries

As the neck moves into hyperextension, the anterior longitudinal ligament prevents the separation of the cervical disks' anterior margins. As the distraction force continues, the ligamentous structures sustain some degree of damage. This injury may occur during violent muscular action that throws the head back, as during discus or javelin throwing or pitching. The structure itself may tear or cause a facet or spinous process **avulsion fracture.** The ligament may tear partially or completely. If the tear is complete, it will cause **dislocation** of a cervical vertebra; the vertebra will be displaced backward over the vertebra below. This dislocation is extremely serious and could cause spinal injury and paralysis below the injured level. Fortunately, this injury does not frequently occur in athletic events.

The face mask of a football helmet has often been implicated in the etiol-

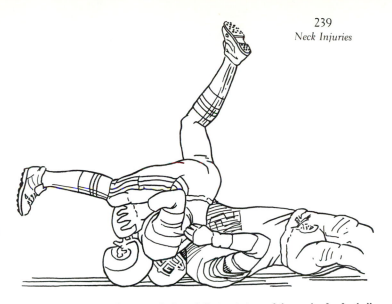

Figure 15-5 Mechanism of a lateral flexion injury of the neck of a football player.

ogy of hyperextension injuries. It is thought that the mask acts as a lever, pushing the back edge of the football helmet against the cervical spine like a "knife edge." There is no radiographic, biomechanical, or epidemiologic evidence to prove this theory.

Rotary Injuries

Most neck injuries stem from some degree of excessive rotary force rather than isolated linear flexion, lateral flexion, and extension motions. Excessive neck rotation may cause sprains, strains, subluxation, and dislocation. A combination of excessive rotary and linear forces usually results in serious injury. The extent of injury will vary according to the position of the cervical spine and the strength and duration of the force applied through the spinal segments.

Evaluation

When a serious neck (or head) injury is suspected, the first step in **evaluation** is to check the **vital signs** (see Chapter 10). If the athlete is unconscious, **splint**

Stinger: A lateral flexion neck injury characterized by a burning and stinging sensation. Also called cervical nerve pinch syndrome or a burner.

Avulsion fracture: A fracture caused by a small fragment of bone breaking away at the site of attachment of a ligament or tendon.
Dislocation: Displacement of bone(s) from a joint.
Evaluation: Assessment of an injury; the process typically includes past and present history, inspection, and testing.
Vital signs: Heart rate, ventilatory rate, level of consciousness, blood pressure, and body temperature.
Splinting: Immobilization of a joint or body part with a rigid device.

Table 15-2 *Signs and Symptoms of the Stinger*

Grade 1

1. Severe burning pain down the arm, present after attempting blocking or tackling.
2. Pain in shoulder radiating down the arm and into the hand.
3. Numbness and tingling through the arm and into the hand.
4. Palpable tenderness in midportion of the anterior aspect of the trapezius.
5. Recovery time is usually same day, and return to competition is allowed if pain symptoms do not persist and muscle weakness is not present.

Grade 2

1. Burning pain as in symptoms 1 to 3 of grade 1 stinger. Subjective complaint of burning pain "shooting down the arm."
2. Complete loss of function of arm for several minutes.
3. Failure to regain normal strength in deltoid, infraspinatus, supraspinatus, and biceps brachii muscles for 2–3 weeks.
4. Possible abnormal EMG readings.

Grade 3

1. All the previous signs and symptoms plus failure to regain normal use of the arm and supporting musculature for times up to and beyond 1 yr.
2. Definite abnormal EMG readings.

the head, check and restore the airway (if necessary), and check the pulse (and indirectly monitor blood pressure by the strength of the pulse). If there is no pulse, initiate **CPR** and check the pupils. See Putting It into Practice 15-2.

History and Observation

The initial evaluation should include a thorough **history** of the events leading to the incident. Ask the athlete to describe the circumstances of the injury. Determine if there was a sudden head movement or if the person was hit from behind or struck head-on. Ask whether the athlete felt or heard a snapping in the neck. Establish the degree of pain (mild, moderate, or severe) or the existence of numbness.

Closely observe the athlete while taking the history. Look for signs of head injuries (described in Chapter 14). Look for swelling, **ecchymosis,** and muscle spasm. Note any areas of **point tenderness** (especially over the cervical processes), bony deformity (which may indicate dislocation), **crepitus, indentation** caused by a break in or separation of tissues, and hematoma. If you suspect a fracture or dislocation, take appropriate action to prevent potentially disabling injuries. An athlete with a severe neck injury will say "I heard something snap" or "Something gave way" and will be afraid to move. He or she may also describe numbness, burning, and labored breathing.

Palpation and Neurological Evaluation

After completing the history and observation, **palpate** the injured area to determine the physical signs of the injury. Next, perform neurological tests to evaluate sensory and motor function. Perform sensation testing to determine sensory level and reflex testing of the biceps, brachioradialis, and triceps (see Chapter 8). Test motor function for

CPR (cardiopulmonary resuscitation): Mechanically compressing the heart of a pulseless, nonbreathing person to increase cardiac output and blowing air into the mouth to increase lungs' oxygen content.

History: Review of present health status, past injuries and illness, or circumstances surrounding a specific injury.

Ecchymosis: Black and blue coloring under the skin, caused by blood escaping from the vasculature as a result of injury.

Point tenderness: Pain elicited at a specific anatomical location.

Crepitus (crepitation): A grinding, crackling sound produced by friction of adjacent tissues.

Indentation: The recession of a tissue.

Palpation: Touching an area with the hands.

Managing Serious Cervical Injury

Neck injuries can be life-threatening or cause lifelong disability. The athletic trainer should always assume that a neck injury is extremely dangerous and act accordingly. A primary rule when dealing with neck injuries is to not do any more damage. Movement may cause fractured or dislocated vertebrae to move and damage nerve roots or the spinal cord. It is critical that the athletic trainer identify the spinal injury.

- *Preinjury planning:* Anticipate the possibility of serious neck injury in sports like rugby, football, and gymnastics and formulate an injury plan. Have all necessary equipment, including spine board and bolt cutter (for cutting off helmet faceguard), readily available. Be sure personnel know their assignments so there is no indecisiveness when an injury occurs.
- *Symptoms:* Pain (if athlete is conscious), loss of feeling and function in muscles below the shoulder, tingling in the extremities, pain when moving the neck. *Never* encourage the injured athlete to move his or her neck!
- *Signs:* Cervical deformity (not always), point tenderness (particularly at the base of the neck), lacerations and contusions on the face or head (not always), diaphragmatic breathing, and paralysis. A male may have a penile erection.
- *Evaluation and course of action:*
1. Do not move the athlete. Prevent further injury by manually stabilizing the neck in a neutral position. Check vital signs: respiration, pulse, level of consciousness, blood pressure, and temperature.
2. Perform CPR if necessary (see Chapter 10). Use the jawthrust technique if the airway must be opened (see CPR manual for proper technique). The athlete's breathing *must* be satisfactory. If the injured person is a football player, do *not* remove helmet (but *carefully* remove the face mask with bolt cutters). If the athlete is face down and requires CPR, a five-person team should "logroll" the person to a face-up position. The team leader controls the head and directs team movements while the other three members perform the roll. The fifth member helps bear the athlete's weight if necessary.
3. Send for an ambulance. Remember that this is a major medical emergency!
4. If the athlete is conscious and CPR is not necessary, note and record neural and psychological characteristics: emotional state (i.e., oriented, restless, combative, etc.), speech patterns (i.e., clear, incoherent, mumbled, none), reaction to pin pricks administered at the feet and proceeding upward, size of pupils, ability to move extremities. Do not encourage movement; instruct the athlete to lie quietly in one place.
5. Ask the athlete or bystanders about the circumstances of the injury. Question the athlete about all symptoms.
6. Examine and note any contusions or lacerations about the head, face, or neck.
7. Palpate for deformity and point tenderness.
8. When the ambulance arrives, give the physician or medical personnel all pertinent data.

neck, shoulder, arm, and hand motions because these area are innervated by the cervical spinal nerves (see Putting It into Practice 15-3).

Range of Motion

Determine flexion, extension, rotation, and lateral flexion range of motion. Normally, athletes should be able to touch their chins to their chests, look directly at the ceiling or sky, move their heads far enough to both sides so that their chins are almost in line with their shoulders, and tilt their heads about forty-five degrees toward each shoulder. Any limitation or pain while these tests are performed indicates possible muscle or ligament injury.

Inability to perform active ROM tests may be caused by muscle weakness, soft tissue contractures, or bony blockage and may indicate the need for immediate medical attention. Conduct passive ROM tests *very* carefully and only if there is no obviously serious injury. Muscle weakness is usually the cause if the head and neck move through a full ROM under passive conditions but have limited active motions. Bony blockage is generally the cause if restriction is consistent during both active and passive testing.

If active and passive ROM tests have been accomplished with little or no discomfort, conduct resistive testing. Administer these tests in the same manner as the ROM tests, except that the athletic trainer should manually resist the motions. This resistance is an indication of the muscles' and ligaments' functional ability and helps determine if the athlete can return to competition. Do not let athletes return to competition if they exhibit restricted ROM residual tenderness, neurological deficits, and recurrence of pain while performing active motions; pain in the absence of muscle weakness is not as significant as the other factors.

Treatment

Ice, rest, and reduced activity are appropriate for the first twenty-four hours if the injury is mild, followed by heat and strengthening exercises (see Figures 15-6 and 15-7 and Box 15-1,

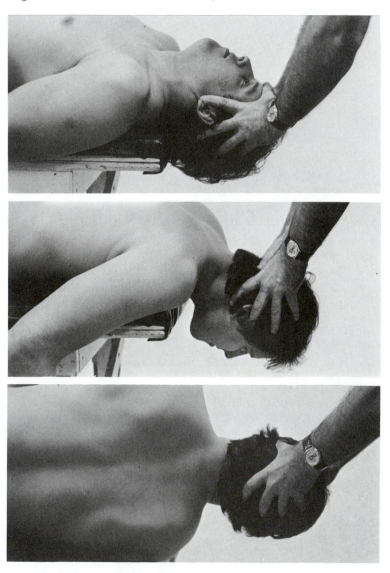

Figure 15-6 Manually resisted neck exercises are an effective and safe way of increasing the strength of neck muscles. Be sure resistance to neck motion is not excessive. Ranges of motion include flexion (top photo), extension (middle), and lateral flexion (bottom).

PUTTING IT INTO PRACTICE 15-3

Signs and Symptoms of Neck Injury: Checklist

Motor Activity and Roots	Normal	Abnormal
Shoulder abduction (C5)	( )	( )
Elbow flexion (C5–C6)	( )	( )
Wrist extension (C6)	( )	( )
Elbow extension (C7)	( )	( )
Finger extension (C7)	( )	( )
Finger flexion (C8)	( )	( )
Finger abduction (T1)	( )	( )

Reflexes and Roots	Positive	Negative
Biceps (C5)	( )	( )
Brachioradialis (C6)	( )	( )
Triceps (C7)	( )	( )

Sensory Level and Roots	Feeling	No Feeling
Lateral upper arm (C5)	( )	( )
Lateral forearm (C6)	( )	( )
Middle finger (C7)	( )	( )
Medial forearm (C8)	( )	( )
Medial arm (T1)	( )	( )

Signs of Fractures	Present	Absent
Localized tenderness	( )	( )
Pain with palpation	( )	( )
Swelling	( )	( )
Inability to move neck	( )	( )

ROM Testing	Active		Passive		Resistive	
	Normal	Limited	Normal	Limited	Normal	Limited
Flexion	( )	( )	( )	( )	( )	( )
Extension	( )	( )	( )	( )	( )	( )
Rotation (right)	( )	( )	( )	( )	( )	( )
Rotation (left)	( )	( )	( )	( )	( )	( )
Lateral bending	( )	( )	( )	( )	( )	( )

pp. 242, 244, 245). If the injury is moderate, use a cotton cervical collar to prevent unnecessary motion (Figure 15-8, p. 244) (some orthopedic physicians do not recommend this practice). Continue protection until the athlete is pain-free through all the ranges of movement.

Severe injury requires careful handling. Medical referral is necessary, to rule out fracture or dislocation. Surgery to remove bony fragments and repair torn ligaments may be required for flexion injuries involving avulsion fractures. Nonsurgical treatment is to immobilize the head in a hyperextended position, thus allowing the ligament to grow back together at near normal length. With extension injuries, immobilize the neck in a slightly flexed position to allow the ligament to heal.

Figure 15-7 The Nautilus neck machine enables athletes to develop extension, flexion, and lateral flexion strength.

Prevention

The incidences of death and total quadriplegia have dramatically decreased since the early 1970s. Clarke stated that the decrease is from such factors as rule changes in tackling technique, improved helmet standards, and continued research into various aspects of contact sports.

Improved materials and equipment design has turned out to be a mixed blessing. Better protection sometimes gives the false impression of invincibility, and equipment then may be used as a weapon.

Over the last 100 years, the art of blocking and tackling has evolved into a technique of body-to-body contact rather than head-to-head contact. Spearing (using the helmet as the initial point of contact) has been outlawed. Spearing requires the athlete to voluntarily splint the neck and meet the opponent head-on. "Voluntary splinting" implies that the tackler has the time, technique, knowledge, and desire to voluntarily splint or tighten the neck and shoulder muscles prior to contact.

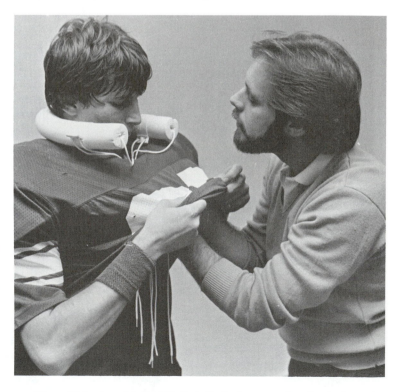

Figure 15-8 A neck collar effectively limits the range of motion in the neck, thus preventing further injury.

**BOX
15-1**

Strengthening the Neck

Strong neck muscles are important for athletes, particularly in football, wrestling, gymnastics, diving, weight events in track and field, and rugby. Yet many athletic teams follow no systematic program for strengthening the neck muscles, even though the neck is vulnerable to serious injury. The intensity of neck exercise should be increased gradually (particularly when rehabilitating a neck injury) because these muscles are relatively small and thus more susceptible than larger muscle groups to the destructive effects of sudden overload. There are various techniques for increasing neck strength and endurance:

- *Manual exercise:* Manually resisted neck exercises provide an exercise load in all neck motions. Manual exercise is an easy, inexpensive way to strengthen neck muscles and can be incorporated into calisthenics. *Caution is essential:* Manual resistance can be very dangerous if the person applying the resistance is unskilled.
- *Neck machines:* Certain machines exercise the neck through the majority of neck motions. (These machines are extremely effective and recommended, but they are expensive.) These machines allow overload of neck muscles during flexion, extension, lateral flexion, and rotation; "shoulder shrug" machines are also available. Shoulder shrugs can also be practiced with a barbell or on the bench press of a Universal Gym.
- *Neck harness exercises:* A neck harness worn about the head enables the athlete to suspend weights from the harness; this weight increases the resistance of the exercise. Although this device is inexpensive and practical, it is difficult to overload the neck muscles during rotation and circumduction.
- *Neck bridges:* These exercises, probably the most known and popular, are mostly static contraction of the neck muscles. Neck bridges are contraindicated during rehabilitation (at least during the early stages and midstages) because they may subject muscles to an intolerable overload. Although the exercises are an acceptable part of the neck-injury-prevention program for healthy athletes, they should be practiced with isotonic and isokinetic exercises to maximally develop dynamic strength and muscle endurance. *Some sports medicine experts feel that athletes should not practice neck bridges.* Certainly, this exercise should not be practiced until the neck is strong enough to handle weight-bearing activities.
- *Progression during rehabilitation:* Initial treatment may include anti-inflammatory and analgesic treatments (see Chapters 8 and 13) and traction. Range of motion and submaximal isometric contractions may be started when most of the pain has subsided. Isotonic exercises (except neck bridges) may be gradually added as range of motion is restored and pain disappears. Neck bridges may be added to the program when the neck muscles are strong enough to handle the load.

The assumption is not always correct. Unfortunately, the regulations against spearing are not consistently enforced; films of games at any level usually reveal numerous incidents of both accidental and deliberate **spearing.**

The coach, officials, and players are all responsible for preventing injury. The coach should teach proper blocking and tackling techniques (i.e., the moment of contact should be preceded by a "setting" or "splinting" of the neck and shoulder muscles) and should be sure the athletes are conditioned to take and deliver a blow. The coach should explain the consequences of poor technique and its relationship to injury in a straightforward, nonthreatening manner so that the athletes know the risks involved.

The officials must control the game and interpret on-field situations as directed by the rule books. Officials should control mismatches in age, size, and ability. Very often officials are asked to assume the responsibility for athletes' on-field behavior and game control, so they should be trained and prepared to handle all these situations.

The athletes must take an active role in their own athletic development and play by the rules. They must learn the correct tackling and blocking techniques and adhere to the coach's teachings as though they were law. Every athlete must "prepare for performance" by developing strength and mass in the supporting musculature of the neck and shoulders. Athletes should also strive to develop quickness, fast reaction and movement time, and agility. All facets of the game must be addressed and covered in any preseason conditioning program. Finally, each player must assess personal reasons for participating. Fear of injury may precipitate injury. An old adage that rings with great truth regarding prevention of injuries is: "If you don't enjoy it, don't do it."

References

Calliet, R. *Neck and Arm Pain*. Philadelphia: F. A. Davis, 1981.

Carter, D., and V. Frankel. Biomechanics of hyperextension injuries to the cervical spine in football. *American Journal of Sports Medicine* 8:302–308, 1980.

Clarke, K. Football fatalities in actual perspectives. *Medicine and Science in Sports and Exercise* 10:1978.

Hoppenfeld, S. *Physical Examination of the Spine and Extremities*. New York: Appleton-Century-Crofts, 1976.

Norkin, C., and P. Levangie. *Joint Structure and Function—A Comprehensive Analysis*. Philadelphia: F. A. Davis, 1983.

O'Donoghue, D. *Treatment of Injuries to Athletes*. Philadelphia: W. B. Saunders, 1984.

Rogers, B. The mechanics of head and neck trauma to football players. *Athletic Training* 132–135, 1981.

Schneider, R. *Head and Neck Injuries in Football*. Baltimore: Williams & Wilkins, 1973.

Strauss, R. H. *Sports Medicine and Physiology*. Philadelphia: W. B. Saunders, 1976.

Torg, J. *Athletic Injuries to the Head, Neck and Face*. Philadelphia: Lea & Febiger, 1982.

Tortora, G. *Principles of Human Anatomy*. San Francisco: Harper & Row, 1977.

Spearing: In football, an illegal blocking technique in which the blocker's head is the first point of contact with an opponent. This technique has caused many serious head and neck injuries.

16 Back Injuries

The difficult and physically demanding routines today's gymnasts practice have increased their risk of back injuries.

BACK injuries are extremely common in athletics, particularly in contact sports like football and hockey and in activities that involve vigorous spinal motions, such as gymnastics and diving. Although strains and contusions are the most common athletic back injuries, back pain may be caused by related factors such as infection, **renal disease,** biomechanical aberrations, and **congenital** anomalies.

Back pain is usually self-limiting, typically clearing up within one or two weeks even without treatment. (However, in some athletes a back injury can become chronically debilitating.) The fact that back injury occurs so often suggests that most athletes have musculoskeletal deficiencies that predispose them to injury. Since the primary causes of back injury are inadequate strength and flexibility, poor technique, and overuse (all causes that are amenable to correction), the athletic trainer and coach should initiate a preventive program that addresses each factor. The athletic trainer and coach must have a knowledge of spinal anatomy and **biomechanics,** know how to evaluate back problems, and be thoroughly familiar with rehabilitative techniques.

Renal disease: Disease of the kidney.
Congenital: Present at birth.
Biomechanics: Study of the physics of motion in humans or animals.

247

248

Anatomy

The vertebral column consists of seven cervical (neck), twelve thoracic (throat), five lumbar (lower back), five fused sacral, and four fused coccygeal vertebrae. The column surrounds and protects the spinal cord, is an attachment site for ligaments and muscles, helps maintain upright posture, and helps support the thorax (Figure 16-1). Neck injuries were discussed in Chapter 15; here we describe the lumbar and thoracic portions of the spine.

Vertebrae

The vertebrae have certain common characteristics, but there are also considerable differences among those in the cervical, thoracic, and lumbar portions of the spine (Figure 16-2). The two essential segments of a vertebra are the anterior (body) (see Figure 16-3, p. 250) and the posterior (arch). The vertebral body is cylindrical, has flattened surfaces for attachments of an intervertebral disk, and has a rim around its circumference.

The vertebral arch is made up of several parts (Figure 16-3). Two short, thick processes called **pedicles** extend posteriorly from the upper border of the vertebral body and join the arch to the vertebral body. Concavities called intervertebral notches lie above and below the pedicles. The notches between two vertebrae form the intervertebral **foramina,** through which pass the spinal nerves. The **laminae** are two broad plates extending posteromedially from the pedicles. They fuse at the midline and form the vertebral foramen with the pedicles. The **spinous process,** which is a site for attachment of muscles and ligaments, is a bony projection which begins at the fused site of the laminae and extends posteriorly from the midline. Also, a pair of **transverse processes** project laterally from the

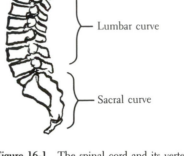

Figure 16-1 The spinal cord and its vertebrae. (From Crouch, J. E. *Introduction to Human Anatomy*, 6th ed. Palo Alto, Calif.: Mayfield Publishing Co., 1983, p. 57.)

point where the lamina joins the pedicle. Finally, pairs of **superior** and **inferior facets,** which serve as articulations for adjacent vertebrae, arise from the junctions of the pedicles and laminae.

Spinal Curves

At maturity, the spine exhibits four characteristic curves. The posteriorly convex thoracic and sacral curves are the primary curves because they form early in life. The posteriorly concave and aligned cervical and lumbar curves are the secondary curves. Together, the cervical and lumbar concavities are called a **lordosis;** the thoracic and sacral convexities are called a **kyphosis.**

A change in one curve causes change in the other. Often, an individual with an increased lumbar lordosis compensates with an increased thoracic kyphosis. Conceivably, a low back injury could eventually manifest itself as pain in the cervical or thoracic area and vice versa.

Pedicles: Two short, thick processes of vertebral bone that connect the vertebral body to the transverse processes.
Foramen (foramina): A natural opening in a bone or tissue.
Laminae: Two broad plates of bone that extend from the pedicles to the spinous processes of the vertebrae.
Spinous process: Portion of a vertebra that projects rearward (dorsally); acts as attachment for spinal muscles and ligaments.
Transverse process: Portion of a vertebra that projects laterally (each side) from the point where the lamina joins the pedicle.
Superior/inferior facets: Articular processes of the vertebrae that project from the junctions of the pedicles and the laminae.
Lordosis: The concavities of the cervical (neck) and lumbar (low back) spine. Often used to refer to an abnormal forward curvature of the back.
Kyphosis: The convexities of the thoracic and sacral spine. Often used to describe an abnormally convex (rearward) thoracic spine.

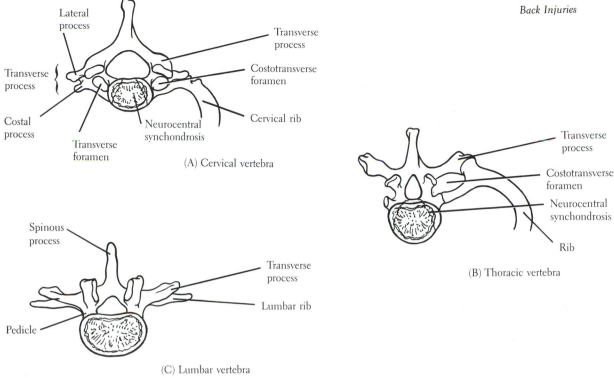

Figure 16-2 Examples of cervical, thoracic, and lumbar vertebrae.

Alignment of the pelvis also affects the curvature of the spine. Normally, the anterior superior **iliac spines** and the **symphysis pubis** lie in an almost vertical plane, while the anterior iliac spines and the posterior inferior iliac spines lie almost along the same horizontal plane. The pelvis is therefore normally aligned in an anterior tilt. Pelvic obliquity can lead to scoliosis (abnormal lateral curvature of the spine), which may cause an increased susceptibility to injury (Figure 16-4, p. 251). As discussed in Chapter 11, spinal malalignment can be easily identified in the preparticipation physical examination and remedial exercises then prescribed.

Intervertebral Disks

The intervertebral disks are the chief structural units between the vertebral bodies and mainly absorb and disperse shock during spinal loading. They also bind the vertebrae yet allow movement. As do the vertebrae, the intervertebral disks exhibit characteristics unique to their location in the spine. The thoracic disks are of equal height both anteriorly and posteriorly. They are also thinner here than in other areas and small in comparison to the size of the vertebral body. Lumbar disks are thicker anteriorly than posteriorly and therefore contribute to the normal lumbar curve.

The disks' shock-absorbing properties derive from the **nucleus pulposus, the annulus fibrosus,** and the cartilaginous end plates. The nucleus of each disk is normally about 80 percent water, which enables the disk to change shape when compressed (although this ability decreases with age). The nucleus also exerts an intrinsic pressure called **preload,** which enhances the disk's resistance to forces. However, the nucleus pulposus'

Iliac spines: One of four short projections of bone from the ilium.

Symphysis pubis: The point in the pelvis where the two pelvic bones are joined by fibrocartilage.

Nucleus pulposus: The central portion of an intervertebral disk; composed of a gelatinous material that contains much water.

Annulus fibrosus: The outer portion of an intervertebral disk; composed of fibrocartilage.

Preload: The stretch the nucleus pulposus imposes on the intervertebral disk to help the disk withstand compressional forces.

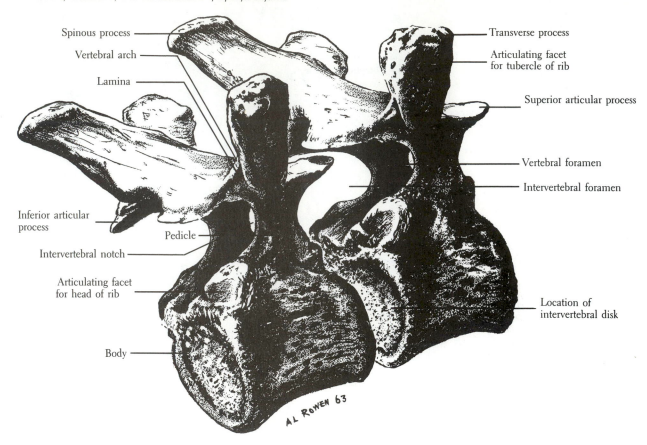

Spinous process

Vertebral arch

Lamina

Inferior articular process

Intervertebral notch

Pedicle

Articulating facet for head of rib

Body

Transverse process

Articulating facet for tubercle of rib

Superior articular process

Vertebral foramen

Intervertebral foramen

Location of intervertebral disk

AL RONEN 63

Figure 16-3 Two thoracic vertebrae—view from below and the right side. (From Crouch, 1983, p. 57.)

central and somewhat posterior location in the disk predispose the disk to injury. Injury to the disk may result in the disk bulging and impinging upon the nerve root, causing back and leg pain (Figure 16-5).

The annulus fibrosus, a strong, fibrocartilaginous structure, surrounds the nucleus pulposus. The annulus' elasticity helps absorb forces while holding the vertebrae together. The parallel alignment and the thickness of the posterior annulus fibers make the disks resistant to torsional stress but structurally vulnerable to anterior stress.

The cartilaginous **end plates** separate the disks from the vertebral bodies; they are composed of hyaline cartilage and act as semipermeable membranes that facilitate the delivery of nutrients to the

disks. Holes within the end plates allow for the diffusion of metabolites but also cause structural weakness.

Ligaments

The inter- and intrasegmental longitudinal ligament track systems form a mechanical unit. The intersegmental system binds several vertebrae and consists of the anterior and posterior longitudinal and supraspinous ligaments. The intrasegmental system binds single, adjacent vertebrae and consists of the interspinalis ligamentum flava and the intertransverse ligaments. The posterior ligaments limit flexion and the anterior ligaments limit extension. See Figure 16-6 (p. 252).

End plates: The cartilaginous articular surface of vertebrae that separates the intervertebral disks from the vertebral bodies.

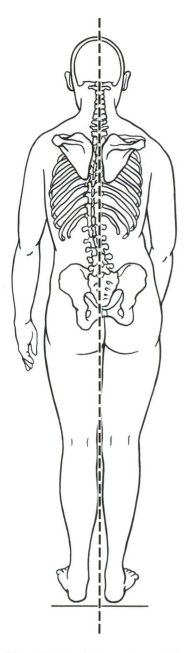

Figure 16-4 Scoliosis, an abnormal lateral curvature of the spine.

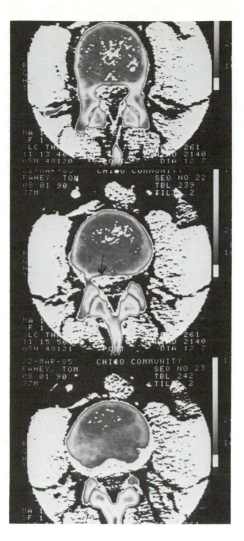

Figure 16-5 CT scan of lumbar vertabrae (L3 and L4) showing ruptured intravertebral disk. This injury was sustained during weight lifting.

Muscles

A number of small muscles combine to form the relatively dense musculature of the back (Figures 16-7 and 16-8, pp. 252, 253). These muscles work with the abdominals to stabilize the thorax, protect the abdominal cavity, and perform the active motions of the spine.

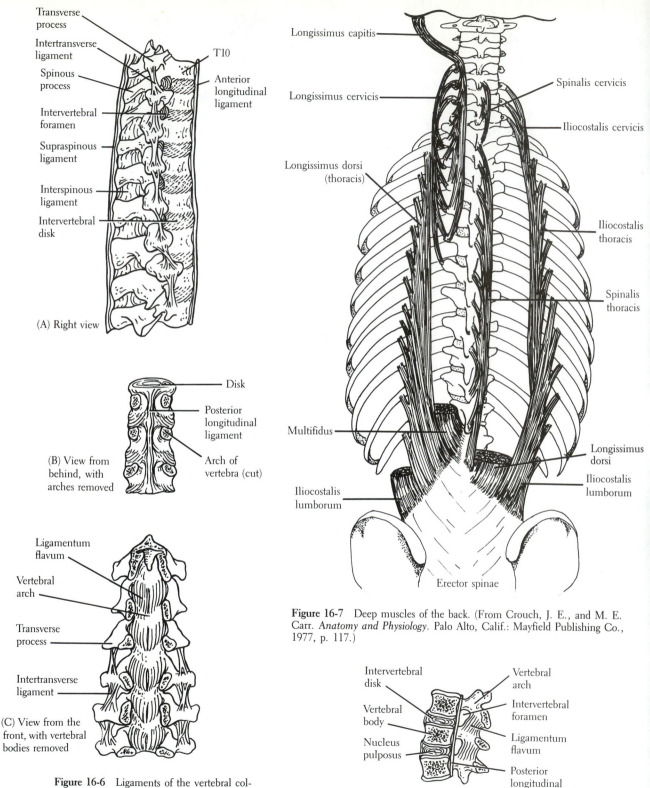

Transverse process

Intertransverse ligament

Spinous process

Intervertebral foramen

Supraspinous ligament

Interspinous ligament

Intervertebral disk

T10

Anterior longitudinal ligament

(A) Right view

Disk

Posterior longitudinal ligament

Arch of vertebra (cut)

(B) View from behind, with arches removed

Ligamentum flavum

Vertebral arch

Transverse process

Intertransverse ligament

(C) View from the front, with vertebral bodies removed

Figure 16-6 Ligaments of the vertebral column.

Longissimus capitis

Longissimus cervicis

Longissimus dorsi (thoracic)

Multifidus

Iliocostalis lumborum

Spinalis cervicis

Iliocostalis cervicis

Iliocostalis thoracis

Spinalis thoracis

Longissimus dorsi

Iliocostalis lumborum

Erector spinae

Figure 16-7 Deep muscles of the back. (From Crouch, J. E., and M. E. Carr. *Anatomy and Physiology*. Palo Alto, Calif.: Mayfield Publishing Co., 1977, p. 117.)

Intervertebral disk

Vertebral body

Nucleus pulposus

Vertebral arch

Intervertebral foramen

Ligamentum flavum

Posterior longitudinal ligament

(D) Left view

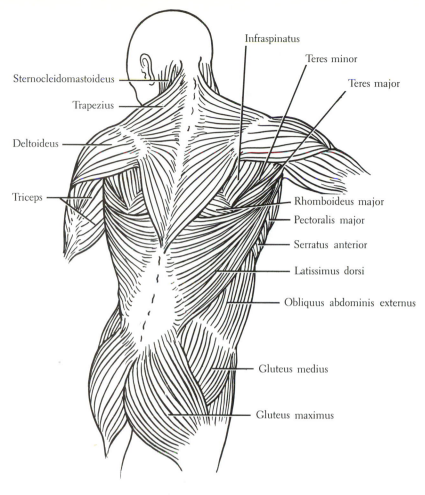

Figure 16-8 Superficial muscles of the back.

Labels on figure:
Infraspinatus
Teres minor
Teres major
Sternocleidomastoideus
Trapezius
Deltoideus
Triceps
Rhomboideus major
Pectoralis major
Serratus anterior
Latissimus dorsi
Obliquus abdominis externus
Gluteus medius
Gluteus maximus

Biomechanics of the Spine and Disks

The **classical movements** of the spine are **flexion, extension,** rotation, and **lateral flexion.** These classical movements are accompanied by more subtle **accessory movements** that are essential to normal range of motion (ROM) and painless function. Accessory movements include joint-play and component motions. The joint-play motions are gliding and compressional, not under voluntary control, and occur only in response to an outside force. These motions are analogous to the small shifts in bridges when the wind blows

heavily; like the spine, bridges are built in segments to accommodate compressional and gliding forces and to "give a little" in response to outside forces. The component motions take place in a joint complex or related joint and facilitate a particular active motion.

For the most part, the size of the intervertebral disks and the direction of the articulating facets determine the spine's movement. If the facets lie in a horizontal plane, more rotation can occur; if they lie in a sagittal plane, more flexion and extension can occur; and if they lie in a frontal plane, more lateral flexion can occur.

Isolated active movement of just one spinal segment is not possible; movement occurs in other segments as well.

Classical movements: The gross, obvious movements of a joint.

Flexion: Bending of a joint, thus decreasing the joint angle.

Extension: Straightening of a joint, thus increasing the joint angle. The opposite of flexion.

Lateral flexion: Sideward bending of a joint; possible in the neck and trunk.

Accessory movements: Subtle joint movements such as "joint play" (an imperceptible gliding motion within the joint).

Furthermore, spinal flexion is a segmental *upward* movement; for example, the fifth lumbar moves before the fourth, which moves before the third, and so on. Spinal flexion is a "pure" movement that does not require vertebral rotation to achieve a full ROM. Extension is also segmental and pure but proceeds downward. Lateral flexion is segmental and proceeds upward but requires rotation of the vertebra to attain complete ROM. Rotation is pure but not segmental and unique; all segments rotate synchronously.

As discussed, the intervertebral disks have the ability to change shape, which helps them absorb forces. With movement, a disk becomes wedge-shaped, with the wider edge toward the convexity of the curve. Pressure to the annulus is greater on the concave side. The articulating facets glide while the disk deforms. The loss of motion in either trunk flexion or extension causes loss of function in the opposite motion.

As the spine flexes, the wider edge of the now wedge-shaped disk is posterior, stretching the posterior fibers of the annulus. There is accompanying compression of the anterior fibers and a posterior gliding of the nucleus. This process is reversed during extension. During left and right lateral flexion, the motion of the wedge is medial and lateral instead of anterior and posterior.

Factors Predisposing Athletes to Back Pain

Although back strain is by far the most prevalent cause of back pain, various congenital and **pathological** factors may be the primary or secondary causes. As discussed in Chapter 19, even though pain in athletes is rarely caused by pathological factors, the factors must be considered because the consequences of neglecting them are so potentially severe. For example,

chronic low back pain, which in most cases is due to such factors as overuse or trauma, may, in an isolated case, be caused by a malignant tumor. Therefore, the point cannot be overemphasized: When in doubt, refer the athlete to the team or family physician.

Nerve-Root Entrapment Syndrome

Nerve-root entrapment, a relatively common problem, may be initiated by a combination of congenital defect and trauma. This **syndrome** may be caused by **subluxation** of facet joints, which results in a synovial capsule reaction (see Chapter 7), cartilage destruction, abnormal bone formation, or enlargement of the articular processes. Injury or pathological changes in the disks may also cause nerve-root entrapment; contributing factors in changing disk characteristics are tears and internal disruption from trauma, spondylolysis (degeneration and resorption of the disk), and **osteoarthritis**. Persons with congenitally narrow spinal canals are particularly prone to nerve-root entrapment syndrome. **Atrophy** of leg muscles is a sign of this disorder.

Spondylolysis and Spondylolisthesis

Spondylolysis and **spondylolisthesis** are fractures of the **pars interarticularis** (isthmus) and thought to be genetic in nature. Spondylolysis is a partial defect in the pars interarticularis with no vertebral slippage; spondylolisthesis is a complete break in the isthmus, in which the body of the affected vertebra slips forward across the vertebra immediately below it. These injuries occur in gymnastics and contact sports, usually from chronic or acute hyperextension of the spine (Figure 16-9). The incidence of these injuries has increased in gymnastics, probably because of the extreme spinal hyperextension movements made popular by Olympic gymnastic champions Olga Korbut and Nadia Comaneci.

Syndrome: A group of signs and symptoms that appear together in a predictable manner.
Subluxation: Partial joint dislocation.

Osteoarthritis: Disease of the joints characterized by degeneration of joint (articular) cartilage and increase in the size (hypertrophy) of local bone.
Atrophy: Decrease in size and function of a muscle.

Spondylolysis: Development of fibrous tissue at the par interarticularis that results from a stress fracture or fracture from a single traumatic incident.
Spondylolisthesis: Forward slipping of one vertebral body in relation to the vertebral segment immediately below it.
Pars interarticularis: The narrow bony isthmus between the superior and inferior articular processes of the vertebrae.
Pathological: Pertaining to the nature, cause, development, and consequences of disease or injury.

Infection

Infection, particularly from staphylococci, may cause back pain, even in young athletes. To rule out infection, the athletic trainer should always take the oral temperature of athletes complaining of back pain. If infection is suspected, the athlete must be referred to a physician.

Unstable Vertebrae

Unstable vertebrae—one vertebra slips backward and forward on another vertebra—may predispose an athlete to back pain. This condition is typically detected by an x-ray of the spine in flexion and extension. Corrective measures include conditioning exercises (see "Rehabilitation and Exercises for the Lower Back," p. 263) and bracing (e.g., the Boston brace; see Chapter 13). Surgery is sometimes necessary in extreme cases.

Hyperlordosis

Hyperlordosis (accentuated low back curve), caused by a congenital defect, protruding abdomen and abnormal pelvic tilt, and poor posture, may predispose an athlete to low back pain. This condition puts pressure on the spinal nerves, causing spasm and disability. This problem, which is difficult to treat, may be managed through weight loss, posture modification, and exercise (see "Rehabilitation and Exercises for the Lower Back," p. 263).

Scoliosis

Scoliosis (abnormal lateral curvature of the spine) may predispose an athlete to back pain (Figure 16-4, p. 251). This condition, which is typically idiopathic (without known cause), tends to worsen with age (back pain and degenerative arthritis), so it is important to identify and correct it in young athletes. The simple posture tests in Figure 11-3 (p. 172) provide a simple screen-

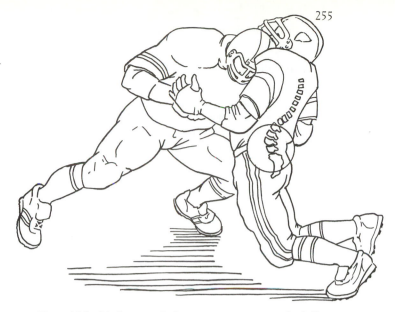

Figure 16-9 Mechanism of a hyperextension injury in football. Hyperextension causes increased stress at the par interarticularis.

ing technique. Scoliosis usually can be corrected without surgery through remedial exercises if identified and treated early. A physician should manage the treatment for scoliosis.

Other Conditions

Various other factors may cause back pain or predispose an athlete to it; fortunately, most are rare. Among these conditions are facet tropism (congenitally asymmetrical facet alignment), transitional vertebrae (variant in the number of mobile vertebrae), differences in leg length (fairly common), benign and malignant **tumors,** chemical toxicity, **osteoporosis** and other metabolic disorders, inflammatory diseases like rheumatoid arthritis, chronic infection, circulatory disorders (e.g., abdominal aortic **aneurysm**), and psychological factors. Pain may also be referred from injuries in other areas, such as the hip. Psychological factors are probably the most common conditions among athletics, who may use minor back pain as a way to malinger or seek sympathy. Anxiety, however, may exacerbate symptoms by causing muscle tension.

Hyperlordosis: Exaggerated or abnormal curvature of the lumbar spine.

Tumor: An overgrowth of a tissue; also called neoplasm.
Osteoporosis: A bone disease characterized by loss of bone matrix; most common in postmenopausal women.
Aneurysm: The bulging of a blood vessel.
Scoliosis: Abnormal lateral curvature of the spine.

Low Back Injuries

Most athletic back injuries are traumatic, and the onset of injury is usually rapid rather than progressive. The athlete may describe the mechanism of injury as "I hit the ground," "I was twisted," "I was torqued," etc. Putting It into Practice 16-1 summarizes the principles of evaluating back injuries.

Contusions

A **contusion** is one of the most frequent injuries in contact sports. The low back areas most susceptible to contusion are (1) the muscles surrounding the low back, (2) posterior iliac crest, (3) posterior superior iliac spine, and (4) the vertebrae spinous processes (Figure 16-10, p. 258).

Mechanism of Injury. Contusions most frequently result from contact with other players and objects. They occur relatively often in sports like basketball, hockey, gymnastics, football, and rugby. Frequently an athlete receives a contusion along the posterior aspect of the iliac crest. Contusion to this area (known in athletic jargon as a "hip pointer") should not be considered a back problem.

Contusion: A bruise.

PUTTING IT INTO PRACTICE 16-1 — Evaluating Low Back Injury

Injuries to the low back include contusions, sprains, strains, and spinal nerve compression. The biomechanical relationships among vertebrae, pelvis, and musculature are extremely complex, so the athletic trainer must determine the precipitating mechanism of the injury. Perform the following steps when evaluating a back injury:

History of Injury

What was the nature of the activity when the injury occurred? Did the injury occur in flexion or extension? Does the athlete have a history of chronic back pain? What motions tend to cause pain? If back pain is chronic, are there any times when the pain or discomfort is more severe?

Visual Examination

Observe the athlete's posture for symmetry and pelvic tilt. Is the pelvis symmetrically aligned, or is one iliac crest higher than the other? Mark spinous processes and assess for scoliosis (see Chapter 11). Is the athlete stooped over? Notice the characteristics of voluntary movements. Do any normal spinal movements (flexion, extension, lateral flexion, rotation, circumduction) cause pain or hesitation? Is the athlete obviously experiencing muscle spasm? Upon inspection, are there any signs of obvious deformity, swelling, or discoloration? Visually inspect the spine as a unit and examine the characteristics of individual vertebrae. Look for obvious differences between right leg and left leg in muscle mass. If you observe differences, measure them.

Palpation

Locate areas of the spine most subject to trauma (i.e., spinous processes, iliac crests) and palpate them for point tenderness. Refer the athlete to a physician if skeletal or ligamentous structures have any point tenderness. Palpate the low back muscles, quadriceps, anterior and posterior lower leg muscles, and buttocks, and look for point tenderness, swelling, and muscle spasm.

Range of Motion

Test the various active and passive ranges of motion of the lower spine. Passive stretching of the muscle to the opposite side of the injury will cause pain if the athlete has a low back strain. Active lateral flexion with or without resistance

(continued on next page)

Evaluation. When evaluating the injured athlete, the athletic trainer should (1) take a thorough history, (2) visually examine (inspect) the spinal column for obvious signs of injury, (3) locate those areas most subject to trauma, and (4) palpate each spinous process, noting areas of **point tenderness.** If palpation reveals an acutely tender area, refer the athlete for x-ray examination.

Treatment and Prevention. Chapter 5 covers treatment of contusions. Contusions are difficult to prevent, although practicing normal injury-prevention methods, such as using good technique and observing the rules, may help.

Ligament Injuries

The anterior-posterior longitudinal ligaments that run along each side of the vertebrae are thick, tough, and not easily injured. The supraspinal ligament that sits on top of all spinous processes is most subject to trauma.

Evaluation. Acute sprain of the supraspinal ligament involves tenderness where the ligament attaches to the spinous process. Active and passive spinal hyperextension will not be painful, and active flexion of the spine will cause pain only when the stress is sufficient to stretch the ligament at the site of injury. Muscle spasm is the most common symptom of this injury.

Point tenderness: Pain elicited at a specific anatomical location.

Evaluating Low Back Injury *(continued)*

toward the injured side will cause pain. Active hyperextension against resistance will be painful. Forward flexion will be painful only when the flexion is sufficient to stretch the muscle involved. Also, measure the flexibility of the hamstrings, hip flexors, quadriceps, and Achilles tendon. Have the athlete touch his or her toes while sitting, and assess segmental flexibility (i.e., upper back, lower back, hamstrings, and calf), and observe pelvic tilt. A symmetrically rounded back with normal ROM indicates a normal length of the back, hamstring, and calf muscles.

Muscle Strength

Manually test muscles of the trunk and lower leg.

1. Test the back extensor muscles by having the athlete raise the trunk while lying on his or her stomach (back hyperextension). Notice the position of the pelvic tilt. The buttocks will appear elevated if the hip extensors are weak or neurologically impaired.

2. Test the strength of the abdominal muscles by having the athlete perform and hold an abdominal curl (partial trunk flexion) with the legs straight. This movement should be performed with hands behind the head. Abdominal weakness is indicated if the athlete must place the hands on the chest or extend the arms in front. A sixty-second bent knee sit up test may be performed when the symptoms are in remission.

3. Manually test muscle strength of knee extensors and flexors, hip flexors and extensors, and ankle plantar and dorsiflexors (the results also provide neurological information).

Neurological Evaluation

Note signs of numbness or radiating pain. Map and cross-check these areas by using a dermatome map to help determine level of disk involvement (see Figure 9-6, p. 143). Remember that referred pain can be manifested by disk problems above or below the actual level of complaint. Perform tests for sciatic nerve irritation (contralateral straight leg raising test, Lasègue's sign test, and the bowstring sign test). Test sensory perception of the lower leg's dermatomes, and test stretch reflexes of the patellar and Achilles tendons.

Treatment and Rehabilitation. After administering acute injury care, the athletic trainer should refer the athlete to a physician. Treatment typically includes rest, bracing to restrict motion, and heat (heat is applied after the acute phase; see Putting It into Practice 13-1, p. 194). See "Rehabilitation Exercises for the Lower Back" (p. 263) for exercises appropriate for this injury.

Muscle Strains

A number of small muscles comprise the musculature of the low back (Figures 16-7 and 16-8, pp. 252, 253). Strain to any one muscle or group of muscles can be caused by overstretching or overuse.

Evaluation. Evaluation of the injured athlete may reveal the following signs and symptoms:

- Visual inspection may reveal swelling or discoloration.
- Palpation may reveal localized or point tenderness and muscle spasm in the involved musculature.
- Passive stretching of the muscle to the opposite side of the injury will cause pain.
- Active lateral flexion with or without resistance toward the injured side will cause pain.
- Active hyperextension against resistance will be painful.
- Forward flexion will be painful only when it is sufficient to stretch the muscle involved.

Treatment and Rehabilitation. Administer acute care for soft tissue injury (see Chapter 5). Refer serious strains to a physician for treatment. It is particularly important to determine the cause of the injury by taking a thorough history. Often, a predisposing factor, such as poor posture, scoliosis, or poor lifting techniques (see Putting It into Practice 16-2) is the root of the problem. Rehabilitation exercises are discussed later in this chapter.

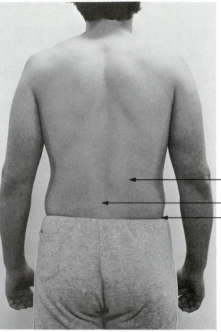

Soft tissue on lateral aspects of spine

Lumbar spine

Iliac crest

Figure 16-10   The three most common sites of contusions to the back.

Neurological Problems

Reduction in joint space is the major cause of neurological disorders in the low back. When the space between two vertebrae narrows, it impinges or pinches a spinal nerve. This pathology is commonly called a **pinched nerve,** but it is actually a compression of a spinal nerve. Once the nerve has been compressed, the athlete may display the following neurological signs: (1) numbness in the involved dermatome, (2) **radiating pain** (pain sensation that travels along the path of a spinal nerve, (3) loss of motor functions, and (4) depressed reflexes. Symptoms vary tremendously among athletes.

Evaluation for Neurological Problems. Carefully evaluate any signs of numbness or radiating pain. Because these signs follow a specific pattern, the areas of numbness or radiating pain can be mapped and cross-checked by using a dermatome map (see Figure 9-6,

Pinched nerve: Injury caused by compression of a nerve. Symptoms may include numbness, radiating pain, loss of motor function, and depressed reflexes.

Radiating pain: Pain that travels from one point to another.

Referred pain: Pain experienced at one location but caused by injury in another location.

p. 143). The dermatome map is useful for determining the level of disk involvement. For example, if an athlete complains of numbness or pain over the anterior portion of the thigh, the second and third lumbar (L2 and L3) are most likely involved. The dermatome map allows the athletic trainer to follow the sensory nerve from the point on the body producing pain, numbness, etc., to the point of injury (point of neural impingement). This phenomenon of experiencing pain at one point from an injury at another point is called **referred pain.** Referred pain is manifested by disk problems above or below the actual level of complaint. The dermatome map can be very helpful for evaluating referred pain.

Three simple tests for determining sciatic nerve irritation are Lasègue's sign test, the contralateral straight leg raising test, and the bowstring sign test (Figures 16-11 to 16-13; see pp. 260, 261). If there is sciatic nerve irritation, these tests produce a sharp pain that may radiate from the leg to the back.

Evaluation of Chronic Low Back Problems

When an athlete complains of chronic low back pain, a spinal examination is necessary to determine the cause. After a complete history of the injury has been obtained, a structural evaluation is necessary. Evaluation procedures are discussed in Chapter 9.

After inspection and palpation have been performed, assess the active movements: (1) flexion, (2) extension, (3) lateral flexion, and (4) rotation. Perform the first three tests with the athlete standing. To test flexion, have the athlete bend forward as far as possible, keeping knees straight and trying to touch the floor. Test extension by having the athlete bend backward as far as possible. Assess lateral flexion by having the athlete slide his or her hand down

PUTTING IT INTO PRACTICE 16-2

Proper Lifting Techniques

Poor lifting techniques are a common cause of many back injuries. To lift properly, follow these techniques:

- Keep your weight as close to your body as possible. The farther you hold a weight from your body, the more strain there is on your back.
- Do most of your lifting with your legs. The large muscles of the thighs and buttocks are much stronger than those of the back, which are better suited for maintaining an erect posture. Keep your hips and buttocks tucked in.
- When picking up an object from the ground, do not bend at your waist with straight legs because this action places tremendous strain on the low back muscles and disks.
- Do not twist while lifting. Twisting places an uneven load on back muscles, which can cause strain.
- Lift the weight smoothly, not with a jerking, rapid motion. Rapid motions place more stress on the spinal muscles.
- Allow adequate rest between lifts. Fatigue is a prominent cause of back strain.
- Lift within your capacity. Athletes should not lift a load beyond the limits of their strength.

the lateral side of the leg as far as possible.

Next, assess lumbar rotation. The configuration of the facets of the lumbar vertebrae are structured to allow flexion and extension but not rotation. However, because no one section of the spinal column works by itself, some lumbar rotation does occur. To test lumbar rotation, have the athlete lie on her or his back, with hips and knees flexed ninety degrees. The athlete then rotates her or his legs from side to side, keeping shoulders flat on the table. If rotation is limited, the athlete will not be able to keep the shoulders flat on the table.

The next concern is the condition of the muscles surrounding the hip joint because they are important stabilizers of the low back and pelvis. Any abnormalities in joint ROM or mobility place undue stress on the spinal column, especially the lumbar area. Athletes often display tight hip flexors and quadriceps because during training they usually do not use the muscles through their full ROM.

To test the tightness of these muscle groups, have the athlete lie on his or her back on a treatment table (**Thomas' sign test**). The athlete flexes the right hip by bringing knees toward the chest. Normally, the left thigh should not come off the table. The tighter the hip flexor muscles, the higher the opposite thigh will rise off the table. Repeat the test on the left side and compare the ROM of both hips.

To assess quadriceps flexibility, have the athlete lie supine with hips flexed ninety degrees. The athlete flexes the knee as far as possible. Normally the athlete will be able to almost touch the heel to the buttock.

Next, test the tightness of the hamstring group. Use the **straight leg raising test.** Have the athlete lie supine and lift a straight right leg to a position ninety degrees of hip flexion, which is the normal ROM for the joint. If the athlete has any neurological abnormali-

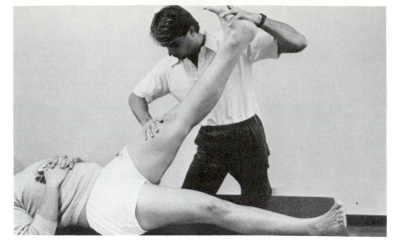

Figure 16-11 Lasègue's sign for determining sciatica. The athlete's straight leg is raised while the foot is in dorsiflexion. Pain is produced along the sciatic nerve pathway if a nerve root is impinged during this procedure.

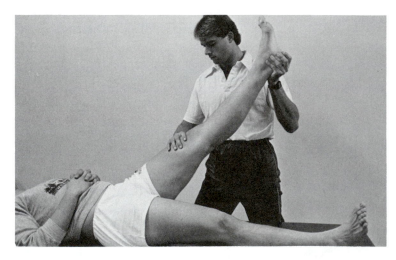

Figure 16-12 Straight leg raising test. This motion produces sciatic nerve symptoms, such as hip, leg, or foot pain, if a nerve root is impinged.

ties, the person will experience sharp and stinging pain while lifting the straight leg because this movement puts pressure on the spinal nerves (Figures 16-11 and 16-12).

The hip abductors are the next group of muscles to assess. Have the athlete lie on her left side while holding her right leg at a forty-five degree angle as hard as she can. Manually push the leg down and estimate the resistance. Repeat the test on the left side and compare the difference in strength. Fre-

Thomas' sign test: Tests the flexibility of the hip flexors.

Straight leg raising test: Tests the flexibility of the hamstrings and helps detect neurological abnormalities in the lumbar (low back) spine.

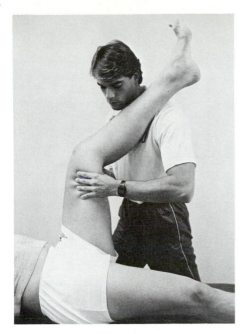

Figure 16-13 Bowstring sign test. The athlete's hip is flexed while the knee is bent. Nerve-root impingement will elicit sciatic nerve symptoms. This test is often more effective if the athlete dorsiflexes the foot.

quently, athletes who complain of low back pain have weaker hip muscles on one side than the other. It is important to have good, symmetrical hip strength because the abductors on the opposite side of the unsupported leg hold the pelvis level. If the abductors are not strong enough, the pelvis collapses to the unsupported side, resulting in the **Trendelenburg gait.**

Most daily activities place the spine in flexion, so many people have limited ability for spinal extension. To further check lumbar extension, have the athlete lie prone on a treatment table and perform a press-up. The athlete places her hands by her shoulder as if she were going to perform a push-up; then she pushes up while leaving her hip on the table.

Manually test the muscles listed in Putting It into Practice 16-3 (under "Muscle Tests"; see p. 262) to help locate the possible level of pathological involvement. Grade each test by using the standard 0 to 5 rating scale: 5 = normal strength, 4 = good strength,

3 = fair strength, 2 = poor strength, 1 = trace strength, and 0 = zero strength. Determine the level of pathology by comparing specific muscular deficiencies with the spinal innervations shown in Putting It into Practice 16-4 (p. 263).

Back pain is related to poor posture and improper body mechanics. Often, instructing athletes in how to properly sit, stand, sleep, and lift will greatly decrease their incidence of chronic back pain.

Sitting, especially for a long time, dangerously increases intradiskal pressure, particularly in posterior portions. Proper lumbar support with a backrest inclined slightly posteriorly reduces the intradiskal pressure. A chair should have arm and thigh supports. Frequent change of position and getting up and walking every hour or so are important ways to reduce compressional stress.

Postural stresses during sleeping often cause chronic back pain. One-third of the day is spent sleeping; poor posture during this time can undo even the most judicious back-rehabilitation program. Lying in a kyphotic posture for a prolonged period (a posture that accentuates the posterior convex curve of the back; can be caused by an overly soft mattress) may increase pressure toward the posterior aspect of the disk. Sleeping on a firm mattress and without a pillow prevents excessive flexion of the spine. Likewise, sleeping supine increases the lumbar lordosis, which can also cause problems. Athletes should sleep on their sides with knees bent (fetal position) or on their backs with pillows propped under their knees.

There are also proper techniques for getting out of bed. The athlete should roll to the side, swing the legs over the side of the bed, and then push himself or herself up with the arms to a sitting position. Sitting up directly while twisting the body at the same time may be dangerous.

Lifting is a common occupational and physical conditioning activity. While an athlete is lifting, the load

Trendelenburg gait: When a person is walking and weight is placed on one leg, the opposite side of the pelvis is elevated to maintain balance.

PUTTING IT INTO PRACTICE 16-3

Evaluating Low Back Pain

Active Movements

_____ Extension
_____ Side flexion (right)
_____ Side flexion (left)
_____ Flexion

Movement	Group	Nerve Root	Findings
	Muscle Tests, Standing		
Plantar flexion of ankle	Gastrocnemius	S1, S2	
	Muscle Tests, Supine		
Hip compression	Sacroiliac joints		_____
Flexion of hip	Hip joint		_____
Extension of hip			_____
Medial rotation			_____
Lateral rotation			_____
Side lateral rotation with neck flexion			_____
Hip flexion	Iliopsoas	L2, L3	_____
Dorsiflexion	Anterior tibialis	L4	_____
Toe extension	Extensor hallucis	L4, L5	_____
Eversion of foot	Peronei	L5, S1	_____
Reflexes	Knee		_____
Plantar response (upper motor neuron sign)	CNS		
	Lumbar Tests, Prone		
Ankle jerk		L5, S1, S2	_____
Quadriceps stretch		L3	_____
Hip flexor stretch		L3	_____
	Muscle Tests, Prone		
Knee flexion		S1, S2	_____
Knee extension		L1, L2	_____

should be kept close to the body, to reduce the bending moment arm at the spinal joints. This requires less muscle force because an object requires more force to lift the farther it is carried from the body. Keeping the object close to the body also reduces intradiskal pressure. A lift should be performed primarily with the legs rather than the back. In addition, when moving an object, pushing is preferable to pulling. In pushing, the rectus abdominis mus-

cle counterbalances the moment arm (the spine acting as a lever), reducing the load on the disk. (See also Putting It into Practice 16-2, p. 259).

A lift involving rotation should be performed in two separate motions: lift, then rotate. Rotation weakens the disks' annulus fibers, and flexion followed by rotation is a particularly dangerous position for the spine. With flexion, the joint opens and places the load on the disk, which is not protected by the facets.

Determining Spinal Innervations: Checklist

Nerve Root	Signs	Present?
L2	Weak psoas; C.A.[a] from groin to front of knee; knee jerk unaffected	
L3	Weak psoas and quadriceps; C.A. from knee to front of ankle; knee jerk absent	
L4	Limited side lateral rotation; weak anterior tibialis and extensor hallucis; C.A. from big toe; knee jerk unaffected	
L5	Limited side lateral rotation; weak extensor hallucis and peronei; first, second, and third toes numb; ankle jerk may be absent	
S1	Limited side lateral rotation; weak peronei, calf, hamstrings, and gluteus maximus; C.A. from outer two toes; ankle jerk absent	
S2	Limited side lateral rotation; weak calf, hamstrings, and gluteus maximus; calf (sometimes thigh) numb; ankle jerk absent	
S3	Full side lateral rotation; no neurological signs	
S4	Full side lateral rotation; weak bladder and anus; numb perineum	

[a]C.A. = cutaneous anesthesia (loss of sensation in skin).

Rehabilitation and Exercises for the Lower Back

The first goal in rehabilitation is to relieve the symptoms. Rest is usually mandatory for most cases of acute and chronic back pain. As discussed, athletes should be taught to appreciate the importance of proper posture and body mechanics. Rest does little good if the athlete slouches while sitting in a chair, sleeps in an incorrect posture, or lifts objects improperly.

Acute soft tissue injuries of the back should be treated with standard injury-management techniques: ice, compression, and immobilization. This phase should be followed by ROM exercises, heat, contrast heat and cold, ultrasound, etc. Bracing with such devices as the Boston brace, which tends to flatten an excessive lumbar lordosis, or a corset that supports the low back, is often indicated for athletes wishing to return to physical activity. Bracing often takes the pressure off sensitive spinal nerves while enabling the athlete to continue rehabilitation exercises (and sometimes sports participation). This brace must be fitted by a physician. The use of back braces is somewhat controversial; some experts believe that braces can contribute to additional atrophy and exacerbate symptoms rather than alleviating the problem.

Musculoskeletal rehabilitation should be aimed at strengthening the muscles of the abdomen, spine, and buttocks

---

BOX 16-1 — Low Back Rehabilitation: Flexion or Extension Exercises?

The ultimate goal of any low back rehabilitation program is to achieve spinal alignment that minimizes pressure on the spinal nerve roots. This goal is accomplished by maintaining an optimum pelvic tilt and low back curve through the use of exercises that stretch and relax back muscles, strengthen abdominal muscles, and increase the strength and flexibility of support muscles around the spine (e.g., iliopsoas group, gluteals, hamstrings, and quadriceps).

The rehabilitation strategy for determining which component (flexion or extension exercise) to emphasize depends upon the mechanism and extent of injury. Flexion exercises have been recommended by back rehabilitation experts for the last thirty years, but currently there is a realization that the exercise program must be tailored to each individual case. For example, an athlete with a back injury who can do 150 sit-ups with weights behind his head and the trunk in flexion will gain very little by doing additional abdominal exercises. In this case, the in-tervertebral disk may be distorted posteriorly from overstretching the annulus fibrosus and vertebral ligaments. This athlete is much more likely to benefit from a program that emphasizes extension exercises because they facilitate the containment of the disk anteriorly.

A candidate for extension exercises typically injured his or her back in flexion, exhibits more pain when sitting than walking, may have difficulty standing upright, and does not have a problem with excessive lordosis. The press-up is probably the most effective extension exercise (Figure 16-14); it is excellent for restoring lumbosacral flexibility and stretching the joint capsule, abdominals, and hip flexors, mobilizing the vertebral facets, and unloading the disk. However, some people have difficulty performing the press-up without some physical preparation. A good progression leading up to this exercise is to

1. Lie prone with a pillow under the abdomen.
2. Do the same exercise without the pillow.

3. Perform the press-up while supporting the body weight with the elbows.
4. Perform the press-up while supporting the body weight with the hands.

In addition, periodically during the day, while standing, the athlete should arch the low back with the hands placed in the small of the back. Other excellent extension exercises are those illustrated in Figure 16-15.

Again, each athlete must be individually evaluated. In our example, if the athlete had sustained a severely herniated disk, extension exercises would only further impinge the disk and exacerbate the pressure on the nerve root. Be flexible enough to eliminate from the program any exercises that appear counterproductive. Also, to be effective, the back rehabilitation program must emphasize good body mechanics while lifting, bending, standing, carrying, sitting, and sleeping.

SOURCE: Valponi, David L. *R.P.T.* Chico, Calif.: Chico Physical Therapy Associates, 1985.

while increasing the flexibility of the spine, hip flexors, hamstrings, and lumbodorsal fascia.

The nature of the back rehabilitation program should be reflected by the mechanism of injury (see Box 16-1). For example, injury caused by excessive hyperextension (Figure 16-9, p. 255) requires emphasis upon flexion exercises, whereas injury that occurred while the athlete was in a flexed position requires some emphasis upon trunk extension exercises. A blanket exercise rehabilitation program for low back injury should be applied with extreme caution. Back exercises may include:

- *Press-ups* (Figure 16-14): Press-ups restore lumbosacral flexibility and stretch abdominals and hip flexors.
- *Abdominal curls* (see Putting It into Practice 4-3, p. 72). Abdominal curls isolate and strengthen abdominal musculature. They should be done with bent knees without hooking the toes under a restraining surface so that the abdominal muscles rather than the powerful iliopsoas muscles are exercised.
- *Extension exercises* (Figure 16-15): Extension exercises isolate and strengthen back, buttocks, and leg muscles.
- *Black cat exercise* (Figure 16-16, p. 266): The black cat exercise strengthens and increases the flexibility of low back muscles.
- *Pelvic thrust* (Figure 16-17, p. 266): Pelvic thrust develops flexibility in the lower back and improves coordination of abdominal and extensor muscles.
- *Lateral shift*: Lateral shift develops lateral flexibility in the lumbar spine when the pelvis is shifted to the left or right. Do the exercise only in the opposite direction of the pelvic shift.
- *Rotational exercises* (Figure 16-18, p. 266): These exercises provide flexibility and strength to the rotational musculature of the low back.

Figure 16-14 The press-up. Press up on your hands while letting your lower back sag and attempting to keep your hips on the floor. Hold the position. Start with five seconds and gradually advance to thirty seconds. This exercise strengthens spinal extensor muscles and maintains a normal lordosis. Stop this exercise if back pain becomes worse.

(A)

(B)

Figure 16-15 Extension exercises. (A) is a unilateral spinal extension exercise. Balance on your right hand and knee. Lift your left leg and left arm. Extend your leg to the rear and reach to the front with your arm. Repeat with your right leg and right arm. Start with five repetitions and advance to fifteen. This isometric exercise is particularly useful when the pelvis is laterally shifted. (B) is a bilateral spinal extension exercise. Balance on your right hand and left knee. Lift your right leg and left arm. Extend your leg to the rear and reach to the front with your arm. Repeat with your left leg and right arm. Hold this position ten to thirty seconds per repetition.

Preventing Back Injuries

Poor strength and flexibility are by far the leading causes of back pain. Athletes must be encouraged to perform exercises to strengthen the abdominal and spinal muscles; develop and maintain flexibility of the hamstrings, quadriceps, and hip flexors; and maintain the proper pelvic tilt. In addition, proper lifting techniques and good posture must be emphasized. Athletes should be encouraged to not become overweight—a problem in sports such as football, weight lifting (heavyweight class), wrestling (heavyweight class), and throwing events in track and field—because a protruding abdomen tends to increase the lumbar lordosis.

References

Cailliet, R. *Soft Tissue Pain and Disability*. Philadelphia: F. A. Davis, 1977.

Edgelow, P. Physical examination of the lumbosacral complex. *Physical Therapy* 59:974–977, 1979.

Garg, A. Lifting and back injuries. *Plant Engineering*. December:67–71, 1983.

Goss, C. M. (ed.). *Gray's Anatomy*. Philadelphia: Lea & Febiger, 1973.

Hoppenfeld, S. *Physical Examination of the Spine and Extremities*. New York: Appleton-Century-Crofts, 1976.

Jensen, G. Biomechanics of the lumbar intervertebral disk: a review. *Physical Therapy* 60:765–773, 1980.

Keim, H. A. Low back pain. *Clinical Symposia* 32:1–35, 1980.

Kent, B. Anatomy of the trunk, a review: *Physical Therapy* 54:722–744, 1974.

McKenzie, R. Manual correction of sciatic scoliosis. *New Zealand Medical Journal* 76:194–199, 1972.

Miller, J. K. The low back problem: flex or extend? *Sports Medicine Digest* 8:3–4, 1981.

Stanitski, C. L. Low back pain in young athletes. *The Physician and Sportsmedicine* 10:77–91, 1982.

Figure 16-16 The "black cat" exercise. This exercise improves spinal flexibility and strengthens spinal extensor muscles. Raise your back and hold the position for approximately ten seconds.

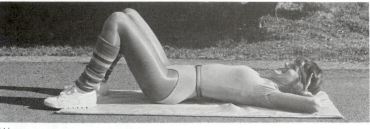

(A)

(B)

Figure 16-17 The pelvic tilt exercise. Flex your pelvis and flatten your lower back. Do not raise your pelvis from the ground. This exercise helps optimize spinal-pelvic alignment. (A) Before tilt, the athlete's waist is off the ground. (B) With pelvic tilt, her waist is pressed to the ground.

Figure 16-18 A rotational exercise. Lie on your back with your hands out to the side and your hips and knees flexed ninety degrees. With your shoulders flat, roll both legs toward the floor and then return to the starting position. Repeat on the opposite side. Begin with ten repetitions and progress to twenty. This exercise develops flexibility and strength in the lower back muscles.

Shoulder Injuries

Swimmers often incur impingement injuries of the shoulder. Conditioning and avoiding overuse may prevent these injuries.

T HE SHOULDER is one of the most complex joints in the body. It involves several articulations and has a highly specialized muscular and connective tissue support system. Unlike the hip (see Chapter 20), the shoulder is poorly reinforced by bone and ligaments, so it depends upon muscles for stability and protection. In addition, because the upper extremity is not attached to the **axial skeleton** by a strong bony connection, the soft tissues of the shoulder must support and secure the limb under a variety of stresses. The shoulder's structural characteristics leave the limb particularly vulnerable to injury.

To understand shoulder injuries, the athletic trainer must be familiar with the anatomy of the shoulder. The term "shoulder injury" is ambiguous because a variety of joints comprise the shoulder, including the sternoclavicular (SC), costoclavicular (CC), coracoclavicular (CC1), glenohumeral (GH), acromioclavicular (AC), and scapulothoracic (ST) joints. Communication between athletic trainers and clinicians will be much easier if *precise* descriptions are used when referring to shoulder injuries.

Axial skeleton: The skeletal structures of the head, neck, and trunk; the skeleton minus its extremities.

267

Anatomy

The shoulder is an intricate structural network of bones, muscles, vasculature, nerves, lubricating elements like bursae and synovium, and supporting structures like tendons from the pectoralis major and biceps brachii muscles.

Many elements of the shoulder are easy to study and can be palpated and visually examined. Figures 17-1 through 17-6 show anatomical landmarks that should be identified as part of every shoulder evaluation. The clavicle (except for its most distal end) and its articulation with the sternum are easy to palpate, even in the most muscular individuals. In most athletes, the coracoid process can be felt below the distal one-third of the clavicle, particularly when the arm is extended. Across the AC joint, which can be felt by following the clavicle distally, the acromion blends with the spine of the scapula, which continues to the scapula's border. In most persons this border can be felt and seen, but in other people borders are often obscured by muscle. Although superficial muscles are easy to identify and palpate, some of the deeper muscles, such as the subscapularis, can also be palpated through the axilla. (Palpation techniques are discussed in the "Evaluation" section, p. 279.)

Skeleton

The bony elements of the shoulder are the clavicle, humerus, scapula, and sternum (Figure 17-2).

Clavicle. The clavicle is an irregularly shaped bone with a proximal curve directed posteriorly and a distal curve directed anteriorly. Muscles attached to the clavicle include the deltoid, trapezius, sternocleidomastoid, sternohyoid, subclavius, and pectoralis major (Figure 17-3).

Some people are born without a

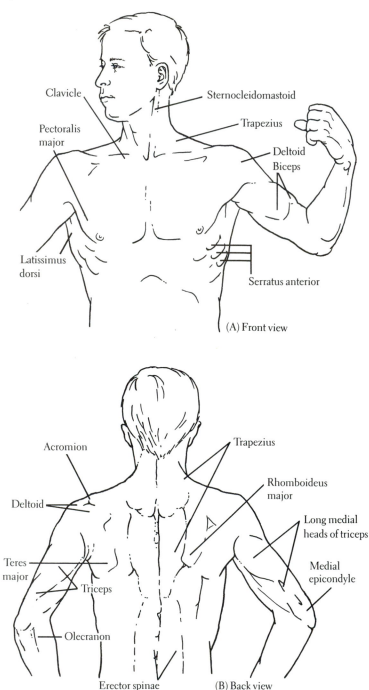

Figure 17-1 The thorax and arms.

clavicle. Typically, these people show no obvious abnormality, but the absent bone causes hypermobility during shoulder elevation and protraction (a condition called hypoplasia of the clavicle).

A very common disorder of the clavicle is malunion of a fracture, which leaves an unsightly and highly visible lump under the skin. The lump is usually absorbed over a long time, even though the clavicle does not remodel itself to the same extent as a weight-bearing bone.

Humerus. The proximal end of the humerus forms a smooth, ball-like surface that loosely fits into the glenoid fossa of the scapula. The greater and lesser tubercles lie laterally and medially, respectively, to the glenohumeral articulation. These bony prominences, which may be palpated, form an intertubercular groove through which runs the tendon of the long head of the biceps brachii to its attachment on the scapula. The tubercles are attachment sites for rotator cuff, pectoralis major, and latissimus dorsi muscles. The surgical neck of the humerus is formed as the tubercles fuse with the humeral shaft. The deltoid tuberosity, which serves as the insertion of the deltoid muscle, lies on the lateral aspect of the humeral shaft. (See Figure 17-4, p. 270.)

Scapula. The scapula is a bone of almost indescribable shape, but it does have specific processes, tubercles, and surfaces that are readily identified. These bony landmarks include the acromion, coracoid process, superior and inferior angles, glenoid fossa, and medial and lateral borders (Figures 17-5 and 17-6, p. 271). The scapula is both origin and insertion for many muscles that provide action at the glenohumeral and scapulothoracic joints (Figure 17-7, p. 272).

Occasionally, during the course of a person's development the scapula fails to descend from its high thoracic posi-

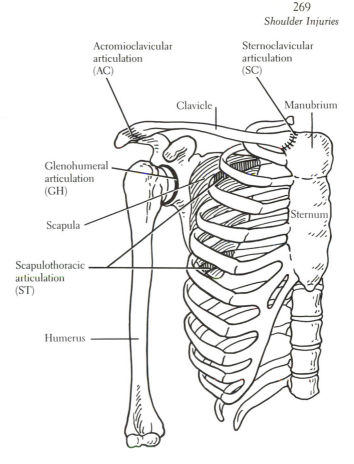

Figure 17-2 The shoulder girdle.

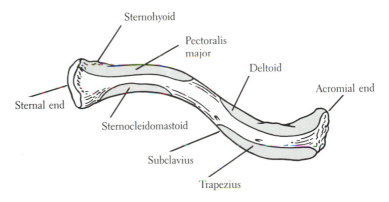

Figure 17-3 The right clavicle from above, with muscular attachments.

Prevention, Treatment, and Rehabilitation of Specific Injuries

tion. Congenital elevation of the scapula is called Sprengel's deformity, which is sometimes associated with thoracic or cervical scoliosis, supernumerary ribs (fused ribs), or shortened clavicles. It typically restricts abduction and in most cases is unilateral.

Cervical Rib. Shoulder examination may reveal a bony prominence called a cervical rib that lies superior and somewhat anterior to the superior border of the scapula. This bony anomaly, which is rare, is typically asymptomatic until the late teens, when certain activities or natural muscular development aggravate the condition, which causes discomfort, decreased range of motion, or neurovascular compression.

Sternum. The sternum is a flat, longitudinally shaped bone that lies in the center of the thorax. Generally, it is not considered part of the shoulder, but it does have a profound effect upon shoulder function because it articulates with the clavicles and ribs and serves as part of the origin of the pectoralis major muscle.

Articulations

The articulations of the shoulder include the sternoclavicular, costoclavicular, coracoclavicular, acromioclavicular, glenohumeral, and scapulothoracic (see Figure 7-2, p. 269).

Sternoclavicular. The clavicle and the manubrium of the sternum form a synovial joint. Actually, two synovial cavities are formed by an intervening articular disk of fibrocartilage attached peripherally to the joint capsule. The joint is stabilized and protected by anterior and posterior sternoclavicular ligaments. These ligaments in turn protect against anterior, posterior, and medial displacement. The interclavicular ligament provides lateral stability. The capsule of the SC joint is very thick anteriorly and posteriorly but thin superiorly and inferiorly.

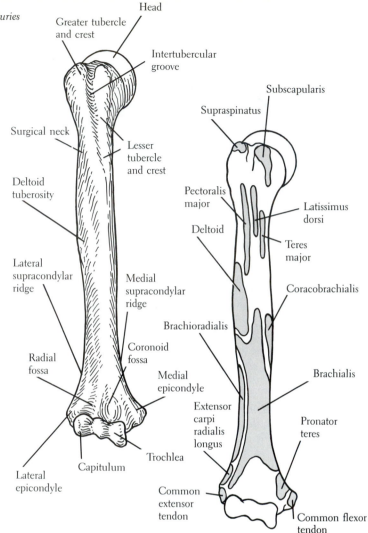

Figure 17-4 Anterior humerus with muscular attachments.

Costoclavicular. This fibrous joint is formed between the first rib and the clavicle by the costoclavicular ligament. The CC ligament resists lateral displacement of the clavicle.

Coracoclavicular. The coracoid process and the clavicle form a fibrous joint with the coracoclavicular ligament. This ligament resists upward movement of the clavicle (relative to the scapula) and downward movement of the scapula (relative to the clavicle). It is a major bracing ligament for the acromial end of the clavicle. As long as the CC1 is intact, the acromion cannot be

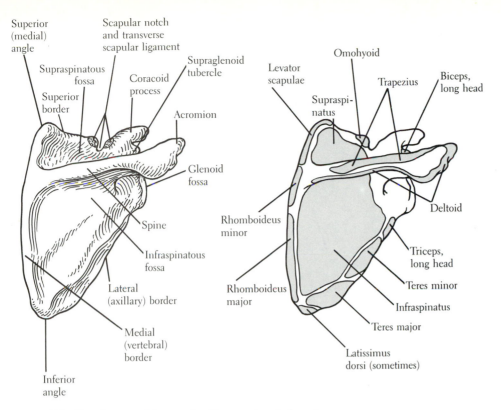

Figure 17-5 Dorsal aspect of the scapula with muscular attachments.

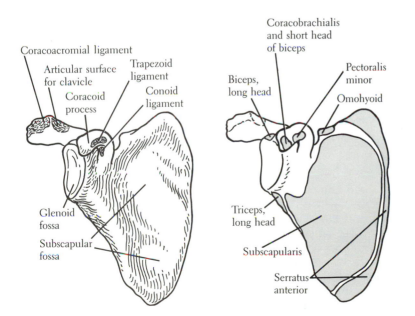

Figure 17-6 Costal surface of the scapula with muscular attachments.

driven under the clavicle. Some authorities believe that this ligament provides much of the AC joint stability traditionally ascribed to the AC ligament.

Acromioclavicular. The articular surface of the clavicle faces laterally, and the corresponding surface of the acromion faces medially. Joint surfaces are separated by a small articular disk that, together with a somewhat lax capsule, allows some motion between the bones. The AC ligament resists distraction of the joint, but it cannot prevent protraction or retraction of the scapula on the clavicle. Thus, a **shoulder separation** (subluxation) of the AC joint is frequently due to forces acting to protract or retract the scapula on the clavicle.

Glenohumeral. The glenohumeral joint's remarkable mobility is mainly caused by the shallow socket formed by the glenoid fossa and its **labrum** and the loose capsule and ligaments that enclose the joint. The fossa is lined with hyaline cartilage that becomes quite thin at the edges (see Chapter 7). A ring of fibrocartilage is attached to the rim of the fossa, at the edges of the hyaline cartilage, forming a labrum. The labrum adds diameter and depth to the socket and thus encloses the humeral head to a greater degree. Painful labrum separations do occur and may predispose an athlete to GH subluxation.

The GH ligaments (also called coracohumeral ligaments) are essentially thickened portions of the anterior joint capsule. These ligaments retard downward displacement of the humerus and loosely hold the humeral head in the socket. The remainder of the capsule is thin and much less structurally significant.

An additional structural element is the tendon of the long head of the biceps, which crosses the GH joint anteriorly and attaches to the supraglenoid tubercle. This tendon originates within the capsule (rather than crossing it ex-

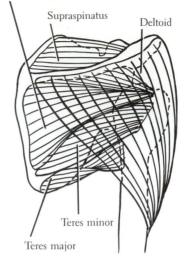

(A) Back view

Shoulder separation: Subluxation of the acromioclavicular joint.

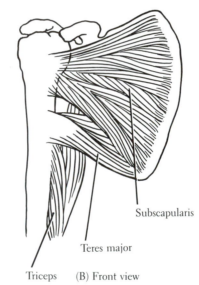

(B) Front view

Labrum: A liplike structure.

Figure 17-7 Intrinsic muscles of the shoulder.

ternally), so it provides muscular support and reinforcement for the joint. Biceps activity also compresses the joint and seats the humeral head deeper in the socket (in certain positions the deltoid also performs this function). The muscles of the rotator cuff provide additional muscular support.

The subacromial bursa, located on the superior surface of the supraspinatus, under the acromion and partly under the coracoacromial ligament, plays a vital role in protecting the underlying structures from abrasion (see Chapter 7). The bursa is subject to **impingement** because of its position.

Scapulothoracic. The scapula forms a muscular joint with the thoracic cage through the trapezius, rhomboideus major and minor, latissimus dorsi, and serratus anterior (Figure 17-8). This is a particularly mobile joint because there are no ligaments, bony elements, or cartilage. In addition, the ST is remarkably resistant to injury (muscular strains around this joint are uncommon). The ST joint contributes significantly to abduction of the arm, a motion often attributed solely to the GH joint.

Nerves

The muscles of the shoulder joints are innervated by the **brachial plexus** and the accessory nerve. The nerves of the brachial plexus arise from the fifth cervical (C5) to first thoracic (T1) segments. The brachial plexus carries motor, autonomic, and sensory nerves to the shoulder. The accessory nerve is the eleventh cranial nerve; it innervates the trapezius. Pain in shoulder structures can be misleading and often results in misdiagnosis because of the complex nature of shoulder innervation.

Elements of the brachial plexus and the blood vessels that accompany these nerves may be compressed by structures along their route, causing pain, **paresthesia,** numbness, weakness, paralysis, swelling, discoloration, and atrophy in the hand, forearm, arm, or shoulder. These disorders are collectively called **thoracic outlet syndrome,** regardless of the site or mechanism of compression.

Vasculature

The axillary artery is the major artery of the shoulder. (See Chapter 18.) It passes under the coracoid process and pectoralis minor tendon and runs

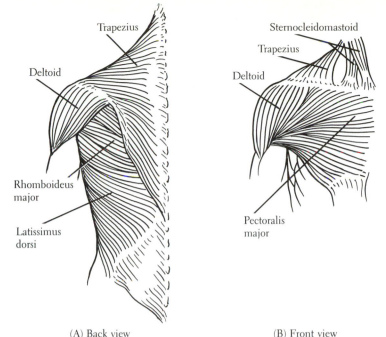

Trapezius
Deltoid
Rhomboideus major
Latissimus dorsi

Sternocleidomastoid
Trapezius
Deltoid
Pectoralis major

(A) Back view   (B) Front view

Figure 17-8   Superficial muscles of the shoulder.

through the axilla to the inferior edge of the teres minor, where it becomes the brachial artery. Four major branches arise from the axillary artery to supply the shoulder's bones and soft tissues. The cephalic vein is the principal vein of the upper extremity.

Blood supply to the scapula and scapular muscles is quite extensive through **anastomoses.** The vascular network arises from four arteries that constitute backup systems in case a vessel is injured or compressed.

All arteries are important, but two deserve particular attention with regard to shoulder injuries. The surgical neck of the humerus is encircled by an anterior and a posterior humeral circumflex artery arising from the axillary artery. These circumflex arteries are readily disrupted in humeral fractures, and the impaired blood supply may significantly prolong healing time and the quality of healing. Similarly, the acromial branch of the thoracoacromial artery supplies the distal acromion and the AC joint. This vessel may be injured from ante-

Impingement: Entrapment of tissue.
Brachial plexus: A network of nerves formed by the fifth to eighth cervical and first thoracic nerves; the network extends from the lateral neck to the axilla.

Anastomoses: Connection between tubular structures such as blood vessels.

Paresthesia: Abnormal sensation or feeling, such as tingling or burning.

Thoracic outlet syndrome: Abnormal sensation in the hand, forearm, arm, or shoulder caused by nerve compression.

rior blows to the shoulder; the blows may also disrupt the AC joint. Consequently, healing may be retarded and be less than optimal.

Shoulder Muscles and Motions

Table 17-1 summarizes the muscles of the shoulder and their actions. The kinesiology of the shoulder involves much more than motion and muscle of the glenohumeral joint. All the shoulder joints can be involved in shoulder motion. When all possible motions of the shoulder joints and their muscles are considered, the kinesiology of the region is extremely complex because certain shoulder muscles are active in several motions (Figure 17-8, p. 273). Furthermore, selective motion is carried out at the motor unit level rather than at the relatively gross level of the whole muscle (see Chapter 5). Finally, the action of one muscle can significantly modify the action of another muscle, thus channeling the force of the first muscle in a direction that may not be readily anticipated. For simplicity, this discussion is restricted to the motion of the GH and ST joints.

Movements of the Scapula. Scapular movements usually complement humeral movements, to give greater range of motion to the upper limb than is possible at the GH joint alone. In some instances, scapular movement is a result of humeral movement. Extrinsic muscles acting upon the humerus can cause scapular movement, relative to the thorax, if intrinsic muscles hold the humeral head in place on the scapula. In addition, extrinsic muscles that attach to the scapula can move this bone independent of humeral movements.

Scapular movements are upward and downward rotation, elevation, depression, protraction, and retraction. Upward rotation of the scapula, an important aspect of abducting the arm, is accomplished by the serratus anterior

and upper trapezius. Downward rotation is accomplished by the rhomboids, levator scapulae, pectoralis minor, and latissimus dorsi. Scapular elevation, called a **shoulder shrug** by athletes, is performed by the trapezius, elevator scapulae, and rhomboids. Depression, which can be achieved by gravity if tone in the elevators is minimal, is accomplished by the lower trapezius, pectoralis minor, serratus anterior, and latissimus dorsi.

Scapular protraction is an anterior movement of the scapula over the thorax and is performed by the serratus anterior and pectoralis minor and major. Such protraction is important when reaching for distant objects because it effectively lengthens the upper limb. It is also a stabilization motion when pushing a heavy object; it is readily seen when a push-up is being performed. Retraction is the movement of the medial border of the scapula closer to the midline of the body. The muscles involved are the trapezius, rhomboids, and latissimus dorsi.

Movements of the Glenohumeral Joint. Movements at the GH joint seldom can be isolated from movements of the scapula on the thorax; indeed, the movements of the two joints are typically coordinated. The scapula provides a stable base during humeral motion, whether or not the scapula shows overt movement. GH motions are usually combined with ST motions to add versatility, range, and efficiency to the shoulder as a whole.

GH joint movements are flexion, extension, abduction, adduction, internal rotation, and external rotation. These movements can be combined to produce circumduction. Flexion is performed by the anterior deltoid, assisted by the pectoralis major, coracobrachialis, and biceps. Extension is performed by the latissimus dorsi and posterior deltoid. Abduction is accomplished by the deltoid and supraspinatus, with help from the biceps when the humerus is

Shoulder shrug: Athletic jargon for an elevated scapula.

Table 17-1 *Actions of the Shoulder Muscles*

Muscles That Elevate and Depress the Scapula

Muscle		Nerve	Segmental Innervation	
			Reported Range	Probable Most Important Segment(s)
Chief elevators	Trapezius, "middle" part	Accessory	—	—
	Levator scapulae	C3 and C4, perhaps dorsal scapular	C3–C5	C3, C4
	Rhomboideus major and minor	Dorsal scapular	C4–C6	C5
Accessory elevators	None			
Chief depressors	Latissimus dorsi	Thoracodorsal	C6–C8	C7
	Pectoralis major, lower part	Pectorals	C6–T1	C7, C8
Accessory depressors	Serratus anterior, lower part	Long thoracic	C5–C8	C6
	Pectoralis minor	Medial pectoral	C8–T1	C8, T1
	Subclavius	N. to subclavius	C3–C8	C5
	Trapezius, lower part	Accessory	—	—

Muscles That Rotate the Scapula

Muscle		Nerve	Segmental Innervation	
			Reported Range	Probable Most Important Segment(s)
Chief upward rotators	Trapezius, esp. "middle" part	Accessory	—	—
	Serratus anterior	Long thoracic	C5–C8	C6
Accessory upward rotators	None			
Chief downward rotators	Levator scapulae	C3 and C4, perhaps dorsal scapular	C3–C5	C3, C4
	Rhomboideus major and minor	Dorsal scapular	C4–C6	C5
	Pectoralis minor	Medial pectoral	C7–T1	C8, T1
Accessory downward rotators	Pectoralis major, lower part	Pectorals	C6–T1	C7, C8
	Latissimus dorsi	Thoracodorsal	C5–C8	C7

(continued on next page)

Table 17-1 (*continued*)

Innervation of the Muscles Flexing the Arm

	Muscle	Nerve	Segmental Innervation	
			Reported Range	Probable Most Important Segment(s)
Chief flexors	Deltoid, anterior part	Axillary	C4–C7	C5, C6
	Pectoralis major, clavicular part	Lateral pectoral	C5–C6	C5, C6
	Coracobrachialis	Musculocutaneous	C5–C8	C6, C7
From hyper-extension only	Pectoralis major, sternal part	Both pectorals	C6–T1	C6, C7, C8
Accessory flexor	Biceps (?)	Musculocutaneous	C5–C6	C5, C6

Innervation of the Muscles Extending the Arm

	Muscle	Nerve	Segmental Innervation	
			Reported Range	Probable Most Important Segment(s)
Chief extensors	Latissimus dorsi	Thoracodorsal	C5–C8	C7
	Deltoid, posterior part	Axillary	C4–C7	C5, C6
From flexion only	Pectoralis major, sternal part	Both pectorals	C6–T1	C6, C7, C8
Accessory extensors	Teres major	Lower subscapular	C5–C7	C5, C6
	Triceps, long head	Radial	C6–C8	C7, C8

Innervation of the Muscles Abducting the Arm

	Muscle	Nerve	Segmental Innervation	
			Reported Range	Probable Most Important Segment(s)
Chief abductors	Deltoid	Axillary	C4–C7	C5, C6
	Supraspinatus	Suprascapular	C4–C6	C5
Accessory abductor	Biceps, long head (?)	Musculocutaneous	C5–C6	C5, C6

(*continued on next page*)

Table 17-1 *(continued)*

Innervation of the Muscles Adducting the Arm

Muscle		Nerve	Segmental Innervation	
			Reported Range	Probable Most Important Segment(s)
Chief adductors	Pectoralis major	Pectorals	C5–T1	C6, C7, C8
	Latissimus dorsi	Thoracodorsal	C5–C8	C7
	Teres major	Lower subscapular	C5–C7	C5, C6
Accessory adductors	Deltoid, posterior part	Axillary	C4–C7	C5, C6
	Coracobrachialis	Musculocutaneous	C5–C8	C6, C7
	Triceps, long head	Radial	C6–C8	C7, C8

Innervation of the Muscles Externally and Internally Rotating the Arm

Muscle		Nerve	Segmental Innervation	
			Reported Range	Probable Most Important Segment(s)
Chief external rotators	Infraspinatus	Suprascapular	C4–C6	C5, C6
	Teres minor	Axillary	C4–C7	C5, C6
Accessory external rotator	Deltoid, posterior part	Axillary	C4–C7	C5, C6
Chief internal rotator	Subscapularis	Subscapulars	C5–C7	C5, C6
Accessory internal rotators	Teres major	Lower subscapular	C5–C7	C5, C6
	Deltoid, anterior part	Axillary	C4–C6	C5, C6
	Pectoralis major	Pectorals	C5–T1	C5, C6, C7, C8
	Latissimus dorsi	Thoracodorsal	C5–C8	C7
	Supraspinatus (?)	Suprascapular	C4–C6	C5

SOURCE: Modified from Hollingshead, W. H. *Textbook of Anatomy,* 4th ed. New York: Harper & Row, 1974, pp. 201–213.

externally rotated. Adduction is performed principally by the sternocostal part of the pectoralis major, latissimus dorsi, and teres major. External rotation can be created by the infraspinatus, teres minor, and posterior deltoid. Internal rotators are the subscapularis and teres major. Latissimus dorsi, anterior deltoid, pectoralis major, and possibly supraspinatus may also internally rotate, depending upon the limb position and degree of force required.

Rotator Cuff. The so-called **rotator cuff,** more correctly known as the musculotendinous cuff, is composed of the supraspinatus, infraspinatus, teres minor, and subscapularis muscles. Injuries to these muscles are common in baseball, javelin throwing, and tennis. These muscles are important as shoulder rotators, but they also play an extremely important role in joint stabilization. The supraspinatus in particular seats the humeral head in the glenoid

Rotator cuff: Muscles that rotate the humerus.

fossa; the other muscles provide antero-posterior stability. This vital function of joint stabilization allows the creation of a "fixed fulcrum," which enables extrinsic muscles to move the humerus on the scapula.

The subscapularis is important in preventing anterior subluxation of the GH joint. Weakness or laxity of this musculotendinous unit leaves the anterior margin of the joint less stable and more vulnerable to the actions of powerful muscles acting on a long lever arm (i.e., the entire length of the arm).

Scapulohumeral Rhythm (SHR). The synchronous movements of the humerus and scapula are referred to as **scapulohumeral rhythm.** As a rule of thumb, every two to three degrees of humeral abduction is accompanied by one to two degrees of scapular rotation. SHR should be considered when the shoulder is being evaluated: Shoulder movements should always be observed from several different viewpoints, including posteriorly, with the athlete unclothed, to assess scapular motion. In cases of adhesive capsulitis (this topic is discussed later in the chapter), when attempts are made to abduct the shoulder, there is little or no GH motion. Any movement that does occur may be completely scapular. Conversely, a "bound down" (range of motion limited by formation of an adhesion) scapula, secondary to a long period of immobilization, may prevent a scapulohumeral rhythm and limit abduction to near horizontal.

Evaluation

Although all joints may sustain injuries that are difficult to evaluate, the shoulder, by virtue of its mechanical versatility, complex muscle actions, and soft tissue vulnerability, is particularly challenging. The athletic trainer must approach shoulder problems without presumption and observe a primary

maxim of this book: Only a physician may make a diagnosis; other clinicians make assessments and evaluations.

Observation

Often valuable information is obtained simply by watching the athlete walk into the athletic training room. Note the absence of the arm swinging or the presence of a drooping shoulder. Is the athlete stiff and uncomfortable? Is there a sign of bothersome irritation on the athlete's face, or even a painful grimace? You may get some idea of the functional range of motion by observing the manner in which the athlete undresses and lies down.

History

A thorough history may be the athletic trainer's most potent tool in the evaluation of shoulder injuries. Follow the procedures described in Chapter 9 for taking a history, and also pay particular attention to (1) events surrounding the injury, (2) involvement of other body parts, such as the wrist or neck, (3) other injuries to the shoulder, (4) whether the injury is a recurrent one, and (5) numbness, burning, paresthesia, unexpected weakness, or paralysis.

Also note when symptoms are experienced. A relatively minor injury ("microtrauma") may be painful only after activity. A more extensive or serious shoulder injury may be painful both during and after activity. Severe injuries may be painful all the time. Try to characterize the pain (dull, sharp, deep, or throbbing) and localize it. Pain that cannot be localized often arises from injuries to deep structures. Furthermore, deep injuries often refer pain to other areas. For example, the pain of rotator cuff tears is sometimes referred to the upper arm. Structurally, if the injury is clearly limited to the shoulder but pain radiates below the elbow, there may be a nerve injury or **neurovascular compression.**

Scapulohumeral rhythm (SHR): The synchronous movements of the humerus and scapula.

Neurovascular compression: Compression of nerves and blood vessels.

List factors that aggravate and alleviate the symptoms. If the injury is a microtrauma (a low-grade, persistent irritation), aggravating factors may be quite subtle. For example, a breast-stroke swimmer may work on the butterfly stroke on Fridays and Saturdays and then, over a period of several weeks, feel a shoulder ache Sunday through Tuesday. The athlete may not make a connection between the change in workout strokes and the appearance of symptoms.

Inquire about shoulder noises (clicks, pops, etc.), sticking of the joint in motion, blocks to motion, and sensations of apprehension or fears that the joint will dislocate. Noises usually indicate cartilage problems like inflammation, loose bodies, or a labral separation.

Understanding Physician's Diagnosis of the Injured Shoulder. Often, the athlete will have seen a physician before you make your evaluation. A diagnosis may have been made, and thus your evaluation and assessment may be functionally oriented to determine the effects of the injury on athletic performance and the implications for treatment and rehabilitation.

Results of sophisticated tests may be available from the physician. For example, a **roentgenographic** (x-ray) examination may reveal calcium deposits in soft tissue, such as the rotator cuff tendons, a high-riding humeral head, hardening (sclerosis) of the AC joint, degenerative joint disease, or bone spurs. **Arthroscopy** is sometimes performed if specific damage to structures inside the joint capsule is suspected. This procedure allows visual access to the glenoid and humeral head, the labrum and biceps tendon, and the inner surface of the capsule. The arthrogram may reveal thickening of structures and narrowed spaces consistent with impingement syndrome, partial or complete rotator cuff tears, or reduced joint volume, possibly caused by adhesive capsulitis. Arthroscopy is

not useful in evaluating rotator cuff problems unless the involved structures are intracapsular. Some sports medicine specialists occasionally use a CT scan to evaluate certain types of shoulder injuries. Arteriograms (x-rays of arteries), although rarely used, may be helpful in diagnosing vascular disorders, particularly those associated with thoracic outlet syndrome.

Palpation of Bony Tissue

Palpation techniques are fully discussed in Chapter 9. When palpating the shoulder, press gently and slowly. The objective is not to re-create symptoms, such as pain or a sensation of impending subluxation, but to understand the status of the shoulder's tissues. During palpation, look for swelling, subtle displacement, abnormal hardening or thickening of the tissues, increased muscle tone, unusual or abnormal bony formations, changes in tissue pliability, tenderness, **crepitus,** and joint instability.

Palpating SC and AC Joints. After visually examining the shoulders from all sides, perform most of the palpation from behind the athlete. The SC joint is a good starting place. Proceed along the clavicle toward the AC joint, feeling for lumps, bone deformities, and pliability of attaching soft tissues. At the anterior cavity, slip your fingers inferiorly to find the coracoid. This structure is easier to palpate if the shoulder is passively extended. Return to the clavicle and find the AC joint. This articulation has an anteroposterior axis and can be mobilized by pulling posteriorly on the acromion while stabilizing the clavicle. Active shoulder flexion, if the nature of the injury permits and if it is not too painful, makes the AC joint easier to find and palpate. In cases of recurrent separation, look for thickened tissue, particularly around the AC ligament. Always compare the injured shoulder with the uninjured one.

Crepitus: A grinding, crackling sound produced by friction of adjacent tissues.

Roentgenogram (roentgenographic): An x-ray; x-rays strike a film after passing through a portion of the body. Also called a radiograph.

Arthroscopy: Surgical technique using an arthroscope, an instrument that enables the physician to visualize the interior of a joint. Arthroscopy often lets athletes return to participation much faster than they could with other surgical procedures.

Palpating the Scapula. Follow the acromion to the scapular spine. Note the relative elevation of the scapula and any "winging" (protrusion of the scapula posteriorly). Palpate the angles and borders; the scapular spine should lie at the level of the spinous process of the third thoracic vertebra.

Palpating the GH Joint and the Humerus. Return to the acromion, cross the GH joint, and through the substance of the anterior deltoid find the greater tubercle of the humerus. Identify the tendon of the long head of the biceps brachii in the intertubercular groove by passively rotating the athlete's arm externally while slipping your fingers medially from the greater tubercle. Do not apply excessive pressure because most people will report some discomfort or pain over the tendon even when there is no injury or disorder. If the transverse humeral ligament is defective, the tendon will be unstable and slip medially as you externally rotate the limb while resisting the athlete's attempt to flex the elbow from ninety degrees. This maneuver is called the Yergason test.

Palpation of Soft Tissue

Three primary divisions of soft tissue should be systematically palpated during the examination: (1) superficial muscles of the shoulder girdle (Figure 7-8, p. 273), (2) the axilla, and (3) rotator cuff structures (Figure 17-9). (Our division of bony and soft tissue is arbitrary; most skilled clinicians examine bony and soft tissues together.)

Palpating Superficial Muscles of the Shoulder Girdle. Begin by visually inspecting the muscles from all sides for typical signs of atrophy, tone, etc. Begin palpation at the sternocleidomastoid (bilaterally, standing behind the athlete). Move to the pectoralis major and follow it to its insertion on the humerus. Examine its origin on the

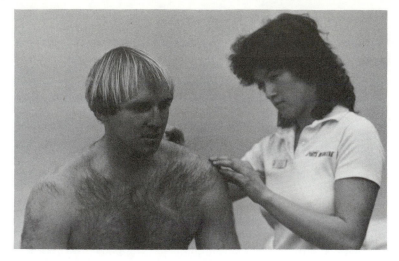

Figure 17-9 Palpating the shoulder. Look for anatomical defects, point tenderness, and increased skin temperature.

sternum and clavicle. Palpate the biceps brachii and follow its two tendons.

Inspect the three portions of the deltoid, and then proceed medially to the trapezius. The upper, middle, and lower trapezius should be examined as three muscles. The upper trapezius in particular is frequently tight in neck and shoulder disorders. Examine its origin on the skull; "trigger points" (specific points at or near soft tissue injuries that are hypersensitive to touch or pressure), associated with headaches, are often found near this location.

The rhomboids are covered by the trapezius; but, to make them prominent, have the athlete put his arm behind his back, with his elbow flexed ninety degrees. The athlete then attempts to extend his shoulder while you resist the effort at his wrist. This maneuver, done bilaterally but not simultaneously, reveals differences in muscle bulk, and the muscle may become tender during palpation.

Follow the latissimus dorsi and teres major across the posterior axillary wall to the ridge of the lower tubercle. Finally, cross the axilla to the chest wall and palpate the serratus anterior. In relaxed individuals, this muscle can be followed medially to the ventral surface of the scapula. Palpation of the superficial long thoracic nerve by an experienced examiner may elicit tenderness or pain if the nerve is inflamed. Insertions of the serratus on the ribs are easily palpated. Tenderness at any insertion point should prompt a search for rib fractures.

Palpating the Axilla. Palpation of the axilla can cause the athlete discomfort if the athletic trainer probes too forcefully (particularly with long fingernails). Look for swollen lymph nodes, asymmetry in the shape of the axilla, and position of the humeral head. Palpate the brachial artery for patency (exposure) and pulse, and try to locate the major nerves of the arm adjacent to the artery.

Palpating Rotator Cuff Structures. The tendon and musculotendinous junction of the supraspinatus are the portions of the rotator cuff most often involved in athletic injury. To palpate these structures, stand behind the athlete and passively extend the shoulder. When the shoulder is in full extension, portions of the tendons of the infraspinatus and teres minor may be palpated. During palpation, tears or defects in these structures will cause complaints of tenderness. Some examiners attempt to reproduce symptoms (create a **similar sign**) by pinching the supraspinatus tendon between the inferior surface of the acromion and the greater tubercle while the arm is in abduction without external rotation. In addition, palpate the subscapularis for tenderness and laxity, especially in cases of anterior subluxation.

Palpating Related Structures. The subdeltoid bursa and its subacromial extension should be examined at the time the supraspinatus tendon is palpated. Look for thickening and tenderness that may be present with bursitis. Sensations of friction and stiffness with occasional pain and discomfort in cer-

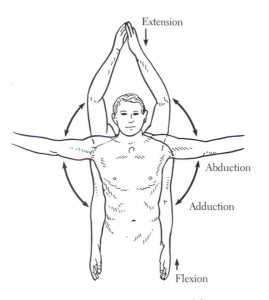

Figure 17-10 Flexion, extension, abduction, and adduction of the shoulder.

tain scapular motions should prompt a search for bursitis outside the GH joint.

Range of Motion

As discussed in the earlier anatomy section, most shoulder motions are principally a combination of glenohumeral and scapular motions. These complex motions are difficult to describe and more difficult to measure during a clinical examination. Therefore, range of motion measurements are usually rudimentary when compared to the shoulder's capability.

Unless the athlete has an obvious serious injury, such as a fracture or subluxation, range of motion should first be assessed in combined, bilateral motions without attempts at measurement. Stand in front of the athlete and instruct him or her to follow your motions. Have the athlete raise both hands directly over the head, with elbows extended, until the hands touch. The athlete should remain in this position and rotate the arms internally so that the palms touch each other (Figure 17-10). Next, the athlete should adduct the arms, with internal rotation, and bring the hands to the midline behind the back until they touch dorsal sur-

Similar sign: Initiating the symptoms by attempting to mimic the mechanism of injury.

faces. To test extension, have the athlete move the arms posteriorly away from the back. The athlete should demonstrate flexion by reaching forward and raising the arms over the head once again. If you find a deficit in motion, carefully measure with a goniometer both active and passive motion.

Apley Scratch Test. The Apley scratch test tests external rotation and abduction. The athlete reaches behind the neck and attempts to "scratch" the superior angle of the opposite scapula. In a similar test for internal rotation and adduction, the athlete tries to "scratch" the inferior angle of the opposite scapula.

Measuring Scapulohumeral Rhythm. Scapulohumeral rhythm is evaluated by a combination of palpation and active range of motion tests. Movement at the inferior angle of the scapula should be followed through active abduction with a finger lightly in contact with it. Pure glenohumeral motion will yield ninety degrees of abduction. The first twenty to twenty-five degrees require no scapular motion, and thus the inferior angle will remain stable while the humerus passes through the initial part of abduction. Beyond this point, the scapula and humerus move together in a 2:1 ratio. The rhythm is typically disturbed in cases of adhesive capsulitis: Passive shoulder abduction may reveal a scapula that moves in upward rotation during the first few degrees of abduction. In addition, anchoring the scapula during active abduction may reveal range limitation from a capsular disorder or weak humeral abduction muscles.

Hesitation Tests. "Hesitation tests" determine if certain movements generate hesitation or apprehension in the athlete. For example, a motion that makes an athlete feel that her shoulder is subluxating will cause apprehension and a break in rhythm because she knows continued motion will cause pain.

A break in rhythm during active abduction as the arm reaches ninety degrees may be the result of **painful impingement syndrome.** Apprehension during abduction with external rotation suggests a recurrent subluxation or a tear of the glenoid labrum. This maneuver must be *carefully* performed; the examiner should not cause a subluxation, particularly in an athlete who has previously complained of subluxation. Hesitation may also be found when the AC joint is examined. As the arm is passively moved in horizontal adduction, the joint is mobilized, and injured tissues may create pain, hesitation, or even refusal to make further movement.

Manual Tests for Muscle Strength

Manual muscle tests are usually performed using the nine GH and scapular motions. Review Table 17-1 for the muscles involved in these motions and Figure 17-11 for the correct position for testing strength in the shoulder. Strength in these motions can be quickly assessed, bilaterally, if the examiner stands behind the athlete and tests corresponding muscles of both shoulders simultaneously. See Table 9-2 (p. 144) for the muscle-testing grading scale.

Drop Arm Test. Some experts consider the "drop arm" test a diagnostic procedure for determining rotator cuff tears. The athlete actively abducts the arm to ninety degrees. The athlete is then ordered to slowly return the arm to neutral. The test is positive if the arm drops to the side from ninety degrees of abduction. The test is also positive if the athlete tries to hold the arm in some degree of abduction and a tap to the wrist causes the arm to drop.

Empty Can Test. Electromyographic studies have shown that the "empty can" test may be a better diagnostic procedure than the drop arm test for

Painful impingement syndrome: Impingement of the subacromial bursa and rotator cuff between the acromion and humerus.

Electromyography (electromyographic): A procedure that detects the electrical activity of muscle; used to assess neurological status and specific muscle activity during motion.

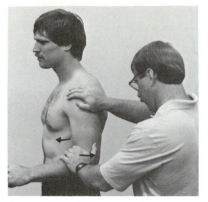

(A) Shoulder flexion. The athlete attempts to flex his shoulder while the athletic trainer provides resistance at or slightly above the elbow.

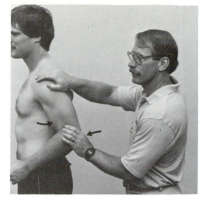

(B) Shoulder extension. The athlete attempts to extend his shoulder while the athletic trainer provides resistance at the elbow.

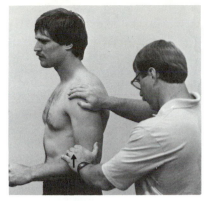

(C) Shoulder abduction. The athlete attempts to abduct his shoulder while the athletic trainer provides resistance on the lateral aspect of the elbow.

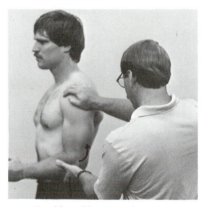

(D) Shoulder adduction. The athlete attempts to adduct his shoulder while the athletic trainer provides resistance at the medial aspect of the elbow.

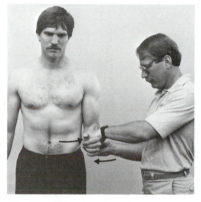

(E) Shoulder external rotation. The athlete attempts to externally rotate his shoulder while the athletic trainer provides resistance to the forearm.

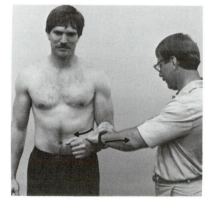

(F) Shoulder internal rotation. The athlete attempts to internally rotate his shoulder while the athletic trainer provides resistance to the forearm.

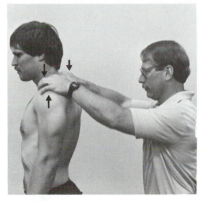

(G) Scapular elevation. The athlete shrugs his shoulders as the athletic trainer pushes downward.

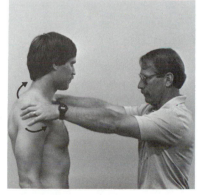

(H) Scapular retraction. The athlete attempts to retract the scapulae in the "position of attention" as the athletic trainer pulls forward on the shoulders.

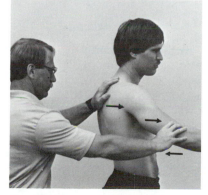

(I) Scapular protraction. The athlete reaches as the athletic trainer provides resistance along the longitudinal axis of the upper arm.

Figure 17-11 Manual tests for shoulder strength.

determining rotator cuff injury (Figure 17-12). The empty can test isolates the supraspinatus from the remaining portion of the cuff at a position that minimizes involvement of the deltoid. In this test, the arm is passively moved to ninety degrees of abduction, thirty degrees of horizontal adduction, and full internal rotation. Imagine a can held in the hand: Its contents spill as this test is performed, and the can is then empty. The athlete resists as the examiner applies force in adduction to the distal end of the forearm. A weak or torn supraspinatus will give way quite easily, thus eliciting a positive response.

Winging of the Scapula. The long thoracic nerve, which innervates the serratus anterior, lies superficially and may be injured relatively easily. When this occurs, the scapula cannot be maintained in the proper position when the shoulder is flexed or when the athlete attempts to push against a wall or perform a push-up. The serratus anterior is a scapular protractor. Resistance applied to a flexed elbow, in the horizontal plane, as the athlete attempts to reach forward (protracting the scapula), may reveal a strength deficit. If the muscle is significantly weakened, the scapula may protrude posteriorly, a phenomenon known as winging.

Neurological Evaluation

A thorough neurological evaluation tests the function of peripheral nerves, brachial plexus, nerve roots, and spinal segments. The examination may also include tests of reflexes, cutaneous sensation, and **proprioception.** Review the muscles and their innervation in Table 17-1 (p. 275). A well-performed neurological evaluation requires a good understanding of the action, origin, and insertion of muscles, methods of testing for strength, the muscles' innervation (including which portion of the brachial plexus and the muscles' segmental innervations). Touch tests using derma-

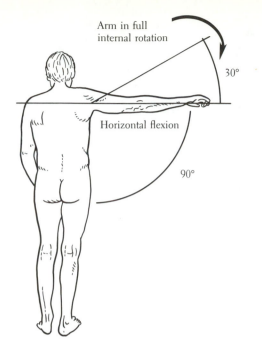

Figure 17-12 The empty can test. This test isolates the supraspinatus muscle from the other muscles of the rotator cuff.

tomes (Figure 9-6, p. 143) are valuable for evaluating possible abnormalities of sensory fibers. Reflex tests, generally valuable in neurological evaluation, are less helpful for shoulder injuries because the muscles in this area do not readily lend themselves to this type of testing. Proprioception is easily tested: Have the athlete close the eyes as you passively move the upper extremity in specific, simple motions; then ask the athlete to repeat the movement pattern.

Continued Evaluation of Shoulder Injuries

Evaluation must be ongoing, performed every time the athlete reports for treatment. Reevaluation is usually cursory and may be limited to assessment of range of motion, intensity and locality of pain, degree of edema, and extent of crepitus.

The evaluator must consider possible injury mechanisms that are not obvious. For example, symptoms localized to the shoulder are not invariably caused by shoulder pathology. They may be from **angina pectoris,** caused by

Proprioception: Spatial awareness caused by sensory input from muscles, tendons, and joints.
Angina pectoris: Deep, visceral pressure or discomfort, typically substernally in the chest, that may radiate to the neck and left arm. Caused by lack of blood flow to the heart muscle, possibly from atherosclerosis or coronary artery vasospasm.

coronary artery disease (see Chapter 24). Irritation of the diaphragm or phrenic nerve may refer pain to the shoulder since these structures share the same segmental innervation (see Chapter 19). Cervical spine disorders, including prolapsed disks, can put pressure upon nerves that innervate shoulder structures and the skin (see Chapters 15 and 16). Finally, carpal tunnel syndrome can create pain, which is typically referred to the shoulder (see Chapter 18).

Common Shoulder Injuries in Sports

Common shoulder injuries in sports can be classified as (1) impingement syndrome (including bursitis, tears of the rotator cuff, and tendinitis), (2) anterior subluxation of the glenohumeral joint, (3) posterior subluxations with multidirectional instability, and (4) injuries to shoulder joints other than the GH joint (including separation or ligamentous sprain of the AC joint, bound down syndrome in the ST joint, and SC joint disorders). Subordinate categories include adhesive capsulitis and fractures of the humerus or clavicle. Putting It into Practice 17-1 covers principles of managing shoulder injuries.

Impingement Syndrome

Another name for impingement syndrome is "painful arc" syndrome (see Putting It into Practice 17-2, p. 286). This disorder ranges from mild to moderate (irritation of the subacromial bursa to tendinitis or tears of the rotator cuff). The subacromial bursa and rotator cuff are impinged between the superiorly located acromion process and coracoacromial ligament and the inferiorly located greater tubercle of the humerus. Occasionally, the tendon of the long head of the biceps brachii is also impinged. The supraspinatus is the portion

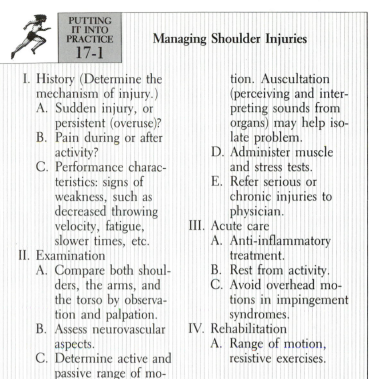

PUTTING IT INTO PRACTICE 17-1

Managing Shoulder Injuries

I. History (Determine the mechanism of injury.)
   A. Sudden injury, or persistent (overuse)?
   B. Pain during or after activity?
   C. Performance characteristics: signs of weakness, such as decreased throwing velocity, fatigue, slower times, etc.
II. Examination
   A. Compare both shoulders, the arms, and the torso by observation and palpation.
   B. Assess neurovascular aspects.
   C. Determine active and passive range of motion. Auscultation (perceiving and interpreting sounds from organs) may help isolate problem.
   D. Administer muscle and stress tests.
   E. Refer serious or chronic injuries to physician.
III. Acute care
   A. Anti-inflammatory treatment.
   B. Rest from activity.
   C. Avoid overhead motions in impingement syndromes.
IV. Rehabilitation
   A. Range of motion, resistive exercises.

of the rotator cuff most often injured, and the condition most often manifests itself during 60 to 120 degrees of shoulder abduction (hence the name painful arc syndrome). Symptoms may be minimal or nonexistent outside this range.

Mechanism of Injury. Impingement syndrome begins with mechanical irritation of the soft tissue and typically occurs from overuse. This condition is relatively common among athletes and people who excessively perform overhead movements, such as baseball pitchers, tennis players, swimmers, and construction workers who install ceilings. Weakness of the rotator cuff muscles is believed to be the basic cause of the mechanical irritation. Rotator cuff weakness allows the head of the humerus to move more than usual during abduction, resulting in a pinching of the soft tissues between the greater tubercle and the overlying acromion and coracoacromial ligament.

**PUTTING
IT INTO
PRACTICE
17-2**

Managing Impingement Syndrome and Rotator Cuff Strain

Stages of Disability

Stage 1: Tendinitis that could lead to atrophied muscles.

Stage 2: Some fiber dissociation in the tendon that can resolve itself with proper treatment.

Stage 3: Rotator cuff tear less than 1 cm (surgery).
Stage 4: Rotator cuff tear greater than 1 cm (surgery).

*Exercises to Stretch the Rotator Cuff**

(A) The athlete lies on his back with his arm over the edge of the table. He places his elbow and shoulder at 90 degrees and passively stretches his shoulder in external rotation. Begin with a 1- to 5-lb weight.

(B) The athlete lies on his back with his arm over the edge of the table. He places his shoulder at 170 degrees and his elbow at 45 degrees and passively stretches his shoulder in external rotation.

(C) The athlete lies on his back with his arm over the edge of the table. He places his shoulder at 135 degrees and his elbow at 45 degrees and passively stretches his shoulder in external rotation.

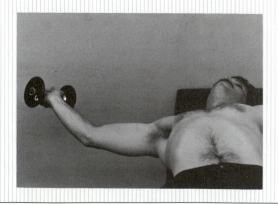

Managing Impingement Syndrome and Rotator Cuff Strain (*continued*)

*Exercise to Strengthen the Infraspinatus and Teres Minor**

(D) The athlete lies on his side on a table, resting on one elbow. He flexes his other elbow 90 degrees, keeping the elbow tight to the rib cage. He slowly lowers the weight and then lifts it back to the starting position.

*Exercise to Strengthen the Subscapularis**

(E) The athlete lies on a table with his elbow flexed 90 degrees and held closely to his thorax. He slowly lowers the weight in external rotation and then slowly lifts it back to the starting position.

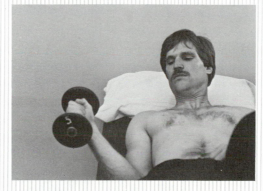

*Empty Can Exercise to Strengthen the Supraspinatus**

(F) The athlete stands upright and holds a weight in each hand. He positions his shoulders in 90 degrees of abduction, 30 degrees of horizontal adduction, and full internal rotation. He then slowly lowers and raises the weights through a 45-degree arc.

*Adapted from Jobe, R., and C. Jobe. Painful athletic injuries of the shoulder. *Clinical Orthopaedics and Related Research* 173:117–124, 1983.

(*continued on next page*)

Managing Impingement Syndrome and Rotator Cuff Strain (*continued*)

Bent-over Arm Pendulum

(G) The athlete lies on his back on a table and lets his arm dangle. He then moves his arm in a circular motion—first clockwise, then counterclockwise, then forward and backward. *Note:* Initially perform this exercise *without* a weight.

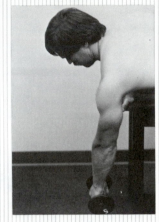

Standing Arm Pendulum

(H) The athlete stands upright with his arms at his sides. He then raises his arms to slightly below shoulder level and then swings them back behind his body.

Arm Circle

(I) The athlete stands upright with his arms extended to the sides and then makes small arm circles both clockwise and counterclockwise. This exercise should be practiced with the forearms pronated and then supinated.

Managing Impingement Syndrome and Rotator Cuff Strain *(continued)*

Elbow Circle

(J) The athlete stands upright with his elbows flexed and shoulders adducted 90 degrees. He then makes small elbow circles both clockwise and counterclockwise.

Saw Exercise

(K) The athlete stands upright with his arms at his sides. He then lifts his arms and reaches forward *(left)*. He then fully flexes his elbows and extends his shoulders in a motion similar to that used when operating a saw *(right)*.

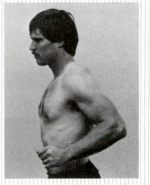

Wall Climber

(L) The athlete stands approximately two feet from a wall. He then places one hand over the other hand on the wall until his arms and hands are fully extended overhead.

This condition typically manifests itself as inflammation of the supraspinatus tendon or subacromial bursa, or both. The athlete complains of shoulder soreness that becomes progressively worse and eventually causes extreme discomfort and inability to perform. If the tendinitis or bursitis is left untreated, the supraspinatus becomes atrophied and perhaps contracted while the surrounding tissues swell. At this point the prognosis is good, but continued use leads to tendon fiber dissociation, increased inflammation, and ultimately a cuff tear. If the athlete attempts self-treatment by laying off a few weeks, scarring and **ossification** may occur, leaving weak tissue that predisposes the athlete to recurrent injury.

Occasionally, the supraspinatus and its tendon are not involved, and the problem is limited to subacromial bursitis or tendinitis of the tendon of the long head of the biceps brachii. The latter injury is particularly likely to occur if the coracoacromial ligament is thickened from previous injury coupled with excessive and repetitive overhead use of the limb.

Although degenerative disease or disorder is the principal cause of rotator cuff tears, the supraspinatus can be injured acutely. Strain may occur from falling on the extended shoulder in sports like wrestling, judo, football, volleyball, or basketball. Shoulder hyperextension, as may occur in wrestling, may tear the muscle or severely stretch the tendon and lead to inflammation.

Evaluation. First check the athlete's history; previous AC joint pathology can lead to thickening of the local tissues and predispose the person to impingement. Next, palpate the subacromial bursa and supraspinatus tendon; palpation usually causes tenderness and pain in athletes with this syndrome. Impingement syndrome can be identified using a hesitation test to create a similar sign. Try to create a similar sign by passively abducting the arm without external rotation, thus forcing the rotator cuff against the underside of the acromion. Evaluate muscle weakness by using the empty can test illustrated in Figure 17-12 (p. 284).

To evaluate a possible associated AC joint disorder, have the athlete bring his elbow across his chest (shoulder horizontal adduction), palpate the AC ligament, and check for joint stability. Look particularly for thickening of the AC ligament.

Treatment and Rehabilitation. Prognosis depends upon the extent of damage and the amount of scarring that might have occurred while the athlete tried to work through the period of discomfort. Prognosis is worsened by an injury that becomes painless when the rotator cuff is loaded while continuing to show abduction weakness, which is characteristic of a true cuff tear.

Treatment initially must be directed at reducing inflammation, to maintain the normal width of the bony gap. This is followed by strengthening the cuff muscles, particularly the supraspinatus, to control the humeral head in abduction and thus prevent recurrence. Specifically, inflammation can be reduced with applications of ice, local rest, and anti-inflammatory medication taken orally or by injection (see Chapters 13 and 27). Strengthening is initially done through isometric exercise, avoiding the type of activity that led to the injury. Later, low-resistance, isotonic exercise can be performed in the empty can position to strengthen the supraspinatus (see Figure 17-12).

Anterior
Glenohumeral Subluxation

Anterior glenohumeral subluxation occurs primarily from forcing the GH joint into abduction, extension, and external rotation. The humeral head is driven anteriorly, stretching the joint capsule and subscapularis tendon. The labrum may be damaged as the hu-

Ossification: The process of formation of the organic matrix (osteoid) of bone.

merus slides forward, or it may be avulsed (separated) from the anterior lip of the glenoid (this is called a Bankart lesion). The athlete is usually quite aware that a displacement has occurred, particularly since spontaneous reduction is rare.

Evaluation. There is an obvious visual difference between the athlete's two shoulders; the subluxed one looks "squared off" at the lateral edge of the acromion, the deltoid is flattened, and the arm is held in twenty to thirty degrees of abduction (Figure 17-13). Radiographically, the humeral head is displaced anteromedially, and it lies in the "subcoracoid space." Palpation will reveal a rather full axilla. The evaluation should always include both a test of axillary nerve function since this structure is particularly vulnerable to injury and an assessment of brachial artery patency.

Treatment and Rehabilitation. Anterior GH subluxation involves much more than a bony displacement. Soft tissues are stretched or torn, and immediate reduction of the subluxed humeral head does not restore normal functional status. These tissues will require protection, reinforcement by strengthening of supporting muscles, and time to become contracted and thus regain their original length. Since an anterior subluxation is a medical emergency, a physician should perform reduction as soon as possible. In fact, if done immediately, reduction may be accomplished with minimal pain. Once the surrounding muscles have gone into spasm, reduction is seldom possible without anesthesia.

The simplest method of reduction, usually performed without anesthesia, requires that the athlete lie supine on a table, with the subluxed shoulder and arm hanging over the edge. The athlete holds a weight in the hand until the muscles relax sufficiently to allow the humeral head to slip back into place.

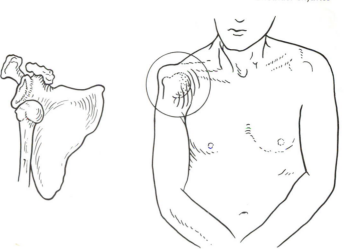

Figure 17-13　Dislocation of the shoulder.

Kocher's maneuver, performed under anesthesia, is (1) distraction of the joint with the elbow flexed; (2) external rotation of the humerus, adduction with flexion at the shoulder, bringing the elbow to midline; and (3) internal rotation until the humeral head slips into place. A variation of this method requires **distraction,** with the hands on the athlete's forearm while stabilizing the trunk with the foot in the axilla. Reduction must be confirmed radiographically. Arthroscopy may be used later to examine the labrum.

GH subluxation often results in a stretched or torn joint capsule, an avulsed labrum, and a stretched subscapularis tendon accompanied by torn muscle fibers. Often these structures have to be surgically repaired. If the physician elects to perform surgery, rehabilitation initially involves three to six weeks of shoulder immobilization, with the arm held against the chest wall in internal rotation. Immobilization is followed by careful strengthening exercises for the shoulder internal rotators, adductors, and flexors. Extension and external rotation must be avoided during this time. Tissues around the joint,

Kocher's maneuver: A technique, performed under anesthesia, for reduction of a glenohumeral dislocation.

Distraction: Separation of a joint surface.

such as the pectoralis major, upper trapezius, and posterior shoulder muscles, should be stretched and massaged. Young, healthy athletes do not run much risk of developing **frozen shoulder.** However, local muscle contractures are common, and considerable care and patience are necessary to restore normal tissue tone and pliability.

Caution the athlete who experiences recurrent GH subluxation against forcing joint displacement as a locker room trick. The athlete should be evaluated for strength of the shoulder girdle muscles and placed on a strengthening program to reinforce the anterior shoulder muscles. Tape or strap the shoulder to protect it in practice or competition. Caution the athlete against moving into external rotation and extension. If anterior subluxation is accomplished easily and if there is crepitus, refer the athlete to a physician for an in-depth evaluation of the labrum, possibly through arthroscopy.

Posterior Subluxation

Posterior subluxation is far less common than anterior displacement. It may occur from a fall on, or blow to, the anterior surface of the shoulder or a fall on the outstretched arm while it is internally rotated and adducted.

Evaluation. The injury is often not recognized because typically there is no gross shoulder deformity. The coracoid may appear more prominent because the humeral head is posteriorly displaced, but this will go unnoticed unless the athlete's uniform (e.g., a football player's shoulder pads) is removed for adequate visual inspection of the shoulder. Palpation may reveal increased fullness and hardness of the posterior surface of the shoulder, with decreased fullness anteriorly. In well-established posterior subluxation, the athlete's arm may be seen locked in adduction and internal rotation. Even a

radiograph may be inadequate for accurate diagnosis because the humeral head slips posteriorly without medial displacement. This posterior movement cannot be seen in an anteroposterior x-ray.

Treatment and Rehabilitation. As in anterior subluxation, reduction can be achieved without anesthesia if it is performed immediately, before significant muscle spasm and pain develop. Again, a physician should perform reduction. The reduction is typically executed under anesthesia if considerable time has passed since the injury or if the athlete is experiencing severe pain and muscle spasm. Reduction is accomplished by distracting the humerus anterolaterally with pressure upon the posterior aspect of the humeral head.

Unfortunately, fracture of the posterior portion of the glenoid lip is a relatively common complication of posterior subluxation. Surgery may be required if this fragment is not reduced to its proper position after reduction of the humeral head. Most likely the capsule will also have to be repaired. Rehabilitation is directed at restoring normal tone and pliability to tissue around the joint that became contracted during immobilization, strengthening the muscles that restrain posterior subluxation, and restoring normal capsule pliability.

Acromioclavicular Separation

The AC ligament is usually sprained by a downward-directed force applied to the most lateral end of the shoulder girdle (Figures 17-14 and 17-15). This moves the acromion downward while the clavicle remains behind. There are three degrees (first, second, and third) of injury to this joint and its ligament. Third degree clearly specifies a joint separation; all three degrees may involve the coracoclavicular ligament as well as the AC ligament.

First degree injury is a sprain with

Frozen shoulder: Loss of range of motion in the shoulder; caused by the formation of fibrous adhesions. Rarely occurs in young athletes.

no separation of the joint. During evaluation, typically there is a normal joint space and only a slight instability, with virtually no shoulder disability, beyond some tenderness to touch. If the fibers of the AC ligament are torn, usually there will be pain directly over the structure. Pain will be localized medially and inferiorly to the joint between the coracoid and clavicle if the coracoclavicular ligament is involved. Treatment is usually limited to protective taping, limitation of activity, and cryotherapy to reduce contusions and pain.

A second degree injury severely damages the AC ligament, and there is considerable pain when the joint is mobilized. Hypermobility is typically not a feature of second degree injuries, but pain and swelling are greater than in the first degree AC sprain. Bringing the elbow across the chest will elicit great pain. This injury may recur if the athlete returns to full activity too soon. Rehabilitation is directed at maintaining strength without widening the injury. Remember that connective tissue heals slowly and is particularly vulnerable to reinjury.

A third degree injury is a complete separation of the AC joint from rupture of the AC ligament alone or combined rupture with the coracoclavicular ligament. The joint is extremely unstable. The athlete typically exhibits a high-riding clavicle that, in radiograph, creates a wide space between the coracoid and clavicle. Pain is localized to the AC joint, and to the area slightly below it if the coracoclavicular ligament is also involved. This injury often requires internal fixation for satisfactory reduction and protection from recurrence.

Adhesive Capsulitis

Adhesive **capsulitis** is an inflammation of the glenohumeral capsule. It may result from intrinsic factors, such as calcific supraspinatus tendinitis, bi-

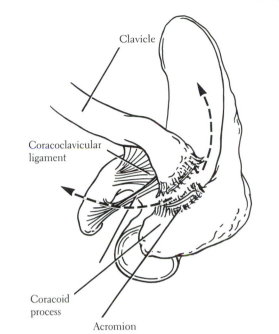

Figure 17-14 Subluxation of the acromioclavicular joint is frequently caused by forces that protract or retract the scapula on the clavicle.

Clavicle

Coracoclavicular ligament

Coracoid process

Acromion

Figure 17-15 Common mechanism of acromioclavicular separation.

cipital tendinitis, or prolonged immobilization of the joint. However, immobilization rarely leads to capsulitis in young, healthy athletes (this syndrome may occur in masters athletes). Extrinsic factors include voluntary immobility that occurs secondary to pain in or around the shoulder from cervical spine disorders, angina pectoris, or phrenic

Capsulitis: Inflammation of a capsule.

nerve inflammation. Regardless of the cause, the inflamed capsule adheres to the humeral head and becomes contracted or tight. This restrains or prevents glenohumeral motion, creating a frozen shoulder. During the inflammatory stage, the athlete will complain of pain, and the evaluation will reveal spasms in shoulder girdle muscles, with an obvious disturbance of the scapulohumeral rhythm.

Treatment and Rehabilitation. Early treatment is local rest and analgesics (pain-reducing substances). Stretching or joint mobilization should not be attempted yet, but the athlete should be encouraged to use the joint in normal motion. Gentle stretching with exercise to maintain muscle tone around the shoulder girdle may begin when inflammation and pain have subsided. If therapy is unsuccessful, inflation of the joint with saline or surgical manipulation may be attempted.

Fractures

Fractures of the humerus are discussed in Chapter 18; here we discuss fractures of the greater tubercle. This is an uncommon injury in young athletes, although avulsion of this traction epiphysis can occur. In older, active people, a fall directly on the point of the shoulder may cause an undisplaced fracture of the greater tuberosity. In either instance, the sensation is similar to subluxation, and the athlete believes he has dislocated his shoulder. However, the pain and symptoms may be more intense than with a subluxation. Careful palpation may reveal a mobile bony fragment at the end of the supraspinatus tendon. Surgical reduction is seldom necessary, but the athlete will require an x-ray and treatment by a physician.

The clavicles of children and adolescents are more easily fractured than those of adults. Typically, an attempt to break a fall with an outstretched arm causes clavicular fractures. Forces are transmitted across the GH and AC joints through the clavicle. The most common fracture site is the middle third of the bone; the lateral piece is pulled downward and medially. In addition, a lateral fracture may occur at the distal end of the clavicle, immediately proximal to the AC joint but distal to the insertion of the coracoclavicular ligament. In this case, the coracoclavicular ligament holds the clavicle in place on the scapula, and the injury may be more difficult to accurately assess.

References

Anderson, J. *Grant's Atlas of Anatomy*. Baltimore: Williams & Wilkins, 1978.

Brunet, M., R. Haddad, and E. Porche. Rotator cuff impingement syndrome in sports. *The Physician and Sportsmedicine* 10(12):86–94, 1982.

DePalma, A. *Surgery of the Shoulder*. New York: Lippincott, 1983.

Hollingshead, W. H. *Textbook of Anatomy*, 4th ed. New York: Harper & Row, 1974.

Kendall, H., F. Kendall, and G. Wadsworth. *Muscles: Testing and Function*. Baltimore: Williams & Wilkins, 1971.

Lord, J., and L. Posati. *Thoracic-Outlet Syndromes*. Summit, N.J.: CIBA-Geigy Corp., 1971.

O'Donoghue, D. *Treatment of Injuries to Athletes*. Philadelphia: W. B. Saunders, 1984.

Post, M. *The Shoulder: Surgical and Nonsurgical Management*. Philadelphia: Lea & Febiger, 1978.

Salter, R. *Textbook of Disorders and Injuries of the Musculoskeletal System*. Baltimore: Williams & Wilkins, 1970.

Wells, K. *Kinesiology*. Philadelphia: W. B. Saunders, 1971.

18

Upper Extremity and Hand Injuries

U PPER EXTREMITY and hand injuries are prevalent in sports that require manipulative skills, such as baseball, basketball, and football. Catching, throwing, and otherwise handling the ball place the hands and arms at increased risk because these anatomical structures are relatively fragile. As humans' upright posture evolved, the upper extremity became more instrumental in dexterous, manipulative skills and less involved in bearing weight. The upper extremity also became smaller and more mobile in all its joints; however, this mobility was gained at the expense of stability and led to increased vulnerability.

Hand and upper extremity injuries can be difficult to evaluate because pain in these areas is often **referred pain** from the spine or shoulders. To properly evaluate and treat arm and hand injuries, the athletic trainer must be acutely aware of the anatomy and the biomechanical interactions of the various regions of the upper **torso.** This chapter examines the structure, functions, and injuries of the upper extremity and hands, excluding the shoulder joint, which is covered in the preceding chapter.

Elbow injuries occur frequently in tennis. The most common causes of tennis elbow are overuse, poor technique, and inadequate conditioning.

Referred pain: Pain experienced at one location but caused by injury in another location.

Torso: The trunk; the area of the body between the hips and neck; the body minus its extremities and head.

295

Prevention, Treatment, and Rehabilitation of Specific Injuries

Anatomy

Upper Arm

The humerus, the skeletal structure of the upper arm, is a long bone with numerous projections for muscular attachment (Figures 18-1 and 18-2). The greater **tuberosity** (GT) lies immediately inferior to the acromioclavicular joint and is a point of insertion for the supraspinatus, infraspinatus, and teres minor (see Figure 17-4, p. 270). Often, this area is very tender during palpation, particularly when the **rotator cuff** has been injured. The lesser tuberosity (LT) lies anterior and medially to the GT and is the point of attachment for the subscapularis muscle.

The GT and LT are separated by the bicipital groove. The tendon of the long head of the biceps passes through this groove and attaches to the superior lip of the glenoid fossa. The tendon is secured within the groove by the transverse humeral ligament. This ligament is subject to overuse injuries, particularly in swimmers (see Chapter 17). The ligament can become painful and inflamed; the biceps tendon may exhibit **impingement syndrome.** As the tendon becomes more irritated and swollen, the space for movement within the biceps' groove decreases, possibly causing compression upon the tendon and subsequent **synovitis** (bicipital tenosynovitis) of the anterior region of the shoulder. Similarly, during horizontal adduction, this tendon may also impinge against the coracoacromial ligament and eventually the supraspinatus muscle.

The latissimus dorsi and teres major muscles (Figure 17-4) are attached to the medial border of the bicipital groove. These muscles act in unison to internally rotate and adduct the arm and are important in lifting the body toward a fixed arm in movements like rope climbing and pull-ups. The pecto-

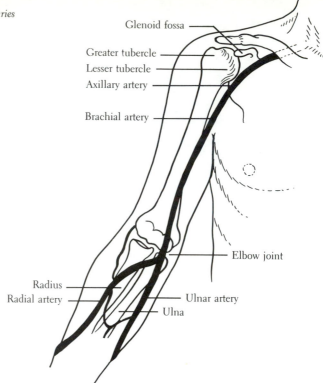

Figure 18-1   The humerus and major arterial blood vessels.

ralis major, an important muscle in humeral internal rotation and adduction of the humerus, is attached to the lateral border of the bicipital groove.

Elbow

The triceps spans the entire length of the posterior humerus and inserts on the posterior surface of the olecranon process of the ulna and the antebrachial fossa of the forearm (Figure 18-2). The long head of the triceps originates from the infraglenoid tubercle of the scapula. The lateral head forms the posterolateral surface of the proximal one-half of the humerus. The medial head forms the distal two-thirds of the posterior medial surface. The triceps' primary function is to extend the elbow; it is also an accessory shoulder extensor muscle.

Tuberosity: A rounded protrusion from the surface of a bone.
Rotator cuff: Muscles that rotate the humerus.
Impingement syndrome: Entrapment of tissue; it causes inflammation.

Synovitis: Inflammation of a synovial (joint) membrane.

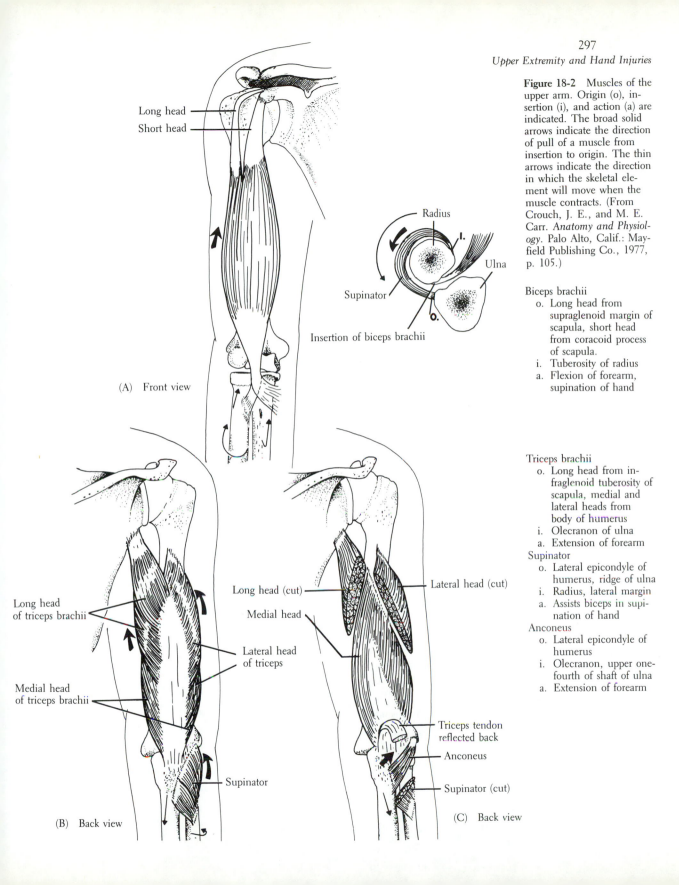

Long head
Short head

Radius

Supinator

Ulna

Insertion of biceps brachii

(A)   Front view

Long head
of triceps brachii

Medial head
of triceps brachii

(B)   Back view

Long head (cut)

Medial head

Lateral head
of triceps

Supinator

Lateral head (cut)

Triceps tendon
reflected back

Anconeus

Supinator (cut)

(C)   Back view

Figure 18-2 Muscles of the upper arm. Origin (o), insertion (i), and action (a) are indicated. The broad solid arrows indicate the direction of pull of a muscle from insertion to origin. The thin arrows indicate the direction in which the skeletal element will move when the muscle contracts. (From Crouch, J. E., and M. E. Carr. *Anatomy and Physiology.* Palo Alto, Calif.: Mayfield Publishing Co., 1977, p. 105.)

Biceps brachii
  o. Long head from supraglenoid margin of scapula, short head from coracoid process of scapula.
  i. Tuberosity of radius
  a. Flexion of forearm, supination of hand

Triceps brachii
  o. Long head from infraglenoid tuberosity of scapula, medial and lateral heads from body of humerus
  i. Olecranon of ulna
  a. Extension of forearm
Supinator
  o. Lateral epicondyle of humerus, ridge of ulna
  i. Radius, lateral margin
  a. Assists biceps in supination of hand
Anconeus
  o. Lateral epicondyle of humerus
  i. Olecranon, upper one-fourth of shaft of ulna
  a. Extension of forearm

298

The numerous **bursae** in and about the shoulder and elbow joints decrease friction and provide freedom of movement between the lubricated areas. Both the bursa and the synovium, which also lubricates the joints, can become painfully irritated when they are abnormally or excessively stressed.

Forearm

The forearm, comprised of the radius and ulna, can be supinated and pronated and gives the hand a mobile base from which to function (Figure 18-1, p. 296). The radius, named because of its rotating function, is always on the thumb side of the forearm. The radius moves about the ulna during **pronation** and **supination**. The ulna is a stationary bone (during supination and pronation) that proximally articulates with the humerus to form a uniaxial hinged (ginglymoid) joint. Distally, it articulates with the wrist's proximal row of carpals. The radius is proximally stabilized by the annular ligament, which allows for rotation of the radial head about its articulation with the capitulum of the humerus and the proximal radioulnar joint. Distally, the radius forms a large articulation with the proximal carpals.

The forearm has many two-joint muscles that function at both the elbow and the wrist (Figure 18-3). Medially, the common flexor tendon attaches to the medial epicondyle of the humerus and the pronator teres, which attaches just proximally to the medial epicondyle on the humerus (Figure 17-4, p. 270). Extreme and repetitive elbow extension and supination irritate this area. This syndrome is sometimes called golfer's or pitcher's elbow because it so often afflicts these athletes. Laterally, the common extensor tendon attaches to the lateral **epicondyle** of the humerus. In racket sports, the overuse and irritation syndrome of this area from severe and repetitive pronation and wrist flexion combined with elbow

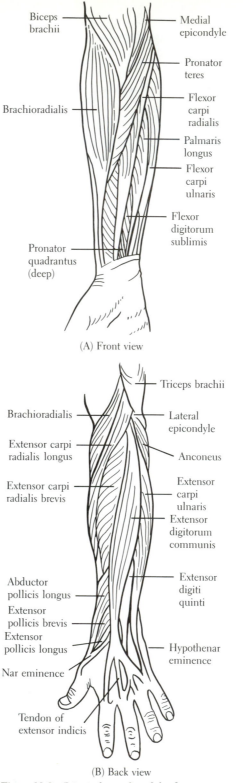

(A) Front view

(B) Back view

Figure 18-3 Principal muscles of the forearm.

Bursae: Connective tissue sacs over bony prominences and near tendons that facilitate movement by reducing friction.

Pronation: Rotation of the forearm so the palm faces downward.
Supination: Rotation of the forearm so the palm faces upward.

Epicondyle: A bony protuberance found above or upon a long bone's smooth articular eminence.

extension is commonly called tennis elbow; the medical terms for these lesions are medial or **lateral epicondylitis.** Although the forearm muscles' primary function is to flex and extend the wrist, they also have an accessory elbow function. The pronator quadratus and supinator are intrinsic to and act solely upon the forearm.

Wrist and Hand

The wrist is composed of eight carpal bones (Figure 18-4). The proximal row of carpals includes the scaphoid (navicular), lunate, triquetrium, and the pisiform. There are two portions to the distal row: the medial aspect, comprised of the hamate and the capitate, and the lateral aspect, comprised of the trapezoid and trapezium. These rows of carpals form two basic joints: the radiocarpal, which moves mainly in extension, and the midcarpal, which moves mainly in flexion (both joints do move in both flexion and extension). Additionally, the wrist is capable of lateral and medial flexion.

The scaphoid and lunate are the most commonly injured carpals. A fall on an outstretched hand with the wrist extended may fracture the scaphoid or dislocate the lunate. Because it is difficult to distinguish between a severe sprain and fracture of the wrist, refer serious wrist injury for medical evaluation and x-ray.

The hand's five metacarpals articulate with the wrist carpals and the fingers' and thumb's proximal phalanges. The metacarpals' structural arrangement allows for numerous types of grips. The metacarpals and their intricate ligamentous support system form longitudinal and transverse arches. The two lateral metacarpals form the mobile segment of the hand; the second and third metacarpals form the stable segments. When gripping, the hand wraps around the object, with the two lateral metacarpals moving toward the thumb. The first metacarpal is covered by strong intrinsic

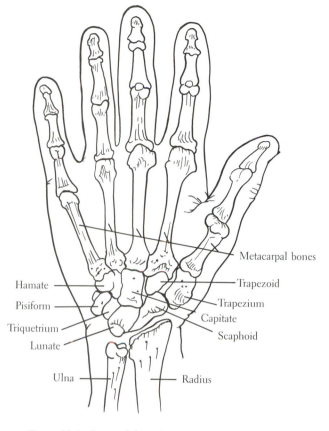

Figure 18-4 Bones of the wrist.

muscles of the hand (Figure 18-5, p. 300); this region is known as the **nar eminence.** The medial aspect of the palm is also important because the intrinsic muscles for apposition and opposition are located there; this area is the **hypothenar eminence.**

Each finger is composed of three phalanges; the thumb is composed of only two. The thumb, which is extremely mobile and has a diverse and extensive range of motion, has evolved primarily for **prehensile** activities. The fingers, which are adept at fine manipulative skills, are controlled by a complex tendinous and ligamentous structure. The hands are among the most commonly injured portions of the body because of their extensive use and relatively small anatomical structure.

Lateral epicondylitis: Pain and tenderness of the tendons near the lateral epicondyle of the humerus, caused by microtrauma and tendinitis. Also called tennis elbow.
Eminence: An elevated area of a bone.
Nar eminence: The eminence formed by the fleshy part of the palm on the thumb side.
Hypothenar eminence: An eminence formed on the medial part of the palm by the muscles of the little finger.
Prehensile: Grasping.

Prevention, Treatment, and Rehabilitation of Specific Injuries

Upper Extremity Blood Supply

The blood supply to the upper extremity emanates from the subclavian artery, which becomes the axillary artery and the brachial artery (the artery has three different names along its course; see Figure 18-1, p. 296). The large subclavian artery has several branches that serve the various regions of the upper extremity. The principal veins of the upper extremity are the cephalic and basilic. In cases of profuse bleeding, pressure applied to the axillary artery will slow the bleeding to the entire upper extremity.

Upper Extremity Nerves

The major nerves of the upper extremity are closely aligned with the major arteries. The hand and arm are controlled by nerves from the **brachial plexus,** which emanates from the fifth through eighth cervical and first thoracic nerves. These nerves form three cords in the extremities that branch into the five major nerves of the upper extremities: radial, axillary, ulnar, median, and musculocutaneous.

It is important to evaluate the neurological status of the limb whenever the upper extremity is injured, particularly in the cases of fractures and dislocations. Any changes in sensation or distinct muscle weakness must be evaluated. The athletic trainer must use a process of elimination to distinguish specific neurological involvement since the five major nerves are formed by the same five spinal segments. The athletic trainer should evaluate superficial and deep sensation, strength, and the ability to perform various movements (Figure 18-6).

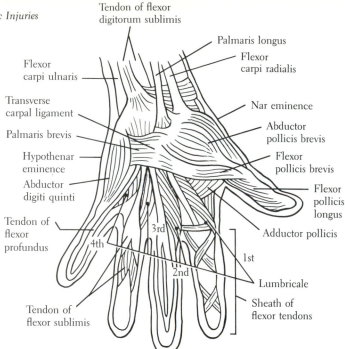

Figure 18-5 Anterior view of the muscles of the surface of the hand.

Brachial plexus: A network of nerves formed by the fifth to eighth cervical and first thoracic nerves; the network extends from the lateral neck to the axilla.

(A)

(B)

(C)

Figure 18-6 Sensation tests of the (A) radial, (B) median, and (C) ulnar nerves. These tests sometimes help the athletic trainer recognize injuries with neurological involvement.

Upper Arm Injuries

Contusions, strains, and fractures are the most frequent soft tissue injuries to the upper arm because this area is often exposed to repeated trauma, especially in contact sports. Overuse injuries to soft tissues are also common in sports like baseball (pitching), javelin, weight lifting, and swimming.

Contusions

The tremendous mobility of the shoulder allows the upper extremity to be involved in a variety of motor skills. However, the versatility of the arms also makes them vulnerable to direct contact with opposing players and objects.

Evaluation and Treatment. Contusions are indicated by skin discoloration and swelling but rarely any significant loss of function. Treatment is early application of ice and compression combined with maintaining the injured soft tissue in a stretched position. Some authorities recommend the application of ice for only the first twenty-four to seventy-two hours, but each injury should be treated on an individual basis. Continue the application of cold until the pain and swelling subside, and properly pad the area to avoid further trauma.

Rehabilitation. Contusions are typically benign, and the athlete can usually return to participation after first aid and protective padding have been administered. In rare instances, myositis ossificans (calcification of a portion of a muscle) may develop secondary to a contusion. When this occurs in the arm, the condition is known as **blocker's exostosis.** It is important to protect a contusion, particularly one that has become calcified, from further trauma

by using an appropriate pad or modifying the activity.

Prevention. Contusions of the upper extremity are difficult to prevent. If allowed, appropriate protective padding may be considered.

Strains

The muscle bellies of the biceps and triceps are susceptible to overuse strains, which cause various degrees of disability. Usually, strains occur at the tendinous insertion of the muscles, occasionally at the musculotendinous junction. Strains often occur in sports that require vigorous throwing motion (e.g., baseball, javelin, discus) or during severe muscular overload (e.g., weight lifting). This discussion is restricted to strains of those upper arm muscles and tendons associated with elbow flexion and extension. Chapter 17 discusses shoulder injuries.

Evaluation and Treatment. As with any strain, evaluation should begin with a history, followed by inspection and palpation. Be sure to compare the injured limb with the **contralateral** side. Strains are characterized by pain, swelling, tenderness, and loss of strength and range of motion.

Treatment for a first degree strain (mild discoloration and swelling but no significant functional loss; see Chapter 5) is the application of ice and gentle stretching exercises. Normally, the athlete is able to participate with minimal discomfort. Rehabilitation of a first degree strain consists of progressive stretching and strengthening exercises combined with continued intermittent application of cold and heat.

A second degree strain is more serious and involves greater muscular injury than a first degree strain. It is treated much the same as a mild strain. However, regularly reevaluate the athlete to determine if he or she can continue playing. Allowing an athlete with

Contralateral: On the opposite side of the body.

Blocker's exostosis: Myositis ossificans occurring in a football player's upper arm; caused by repeated trauma.

a severe strain to continue playing may cause extensive muscle damage, permanent dysfunction, and disfiguration.

Treat a third degree strain—complete rupture of the contractile tissue—with an application of ice and immobilization. This type of strain occurs more often in the biceps, especially at the attachment of the long head on the glenoid fossa. A muscle is ruptured when the structure is exposed to extreme stresses. Gymnasts incur this injury because of the positions and activities inherent in the sport. This injury will typically reveal a palpable defect. Following these severe injuries, early surgical intervention is necessary to reattach the tendon to its attachment site.

Rehabilitation. After administering the standard anti-inflammatory procedures (see Chapter 8), the first priority is to restore normal range of motion. Stretch elbow flexors and extensors by placing the shoulder at the limits of extension and flexion. For example, a good stretching exercise for the triceps is to flex the elbow and shoulder and attempt to reach down the spinal column as far as possible.

Strengthening exercises can begin with manually resisted flexion and extension of the elbow and shoulder. As the affected muscles become stronger, to further strengthen them, institute standard weight-training exercises.

Prevention. Upper arm strains can be prevented by warm-up, avoiding severe overload (unless physically prepared), and emphasizing both flexibility and strength exercises during conditioning.

Fractures

Fractures of the humerus are usually **transverse** or **comminuted** (see Chapter 6). The surgical neck of the humerus is the most common site for a fracture. If the suspected fracture is in the mid-shaft, the athletic trainer must closely evaluate the neurological and vascular competency distal from the site of injury because the radial nerve is easily traumatized. Signs of radial nerve trauma are inability to extend the wrist or supinate the forearm.

Epiphyseal fracture may occur in adolescent athletes, especially at the distal **epiphyseal plate** just proximal to the epicondyles of the humerus (see Chapters 6 and 28). Fractures in this area may lead to abnormal osseous maturation and subsequent malformed distal humerus. This deformity may prevent the athlete from attaining complete elbow extension. Epiphyseal fracture may also lead to nerve entrapments and circulatory problems.

Evaluation and Treatment. Pain is a prevalent sensation following fracture, especially when the injured area is palpated and moved. However, **greenstick fracture,** which occurs in child athletes, is an exception; movement may not be uncomfortable since portions of the bone are not completely separated.

If the athletic trainer suspects a fracture, the injured extremity should be immobilized from one joint below to one joint above the site of trauma. Treat the athlete for shock and transport her or him immediately to a physician for proper diagnosis and care. Depending upon the severity of the fracture, the athlete may miss up to four months of participation.

Rehabilitation. Rehabilitation involves restoring range of motion and muscle strength to the forearm, upper arm, and shoulder muscles.

Prevention. Fractures of the humerus are difficult to prevent. Because a fall on an outstretched arm sometimes causes a fractured humerus, teaching proper falling technique (rolling) may prevent the injury.

Epiphyseal plate: The growth area of bones.

Greenstick fracture: An incomplete fracture that occurs only in children; the break passes only partially through the bone.

Transverse fracture: A bone break in which the fracture line runs perpendicular to the axis of the bone.
Comminuted fracture: A splintering or fragmentation of a bone.

Forearm and Elbow Injuries

The forearm and elbow areas are easily injured, particularly in racket sports like tennis and lacrosse and in throwing sports like baseball and javelin. The relatively small muscles of this region can be overwhelmed by the tremendous forces developed during participation in high-intensity upper body sports.

Soft Tissue Lesions

The elbow region is very susceptible to injury. Elbow pain may be referred from the cervical spine, the shoulder, or the hand, or it can be caused by direct trauma. Many soft tissue components are responsible for the normal function of the joint. Elbow injuries may also debilitate distally located structures. Test the elbow and wrist for range of motion to determine which structures are involved.

Epicondylitis

Epicondylitis is a common disability among such athletes as tennis players, pitchers, and javelin throwers (Figure 18-7; Putting It into Practice 18-1, p. 304; and Box 18-1, p. 305). The injury elicits pain along the brachioradialis or the lateral epicondyle (tennis elbow). Pain occurs when the tendinous attachments become irritated from overuse; pain may also be elicited at the lateral epicondyle with extension and medially with flexion, depending upon the respective injury. Among tennis players, skilled and experienced players most exhibit symptoms on the medial side; both experienced players and novices may exhibit symptoms on the lateral side.

Evaluation and Treatment. An athlete with lateral epicondylitis typically

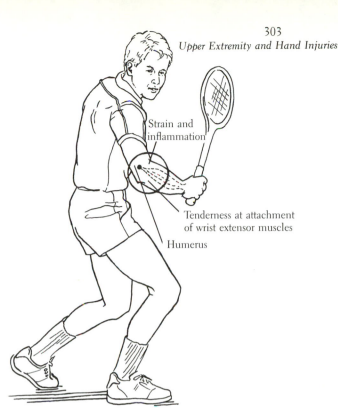

Figure 18-7 Tennis elbow (lateral epicondylitis). A strain or inflammation of the common extensor tendon of the forearm muscles causes this injury. Preventive measures are improved conditioning, better technique, and appropriate equipment. Strapping the forearm can sometimes help prevent and manage the injury.

Strain and inflammation

Tenderness at attachment of wrist extensor muscles

Humerus

will complain of pain over the forearm's common extensor tendon. Often the history will reveal a pattern of poor technique, weak muscles, or overuse. Immediate treatment is reducing inflammation and rest (see Chapter 8). A tennis elbow brace, a two- to three-inch-long strap placed about two to three inches distal to the elbow joint, is often enough support to eliminate symptoms in minor cases.

An athlete with medial epicondylitis manifests pain about the medial epicondyle; sometimes the injury is accompanied by calcification of soft tissue. This injury occurs in better players who serve the ball hard or use the American twist serve. Although this injury involves the wrist flexors, the pattern of overuse and injury is the same as in lateral epicondylitis.

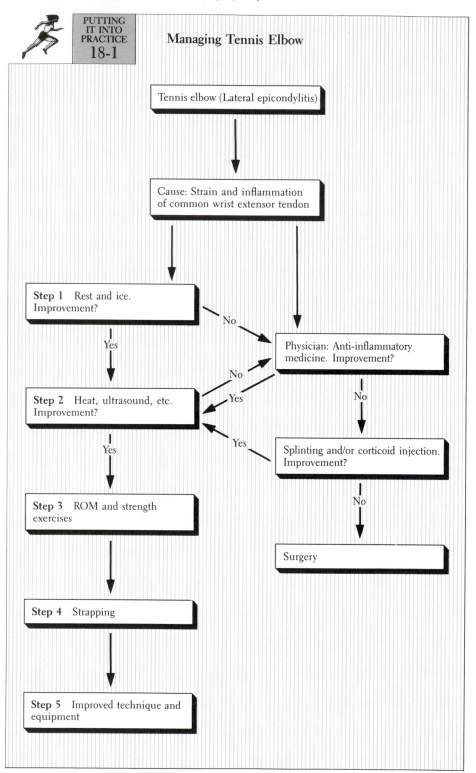

PUTTING
IT INTO
PRACTICE
18-1

Managing Tennis Elbow

Tennis elbow (Lateral epicondylitis)

Cause: Strain and inflammation
of common wrist extensor tendon

Step 1 Rest and ice.
Improvement?

No

Step 2 Heat, ultrasound, etc.
Improvement?

Yes

No

Yes

Physician: Anti-inflammatory
medicine. Improvement?

No

Yes

Step 3 ROM and strength
exercises

Yes

Splinting and/or corticoid injection.
Improvement?

No

Step 4 Strapping

Surgery

Step 5 Improved technique and
equipment

BOX 18-1 Tennis Elbow

Most serious tennis players experience tennis elbow at one time or another. The incidence of injury increases with the frequency of play: Individuals who play tennis six to seven days per week have a 50 percent chance of sustaining the injury, whereas those who play only once a week have a 26 percent chance. Expert players are by no means immune—although they are less likely than intermediate recreational players to incur tennis elbow, they are more likely than beginning players to experience the injury.

Tennis elbow may be prevented by proper conditioning, improving technique, and playing with appropriate equipment. Good strength, flexibility, and endurance in the arms and shoulders help the arm sustain the forces generated during play.

Improperly executed backhands are the root of many elbow problems in tennis players. An incorrect stroke typically requires that most of the power come from the relatively weak forearm and shoulder muscles rather than from momentum created by the legs. Encourage athletes to "step into the ball" and use their shoulder and body weight in a smooth transition of force. The elbow should be straight, with the weight on the front foot as contact is made with the ball. Because the two-handed backhand places less strain on the elbow and almost never results in tennis elbow, athletes with persistent elbow problems should consider this technique.

Good and appropriate equipment helps prevent this injury, so encourage athletes to use lighter, more flexible rackets made of aluminum, steel, fiberglass, or graphite rather than wood. Athletes should use an appropriate grip; a small grip places too much torque on the forearm and may cause injury. Recreational players should not have their strings strung too tightly; fifty-five to sixty pounds is appropriate for most people. (Large rackets, such as the Prince, can be strung tighter, with no apparent increase in the incidence of tennis elbow.) Some experts suggest using strings made of gut because gut gives more than nylon, thus placing less stress on the elbow.

A physician often treats epicondylitis with an injection of **corticosteroids** into the inflamed area. However, this should be a last-ditch procedure, to be used only if more conservative methods such as stretching and strengthening exercises, ice, and deep friction massage have failed. Many authorities believe that steroid injections should be avoided if possible.

Rehabilitation. To stretch the wrist extensors, have the athlete pronate the forearm and then statically flex the wrist (Figure 18-8). The athlete can accomplish this through passive stretching or by pressing the palmar aspect of the hand over the end of a tabletop. Hold these static stretches for approximately thirty seconds; repeat the stretches three to five times.

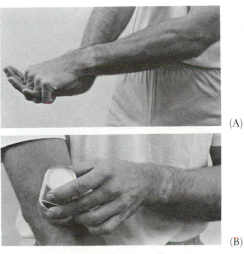

(A)

(B)

Corticosteroids: Adrenal cortex hormones. Synthetic substitutes are sometimes injected to decrease inflammation.

Figure 18-8 Treating tennis elbow.
(A) Passively stretching the extensor carpi radialis (of the right arm here) is an important method.
(B) Ice massage around the insertion of the forearm extensors helps contain the inflammation.

The wrist extensors and flexors should be strengthened both concentrically and eccentrically (Figure 18-9). Have the athlete place the pronated forearm on a table, with the hand protruding off the table's edge. Then, while grasping a weight, the athlete should extend and slowly flex (eccentrically contracting the wrist extensors) the wrist through a full range of motion.

If the injury does not respond to conservative treatment, the wrist may need to be splinted in extension for lateral epicondylitis or in flexion for medial epicondylitis for three to four weeks. This treatment allows the tendinous attachment to heal without any stress. If all methods of treatment fail, surgery may be necessary to either complete or modify the tear in the tendinous attachment, ensuring the formation of normal scar tissue. Treatments for lateral and medial epicondylitis following surgery or splinting include specific stretching with the elbow fully extended, resistive exercise, and the application of such modalities as ice, heat, ultrasound (high-frequency sound waves used as heat therapy), and electrical muscle stimulation. For lateral epicondylitis, the forearm muscles are stretched with the forearm fully pronated and the wrist flexed; for medial irritation, the forearm is supinated and the wrist extended.

Prevention. Many factors have been implicated in the development of epicondylitis, including sudden overload of the extensor (lateral) or flexor (medial) muscles; overuse; quality of the tissue; age; hormonal imbalances in females; lack of strength, endurance, and flexibility; poor joint mechanics; improper equipment; and skill level (see Box 18-1, p. 305). Preventive measures include improving strength (Figure 18-10) and flexibility, using proper technique, and using a racquet with the proper grip size, string tension, and weight. Almost all exercises that strengthen the

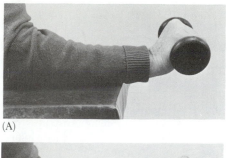

(A)

(B)

Figure 18-9 Wrist exercises using a dumbbell.
(A) This extension exercise helps develop strength and range of motion in the wrist extensors. Begin with a 2.5- to 5-pound weight, slowly progressing to 10 to 15 pounds, as tolerated. Practice this exercise through a full range of motion.
(B) This flexion exercise, although not as effective as extension exercise for treating tennis elbow, helps develop strength and range of motion in forearm muscles.

(A)

(B)　　　　　　　　　　　　　　　　　(C)

Figure 18-10 Triceps exercises.
(A) Supine "French curl." Lie supine on a bench with your shoulders flexed ninety degrees. Grasp the bar at shoulder width, flex your elbows, and lower the bar toward your forehead. Use a spotter for this exercise, particularly if you are working with a relatively heavy weight.
(B) The Nautilus triceps machine, which is excellent for isolating the elbow extensor muscles.
(C) Triceps exercise on a "lat" machine. With your elbows fixed slightly above the anterior iliac crests of your pelvis, grasp the bar with a narrow grip and flex your elbows ninety degrees. Fully extend your arms, pushing down on the bar. Return to the starting position.

muscles of the upper body are appropriate for preventing tennis elbow, but emphasis should be upon the wrist extensors and flexors, elbow extensors, and shoulder extensors (see Chapter 4).

Sprains

Elbow sprains are common injuries in such athletes as gymnasts and throwers, who place great amounts of stress upon their elbows. Ligamentous injuries of the elbow are rated like all other sprains: first, second, and third degree.

Evaluation and Treatment. Pain is often produced while the injured ligaments are being palpated. Test the integrity of the medial and lateral collateral ligaments with the elbow in full extension (Figure 18-11). Any increase in laxity of the joint (compared to the contralateral elbow) is significant. Repeated stress may lead to a functional lengthening of the medial collateral ligament.

The head of the radius is stabilized primarily by the annular ligament, which forms a ring around the radial head to allow necessary rotation of the radius during forearm pronation and supination. The radius must be quite mobile to perform its function, so it is more susceptible to injury than the more stable ulna.

Rehabilitation. Rehabilitation consists of increasing the strength and flexibility of the forearm and upper arm muscles. Exercises include triceps extensions, biceps curls, forearm pronation and supination, wrist flexion and extensions, and forearm stretching exercises. Athletes should avoid any activities that place unnecessary stress upon the elbow ligaments.

Prevention. Strains and sprains occur quite often in novice javelin throwers, who try to generate most of the power of the throw with their arms rather

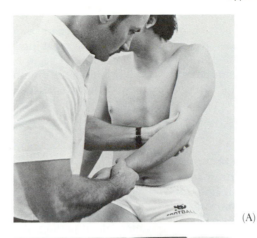
(A)

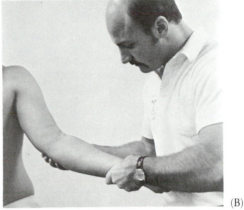
(B)

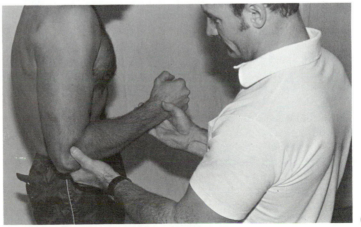
(C)

Figure 18-11 Elbow stress tests. Compare with the opposite side.
(A) With athlete's arm straight, apply varus force to test the stability of the elbow's lateral collateral ligament.
(B) With athlete's arm straight, apply valgus stress to test the stability of the elbow's medial collateral ligament.
(C) Palpation of the humerus' lateral epicondyle will elicit tenderness in this area if the athlete has lateral epicondylitis (tennis elbow).

than their legs. No amount of conditioning will protect an athlete from the effects of improper technique. Javelin throwers must be well schooled in proper throwing techniques and avoid taking an excessive number of "all-out" throws.

Dislocations

Dislocations of the elbow occur in gymnastics, contact sports, and weight lifting. The injury may result from an athlete falling on an outstretched arm with the elbow fully extended or be caused by hyperextension forces during overhead Olympic weight lifting. Most dislocations occur posteriorly, but they can occur medially, anteriorly, or divergently (humerus slips between separated forearm bones).

Evaluation and Treatment. Dislocation reveals itself as an observable and palpable defect accompanied by swelling and discoloration. Evaluation should include assessment of the neurovascular status. Neural aberrations may occur distal to the injury from the numerous neural and circulatory structures in the area. Symptoms (which may manifest themselves before or after the dislocation has been reduced) are numbness, tingling, loss of radial artery pulse, and weakness in the wrist and hand.

Treatments for dislocations include immediate immobilization, compression, and application of ice. The dislocation should be reduced as soon as possible by qualified medical personnel; reduction by untrained people may cause permanent injury.

Rehabilitation. A dislocated elbow is a severe injury that takes many months to heal. After the cast has been removed (four to six weeks), active range of motion exercises may begin. Passive range of motion exercises, elbow manipulation, and resistive exercises to full extension are contraindicated because

they delay healing. Often, the secondary condition of myositis ossificans develops during rehabilitation. Resistive exercises should begin cautiously and only when almost normal range of motion is restored and the athlete is almost pain-free.

Nerve Entrapment

Peripheral nerve entrapments may occur secondary to trauma and involve pressure upon the nerve by connective tissue, muscle, or bone. The radial nerve is most commonly trapped at the anterolateral portion of the elbow joint, where the nerve becomes more superficial. At this point the nerve is more susceptible to trauma and subsequent formation of scar tissue **adhesion** about the nerve. The ulnar nerve courses between the humerus' medial epicondyle and the ulna's olecranon process at the elbow and is easy to palpate (palpation may cause irritation). **Carpal tunnel syndrome** is the entrapment of the median nerve on the **volar** aspect of the wrist (Figure 18-12).

Evaluation and Treatment. Radial nerve entrapment may cause radial nerve **palsy,** whereby the athlete cannot extend the wrist or supinate the forearm. Ulnar nerve entrapment may cause formation of scar tissue adhesions, which may bring about sensory changes along the ulnar border of the forearm, the little finger, and the medial border of the ring finger. Ulnar nerve palsy causes weakness in the hand interossei and fourth and fifth lumbricals. In addition, the hypothenar muscles become weak and atrophied. In complete paralysis of the ulnar nerve, the muscles between the metacarpals on the dorsal aspect of the hand may become extremely atrophied. Carpal tunnel syndrome occurs frequently in older people, but it may occur in athletes who traumatize the volar wrist. The distinguishing sign of carpal tunnel syndrome is atrophy of thenar musculature.

Dislocation: The displacement of a bone or organ from its normal position.

Adhesion: The binding of adjacent tissue surfaces; caused by the formation of fibrous (dense) connective tissue.

Carpal tunnel syndrome: Compression of the median nerve, or its circulation, on the volar aspect of the wrist.

Volar: The palmar surface of the wrist.

Palsy: Paralysis.

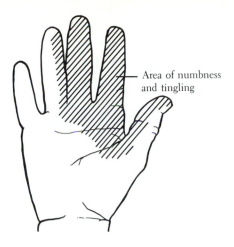

Area of numbness
and tingling

Transverse carpal ligament
Median nerve compressed
Carpal bones

Figure 18-12 Carpal tunnel syndrome. This injury is caused by compression of the median nerve, or its circulation, and characterized by numbness and tingling in the fingers. The syndrome is somewhat common in weight lifters and gymnasts but may also occur in other athletes.

Entrapment syndromes are usually treated surgically because adherent scar tissue or compressing structures on the nerve have to be released. If these syndromes are treated early, the symptoms usually resolve themselves following rehabilitation exercises once the surgical wound has healed.

Rehabilitation. The athletic trainer can help prevent formation of postsurgical adhesions by initiating a program of scar and soft tissue stretching during rehabilitation

Initially, normal range of motion should be restored for elbow extension and flexion, forearm pronation and supination, and wrist flexion, extension, and circumduction. This is accomplished by statically holding specific positions at the end of the range of motion (e.g., flex wrist as much as possible for ten seconds) and performing repetitions of specific motions. When range of motion is restored, joint motions can be resisted manually or with weights so that the muscles can be strengthened.

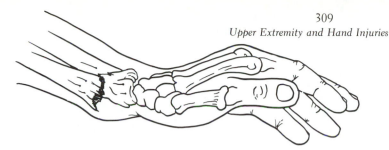

Figure 18-13 Colles' fracture (extension and compression fracture of the lower end of the radius). This injury commonly occurs when an athlete falls on an outstretched hand.

Forearm Fractures and Colles' Fracture

Fractures of the forearm create severe pain and swelling and impair the forearm's functional capacity. Because early recognition of all fractures is essential for proper healing, any questionable serious injury should be referred for medical evaluation.

Colles' fracture is somewhat common among athletes. It occurs at the lower end of the radius, with displacement of the hand backward and outward, and is usually caused by the athlete falling on an outstretched hand (Figure 18-13). A fracture in the same location but with the wrist in flexion is called a reverse Colles' fracture (or Smith's). In an adolescent, an injury similar to Colles' fracture may occur at the distal epiphyseal plates of the radius and ulna.

Treatment. Treatment includes immobilization, ice, and immediate referral to a physician. Barring complications, this injury prevents participation for approximately four to six weeks.

Rehabilitation. Rehabilitation involves restoring range of motion and strength.

Exercises include wrist flexion and extension, squeezing a rubber ball, using "wrist rollers" (rolling up a weight that is attached to a rope and cylindrical piece of wood), and wrist lateral flexion and extension.

Colles' fracture: Fracture of the distal end of the radius.

Prevention. Prevention is difficult but possible if athletes know how to fall. Injury is less likely to occur if athletes "roll" as they hit the ground, progressively absorbing the impact with the shoulder, torso, and hip rather than abruptly absorbing impact with an outstretched hand.

Wrist and Hand Injuries

Sprains and fractures are the most common wrist and hand injuries. These injuries occur often in contact sports and sports requiring vigorous grasping or ball-handling skills, such as gymnastics, basketball, and indoor handball.

Carpal Fractures

Fractures to the scaphoid are the most common sports fractures; fractures to other carpal bones occur much less frequently. Most carpal fractures are caused by a fall on an outstretched arm.

Evaluation and Treatment. Signs and symptoms include swelling and distinct local pain in the "anatomical snuffbox" (Figure 18-14), which is formed by the tendons of the extensor pollicis longus and abductor pollicis longus on the lateral border of the wrist. Radial deviation and movement of the thumb may elicit pain. Additionally, traction or compression along the thumb's axis will cause extreme tenderness.

Because it is difficult to differentiate between a sprained and fractured wrist, all injuries to this area should be x-rayed. If a fractured scaphoid is untreated, bony necrosis (death) may result from an inadequate blood supply to the area. If necrosis occurs, the wrist's function will be severely compromised because the scaphoid helps allow full

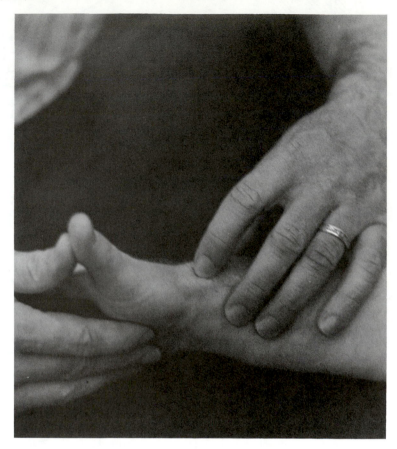

Figure 18-14 The "anatomical snuffbox" is a depression on the lateral wrist as the thumb is flexed. Point tenderness during palpation may indicate a fracture of the carpal navicular.

wrist mobility. A fractured scaphoid can be immobilized for six weeks and often longer.

Rehabilitation. Rehabilitation is similar to that following Colles' fracture: Reestablish normal range of motion in the hand, wrist, and elbow and then begin resistive exercise. If the immobilization period has been particularly long (more than six weeks), the rehabilitation program should begin conservatively, to avoid damaging articular surfaces.

Prevention. Again, teach athletes to fall correctly. Proper falling must become an automatic reflex in athletes such as football players, skiers, and volleyball players.

Metacarpal and Phalange Fractures

Fractured metacarpals are common in sports like basketball and baseball and are often caused by direct blows to the hand. Fractured phalanges result from the tip of a finger or thumb being struck by an object or the phalanges being struck a crushing blow.

Evaluation and Treatment. Symptoms of metacarpal fracture are pain, tenderness when the finger and hand are palpated, local swelling, and discoloration. Metacarpal fracture can sometimes be detected by the metacarpal percussion test shown in Figure 18-15. The function of the fingers may also be impaired. A metacarpal fracture may be accompanied by neural and vascular injuries. A phalangeal fracture may be accompanied by injury to the extensor tendon, which attaches to the base of the distal phalanx. This injury is sometimes called mallet finger or baseball finger (Figure 18-16).

Treatment includes immediate splinting of the joint in an extended position and application of ice to control pain. After the injury has been x-rayed, the finger should be properly immobilized by a physician. Fracture should always be suspected following a traumatic injury to the fingers because it is such a common athletic injury.

Rehabilitation. The immediate goal of rehabilitation following immobilization is to restore normal range of motion. This process may be facilitated with heat (range of motion exercises in the whirlpool) or ice (cryokinetics). Strengthening exercises should be aimed at improving grip as well as the various ranges of motion of the wrist and upper extremity.

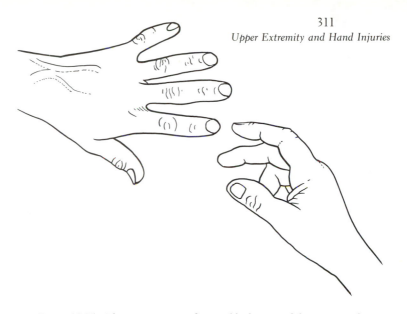

Figure 18-15 The percussion test for possible fracture of the metacarpal. Tap the end of the outstretched finger: If fracture is present, pain results.

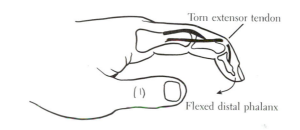

Figure 18-16 Mallet finger often occurs when a thrown ball strikes the tip of a finger and tears the extensor tendon.

Wrist and Hand Soft Tissue Injuries

The wrist is prone to dislocation and sprain because of its extreme mobility and extensive use in sports. The lunate bone is the one most often dislocated. This injury occurs when an athlete falls on a fully extended wrist, creating an anterior gap between the distal and proximal rows of carpals. The lunate dislocates anteriorly when the pressure is released. The distal radio-ulnar joint is also susceptible to dislocation: A severe twist of the forearm may disrupt the integrity of the joint. However, this is not a common athletic injury.

Dislocated fingers are quite common

Prevention, Treatment, and Rehabilitation of Specific Injuries

in sports involving ball handling, such as basketball, baseball, and football (Figure 18-17). The fingers may also be hyperextended (sometimes resulting in boutonniere deformity—see Figure 18-18). The thumb is often injured in sports and should receive special consideration because of its extreme importance. Wrist and hand injuries typically involve soft tissue. Strains in the hand often occur in sports like discus throwing, shot put, and volleyball.

Evaluation and Treatment. A dislocated wrist is characterized by difficult wrist movement and palpable protrusion on the volar surface. Dislocated fingers are characterized by obvious deformity of the structures, pain, and loss of function; soft tissue injury generally reveals a significant loss of muscle strength in the hand (Figure 18-19). Dislocations and sprains heal rapidly *if* they are uncomplicated and treated immediately. With a serious injury, immediately apply ice, immobilize the affected digit(s), and have a physician examine the injury.

Improper management of wrist and hand injuries may cause **hypertrophic scarring** or neural and vascular incompetency. Any loss of sensation or any formation of excessive scar tissue that prevents normal function could be catastrophic to an athlete who depends upon the hand for fine movements.

Rehabilitation. Rehabilitation of hand and wrist injury involves restoring range of motion and strength. Manual resisted motions of the wrist should include flexion, extension, lateral flexion and extension, and circumduction. These exercises can also be accomplished by using small dumbbells. Wrist rollers are good for rehabilitating both the wrists and the hands. Forearm pronation and supination exercises are also indicated. Hand exercises include squeezing a rubber ball and handgrip exercisers.

Figure 18-17 Compression injury of the digits, caused by a ball striking the ends of the fingers.

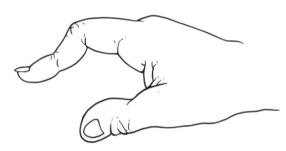

Figure 18-18 Boutonniere deformity occurs when a blow to the top of the middle phalanx ruptures the extensor tendon.

Prevention. The hands play a critical role in essentially all upper body sports, yet most athletes do little to condition them. Exercises that strengthen the hands include squeezing a rubber ball, using finger spring devices (finger flexion is resisted by springs), fingertip push-ups, and barbell cleans.

Soft tissue injuries to the hands can be prevented in contact sports by wearing hand pads. Superficial abrasions can be prevented in golf, baseball, hammer throwing, and weight lifting by wearing gloves.

Hypertrophic scarring: Excessive scarring that may limit range of motion.

References

Bergfield, J. A., G. G. Weiker, J. T. Andrish, and R. Hall. Soft playing splint for protection of significant hand and wrist injuries in sports. *American Journal of Sports Medicine* 10:293–296, 1982.

Burke, E. R. Ulnar neuropathy in bicyclists. *The Physician and Sportsmedicine* 9:53–56, 1981.

Burkhart, S. S., M. B. Wood, and R. L. Linscheid. Posttraumatic recurrent subluxation of the extensor carpi ulnaris tendon. *Journal of Hand Surgery* 7:1–3. 1982.

Calliet, R. *Neck and Arm Pain.* Philadelphia: F. A. Davis, 1969.

Calliet, R. *Hand Pain and Impairment.* Philadelphia: F. A. Davis, 1975.

Carr, D., R. J. Johnson, and M. H. Pope. Upper extremity injuries in skiing. *American Journal of Sports Medicine* 9:378–383, 1981.

Conwell, H. E. Injuries to the elbow. *CIBA Clinical Symposia* 21:35–62, 1969.

Conwell, H. E. Injuries to the wrist. *CIBA Clinical Symposia* 22:3–30, 1970.

Curwin, S., and W. D. Stanish. *Tendinitis: Its Etiology and Treatment.* Lexington, Mass.: Callamore Press, 1984.

Dawson, W. J., and N. Pullos. Baseball injuries to the hand. *Annals of Emergency Medicine* 10:302–306, 1981.

Hang, Y. Tardy ulnar neuritis in Little League baseball player. *American Journal of Sports Medicine* 9:244–246, 1981.

Iversen, L. D., and D. K. Clawson. *Manual of Acute Orthopaedic Therapeutics.* Boston: Little, Brown, 1982.

Kristiansen, B. Athletic injuries of the volar plate in the proximal interphalangeal finger joints. *Italian Journal of Sports Traumatology* 3:57–61, 1981.

Mutoh, Y., T. Mori, Y. Suzuki, and U. Sugiura. Stress fractures of the ulna in athletes. *American Journal of Sports Medicine* 10:365–367, 1982.

Nirschl, P., and J. Sobel. Conservative treatment of tennis elbow. *The Physician and Sportsmedicine* 9:43–54, 1981.

Norwood, L. A., J. A. Shook, and J. R. Andrews. Acute medial elbow ruptures. *American Journal of Sports Medicine* 9:9–16, 1981.

Routson, G. W., and M. Gingras. Surgical treatment of tennis elbow. *Orthopedics* 4:769–772, 1981.

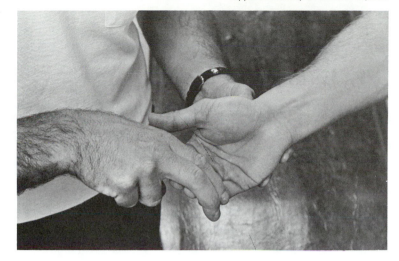

Figure 18-19 Testing the hand's flexor tendons. Stabilize the wrist and provide resistance to distal aspects of the fingers as the athlete attempts to flex them. Pain or weakness indicates strain.

Thoracic, Abdominal, and Pelvic Injuries

THE **thorax, abdomen,** and **pelvis** are injured less frequently than the extremities, but certain of these injuries are life-threatening, which makes them of critical concern to the athletic trainer. These anatomical areas house such vital structures as the heart, lungs, liver, kidneys, and gastrointestinal tract. The symptoms of injuries to these organs often can be mistaken as symptoms of more benign musculoskeletal injuries. *Never* take for granted any injuries that may involve these critical internal organs.

Injuries to the trunk may involve multiple musculoskeletal and visceral structures, so it is often difficult to recognize and manage the problems. The athletic trainer must pay particular attention to the athlete's physical and vital signs in addition to the anatomical aberrations of the thorax, abdomen, and pelvis. The athletic trainer must recognize potential danger and quickly refer or transport the athlete to an appropriate medical facility. It is always better to err on the side of safety. Any suspicion of significant injury to the trunk region is a signal to seek speedy and accurate medical evaluation.

This chapter concisely discusses the anatomy and common injuries of the trunk region. Injuries are subdivided

into those involving superficial tissues and those to deep structures.

Anatomy

The thorax, abdomen, and pelvis represent the largest portion of the body's surface area. This area is relatively well protected by skeletal and soft tissues.

Thorax

The thorax is bounded posteriorly by the midspine, superiorly by the musculoskeletal components of the shoulder girdle and neck, laterally by the rib cage, and anteriorly by the ribs, sternum, and the costocartilage that connects the ribs to the sternum (Figure 19-1). The shoulder, neck, and upper torso muscles lie on the exterior of the thoracic cavity. However, the intercostal muscles (important muscles in breathing), which lie between the first and twelfth ribs, are integral parts of the thoracic cavity. Inferiorly, the cavity is bordered by the **diaphragm,** which plays a critical role in breathing by helping regulate pressures within the thoracic cavity.

Thorax: The chest.
Abdomen: The region between the thorax and pelvis.
Pelvis (cavity): The canal within the skeletal pelvis that contains the bladder, rectum, pelvic colon, and some reproductive organs.

Diaphragm: The main muscle of ventilatory inspiration. Its contraction causes increased volume in the thorax, resulting in a negative pressure and the movement of air into the lungs.

314

Young, healthy athletes are not immune to serious internal medical disorders. The athletic trainer should always consider the possibility of the unusual, particularly when presented with an athlete who has pain but no obvious history of trauma.

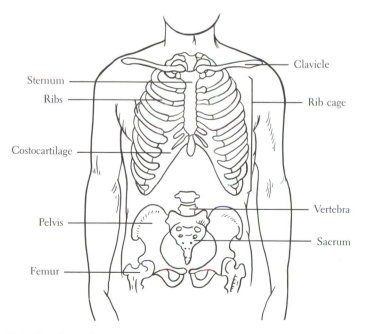

Figure 19-1 The thorax (front view).

The principal structures housed in the thoracic cavity are the heart and lungs (Figure 19-2). The heart is located slightly to the left and deep beneath the sternum; the lungs occupy the space on each side of the thoracic cavity lateral to the heart. Superiorly, the lungs are bounded by the upper ribs and inferiorly by the diaphragm.

The remainder of the thoracic space is occupied by the **trachea, bronchi, esophagus,** nerves, and the great blood vessels leading to and from the heart. Major vessels lead superiorly to the neck, head, and upper extremities. Inferiorly, the vessels descend to supply the abdomen, pelvis, and lower extremities. Large vessels also descend inferiorly along the anterior portion of the thoracic cavity and may be damaged by trauma to this region.

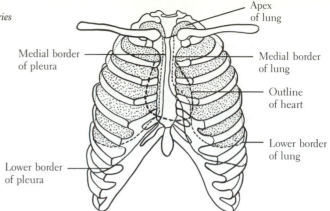

Figure 19-2 The lungs, pleural borders, and heart (front view).

Abdomen

The abdominal cavity extends from the base of the ribs and costocartilage superiorly to the crest of the iliac spine in the pelvic region (Figure 19-3). The cavity is bordered laterally and anteriorly by the abdominal musculature. Posteriorly, the abdominal cavity is supported by the spine.

The abdominal region may be divided into four distinct quadrants. The upper right quadrant is associated with deep **viscera,** which include the liver, gallbladder, stomach, and components of both the large and the small intestines. The upper left quadrant contains portions of the stomach, pancreas, and spleen. The kidneys and adrenal glands lie along the posterior wall of each of these two quadrants and lateral to the spine and the great vessels that continue to descend inferiorly through this region. The lower right and left quadrants primarily contain components of the large and small intestines. The appendix lies within the lower right quadrant at the junction of the small intestines and the large ascending colon. The descending colon lies in the lateral

portion of the lower left quadrant and leads to the rectum, which is housed within the pelvic cavity. Inferiorly, the abdominal cavity merges with the pelvic cavity. Here lie the urinary bladder and reproductive organs.

Pelvis

The true pelvic cavity houses the reproductive organs, the urinary bladder, and portions of the lower digestive system (Figures 19-4 and 19-5, pp. 318, 319). Superiorly, there is little distinction between the abdominal and pelvic regions. Laterally, the pelvis is bordered by the iliac components of the pelvis; posteriorly, the cavity is composed of the spine, sacrum, and coccyx. The **peritoneum** covers the pelvic floor and the associated structures. Anteriorly, the peritoneum is defined by the pubic symphysis, laterally by the ischial tuberosities, and posteriorly by the anterior portion of the sacrum and coccyx.

The bladder and rectum lie along the midsagittal plane, deep within the protection of the pelvic girdle. At the posterior junction of the pelvis and abdomen is the **bifurcation** of the great vessels, which supply and retrieve nutrients from the lower extremities.

The reproductive system is generally considered housed within the pelvic cavity. In males, significant components of the reproductive system are

Trachea: A tube, mainly of cartilage, that extends from the larynx to the bronchi. Also called windpipe.

Bronchi: The trachea's two main branches; they move air into and out of the lungs.

Esophagus: A muscular tube that extends from the pharynx to the stomach.

Peritoneum: The membrane that lines the abdominal and pelvic cavities; it encloses the viscera. Inflammation of the peritoneum is called peritonitis.

Viscera: The internal organs of the body.

Bifurcation: Division into two parts.

external to the inferior margin of the pelvis. However, in both males and females, the lower pelvic region contains a complex of sexual organs and reproductive glands. Many of these structures lie deep to the urinary bladder and anterior to the rectum.

The pelvis' muscular components are few yet significant. The posterior floor of the pelvis incorporates a group of muscles generally referred to as the *Kagel muscles*. These structures help control urinary and bowel functions and provide support to the internal pelvic contents. Anteriorly, the musculature is a continuation of the abdominal components. Laterally, the primary muscular components are external to the pelvis and control hip and lower extremity function. Finally, a group of muscles controlling hip movement lies along the posterior floor of the pelvic cavity. The most important is the psoas major.

Superficial Thoracic Injuries

Contusions and strains are the most common superficial thoracic injuries. The athletic trainer should consider the possibility of these usually benign injuries being much more serious.

Soft Tissue

Contusions of the chest are common injuries in sports. A blow can damage tissue in the overlying skin, ribs, and muscle. There may be pain, swelling, and hematoma formation (a severe blow may cause dyspnea—difficult breathing—or even cardiac arrest). Treatment is the same as for other soft tissue injuries (see Chapter 5) and includes the immediate application of ice.

Muscle strains in the chest may result from participation in strenuous activities like weight lifting, wrestling, and football. Localized pain and swelling

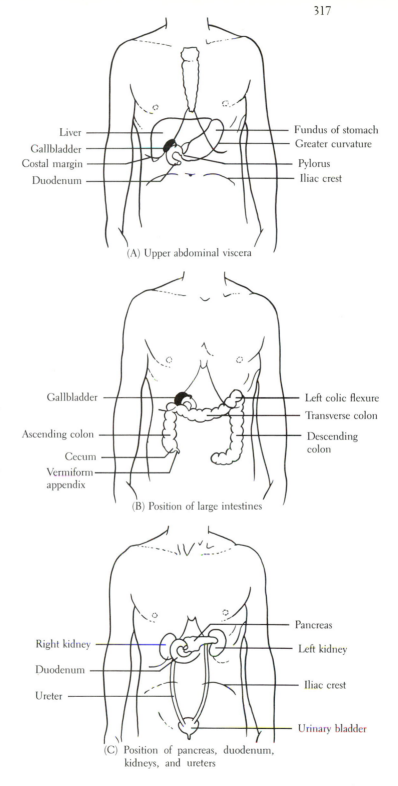

Liver
Gallbladder
Costal margin
Duodenum
Fundus of stomach
Greater curvature
Pylorus
Iliac crest

(A) Upper abdominal viscera

Gallbladder
Ascending colon
Cecum
Vermiform appendix
Left colic flexure
Transverse colon
Descending colon

(B) Position of large intestines

Right kidney
Duodenum
Ureter
Pancreas
Left kidney
Iliac crest
Urinary bladder

(C) Position of pancreas, duodenum, kidneys, and ureters

Figure 19-3 Abdomen with organs superimposed.

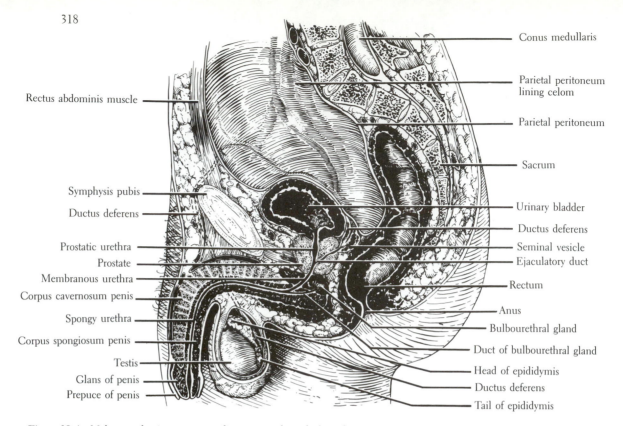

Rectus abdominis muscle

Symphysis pubis
Ductus deferens

Prostatic urethra
Prostate
Membranous urethra
Corpus cavernosum penis
Spongy urethra
Corpus spongiosum penis
Testis
Glans of penis
Prepuce of penis

Conus medullaris
Parietal peritoneum lining celom
Parietal peritoneum
Sacrum
Urinary bladder
Ductus deferens
Seminal vesicle
Ejaculatory duct
Rectum
Anus
Bulbourethral gland
Duct of bulbourethral gland
Head of epididymis
Ductus deferens
Tail of epididymis

Figure 19-4 Male reproductive organs: median section through the pelvis. (From Crouch, J. E. *Introduction to Human Anatomy*, 6th ed. Palo Alto, Calif.: Mayfield Publishing Co., 1983, p. 245.)

are common symptoms that can be partially controlled by ice. Occasionally the muscle is injured severely enough that it tears; surgical repair is then necessary. Stretching and gradual strengthening are critical after chest muscles have been strained. Typically, well-trained weight-trained athletes resume their training program at a level that the recovering muscles cannot tolerate. Such athletes should resume their weight-training program using high repetitions (eight to fifteen) and relatively low resistance (60 percent of one repetition maximum). Increase the intensity of the program *very slowly*.

Breast Injuries

The female breasts are particularly susceptible to direct blows. Treat breast injuries promptly with ice, support, and rest. Refer any contusion not respond-ing readily to such treatment to a medical specialist. The female breast can also be injured by excessive movement during exercise. Biomechanical studies have shown that during running the breasts may create a force from 50 to 100 pounds against the chest wall. These forces can be greatly diminished by wearing a supportive sports brassiere.

Rib Fractures

A rib fracture is a common injury resulting from a direct blow to or forceful compression of the chest. The direct blow typically fractures no more than one or two ribs, whereas the forceful compression may fracture numerous ribs. Indirect forces caused by the violent pull of muscles can also cause fractures.

The player with a rib fracture will complain of severe localized pain at the

Point tenderness: Pain elicited at a specific anatomical location.

Crepitation (crepitus): A grinding, crackling sound produced by friction of adjacent tissues.

Flak vest: A protective rib covering.

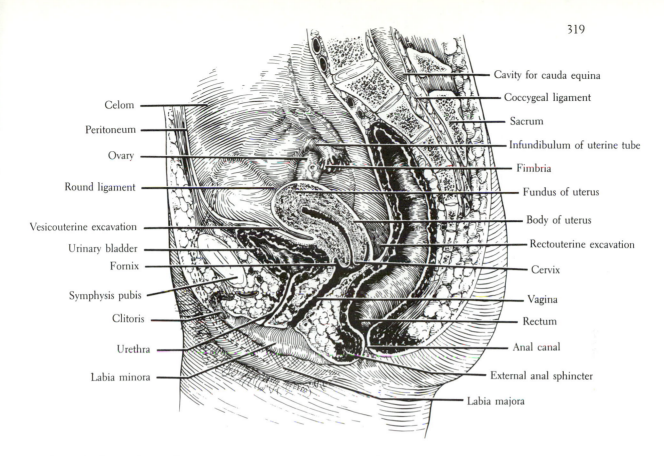

Celom

Peritoneum

Ovary

Round ligament

Vesicouterine excavation

Urinary bladder

Fornix

Symphysis pubis

Clitoris

Urethra

Labia minora

Cavity for cauda equina

Coccygeal ligament

Sacrum

Infundibulum of uterine tube

Fimbria

Fundus of uterus

Body of uterus

Rectouterine excavation

Cervix

Vagina

Rectum

Anal canal

External anal sphincter

Labia majora

Figure 19-5 Female reproductive organs: median section through the pelvis. (From Crouch, 1983, p. 241.)

site of injury and demonstrate **point tenderness** during palpation (a contusion does not usually cause pain with isolated movement of the rib). Deep inspiration will be uncomfortable. Palpation will usually reveal **crepitation** and, if the fracture is complete, a structural defect at the site.

Rib fractures can seriously damage the underlying tissues and organs, so all suspected cases should be examined by a physician and x-rayed. The initial goal of treatment is to make the athlete comfortable. Activity can be continued if the athlete is not experiencing too much pain and there are no underlying complications. Return to play sometimes can be facilitated by taping the area to reduce the motion of the ribs (taping the ribs is minimally effective) and by wearing protective padding such as **flak vests** (Figure 19-6).

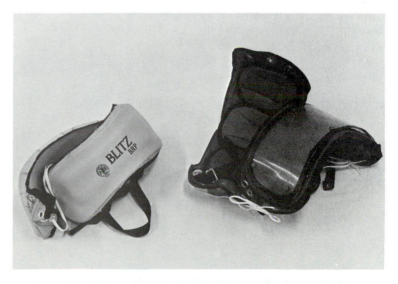

Figure 19-6 Two types of flak vests. The vests protect injured ribs and surrounding soft tissue. The smaller one (left) is generally used for athletes needing maximum mobility, such as quarterbacks; the larger vest at the right is more popular with linemen.

Ligamentous Rib Injuries

The costochondral cartilage, which attaches the ribs to the sternum, may be separated by a blow to the chest (e.g., in sports like football and wrestling). This injury can be most painful and debilitating and may require three to six weeks recovery time. As with rib fractures, rib belts and padding may help decrease discomfort and speed the resumption of play.

Sternum Injuries

A blow to the sternum can sprain or dislocate the sternum manubrium and body. Such an injury may potentially jeopardize the heart, lungs, and some major blood vessels. If sternum fracture is suspected, prompt evaluation by a physician is necessary.

Deep Thoracic Injuries

Injuries to the contents of the chest cavity (lungs and heart) can be immediately life-threatening (see Putting It into Practice 19-1). Trauma is not the only cause of injury to these organs; any underlying disease of the cardiac and pulmonary systems can present itself during the increased demands of sporting activity. For example, the first "symptom" in one-third of people with coronary artery disease is sudden death! Prompt medical attention is essential because of the possible catastrophic consequences of injury or symptomatic manifestation of disease in these deep structures.

Lung Injuries

A direct blow to the chest may not only injure soft tissue and ribs but may contuse the lung itself, resulting in the athlete coughing up frothy, bright red blood (hemoptysis). Such a blow may fracture a rib, thus puncturing the cavity (pleural space) surrounding the lung. This puncture causes **pneumothorax,** partial or full collapse of the lung. A collapse can also occur without direct trauma (spontaneous pneumothorax) when alveoli, the terminal branches of the lung's airway, rupture and allow air into the pleural space. Trauma can cause bleeding into the lung cavity (**hemothorax**), which can also cause collapse of a lung. The athlete may experience only mild shortness of breath and chest discomfort if there is a minimal collapse of the lung. However, with more damage, shortness of breath and chest pain can be acute. Diagnosis of contusion or collapse of the lung is made by percussing the chest and listening to the breath sounds and determining their significance. X-rays will reveal if the injury is present. Medical treatment varies according to the degree of involvement of the lungs.

Any of these injuries is a medical emergency. The athletic trainer should elevate the thorax to approximately forty-five degrees, treat for shock (see Chapter 10), provide oxygen, and arrange for immediate transport to a medical facility.

Heart Injuries

Injury to the heart can be caused by a direct blow to the overlying tissue and bones. The heart tissue can be contused, or the heart's regular rhythm can be interrupted. Indeed, there have been reports of heart attack (**myocardial infarction**) and even sudden death resulting from seemingly trivial injuries caused by, for example, a softball or football striking an athlete's chest. Indications of cardiac damage are chest pain, pain radiating into the neck or upper extremities (particularly the left shoulder and arm), shortness of breath, nausea, vomiting, indigestion, or clammy sweat. Immediate medical attention is indicated.

Pneumothorax: A collection of air in the pleural space resulting in partial or complete collapse of the lung.

Hemothorax: Bleeding into the pleural cavity.

Myocardial infarction: A heart attack; death of part of the myocardium (heart muscle).

Evaluating Critical Thoracic and Abdominal Disorders

Although most athletic injuries to the thorax and abdomen are minor, serious internal disorders can be life-threatening. It is better to err on the side of caution. Seek immediate medical attention if you suspect any of the following critical internal disorders.

Appendicitis (inflammation of large intestinal appendix)
Symptoms: Pain in lower right abdominal quadrant, vomiting, constipation or diarrhea, local tenderness, spasm, and fever.

Diverticulitis (inflammation of diverticuli, small outpouchings in the colon wall present in some people)
Symptoms: Constipation or diarrhea, abdominal cramping in lower left quadrant, fever, rectal bleeding, and nausea. Presence of diverticuli alone do not cause symptoms; the diverticuli must be inflamed.

Myocardial infarction (heart attack)
Symptoms: Angina (chest pain under the lower sternum that may radiate to the neck and left arm),
dyspnea (labored breathing), cold sweat, and "indigestion."

Pancreatitis (inflammation of pancreas)
Symptoms: Severe abdominal pain that may radiate to the back. May be accompanied by fever, vomiting, increased heart rate, cold sweat, decreased blood pressure, and shock.

Pneumothorax (collection of air in thorax that prevents expansion of adjacent lung)
Symptoms: Sudden onset of pain in the chest, dyspnea, and coughing.

Superficial Abdominal Injuries

Fortunately, the incidence of serious visceral injury within the abdominal cavity is low. However, since many of these intraabdominal injuries are serious and require medical or surgical intervention, the athletic trainer must always be on guard. Most injuries to the abdomen occur in the superficial soft tissue.

Perhaps the most common abdominal injury is a blow to the thorax, causing diaphragmatic spasm and the athlete to "lose his wind." Recovery is usually rapid, although for a short time the individual may feel a sense of danger or panic. The athletic trainer should make sure the airway is clear of obstruction. Loosen constrictive clothing and slightly flex the knees. Reassure the athlete of rapid recovery while observing for signs of more serious injury to internal structures. If local pain persists or if recovery is not steady and rapid, get immediate medical attention.

Athletes frequently incur side aches (a "stitch in the side"). Generally the aches occur during endurance activities and under the ribs on the right side. The etiology of exercise-induced side pains is not completely understood, but they are believed to be caused by such factors as gas in the large intestines, diaphragmatic spasm, and congestion of the liver with blood. Resolution is usually spontaneous. Occasionally, stretching the trunk, bending backward or forward, or forcefully exhaling may help relieve symptoms. Once pain subsides, the athlete should be able to resume exercise. The athletic trainer should explore whether the side pain was traumatically induced; trauma to this region may cause visceral damage.

Most of the remaining injuries to the abdomen can be classified as contusions of the abdominal wall: The rectus abdominus or the abdominal oblique musculature are bruised. Frequently these injuries initially manifest themselves as local pain. However, they rapidly resolve into dull, aching annoyances that may restrict motion at the trunk, and they usually exhibit themselves as bruises.

A contusion at the insertion of the abdominal muscles on the iliac crest is commonly called a **hip pointer.** Although not life-threatening, this injury may be extremely debilitating. In severe cases, it may be necessary to surgically reattach the severed abdominal muscular attachments to the iliac crest. Severe **hematoma** may accompany this injury. The patient may also have difficulty with ambulation, trunk mobility, and breathing.

Initial treatment for both the contusion of the abdominal wall and contusion over the iliac crest is similar. First, obtain a good history with regard to the mechanism of injury. Undertake a physical examination; if any questions about the patient's status are unresolved, transport the athlete for medical attention. Immediate ice application with mild compression is appropriate. Use ice exclusively for forty-eight to seventy-two hours, or until the initial bleeding is well controlled. **Transcutaneous neural stimulation (TNS)** (high-voltage direct current) modality may help control pain and encourage healing. Subsequent days or weeks of treatment are required; moist heat, ultrasound, electrical stimulation, ice, and flexibility and strengthening exercises may be required. Protective padding in this region is minimally helpful because padding is difficult to stabilize over the injured area and generally is not comfortable.

The final category of superficial injuries is the abdominal wall musculature. Strains of the musculotendinous network are common. Usually the strains are minor and only mildly annoying to an athlete. Occasionally, however, strains of the abdominal muscles may become chronic and debilitating. Such strains often occur in athletes who are

required to rotate quickly and forcefully at the trunk, such as wrestlers, discus throwers, gymnasts, divers, and hammer throwers. The onset of injury may be sudden or insidious. Sudden injuries are characterized by acute pain, muscle spasm, rigidity, and rapid loss of function. Insidious onset is usually caused by overuse or a neglected mild injury. These symptoms may be as significant as when the injury strikes suddenly.

Treatment of strains to the abdominal wall includes heat and ice modalities; ultrasound and electrical stimulation may also be helpful. The most significant component of treatment is gradual stretching and reconditioning of the area. There should be emphasis upon not only resolving the symptoms but upon establishing a proper flexibility and strengthening routine for the athlete to avoid further injury.

Deep Abdominal Injuries

Serious injury may result from direct trauma to the abdominal region. Many of these deep visceral injuries require immediate emergency medical treatment that, at times, includes emergency surgical treatment. The athletic trainer *must* keep any athlete who has suffered abdominal injury under close observation. Reexamine this athlete frequently to determine any change in vital signs; a change may indicate that internal viscera have been damaged. Table 19-1 shows the site of pain from specific organs.

Spleen

The **spleen** is particularly susceptible to rupture. When blood loss from a ruptured spleen is extremely profuse, the athlete rapidly develops the following signs: elevated pulse rate, low blood pressure, faintness, and indications of impending shock. Injury to the spleen

Hip pointer: Contusion of the iliac crest.

Hematoma: A bruise; a mass of partially clotted blood outside the vascular space, typically formed from trauma.

Transcutaneous neural stimulation (TNS): Therapeutic modality involving the application of electrical nerve impulses to decrease pain.

Spleen: A large abdominal lymphatic organ that filters blood.

Table 19-1 *Pain from Specific Organ*

Organ	Location
Esophagus	Substernal; occasionally neck, jaw, arm or back
Stomach	Epigastrium; occasionally left upper quadrant and back
Duodenal bulb	Epigastrium; occasionally right upper quadrant and back
Small intestine	Periumbilical; occasionally above the lesion
Colon	Below umbilicus, on the side of the lesion
Splenic flexure	Left upper quadrant
Rectosigmoid	Suprapubic region
Rectum	Posteriorly, over the sacrum
Pancreas	Epigastrium or back
Liver and gallbladder	Right upper quadrant, right shoulder, and posterior chest

SOURCE: Friedman, H. H. *Problem-Oriented Medical Diagnosis*. Boston: Little, Brown, 1979, p. 144.

with accompanying hemorrhage may also be quite insidious, with symptoms of splenic injury developing over a period of hours or days.

Injury to the spleen is most frequently caused by a direct blow at the lower border of the posterior left thorax. Usually, the athlete has the arms extended overhead, which elevates the thorax, thus decreasing its protection to the spleen. Initial symptoms of splenic injury are tenderness and dull pain over the upper left abdominal quadrant. Some pain in the left shoulder (Kehr's sign) may develop; this is referred pain from irritation of the diaphragm.

Occasionally, the spleen may rupture from mild trauma or even spontaneously. Pay particular attention to any athlete who has been diagnosed as having mononucleosis. Mononucleosis enlarges the spleen, thus increasing its susceptibility to injury. Any athlete diagnosed as having mononucleosis should be excluded from athletic activities until given medical clearance.

Hepatic System

Trauma to the upper right quadrant of the abdomen may damage the **hepatic** system. Usually, injury to the

liver is minimal, typically restricted to a small hematoma or hemorrhage. Severe injury to the liver may produce symptoms similar to those of the severely damaged spleen. Dull aching pain is often reported in the upper right quadrant of the abdomen. Occasionally, right-sided shoulder pain accompanies significant liver injury. Because injuries to the liver carry a high mortality rate, the athletic trainer should immediately seek proper medical evaluation if he or she suspects that any liver damage has occurred. Substantial liver rupture, typically accompanied by extreme pain and rapid blood loss, must be surgically corrected without delay.

Pancreas

The pancreas lies sagittally at the midline of the upper right and left quadrants. Injuries to the pancreas are rare, although occasionally extensive injury may occur. Damage to this organ may be indicated by tenderness, rigidity, and increased pain during palpation of the midupper abdominal region. A palpable mass or **pseudocyst** may accompany trauma to this organ. Medical management is mandatory. A variety of laboratory and radiological

Liver: A large abdominal organ that plays a critical role in metabolism.

Pseudocyst: A mass of fluid that can often be palpated; it is not enclosed by a membrane.

Hepatic: Pertaining to the liver.

procedures will confirm the diagnosis. The physician may use both surgical and nonsurgical techniques to manage this injury, depending upon the extent of damage to the organ.

Hollow Organs

Infrequently, the hollow viscera of the abdominal cavity are damaged. Hollow organs include the stomach, **duodenum,** jejunum, ileum, and colon. The stomach is the most frequently injured hollow organ. Also, the duodenum is susceptible to injury as it passes over the spine in the posterior abdominal wall. Injuries to the other soft, hollow organs are less frequent. However, forces relayed through the abdominal wall that appear to cause only contusion may actually cause more visceral damage than at first suspected.

Digestive Organs

Although not a common occurrence, severe injury to the digestive organs is extremely dangerous. Usually, symptoms are insidious. Rapid onset of abdominal pain, nausea, **rigidity,** and muscular spasm signal a significant and dangerous injury. Vomiting of blood or passing dark, **tarry stools** also signals digestive tract injury or disease. More typically, the athlete suffers dull, diffuse abdominal pain for hours and even days following significant injury. Some protective rigidity of the abdominal wall may be apparent. Symptoms of shock may appear. The athletic trainer should pay particular attention to abdominal sounds: When decreased or absent, they may indicate intestinal rupture. Due to the complexity of symptoms and the ever-present possibility of peritonitis that accompanies intestinal ruptures, the athletic trainer should always be highly suspicious when an athlete reports persistent abdominal discomfort.

Kidney

Hematuria (blood in the urine) and renal injury must be considered concurrently. Hematuria is frequently associated with vigorous athletic activities. It does not necessarily accompany significant renal injury. During extreme exercise, blood flow is directed toward the muscles and away from the kidneys. This leads to renal **ischemia** and blood loss in the urine. Occasionally, damage to the renal pelvis or ureter may not be accompanied by blood loss into the urine. However, once blood is present, a full medical evaluation with proper laboratory and other appropriate diagnostic procedures is indicated.

Direct renal injury may occur with trauma to the posterior or lateral abdominal areas. More frequently, renal injury is caused by a direct blow to the abdominal region. Again, pain and tenderness over the posterior abdominal area are prime indications of renal injury. Occasionally, signs of bleeding (hematoma) may be present at the posterior or lateral abdominal regions. As with other abdominal disorders, proper medical attention is necessary to determine the extent of the injury and the proper medical management. The athletic trainer should exclude the athlete from further competition until proper medical evaluation is obtained.

Ischemia: Inadequate blood flow.

Duodenum: The first part of the small intestines.

Rigidity: Stiffness.

Tarry stool: Bloody stool.

Superficial Pelvic Injuries

The skin in the genital area is often infected as a result of athletic participation. The skin is moist and warm and can become macerated from undergarments or protective clothing rubbing against it. This macerated condition creates a conducive climate for infection. Most commonly, the infections are fungal (dermatophytes) or yeastlike (candidiases) in nature. Proper medical evaluation is necessary to determine which organism is causing the infection and to ensure that the proper medication is administered. Skin infections in the pelvic area can be prevented by keeping the skin dry and clean. Skin disorders and injuries are discussed extensively in Chapter 23.

Deep Pelvic Injuries

Deep pelvic injuries happen infrequently, but they can be painful and debilitating when they do occur. Injuries encountered in sports include inguinal hernia, bladder and testicle contusion, forceful entry of water into the vagina, and penile frostbite. This discussion is limited to traumatic injury, but note that pelvic infections from venereal disease or other causes occur in athletes and should be suspected when there is no obvious cause of pelvic pain.

Inguinal Hernia

Inguinal hernia is somewhat common in athletes. The indirect inguinal hernia results from a weakness or defect in the fascial coverings of the abdomen, where they form the internal abdominal ring (Figure 19-7). The lining of the abdominal cavity (peritoneum) protrudes through this ring. The abdomen's intestinal contents can be carried into the sac formed by the peritoneum. This sac, with its associated contents, can become trapped, damaging the contents. Often, the athlete is not aware of a hernia. However, there can be symptoms of pain in the abdomen or pelvis. Also, a mass felt in the lower abdominal area or a fullness in the testicle can be palpated. If the hernia becomes trapped, the athlete can experience severe abdominal or pelvic pain. The presence of a hernia should be dis-

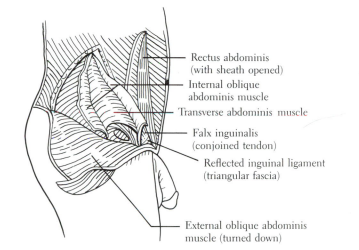

Rectus abdominis (with sheath opened)
Internal oblique abdominis muscle
Transverse abdominis muscle
Falx inguinalis (conjoined tendon)
Reflected inguinal ligament (triangular fascia)
External oblique abdominis muscle (turned down)

Figure 19-7 The inguinal canal and the lateral abdominal wall. Inguinal hernias are caused by weaknesses of the abdominal wall at the inguinal canal.

covered during the preparticipation physical examination (see Chapter 11). When the hernia is identified, proper management, including possible surgical repair, can be discussed with the physician.

Bladder

Bladder injuries occur infrequently in contact sports because the organ is usually empty (or nearly so) during competitions and a collapsed bladder is practically never damaged by direct force. Some blows, however, can contuse the bladder, causing blood cells in the urine and tenderness above the pubis. Very rarely, the bladder may rupture. This is an extremely serious injury, with marked lower abdominal pain and even signs of shock (falling blood pressure, dizziness, loss of consciousness, etc.). Immediate medical attention is needed.

Bladder injuries can also occur in noncontact sports. Distance runners can suffer bladder contusions. During running, the muscles of the pelvic floor contract and simultaneously the pressure in the abdominal cavity increases.

Inguinal hernia: Protrusion of peritoneum through the abdominal wall or inguinal canal.

In the empty bladder, the mobile posterior wall and base of the bladder are forced against each other. This repetitive occurrence produces small areas of trauma in the bladder that can cause blood cells and clots in the urine. This condition should resolve itself within forty-eight hours; if it does not, seek medical attention.

Urethra

The urethra may rupture in male athletes from a fall from a fixed object like parallel bars or a bicycle frame. This injury is characterized by immediate pain, swelling, and hematoma. Urine may leak into the scrotum or soft tissue. Prompt medical attention should be obtained.

Male Genital Organs

Penis injuries occur infrequently. In cyclists, the seat can press on the perineum, irritating the pudental nerve and causing persistent, painful erection (priapism). If there is no relief after bicycling has been stopped, medical attention should be sought immediately.

The incidence of penile frostbite is increasing because of the large number of runners who train even in extremely cold weather. Treatment is the same as for frostbite in other parts of the body (see Chapter 25). Athletes can prevent the injury by wearing adequate clothing when training in cold weather.

A blow to the scrotum can injure one or both testes. Blood can collect around the testicles in the tunica vaginalis, producing a swollen, painful mass (hematocele). Also, the testicle itself can be ruptured. If damage is severe, prompt surgical repair may be needed to preserve the testicular viability. Testicular spasm is common following trauma to the testicles. This injury, characterized by intense pain, may be treated by rest, ice, and testicular support. Having the athlete perform the valsalva procedure (expiration against a closed glottis) can often reduce testicular spasm. Use of a proper athletic supporter is the major factor in preventing these injuries.

Torsion of the spermatic cord is another category of testicular injury, which is characterized by a twisting of the spermatic cord. The symptoms manifest themselves after a sporting activity as groin pain that develops either rapidly or slowly. Examination may reveal swelling, tenderness, and adherence of the scrotal contents to the scrotal sac. Prompt medical attention may save the testicle.

Female Genital Organs

Direct trauma to the female athlete may cause hematoma or laceration of the vulva. The female sex organs are internal and usually well protected but can be injured by forceful entry of water into the vagina during participation in sports like water skiing. These accidents may injure or infect the vagina, uterus, or Fallopian tubes. There may be immediate pain and bleeding; however, symptoms of infection can develop over a few days. To avoid these injuries, rubber pants or a shield should be worn while water skiing. Proper gynecologic care should be obtained if these injuries occur.

References

Eichelberger, M. R. Torso injuries in athletes. *The Physician and Sportsmedicine* 9:87–92, 1981.

Gehlsen, G., and M. Albohm. Evaluation of sports bras. *The Physician and Sportsmedicine* 8:89–96, 1980.

Haycock, C. E. How I manage hernias in the athlete. *The Physician and Sportsmedicine* 11:77–79, 1983.

McIntyre, O. R., and F. G. Edaugh. Palpable spleens in college freshmen. *Annals of Internal Medicine* 66:301–306, 1967.

Maki, D. G., and R. M. Reich. Infectious mononucleosis in the athlete: diagnosis, complications, and management. *American Journal of Sports Medicine* 10:162–173, 1982.

Salem, D. N., and J. M. Isner. Cardiac screening for athletes. *Orthopedic Clinics of North America* 11:687–695, 1980.

Strauss, R. H., and R. R. Lanese. Injuries among wrestlers in school and college tournaments. *Journal of the American Medical Association* 248:2016–2019, 1982.

West, C. D., F. L. Shapiro, C. D. Swartz, and A. J. Ryan. Proteinuria in the athlete. *The Physician and Sportsmedicine* 7:45–55, 1978.

Williams, J. G. P. *Color Atlas of Injury in Sport*. Chicago: Year Book Medical Publishers, 1980.

Hip and Thigh Injuries

Sprinters often suffer hamstring injuries. This athlete has wrapped his thigh to support his injured hamstrings.

T HE HIP and thigh are critical anatomical structures in sports. The large and powerful muscles of these areas are prime movers in such important athletic movements as running and jumping. Fractures of the hip and thigh are rare in athletics, but strains and contusions are common because of the powerful forces the muscles generate and the large surface area of exposed soft tissue. This chapter discusses the anatomy and biomechanics of the hip and thigh and describes the principal injuries the athletic trainer is likely to encounter.

Anatomy and Physiology of the Hip Joint

The hip joint is formed by the articulation of the femur with the ilium. The spherical head of the femur fits into the acetabulum of the ilium, forming a ball-and-socket joint (Figures 20-1 and 20-2, pp. 329, 330). The rim of the acetabulum is extended by a band of fibrocartilage called the acetabular **labrum,** which deepens the acetabulum and increases the stability of the joint.

Labrum: A liplike structure.

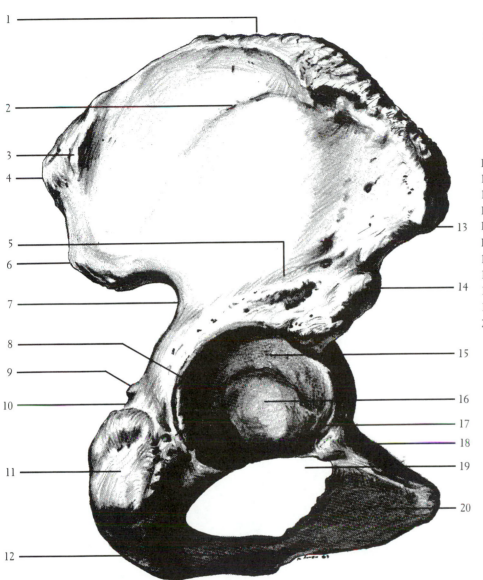

1. Crest of ilium
2. Anterior gluteal line
3. Posterior gluteal line
4. Posterior superior iliac spine
5. Inferior gluteal line
6. Posterior inferior iliac spine
7. Greater sciatic notch
8. Body of ischium
9. Ischial spine
10. Lesser sciatic notch
11. Ischial tuberosity
12. Ramus of ischium
13. Anterior superior iliac spine
14. Anterior inferior iliac spine
15. Body of ilium
16. Acetabulum
17. Body of pubis
18. Superior ramus of pubis
19. Obturator foramen
20. Inferior ramus of pubis

Figure 20-1 Adult right hip bone. (From Crouch, J. E. *Introduction to Human Anatomy*, 6th ed. Palo Alto, Calif.: Mayfield Publishing Co., 1983, p. 68.)

The hip's functional stability almost entirely depends upon the muscles surrounding the joint. The **joint capsule,** the iliofemoral ligament (Y ligament of Bigelow), pubofemoral ligament, and ischiofemoral ligament (Figure 20-3, p. 331) provide additional support. The ligamentum teres is loosely attached from the head of the femur to the acetabulum. It provides little support but acts as a channel to carry the vasculature to the femur.

The internal and external iliac arteries supply blood to the hip region. The internal iliac carries blood to the pelvic walls, gluteal muscles, skin, and

Joint (articular) capsule: A structure composed principally of connective tissue and synovial membrane and that surrounds diarthroidal joints.

muscles of the genital region. The external iliac artery carries blood for the lower limbs, and it becomes the femoral artery as it passes behind the inguinal ligament.

The lumbosacral plexus innervates the hip and pelvic regions and gives rise to the femoral, obturator, and sciatic nerves. The sciatic nerve is vulnerable to injury because it passes close to the hip joint and can be damaged when the hip is dislocated or fractured.

There are many **bursae** about the hip joint, but the iliopsoas and the greater trochanteric bursa are most susceptible to sports injury. The iliopsoas bursa is the largest bursa about the hip and is located on the anterior aspect of the hip joint between the iliopsoas muscle and the articular capsule of the joint. The greater trochanteric bursa lies between the greater trochanter and the gluteus maximus muscle.

Movements of the hip joint are flexion, extension, adduction, abduction, outward rotation, and inward rotation. The movements are performed by the twenty-one muscles listed in Table 20-1; the muscles are grouped by primary function. Figure 20-4 shows various views of the muscles that move the femur (see pp. 332–333).

Avulsion Fractures

An avulsion fracture is a tearing away of a bone fragment from a bone. Avulsion fractures of the **apophyses** of the pelvis and proximal femur are usually caused by violent or explosive muscular activity, such as kicking, running, or jumping. There is a strong pull on the tendinous attachment to the bone, which causes a bone fragment to break away (Figure 20-5, p. 334). The fracture is complete or incomplete. The anterior superior iliac spine (ASIS), anterior inferior iliac spine (AIIS), ischial tuberosity (IT), pubis, greater trochanter

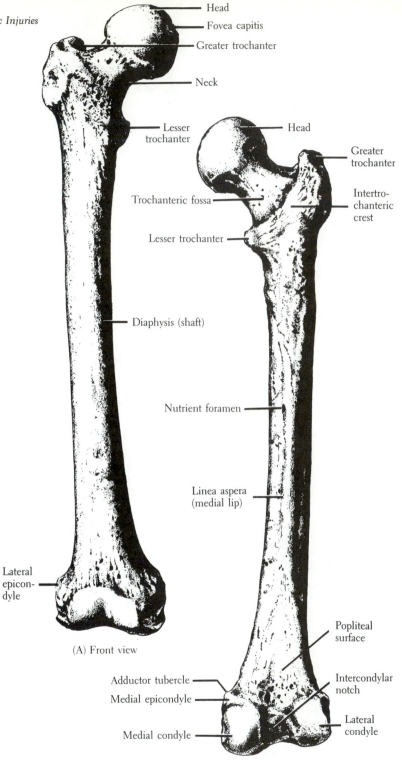

(A) Front view

(B) Rear view

Figure 20-2 Adult right femur. (From Crouch, 1983, p. 70.)

(GT), and lesser trochanter (LT) can incur an avulsion fracture.

In children and adolescents, avulsions often accompany tendon strains that occur at the tendinous attachment on the pelvis and proximal femur region. Most apophyses in this region do not unite with the shaft or bony structure until the ages of eighteen to twenty-five, which explains the increased susceptibility to avulsion fractures in these age groups.

Mechanism of Injury. ASIS avulsions can occur when powerful movements of the sartorius and tensor fasciae latae muscles (they originate on the ASIS) are interrupted, resulting in overload and fracture of the bony origin. This occurs in soccer when a player's leg collides with an opponent, or the soccer player's shoe catches the turf while attempting a lateral **power shot** on the goal, forcing the player's leg into a hyperextended and adducted position (Figure 20-6, p. 334). This injury can also be caused by direct trauma to the ASIS or by indirect trauma induced by, for example, jumping from a height.

AIIS fractures, although rare, can easily be mistaken for a contusion or tendon strain because of the AIIS location (the AIIS is the origin of the rectus femoris, a frequently injured muscle in sports). This injury may be caused by direct trauma or occur when a place-kicker's cleats catch in the turf, disrupting the rectus femoris from its attachment on the pelvis. Sudden or violent movements may also cause this avulsion in the nonfused apophysis of an adolescent.

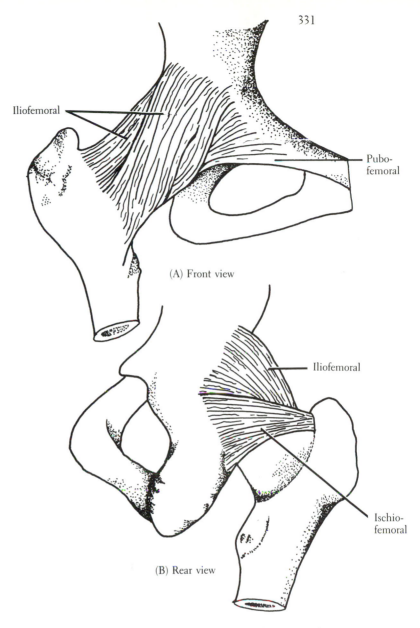

Figure 20-3 Ligaments of the hip joint. (From Crouch, J. E., and M. E. Carr. *Anatomy and Physiology*. Palo Alto, Calif.: Mayfield Publishing Co., 1977, p. 73.)

Table 20-1 *Primary Movers of the Hip*

Flexion: Psoas, iliacus, rectus femoris, pectineus, sartorius
Extension: Biceps femoris, semitendinosus, semimembranosus, gluteus maximus
Adduction: Pectineus, gracilis, adductor longus, adductor brevis, adductor magnus
Abduction: Gluteus medius
Inward rotation: Gluteus minimus
Outward rotation: Gluteus maximus, piriformis, obturator externus, obturator internus, gemellus superior, gemellus inferior, quadratus femoris

Bursae: Connective tissue sacs over bony prominences and near tendons that facilitate movement by reducing friction.

Apophysis: A projection from a bone.

Power shot: In soccer, an explosive, high-speed shot on the goal.

332

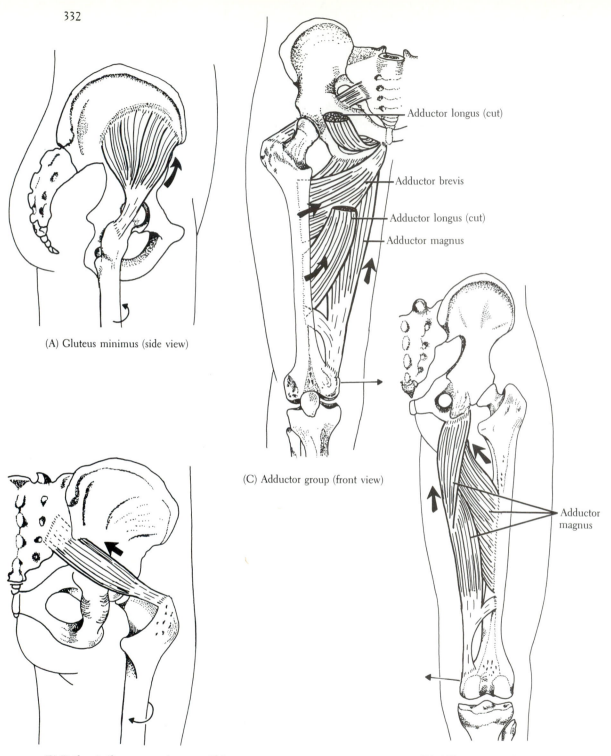

(A) Gluteus minimus (side view)

Adductor longus (cut)

Adductor brevis

Adductor longus (cut)

Adductor magnus

(C) Adductor group (front view)

Adductor magnus

(B) Piriformis (from rear and to one side)

(D) Adductor group (rear view)

Figure 20-4 Muscles that move the femur. The broad solid arrows indicate the direction of pull of a muscle from insertion to origin. The thin arrows indicate the direction in which the skeletal element will move when the muscle contracts. (From Crouch and Carr, 1977, pp. 108, 109.)

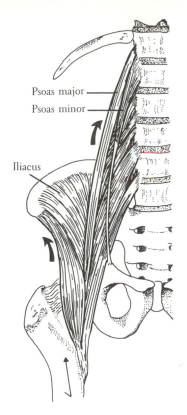

Psoas major

Psoas minor

Iliacus

(E) Psoas major and iliacus (front view)

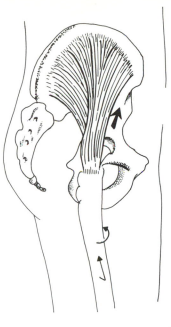

(G) Gluteus medius (side view)

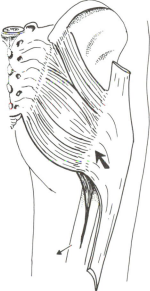

(F) Gluteus maximus (from rear and to one side)

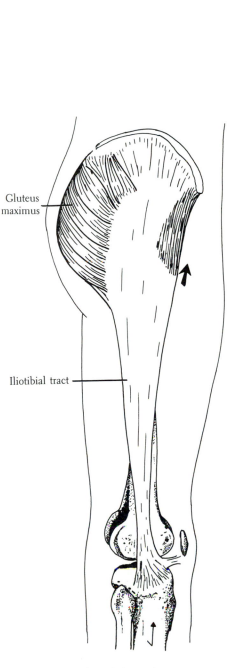

Gluteus maximus

Iliotibial tract

(H) Tensor fasciae latae (side view)

Figure 20-5 Palpating the hip for avulsion fracture. Point tenderness is usually a result of contusion, but an accompanying palpable defect may indicate avulsion fracture.

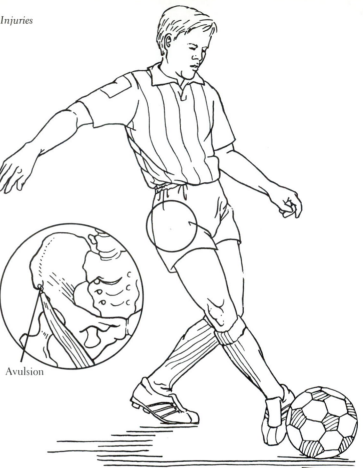

Avulsion

Figure 20-6 Mechanism for avulsion of the sartorius muscle. When a soccer placekicker catches the foot on the turf, the sartorius muscle may tear away from the pelvis.

The ischial tuberosity is the origin of the hamstring muscles. IT avulsion can be caused by direct trauma or powerful muscular overload. For example, this injury may occur when a rodeo rider is thrown from the back of a bull and lands bluntly on his buttocks. A football player might suffer IT avulsion by forcefully flexing his hip with his knee extended while high-stepping to avoid a tackle (Figure 20-7). This high-stepping distributes a tremendous pull on the origin of the long head of the biceps femoris.

Other hip avulsions may also be caused by trauma or violent muscular overload. The pubis may be avulsed during a forceful abduction or adduction of the thigh (Figure 20-8), the greater trochanter during a forceful change of direction while sprinting, and the lesser trochanter from forced extension of the thigh when the hip is in a contracted flexed position.

Evaluation. The complete avulsion fracture is characterized by an obvious and palpable defect between the tendon's origin or insertion and the muscle belly. However, the large girth of muscle in the hip and thigh often makes recognition of this defect difficult. The lesion may be more distinguishable by a tender bulge of tissue adjacent to the involved tendon's original attachment. This is particularly evident during active resistive muscle testing.

Avulsion fractures of the hip and pelvis are rare. However, they do occur and can easily be mistaken for other injuries. The athletic trainer should consider the possibility of this injury, particularly among young athletes involved in high-intensity or contact sports.

Treatment and Rehabilitation. Acute field treatment for complete avulsions may require immobilization by splinting with a full-length **spine board** while the athlete lies in a comfortable position. Transport the athlete to a local medical facility for x-ray and medical evaluation. An athlete with a suspected incomplete avulsion should also be evaluated by a physician as soon as possible.

Treatment typically consists of rest and immobilization. Ice, compression, and elevation are beneficial during the acute stages of injury, followed by heat seventy-two to ninety-six hours afterward. Serious cases may require surgery with internal fixation. Range of motion exercises are contraindicated until the fracture has healed, but muscular conditioning by isometrics and electrical stimulation may be appropriate during the early stages of recovery.

After the fracture has healed, the rehabilitation program can include range of motion and strengthening exercises. Initially, these strength exercises should consist of manual resistance training through all ranges of motion of the hip joint. Gradually, other forms of resistive exercises that use weights and weight machines can be introduced.

Figure 20-7   High-stepping to avoid a tackle may result in avulsion fractures of the hip.

Spine board: A wooden board used mainly to extricate and transport people with suspected spinal injury.

Figure 20-8 Basketball player suddenly changing direction. This movement could be the mechanism of hip adductor strain or avulsion fracture of the pubis.

Displaced and Nondisplaced Fractures

Displaced and nondisplaced fractures of the hip and thigh occur in sports involving extraordinary forces, such as motorcycle, automobile, and downhill racing, ski jumping, and football. Here we discuss fractures to the crest of the ilium, femoral shaft, femoral neck, and capital femoral epiphysis.

Figure 20-9 Fracture to the wing of the ilium. This injury could be caused by a severe blow to the ilium. It could be confused with a hip pointer.

Crest of the Ilium

Fracture of the crest of the ilium is rare but is devastating when it does occur (Figure 20-9). The accompanying soft tissue injury can be more debilitating than the fracture itself, and the pain is tremendous, often lasting many weeks.

Evaluation. Physical examination is usually difficult because of the pain and lack of local musculature. Palpation typically reveals extreme tenderness on the iliac crest and ilium. When both hands are placed on the anterior superior iliac spines and slight downward and outward pressure is applied, pain will result. Pressure in the opposite direction will also cause pain if the ilium is fractured. This injury can be easily overlooked and mistakenly considered a severe contusion or "hip pointer" because the two injuries are so similar. (The hip pointer injury is discussed in the "Contusions" section, p. 344.)

Treatment and Rehabilitation. Immediate treatment includes immobilization of the leg and upper body on a stretcher, preferably a spine board. Place the athlete on the stretcher in the position the athlete was found in. Get medical attention for the athlete as soon as possible. Watch for signs of shock; if there are any, treat accordingly

(see Chapter 10). Bed rest is the treatment of choice, with ambulation permitted as soon as pain is tolerable. Because it takes six to eight weeks for the fracture to heal, an athlete with the injury is usually eliminated from sports for the season.

Femoral Shaft

A fractured femoral shaft is caused by a large force, typically from excessive rotary motions, as in alpine skiing, or a direct blow, as in football, rugby, and hockey. The middle third of the femur is the most common site of fracture because it is the most exposed and the femur is curved slightly at this point, making it structurally weaker.

Evaluation. The **displaced fracture** reveals itself by deformity, loss of function, shortening of the thigh, pain, and swelling. Shock is very common following femoral fractures because of the severe trauma and pain. Seek medical attention immediately.

Nondisplaced fractures of the femur are more difficult to evaluate and require x-ray examination for an accurate diagnosis. Physical examination may reveal point tenderness, pain on weight bearing, **crepitation,** weakness, spasm, and swelling. Palpating the uninjured

Displaced fracture: A break in a bone; the bone fragments are not aligned.

Nondisplaced fracture: A break in a bone; the bone fragments are aligned.

Crepitation (crepitus): A grinding, crackling sound produced by friction of adjacent tissues.

leg can help differentiate between a nondisplaced fracture and a severe contusion of the quadriceps. If palpation produces pain, suspect a fracture. Another test is to immobilize, elevate, and relax the leg and then apply slight pressure to the heel and foot along the longitudinal axis of the injured femur. Pain may indicate fracture.

Treatment and Rehabilitation. Promptly and properly immobilize the displaced fractured femur (see Chapter 10). In addition, splint the hip and knee joint to ensure that the fracture is immobilized. A good rule to remember is "Splint them as they lie"; this helps minimize further complications with both nondisplaced and displaced fractures. Rehabilitation of displaced and nondisplaced fractures may start as soon as possible by exercising the *noninjured* extremity and the available muscles of the involved leg. Resume full activity when the fracture has healed, the muscles of the involved leg become as strong as those in the uninvolved leg (and the strength of both legs is appropriate for the sport), and full range of motion has been restored in both the knee and hip joints.

Femoral Neck

The hip usually dislocates before the femoral neck fractures because of the bone's tremendous tensile strength. A displaced femoral neck fracture, which may be caused by direct forceful trauma, is very serious because of possible long-term complications, such as **avascular necrosis** and degenerative arthritis.

Evaluation. Symptoms of a displaced fracture of the femoral neck are an externally rotated, adducted, and slightly flexed thigh. This injury is immediately disabling and accompanied by severe pain in the groin that may be referred to the medial side of the thigh and knee.

The signs of nondisplaced femoral neck fracture are less obvious and require x-ray examination for confirmation. The usual signs are pain with walking, point tenderness over the greater trochanter, and decreased leg mobility. This injury typically results from a great force exerted along the axis of the femur toward the pelvis while the knee and hip are flexed (in a position such as sitting). The most common cause of femoral neck fractures (displaced and nondisplaced) are automobile accidents.

Treatment and Rehabilitation. Initial treatment is checking and caring for probable shock, immobilizing the athlete's hip and thigh on a full-length stretcher or spine board (in the position the athlete was found in or as comfortably as possible), and obtaining medical assistance as soon as possible (see Chapter 10). Medical treatment includes fracture immobilization and non-weight-bearing reduction (with or without open reduction, depending upon the severity of injury). Solid union takes three to five months (less time in children), after which active rehabilitation may begin.

Rehabilitation involves restoring range of motion and then strength, endurance, and normal functional capacity.

Capital Femoral Epiphysis

Hip dislocations or subluxations in the young athlete can result in a fractured capital femoral **epiphysis**. The signs, symptoms, and history are usually similar to those for fractured femoral neck and include a shortening of the limb with the thigh in internal rotation, flexion, and adduction. Pain may be referred to the knee because the obturator nerve is involved, so always examine the hip whenever a child complains of knee pain. This is a serious injury that must receive immediate medical attention if suspected.

Epiphysis: The end of a long bone. During growth it is separated from the shaft by a cartilaginous growth plate.

Avascular necrosis: Death of bone from the absence of a blood supply.

Stress Fractures

Stress fractures of the pelvis and femur are common among the elderly and people with osteoporatic problems but seldom occur in young, healthy athletes. The increased popularity of jogging has been accompanied by an increased incidence of stress fractures. Evidence is mounting that the rhythmic, repetitive action of jogging produces the forces necessary to cause a stress fracture in the pelvis and femur.

Femoral Neck

Symptoms of a femoral neck fracture are pain in the groin, with referred pain to the anterior thigh and knee; painful walking; point tenderness over the greater trochanter; and decreased range of motion, particularly internal rotation of the thigh. Pain may occur only when weight is borne, or it may progressively increase during activity.

Osteitis Pubis

Osteitis pubis is a stress fracture of the pubic symphysis and is caused by repeated trauma to the tendinous origin of the thigh's adductor muscles. It occurs most frequently in contact sports like soccer, rugby, and lacrosse and sometimes in track and field, bowling, and automobile racing.

The initial physical examination typically reveals little point tenderness. The athlete usually complains of a gradual onset of pain in the groin area, and the injury may be mistaken for an adductor strain. As the athlete continues to participate in the sport, pain is experienced when the region of the pubic symphysis is palpated and may radiate distally along the region of the thigh's medial aspect (following the course of the adductor muscles). This injury may occur when an athlete is passing a soccer ball: The leg is externally rotated and adducted and the hip is violently flexed.

Treatment

Athletes should be treated with ice, rest, and anti-inflammatory drugs. If the symptoms continue for more than two or three weeks after conservative anti-inflammatory therapy, refer the athlete to a physician, who may order an x-ray, a bone scan, or even a metabolic examination to rule out thyroid disorders.

Pelvic and femoral stress fractures can keep an athlete out of activity for an entire season or more if not properly cared for. For example, a professional football player who was instrumental in his team's Super Bowl victory the previous season was diagnosed as having an adductor strain and treated accordingly. He elected to continue playing, but his symptoms became more severe. After follow-up x-ray examination, the injury was finally diagnosed as osteitis pubis. At that point the player was instructed to terminate all activity for four months, after which he could begin a progressive running program. By the time the player recovered, he had missed the second half of the season and the first half of the following season. Of all the therapies and treatments this athlete received, rest was probably the one most responsible for his recovery.

Dislocation of the Hip

Dislocation of the hip is a disabling and severely painful injury. The forces necessary to produce a hip dislocation are usually absent in athletic competitions, but they may be present in certain circumstances and affect adolescent athletes. A dislocation is usually caused by a powerful blow to the knee while both the knee and the hip are flexed (Figure 20-10). The force follows an anteroposterior direction along the shaft of the femur and pushes the femur through the posterior aspect of the joint

Stress fracture: A fracture induced by a muscle repetitively stressing a bone (such as at a site of muscle attachment). With continued stress, the fracture may progress from a micro state to a complete displacement.

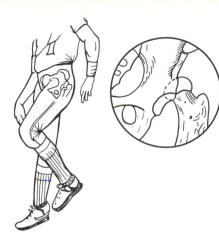

Figure 20-10 Dislocation of the hip. The hip may be posteriorly dislocated when it is severely flexed and adducted. This injury could occur during a pileup in football or in high-force activities like downhill skiing and motorcycle racing.

capsule, producing a posterior dislocation. The injury may be accompanied by a fractured acetabulum.

Evaluation. Physical examination usually shows the affected leg shortened, internally rotated, slightly flexed, and adducted. During palpation, the head of the femur lies posterior to the acetabulum and the greater trochanter appears prominently on the anterior aspect of the hip. The athlete experiences severe pain when attempting to move the dislocated hip. Do *not* attempt to reduce the injury. X-rays must be taken to determine evidence of further injury, such as bone fragments.

Treatment. Obtain medical attention as soon as possible because of the danger of shock and the development of avascular necrosis from the ruptured ligamentum teres. The hip must be totally immobilized and constantly checked for adequate blood supply to the lower leg and for nerve damage. Treatment for dislocations after reduction is immobilization for four to six weeks, after which physical rehabilitation may begin. Do not permit vigorous sports activities for at least three months, to give the joint capsule time to heal.

Vascular System

A direct blow to a vulnerable area such as the femoral triangle, where the femoral artery, nerve, and vein are fairly subcutaneous, can cause **vascular** injury. These injuries seldom occur in sports because of athletes' protective response prior to being hit (e.g., in football or rugby the player flexes his trunk and lowers his head as he is about to be tackled). But when an athlete does receive a direct blow, **phlebitis** or even **phlebothrombosis** can occur, a possibility the athletic trainer should consider if disability and irritation persist for several hours.

Phlebitis is inflammation of a vein; phlebothrombosis is the formation of a blood clot in the vein. The symptoms of these disorders include pain (may be extreme in severe cases) and edema. Athletes may develop these conditions by becoming excessively inactive (e.g., from bed rest) following soft tissue trauma. Therefore, the best way to prevent the problems is to have athletes avoid excessive inactivity following an injury such as a severe contusion.

Treatment includes rest and wearing elastic wraps or stockings. Anticoagulant therapy may be indicated for phlebothrombosis. The danger of phlebothrombosis is that the clot may travel through the circulation and cause pulmonary embolism.

Lymphatic System

Irritated lymph nodes can cause damage to the **lymphatic system.** Inflamed inguinal lymph nodes cause swelling and irritation in the groin area. The athletic trainer must consider factors other than orthopedic disorders when an athlete complains of pain. If there is no history of traumatic injury in the groin region but there is considerable pain and swelling, consider in-

Vascular: Pertaining to blood vessels.

Phlebitis: Inflammation of a vein.
Phlebothrombosis: Formation or presence of a thrombus (blood clot) in a vein without accompanying inflammation.

Lymphatic system: The system composed of lymph (clear liquid containing white blood cells), lymph nodes, and lymph vessels; it is important for filtering the blood and protecting the body from foreign material.

339
Hip and Thigh Injuries

fection as the cause of irritation. For example, an infected blister on the bottom of the foot can irritate lymph nodes that are particularly visible in the groin area.

Treatment. Treatment consists of cleaning the infected area and protecting it from further contamination with a sterile dressing and antibiotic ointment. Oral antibiotics may be necessary, so refer the athlete to a physician for further examination.

Sprains

The hip ligaments are rarely sprained because of the hip joint's large range of motion. The vast amount of muscles surrounding this joint adds greatly to its stability, and an injury to the muscles usually precedes injury to the ligaments.

Symptoms of hip sprain typically are vague and include pain in the groin area and loss of function, especially rotation of the hip. Treat this injury like any sprain, emphasizing ice and rest. Activity may begin when the athlete has pain-free range of motion.

Strains

Strains to the hip and thigh are common and can be extremely debilitating. Prevention includes the encouragement of a year-round stretching, strengthening, and conditioning program. Athletes should be taught to condition the joints through all the joints' ranges of motion.

Quadriceps

Quadriceps muscle strains occur frequently in most sports, although the quadriceps are less prone to strain than the hamstrings because of their great strength and size. The rectus femoris is the most commonly injured quadriceps

muscle. This injury usually occurs during sprinting (particularly during the early season) or during explosive knee extension or hip flexion movements, as when a soccer player is making a shot on the goal and the lower leg is blocked. The mechanism of this injury is the same as for an avulsion fracture of the anterior inferior iliac spine. The most common site of injury is the musculotendinous junction, either at the origin or insertion of the muscle.

Evaluation. Physical examination may reveal point tenderness with possible **palpable defect,** swelling, discoloration, weakness, and pain during active contraction and passive stretch of the involved muscle. The athlete may experience a "snapping" or "popping" sensation immediately followed by pain and loss of function.

Occasionally, the muscle may completely rupture. This usually happens when the muscle is maximally contracted and then receives a direct blow to the muscle belly. A rugby player may sustain this injury when he is driving his leg and his unprotected thigh receives a blow. The rupture is followed by a complete loss of function. A defect can often be palpated if the injury is examined before swelling becomes significant. A bulge, which represents the loose end of the muscle, may be present. Early evaluation can lead to very satisfactory results, but if swelling becomes very significant, the injury can be disguised and often mistaken for a contusion or hematoma.

Treatment and Rehabilitation. When the quadriceps muscle has been ruptured, repair is extremely difficult if the injury is not treated for a long time. A ruptured muscle *must* be immediately evaluated and treated by a physician. Immediate first aid is ice, compression, and immobilization.

Rehabilitation of quadriceps strains is similar to that for other muscles. Depending upon the severity of the injury,

Palpable defect: A structural abnormality that can be palpated.

active rehabilitation may begin after acute inflammation and pain have subsided. Start with static stretching of the quadriceps and passive range of motion exercises. Progress to active range of motion and resistive exercises, practicing both knee extension and hip flexion. Swimming with fins is a good quadriceps exercise during the late pre-weight-bearing phase of rehabilitation. Active weight bearing may begin when the injured leg is at least 90 percent as strong as the uninjured leg. Weight-bearing exercises may initially include walking, followed by slow jogging, then sprinting, and finally "broken-field" sprinting.

Hamstring

Hamstring strains are one of the most common injuries in sports. Athletes participating in any sport that requires explosive movement are susceptible to this injury. The hamstring muscles are the most frequently injured muscles in the leg and can be the most difficult to treat and rehabilitate because athletes tend to reinjure them before the injury completely heals. Hamstring strain is caused by weak or fatigued muscles, lack of flexibility, lack of neuromuscular control, improper technique, and strength imbalances between knee and hip flexors and extensors.

Athletes with imbalanced strength between the knee flexors and extensors or significant strength differences between legs are at high risk of receiving a strain. The best treatment for hamstring strains is prevention by developing strength, flexibility, and neuromuscular control.

Approximately half of the athletes who suffer a severe hamstring pull will never perform as well as they did before they were injured. The injured muscle repairs itself with nonelastic **scar tissue** (see Chapter 8). Without careful and proper rehabilitation, there is a high rate of recurrence, which can create considerable apprehension in the ath-

lete. The fear of reinjuring the hamstring can hinder performance as much as the injury itself. Proper guidance, treatment, rehabilitation, and moral support from the athletic trainer can save an athlete from a very frustrating experience and allow full return to activity in a relatively short time.

Evaluation. During evaluation, the signs of a hamstring strain are very clear. There is point tenderness at the site of muscle injury, with a palpable defect in moderate to severe strains. Pain is elicited with passive stretching and active contraction of the hamstring muscles, and there is swelling shortly after the injury has occurred. Ecchymosis (bluish discoloration) occasionally occurs in the popliteal fossa at the back of the knee.

Treatment and Rehabilitation. If the strain is not properly treated, the increased extracellular fluid from the hamstring will accumulate around the knee joint and delay recovery. Immediate care is ice, compression, elevation, and immobilization. Proper support of the hamstring by use of a spica wrap can decrease aggravation to the injured muscle, which will decrease pain and irritation (Figure 20-11).

Scar tissue: Fibrous tissue formed in response to trauma.

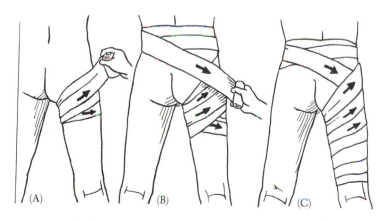

Figure 20-11 A spica wrap for hamstring injury.
(A) Begin at the groin and wrap tightly.
(B) Extend wrap around the waist.
(C) Extend wrap to the lower hamstring.

After the acute inflammatory phase of the injury has passed, rehabilitation should begin with gentle static stretching and isometric contractions of the hamstrings. As pain and disability subside, manually resisted knee flexion and hip extension exercises may be instituted. These exercises can be supplemented with isokinetic exercise, initially conducted at moderate speeds of approximately 120 degrees per second. Speeds can be increased according to the athlete's tolerance. As with quadriceps strains, swimming with fins also strengthens hamstrings without subjecting them to the burden of bearing weight.

Do not let athletes return to full participation until their hamstring strength is at least 60 percent of their quadriceps strength (i.e., knee extension-flexion strength measured at sixty degrees per second on a Cybex isokinetic dynamometer), they have achieved normal flexibility (see Chapter 8), and they have normal strength symmetry in the hamstring and quadriceps muscles between the left and right sides of the body. When active weight bearing is permitted, exercise should progress from walking to jogging or pool running, striding, sprinting, and broken-field sprinting.

Groin

Groin strains are very common and can severely limit the athlete (see Putting It into Practice 20-1). The groin consists of the iliopsoas group, rectus femoris, and hip adductors (Table 20-1, p. 331). These muscles are very active during athletic performance and are required for a tremendous variety of movements. Overuse or acute overload can cause injury. As with other strains, the athlete usually experiences a pull during a particular movement, especially when changing direction and moving forward rapidly. After suffering a groin strain, the athlete can usually tolerate straightahead running, but any lateral movement will cause severe pain. For example, the crossover step in football (defensive backs and linebackers) and pivoting in basketball are painful and difficult for an athlete with a pulled groin. Adductor contractions required for horseback riding or **snow plowing** in skiing or passing the ball in soccer can cause a groin strain. Splits performed in gymnastics and cheerleading can also precipitate groin strain.

Evaluation. All the groin muscles are very susceptible to injury, so functional muscle testing must be used to locate the exact site of injury. Physical findings include point tenderness, swelling, palpable defects, and loss of function.

Treatment and Rehabilitation. After initial treatment with ice, compression, and rest, activity can be gradually started as the strength and flexibility rehabilitation program progresses. Rehabilitation should begin with isometric exercises and gentle static stretching (see Chapter 4). Gradually, introduce manual resistance exercises, followed by more vigorous weight-training techniques such as adduction weight machines and squats. As discussed, running in a straight direction may pose few problems, even during the acute phase of injury, but introduce lateral running very gradually and only when the athlete is pain-free and has adequate strength. Use a spica or spiral wrap for support and to limit range of motion.

Gluteal Muscles

The gluteal muscles are rarely injured because of their size. Contusions are the most common injury, but they seldom lead to loss of playing time. Gluteal strains usually occur from muscular overload in movements such as squats in **power lifting** or rowing in crew. Muscle testing must be used to distinguish between injury to the hamstrings and to the gluteal muscles.

Snow plow: An alpine skiing technique in which the skis are placed in a wedge. Principally used by beginning skiers.

Power lifting: A type of competitive weight lifting involving the squat, bench press, and deadlift.

Managing Hamstring and Groin Injuries

The following rehabilitation periods are arbitrary and vary with the severity of injury. Symptoms dictate when an athlete can progress from one stage to the next.

Acute Stage (first 48–72 h, depending upon severity)

- Ice, compression, elevation, rest.
- Possible use of nonsteroidal anti-inflammatory drugs (prescribed by physician).

Early Rehabilitation Stage (2–3 days after injury)

- Continue rest from active participation; ice.
- Apply other modalities: ultrasound, transcutaneous nerve stimulation, electrical muscle stimulation.
- Begin progressive static stretching. Progressive manually resisted exercise can begin when tolerated.

Rehabilitation Stage (2 weeks after injury, depending upon severity)

- Continue rest from active sports participation.
- Vigorous flexibility and resistive exercise training. Athletes may supplement this training with flexion or adduction exercise machines.
- Athletes can begin slow jogging if they are pain-free. They should initially avoid sprinting or abrupt changes in direction.
- Friction massage to break up adhesions (not recommended by some experts).

Late Rehabilitation Stage

- Continue active flexibility and resistive exercise programs.
- Athletes should wear spica or groin wrap during field drills. The benefits of these wraps are debatable, but the wraps do provide psychological support.
- Institute controlled sprint drills, such as figure eight running patterns, high-knee exercise, high-bounding exercise, gradually accelerating sprints, run-and-cut drills, etc. Begin these drills at half speed, gradually increasing the tempo.
- Athletes should not return to competition until they are pain-free, have good strength and flexibility (as good or better than before they were injured), and can use the muscles in the same manner as required in competition. These injuries often recur because they are seldom fully rehabilitated.

Factors Predisposing Athletes to Groin and Hamstring Injuries

- Poor strength and flexibility.
- Strength imbalances between opposing muscle groups. For example, the hamstrings should be approximately 60 percent or more as strong as the quadriceps (measured isokinetically at speed of approximately sixty degrees per second).
- Poor technique. For example, groin strains from discus throwing are sometimes caused by an athlete's failure to place weight squarely over the left leg at the back of the circle during the first turn. Many athletes attempt to drive an abducted thigh around the left leg as a compensation for an unbalanced position, which often causes groin strain.

Treatment and Rehabilitation. Early treatment is limited to rest and, after forty-eight to seventy-two hours, deep, penetrating heat from such modalities as ultrasound or diathermy. Superficial heat and cold treatments have little therapeutic effect because the muscle tissue is so thick. However, there is no harm in using ice during rehabilitation because a portion of the injury may be superficial and may benefit from this modality. Do not use heat prematurely because it may exacerbate the inflammatory process (see Chapters 8 and 13).

Supportive wraps are of little value because they are difficult to apply and it is hard to maintain the position of the wrap once it is applied. Start range of motion exercises within a few days after the injury. Gluteal flexibility, which is usually neglected by healthy athletes, should be included in the injury-prevention program.

Contusions

Contusions about the hip and thigh occur frequently in athletics because these tissues have such a large surface area. Contusions may result from direct blows from balls or racquets, collisions with equipment or other athletes. This injury can significantly reduce the athlete's playing time if not managed properly. Probably the most effective treatment is to protect the athlete from further injury by having the athlete wear pads or by modifying activity.

The Iliac Crest: The Hip Pointer

The iliac crest is prone to injury because of its exposure and lack of soft tissue protection. The hip pointer is an extremely debilitating and frustrating injury. A direct blow to the iliac crest forces the muscles against the bone, pinching the surrounding soft tissue and sometimes the bone itself. Because numerous upper and lower body muscles attach to the iliac crest, virtually any movement of the trunk will cause pain when an athlete has this injury. In fact, an athlete may be so sensitive to trunk movements that sneezing, coughing, laughing, and even bowel movements are painful.

Mechanism of Injury. The injury occurs most often in contact sports, although it can occur in noncontact sports like baseball (poor sliding technique) or volleyball (diving for a ball and landing on the hip). An athlete can receive a hip pointer fairly easily, even when wearing hip pads.

Evaluation. Physical examination reveals point tenderness over the iliac crest, anywhere from the anterior superior iliac spine to the posterior superior iliac spine. There is swelling, discoloration, spasm with loss of function, difficulty with walking, and the trunk laterally flexed toward the injured hip. If the contusion is severe, the athlete may not be able to bear weight at all or even walk on crutches. Some experts feel that a severe hip pointer is more painful and handicapping than a fractured ilium.

Careful and complete evaluation should consider the possibility that more serious injuries have occurred, such as femoral neck fracture or avulsion fracture of the muscle attaching to the iliac crest. If the contusion is on the posterior aspect of the hip, the athletic trainer should note any numbness, tingling, or muscle weakness in the leg or foot or the development of cold toes; all these are signs of neural and circulatory deficiencies. If such signs are present, the athlete must immediately go to an emergency facility. The athlete can usually continue to play after sustaining a mild hip pointer, but the pain often becomes more severe and swelling increases after the activity stops.

Treatment and Rehabilitation. Immediate treatment includes ice and compression and should be continued for at least three days. Heat therapy may begin with very mild range of motion exercises when there are no signs of hemorrhage (decreased swelling). Once the athlete can perform activities with confidence, agility, and minimal pain, he may return to activity if he wears a protective pad to prevent further injury.

Protecting the hip pointer can be difficult. A custom-formed plastic shell with a dense foam donut pad fitted to its inside helps protect the iliac crest from further injury, if the injury is small and well-defined (Figure 20-12). This protective padding can be held on with a figure eight elastic wrap. Unfortunately, the contusion is usually diffused and covers an area where there is a variety of movements. In these cases, protective padding is not as effective, and the pressure of the pad may even increase pain.

Greater Trochanter

A small amount of soft tissue overlays the greater trochanter, which includes the greater trochanteric bursa, iliotibial band, and skin. As with the hip pointer, a blow to this area creates a pinching effect and produces a painful injury that can irritate bone, bursa, and muscle. This injury may develop into chronic bursitis of the greater trochanteric bursa if not properly treated and protected from further damage.

Physical evaluation and treatment are similar to those for the hip pointer. There are rarely any complications to this injury. Carry out rehabilitation as soon as possible, but within the athlete's pain tolerance.

Quadriceps

The quadriceps muscles are often contused from sports like football, ice and field hockey, and soccer. Although the quadriceps are very strong and thick, they often suffer contusions because of the great forces they receive during movements such as blocking and tackling. Upon impact, the athlete experiences some pain and momentary loss of function; this is commonly called a **charley horse.** Usually the player can return to competition within a few minutes after the injury has occurred.

Evaluation. Typically, symptoms develop when the activity has stopped and the athlete has cooled down. Symptoms

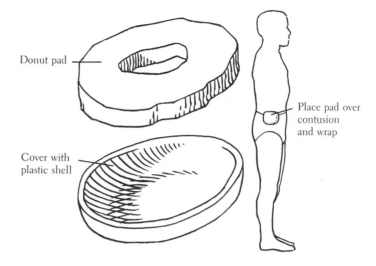

Figure 20-12 Protective padding for a hip pointer. This technique is effective only if the injury is small and well defined. Construct a donut pad and plastic protective shell according to the characteristics of the athlete and affix them to the injury site with an elastic wrap.

include pain, spasm, swelling, weakness, loss of function (especially hip flexion), and difficulty in walking. The athlete should be told to report signs of excessive swelling, which can manifest itself as tingling, numbness, and difficulty in maintaining the foot in dorsiflexion. If these signs are present, immediately refer the athlete to a physician or emergency facility. Swelling can become so severe that surgery to reduce the swelling may be necessary to release the fascia surrounding the muscle.

Treatment and Rehabilitation. Treatment includes ice, compression, elevation, and immobilization to prevent further irritation. Continue this therapy for three to five days, until swelling and pain have subsided. After that, heat and mild stretching can be used to minimize contractures and prevent excessive scarring.

Rehabilitation should start as soon as possible, with mild quadriceps stretching and resistive exercise. Resistive exercises should include knee extension and hip flexion. All rehabilitation should be

Charley horse: A contusion of the quadriceps muscles.

nearly pain-free. The athlete can return to activity when normal range of motion has been restored and the pain is gone. The athlete should wear a protective pad to prevent reinjury.

Myositis Ossificans

Myositis ossificans is mineralization within the muscle; it sometimes occurs during a hematoma's healing process. With continued irritation of the hematoma, bone develops (ossification) within the muscle. After three to four weeks of such development, a hard, immovable, painful mass may be palpated and confirmed by x-ray.

In mild to moderate contusions of the thigh, most athletes have a tendency to "run off" the injury, massage or "knead out" the spasm, or begin active rehabilitation too early. Such activity must be discouraged because it may cause further irritation and lead to long-term complications like myositis ossificans. Myositis ossificans is self-limiting unless reaggravated, and it may not significantly affect physical performance if the bony mass is small.

Treatment and Rehabilitation. Treatment is immobilization for approximately six weeks, with gradually increasing, pain-free exercise. Avoid manipulation and massage, to prevent inflammation from increasing. The bony plaque is usually surgically excised if it is significantly large and disabling, but only after it has completely matured. Early biopsy and microscopic examination of myositis ossificans reveal an almost exact resemblance to ostogenic sarcoma. Patience and time are necessary when treating this condition to avoid the tragic consequence of a malignant bone tumor. After the bony mass has been surgically removed, the athlete can begin active rehabilitation in three weeks. It may be five to six months before the athlete's knee regains normal flexion. Treatment is long and painstaking; the athletic trainer must provide encouragement and support during rehabilitation.

Gluteal Muscles

Usually the gluteal muscles are not severely contused because of their size and natural protective padding of fat. Since athletes rarely wear protective pads for the buttocks, a minor or moderate contusion can occur frequently, but it is rarely disabling. The most common cause of gluteal contusions is a direct blow. As with any uncomplicated contusion, there is tenderness, discoloration, and swelling. Treatment is the same as for other contusions and includes ice and wearing pads as protection from further injury.

Sciatic Nerve

A direct blow to the gluteal muscles may contuse the sciatic nerve. The sciatic nerve is located between the greater trochanter and ischial tuberosity. An injury to this area may cause radiating pain down the back of the hamstrings into the calf and foot. Sciatic pain can be easily confused with ischial bursitis, so the two structures must be isolated and the areas of tenderness identified to avoid errors in recognition and treatment. Symptoms of a contused sciatic nerve are shooting, tingling, or a burning sensation radiating down the nerve pathway. Hamstring stretching or palpation usually elicits these symptoms. The history of the injury is the primary factor for distinguishing sciatic nerve contusion from vertebral disk injury.

Ischial Tuberosity

The ischial tuberosity can be easily contused by a fall on the buttocks when the hip is flexed. This position moves the gluteus maximus upward and exposes the tuberosity. This injury can make even simple tasks, such as sitting, difficult and painful; it can be accompanied by ischial bursitis and become a long-lasting ailment.

Myositis ossificans (muscular ossification): Formation of bone within a muscle, usually caused by trauma.

Bursitis

Bursa are physiologically and developmentally related to tendon sheaths and synovial membranes and are subject to similar diseases and injuries. Bursitis is an inflammation usually caused by a direct blow or from overuse. It is best treated by rest, hot and cold therapy, compression, and protection from reinjury.

Greater Trochanteric Bursitis

Bursitis of the greater trochanteric bursa is common in female athletes who have a wide pelvis and large Q angle (see Chapter 21). These factors cause the tensor fasciae latae muscle to slide back and forth excessively over the greater trochanter and its bursa during flexion, extension, and rotation of the hip, which inflames the bursa. This injury also occurs in runners who effectively increase their Q angle by crossing their feet over their midline as they run. There is pain between the gluteus maximus and posterolateral aspect of the greater trochanter. Contraction of the gluteus maximus or tensor fasciae latae also causes pain because of the pressure applied to the underlying bursa.

Chronic bursitis of the greater trochanteric bursa can cause **snapping hip,** which is characterized by a snapping that can be heard or felt each time the tensor fasciae latae glides over the greater trochanter. Snapping hip sometimes occurs in female dancers with bursitis who continue to dance. This condition has a high tendency to recur, and surgery may be necessary for complete recovery.

Iliopsoas Bursitis

The iliopsoas (iliopectineal) bursa is located deep in the groin, between the iliopsoas and pectineus muscles, and is the largest bursa in the body. When this bursa is inflamed, there are pain and swelling along the inner edge of the sartorius muscle on the lateral aspect of the femoral triangle. The swelling can be so significant that it obscures the inguinal groove. Pain may radiate down the anterior aspect of the thigh toward the knee, probably from femoral nerve compression. Contracting or stretching the iliopsoas muscle causes pain.

It is very difficult to properly recognize this injury, and it is beyond our scope to describe the correct procedure. It is mentioned here to emphasize the fact that the groin can be injured from factors other than muscle strain or avulsion fracture. The athletic trainer must monitor the swelling and note the characteristics of the pain.

Hip Synovitis

Hip synovitis, inflammation of the synovial membrane of the hip, is difficult to identify because the joint is large and has such a great quantity of surrounding musculature. This injury usually results from overuse or accompanies an acute condition, such as sprain. Treatment is rest, ice, and compression; implement heat therapy as swelling diminishes. Resume activity when pain is tolerable. This can be a very frustrating injury because the symptoms are usually minimal but long-lasting. If the condition remains unchanged for more than two weeks, refer the athlete to a physician for examination.

Congenital Defects

Any congenital defects (abnormal conditions present since birth) that may present themselves in sports are usually seen in children and adolescents. Most of these conditions are self-limiting and

Snapping hip: A condition caused by the tensor fasciae latae gliding over a greater trochanteric bursa that has experienced fibrous hypertrophy from repeated trauma. Common in dancers.

need treatment only to prevent deformity until the condition runs its course.

Slipped Capital Femoral Epiphysis

Slipped capital femoral epiphysis is most common in children who are large and obese or rapidly growing and slender. This condition is different from a fracture of the unfused capital epiphysis in adolescents, which tends to occur as a direct result of trauma (discussed earlier). The slipped capital epiphysis is more common in boys than girls and is usually initiated by a traumatic incident. Typically, there is some underlying deficiency in calcium metabolism; sometimes pituitary and thyroid dysfunction contributes to the problem. Any child who complains of hip or knee pain should be examined by a physician. Symptoms are very general and similar to that of acute fractures of the femoral neck and other diseases of the hip, such as Legg-Perthes disease.

Legg-Perthes Disease

Legg-Perthes disease is self-limiting and usually found in male children five to ten years old. It is an **osteochondritis** of the femoral head caused by a vascular disturbance that diminishes blood flow to the capital area of the femur. Symptoms are muscle spasm, restricted abduction and rotation of the thigh, and hip pain that is sometimes referred to the knee. X-ray examination must be performed for accurate diagnosis. Treatment consists of preventing deformity of the femoral head during the period of avascular necrosis by immobilization, non-weight bearing, and sometimes surgery. Treatment takes one to two years.

References

Blauvelt, C. T, and F. Nelson. *A Manual of Orthopaedic Terminology.* St. Louis: C. V. Mosby, 1977.

Burkett, L. N. Causative factors in hamstring strains. *Medicine and Science in Sports and Exercise* 2:39–42, 1970.

Butler, J. E. Subtrochanteric stress fractures in runners. *American Journal of Sports Medicine* 10:228–232, 1982.

Carter, M. C. A reliable sign of fractures of the hip or pelvis. *New England Journal of Medicine* 305:1220, 1981.

Clemente, C. D. *Anatomy: A Regional Atlas of the Human Body.* Baltimore: Urban and Schwarzenberg, 1981.

Craig, C. L. Hip injuries in children and adolescents. *Orthopedic Clinics of North America* 11:743–753, 1980.

De Palma, A. F. *The Management of Fractures and Dislocations: An Atlas.* Philadelphia: W. B. Saunders, 1980.

Fernbach, S. K., and R. H. Wilkinson. Avulsion injuries of the pelvis and proximal femur. *American Journal of Rehabilitation* 137:581–584, 1981.

Foster, B. K. Perthes disease: returning children to sports. *The Physician and Sportsmedicine* 10:69–74, 1982.

Grana, W. A., and E. Schelberg-Kaines. How I manage deep muscle bruises. *The Physician and Sportsmedicine* 11:123–127, 1983.

Grindulis, K. A., and B. McConkey. Iliopsoas bursitis—a surgically correctable cause of lower limb oedema. *The Practitioner* 226:1336–1337, 1982.

Hajek, M. R., and H. B. Nobel. Stress fractures of the femoral neck in joggers. *American Journal of Sports Medicine* 10:112–116, 1982.

Hopenfeld, S. *Physical Examination of the Spine and Extremities.* New York: Appleton-Century-Crofts, 1976.

Lagier, R., and B. Jarret. Apophysiolysis of the anterior inferior iliac spine. *Archives of Orthopaedic and Traumatic Surgery* 83:81–89, 1975.

Larson, C. B., and M. Gould. *Orthopedic Nursing.* St. Louis: C. V. Mosby, 1974.

Osteochondritis (osteochondrosis): Inflammation of bone and its cartilage, typically associated with avascular necrosis.

Lombardo, S. J., and D. W. Benson. Stress fractures of the femur in runners. *American Journal of Sports Medicine* 10:219–227, 1982.

O'Donoghue, D. H. *Treatment of Injuries to Athletes*. Philadelphia: W. B. Saunders, 1984.

Rasch, P. J., and R. K. Burke. *Kinesiology and Applied Anatomy*. Philadelphia: W. B. Saunders, 1978.

Turek, S. L. *Orthopaedics: Principles and the Application*. New York: Lippincott, 1980.

Schlonsky, J., and M. L. Olix. Functional disability following avulsion fracture of the ischial epiphysis. *Journal of Bone and Joint Surgery* 54a:641–644, 1972.

Skinner, H. B., and S. D. Cook. Fatigue failure stress of the femoral neck. *American Journal of Sports Medicine* 10:245–247, 1982.

Wiley, J. J. Traumatic osteitis pubis: the gracilis syndrome. *American Journal of Sports Medicine* 11:360–363, 1983.

Knee Injuries

Knee injuries, common in skiing, may be prevented by improving strength, endurance, and skill and by skiing runs that are not beyond the skier's ability.

THE KNEE is the most commonly injured body structure in athletes. Data from the National Athletic Injury Reporting System (located at Pennsylvania State University) showed that in football the knee accounted for twice the number of serious injuries as the ankle, the next most injured site. In skiing, 22 to 26 percent of all injuries affect the knee, and of these injuries, 5 percent are major, which is an incidence similar to that in college football. Knee injuries are the most common ones in running, soccer, and wrestling and the most common major injuries in volleyball, basketball, and gymnastics.

The demands of athletics sometimes exceed the knee's anatomical limits. The joint lies in the middle of a long lever arm with no soft tissue to protect it, making the knee more susceptible to injury. In addition, the knee's functional position (thirty to sixty degrees of flexion) provides the least stability and places both the femorotibial and patellofemoral joints at risk.

The etiology of knee injuries is complex. Understanding the foundational mechanisms requires a pervasive awareness of the knee's anatomy, physiology, and biomechanics. The athletic trainer must be capable of properly collaborating with the orthopedic surgeon to handle all knee injuries, from routine to severe.

Anatomy

The knee is composed of the femorotibial and patellofemoral joints, articulating the femur, tibia, and patella (Figure 21-1). Although it is usually considered a hinge joint, the knee is more correctly classified as a bicondyloid joint because each femoral and tibial condyle has a different shape and therefore a different center of rotation and different radius of curvature (Figure 21-2, p. 352). Biomechanical engineers use the term **polycentric joint** to precisely describe the knee.

The knee joint is surrounded by a capsule composed of fibrous tissue and lined by synovial membrane that secretes the lubricant called **synovial fluid.** This capsule provides integrity to the joint as well as lubrication and nutrition for the knee's tissue (Figure 21-3, p. 353).

Flexion and extension are the knee's principal motions. The normal range of motion (ROM) is from 0 to 160 to 170 degrees and is expressed in degrees of flexion. Extension beyond 0 degrees is possible in people who have **hyperelastic joints** and can occur up to approximately 10 degrees without being abnormal, provided it is present on both sides. This excess extension is called **hyperextension** or **genu recurvatum.**

The knee joint is also capable of a small amount of rotation, which can be performed only when the knee is flexed. Active internal rotation is approximately thirty degrees; active external rotation is approximately forty degrees. The passive motion is an additional five degrees in both directions and is greater than the active ROM because the internal and external rotators on the proximal tibia have poor

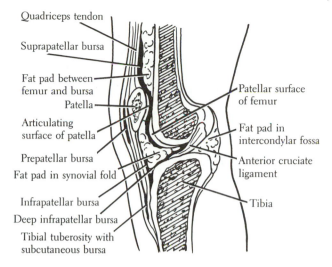

Figure 21-1 Sagittal section through the knee joint.

mechanical advantage. At terminal extension, there is an automatic five degrees of external rotation of the tibia, which is sometimes called the **screw home mechanism.**

The Femorotibial Joint

The femorotibial joint is the articulation of the two femur condyles with the concave tibial plateaus. The intercondylar notch between the femoral condyles provides enough space for the cruciate ligaments and the two tibial spines. These spines, as well as the irregular shape of the tibial plateaus, help control the **axial rotation** of the tibia on the femur. The knee's center of the rotation lies between these two tibial eminences.

The anterior-posterior profile of the tibial condyles or plateaus shows incongruent surfaces (Figure 21-2). This incongruity is compensated by the **menisci** (interarticular fibrocartilages). The tibial spines also control movement. The medial spine is higher than the lateral and impinges against the medial femoral condyle, restricting its movement. Damage to the knee's gliding surfaces will disrupt normal function.

Polycentric joint: A joint with articulations that have different radii of curvature and different centers of rotation.

Screw home mechanism: An automatic five degrees of external rotation of the tibia on the femur during terminal extension of the knee joint.

Synovial fluid: Fluid secreted by the joint synovium; it lubricates and nurtures the joint.

Hyperelastic joint: A joint with a range of motion greater than normal.

Axial rotation: Rotation of a body around its axis.

Hyperextension: Extension beyond the normal limit or beyond 180 degrees.

Genu recurvatum: Hyperextended knee.

Menisci: Interarticular fibrocartilages.

Prevention, Treatment, and Rehabilitation of Specific Injuries

Ligaments. The ligaments of the knee lie both within and outside the joint capsule. They are at least as important as the bony configuration in controlling normal motion. In addition, ligaments provide the knee joint's principal support. Ligament damage is perhaps the most serious type of knee injury. An understanding of the biomechanics of ligaments is mandatory to understanding the mechanism of knee injuries and initiating the proper rehabilitation procedures.

The anterior and posterior cruciate ligaments give the joint rotary and anterior-posterior stability (Figure 21-4, p. 354). As the name implies, the cruciate ligaments "cross" each other. Injury to these structures is perhaps the most disabling ligamentous injury.

The anterior cruciate ligament (ACL) is surrounded by a synovial sheath but is included in the joint capsule. It attaches anteriorly on the tibia and runs obliquely posteriorly to attach at the articular margin of the posterior aspect of the lateral femoral condyle in the intercondylar notch. ACL instability is characterized by excessive rotation of the knee joint and progressive degeneration of the articular surfaces. The deficient anterior cruciate is more incompetent following loss of the medial meniscus because the meniscus gives the joint secondary support. The posterior cruciate ligament (PCL) arises from the posterior aspect of the tibia outside the capsule and runs obliquely and anteriorly, inserting on the medial femoral condyle in the intercondylar notch.

Both the ACL and PCL are subdivided into bundles that tend to keep each ligament tight throughout the knee's ROM. However, the ACL as a whole is tightest in extension and the PCL is tightest in flexion. Therefore, hyperextension stresses the ACL before the PCL. The ACL can rupture when it is subjected to hyperextension with external or internal rotation of the femur on a fixed tibia. The PCL is at risk when the knee receives a blow to

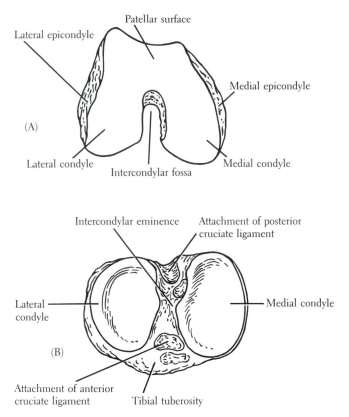

Figure 21-2 (A) Distal end of the right femur and (B) proximal end of the right tibia.

its anterior aspect with the joint flexed (a time when the PCL is tightest), driving the tibia posteriorly.

The medial and lateral collateral ligaments give the knee medial-lateral and external rotational support. The ligaments tighten as the tibia externally rotates. The medial collateral ligament (MCL) is divided into the deep capsular and superficial portions. The MCL runs in a posterior to anterior direction.

The lateral collateral ligament (LCL) is not a capsular structure; it is a completely separate, well-defined, ropelike ligament extending from the posterior one-third of the lateral femoral condyle down to the fibular head. The LCL runs in an anterior to posterior direction.

The arcuate ligament complex is composed of the arcuate ligament and

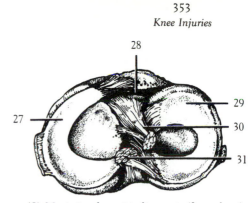

(C) Menisci and cruciate ligaments (from above)

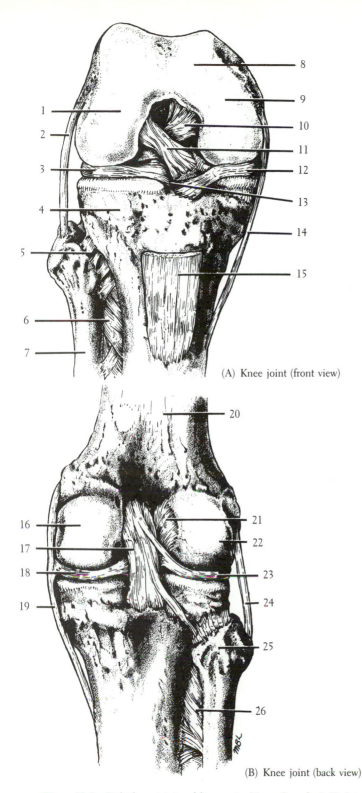

(A) Knee joint (front view)

(B) Knee joint (back view)

1. Lateral condyle of the femur
2. Fibular collateral ligament
3. Lateral meniscus
4. Head of tibia
5. Tibiofibular articulation
6. Interosseous membrane
7. Fibula
8. Patellar surface
9. Medial condyle of the femur
10. Posterior cruciate ligament
11. Anterior cruciate ligament
12. Medial meniscus
13. Transverse ligament
14. Tibial collateral ligament
15. Patellar ligament
16. Medial condyle of femur
17. Posterior cruciate ligament
18. Medial meniscus
19. Tibial collateral ligament
20. Femur
21. Anterior cruciate ligament
22. Lateral condyle of femur
23. Lateral meniscus
24. Fibular collateral ligament
25. Head of fibula
26. Interosseous membrane
27. Medial meniscus
28. Transverse ligament
29. Lateral meniscus
30. Anterior cruciate ligament
31. Posterior cruciate ligament

Figure 21-3 Right knee joint and ligaments. (From Crouch, J. E. *Introduction to Human Anatomy*, 6th ed. Palo Alto, Calif.: Mayfield Publishing Co., p. 72.)

Prevention, Treatment, and Rehabilitation of Specific Injuries

ligaments of Humphrey and Wrisberg and is located in the knee's posterolateral aspect. These ligaments give excellent support to the knee's posterolateral aspect and tighten as the tibia internally rotates on the femur. The drawer test, which measures anterior-posterior instability, can render a false-negative result in an unstable knee due to the support the arcuate ligament complex provides.

Menisci. There are two semilunar-shaped cartilages (menisci) in the knee (Figure 21-5). Their three main functions are to (1) help stabilize the joint (assisting the ligaments); (2) cushion the joint on weight bearing, distributing the forces more evenly around the curved, nonarticulating joint surfaces and smoothing out the otherwise incongruous tibiofemoral joint, and (3) lubricate joint surfaces. The medial meniscus is half-moon-shaped; the lateral meniscus is closer to a complete circle in shape. Both menisci are peripherally attached to the capsule by a coronary ligament and divided into a superior and inferior or a femoral and tibial surface (Figure 21-2, p. 352). The superior surface is concave and comes in contact with femoral condyles; the inferior surface is flat and lies against the tibial condyles.

The menisci's loose attachment allows them to move during flexion, extension, and rotation (note that the medial meniscus is more stationary than the lateral meniscus). Upon flexion, the menisci are only partially in contact with the condyles; this "position of function" makes them more susceptible to injury. During axial rotation, the menisci follow femoral condyle displacement, moving in an opposite direction to the tibial condyle. During external rotation of the tibia, the lateral meniscus remains anteriorly with the lateral femoral condyle and the medial meniscus moves posteriorly in relation to the medial tibial plateau. Conversely, upon internal rotation of the tibia, the medial meniscus stays with the medial femoral condyle and re-

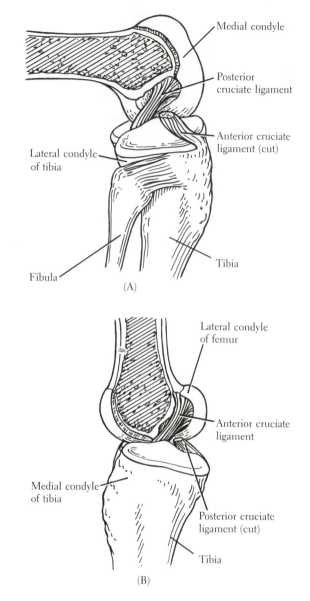

Figure 21-4 The anterior and posterior cruciate ligaments with the knee in (A) flexion and (B) extension.

mains anterior to the tibial plateau, and the lateral meniscus stays with the lateral femoral condyle and moves posterior to the lateral tibial plateau. If there is a sudden movement that does not let the menisci follow these normal relationships, the menisci can be caught between the femur and tibia and torn.

The Patellofemoral Joint

The **patellofemoral joint** plays a significant role in the pathomechanics of the knee, to the great consternation of athletes and their medical providers. The femoral articular surface is divided into the anterior patellofemoral and posterior tibiofemoral surfaces (Figure 21-6). The patella sits in the trochlear notch during flexion of the knee and is guided by the contour of this notch. The patella is a **sesamoid bone** superiorly attached to the quadriceps tendon and inferiorly attached to the patellar ligament. It acts as a changing fulcrum during flexion, maximizing the mechanical advantage throughout the range of motion. The loss of the patella or disruption of its function adversely affects the strength of the quadriceps; the loss causes a 20 to 30 percent decrease.

Variations in skeletal mechanical alignment can cause patellofemoral and other lower extremity injuries. The lower limb's longitudinal mechanical axis is measured from the center of the femoral head at the hip joint through the middle of the femoral condyles to the center of the ankle joint. In most people this axis forms a three-degree oblique angle from vertical (called degrees of valgus) because the hips are wider than the ankles. Extreme exaggeration of this angle is called **genu valgum** (knock-kneed); the reverse condition (an acute angle of the hips, knees, and ankles) is called **genu varum** (bowlegged).

The degree of **valgus** is greater in women than men because their pelvises are broader. The longitudinal axis is similar between the sexes before puberty. The widening of the pelvis in females during puberty accounts for many of the patellofemoral problems that develop in adolescent girls.

The patellar ligament attaches to the tibial tubercle. The position of the tubercle on the tibia's frontal plane determines the direction of pull on the pa-

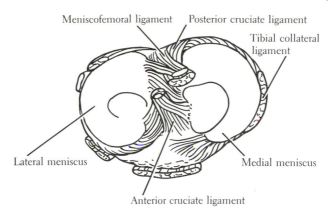

Figure 21-5   The proximal surface of the right tibia with menisci and cruciate ligaments.

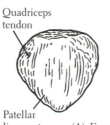

(A) Front surface

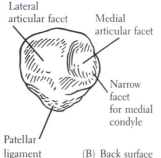

(B) Back surface

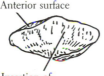

(C) Side view

Figure 21-6   The left patella.

Patellofemoral joint: A joint formed by the femur and patella.

Sesamoid bone: A bone within a tendon. Sesamoid bones are located within the patellar tendon (patella) and within the tendon of the flexor hallucis brevis.

Genu valgum (knock-kneed): When the angle formed by the hips, knee, and ankle exceeds three degrees.

Genu varum (bowlegged): When the angle formed by the hips, knees, and ankles is acute.

Valgus: Deviating away from the midline.

Prevention, Treatment, and Rehabilitation of Specific Injuries

tella during flexion and extension. The bias of patellar tendon attachment is called the **Q angle** and is the deflection of the long axis of the femur with an imaginary line drawn between the tibial tubercle and central portion of the patellar tendon (Figure 21-7). A Q angle greater than twenty degrees is considered abnormal.

An abnormally large Q angle increases the risk of patellar **subluxation** and complete dislocation. The patella tends to be displaced laterally as the tibia externally rotates and the quadriceps muscles tighten. If valgus stress (lateral) is placed on the knee at the same time, there is even further tendency for the patella to dislocate over the lateral femoral condyle. Women experience more lateral patellar subluxation and dislocation than men because of their broader hips and greater degree of valgus. Medial patellar dislocation is extremely rare because of the direction of pull of the quadriceps muscles and the limited amount of the tibia's internal rotation.

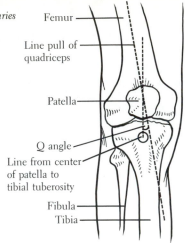

Figure 21-7 The Q angle.

Q angle: The angle between a line formed by the tibial tubercle and the center of the patella and a line formed by the anterior superior iliac spine and the center of the patella.

Subluxation: Partial joint dislocation.

Muscles

Three major muscle groups control and support the knee joint: quadriceps, hamstrings, and gastrocnemius (Figure 21-8, pp. 358–359). The quadriceps consist of four muscles—vastus medialis, vastus intermedius, vastus lateralis, and rectus femoris—inserted by a common tendon into the patella's superior pole. The quadriceps are not required to stabilize the knee at full extension, but they must contract with the slightest degree of flexion as the center of gravity shifts behind the knee's vertical axis. These muscles supplement the posterior cruciate ligament in preventing posterior displacement of the tibia and are extremely important in the rehabilitation of posterior cruciate-deficient knees.

All four quadriceps muscles extend the knee; the rectus femoris also flexes

the hip. Following knee injuries and corrective surgery, when flexion-extension exercises may be contraindicated, hip flexion exercises can, to a certain extent, prevent **atrophy** of the quadriceps. The gluteus maximus is **synergistic** to the rectus femoris and should not be neglected during rehabilitation.

The hamstrings consist of the semimembranosus, semitendinosus, and biceps femoris and are knee flexors and hip extensors. The hamstrings' function as hip flexors is why they are less susceptible to disuse atrophy following injury than the knee extensors: They continue to work even when knee flexion is impossible. Other knee flexors are the popliteus, sartorius, gastrocnemius, and gracilus. The tensor fasciae latae, a weak hip abductor and tibial external rotator, is involved in the screw home mechanism.

Strength balances among the muscles controlling the knee are important prognosticators of **pathology** and the risk of injury. The quadriceps-hamstring strength ratio is typically 3:2. Decrements in quadriceps strength may indicate patellar pathology; deficiency in hamstring strength may indicate an increased risk of injury in those muscles. A balanced action of the three vasti muscles is important in controlling patellar displacement. Typically, in an individual predisposed to patellar dislo-

Atrophy: Decrease in size and function of a muscle.
Synergists: Muscles that assist prime movers.

Pathology: The nature, cause, development, and consequences of disease or injury.

cation, the vastus medialis (especially the oblique portion) is underdeveloped or congenitally hypoplastic. This problem often must be surgically corrected by releasing the tethering effect of the vastus lateralis.

Rheology of the Knee Joint

Rheology is the study of the flow of liquids. In the context of this chapter, rheology refers to lubrication of the knee joint and its effect upon movement and tissue nutrition (see Chapter 7). The knee joint receives lubrication and much of its nutrition from the synovial membrane and the bursae. Proper lubrication requires motion, a fluid of normal composition and viscosity, and a wedge-shaped environment to propagate the lubricant. The knee fulfills all three criteria.

Deviations from the ideal lubrication milieu lead to potential articular surface damage. Since the hyaline cartilage has little regenerative power, significant damage is permanent. Increased understanding of joint rheology has changed many traditional orthopedic procedures. For example, total removal of the menisci is now avoided because of the menisci's effects upon stabilization and their role in lubrication.

Joint immobilization prevents contact of articular surfaces, which causes local malnutrition and degeneration. This fact illustrates the importance of maintaining joint range of motion; even a short period in a cast changes the articular chondrocytes and makes them more susceptible to further injury. A normal patellofemoral joint immobilized in a long cast tends to be inadequately lubricated. Overly vigorous therapy can permanently damage the articular surface if rehabilitation begins before adequate nourishment and lubrication of the joint surface have been reestablished.

Effusion (swelling) of the knee causes a reflex inhibition of the quadriceps due to the action of the **Golgi tendon apparatus.** It is nearly impossible to fully rehabilitate the quadriceps until the effusion in the knee has subsided. For this reason, a person with swelling in the knee should not be encouraged to participate in strenuous activities. Strong muscles not only support the menisci and ligaments but protect the articular surfaces.

Knee Injuries

As mentioned at the beginning of the chapter, the knee is the most frequently injured body structure in sports. Injuries to the knee include fractures, sprains, strains, osteochondrosis, tendinitis, patellofemoral tracking disorders, dislocation, and meniscal tears.

Fractures

Knee fractures can be both extraarticular and intra-articular; the latter type involves cartilage of both bone and joint surfaces. The intra-articular fracture extends into the knee joint and causes tremendous hemarthrosis from bleeding within the bone. This fracture always causes disruption of the smooth joint surface, even with perfect reduction.

A chondral fracture is intra-articular and involves only the articular surface; an osteochondral fracture involves both bone and cartilage. These fractures can create loose bodies that can cause the knee to lock, catch, or give way. These loose bodies may not be detected or their size may be grossly underestimated because articular surface and meniscal cartilages are not visible on x-rays. These loose fragments are frequently palpated by the injured person and can be moved around in the knee.

Extra-articular fractures about the knee involve the femur, tibia, or fibular

Effusion: Swelling.

Golgi tendon apparatus: Receptors within skeletal muscle that sense and inhibit tension.

Rheology: Study of the flow of fluids and semisolids.

358

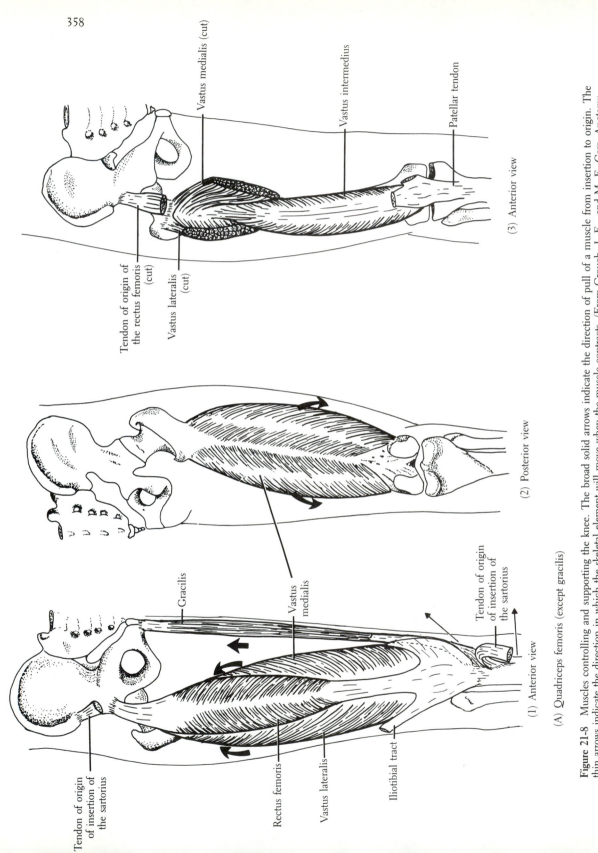

Figure 21-8 Muscles controlling and supporting the knee. The broad solid arrows indicate the direction of pull of a muscle from insertion to origin. The thin arrows indicate the direction in which the skeletal element will move when the muscle contracts. (From Crouch, J. E., and M. E. Carr. *Anatomy and Physiology*. Palo Alto, Calif.: Mayfield Publishing Co., 1977, pp. 110, 111, 114.)

Vastus medialis (cut)

Vastus intermedius

Patellar tendon

Tendon of origin of the rectus femoris (cut)

Vastus lateralis (cut)

(3) Anterior view

(2) Posterior view

Gracilis

Vastus medialis

Tendon of origin of insertion of the sartorius

(1) Anterior view

(A) Quadriceps femoris (except gracilis)

Tendon of origin of insertion of the sartorius

Rectus femoris

Vastus lateralis

Iliotibial tract

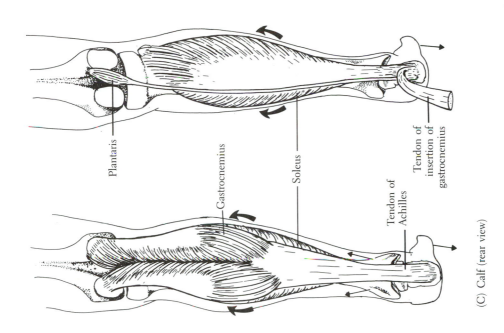

Plantaris

Gastrocnemius

Soleus

Tendon of insertion of gastrocnemius

Tendon of Achilles

(C) Calf (rear view)

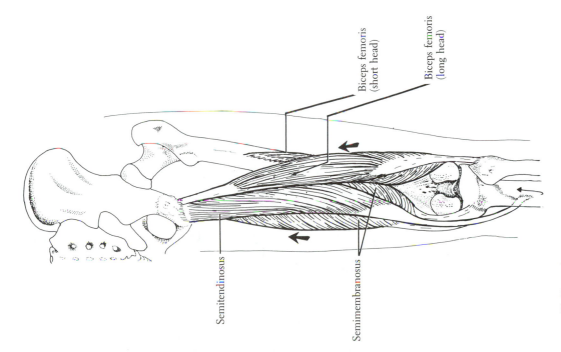

Biceps femoris (short head)

Biceps femoris (long head)

Semitendinosus

Semimembranosus

(B) Hamstrings

Figure 21-8 *(continued)*

head. Any angulation, rotation, or depressed deformity in the tibiofemoral joint has to be corrected if normal biomechanical function is to be restored. The necessity for early motion of the joint to maintain the integrity of the articular surface and prevent the formation of adhesions complicates the treatment of these injuries. Fortunately, serious fractures about the knee are uncommon in athletes.

Avulsion Fractures. Avulsion fracture is a tearing away of a skeletal structure. A typical example is the lateral tibial plateau avulsion fracture, caused by excessive stress upon the lateral capsule when the femur is externally rotated on the fixed tibia. This injury also puts stress upon the anterior cruciate ligament, causing a high incidence of ACL failure. Patellar dislocation can also cause an avulsion fracture of the patella (called a medial marginal fracture).

Stress Fractures. Stress fractures are known to occur in the patella, but they are more common in the proximal fibular shaft. They rarely occur in the proximal tibia and the distal femur. It is difficult to diagnose a stress fracture because usually it is not apparent on x-ray until some bone about the fracture line has been resorbed, which can take two or more weeks. Bone scans can facilitate early diagnosis.

Epiphyseal Fracture. The **epiphyses** are the bone-growth centers and a weak link in the skeletal structure of developing children. Always consider epiphyseal fractures following injuries about the knee in adolescents, particularly if the injuries exhibit varus or valgus stress. These injuries often do not appear on an x-ray unless the epiphysis is placed under stress during filming. A child who has tenderness at or above the femoral attachment of the collateral ligaments should be considered as having an epiphyseal injury until proven otherwise. If an epiphyseal fracture is

recognized and properly immobilized, prognosis is excellent.

Ligament Injuries

In a first degree knee sprain, swelling is minimal, but palpation generally causes tenderness. The athlete can usually return to activities demanding twisting, jumping, and running within three weeks, but the knee should be supported with a brace or tape for the remainder of the season.

A second degree knee sprain is accompanied by significant swelling, tenderness, loss of function, and usually some instability. Proper management is very important to prevent the remaining fibers from tearing and includes early diagnosis, rest, and immobilization to prevent additional stress. This injury usually requires a minimum of six weeks to heal, and the athlete is usually out for the season.

In third degree knee sprain there is complete disruption of the ligament, with a marked loss of function, gross instability, pain, and tenderness. These injuries require surgical repair within the first week (no later than two weeks) because ligaments rapidly atrophy and are resorbed, at which time it is impossible to restore their normal attachments.

Establishing the mechanism of injury can help determine which structure was damaged. For example, rotary instabilities are typically caused by the application of torque about a fixed leg or foot. In downhill skiing, the ski sometimes continues in a constant direction or becomes embedded in deep snow while the thigh rotates on a fixed tibia (Figure 21-9). Cleats or spikes sometimes fix the lower limb while the body excessively rotates in one direction or the other. Wrestling injuries often involve a fixed upper body and an excessively rotated lower extremity, caused by an opponent's grasping and twisting. One part of the lever arm has to be fixed in all significant ligament injuries of the

Epiphysis: The end of a long bone. During growth it is separated from the shaft by a cartilaginous growth plate.

knee. Instabilities are straight, rotational, or a combination of straight and rotational.

Straight Instabilities. Straight anterior instability is indicated by excessive motion of the tibia anteriorly on the femur and is caused by ACL injury. Straight posterior displacement of the tibia on the femur indicates PCL deficiency. Valgus (abduction) instability is due to a tear of the medial collateral ligament; **varus** (adduction) instability is due to a tear of the lateral collateral ligament. Straight instabilities are rarely associated with rotational forces and usually occur with the knee in full extension. Isolated medial or lateral collateral ligament injury can be caused by blows to an extended leg during blocking or tackling in football or by sliding into an extended knee in baseball.

Straight hyperextension of the knee is common in soccer, football, skiing, wrestling, and judo. Typically, the posterior capsule and anterior cruciate are sprained. The posterior cruciate is the last structure torn in hyperextension. At that point, the knee is essentially dislocated, which is a very serious injury.

Straight posterior instability of the knee indicates posterior cruciate injury and is usually caused by a blow against the tibial tubercle when the knee is flexed ninety degrees. Typically, the athlete falls on the knee, landing with all the weight on the tibial tubercle and driving the tibia posteriorly. The ankle is usually plantar flexed; otherwise, the forces are directed onto the patella, causing problems there instead.

Rotational Instabilities. Rotational forces are usually involved in ligament injuries sustained in athletics. As discussed, the knee is most functional when flexed, but then it is considerably less stable than when fully extended. The foot is usually fixed, with the forces applied directly by a blow to the knee or indirectly by the body twisting. Rotary instabilities are named according

Figure 21-9 Mechanism of skiing injury resulting in rotary instability. Left ski continues in a constant direction while right thigh rotates on a fixed tibia.

to the direction that the tibia rotates on the femur. In posterolateral instability, the lateral tibial plateau rotates excessively posteriorly. In anteromedial rotary instability, the medial tibial plateau rotates excessively anteriorly. In anterolateral rotary instability, the lateral tibial plateau rotates excessively anteriorly. The two most common rotary instabilities are anterolateral and anteromedial.

One of the most common causes of ACL sprain is hyperextension of the knee with external rotation of the femur on the fixed tibia. Another mechanism of ACL tearing is the application of valgus stress against a flexed knee with excessive internal rotation of the femur on a fixed tibia. This mechanism is always associated with the tearing of other structures, mainly the medial collateral ligament and posterior medial one-third capsular ligament. It is also thought to be responsible for the **unhappy triad,** which is a tear of the ACL, MCL, and medial meniscus (Figure 21-10, p. 362). This injury is particularly common in football and stems from blocking and tackling into the lateral aspect of the knee. The medial

Varus: Deviating toward the midline.

Unhappy triad: A tear of the anterior cruciate ligament, medial collateral ligament, and medial meniscus.

Prevention, Treatment, and Rehabilitation of Specific Injuries

side of the knee presents a higher risk of ligament injury because it is more vulnerable (blows to the lateral knee tend to cause medial ligament injuries) and lacks the strong iliotibial band of the lateral side.

In most cases, an individual with an anterior cruciate-deficient knee who initially has minimal instability later develops rotary instabilities. The secondary restraints stretch out as they perform functions for which they were not designed (preventing rotation). ACL damage must be quickly diagnosed and treated to prevent damage to the articular surface and menisci. Approximately 70 percent of all ACL injuries are accompanied by meniscal injury.

Athletes with anterior cruciate injuries should wear derotation braces (e.g., Lennox Hill or Can-Am) that have a hyperextension stop (Figure 21-11). However, with acute injury, immobilization in a hinge brace that restricts motion is standard care before functional bracing is indicated. A hinge brace allows early mobilization, prevents disuse atrophy, facilitates the use of electrical muscle stimulation, and permits normal nourishment of the articular surface.

Varus stresses associated with rotation of the knee injure the lateral collateral ligament as well as the posterolateral aspect of the knee. There is some associated hyperextension and internal rotation of the femur on a fixed tibia. The injury usually includes the popliteus, arcuate ligament complex, and often the lateral head of the gastrocnemius and the insertion of the biceps femoris on the fibular head. The PCL can also be torn if the forces are great enough, leading to posterolateral rotary instability.

Strains

The significant strains about the knee involve the quadriceps unit, mainly the quadriceps tendon and patellar ligament (tendon), the three hamstring tendons,

Figure 21-10 Mechanism of the unhappy triad. The player is struck on the side of the knee, causing valgus stress against a flexed knee and fixed tibia.

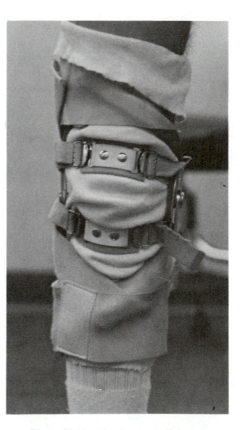

Figure 21-11 The Lennox-Hill derotation brace. Proper fit, essential in active athletes, may be achieved only through a series of adjustments.

the popliteus tendon, the two heads of the gastrocnemius, and the iliotibial tract. Strains are often more painful than sprains and can be quite disabling.

Strains commonly occur when abnormal body mechanics and excessive forces overcome the musculotendinous unit. Strains of the distal hamstrings are most common and frequently occur from strength imbalances between the quadriceps and hamstrings and between the muscles of the left and right legs. These imbalances should be assessed during the preparticipation physical examination.

Osteochondrosis. Osteochondrosis is an inflammation of the developing bone and typically occurs at the bone-tendon or bone-cartilage interface. **Osgood-Schlatter** (OS) (Figure 21-12) and Sinding-Larsen-Johansson (SLJ) diseases are two types of osteochondrosis in the knee. OS occurs during adolescence and is caused by excessive stress on and disruption of the attachment of the tibiopatellar tendon (ligament). It is more common in males than females and usually follows a rapid growth period in which the length of the bone exceeds the tendon's ability to lengthen. The tendon pulls on its apophyseal attachment where it stimulates the development of excessive bone and, in some cases, prevents the entire apophysis from fusing with the underlying bone at maturation. A small piece of bone may remain in the patellar tendon if any ossicle of bone fails to unite. This bone may become a source of patellar tendinitis, especially upon squatting or kneeling, and may have to be removed when growth has stopped.

SLJ disease is similar to OS and occurs when the origin of the patellar ligament (tendon) at the inferior pole of the patella is stressed. These stresses can prevent the patellar ossification centers from uniting and cause pain and inflammation. Occasionally, as in OS, a residual ossicle of bone can be

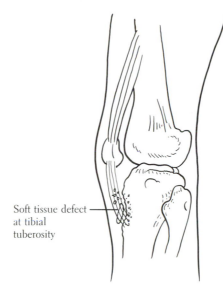

Figure 21-12 Osgood-Schlatter disease is a soft tissue defect at the tibial tuberosity.

embedded in the patellar tendon and create further irritation.

Tendinitis. Patellar tendinitis (PT) is extremely common and tends to occur in athletes who overuse the quadriceps and are involved in high-intensity activities like jumping, shot put, weight lifting, discus throwing, football, and basketball. Chronic PT is difficult to cure and is usually complicated by athletes who refuse to rest enough to let the injury heal. Treatment sometimes includes braces to take the strain off the quadriceps mechanism and surgery to excise scar tissue or degenerative tendon tissue.

Tendinitis (in the knee or any other joint) can be prevented by developing adequate strength and flexibility in the musculotendinous unit. Quadriceps stretching is often overlooked in the training program. Check the ability of anyone with a problem in the patellofemoral joint, quadriceps, or patellar tendon to bring their heel to their buttocks. Correct deficiencies through a passive stretching program.

Popliteus tendinitis commonly results from downhill running or hiking and

Osteochondrosis: Inflammation of bone and its cartilage, typically associated with avascular necrosis.
Osgood-Schlatter disease: Excessive stress and disruption of the attachment of the tibial patellar tendon, usually accompanied by a painful bump over the tibial tubercle.

usually occurs bilaterally in the knee's posterolateral aspect. The popliteus is under strain in extension and acts as a deaccelerator, preventing sudden extension-hyperextension of the knee.

Iliotibial tract inflammation and bursitis are common in runners and result from excessive internal rotation of the tibia on the femur. This excessive motion frequently can be reduced by wearing proper running shoes and inserting an orthotic device into the shoe(s). A pronated foot or a heel in a calcaneovalgus position allows more internal rotation of the tibia on the femur, placing a strain on the iliotibial tract. This can also strain the biceps tendon that is resisting this internal rotation or strain the patellar tendon and patellofemoral joint.

Patellofemoral Disorders

Patellofemoral (PF) disorders can be subdivided into congenital and traumatic. Congenital disorders include patellar hypoplasia (underdevelopment), trochlear notch hypoplasia, vastus medialis obliquus hypoplasia, genu valgum, patella alta (high-riding patella), and miserable malalignment syndrome. Traumatic injuries include acute dislocations, acute or chronic subluxations, chondral fractures, patellar fractures with intra-articular involvement, and femoral condylar fractures with intra-articular involvement.

Miserable Malalignment Syndrome (MMS). MMS is caused by congenital and developmental abnormalities and consists of femoral neck anteversion (forward displacement), external tibial torsion, and pronated feet; the syndrome presents the appearance of squinting patellae and knock-knees. MMS places excessive stresses on the patellofemoral joint, causing chronic inflammation and even chondrosis of the patellofemoral articular surfaces. People with MMS should not participate in jogging or distance running.

Chondrosis. Chondrosis is disease of the articular cartilage, often caused by congenital disorders. Chondromalacia is the early (stage 1) form of this disease in the patellofemoral joint; it is softening of the cartilage. Stage 1 is not necessarily symptomatic. It is incorrect to classify all patellofemoral joint symptoms as chondromalacia because this is but one stage of the degenerative process. In stage 2, the columns of hyaline cartilage cells split, resulting in articular surface incongruities that look like peach fuzz or a shag rug. Further progression into stage 3 leads to deeper fissures and splitting in the larger portions of the cartilage, sometimes with flaps of full-thickness cartilage forming. These flaps can break off into loose chondral fragments that can catch or lock the knee. In stage 4, the subchondral bone is significantly exposed; this represents permanent damage and the probable formation of traumatic arthritis.

Crepitation (grinding and grating) accompanies all stages of chondrosis. It is often difficult to descend stairs because of the increased compression on the patellofemoral joint; ascending stairs is better tolerated. Initially, the pain may manifest itself in the subpatellar area from excessive pressure of the patella on the underlying trochlear notch. The increased sensitivity is usually due to the presence of chondromalacia or more severe chondrosis. The "theater sign" pain experienced when sitting with a bent knee for a prolonged period (as in a theater) is typical in people with chondrosis in the patellofemoral joint. Subpatellar pain is such an enigma that an accepted diagnosis is "peripatellar pain," implying no known reason for it.

Initial treatment involves strengthening the vastus medialis, which can help align a laterally sliding patella, and stretching the quadriceps and hamstrings to take the tension off the patellofemoral joint (Figure 21-13). Sometimes splints with pads to control patellar motion can help, but they should not impose excessive downward pressure against the joint. Correcting improper foot posture with orthotics may be helpful. Surgical intervention, although not a cure-all, may be necessary if more conservative approaches fail.

Significant chondrosis of the patellofemoral joint is a poor prognosis for return to high-level competition. This is a very common problem that prevents many young gymnasts and dancers from achieving their career goals. The athletic trainer can certainly help ease the blow when it is necessary for a young athlete (usually female) to be excluded from the activity.

Subluxation and Dislocation. These two types of injuries are particularly traumatic when not caused by congenital factors. Any severe valgus stress with internal rotation of the femur on the tibia can dislocate the patella as well as tear the anterior cruciate and medial collateral ligaments. The patella can also dislocate from medially placed forces associated with external rotation of the tibia on the femur. Sudden external rotation of the knee with the foot fixed can dislocate an otherwise normal patella.

Patellar dislocation is often accompanied by hemarthrosis from the patellofemoral ligament tearing, osteochondral fracture, or medial marginal avulsion fracture of the patella. Significant injury can occur during sudden, forceful reduction of the dislocation. Acute dislocations of the patella usually reduce spontaneously, or they can be fairly easily reduced if they are immediately treated.

Recovery time following a lateral parapatellar release for subluxating patella is a minimum of six weeks, closer to three months. The length of time partially depends upon the extent the vastus medialis muscle is developed during rehabilitation. A patellar splint with a horseshoe pad holding the kneecap medially is required when returning to activity.

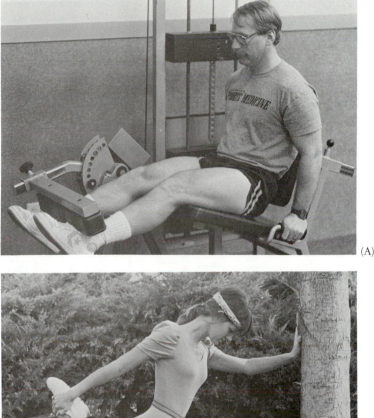

(A)

(B)

Figure 21-13 Most patellofemoral joint problems are thought to be caused by abnormal tracking of the patella. Tracking may be improved in some cases by strengthening the vastus medialis (VM) muscle and increasing the flexibility of the quadriceps and hamstrings.

(A) Restricted range of motion knee extension (last twenty degrees of extension) strengthens the VM while minimizing patellofemoral compression.

(B) Stretching the quadriceps. Grab the instep and attempt to flex your knee and extend your hip until you feel stretch in your quadriceps.

Meniscal Damage

Meniscal tears are relatively common in adults but rare before the teenage years. They tend to occur posteriorly because of the increased stress on the posterior horn of both menisci when the knee is flexed. Rotation of the femur on the tibia produces shearing forces that tear the meniscus. The menisci are more frequently torn without any associated injury, but this injury often accompanies tears to the ACL.

The menisci cannot be seen on an x-ray and are difficult to visualize, even with large arthrotomy incisions made during reconstructive ligament repair. In the past, arthrograms—contrast media that visualize the joint—were used to detect meniscal damage. Today fewer arthrograms are being performed because of the advent of the arthroscopic examination and the increased skill of the arthroscopist.

The menisci have limited blood supply, except at their peripheral attachment, so tears in their substance usually do not heal, and the torn portion has to be excised. There is a trend toward repairing peripheral tears rather than removing the entire structure. Total meniscectomy, especially of the medial meniscus, removes an important secondary knee restraint and hastens the onset of degenerative changes in the knee.

Meniscal injuries frequently can be treated at the end of the season if the person is not markedly disabled. The only exception is the "bucket handle" displaced tear, which locks the knee. Even loose bodies, which occasionally impinge the knee, usually can be tolerated enough to delay surgical intervention until the end of the season. The advent of arthroscopic surgery has hastened recovery from meniscal injury, often allowing the athlete to return to competition in the same season the injury occurred.

Average recovery time following a partial meniscectomy performed arthroscopically is four to six weeks. Although most meniscal procedures are performed on an outpatient basis, and frequently with local anesthetic, there is still enough surgical trauma and swelling to prevent the athlete's high-intensity training for a month. During this period, stationary cycling, swimming, and weight training can be practiced as tolerated. Recovery may be prolonged if this injury is accompanied by articular cartilage damage (the knee may never be totally asymptomatic).

Synovial Plica Syndrome

Synovial plica syndrome (SPS) is frequently confused with medial meniscus injury. The synovial plica is a rudimentary fold of the synovial wall that extends from the anterior fat pad along the medial wall and is present in most people (see Chapter 7). SPS can become symptomatic if it hypertrophies or is congenitally excessive. A fall or blow that affects the knee's anteromedial aspect can lead to hypertrophic changes and scar the otherwise pliable and thin synovial plica. This in turn can lead to patellar chondrosis as well as symptoms that resemble medial meniscal tears, such as clicking with pain, catching, and sudden instability. Diagnosis is frequently made during arthroscopic surgery, but it sometimes can be made by palpating the fibrous band extending from the patellar tendon region to the medial femoral condyle above the joint line, thereby differentiating it from meniscal injury. Arthroscopically excising a symptomatic medial plica synovialis is usually satisfactory.

Inflammatory Processes of the Knee

Arthritis is inflammation of a joint and can be caused by trauma, infection, degeneration, metabolic abnormality, and rheumatoid or other collagen disorder. This discussion is limited to those conditions commonly observed in athletes.

Effusion. Significant inflammation of the knee is usually accompanied by effusion (swelling) from reactive synovial fluid. Spontaneous effusion without any history of trauma frequently responds to appropriate rest and does not need immediate aspiration. However, recurrent effusions require that the knee be aspirated to determine the cause if not known. With acute trauma it is important to aspirate the knee to relieve pressure created by bloody fluid. The proper treatment is immobilization of the knee, to prevent further bleeding.

Effusion places the knee at increased risk during vigorous activity because the quadriceps lose approximately 10 to 20 percent of their strength from reflex inhibition. This does not mean that every knee with swelling needs to be repeatedly aspirated. In fact, repeated aspirations of the knee should be avoided because of the increased chance of infection. Ice often very effectively controls chronic effusion.

Bursitis. Bursitis is swelling and inflammation of the bursae. The prepatellar bursa is commonly traumatized by blows or injury to the kneecap's anterior aspect. Chronic kneeling, as occurs in surfing, wrestling, or certain occupations, can cause chronic prepatellar bursitis (sometimes called "housemaid's knee"). This injury can be prevented with protective padding.

The pes anserinus bursa, located between the pes anserinus tendons and medial collateral ligament, can become irritated from abnormal rotation of the tibia. This type of bursitis is seen more in nonathletes but does occur in dancers. Bursae between the lateral collateral ligament and lateral capsule and between the iliotibial tract and lateral capsule can become irritated in runners and joggers who have abnormal gaits characterized by excessive rotation of the tibia on the femur.

Osteochondritis Dissecans

Osteochondritis dissecans (OD) is a vascular disease distinguished by inadequate blood supply to the subchondral bone (see Chapter 6). The disease causes bone death and, eventually, articular cartilage cracking where the cartilage is not receiving underlying support. The articular cartilage can loosen and break off, creating loose bodies. In the knee, OD most often occurs in the medial femoral condyle and is the most common cause of sudden locking of the knee in teenage boys. Locking is typically preceded by nondescript feelings of discomfort and pain and reactive fluid in the knee following activity. The sudden appearance of a palpable loose body usually precipitates a visit to the physician. OD usually heals with rest without intervention, although this may take one or two years.

Evaluation of Knee Injuries

Injury evaluation involves the history, physical examination, and diagnostic testing. Putting It into Practice 21-1, 21-2, and 21-3 summarize these procedures and their expected outcomes (see p. 368). Chapters 9 and 11 discuss general procedures. This section deals with methods specific to the knee.

History

The first step is to determine the mechanism of injury: How did the injury occur? Establish whether it was an indirect injury (e.g., occurring during twisting or jumping) or a direct injury caused by a direct blow. What was the shoe-surface interface? Did the injury occur on ice or in deep powder snow? Did the bindings release? Were the cleats long or short? Was the turf muddy or tartan? Determine the degree

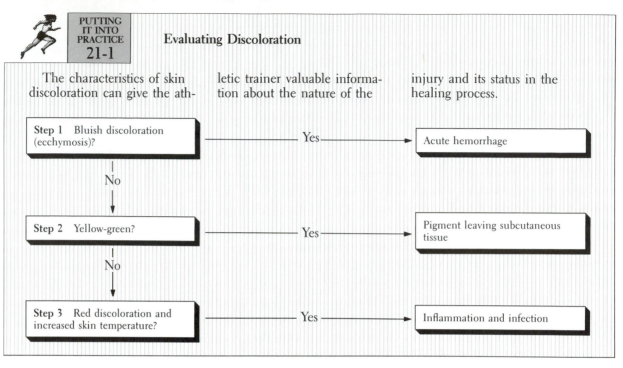

PUTTING IT INTO PRACTICE 21-1

Evaluating Discoloration

The characteristics of skin discoloration can give the ath- letic trainer valuable information about the nature of the injury and its status in the healing process.

Step 1 Bluish discoloration (ecchymosis)? ——— Yes ———→ Acute hemorrhage

No ↓

Step 2 Yellow-green? ——— Yes ———→ Pigment leaving subcutaneous tissue

No ↓

Step 3 Red discoloration and increased skin temperature? ——— Yes ———→ Inflammation and infection

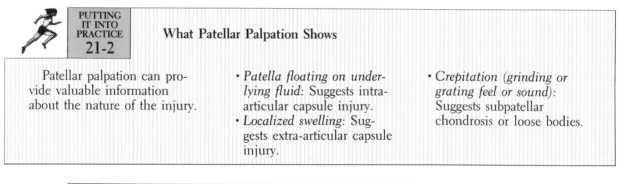

PUTTING IT INTO PRACTICE 21-2

What Patellar Palpation Shows

Patellar palpation can provide valuable information about the nature of the injury.

- *Patella floating on underlying fluid*: Suggests intra-articular capsule injury.
- *Localized swelling*: Suggests extra-articular capsule injury.

- *Crepitation (grinding or grating feel or sound)*: Suggests subpatellar chondrosis or loose bodies.

PUTTING IT INTO PRACTICE 21-3

What Stress Tests Show

Stress tests of the knee can help identify the location of ligament injury. Muscle spasm and involuntary splinting can mask instability. Always compare the injured and uninjured knee to account for normal individual differences in joint laxity.

- *Lachman test*: Positive test indicates anterior cruciate ligament (ACL) tear.
- *Valgus stress test*: Positive test indicates medial collateral ligament (MCL) tear.
- *Varus stress test*: Positive stress test indicates lateral collateral ligament tear.

- *Anterior drawer test*: Positive neutral test—ACL tear; external rotation—MCL tear; internal rotation—tear to iliotibial tract, ACL, and posterior cruciate ligament.
- *Pivot shift test*: Positive test indicates injury to ACL.

of tibial fixation and the direction that the femur moves on it. For example, if the body externally rotated with the knee flexed and the blow came from the outside and was against the knee, forcing it into valgus, the anterior cruciate, and perhaps the medial structures, could be damaged. A direct frontal blow that forces the knee into hyperextension may damage the anterior cruciate and perhaps the posterior cruciate and posterior capsular structures.

Determine the location of pain and its relationship with swelling, both at the time of examination and time of injury. For example, swelling occurs rapidly following ACL injury. A serious ACL injury is less likely if the swelling developed more gradually. Immediate swelling is common in fractures and significant synovial membrane disruptions but more gradual following meniscal injury.

Identify the location of swelling. The anterolateral joint line (lateral to the patellar tendon) is the most common site of intraarticular effusion. Significant swelling requires an intact joint capsule or the fluid will drain out of the knee. Often there is no visible swelling, but the athlete relates a feeling of stiffness upon flexion, an indication that fluid in the knee is compressed.

Establish how the symptoms interfere with performance. Is function affected while the athlete walks up and down stairs or rises from a chair, or does it take fifteen miles of running for function to be affected? The knee locking, catching, giving way, or collapsing are symptoms of irregular joint surface or impingement of tissue between joint surfaces. Locking can result from bucket handle tears of the menisci, spasm, loose bodies, or a dislocated patella. The knee gives way due to a sudden reflex inhibition of the quadriceps in an effort to minimize pain and occurs at a subconscious level. A complete avulsion of the quadriceps mecha-

nism is the only time that the knee truly gives way.

As with other injuries, the history should include level of conditioning, any protective clothing worn, past injuries, and the nature of initial treatment.

Physical Examination

Conduct the physical examination with attention to detail, an air of confidence, and empathy. The athlete is often experiencing a great deal of pain and apprehension, so the examiner should try to place the person at ease. Always examine the opposite (uninjured) knee first, to give the athlete an indication of what to expect. Ideally, the pants, shoes and socks should be removed. Repeated examinations are indicated because a change in status can provide additional information.

Inspection. Look for alignment abnormalities, especially of the patellofemoral joint. Check for genu varum, genu valgum, or recurvatum with the athlete in a standing position. Recurvatum is common in hyperelastic joints but should be present on both sides. A person with an anterior cruciate deficiency will experience a feeling of recurvatum on the involved side.

Alignment abnormalities can play a role in a variety of overuse injuries. Pay attention to the alignment of the entire lower extremity when evaluating these injuries. Note factors such as patellar alignment, foot posture, and symmetry between left and right sides. Evaluate patellofemoral alignment by having the person actively flex and extend the knee and watch the excursion of the patella. A person with a tendency toward lateral subluxation will have a "reverse J sign," which means that the patella suddenly moves diagonally to the lateral side at terminal extension. A Q angle over twenty degrees is significant when associated with other findings.

Bluish discoloration (ecchymosis) occurs from acute hemorrhage; blood from previous bleeding is yellow-green, caused by pigment leaving the subcutaneous tissue. Red discoloration accompanied by increased skin temperature indicates inflammation, especially infection.

Palpation. Determine the nature of injury by locating points of tenderness and increased temperature. Determine if swelling is from intra- or extra-articular fluid. If there is effusion (fluid within the knee), the patella will float on the fluid and can be balloted on the underlying femur, accompanied by a clicking sound. Do this with the knee in extension and the quadriceps relaxed. One hand pushes down and closes off the suprapatellar pouch, forcing the fluid into a smaller volume, making it easier to ballotte the patella. It is impossible to create this sensation of a floating kneecap in a normal knee because there are only one or two milliliters of synovial fluid. Extra-articular swelling is more localized, and there is no ballottement of the patella.

Patellofemoral (PF) compression tests provide information about the integrity of the PF articular surfaces. Watch for signs of discomfort while directly pressing down on the patella (with and without motion). A person with chronic PF incongruity problems will frequently grab your hand and push it away from the patella (positive apprehension test). To determine the degree of roughness of the PF articular surfaces, place your hand over the patella while the athlete is flexing and extending the knee. Often crepitation is not audible but is palpable during this test.

Diagnostic or Stress Tests

A number of tests have been devised to evaluate the stability of specific ligaments and capsular structures. These tests are helpful in making an early diagnosis. Perform these tests on both legs to account for individual differences in joint laxity.

Ligament stability tests can be painful and should be performed carefully. They must be correctly administered the first time because the athlete usually will be extremely apprehensive of further tests because of the pain experienced during the initial examination. First examine the uninjured leg, to familiarize the athlete with the test and reduce apprehension. The athletic trainer's initial evaluation is invaluable because later medical examinations may be hampered by muscle spasm and effusion.

Lachman Test. See Figure 21-14. Of all the ligament laxity procedures, this test produces the least pain and should be performed first. The Lachman test examines the integrity of the anterior cruciate ligament. A slightly positive test indicates torn anteromedial bundles of the ligament; a highly positive test indicates that the entire structure is torn.

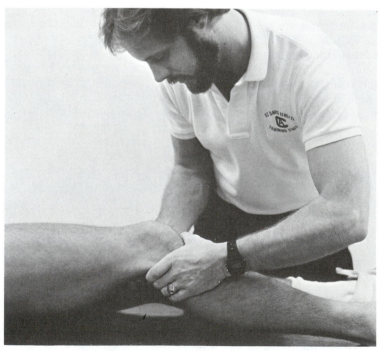

Figure 21-14 The Lachman test measures the integrity of the anterior cruciate ligament. While stabilizing the athlete's femur with one hand, grasp the lower leg (at the tibial tubercle) with your other hand and draw it forward.

Perform the Lachman test with the tibia in neutral rotation. Stabilize the femur by grasping it with one hand just above the suprapatellar pouch and with the other hand at the level of the tibial tubercle. The tibia is then drawn forward as the femur is stabilized. Two people may be required to perform this test if the athlete has large thighs or the examiner has small hands.

Valgus (VAL) and Varus (VAR) Stress Tests. See Figure 21-15. VAL measures medial collateral ligament instability; VAR determines the stability of the lateral collateral ligament. Perform these tests by abducting (VAL) and adducting (VAR) the tibia on the fixed femur with the knee flexed twenty to thirty degrees. Any opening greater than one centimeter compared to the opposite knee is considered significant.

Also perform these tests with the knee in full extension. An opening with VAL stress indicates a posteromedial corner tear and perhaps involvement of the posterior capsule and posterior cruciate ligament. A lateral opening during VAR stress indicates involvement of posterolateral corner structures and the lateral collateral ligament. The posterolateral structures include the popliteus tendon, arcuate ligament complex, and possibly the posterior cruciate ligament. The lateral head of the gastrocnemius and biceps tendon may also be involved.

External Rotation Recurvatum Test. See Figure 21-16. This test measures posterolateral rotary instability. With the athlete's knee fully extended, grasp the foot with one hand and the tibia at the tibial tubercle with your other hand and externally rotate and hyperextend the tibia on the femur. Improved stability when internally rotating this same knee indicates that the ligaments of Humphrey and Wrisberg are still intact.

Anterior Drawer Tests (ADT). See Figure 21-17 (p. 372). Have the ath-

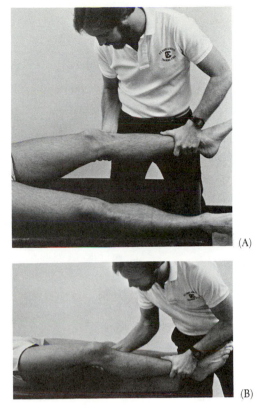

(A)

(B)

Figure 21-15   Valgus and varus stress tests.
(A)   The valgus stress test measures the integrity of the medial collateral ligament. With the athlete's leg slightly flexed, grab the lower leg or foot with one hand and apply lateral stress to the knee with your other hand.
(B)   The varus stress test measures the integrity of the lateral collateral ligament. With the athlete's leg slightly flexed, grab the lower leg or foot with one hand and apply medial stress to the knee with your other hand.

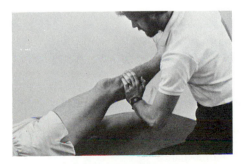

Figure 21-16   The external rotation recurvatum test. With the athlete's knee extended, grasp the foot with one hand and the tibia (at the tubercle) with your other hand and externally rotate and hyperextend the tibia on the femur.

lete's knee flexed seventy to ninety degrees, the foot fixed, and the hamstrings relaxed. The tibia is pulled forward on the femur with the tibia placed in neutral, internal, and external rotation.

Laxity during the straight (neutral) ADT indicates injury to the anterior cruciate ligament; laxity during external rotation implies medial collateral ligament injury, with perhaps some anterior cruciate ligament involvement. Instability during the internal rotation ADT may indicate disruption of the iliotibial tract, anterior and posterior cruciate ligaments, and posterolateral corner structures.

Pivot Shift Test. See Figure 21-18. This test is positive when the lateral tibial plateau subluxes anteriorly on the femur in extension and, as the knee is flexed, it snaps back into the reduced position, causing a shifting sensation (called a "jerk"). The pivot shift test measures anterior cruciate stability. This examination is not easily tolerated following an acute injury.

Posterior Drawer Test. See Figure 21-19. This test is similar to the anterior drawer test except that the tibia is pushed posteriorly instead of anteriorly. This test measures posterior cruciate ligament stability.

Drop Back Sign. This test is basically a passive posterior drawer test. Have the athlete's knee bent ninety degrees, with the foot held by the heel. This test is positive if there is posterior motion of the tibia on the femur (the knee sags). Repeat this test with the knee in full extension to determine if there is any recurvatum. Passive recurvatum exhibited while the athlete's heel is held and the knee is allowed to sag backward or while the athlete is standing and the knee is forced backward indicates posterior cruciate deficiency. A feeling that the knee wants to go into hyperextension is frequently associated with anterior cruciate ligament injury.

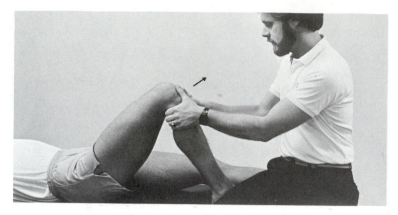

Figure 21-17 Anterior drawer tests. With the athlete's knee flexed seventy to ninety degrees, foot fixed, and hamstrings relaxed, pull the tibia forward on the femur. This test should be performed with the tibia in neutral, internal, and external rotation.

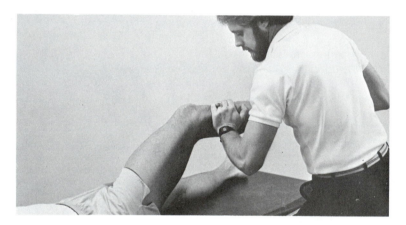

Figure 21-18 The pivot shift test. With the athlete's knee slightly flexed, apply lateral and anterior stress to the knee.

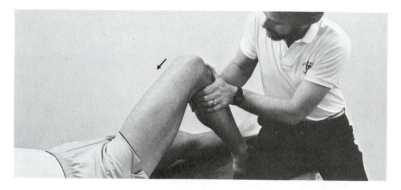

Figure 21-19 Posterior drawer test. With the athlete's knee flexed, foot fixed, and hamstrings relaxed, apply posterior pressure to the upper tibia.

Patellar Laxity. Have the knee fully extended and flexed forty-five to fifty degrees. Place lateral forces on the medial side of the patella. The test is positive if the patella tends to dislocate.

Menisci Tests. The McMurray test (MT) and Apley compression and distraction test (AT) measure meniscal injury. During the MT, grasp the tibia and internally and externally rotate it as the athlete brings the knee from full flexion into extension (Figure 21-20). A clunk, thud, or click (with or without pain) suggests meniscal injury. For the AT, the athlete lies prone and bends the knee ninety degrees. Lift the bent knee up by the foot and internally and externally rotate it to distract the knee. Then press down again with internal and external rotation in an attempt to catch the loose meniscal tissue between the articular surfaces (Figure 21-21, p. 374). Squats, performed with the tibia internally and externally rotated, are another way to measure meniscal integrity. Pain experienced during internal rotation indicates lateral meniscus damage; pain during external rotation indicates medial meniscus damage. An athlete who can duckwalk probably has minimal meniscal damage. One-legged squats can be valuable for comparing the strength of one leg with the other.

Range of Motion. Record active and passive range of motion. These measures are particularly valuable in overuse injuries. More specific functional tests include running and cutting (e.g., forty-yard dash and shuttle run). A drop in performance from preseason or other tests may indicate an underlying problem or incomplete rehabilitation.

Circumference. Measurements should include the thigh, midpatella, calf, and leg length. Circumference measurements determine the degree of atrophy, and the midpatellar measurement helps determine the amount of swelling in the knee. Measure thigh circumference seven and fifteen centimeters above the patella in both legs. Measure the calf at its largest circumference. The return of normal muscle bulk will usually lag behind the return of strength (as measured by the isokinetic dynamometer).

Isokinetic Evaluation. Isokinetic evaluations, in which the injured and uninjured limbs are compared, are helpful in assessing strength. Absolute scores are often misleading because of the variability in standardization among instruments.

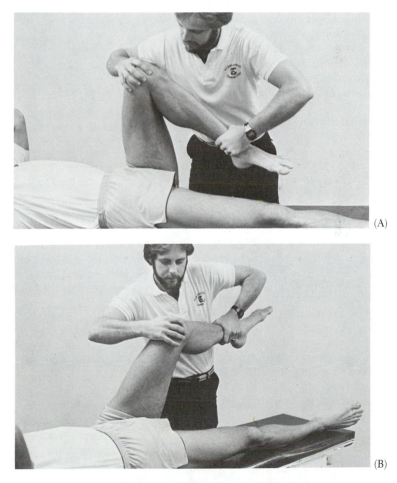

(A)

(B)

Figure 21-20 The McMurray test.
(A) Grasp the lower leg with the knee in flexion.
(B) Internally and externally rotate the tibia as the knee is extended.

Rehabilitation

Treatment and rehabilitation are difficult to separate and begin simultaneously (see Putting It into Practice 21-4, p. 375). Treatment is surgical and nonsurgical. Surgical intervention is frequently indicated for ligamentous tears, menisci injury, loose bodies, severe chondrosis of the articular surfaces, benign tumors about the knee, and some chronic inflammatory disorders. Nonsurgical treatment covers most injuries, including first and second degree sprains and strains, contusions, bursitis, overuse syndromes, and uncomplicated fractures. Specific treatments were briefly discussed; this discussion is specific to the knee. See Chapters 4 (training), 10 (emergency care), 12 (philosophy of rehabilitation), and 13 (modalities) for universal rehabilitation procedures.

Rehabilitation depends upon appropriate first aid, proper evaluation, accurate diagnosis, and treatment. First aid should be aimed at controlling swelling and preventing further injury; treatment should restore damaged structures, if at all possible. Athletes, coaches, and parents must have realistic expectations about the outcome of treatment and rehabilitation procedures.

There are five stages in the knee rehabilitation program. Progression from one stage to the next depends upon the results of ongoing testing and evaluation. The following discussions are general guidelines. Successful rehabilitation depends upon communication and cooperation among the athletic trainer, coach, and orthopedic surgeon. Exceptions or clarifications regarding specific injuries are noted.

Stage 1: Presurgical

This stage is appropriate before surgery or after an acute injury. It is a continuation of the first aid measures of controlling edema by ice, elevation,

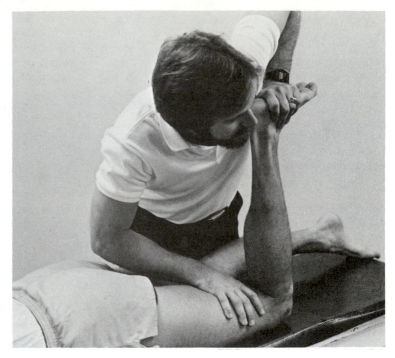

Figure 21-21 The Apley test. Lift the bent knee (ninety degrees) by the foot, internally and externally rotate the tibia, then press down while again internally and externally rotating the tibia. Clicks or thuds imply that loose meniscal tissue has been caught between the articular surfaces.

compression, and appropriate immobilization. A major goal of this stage is to "do no harm"—never extend the degree of injury by excessive treatment.

If surgery is not indicated, treatment should prevent disuse atrophy, improve circulation, and maintain proprioceptive responses about the knee. Procedures may include isometrics, range of motion, electrical stimulation, and resistive exercise (as tolerated). It is particularly important to maintain the range of motion in uninvolved joints. If surgery is necessary, proceed to stage 2; otherwise, proceed to stage 3 when the range of motion and strength have reached 50 percent of the uninvolved knee. Evaluation criteria include strength (measured isokinetically, isometrically, or manually), range of motion, and swelling.

Take care to protect the patellofemoral articular surface throughout all

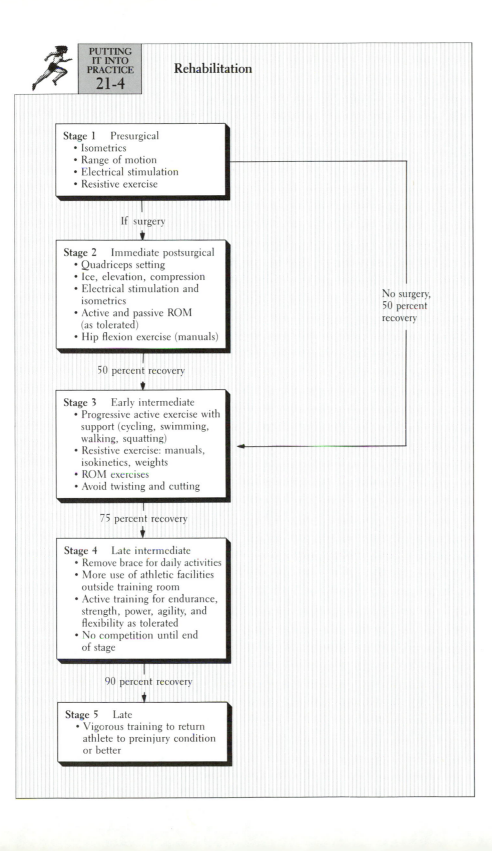

PUTTING IT INTO PRACTICE 21-4

Rehabilitation

Stage 1 Presurgical
• Isometrics
• Range of motion
• Electrical stimulation
• Resistive exercise

If surgery

Stage 2 Immediate postsurgical
• Quadriceps setting
• Ice, elevation, compression
• Electrical stimulation and isometrics
• Active and passive ROM (as tolerated)
• Hip flexion exercise (manuals)

50 percent recovery

No surgery, 50 percent recovery

Stage 3 Early intermediate
• Progressive active exercise with support (cycling, swimming, walking, squatting)
• Resistive exercise: manuals, isokinetics, weights
• ROM exercises
• Avoid twisting and cutting

75 percent recovery

Stage 4 Late intermediate
• Remove brace for daily activities
• More use of athletic facilities outside training room
• Active training for endurance, strength, power, agility, and flexibility as tolerated
• No competition until end of stage

90 percent recovery

Stage 5 Late
• Vigorous training to return athlete to preinjury condition or better

phases of rehabilitation. Proper nourishment of the chondrocytes requires motion and lubrication. Extended immobilization of the patella can cause drying and stickiness of the articular surface; excessive compression can cause patellar chondrosis. Short arc knee extensions, beginning twenty degrees from full extension, maximize the development of the vastus medialis muscle while minimizing patellofemoral compression. The orthopedic surgeon must inform the athletic trainer of the location of articular surface defects so that sensitive points in the range of motion can be avoided during rehabilitation.

Stage 2: Immediate Postsurgical

The duration of this stage depends upon the severity of injury and the type of surgery but should last until the injured knee has regained 50 percent of its function. The amount of postsurgical activity varies.

Begin isometric exercises, such as quadriceps setting, immediately after surgery, although rest is often indicated for twenty-four hours. Increase the frequency, intensity, and duration of these exercises with time. Use measures to control swelling, such as ice, elevation, and compression. Swelling sometimes can be contained by active and passive motion, but vigorous active motion can increase bleeding. Electrical muscle stimulation may be indicated with isometrics to maintain tone and decrease edema, especially where pain-induced inhibition prevents motion. If available, continuous passive motion (CPM) may help reduce swelling. Isokinetic exercise or testing must be reserved for when sufficient ROM is present, to prevent ballistic stretching of antagonistic muscles.

A cast hinge or a commercial hinge brace needs frequent adjustment to keep it tight because of atrophy of the quadriceps and calf muscles. Atrophy will always occur, despite isometric exercises and electrical stimulation.

Initiate manual hip muscle exercises within one week following surgery (Figure 21-22). As discussed, the rectus femoris can be exercised through hip flexion exercises. Take care to not use the lower leg as a lever because of the inappropriate forces placed across the knee. An exercise machine like the Nautilus hip and back machine may be useful.

No weight bearing is allowed for two to three months with anterior cruciate ligament repairs and reconstructions. Rehabilitation of the anterior cruciate should stress the hamstrings because they are an active complement to this structure, and hamstring exercises do not affect the surgical repair. Bicycle riding may be allowed at six weeks and weight bearing at two months. Isometric exercises can be started at approximately eight weeks at forty-five, sixty, and ninety degrees of flexion.

Stage 3: Early Intermediate

This stage involves active exercise while continuing support for the injured structure. Appropriate support may include tape for mild sprains and a derotation brace with a hyperextension stop for an anterior cruciate repair. The brace should be worn at all times, particularly during the exercise program. (The brace is worn during swimming, but trustworthy athletes can remove it during the later parts of this stage.) Power and endurance should be developed in addition to strength and range of motion. The athlete should remain in this phase until 75 percent of function has been restored.

Progressive functional activities may include stationary cycling (avoid street bike riding), swimming, walking, and squatting. These activities are appropriate five to six months after anterior cruciate ligament repair and approximately three to four months following collateral ligament repair.

You can allow squatting to ninety degrees with knees protected and feet

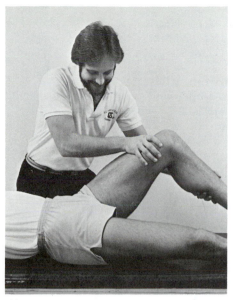 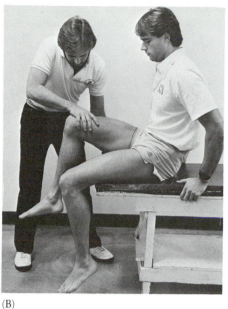

(A)   (B)

Figure 21-22 Manual hip exercises. These exercises can strengthen the rectus femoris without excessively straining the knee joint.
  (A) The athlete lies supine, and the athletic trainer resists attempt to flex the hip.
  (B) With the athlete seated, the athletic trainer manually resists hip flexion.

pointing straight ahead. Squats place less stress on the anterior cruciate ligament than leg extensions, and they develop the gluteus maximus muscle as well as the muscles of the other leg.

In knees whose anterior cruciate ligaments have been repaired, the active quadriceps function is still limited in the last thirty degrees of flexion during this entire period. (With other ligament repairs, active quadriceps function through a full range of motion was started in stage 2.) With posterior cruciate repairs, full range quadriceps exercises were encouraged from the very beginning because they contributed to posterior stability.

With medial collateral ligament repairs, swimming can actually be started in stage 2, where a full range of motion is encouraged. Fast walking, and even jogging and rope skipping, may be practiced later in this stage. Sprinting can be started late in this phase because

it actually places less impact on the knee than slow jogging. Avoid twisting and cutting.

Stage 4: Late Intermediate

The goal during this phase is to gain full range of motion without any swelling or pain except in anterior cruciate (AC) repairs. The number of visits to the athletic trainer or therapist greatly decreases, and resources outside the training room are increasingly used for conditioning and rehabilitation. Endurance activities (cardiovascular as well as specific muscle endurance) are encouraged, especially cycling and swimming. Graduation to stage 5 requires 90 percent function.

Athletes with collateral ligament repairs may begin agility and high-intensity exercises. Rehabilitation should be nearly complete at the end of this phase for these athletes.

With AC repairs or reconstructions, the last twenty degrees of extension is still limited, but full flexion should be obtained. The derotation brace may be removed for daily activities but worn during exercise. Competitive athletics are prohibited for athletes with anterior and posterior cruciate repairs. Athletes with cruciate repairs may begin agility and high-intensity exercises only at the end of this phase.

Stage 5: Final

The purpose of this phase is to return the athlete to preinjury condition or better. It may take as long as eight to twelve months for those with some injuries to reach this stage. Objective measures such as the isokinetic dynamometer, shuttle run, standing long jump and high jump, forty-yard dash, and 1½-mile run should be used to measure the extent of rehabilitation. This phase involves intensive training to maintain or further develop strength, power, endurance, flexibility, skill, and coordination. Protective devices, such as bracing, tape, and padding, should be used to prevent further injury.

Preventing Knee Injuries

Knee injuries can be prevented by maximizing the fitness of the leg muscles, wearing proper equipment, using proper sports techniques, and fully rehabilitating injuries when they occur.

Conditioning

Improving the strength, endurance, and flexibility of the leg muscles is probably the best method of preventing knee injuries. Although the leg muscles are vital to most sports, it is indeed odd that many athletes stress upper body exercises (sometimes to the exclusion of lower body exercises) in their strength and conditioning programs. Too often, athletes overemphasize arm, shoulder, and chest exercises, such as biceps curls and bench presses, and neglect important lower body exercises, such as leg presses and squats.

Every athlete involved in sports where the knee is at increased risk should regularly practice lower body exercises that maximally stress the leg muscles. These exercises may include squats, leg presses, step-ups, and variations of these basic exercises. Athletes should avoid those exercises that seem to place excessive stress on the articular surfaces of the knee joint. For example, full squats are contraindicated, but parallel squats (thighs parallel with the ground) may be practiced by most athletes. However, even parallel squats may be contraindicated in athletes with patellofemoral malalignment problems.

Athletes should also practice exercises that isolate specific muscle groups, such as the quadriceps, hamstrings, and calf. Knee extension exercises are particularly good for developing the vastus medialis muscle, an important muscle for knee stability and optimal patellofemoral tracking. Athletes with patellofemoral problems should practice restricted range knee extension to minimize compression of the patella on the underlying surfaces. (However, athletes should avoid the forty to sixty degree range because it produces the greatest amount of patellofemoral compression.) Knee flexion exercises (leg curls) and calf exercises (calf raises) also contribute to the knee's stability.

Flexibility of the quadriceps, hamstrings, and calf muscles should not be neglected. Inflexible quadriceps may contribute to patellofemoral disorders, and inflexible hamstrings and calf muscles may create muscle imbalances that could set the stage for knee injury.

Athletes should strive to develop both cardiovascular and specific-muscle endurance. Fatigue seems to precipitate sports injuries throughout the body. For example, the incidence of knee injuries in downhill skiing is much higher when the skier is fatigued. Specific lower body and cardiovascular fitness can be developed through exercises such as running, cycling, or cross-country skiing. Specific muscle endurance can be developed through exercises such as the phantom chair (wall sits without support) and high-repetition knee extensions and knee flexions.

Equipment

Proper equipment helps prevent knee injuries. Ill-fitting or worn shoes may cause the foot to excessively pronate, which may place aggravating tortional stresses on the articular surfaces of the knee. Excessively long football cleats may increase the risk of ligament and meniscal injury. Improperly serviced ski bindings may not release when they are subjected to critical forces during a fall on the ski slope.

Technique

Some sports techniques contribute to knee injuries. Blind-side blocks (blocking on the lateral side of the knee) in football are dangerous and should not be tolerated. Incomplete instruction in rotary motions, such as the discus and rotational shot put, may place the inexperienced athlete at risk of injury.

Complete Rehabilitation

Incomplete rehabilitation may contribute to reinjury. Athletes should not be allowed to resume participation until they can demonstrate that they are recovered, or better yet, playing at or near optimal fitness. Most athletes want to return to play as soon as possible after an injury. However, some knee injuries take a year or longer to become fully rehabilitated. The athletic trainer is not doing the athlete any favors by allowing premature return to practice.

The rehabilitating athlete should be protected from further injury. This protection may include protective taping (see the appendix), bracing (see Figure 21-23), or modification of the activity. The risk of reinjury can be minimized if rehabilitation is complete.

 (A)  (B)  (C)  (D)

 (E)

Figure 21-23 Protective braces for the knee.
(A) Neoprene patella stabilization sleeve helps ensure proper patellar tracking within the intercondylar groove between the lateral and medial femoral condyles. This is very important for the athlete with a chronic subluxing patella.
(B) Anderson knee stabilizer is a double-hinged prophylactic knee brace that also incorporates a hyperextension stop. The brace is attached to the lateral aspect of the knee by the wrap-on Neoprene cuff. The brace protects against the valgus force that results from a blow to the lateral aspect of the knee. This is the most common mechanism of knee injury in football.
(C) McDavid knee guard is a single-hinged prophylactic knee brace that also incorporates a hyperextension stop. The brace is located on the lateral aspect of the knee only. It too protects against valgus force.
(D) The extension control knee orthosis (ECKO) is used on the athlete with anterior cruciate ligament damage. This brace is equipped with a hinge lock and a posterior pad that keeps the knee from backing into extension, which can lead to lateral pivot shift.
(E) An adaptation of the ECKO brace for posterior cruciate ligament-deficient athletes. The patellar kneecap pad tightens during flexion, which stabilizes the tibia and prevents posterior displacement of the tibia on the femur.

References

Albright, J. A., and R. A. Brand. *The Scientific Basis of Orthopaedics*. New York: Appleton-Century-Crofts, 1979.

Balkfors, B. *The Course of Knee Ligament Injuries*. Malmo, Sweden: University of Lund, Department of Orthopedic Surgery, 1982.

Brody, D. M. Running injuries. *CIBA Clinical Symposia* 32:1–36, 1980.

Ellison, A. E. Skiing injuries. *CIBA Clinical Symposia* 29:1–40, 1977.

Ficaty, R. P., and D. S. Hungerford. *Disorders of the Patello-Femoral Joint*. Baltimore: Williams & Wilkins, 1977.

Hoshikawa, Y., H. Kurosawa, T. Fukubayashi, H. Nakajima, and K. Watarai. The prognosis of meniscectomy in athletes. *American Journal of Sports Medicine* 11:8–13, 1983.

Houston, M. E., and P. H. Goemans. Leg muscle performance of athletes with and without knee support braces. *Archives of Physical Medicine and Rehabilitation* 63:431–432, 1982.

Kapandji, I. A. *The Physiology of Joints*. Edinburgh: Churchill Livingston, 1978.

Kurosawa, H. Diagnosis and treatment of meniscus lesions with anterior cruciate insufficiencies. *Orthopedic and Traumatic Surgery* 13:481–488, 1980.

Larson, R. L., and K. M. Singer (eds.). The knee. *Clinics in Sportsmedicine* 4(2):207–401, 1985.

McGinty, J. B. Arthroscopic surgery in sports injuries. *Orthopedic Clinics of North America* 11:787–799, 1980.

Mital, M. A., and L. I. Karlin. Diagnostic arthroscopy in sports injury. *Orthopedic Clinics of North America* 11:771–785, 1980.

Muller, W. *The Knee: Form, Function, and Ligament Reconstruction*. Berlin: Springer-Verlag, 1983.

Nilsson, S. Jogging injuries. *Scandinavian Journal of Social Medicine* suppl. 29:171–178, 1982.

O'Donoghue, D. H. *Treatment of Injuries to Athletes*. Philadelphia: W. B. Saunders, 1984.

Walker, P. S., and J. V. Hajek. The load-bearing in the knee joint. *Journal of Biomechanics* 5:581–589, 1972.

Williams, J. G. P. *Color Atlas of Injury in Sport*. Chicago: Year Book Medical Publishers, 1980.

Zimbler, S., J. Smith, A. Scheller, and H. H. Banks. Recurrent subluxation and dislocation of the patella in association with athletic injuries. *Orthopedic Clinics of North America* 11:755–770, 1980.

Calf, Ankle, and Foot Injuries

T HE LOWER LEG and foot are among the most common sites of sports injuries. Because these structures must bear weight, they are at greater risk of injury and are very difficult to rehabilitate when they have been injured. The lower leg and foot are particularly susceptible to overuse injury in addition to their vulnerability to direct trauma. This chapter explores the causes, treatment, and rehabilitation of major leg and foot injuries sustained in sports.

Anatomy and Physiology of the Lower Leg

The lower leg is defined as the area between the knee and ankle. The bones of the leg are the tibia (medially) and the fibula (laterally). Proximally the tibia is large, strong, and triangular where it articulates with the condyles of the femur. It becomes wider at its distal end, where it forms the medial malleolus and articulates with the talus of the foot. Injuries to the tibia are very common because it is the lower leg's only weight-bearing bone.

Ankle injuries frequently occur in sports such as field hockey that involve rapid changes of direction.

The fibula is a long, slender bone that (1) is the origin of muscles, (2) acts as a pulley for tendons passing behind it at the ankle, and (3) is a lateral "splint" for the ankle joint. The fibula's function as an ankle stabilizer is vital to the ankle joint's security. The area between the tibia and fibula is occupied by the interosseous membrane, which is similar to the membrane between the ulna and radius in the forearm. The tibia and fibula articulate proximally and distally to form two tibiofibular joints. Both joints are secured by strong anterior and posterior ligaments that are expansions of the interosseous membrane.

The muscles of the lower leg are responsible for the movements of the ankle and toes. Table 22-1 lists the muscles by their primary movement; Figures 22-1 and 22-2 illustrate the muscles. These muscles are innervated by the tibial, common, superficial, and deep peroneal nerves.

The popliteal artery, which arises from the femoral artery, divides into the anterior and posterior tibial arteries and supplies blood to the leg. The anterior branch of the tibial artery supplies the anterior aspect of the lower leg. The posterior tibial artery travels beneath the soleus and gastrocnemius to supply the posterior lower leg. The peroneal artery branches off the posterior tibial artery to supply the lateral aspect of the lower leg.

The lower leg is divided into the anterior, posterior, and lateral compartments (Table 22-2, p. 384). These compartments are tightly surrounded by heavy **fascia**—loose connective tissue that can be the site of severe injury, especially in the anterior compartment.

The lower leg is susceptible to a variety of injuries, including fractures, strains, sprains, and contusions. Overuse injuries are particularly common in the lower leg. The following section discusses leg injuries.

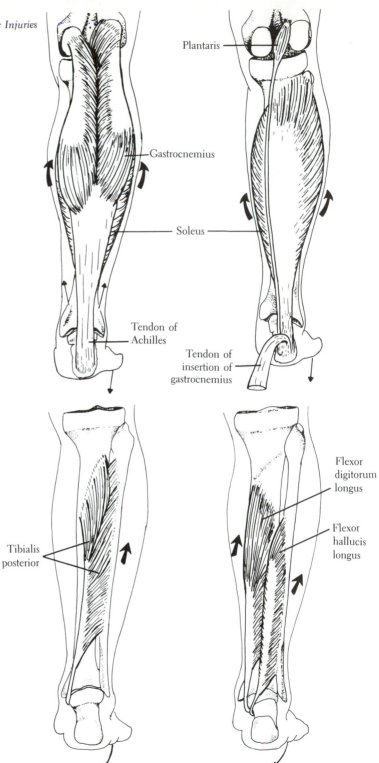

Figure 22-1 Muscles that move the foot (rear views). The broad solid arrows indicate the direction of pull of a muscle. The thin arrows indicate the direction in which the skeletal element will move when the muscle contracts. (From Crouch, J. E. *Introduction to Human Anatomy*, 6th ed. Palo Alto, Calif.: Mayfield Publishing Co., 1983, p. 101.)

Table 22-1 *Primary Movers of the Ankle, Foot, and Toes*

Ankle and Foot

Dorsiflexion: Tibialis anterior, extensor digitorum longus, peroneus tertius
Plantar flexion: Gastrocnemius, soleus
Inversion: Tibialis anterior, tibialis posterior
Eversion: Extensor digitorum longus, peroneus tertius, peroneus longus, peroneus brevis

Toes

Flexion: Flexor digitorum longus, flexor hallucis longus
Extension: Extensor digitorum longus, extensor hallucis longus

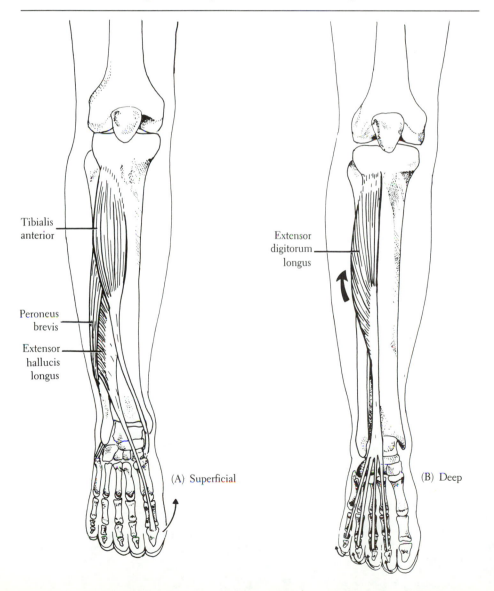

Tibialis anterior

Peroneus brevis

Extensor hallucis longus

(A) Superficial

Extensor digitorum longus

(B) Deep

Figure 22-2 Muscles that move the foot (front views). The broad solid arrows indicate the direction of pull of a muscle. The thin arrows indicate the direction in which the skeletal element will move when the muscle contracts. (From Crouch, 1983, p. 100.)

Table 22-2 *Compartments of the Leg*

Anterior	Posterior	Lateral
Tibialis anterior	Gastrocnemius	Peroneus longus
Extensor hallucis longus	Soleus	Peroneus brevis
Extensor digitorum longus	Deep peroneal nerve	Peroneus tertius
Anterior tibial nerve	Flexor digitorum longus	Superficial peroneal nerve
Tibial artery	Flexor hallucis longus	
	Tibialis posterior	

Fractures

Fractures to the leg—infrequent but not rare—tend to occur in a contact activity such as skiing, which places high rotatory stress on the leg. Types of leg fractures are open, closed, stress, and epiphyseal.

Open and Closed Fractures

In a **closed fracture** the bone is broken, but the bone ends do not penetrate the skin (see Chapter 6). In an **open fracture** the bone is broken, and an external wound leads down to the site of the fracture or fragments of bone protrude from the skin. Open and closed fractures, which occur along the shafts of the tibia and fibula, are caused by direct or indirect trauma.

Tibia. A fractured tibia usually costs the injured athlete the remainder of the season because the tibia is the only weight-bearing bone in the leg. The tibia is most commonly fractured along the distal third of its shaft. Fractures of the tibia and fibula sometimes occur simultaneously.

Mechanism of Injury. There are numerous mechanisms of tibial fracture. In soccer, the tibia can be fractured when a defensive player attempts to block or steal the ball and accidentally kicks the offensive player in the shin. In alpine skiing, the injury usu- ally occurs from excessive rotary forces and is typically a unilateral or bilateral spiral fracture. Tibial fractures in skiing most commonly occur in slower moving skiers who are using shorter skis, lower boots, and tighter bindings than recommended for their skill level. Typically the injury occurs immediately after the skier starts down the slope and unintentionally begins to snowplow (wedging the skis outward); the skier cannot stop or control the maneuver, and one or both legs is forced into extreme internal rotation (Figure 22-3).

Closed fracture: The bone is broken, but the skin is not penetrated.
Open fracture: The bone is broken, and the skin is penetrated.

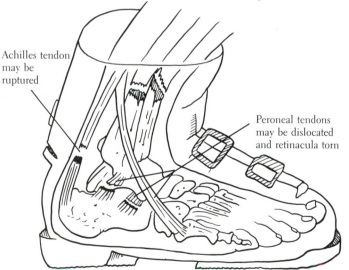

Achilles tendon may be ruptured

Peroneal tendons may be dislocated and retinacula torn

Figure 22-3 Boot top fracture of the tibia and fibula. This injury may be accompanied by Achilles tendon rupture, dislocated peroneal tendons, and retinacula tears.

Evaluation. Signs and symptoms of tibial fractures are often obvious but not always straightforward. It is extremely important to determine at once whether the fracture is open or closed. Open fractures are much more serious than closed ones because more blood is lost and open fractures can become easily infected. See Chapter 6 for discussion of fractures and Chapter 10 for emergency procedures.

Typical signs of tibial fracture are (1) deformity—the tibia may lie in an unnatural position or be angulated where there is no joint; (2) tenderness—there is point tenderness at the site of the break, and it can be located by gently palpating along the shaft of the tibia; (3) crepitus—a sensation that often can be heard or felt when the broken ends of the bone rub together; and (4) swelling.

Examine the athlete with a tibial fracture for numbness or paralysis in the lower leg (from pinched or cut nerves) and for loss of pulse distal to the fracture site (from pressure, pinching, or cutting of blood vessels). To examine the athlete, ask him or her to move the toes; stroke or pinch the athlete's leg below the fracture site to determine responsiveness to the stimulus, and palpate the posterior tibial artery (lies immediately posterior to the medial malleolus) with your index and middle fingers to determine distal pulse.

Treatment. Immobilize the leg with splints; remember to include *both* the knee and ankle joints. Transport the athlete to a local medical facility for further evaluation and x-rays. Keep the athlete calm and reassured because this is a highly emotional and painful experience that can easily cause shock.

Most tibial fractures are treated by closed reduction and manipulation. The leg is usually immobilized in a long cast; eventually the long cast is replaced by a short leg cast as the fracture heals. Healing rate is often difficult to determine, but the leg may be in a cast two to five months, depending upon the physician's philosophy and the severity of the fracture.

Fibula. Fibular fractures are typically less serious than tibial fractures because the fibula does not bear weight. Research and clinical experience indicate that open fractures occur more commonly in the fibula than in the tibia. This injury does not necessarily cause the athlete to miss the remainder of the season. However, a fibular fracture can become chronically debilitating if it is associated with a rupture of the ankle's lower tibiofibular ligament and results in instability or separation of the ankle mortice. The physician must determine the stability of the ankle joint when managing the fractured fibula, particularly if the fracture occurred at the distal end of the bone.

Mechanism of Injury. Fibular fractures are usually caused by direct blows to the lateral side of the leg, as in soccer when a defensive player tries to block or steal the ball and kicks the offensive player in the shin. An athlete with a fibular fracture often returns to play complaining only of a bruiselike aching pain in the leg. It may be necessary to refer the athlete to the team physician for a follow-up examination and x-rays.

Treatment. Management of a fibular fracture depends upon the severity of the injury but is similar to that for a tibial fracture. If an incomplete fracture of the fibula is suspected and the athlete is able to walk with only moderate discomfort, the suggested procedure is to apply ice and a compression bandage, provide crutches for ambulation, and refer the athlete to the team physician.

Stress Fractures

The increased emphasis upon physical fitness and the popularity of distance running among the general public have been accompanied by an increased incidence of leg pain and **stress fractures.** Stress fractures of the tibia and fibula are not exclusive to distance running; they may occur in almost any sport. In a stress fracture, a bone loses its capacity to withstand repetitive microtrauma. A stress fracture can become a complete fracture, but it differs from an acute fracture in that it is a *repetitive* accumulation of stresses over time rather than a single stress. The tibia is a much more common site of stress fracture than the fibula, particularly in distance runners.

Mechanism of Injury. There are four principal causes of stress fracture: (1) simple overload, brought about by muscle contraction; (2) alteration in the stress distribution in the bone, from continued activity while fatigued; (3) changes in the running surface; and (4) high repetition of stress, even when the stresses are relatively low.

The most common signs of stress fractures of the tibia and fibula are focal swelling and point tenderness. Additional symptoms include alteration of gait, muscular atrophy (particularly of the anterior tibialis and gastrocnemius muscles), full and painless range of motion in adjacent joints, and a callus three to six weeks from onset of symptoms). Always suspect stress fracture when these symptoms are present in athletes involved in sports like distance running and when the symptoms are relieved with rest. Stress fracture must be differentiated from other causes of shin splints as soon as possible to avoid more serious bone injury from developing (see Chapter 6). At the onset of leg pain in an athlete, the examiner should pay particular attention to the athlete's training program (history). Many times the athlete will relate an increase in activity or a sudden change in training that can increase strain, such as running on a harder sur-

face, running longer distances, running at faster speeds, or wearing a different pair of shoes.

Skeletal malalignment of the leg and foot can increase the incidence of stress fracture when accompanied by the repetitive stress of activities like distance running (see Chapter 6). For example, excessive varus alignment of the lower leg and foot causes the tibia to internally rotate and predisposes it to stress fractures, particularly in the lower leg's mid and distal portions. Soft and semi-rigid orthotics may be indicated to correct and balance foot abnormalities. For example, an **orthotic** maintains a pronated foot in a neutral position by supporting its medial side.

Evaluation and Treatment. Stress fractures must be treated early because they can progress to complete fractures with displacement. If you suspect a stress fracture, immediately refer the athlete to a physician for further evaluation. Early x-rays are often negative. If a stress fracture is suspected and clinical x-rays are normal, the physician may perform a radionuclide bone scan, which will demonstrate the defect.

Treatment for stress fracture includes rest, ice massage, and exercises to increase muscle strength, endurance, and flexibility in the ankle's dorsi- and plantar flexors. In addition, the quadriceps and hamstrings should be exercised to prevent disuse atrophy. Use non-weight-bearing exercises such as swimming and cycling to maintain cardiovascular fitness. When the athlete returns to training, the intensity of the exercise program should be increased gradually.

Epiphyseal Fractures

Epiphyseal fractures of the tibia and fibula are not uncommon in the child athlete (see Chapter 28). Most epiphyseal injuries associated with sports occur in the athlete's later years of growth,

Stress fracture: A fracture induced by a muscle repetitively stressing a bone (such as at a site of muscle attachment). With continued stress, the fracture may progress from a micro state to a complete displacement.

Orthotics: Orthopedic devices.

Epiphyseal fracture: Fracture at the epiphyseal-metaphyseal junction.

approximately at the onset of adolescence. Epiphyseal fractures in sports are usually not severe, and most epiphyseal injuries do not cause major length discrepancies or angular deformities. With close observation, all growth variances can be identified and treated.

The points of ligament insertion play a major role in the location of epiphyseal injuries. Ligaments and their insertions are stronger than the epiphyseal-metaphyseal junction, so a stress applied to a child's long bone will more likely cause a fracture at the epiphyseal-metaphyseal junction than a torn ligament. Adults are more susceptible to ligamentous injury because their epiphyses are fused. For example, an eversion ankle sprain in an adult most often causes the deltoid ligament to be partially torn. However, in a child's ankle, the deltoid ligament inserts into the bony medial portion of the tibia's distal epiphysis. Since the child's growth plate is not fused, it is more susceptible to an epiphyseal fracture. However, even adults can suffer an avulsion fracture of the medial malleolus as a result of an eversion sprain.

Evaluation. The athletic trainer should suspect an epiphyseal fracture and refer the athlete to a physician whenever a child or adolescent athlete presents evidence of dislocation, fracture, or moderate to severe sprain.

Vascular Disorders

Vascular disorders of the leg rarely occur in athletes, but when they do, there may be associated complications such as pulmonary emboli and subsequent pulmonary infarctions or loss of leg function. Consider circulatory abnormalities whenever a healthy, young athlete complains of leg pains or "shin splints" that subside with rest. Deep vein thrombosis and popliteal artery entrapment syndrome are the most common vascular disorders in athletes.

Deep Vein Thrombosis

Deep vein thrombosis (DVT) usually occurs in patients recovering from surgery or those who are restricted to bed for prolonged periods. The thrombosis may be from surgery, overproduction of fibrinogen, heredity, or trauma.

Evaluation. Signs include point tenderness when the popliteal fossa or gastrocnemius muscle is deeply palpated; pain when weight is borne and that increases with activity; tightness and weakness in the leg and ankle; paresthesia (a feeling of tingling, crawling, burning of the skin); and shooting, burning pain radiating from the popliteal fossa. Physical examination may reveal general signs of inflammation (swelling, redness, increased tissue temperature—see Chapter 8), distended superficial veins, formation of a lump in the calf, and pain during forced ankle dorsiflexion (positive Homans' sign). A careful history may reveal changes in training (e.g., increased intensity, changed terrain, etc.), recent hamstring or ankle sprain, contusion, dehydration, and difficulty in breathing at rest and during activity. DVT is difficult to identify and may be misdiagnosed as Baker's cyst or a hematoma.

Treatment. Treatment consists of hospitalization with (1) bed rest and elevation and compression, (2) anticoagulation therapy, and (3) monitoring clotting times and clotting factors. Treatment is usually two to three weeks long. Rehabilitation starts as soon as possible, beginning with very mild cycling and swimming, graduating to running only when decomposition of the thrombus has been confirmed by an angiogram (radiographic depiction of blood vessels). The athlete can usually return to normal activity in three to four months, barring further complications.

Popliteal Artery Entrapment Syndrome

Popliteal artey entrapment should be considered when a young athlete complains of leg pain that diminishes with rest. This vascular abnormality occurs in the popliteal fossa and can be detected by a noninvasive blood flow test; however, the diagnosis must be confirmed by angiography. See Table 22-3 for the causes of this syndrome.

Evaluation and Treatment. History and physical examination reveal claudication (leg pain), decreased tissue temperature, numbness, paresthesia, absence of distal pulse, and cyanosis. Surgery is the treatment of choice to relieve the symptoms and prevent further possible complications of arterial thrombosis and occlusion. Surgery produces excellent results and allows the athlete to continue to participate asymptomatically.

Sprains and Strains

Leg sprains and strains are common in sports and have a high rate of recurrence. Sprains and strains should be prevented through proper conditioning and fully rehabilitated when they do occur.

Superior Tibiofibular Joint

A leg sprain occurs predominately in the superior tibiofibular joint. It is an uncommon injury, so it may be overlooked when other injuries such as meniscal damage or collateral ligament sprain occur concurrently. The superior tibiofibular joint may be sprained from a direct blow to the lateral aspect of the knee, a pull of the biceps femoris upon the head of the fibula, or indirectly

Table 22-3 *Causes of Popliteal Artery Entrapment*

1. Medial deviation of the popliteal artery through the medial head of the gastrocnemius muscle.
2. An accessory slip of muscle or tendon from the gastrocnemius muscle, bridging the artery.
3. Trapping of the popliteal artery between the femur and popliteus muscle.
4. Compression of the popliteal artery by a cyst.

from severe ankle stress during knee flexion. Varus stress is also produced in the knee joint, which may sprain the lateral collateral ligament (see Chapter 21). Damage to the lateral collateral ligament increases the superior tibiofibular joint's risk of injury.

Mechanism of Injury. The injury occurs when the ankle is inverted during dorsiflexion, the knee is flexed, and the extremity is bearing weight; this puts abnormal stress on the fibula and the tibiofibular joint. Pathology may range from a mild sprain to a subluxation or dislocation. This injury may occur in activities that place severe stress on the leg and ankle, such as parachuting or gymnastics. A quick change in direction or movement that inverts the ankle while it is in dorsiflexion may also precipitate this injury.

Evaluation. Physical examination shows inflammation, pain around the superior head of the fibula and posterolateral calf, pain with resisted knee flexion, and a prominent fibular head. Movements such as "toe walking" or "hopping" on a flexed knee produce pain. "Rocking" the fibular head while the knee is flexed elicits pain.

Treatment. Treatment is the same as for sprains of other joints: ice, elevation, compression, and immobilization.

If the fibular head has dislocated and not spontaneously reduced, immobilize the knee joint from above the ankle to the groin. *Caution:* Closely monitor distal blood flow and nerve function when using spiral wraps to secure splints or compress the leg. Extreme laxity resulting in chronic dislocation or disability usually requires correction by surgery.

Shin Splints

Shin splints is a nonspecific term for pain between the knee and ankle. Proper treatment requires an understanding of the mechanism of injury, the structures involved, and the biomechanics of the lower leg.

Mechanism of Injury. Shin splints usually result from excessive stresses to the lower leg, such as overzealous training during the early phases of an exercise program, running on hard or uneven surfaces, sprinting, uphill or downhill running, or training in stiff or broken-down shoes. Other causes of shin splints are faulty posture, fallen arches, muscle fatigue, overuse, and lack of flexibility. Putting It into Practice 22-1 lists predisposing factors and symptoms of shin splints.

Evaluation. An athlete complaining of shin splints may state that pain increases with deceleration or pain increases after running and decreases with rest. The pain is usually sharp and throbbing. Occasionally the athlete complains of weakness and tightness in the leg and possibly tingling and coolness in the foot. These may be symptoms of anterior compartment syndrome; refer the athlete to the team physician. Physical examination of an athlete with shin splints may show a weak tibialis anterior muscle, a tight Achilles tendon, a pronated foot, poor running technique, swelling, and increased tissue temperature. An accurate history and complete physical evalua-

PUTTING IT INTO PRACTICE 22-1	**Recognizing Shin Splints**
Condition	*Symptom*
• Irritation of origin of tibialis posterior muscle on the tibia (periostitis)	• Tenderness along posterior medial aspect of tibia. Pain with active contraction or passive stretch of tibialis posterior muscle.
• Irritation of the origin of the tibialis posterior muscle on the interosseus membrane	• Deep posterior pain in calf muscles.
• Irritation of the tibialis anterior muscle	• Pain tightness on proximal lateral border of tibia and distal third of medial aspect of tibia. Pain with active contraction and passive stretch of tibialis anterior muscle.
• Stress fracture of the tibia	• Pain on distal, medial aspect of tibia (local, not diffuse).

tion are important for treating and preventing further injury.

Treatment. The primary treatment for shin splints is ice, compression, elevation, and rest. Monitor swelling if heat is used because of the danger of anterior compartment syndrome developing.

A mild strength and flexibility program should be instituted, and antiinflammatory therapy should continue after the pain and swelling have diminished. When the athlete returns to activity, the program should be conducted cautiously, never to the point of pain. A program of walking, then walking-running, and finally jogging on soft surfaces is the best approach for returning to activity and minimizing recurrence. Shin splints can be frustrating because of the high incidence of recurrence. The recovery period may be quite lengthy and seldom complete if the bone and periosteum are involved. To reduce symptoms during rehabilitation, use support taping and wraps (see

Shin splints: Pain between the knee and ankle, mainly from overuse. Course of the injury may include strain, stress fracture, and vascular entrapment.

the appendix). The longitudinal arch support and the application of $\frac{1}{2}$-inch felt strips along the medial border of the tibia (held in place with spiral strips of tape) are the most useful supports. Rest is the most beneficial treatment and should be strongly encouraged.

Prevention. Conditioning is the best preventive measure, as it is with most other soft tissue injuries. Encourage athletes to progressively strengthen the anterior and posterior leg muscles as well as develop lower leg flexibility. Structure the training program to avoid overstressing soft tissue of the lower leg. In addition, the athlete should wear shoes with good shock-absorbing qualities and that help avoid excessive pronation. Refer athletes with severely pronated feet to a podiatrist. Athletes should avoid running on hard surfaces.

Calf: Gastrocsoleus Complex

The gastrocnemius muscle has two heads that originate at the posterior aspect of the femur's medial and lateral condyles (Figure 22-1, p. 390). The soleus muscle originates on the posterior aspect of the proximal tibia and fibula. Both muscles come together to form the Achilles tendon and insert on the posterior surface of the calcaneus. Strains to this musculotendinous complex occur frequently in sports that require explosive starts and stops or quick changes of direction, such as tennis, racquetball, or basketball (Figure 22-4). Because the gastrocnemius is a two-joint muscle, it is injured more often than the soleus. It crosses both the knee and ankle joint and may be overstressed during knee extension or ankle dorsiflexion.

Mechanism of Injury. The muscle is most commonly strained at the musculotendinous junction. Strain typically results from overuse or acute overload of the muscle. This injury, popularly called "tennis leg," occurs more often

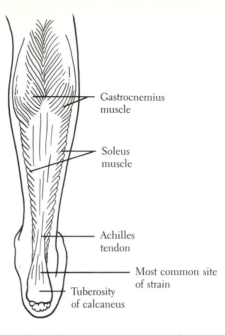

Figure 22-4 Most common site of strain of the gastrocsoleus complex is near the insertion of the Achilles tendon.

in older athletes who have not maintained this muscle group's strength and flexibility. Injury is produced by sudden dorsiflexion of the ankle from a dorsiflexed position, with simultaneous knee extension. Pain may be immediate and disabling when the strain is moderate to severe. The athlete may state that "It felt as if a ball struck my calf." A snap is frequently heard if the tendon ruptures.

Evaluation. Examination of the leg reveals swelling, point tenderness, ecchymosis, and pain with active contraction and passive stretch of the calf. A thorough evaluation of the injury should include functional muscle testing to differentiate between injury to the gastrocnemius and to the soleus. If the injury is mild, usually there will be only a general aching in the calf, with perhaps tenderness when the muscle belly is palpated. Consider this soreness a warning that continued play could cause a rupture (see the following discussion of Achilles tendon). A moderate or severe strain reveals a palpable defect in the tendon when the tendon is stretched. A rupture shows a defect even when the muscle is relaxed. A large mass may appear in the calf when the muscle is actively contracted. If this occurs, the athlete should seek medical attention as soon as possible.

Treatment. Treatment consists of the usual anti-inflammatory therapy along with rest and the use of a heel lift to relieve stress upon the tendon (by shortening it). Rehabilitation can begin as soon as the acute symptoms of pain and swelling diminish. Use Achilles tendon strength and flexibility exercises (Figure 22-5) (and continue to use them as a preventive measure). Once the athlete resumes activity, tape the Achilles tendon (see the appendix); the athlete should continue to wear the heel lift. Taping support can be eliminated as soon as strength and flexibility increase significantly.

Achilles Tendon

Achilles tendon injury is common in sports that involve a large amount of jumping, deceleration, cutting maneuvers, interval training, and prolonged running, such as volleyball, basketball, and track.

Mechanism of Injury. Achilles tendon injury may be initiated by subtle changes in the training program, such as a change in the running surface (e.g., from road to track), the shoes, or the sport (e.g., from cross-country to track or from water polo to baseball). The injury results from the tendon being overloaded during dorsi- and plantar flexion. The athlete usually does not experience a definite tearing sensation because the inflammatory condition generally develops gradually, although sometimes the symptoms are initiated by a direct blow to the posterior leg (e.g., being kicked by an opponent in soccer or hit by a foul-tipped baseball).

Figure 22-5 (A) and (B) Stretching exercises for the gastrocsoleus complex and Achilles tendon. (C) Slant board for stretching the Achilles tendon. The greater the angle of the slant, the greater is the stretch.

Evaluation. An athlete suffering from a mild or first degree Achilles tendon strain may complain of pain after the activity or immediately after the injury has occurred. The athlete may limp to prevent dorsi- or plantar flexion or may complain of pain and stiffness in the morning that diminishes with activity. The pain and stiffness are probably caused by a breakup of adhesions between the tendon and its sheath or the tendon and bursa (see Chapter 8). Physical examination reveals pain directly over the Achilles tendon, swelling, crepitation, discoloration, and weakness during plantar flexion. The Achilles tendon can become calcified from chronic **tendinitis,** so an x-ray may be indicated if the injury is chronic.

Treatment. Immediate care and rehabilitation for mild Achilles tendon strains is the same as for gastrocnemius strain. The injury should be treated conservatively to avoid chronic tendinitis. Treatment includes using heel pads on both feet, Achilles tendon support

Tendinitis: Inflammation of a tendon.

taping (see the appendix), wearing high-heeled shoes (*note:* chronic use of high-heeled shoes may predispose the athlete to this injury by decreasing normal range of motion), decreasing activity, and frequent anti-inflammatory treatments. Once the athlete has returned to activity, he or she should minimize irritation by warming up the tendon via hydrocollator pads, a warm whirlpool, or ultrasound; wearing heel lifts and Achilles tendon taping; and icing down immediately after the activity has terminated. Avoid **corticosteroid** injections into the tendon because they eventually weaken the tendon's structure and predispose it to rupture.

Moderate and Severe Strains. Moderate and severe strain (partial and complete rupture) of the Achilles tendon is very common among runners and joggers, particularly in men thirty to fifty years old. This injury usually follows a history of chronic inflammation and gradual degeneration of the tendon. This rupture can occur during a motion involving sudden dorsiflexion when the knee is extended (e.g., fast start or sudden change in direction) or during a motion that places the ankle in extreme dorsiflexion (e.g., in snow skiing the skier falls forward and the heel binding does not release, which places severe stress on the gastrocsoleus complex).

Evaluation. With a moderate or severe strain, the athlete may have heard or experienced a loud "pop," felt a sudden sharp pain during an explosive movement, and state that the back of the calf feels as though it had been hit by a golf ball. Complete ruptures do not cause as much pain as one would expect: The initial pain gradually diminishes, and the athlete can usually walk. This can cause problems because the injury is believed to be less severe than it actually is, so sometimes medi-

cal attention is not sought until days later.

Physical examination of an acute rupture reveals a palpable gap two to five centimeters above the tendon's insertion on the calcaneus, swelling, ecchymosis, inability to actively **plantar flex** the foot, calf muscles bunching during contraction (displaying an obvious mass), and a positive Thompson test (Figure 22-6). The defect is hard to locate if the athlete is not examined soon after the injury because blood fills the defect. The posterior tibial, peroneal, and toe flexor muscles can plantar flex the foot even when the Achilles tendon is completely ruptured, so tests to determine a ruptured Achilles tendon may yield false negative results.

Treatment. Treatment for a moderate or second degree strain consists of decreased activity, immobilization, heel lifts, and anti-inflammatory therapy. Surgery may be required if the symptoms remain unchanged or increase in severity after one to two weeks. Some surgeons believe that surgery should be performed on all significant Achilles strains (second or third degree) in athletes to ensure return to competition with minimal complications and prevent recurrence. Surgery is almost always indicated for complete Achilles tendon ruptures, although some nonsurgical techniques have been successful. Following surgery and immobilization, treatment should consist of electrical muscle stimulation. Cryotherapy should graduate into heat therapy (see Chapter 13), and flexibility and strength exercises should begin approximately three months after surgery.

Peroneal Muscles

Several factors may strain the peroneal muscles (PM), including foot structure, ankle fractures, overuse, and inversion ankle sprains (as the ankle inverts, it stresses the tendons of the peroneal muscles). Of the three pero-

Plantar flexion: Downward flexion of the ankle by pointing the toes away from the shin.

Corticosteroids: Adrenal cortex hormones. Synthetic substitutes are sometimes injected to decrease inflammation.

neal muscles, the peroneus longus is the one most commonly injured. The frequency of PM strain has significantly risen with the increased popularity of running and jogging.

Evaluation. This injury is characterized by pain along the length of the tendon, particularly at the inferior angle of the head of the fibula. Active ankle **eversion** and passive ankle **inversion** elicit pain.

Treatment. Initiate treatment as soon as possible to avoid a chronic condition. Treatment includes the use of ice, a whirlpool, ultrasound, and strength and flexibility exercises. Taping helps prevent inversion of the ankle when the athlete is ready to resume activity (see the appendix). Felt pads applied over the lateral side of the ankle also provide support. Orthotics may help relieve symptoms in athletes with abnormal foot structure. Chronic peroneal tendinitis may require immobilization or surgery to relieve the irritation or correct the structural defect.

*Peroneal
Tendon Dislocation*

Subluxation or dislocation of the peroneal tendons is a rare injury that can easily be mistaken for a simple ankle sprain. If not properly diagnosed and treated, this injury may cause chronic ankle instability. Dislocated peroneal tendons occur most often in snow skiing as a result of digging the tips of the skies into the snow or from movements involving a sudden forward lean, which place severe stress on the muscles that plantar flex and evert the ankle. During the extreme dorsiflexion that accompanies these movements, there is a reflex contraction of the peroneal muscles, which increases the tension of the tendons against the peroneal retinaculum, causing a rupture and subsequent dislocation. This injury can also be caused by the foot being everted with slight

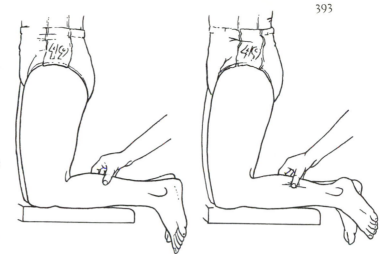

Figure 22-6 The Thompson test to determine complete rupture of the Achilles tendon. Squeeze both calves below the widest part of the muscle belly. The Achilles tendon is probably ruptured if the foot of the injured leg fails to plantar flex.

plantar flexion, as may occur when edging the downhill ski while turning.

Evaluation. The athlete usually experiences a snapping or popping in the ankle's posterolateral aspect, followed by severe but rapidly subsiding pain. Usually the athlete cannot continue to play and may not be able to walk. Physical examination reveals swelling, ecchymosis, and pain on the lateral side of the ankle, with point tenderness in the retromalleolar groove where the tendon passes behind the lateral malleolus (Figure 22-7, p. 394). The location of the pain can help distinguish between a lateral ankle sprain and peroneal muscle dislocation. Pain in the retromalleolar groove indicates injury to the peroneal retinaculum; injury to the anterior tibiofibular or calcaneofibular ligaments elicits pain anterior and inferior to the malleolus.

The injury must be reproduced during the evaluation, particularly if the dislocated tendons reduce spontaneously. There is a positive result if pain is produced during active contraction of the peroneal muscles while the foot is dorsiflexed.

Treatment. Surgery is the treatment of choice for a chronic or an acute

Eversion (foot): Turning the foot outward.
Inversion (foot): Turning the foot inward.

condition. Conservative treatment for athletes has not proven effective. Initiate rehabilitation as soon as possible with the usual therapies of ice, whirlpool, and strength and flexibility exercises.

Plantaris Muscle

The plantaris is a small muscle that lies between the gastrocnemius and soleus muscles and inserts via a long thin tendon into the posterior calcaneus. This muscle, which is absent in about 6 to 8 percent of the population, is a weak assistant for knee flexion and plantar flexion.

Evaluation and Treatment. Plantaris strain, which typically occurs in a manner similar to Achilles tendon injury, is characterized by deep pain in the calf, sometimes around the ankle. Swelling and ecchymosis may also be present in the ankle. This injury is sometimes very painful, but it usually resolves itself in a relatively short time. Symptoms are very similar to gastrocnemius strain, so examination must be carefully performed to distinguish between the two injuries. Treatment is the same as for gastrocsoleus strain. Full participation can begin when the athlete can tolerate activity.

Leg Contusions

Leg contusions are common in sports because the leg is usually unprotected and vulnerable to direct impact. Since the injury does occur frequently, it is often overlooked or managed improperly, which can harm the athlete's performance. This section discusses the pathology, evaluation, and treatment of muscle, tibial, and peroneal nerve contusions (see Chapter 5 for basic contusion care).

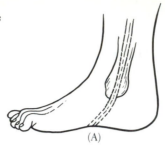

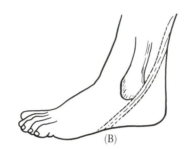

Figure 22-7   Peroneal tendon (A) dislocation and (B) reduction.

Muscle Contusions

Leg contusions tend to occur over the anterior compartment (anterior tibialis) and calf (gastrocnemius-soleus) muscle groups. The athlete may sustain this type of injury by getting kicked by an opponent (soccer) or by getting hit by an object, such as a ball.

Evaluation. Check the function of the knee and ankle joints during the examination. In addition, perform gross sensory tests, such as stroking the dorsal and plantar aspects of the foot and pinching the leg's lateral aspect. Begin palpation proximal or distal to the painful area; palpate both bony and soft tissue. Always suspect fracture with any contusion. Girth measurements help determine the inflammatory status, particularly during the acute stage of injury.

Severe contusions of the calf can be very debilitating, requiring that the athlete use crutches to move about. Contusions usually respond very well to a regimented treatment program. However, severe contusions over the muscle of the anterior compartment may lead to anterior compartment syndrome if the diffuse swelling fills the compartment space. This is a medical emergency that requires immediate **fasciotomy** by a physician to prevent permanent loss of nerve and muscle function. The athlete should be informed about the signs and symptoms of this syndrome and instructed to report to the athletic trainer or team physician *immediately* if the symptoms appear.

Treatment. As discussed in Chapter 5, acute treatment includes ice, compression, and elevation. The athlete should be instructed to apply ice every two hours at home if the contusion is severe. Apply a compression bandage beginning at the distal end of the foot, to prevent edema in the foot and ankle. Inform the athlete to loosen or remove the compression bandage if pain, throbbing, or numbness occurs or increases. Elevate the leg as often as possible, particularly during the acute stage of injury. As discussed in the general treatment chapters, other modalities include continuous high-frequency electrical muscle stimulation; heat (after the acute inflammatory period), which includes ultrasound, diathermy, moist heat, warm whirlpool, and hydrocollator pads; moderate static muscle stretching (provided it is not overly painful); gentle active range of motion exercises (two to three days postinjury, depending upon severity); and resistive exercises (when pain-free active range of motion has been restored).

As the athlete regains functional capacity, moderate-intensity cycling may begin during the later stages of recovery (ice after exercise). A protective pad can be constructed from orthoplast, two strips of Velcro, adhesive foam, and moleskin to protect the leg when the athlete returns to participation.

Tibial Contusions

The tibia's anterior border and subcutaneous medial surface are susceptible to severe contusions from direct blows. These areas are vulnerable because there is no tissue other than the integument and periosteum to absorb the impact.

Evaluation. Trauma to the periosteum causes immediate swelling, pain, and inflammation. Tibial contusions are sometimes called "traumatic tibial periostitis."

Treatment. The first priority is to control swelling and pain by applying ice, compression, and elevation. Crutches for moving about may be indicated if the athlete experiences pain when bearing weight. This injury usually takes a long time to heal, with full return to participation depending upon pain tolerance. When returning to practice, the athlete should wear a durable pad to protect the tibia's anterior and medial aspect.

Peroneal Nerve Contusion

The peroneal nerve arises from the upper sacral plexus and is a component of the sciatic nerve in the thigh as far as the upper part of the popliteal space. There, it descends independently along the posterior border of the biceps femoris, diagonally across the back of the knee joint to the upper lateral portion of the leg behind the head of the fibula, where it turns anteriorly between the peroneus longus and fibula (Figure 22-8, p. 396). Injury may result from direct trauma, especially in the region of the neck of the fibula.

Evaluation. Tenderness in this area during palpation suggests direct impact to the nerve. Peroneal nerve lesions or neuritis can also occur from fractures of the leg and prolonged sitting with crossed knees. This area is vulnerable

Fasciotomy: Surgical incision of a fascia.

396

Prevention, Treatment, and Rehabilitation of Specific Injuries

to direct blows from both the posterior and lateral aspect of the leg. Peroneal nerve contusion sometimes occurs in football linebackers or defensive linemen when the upper lateral aspect of the leg receives a direct blow from the helmet or shoulder pad of an offensive player.

Symptoms range from a stinging or burning sensation down the length of the leg to paralysis of the structures at the nerves' distribution sites. Contusion of the peroneal nerve can cause edema (swelling) within the nerve sheath. Since the nerve is contained within this sheath, the edema's increased pressure on the nerve fiber may cause paralysis. Although necrosis of the nerve fibers may cause irreparable damage and dysfunction, the typical contusion does not cause permanent problems; usually the swelling diminishes and the nerve progresses to normal function.

With severe contusions of the peroneal nerve, pain, numbness, tingling, and associated dysfunction (dropfoot) tend to increase as inflammation increases. Muscle testing of the foot reveals signs of weakness in dorsiflexion and eversion. There could be complete sensory and motor loss throughout the peroneal nerve distribution. This progression may occur within days or weeks, and recovery may not ever be complete.

Treatment. The standard regimen of ice, compression, and elevation is appropriate for most peroneal nerve contusions. The area of contusion should be protected before the athlete returns to participation. Taping or lateral ankle bracing is appropriate to prevent lateral ankle sprain if the anterior tibialis and peroneal muscle groups have been weakened. Refer any moderate to severe peroneal nerve contusion, or one that progressively worsens, to the team physician.

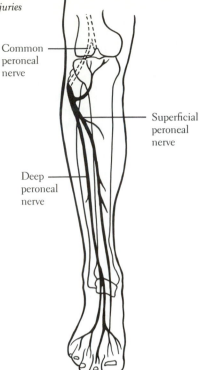

Figure 22-8 The common peroneal nerve.

Anterior Compartment Syndrome

Anterior compartment syndrome (ACS) is relatively rare, but it deserves special attention because permanent paralysis may result from a severe condition not recognized and properly treated within a few hours of the onset of symptoms. The athlete *must* be referred to a physician for evaluation if ACS is suspected. The anterior compartment (AC) is one of the four closed fascial compartments of the leg. The AC is bordered by the crural fascia, anterior intermuscular septum, fibula, interosseous membrane, and tibia. Enclosed within the AC are the tibialis anterior, extensor digitorum longus,

Anterior compartment syndrome (ACS): Development of pressure within the closed fascial compartment, causing local ischemia (inadequate blood flow) and inflammation.

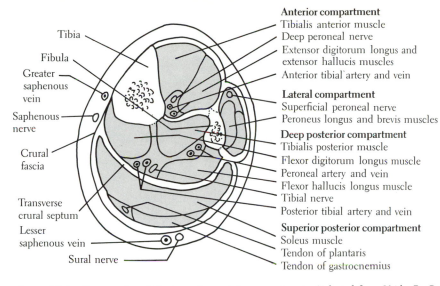

Tibia
Fibula
Greater saphenous vein
Saphenous nerve
Crural fascia
Transverse crural septum
Lesser saphenous vein
Sural nerve

Anterior compartment
Tibialis anterior muscle
Deep peroneal nerve
Extensor digitorum longus and extensor hallucis muscles
Anterior tibial artery and vein
Lateral compartment
Superficial peroneal nerve
Peroneus longus and brevis muscles
Deep posterior compartment
Tibialis posterior muscle
Flexor digitorum longus muscle
Peroneal artery and vein
Flexor hallucis longus muscle
Tibial nerve
Posterior tibial artery and vein
Superior posterior compartment
Soleus muscle
Tendon of plantaris
Tendon of gastrocnemius

Figure 22-9 Cross section of the lower leg and its compartments. (Adapted from Veith, R. G., F. A. Matsen, and S. G. Newell. Recurrent anterior compartmental syndromes. *The Physician and Sportsmedicine* 8:80–88, 1980.)

and extensor hallucis longus muscles (Figure 22-9). The deep peroneal nerve innervates the AC muscles and the extensor digitorum brevis muscles and supplies sensation to the first digital web space. The anterior tibial artery supplies the AC muscles and continues distally as the dorsal pedal artery.

Mechanism of Injury. ACS is caused by pressure developing within the closed fascial compartment; the pressure leads to ischemia (decrease in blood flow) of the structures in the compartment and inflammation. In recurrent ACS, the normal muscles can hypertrophy by as much as 20 percent. The degree of muscle swelling and the distensibility of the fascial wall determine the extent of injury.

In its most severe form, ACS leads to **fibrosis** and ischemic **contractures** (sometimes called Volkmann's ischemic contracture of the leg). In these acute cases, there is often permanent damage to the muscles and nerves if the compartment is not immediately decompressed.

ACS can be chronic or recurrent. In recurrent ACS, tissue pressure remains high between muscle contractions, which impedes blood flow and produces relative muscle ischemia as long as vigorous exercise continues. The symptoms usually dissipate within a few minutes once the exercise is discontinued. Recurrent ACS is the most common form in athletics, particularly among distance runners and athletes who suddenly embark on a heavy, strenuous training program. Contributing factors associated with ACS include fractures, direct contusions, burns, compression dressings, open reduction of fractures, casts, and muscle strains.

Evaluation. Initial symptoms include severe pain and pressure over the involved compartment. The pain develops within twelve hours after exercise. Upon palpation, there is extreme tenderness over the proximal aspect of the AC. Passive flexion of toes elicits pain over the compartment. Weakness of both the extensor hallucis longus and extensor digitorum and **hypesthesia** in the first web space are often present. Pedal pulses of both the dorsal pedal and posterior tibial arteries can usually be palpated.

Fibrosis: The formation of fibrous connective tissue.
Contracture: Shortening of a musculotendinous unit from scar tissue formation, atrophy, or muscle spasm.
Hypesthesia: Lessened sensitivity to touch.

The history is invaluable for evaluating recurrent ACS. For example, the distance runner is usually able to tell the exact distances needed to produce the discomfort and the length of time that pain persists. Typically, the pattern begins as the season starts: The muscle becomes hypertrophied, which decreases the volume of the anterior compartment. The pain usually diminishes completely within a few minutes after exercise, the compartment becomes tense or taut, but peripheral pulses remain palpable. Mild, recurring ACS can become more serious.

The pain over the anterior compartment in recurrent ACS is sometimes described as aching, cramping, or stabbing. The symptoms are bilateral in 95 percent of the cases, with fascial hernias noted in 60 percent (becoming more obvious after exercise). Most of the fascial defects occur in the distal third of the leg between the anterior and lateral compartments, where the superficial peroneal nerve emerges. Hypesthesia may be noted on the dorsum of the foot and be accompanied by toe extensor weakness.

During an evaluation, the examiner should consider other possible conditions, such as deep vein thrombosis, stress fractures of the tibia and fibula, tenosynovitis of the foot dorsiflexors, popliteal artery entrapment, muscle strains in the lower leg, and tibial periostitis.

Treatment. Immediately refer an athlete with ACS to a medical facility or the team physician. The immediate treatment in severe cases is surgical fasciotomy to decompress the compartment.

Treatment of less severe cases of ACS varies, depending upon the physician's philosophy. Modalities include ice, rest, elevation, orthotics, softer insoles, anti-inflammatory agents, local corticosteroid injections, and decompression of the compartment through fasciotomy. Compression bandages are contraindi-cated. Note that the symptoms of ACS can increase in severity from aspirin-induced bleeding, so avoid administering anticoagulant drugs when treating this syndrome.

Ankle Injuries

Ankle injuries are among the most common and recurring in sports. The treatment and prevention of the injuries require a thorough understanding of the anatomy and biomechanics of the ankle joint, lower leg, and foot.

Eighty-five percent of ankle injuries are sprains, most commonly occurring in the lateral aspect of the joint. Ankle sprains typically involve plantar flexion and inversion. The injury often occurs on irregular playing surfaces, such as poorly maintained football or soccer fields. In basketball or volleyball, the injury is frequently caused by landing on top of another player's foot. A less frequent mechanism of injury is hyperplantar flexion or hyperdorsiflexion. All significant ankle injuries should be x-rayed to rule out possible avulsion fractures, tibial or fibular fractures, osteochondral injuries, and ruptured ligaments (when x-rayed under stress).

Anatomy of the Ankle

The ankle joint is the articulation of the talus, tibia, and fibula. It is a hinge joint that moves only in a sagittal plane (extension and flexion). Inversion and eversion are accomplished mainly by the transverse tarsal joint and are possible when the foot is in plantar flexion. The ankle is a very stable joint because of its mechanical design and ligamentous support. The talus fits snugly into a mortice formed by the tibia and fibula. During dorsiflexion, the talus' wide anterior aspect is wedged into the mortice, which allows no lateral movement; in plantar flexion, the talus' narrow portion moves into the mortice, which creates lateral instability.

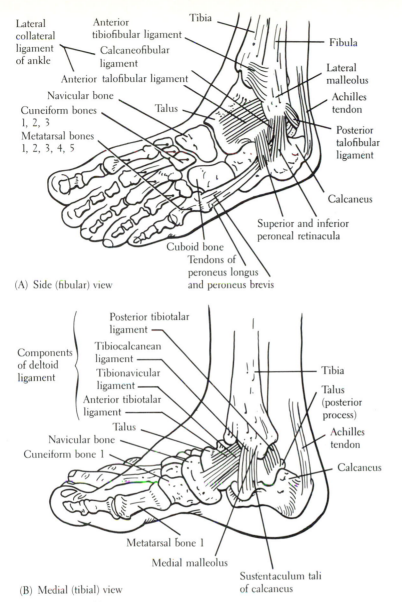

(A) Side (fibular) view

(B) Medial (tibial) view

Figure 22-10 The ankle joint.

The ligaments of the ankle's lateral aspect are the anterior talofibular, calcaneofibular, and posterior talofibular (Figure 22-10). The anterior talofibular and calcaneofibular ligaments are the most frequently injured ligaments in an ankle sprain. The medial aspect of the ankle is supported by the deltoid ligament, which is so strong that severe stress to this structure usually fractures the medial malleolus before the ligament ruptures. Plantar flexion is the ankle's most unstable position. Forceful inversion or eversion while in this position may strain the ligaments and possibly fracture the medial or lateral malleolus.

The muscles that cross the ankle joint are listed in Table 22-1 (p. 383). These muscles add dynamic support to the ankle joint, supporting it only when they are contracted. The muscles also absorb shock, to prevent stress upon the foot, ankle, and leg bones.

Fractures

Fractures result from stresses similar to those that injure the ankle ligaments.

Medial Malleolus. A fracture of the **medial malleolus** is unusual. During ankle inversion, stress is placed upon the lateral ligaments. The talus may be forced against the medial malleolus if the ligaments tear from intolerable stress. The tip of the medial malleolus will impinge against the medial aspect of the talus because of the bony arrangement of the mortice. The tip of the tibia may be fractured if the stress continues. This injury damages both sides of the ankle. The major symptom is point tenderness on the tip of the tibia (from the talus impinging). Treatment is typically immobilization or surgery.

Lateral Malleolus. The mechanism of this injury is similar to that for medial ankle sprain: The talus is forced against the fibula during the early phase of eversion. Usually this in itself terminates the stress, but if the force is severe, the deltoid ligament will rupture or the lateral malleolus will fracture.

Dome of the Talus. Fracture of the dome of the talus is an osteochondral-type fracture that occurs infrequently. This injury occurs during plantar flexion, inversion, and lateral rotation. The injury could occur when a football player is being tackled and his foot is secured to the turf by another player standing on it or by the cleats on his shoe being firmly embedded in the ground. Dome of the talus fracture can also be caused by the **dorsiflexion** compression forces that occur during the descent phase of power squats (weight lifting exercise).

The athlete may not seek medical attention for weeks because the injury is perceived as an ankle sprain. Inadequate treatment of this injury may lead to chronic irritation and ossification of the tibiofibular ligament. The injury may require surgery.

Ankle Sprains

Inversion Sprain. The inversion sprain is the most common ankle injury that occurs when the foot is plantar flexed and the ankle mortice is in an unstable position. As discussed, the anterior talofibular (ATL) and calcaneofibular ligaments (CFL) are the most commonly injured ankle ligaments. See Putting It into Practice 22-2.

Evaluation. If just the ATL is torn, there is lateral instability only during plantar flexion. The ankle is unstable in all positions if both the ATL and CFL are torn. Determining the mechanism of injury (history) usually identifies the type of ankle sprain (Figure 22-11). The entire foot, ankle, and lower leg must be examined to rule out other possible injuries, such as peroneal muscle strain, Achilles tendon strain, fractures of the metatarsals, and midfoot sprains.

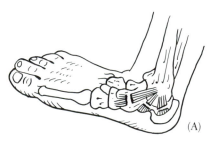
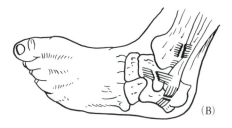

Figure 22-11 Mechanisms of (A) an eversion ankle sprain and (B) an inversion ankle sprain.

Medial malleolus: A large projection on the medial side of the ankle formed by the tibia.

Dorsiflexion: Upward flexion of the ankle by pointing the toes toward the shin.

Perform the physical examination as soon as possible after the injury, to clearly localize the injury. Examination usually shows swelling, ecchymosis, pain on the lateral aspect of the ankle, and point tenderness just anterior and inferior to and posterior to the lateral malleolus. The athlete may relate that a pop or snap was heard and was accompanied by instability. A moderate to severe sprain can cause a gap between the talus and tip of the fibula (may be obscured by swelling) that will not be present in a mild sprain. Perform the **anterior drawer test** or the **talar tilt** test to evaluate the ankle's anterior stability (Figure 22-12, p. 402).

Treatment. Treatment is ice, compression, elevation, and immobilization. Swelling must be controlled because it can further aggravate the joint; use a ¼-inch felt horseshoe compression pad to help control swelling. Contrast baths and mild strength and flexibility exercises may begin when the swelling has subsided (Figure 22-13, p. 403). Increase the intensity of these exercises as the status of the injury improves. An open basketweave taping (see the appendix) is helpful during the early stages of injury because it increases stability yet accommodates changes in lower leg volume due to swelling. Putting It into Practice 22-3 (pp. 402–403) describes a rehabilitation program. The athlete cannot return to field activities until the body weight can be supported and the athlete is capable of hopping ten times on the leg with the injured ankle. The athlete's ankle should be taped with the closed basketweave technique when returning to competition (see the appendix). This taping procedure should include a heel lock to control calcaneal movement.

Eversion Sprain. The eversion ankle sprain rarely occurs. When it does, it is usually accompanied by an avulsion fracture.

PUTTING IT INTO PRACTICE 22-2

Managing Ankle Sprains

I. History (Determine the mechanism of injury.)
II. Examination
   A. Compare and palpate both feet, ankles, and legs. Look for abnormalities, swelling, and signs of ligament damage. *Note:* Point tenderness lateral or medial to the lateral malleolus may indicate fracture.
   B. Perform stress and range of motion tests.
III. Acute care
   A. Ice, compression, elevation (24–48 h).
   B. Anti-inflammatory medication.
   C. Refer to physician if second or third degree sprain or fracture is present.
   D. Crutch ambulation.
IV. Rehabilitation (Continue anti-inflammatory treatment.)
   A. 48 h: Supported weight bearing.
   B. 3–4 days: Limited range of motion exercises, non-weight-bearing endurance exercise (swimming).
   C. When swelling is gone: Warm whirlpool bath.
   D. 1 week (as tolerated): Progressive ROM and resistive exercises.
   E. When tolerated: Walking, running, striding, sprinting, lateral movements.
   F. Return to participation when strength and flexibility are same as on the uninjured side.

Evaluation. Physical examination shows swelling, ecchymosis, and medial pain, particularly inferior and anterior to the medial malleolus. As with the lateral ankle injury, all associated structures must be examined and evaluated.

Treatment and Rehabilitation. Treatment and rehabilitation are the same as with the lateral ankle sprain and include anti-inflammatory procedures, range of motion exercises, strength exercises, taping for protection, and field exercises.

Dorsiflexion Sprains. Severe dorsiflexion can widen the ankle mortice, sprain the inferior tibiofibular and deltoid ligaments, and stress the Achilles tendon complex. This injury can make

Anterior drawer test: A test for a tear of the anterior talofibular ligament.
Talar tilt test: A test for a tear of the calcaneofibular and anterior talofibular ligaments.

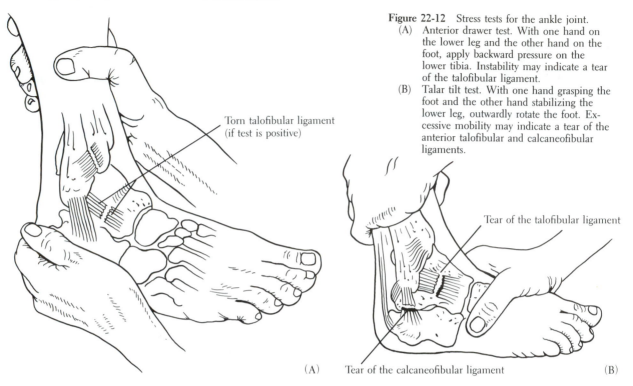

Torn talofibular ligament
(if test is positive)

Figure 22-12 Stress tests for the ankle joint.
(A) Anterior drawer test. With one hand on the lower leg and the other hand on the foot, apply backward pressure on the lower tibia. Instability may indicate a tear of the talofibular ligament.
(B) Talar tilt test. With one hand grasping the foot and the other hand stabilizing the lower leg, outwardly rotate the foot. Excessive mobility may indicate a tear of the anterior talofibular and calcaneofibular ligaments.

Tear of the talofibular ligament

(A)   Tear of the calcaneofibular ligament   (B)

PUTTING IT INTO PRACTICE 22-3

Ankle Exercise Program

I. First stage (Check range of motion.)
A. *Flexion*: Flex the foot as far as possible; point toes upward.
B. *Extension*: Extend the foot as far as possible; point toes downward.
C. *Inversion*: Turn the soles of the feet inward.
D. *Eversion*: Turn the soles of the feet outward.
II. If the ankle performed those exercises in full range of motion and without pain, the athlete should do the following exercises:

A. *Foot circles*: The foot circumscribes a small circle. First bring down the ball of the foot; then bring the foot in, up, and out.
B. *Alphabet*: Sitting on a table with the knee straight and only the ankle extended over the end of the table, the athlete should use the foot to print in capital letters the entire alphabet.
III. If the athlete performed those exercises in full range of motion and without pain, the athlete should do the following exercises:

A. *Towel exercise*: Sit on a chair with the foot on a towel; with the toes, pull the towel up under the foot. After completing that part successfully, the athlete should place a weight on the other end of the towel, to offer resistance.
B. *Pick-up exercise*: Pick up marbles, a small piece of sponge rubber, or a partly used gauze roller bandage. Alternate placing the object in the hand opposite the knee of the good leg and in the hand behind the

(continued on next page)

Figure 22-13 Resistive and range of motion ankle exercises using a towel (A) and surgical rubber tubing (B to D).

Ankle Exercise Program *(continued)*

buttocks of the injured leg.

C. *Toe rises*: Stand with feet 1 ft apart, toeing in. Rise on the toes as high as possible without pain. Repeat this exercise with the toes pointed straight ahead and then pointed out.

IV. If the athlete performed those exercises in full range of motion and without pain, the athlete should do the following exercises:

A. Repeat the range of motion exercises, with the athletic trainer giving resistance with his or her hands.

B. *Hopping exercise*: First, stand on the good leg and hop as high as possible. Then repeat on the injured leg.

V. When the athlete can perform the hopping exercise equally as well as on the good leg and without pain, the athlete

should do the following exercises:

A. *Active jogging and walking with ankle strapped*: *Note*: Any time the athlete limps, stop all running.

1. Walk 25 yd; jog 25 yd.
   Walk 25 yd; jog 50 yd.
   Walk 25 yd; jog 75 yd.

2. *Straight ahead*: Repeat the walk and jog exercises, but at half speed.

3. *Straight ahead*: Repeat the walk and jog exercises, but at three-quarter speed.

4. *Straight ahead*: Repeat the walk and jog exercises, but at full speed.

B. When the athlete can sprint at full speed and without a limp, then have the athlete run clockwise and counterclockwise circles. Start with

large circles, working down in size.

C. When the athlete can run the circles at full speed without a limp and without pain, have the athlete run figure eights.

D. When the athlete can run figure eights at full speed without a limp and without pain, then have the athlete run a zigzag course the length of the football field.

E. The last step is to test the athlete on right angle quick cuts to both the right and the left. When the athlete can do this, he or she is ready for competition and practice.

Repeat all exercises at least ten times daily.

When the athlete starts jogging with the ankle strapped, he or she can do all previous exercises at home and unsupervised, with the trainer checking these exercises twice a week.

Prevention, Treatment, and Rehabilitation of Specific Injuries

a joint unstable and may lead to degenerative changes and chronic irritation if not treated properly. A dorsiflexion sprain must be confirmed by x-ray. When confronted with a dorsiflexion injury, the athletic trainer should be highly suspicious.

Treatment for a mild injury is the usual anti-inflammatory procedure, taping to prevent dorsiflexion (see the appendix), and heel lifts. Severe injuries may require splinting and not bearing weight for up to eight weeks. Start rehabilitation as soon as possible. Do not permit dorsiflexion exercises during the early stages of recovery.

Exostoses (Bone Spurs)

Exostoses (bone spurs) occur frequently in the ankle and foot; Figure 22-14 shows a calcaneal bone spur. An exostosis is a bony growth at the site of irritation on a bone (usually the talus in the ankle). In the ankle, it results from chronic extreme motions of dorsiflexion or plantar flexion, inversion, or eversion. This reaction is analogous to the development of calluses on the hands, except that exostoses are more serious.

Evaluation. Symptoms include sharp pain during extreme dorsiflexion, as may occur in a sprint start or driving from the line in football. Pain is located on the anterior aspect of the talotibial joint. Physical examination may show very little, and there will be little or no pain or swelling during normal ankle movements.

Treatment. Exostoses do not have to be surgically removed unless they are symptomatic, and the prognosis is usually excellent after they are removed. After the surgery, the athlete should begin active use of the ankle as soon as possible in conjunction with anti-inflammatory treatment.

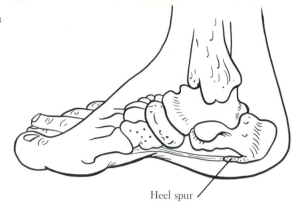

Figure 22-14 Calcaneal heel spur at attachment of plantar fascia.

Foot Injuries

Foot injuries are extremely common in sports because of the foot's role in bearing weight. There is also a high rate of reinjury due to the difficulty of adequately resting this vital structure following injury.

Anatomy and Biomechanics

The foot is a complex structure consisting of twenty-six bones and thirty-three joints. There are five metatarsal bones that articulate distally with the five phalanges (Figure 22-15). Proximally, the metatarsal bones articulate with the tarsal bones. A pair of sesamoid bones located on the plantar surface of the head of the first metatarsal helps relieve and disperse the metatarsal's stress of weight bearing. The tarsal and metatarsal bones form longitudinal and transverse arches. The longitudinal arch runs from the calcaneus to the distal end of the first metatarsal. The transverse arch runs perpendicular to the longitudinal arch (Figure 22-16, p. 406). The arches help the foot absorb the shock of bearing weight. Ligaments, joint capsules, and muscles hold the arches together. Injuries to these soft tissues can weaken the arches and cause disabling conditions.

Exostosis: A bone spur; a bony growth on a bone's surface.

See Table 22-1 (p. 383) for the muscles and movements of the foot. Figure 22-17 (p. 406) shows the muscles of the plantar foot. The anterior tibial artery becomes superficial near the ankle's medial aspect and becomes the dorsal pedal artery, which supplies blood to the foot's dorsum. The posterior tibial artery branches into the peroneal artery, which divides into the medial and lateral plantar arteries that supply blood to the foot and its toes' plantar aspect. The tibial nerve innervates the posterior leg and plantar aspect of the foot, and the common peroneal nerve divides into the deep and superficial peroneal nerves, which supply the dorsum of the foot and toes.

Hindfoot Fractures

The hindfoot includes the calcaneus and talus. Fractures to these bones are relatively rare.

Fracture of the Calcaneus. A fractured calcaneus is usually caused by direct trauma, such as when a person lands on the heels after falling from a height. Often the injury is bilateral and may be associated with compression fractures of the spine.

Evaluation. Upon examination, the heel may look broadened, with swelling apparent distally and posteriorly to the malleoli. Any movement or palpation of the calcaneus is extremely painful, and weight bearing cannot be tolerated. Always suspect a fracture of the calcaneus when there is heel pain after direct impact.

Treatment. Acute care consists of ice (closed fracture); splinting the foot, ankle, and lower leg; elevation; and transportation to a local medical facility or team physician for evaluation.

Stress Fractures of the Calcaneus. Stress fractures of the calcaneus are

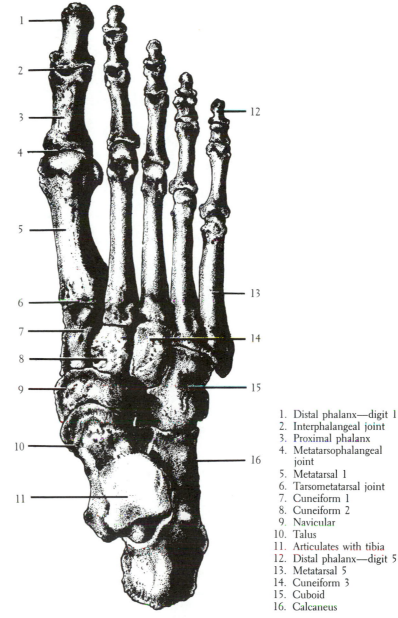

1. Distal phalanx—digit 1
2. Interphalangeal joint
3. Proximal phalanx
4. Metatarsophalangeal joint
5. Metatarsal 1
6. Tarsometatarsal joint
7. Cuneiform 1
8. Cuneiform 2
9. Navicular
10. Talus
11. Articulates with tibia
12. Distal phalanx—digit 5
13. Metatarsal 5
14. Cuneiform 3
15. Cuboid
16. Calcaneus

Figure 22-15 Bones of the foot (dorsal surface). (From Crouch, 1983, p. 73.)

commonly overlooked and may be mistaken for Achilles tendinitis, retrocalcaneal bursitis, or **plantar fascitis.**

Evaluation. Symptoms include gradual onset of pain, swelling at the back

Plantar fascia (PF): The fascia on the plantar (bottom) surface of the foot. Plantar fascitis is injury and inflammation of this structure.

of the heel, and pain upon palpation. The injury may be caused by running excessive distances, particularly on hard surfaces, or from the heel being constantly pounded while running on a basketball court. As with other stress fractures, the acute injury may not appear on x-ray and may require a bone scan or follow-up x-rays for accurate diagnosis.

Treatment. Treat calcaneal stress fractures conservatively. Rest is of the utmost importance, and immobilization with a cast may be indicated. Maintain cardiovascular fitness through bicycling or swimming. A graduated exercise program may be initiated within the sixth or seventh week of the onset of symptoms and treatment. The athlete should wear a heel cushion in the shoe to absorb shock. Discontinue or modify the program if pain reappears.

Talus (Os Trigonum). The os trigonum is an accessory bone located in the posterior aspect of the talus, behind the posterior tubercle, and it may appear as a separate ossicle or be fused to the talus. Fractures of the os trigonum are rare because the bone is not present in every individual. This injury should be considered in athletes with chronic ankle pain and an associated histoy of fracture of the tibia, talus, or calcaneus. Fracture of the fused os trigonum usually occurs in active adults.

Evaluation. Upon evaluation, the athlete may complain of pain in the posterior aspect of the ankle, particularly with weight bearing and plantar flexion. Passive range of motion of the foot may be restricted because of muscle spasm and swelling. Crepitation may be heard or felt upon palpation, just anterior to the Achilles tendon insertion. When reviewing the history, the athlete may recall that the onset of pain occurred after a sudden violent plantar flexion or appeared gradually after repeated extreme plantar flexion.

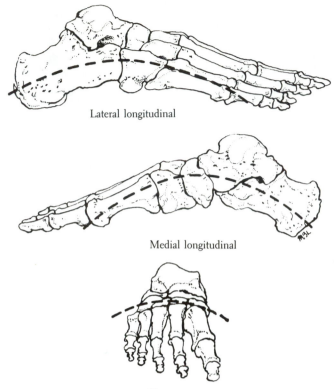

Lateral longitudinal

Medial longitudinal

Transverse

Figure 22-16 Arches of the foot. (From Crouch, 1983, p. 73.)

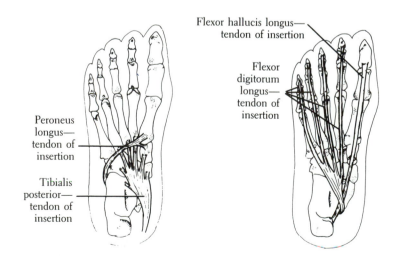

Flexor hallucis longus—
tendon of insertion

Flexor digitorum longus—
tendon of insertion

Peroneus longus—
tendon of insertion

Tibialis posterior—
tendon of insertion

Figure 22-17 Muscles of the foot's plantar surface. (From Crouch, 1983, p. 101.)

In the latter case, the os trigonum is repeatedly pinched between the posterior tibia and calcaneus. Refer the athlete to the team physician if you suspect this injury.

Midfoot Fractures

The midfoot is formed by the navicular, cuboid, and the first, second, and third cuneiform bones. These bones are rarely fractured in athletics. However, the bones are susceptible to avulsion fractures because the tarsal bones are tightly bound to each other with ligaments. These avulsions tend to occur during dislocation or subluxation of a tarsal joint, causing an attached ligament to pull a bone fragment from one of the tarsal bones.

Evaluation. During evaluation, consider the characteristic signs of fracture, including deformity, loss of function, swelling, pain during direct or indirect palpation, and numbing distal to the site of injury.

Treatment. Treatment includes ice (if closed fracture); immobilization of the foot, ankle, and lower leg by splinting; elevation; and transportation to a medical facility or team physician. When the cast is removed, protect and support the foot and arch with orthotics or taping until functional stability has been restored.

Navicular Stress Fracture. Stress fractures of the navicular are rarely documented and may often be unrecognized. This overuse syndrome can occur in any sport that involves repetitive explosive plantar flexion (toe push-offs). Recognition of this injury is extremely important because continued activity may result in a displaced intra-articular fracture.

Evaluation. A common characteristic of this injury is that pain tends to increase during rather than after activity

as in many overuse syndromes. Pain is primarily localized on the dorsomedial aspect of the foot, but it often radiates to the first, second, or third toes. This injury is sometimes misdiagnosed as Morton's neuroma (see p. 412). X-rays may not be diagnostic, so the team physician may use bone scans or **tomograms** for verification.

Treatment. Treatment is conservative if the diagnosis is made before a displaced navicular fracture develops. Rest is essential, and the use of a cast boot or custom-fitted orthotic may be indicated. Once the athlete is given clearance to bear weight on the injured foot, rehabilitation includes reestablishment of functional stability and normal foot motions.

Forefoot Fractures

The forefoot includes the five metatarsals, five phalanges, and the two sesamoids that lie under the first metatarsal head. Fractures in this area occur more often than in other areas of the foot.

Metatarsals. The five metatarsals are sometimes called the long bones of the foot. The foot resembles the hand in that the base of the first and second metatarsals are not connected. The bases of the four outer metatarsals are connected by dorsal, plantar, and interosseus ligaments. The metatarsal heads comprise the anterior arch, which is one of the foot's main weight-bearing surfaces.

Evaluation. Fractures are commonly caused by direct impact (e.g., being kicked or stepped on by another player), repetitive overload, or excessive torsional stress. Signs and treatment of these fractures are similar to those for the other fractures discussed in this chapter.

Tomogram: An x-ray that produces a cross-sectional image of a structure. Also called a CT scan (computer-assisted-tomogram).

Treatment. The usual casting period is four to six weeks. After the cast has been removed, support the arch by taping, arch supports, and firm-soled shoes. The distribution of soft tissue in this area is sparse, so restoration of length and alignment (particularly in the anteroposterior plane) is the most important treatment concern. The rehabilitation program should attempt to gradually increase pain-free functional stability.

Fifth Metatarsal. Fractures of the fifth metatarsal, which are among the most common fractures in sports, may occur at the bone's base (most common), shaft, or head. Fractures to this structure include displaced, nondisplaced, avulsion, and stress.

The fifth metatarsal is recognized by the tubercular eminence on the outer side of its base. It articulates at its base with the cuboid and the fourth metatarsal. The peroneus brevis, cubometatarsal ligament, lateral band of the plantar fascia, and the peroneus tertius insert into the base of this bone. Base fractures are typically caused by forced forefoot inversion, which can cause an avulsion fracture from overload of the peroneus brevis tendon at its insertion. Other common mechanisms include direct or repetitive stresses.

Evaluation. In addition to other common signs of fracture (see Chapter 6), look for pain upon palpation of the base and shaft of the bone. Typically, there is tenderness over the insertion of the peroneus brevis tendon and pain during active resistive eversion or passive inversion. Treatment is the same as for other foot fractures. The athlete may return to participation when pain over the fifth metatarsal has subsided.

Treatment. Treatment for a stress fracture includes ice, taping to prevent forefoot inversion, rest from repetitive stresses to the foot, non-weight-bearing cardiovascular exercise, gradual return

to running, and the use of a soft insert in the shoe, which protects the lateral border of the foot.

Phalanges. Although fractures of the phalanges do not appear serious, this injury can be disabling for many weeks because the area is so vulnerable. The light, flexible footwear used in many sports allows the toes considerable mobility, which tends to irritate the injury and prevent it from healing. In addition, the strong plantar flexion of the foot required for push off causes pain and delays healing.

This injury is typically caused by actions such as kicking a heavy immovable object or stubbing the toe while not wearing a shoe. The injury tends to occur off the playing field. The fracture may be caused by hyperflexion, hyperextension, or compression of the phalanges. In an avulsion fracture of the proximal or distal phalanx, a hammer toe will result if the injury is not treated properly. (*Note:* Hammer toes may also be caused by wearing shoes too short during growth spurts.)

Evaluation and Treatment. Fracture involving the interphalangeal or metatarsaphalangeal joint can cause serious problems, so always refer the athlete to a physician when this injury occurs. This injury is often accompanied by the formation of a hematoma under the nail, which may require a hole drilled in the nail for relief of pain. A plaster cast may be indicated (four weeks) if the patient will not stay off the foot. During rehabilitation, protect the toe by adhesive taping, foam pad, or an insole splint to prevent hypermobility of the injured toe.

Sesamoid Bones. The two sesamoid bones, located in the tendon of the flexor hallucis brevis, are subject to irritation and fracture because of their location and weight-bearing function. Athletes with a high arch or tight plantar fascia are predisposed to this injury because they place increased tension on the sesamoids. This injury may occur from direct pressure, as from a cleat protruding through a worn shoe insole. Relieve the resulting sesamoiditis with padding, orthotics, and anti-inflammatory treatment.

Fracture of the sesamoids usually occurs from a direct blow to the ball of the foot while the great toe is in hyper-dorsiflexion. Stress fractures, while rare, may also occur. This injury is very painful and disabling, and the athlete will not be able to "toe off" while walking or running. A chronic condition that may be corrected only through surgery can develop.

Evaluation and Treatment. Typical symptoms include severe point tenderness on the ball of the foot, localized swelling, pain during active plantar flexion and active and passive dorsiflexion. The foot may require immobilization if the pain is severe. Rehabilitation should begin as soon as possible with non-weight-bearing cardiovascular exercise. When weight bearing is tolerated, the athlete begins "flatfoot" walking, graduating to toe-off walking, to mild jogging. The running program should gradually progress to easy sprinting, figure eight patterns, and finally full-effort start-and-stop sprinting. Stabilize the joint by taping (see the appendix); the athlete should wear stiff-soled shoes.

Foot Contusions

Foot contusions, particularly on the plantar surface, are common because of the foot's weight-bearing requirements. A contusion can be disabling for a long time because of the foot's vulnerability.

Contusions over the calcaneus occur frequently in sports requiring jumping, such as long jump, triple jump, basketball, and volleyball (Figure 22-18). This injury is common even though the area is protected by thick skin and a large fat pad. The contusion is particularly dis-

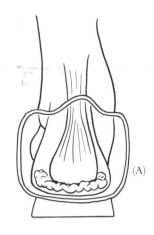

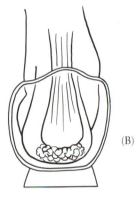

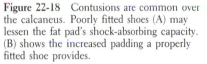

Figure 22-18 Contusions are common over the calcaneus. Poorly fitted shoes (A) may lessen the fat pad's shock-absorbing capacity. (B) shows the increased padding a properly fitted shoe provides.

tressing and frustrating because it appears trivial yet causes so much pain.

Evaluation and Treatment. Symptoms include severe pain in the heel when it is palpated or bearing weight. The athlete may relate that the pain feels like a stone embedded in the heel. If not properly treated, the injury may progress into a chronic periostitis of the calcaneus. Treatment involves the usual therapies for contusions (see Chapter 5), including acute anti-inflammatory procedures and range of motion exercises. Rest and protecting the area with a heel cup, adhesive taping (see the appendix), and the use of felt doughnut pads are also important. Inspect the athlete's footwear to determine if the shoes have adequate shock-absorbing ability.

Midfoot Sprain

The midfoot ligaments can be strained when excessive strain is placed on an unsupported foot. The injury is common among gymnasts who wear only slippers or track athletes who wear racing flats. The injury often results when the foot is severely pronated (sprained metatarsal ligament) or when the longitudinal arch is forced down (sprained calcaneonavicular ligament—"spring ligament"). These sprains can be caused by either acute or chronic overload.

Evaluation and Treatment. Symptoms include swelling and pain deep in the medial aspect of the foot. Treatment is the same as for other strains and includes anti-inflammatory therapy, range of motion and strength exercises, and rest. When returning to competition, the athlete should wear stiff shoes that have arch support. Figure eight arch support taping (see the appendix) or orthotics may support these injured ligaments.

Turf Toe

Sprain of the collateral ligaments of the first metatarsophalangeal (MP) joint **(turf toe)** is relatively common in football and soccer. An increased incidence of turf toe in football has been attributed to artificial turf and light, flexible football shoes, although this injury also occurs on natural grass. Turf toe may be caused by hyperextension, hyperflexion, or valgus stress of the MP joint. These motions can occur during kicking, driving on a block in football, or initiating an explosive lateral movement (e.g., a football lineman pulling down the line of scrimmage).

Evaluation. There is point tenderness during palpation of the collateral ligaments, pain during movement of the joint (particularly in the direction that produced the injury), swelling, and discoloration.

Treatment. Treatment consists of immobilization by splinting, plaster casting, or a lace-up cast boot; use of a crutch or cane for movement, and standard anti-inflammatory treatments and modalities. The rehabilitation program is the same as that for injury to the sesamoid bones. When the athlete resumes active exercises, it is very important that the injured MP joint be stabilized with adhesive tape. A $\frac{1}{4}$-inch felt pad placed under the head of the first metatarsal bone sometimes relieves pain in a hyperextension injury because it decreases the range of motion during push off. Also, the use of orthoplast or metal insole splints running from the front of the heel to the tips of the toes can be beneficial.

Foot Strain

Foot strain from acute or chronic overload is very common in athletes. Untreated foot strain can cause deformity because of the mechanical changes that occur to compensate for weakness and pain. Foot strain may be caused by factors such as obesity, overuse, activity on hard surfaces without adequate support and protection, poor foot mechanics, and poorly fitted shoes. Strains of the Achilles tendon, tibialis anterior, tibialis posterior, and peroneal muscles (which may manifest themselves as foot strains) were discussed previously; here we discuss strains of the hallucis longus and plantar fascia.

Flexor Hallucis Longus (FHL) Tendinitis. The FHL tendon originates on the posterior aspect of the fibula, from the lowest part of the interosseus membrane. The tendon structure occupies almost the entire length of the muscle,

Turf toe: Sprain of the collateral ligaments of the first metatarsophalangeal joint.

passing around the medial malleolus, and courses forward along the medial longitudinal arch toward its insertion on the undersurface of the great toe. The FHL is also protected by a synovial sheath that can become inflamed, resulting in tenosynovitis.

This injury is common in ballerinas who repeatedly stress the FHL tendon when dancing on the tips of their toes. This injury is also prevalent in athletes who perform repetitive forceful push-offs in sports like tennis, basketball, track, and football.

Evaluation. Symptoms include pain and swelling behind the medial malleolus or along the medial longitudinal arch. Passive dorsiflexion of the great toe usually elicits pain. Manually resisted dorsiflexion helps identify the site of pain and injury and differentiate strains of the FHL and Achilles tendon.

Treatment. Treatment is the same as for any strain (see Chapter 5) and includes anti-inflammatory therapy, range of motion and strength exercises, and rest. Helpful aids are adhesive taping to prevent hyperextension of the great toe or orthotics to support the longitudinal arch. Sometimes a hard-soled shoe can alleviate pain during the push-off phase of movement.

Plantar Fascitis (PF). The plantar fascia is a tough ligamentous structure located on the foot's plantar aspect. It extends from the inferior aspect of the calcaneus to the heads of the metatarsal bones (Figure 22-19). Trauma from jumping from heights, chronic jumping, overuse from running, or torsional stress from abnormal foot structures can cause plantar fascitis. These forces overstretch and irritate the plantar fascia.

Evaluation. Symptoms include pain on or about the heel, particularly on its medial aspect. Pain is usually most serious when the athlete gets out of bed in

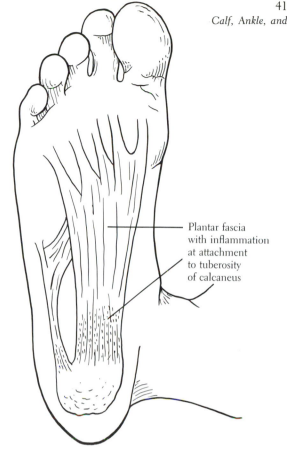

Plantar fascia with inflammation at attachment to tuberosity of calcaneus

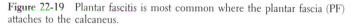

Figure 22-19 Plantar fascitis is most common where the plantar fascia (PF) attaches to the calcaneus.

the morning. While running, the athlete may experience pain during or after activity (depending upon the severity of the injury).

Treatment. In addition to the standard treatment for strains (anti-inflammatory therapy, range of motion and strength exercises, and rest), figure eight arch taping (see the appendix) is satisfactory support. Application of spiral strips of tape around the arch of the foot is contraindicated because it will worsen the overstretch of the fascia and prolong recovery.

Bursitis

The Achilles (located between the Achilles tendon and the skin) and the retrocalcaneal bursae (located between the calcaneus and Achilles tendon) are easily inflamed from trauma or overuse (Figure 22-20). The usual causes of this condition are ill-fitting shoes or stiff, unpadded heel counters.

Evaluation. Bursitis can be mistaken for an injury to the insertion of the Achilles tendon or a plantar ligament. Carefully examine and identify the precise location of the pain and swelling to help differentiate between these injuries. For example, with bursitis, active contraction of the Achilles tendon usually will not elicit pain, but passive stretch will. Chronic irritation of these bursae causes calcification and thickening, producing a "pump bump" or "runner's bump." This bump can impinge on the Achilles tendon during dorsiflexion, causing further inflammation (Figure 22-21).

Treatment. Treatment begins with proper-fitting shoes, padding, and the usual anti-inflammatory treatments. Local corticosteroid injection may be indicated if the injury does not respond well to conservative treatment. Taping to prevent dorsiflexion of the foot may reduce irritation and allow the athlete to return to competition.

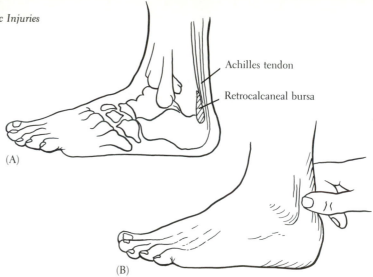

Figure 22-20   To differentiate (A) retrocalcaneal bursitis from (B) Achilles tendinitis, palpate for tenderness in front of the Achilles tendon.

Plantar Neuroma
(Morton's Neuroma)

Plantar neuroma (PN) is an entrapment neuropathy of an interdigital nerve and is not uncommon in athletes, particularly in women. Symptoms include sudden attacks of sharp pain in the transverse arch between the third and fourth metatarsal heads. Often this burning, shooting pain radiates to the dorsum of the foot toward the ankle. In the early stages, there is a burning sensation in the region of the metatarsal heads, which may radiate to the toes and be accompanied by paresthesia and numbness, but the foot will appear normal.

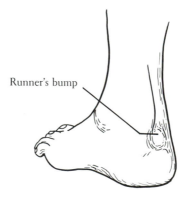

Figure 22-21   Runner's bump is caused by the Achilles tendon bursae calcifying and thickening.

Evaluation. Firm palpation reveals a small area of extreme tenderness usually located in the third metatarsal space. In the later stages, upon palpation this pain will be accompanied by crepitation. The pain of Morton's neuroma is associated with a localized thickening of the nerve at its bifurcation in the interphalangeal space. The enlargement or neuroma is a result of the nerve being repeatedly traumatized by the metatarsal heads.

Treatment. Treatment includes supporting the transverse arch with a felt or rubber pad. If this technique proves unsatisfactory, local injection of a corticosteroid may give temporary relief; surgery is usually required for permanent relief from pain.

Hammer Toes

Hammer toes are characterized by dorsiflexion of the MP joint and plantar flexion contracture of the proximal interphalangeal (IP) joint. Any toe may be affected, but the injury is more prevalent in the second toe. Tender corns and calluses are usually present on the dorsal surface of the proximal IP joint. Hammer toes are occasionally congenital, in which case they occur in more than one toe and are usually associated with other congenital foot deformities. Hammer toes are usually acquired and tend to occur in people with pronated feet. This condition may be caused by new shoes or tight elastic socks that are too short.

Treatment. Simple manipulation, padding, and splinting often relieve discomfort in the early stages of this disorder. More advanced cases may require surgical correction.

Hallux Valgus (Bunions)

Hallux valgus is a lateral angulation of the great toe at its MP joint. Usually the medial side of the head of the first metatarsal bone is enlarged, and a bursa and callus form over this area. The bony prominence and its overlying bursa constitute a bunion. Hallux valgus is frequently congenital and is much more common in women than in men. Medial deviation of the first metatarsal bone may initiate the deforming change; narrow, pointed shoes doubtlessly aggravate bunions.

Treatment. In mild cases, wearing properly fitted shoes and undergoing

repeated overcorrection by stretching may prevent progression of the deformity and relieve discomfort. The individual should sleep with a pad or other device separating the first and second toes. The depression of the metatarsal arch should be corrected by a supportive pad and exercises. Thermal therapy (Chapter 13) can sometimes help reduce inflammation. Corrective adhesive taping may also be beneficial.

Morton's Syndrome

Morton's syndrome is a short first metatarsal. The syndrome causes overpronation, which results in hypermobility of the first and second metatarsal joints and sometimes metatarsalgia (pain and tenderness in the metatarsal area). The second metatarsal develops a thickened shaft from excessive weight bearing. (The first metatarsal takes longer to make contact with the ground, forcing the second metatarsal to undergo more stress.) A painful callus often develops under the head of the second metatarsal, and the ligaments, capsule, and muscles surrounding the joint of the first and second metatarsals and first cuneiform bone may become irritated and hinder performance.

Treatment. Treatment for Morton's syndrome consists of placing pads under the first metatarsal. The pads will share the weight bearing and relieve the second metatarsal.

References

Arrowsmith, S. R., L. F. Lamar, and F. L. Allman. Traumatic dislocations of the peroneal tendons. *American Journal of Sports Medicine* 11:142–146, 1983.

Basmajian, J. V. *Primary Anatomy*. Baltimore: Williams & Wilkins, 1970.

Beall, S., J. Gardner, and D. Oxley. Anterolateral compartment syndrome related to drug-induced bleeding. *American Journal of Sports Medicine* 11:454–455, 1983.

Blatz, D. L. Bilateral femoral and tibial shaft fractures in a runner. *American Journal of Sports Medicine.* 9:322–325, 1981.

Blauvelt, C. T., and F. R. Nelson. *A Manual of Orthopaedic Terminology.* St. Louis: C. V. Mosby, 1981.

Calliet, R. *Foot and Ankle Pain.* Philadelphia: F. A Davis, 1968.

Cassells, S. W., and B. Fellows. Another young athlete with intermittent claudication: a case report. *American Journal of Sports Medicine* 11:180–182, 1983.

Chamey, A. Mechanical and morphological aspects of experimental overload and fatigue in bone. *Journal of Biomechanics* 3:263–270, 1970.

Chusid, J. G. *Correlative Neuroanatomy and Functional Neurology.* Los Altos, Calif.: Lange Medical Publications, 1976.

Coker, T. P., J. A. Arnold, and D. L. Weber. Traumatic lesions of the metatarsophalangeal joint of the great toe in athletics. *American Journal of Sports Medicine* 6:326–334, 1978.

Detmer, D. E. Chronic leg pain. *American Journal of Sports Medicine* 8:141–144, 1980.

Fond, D. Flexor hallucis longus tendonitis—a case of mistaken identity and posterior impingement syndrome in dancers: evaluation and management. *Journal of Sports and Physical Therapy* 5:1984.

Frankel, V. H. Editorial comment. *American Journal of Sports Medicine* 6:396, 1978.

Garrick, J. G. The frequency of injury, mechanism of injury and the epidemiology of ankle sprains. *American Journal of Sports Medicine* 5:241–242, 1977.

Grana, W. A., and E. Schelberg-Karnes. How I manage deep muscle bruises. *The Physician and Sportsmedicine* 11:123–127, 1983.

Halpern, A. A. Compartment Syndromes. Paper presented at Stanford University Medical Center, March 19, 1977.

Harvey, J. S. Effort thrombosis in the lower extremity of a runner. *American Journal of Sports Medicine* 6:400–402, 1978.

Hunter, L. Y. Stress fracture of the tarsal navicular—more frequently than we realize? *American Journal of Sports Medicine* 9:217–219, 1981.

Ihle, C. L., and R. M. Cochran. Fracture of the fused os trigonum. *American Journal of Sports Medicine* 10:47–50, 1982.

Johnson, R. J., and M. H. Pope. Tibial shaft fractures in skiing. *American Journal of Sports Medicine* 5:49–61, 1977.

Kaumeyer, G., and T. Malone. Ankle injuries: anatomical and biomechanical considerations necessary for the development of an injury prevention program. *Journal of Orthopedic Sports and Physical Therapy.* 1:171–177, 1980.

Leach, R. E., E. DiIorio, and R. A. Harney. Pathologic hindfoot conditions in the athlete. *Clinical Orthopaedics and Related Research* 177:116–121, 1983.

Leach, R. E., S. James, and S. Wasilewski. Achilles tendinitis. *American Journal of Sports Medicine* 9:93–98, 1981.

Lysens, R. J., L. M. Renson, et al. Intermittent claudication in young athletes: popliteal artery entrapment syndrome. *American Journal of Sports Medicine* 11:177–179, 1983.

McCarthy, S. Protecting anterior tibial contusions in baseball. *The Physician and Sportsmedicine* 9:122, 1981.

McLennon, J. G. Treatment of acute and chronic luxations of the peroneal tendons. *The Physician and Sportsmedicine* 8:63–64, 1980.

Mackie, J. W., and J. A. Webster. Deep vein thrombosis in marathon runners. *The Physician and Sportsmedicine* 9:91–98, 1981.

Mannis, C. I. Transchondral fracture of the dome of the talus sustained during weight lifting. *American Journal of Sports Medicine* 11:354–355, 1983.

Mubarak, S. J., R. N. Gould, et al. The medial tibial stress syndrome. *American Journal of Sports Medicine* 10:201–204, 1972.

Noble, A. B., and F. H. Selesnick. The Thompson test for ruptured Achilles tendon. *The Physician and Sportsmedicine* 8:63–64, 1980.

Norfray, J. F., L. Schlachter, et al. Early confirmation of stress fractures in joggers. *Journal of the American Medical Association* 243:1647–1649, 1980.

Ogben, J. A. Subluxation of the proximal tibiofibular joint. *Clinical Orthopaedics and Related Research* 101:192–197, 1974.

Pappas, A. M. Epiphyseal injuries in sports. *The Physician and Sportsmedicine* 11:140–148, 1983.

Pearl, A. J. Anterior compartment syndrome: a case report. *The Physician and Sportsmedicine* 9:119–120, 1981.

Quigley, T. B., and A. D. Scheller. Surgical repair of the ruptured Achilles tendon. *American Journal of Sports Medicine* 8:244–250, 1980.

Radakovich, M., and T. Malone. The superior tibiofibular joint: the forgotten joint. *Journal of Sports and Physical Therapy* 3:129–132, 1983.

Reneman, R. S. The anterior and lateral compartment syndrome of the leg due to intense use of muscles. *Clinical Orthopaedics and Related Research* 113:69, 1975.

Roy, S. How I manage plantar fascitis. *The Physician and Sportsmedicine* 11(10):127–131, 1983.

Rudo, N. D., and H. B. Noble. Popliteal artery entrapment syndrome in athletes. *The Physician and Sportsmedicine* 10:105–114, 1982.

Shields, C. L. Achilles tendon injuries and disabling conditions. *The Physician and Sportsmedicine* 10:77–84, 1982.

Smart, G. W., J. E. Taunton, and D. B. Clement. Achilles tendon disorders in runners—a review. *Medicine and Science in Sports Exercise* 12:231–243, 1980.

Staniski, C. L., J. H. McMaster, and P. E. Scranton. On the nature of stress fractures. *American Journal of Sports Medicine* 6:391–396, 1978.

Taunton, J. E., D. B. Clement, and D. Webber. Lower extremity stress fractures in athletes. *The Physician and Sportsmedicine* 9:77–86, 1981.

Van Hal, M. E., J. S. Keen, et al. Stress fracture of the great toe sesamoids. *American Journal of Sports Medicine* 10:122–128, 1982.

Wilcox, J. R., A. L. Moniot, and J. P. Green. Bone scanning in the evaluation of exercise-related stress injuries. *Radiology* 123:699–703, 1977.

Yale, I. *Podiatric Medicine*. Baltimore: Williams & Wilkins, 1980.

Zernicke, R. F. Biomechanical evaluation of bilateral tibial spiral fractures during skiing—a case study. *Medicine and Science in Sports Exercise* 13:243–245, 1981.

Skin Injuries and Diseases

23

S KIN INJURIES and diseases are prevalent in athletics because of the skin's large surface area and the many pathogens in the athletic environment. The athletic trainer should be able to recognize the principal skin disorders and maintain a preventative program that stresses cleanliness in both the athletic training room and the various practice areas. This chapter discusses the anatomy, physiology, and principal skin disorders commonly seen in athletes.

Anatomy and Physiology

The skin, or integumentary system, is the body's first line of defense against invasion from fungal or bacterial agents. Without this barrier, many bacteria, commonly found in the surrounding air, would find their way into the moist, warm environment of the inner body, causing disease, infection, and possibly death. It is therefore important to know how the skin helps keep disease out of the human organism and internal body fluids and heat from escaping.

Athletes frequently exposed to the sun should wear a sunscreen to protect their skin from harmful ultraviolet rays.

416

The skin is divided into the outer, nonvascular epidermis and the vascular dermis. The epidermis consists of five layers; from the highest to the lowest they are the (1) stratum corneum, (2) stratum lucidum, (3) stratum granulosum, (4) stratum spinosum, and (5) stratum basale. The dermis consists of two layers: the reticular and papillary.

Epidermis

The **epidermis** is a nonvascular, layered covering (Figure 23-1, p. 418) whose function is mainly protective (i.e., keeping disease and trauma from injuring deeper tissues). Hair and nails and gland are extensions of the epidermis and are discussed in later sections.

The thickness of the epidermal covering varies from 0.5 millimeter on the eyelids, penis, and eardrum to 5 to 6 millimeters on the soles of the feet and palms of the hands. The average thickness over the rest of the body is 1 to 2 millimeters.

Since the epidermis is devoid of blood vessels, lymphatic vessels, and connective tissue, it is considered parasitic on the underlying dermal layer. Any injury or disease to the dermal layer is usually manifested first as a change in the epidermal layer. In addition, the epidermal tissue heals much slower than the underlying tissue because it lacks adequate blood flow.

The epidermis must be flexible to allow movement. Close examination discloses many visible furrows on the skin's surface that usually run parallel to a joint's movement, allowing smooth movement without the skin overstretching. There are also many nonvisible furrows, called **Langer's lines,** which are important for understanding a puncture wound or cut. If the skin is punctured, it will tear along one of the stress lines, leaving a tear rather than a hole (except in the case of a high-velocity puncture like a gunshot wound). These stress lines have been mapped out using cadavers (see Figure 23-2, p. 419).

Ridges on the fingers and toes, as well as the linear furrows covering the rest of the body, are the result of irregularities in the skin's underlying dermal layer. The epidermal stratum basale adheres to the dermal layer and follows the contours of that layer. The finer contours of the fingers—fingerprints—are unique to each individual, which is why fingerprints are used for identification.

The stratum corneum layer—the outer layer—is actually a layer of dead cells of the fibrous protein **keratin,** a metabolic end product of epidermal cells. As the keratin migrates to the surface, it is sloughed off. Keratin is usually thinner than the actual living epidermis, but in high-stress points (i.e., feet and hands), the layer can build up and become quite thick, as mentioned earlier.

The transition zone between the stratum corneum and the underlying epidermal layers is the barrier to penetration. The tissues on the inside of this barrier contain approximately 70 percent water; the outer, horny layer contains less than 15 percent water. The external environment controls the amount of water in the outer layer. If the air is dry, more water is lost from the stratum corneum, giving the skin a dry, flaky appearance. If the environment is humid or wet (as in bathing), the stratum corneum will pick up additional water, leaving the skin looking white and wrinkled. If the water content drops below 10 percent, the skin chaps and cracks, leaving openings through which bacteria and fungus can pass to the moist, warm environment of the lower skin layers.

Dermis

The dermal layer of the skin is sometimes referred to as the true skin. The dermis is important because it contains the circulatory system that supplies both the dermal and the epidermal layers with nutrients and a lymphatic system

Epidermis: The outer, nonvascular part of the skin; it protects deeper tissue and is a barrier to foreign organisms.

Keratin: A protein comprising the major component of the epidermis.

Langer's lines: Furrows on the surface of the skin that allow the joints to move without significantly stretching the skin.

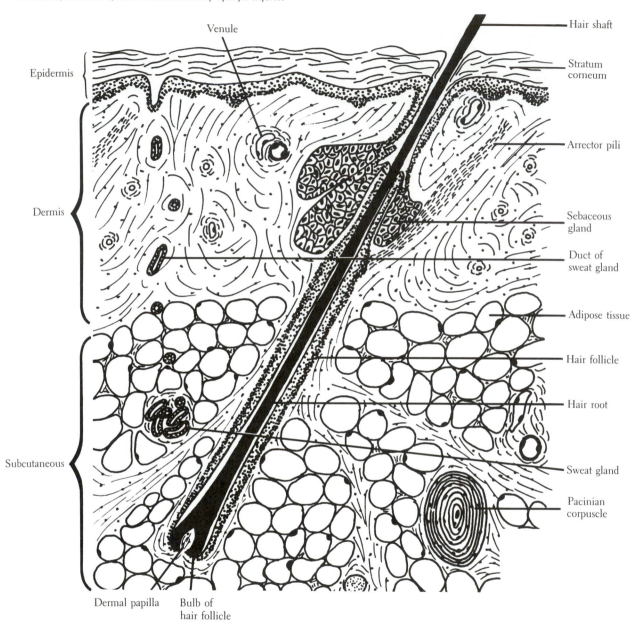

Figure 23-1 Human skin from the abdomen at 35X (adipose tissue shown at 100X for detail). (From Crouch, J. E. *Introduction to Human Anatomy*, 6th ed. Palo Alto, Calif.: Mayfield Publishing Co., 1983, p. 31.)

that removes some waste products (see the "Circulation" section, p. 421). Remember that although many diseases of the skin are diagnosed by changes in the epidermis, the disease may be dermal in nature.

The three main cells in the **dermis** are the fibrocyte, histiocyte, and mastocyte. The fibrocytes form the collagen that makes up the major portion of the dermal layer. Collagen is a structural substance found in connective tissue all over the body (see Chapter 5). It provides the skin's framework. A second type of connective tissue also arises from fibrocytes, an elastic protein called elastin. Both these fibers are held together by a cementlike substance (interfibrillar cement) that provides a strong structural framework. It is believed that this cement is formed or secreted by the mastocyte cells.

Histiocytes are scavenger cells, much like white blood cells; they roam through the dermis, absorbing foreign substances. Mastocytes contain two proteins, histamine and heparin, which can cause local redness or swelling if the mastocytes are damaged, for example, an allergic reaction to a substance like poison oak resin.

The papillary layer of the dermis consists of the two types of fibrocytes tightly intertwined. Most of the sensory nerves are found here. The upper portion of this layer is composed of many minute ridges called papillae, giving rise to its name. These papillae mesh with the epidermal layer and give the skin its ridged, wrinkled appearance.

The reticular layer is under the papillary layer. This layer consists of a much looser organization of collagen and elastin interwoven with smooth muscle, to give the skin its tone. Between the mesh formed by the other fibers is the origin of eccrine and apocrine glands and hair follicles. Beneath this layer is the subcutaneous fat layer.

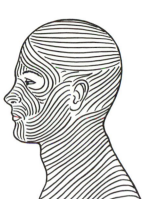

Dermis: The lower layer of skin, largely composed of collagen.

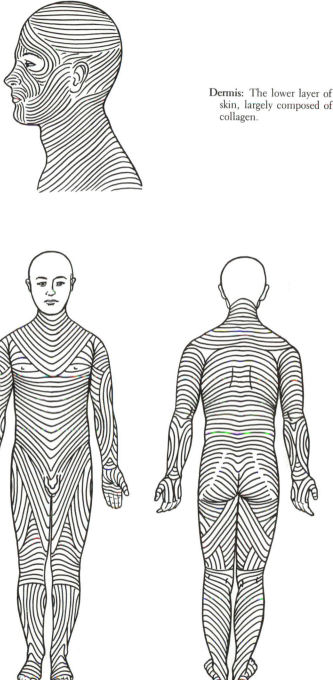

Figure 23-2 Langer's lines (cleavage lines) of the skin.

Hair and Nails

Fingernails and toenails are extensions of the epidermis. The nail is formed from the second epidermal layer, the stratum lucidum; the stratum corneum forms the cuticle around the base of the nail. The nail gets its pink color from the vascular bed in the underlying layers of the skin and the firm attachment of the nail to these layers. The lunula (the moon-shaped area at the base of the nail) is not attached to the lower layers and thus does not reflect the underlying vascularization.

Nails sometimes indicate overall body health. Since nails are made of nonessential material, they shed in times of stress (emotional as well as disease). Vitamin deficiencies do not manifest themselves in the nails of otherwise healthy individuals; in fact, only in the later stages of malnutrition do the nails suffer to a great degree.

Various factors can increase the rate of nail growth, including trauma and stress. In certain occupations and sports, such as farming, wrestling, and basketball, the nails are subjected to constant injury, causing the nails to greatly increase in thickness; nail biting sometimes doubles the rate of growth.

Hair is found all over the body except on the palms of the hands and the bottoms of the feet. Hair is the second fastest-growing tissue in the body—only bone marrow grows faster. Most people have a thin, downy covering of hairs over most of their body, with terminal hairs covering the head, armpits, genitals, and, in males, the face and neck.

In both males and females, the male hormone testosterone controls the terminal hair growth of the axilla, pubic region, beard, and body hair (the secondary sex characteristics). The growth of female facial hair is inhibited by hormones such as estrogen. In postmenopausal women, this hormone inhibition may diminish, and facial hair may grow in. In males, high levels of testosterone are the underlying cause of baldness, even though testosterone enhances the growth of facial hair.

Hair itself is composed of tightly fused keratin cells and grows upward from an epidermal hair follicle that is lodged in the dermis. These hair follicles are formed during fetal development and are not replaced after birth, so any damage to hair follicles is permanent. Plucking a hair usually leaves a few matrix cells in the follicle, which will then regenerate a new hair.

Each hair is associated with a sebaceous gland that secretes an oily substance (sebum), blood vessels that supply the growing hair with nutrients, and a smooth muscle (the erector pili).

Unlike nail growth, hair growth does not continue indefinitely. The length of a hair is determined by **follicular activity,** which is cyclical. Fortunately, not all follicles are dormant at the same time, so hair loss is continuous (from 20 to 100 hairs daily in the scalp) but not noticeable. The shorter hairs of the body may have a growing period of six months or less, whereas scalp hairs can grow up to twenty-five years. Obviously, a disease involving the hair follicles is harder to control in an area of long growth (ringworm infection in the scalp may last years if untreated) than in an area of shorter growth (ringworm spontaneously disappears from the eyelashes in a few months when the follicle becomes dormant).

Follicular activity: Growth activity of the hair follicle.

Glands

There are three types of glands in the epidermis or passing through it: sebaceous, apocrine, and eccrine (sweat) glands. **Sebaceous glands** are multilobed structures found in association with hair follicles. They secrete a fatty substance called sebum into the hair follicle; sebum eventually finds its way to the epidermis. Sebum contains a pro-vitamin D, which is converted to vitamin D in the presence of ultraviolet light and then reabsorbed through the skin. Sebaceous activity is greater in

Sebaceous glands: Glands in the skin that secrete an oily substance called sebum.

young people and males and is responsible for the skin's oily appearance.

The skin's **apocrine glands** have no known physiologic significance. These glands secrete a milky, odorless substance that is acted upon by skin bacteria and leaves a distinct odor. There are many of these glands in the axilla, nipples, anogenital region, and the ear canal, where they are partially responsible for the secretion of ear wax. The mammary gland is the only other physiologically important apocrine gland.

The **eccrine gland** consists of a coiled tube beginning deep in the dermis and passing through the epidermis, ending in a small duct on the skin surface. Sweat glands are all over the body and are responsible for thermal regulation (see Chapter 25). The greatest concentration of eccrine glands is in the palms of the hands, the soles of the feet, the forehead, and the axillae.

Circulating hormones and internal heat production control the secretion of the sweat glands. The hypothalamus is the master control for the circulating hormones and thus the secretion of the glands. Internal heat production from physical activity is the main cause of increased eccrine gland secretion, but emotional stress can also increase sweating. In addition, local reflex sweating can occur, as when eating especially spicy foods.

The composition of sweat is similar to that of distilled water. In most physiological states, there are some salts dissolved in the sweat. In addition, lactate ion, urea, and ammonia are concentrated in sweat. It is especially important to note that in highly acclimated persons, the amount of dissolved ions (especially the chlorine ion) is much less than in an unacclimatized person.

Pigment

A cell called a melanocyte is responsible for skin **pigmentation** (melanin). Melanin's physiologic effect is to protect against the sun's ultraviolet rays, which can cause skin cancer. Skin cancer in the darker races is almost unknown. **Melanocytes** are actually a type of neural cell that has become specialized for melanin production. During fetal development they migrate from the neural crest through the dermis to the stratum basal, where their long protrusions (dendrites) wind around the keratinocytes and inject melanin. As the keratinocytes migrate outward, the malanin disperses into a fine dust, giving the skin its color. The number of melanocytes does not determine the amount of color; it is mainly the amount of activity of the melanocytes that determines the darkness of the skin. There is no evidence of increased numbers of melanocytes in darker races, only larger and harder-working ones. In albinism, there is a normal number of melanocytes, but the production of melanin is somehow blocked.

There are numerous depigmenting agents on the market; most contain monobenzyl ether of hydroquinone, an antioxidant that is applied topically for several weeks. There are also substances that will increase the pigmentation; melanocyte-stimulating hormone (MSH), produced in the pituitary gland, turns the lightest skin black if given over a period of time.

Return of skin color is considered a sign of complete healing. This indicates that melanocytes have recovered from the injury or that new ones have migrated to the injured area.

Circulation

To demonstrate that normal, healthy skin has a good blood supply, press on an area and then release the pressure. The skin first turns white and then quickly regains its original color as the small capillaries fill with blood. It is indeed important that the skin contains such an efficient circulatory system since one of the skin's important functions is to remove metabolic heat from the body.

Apocrine glands: Sweat glands located principally in the axillary and anogenital region. They secrete a milky substance that bacteria act upon, causing a characteristic odor.

Melanocytes: Cells that produce melanin.

Eccrine glands: Sweat glands well distributed throughout the skin. They play a vital role in regulating temperature, particularly during exercise.

Pigmentation: Coloration of the skin by a pigment (any substance in the skin that causes coloration, such as melanin and hemoglobin). It protects underlying tissue from UV radiation.

Prevention, Treatment, and Rehabilitation of Specific Injuries

The rate of blood flow through the skin is more variable here than in any other part of the body (from 400 milliliters per minute at rest in cool temperature to 2.8 milliliters per minute at maximum dilation). Even at rest, the normal blood flow through the skin is ten times greater than the metabolic needs of that tissue, indicating a greater importance than just nutrition. In very cold weather, the body must retain heat, so the blood flow to the skin is restricted, possibly to the point where the nutritional needs of the tissue cannot be met. This of course leads to death of the tissue, as in **frostbite.**

A common practice in injury rehabilitation is to apply ice to an injured tissue. Physiologically, this causes a vasoconstriction until the skin temperature reaches 15°C. From 15°C down to 0°C, vasodilation occurs. Therefore, icing an injury eventually causes circulation in the affected area to increase.

Nervous System

Neural tissue is found mainly in the skin's dermal layers. Recent evidence has demonstrated some free nerve endings in the epidermal layer; these endings are sensitive to fine changes in temperature and sensation (touch).

In the dermal layer, the nervous system is well defined. It is composed of motor nerves and sensory nerves. Motor nerves are part of the autonomic nervous system and control the eccrine and apocrine glands, the smooth muscle that runs through the skin, and the erector pili, which causes the hair to stand up. The sensory nerves are general in nature, specialized only in the palms of the hands and soles of the feet. Sensory nerves send sensations of pain, heat, cold, and touch through the spinal reflex arc, thus essentially protecting the organism from injury.

An obvious, and sometimes irritating, function of the sensory nervous system is the itch reflex (pruritus). Although many diseases, such as contact dermatitis (poison oak), cause itching, many people suffer from itching without having any disease. It is thought that an enzyme found in cells, in bacterial flora, or from outside sources is responsible for the itching feeling. Since itching and burning sensations are passed along the same nerves, the itching feeling may be associated with a burning feeling if left untreated. Local anesthetics (procaine) or cold usually stop the sensation.

Permeability

Unlike systemic disorders, skin diseases are visible, which means that in some cases treatment can be applied directly to the problem area and that the effect of any treatment is readily apparent. However, the ease of detection is offset by the fact that the skin is relatively impermeable to foreign substances, so it is not always possible to topically apply drugs.

The skin is permeable only to certain substances. Water and electrolytes cannot get past the first layer of the epidermis. All gases but carbon monoxide, on the other hand, are permeable. The most permeable substance is lipids. In fact, the skin itself secretes lipids through the sebaceous glands around the hair follicles.

The skin's **permeability** increases if the horny outer stratum corneum is removed or bypassed. There are two ways to remove or bypass this layer. One is to chemically remove or dissolve the keratin from the skin. Dimethylsulphoxide (DSMO—it is illegal for athletic trainers to use DMSO for medical purposes; see Chapter 27) and salicylic acid are two of the most common chemicals used for this purpose. The second method is to abrade the skin by dry shaving or tape stripping (continually applying and removing adhesive tape to the area).

An easier way to get drugs through the outer barrier is to use the "holes" already there: the hair follicles. If the

Frostbite: The partial or complete freezing of tissue.

Permeability: Allowing other substances to pass through.

drug is fat-soluble, it can pass through the sebum secreted into the hair follicle, finally gaining access to the dermal layer below. These drugs are rubbed onto the skin, to force them deep into the hair follicles. They are usually greasy substances that are not easy to rub off.

Care must be taken when applying topical drugs to open wounds. Since the normal barrier to the skin has been removed, the door is open, allowing greater amounts of drugs to enter the dermal layers. This might cause a potentially lethal buildup of the drug inside the body. For example, uninjured skin is impermeable to boron, but in an open wound, the levels of boron (from a boric acid compress) entering the skin could be fatal.

Skin Diseases and Traumas

Because of the extremely contagious nature of most dermatological diseases, when a skin disease is suspected, the athlete should be referred to a dermatologist, family physician, or sports medicine doctor. Early symptoms of disease are

1. Circulation disturbance
2. Pigmentation disturbance
3. Increase in skin abnormalities
4. Skin inflammation
5. Chemical and physical injuries
6. Genetic abnormalities

The remainder of this chapter discusses the various diseases and traumas that affect the skin.

Lesions

Every human body is subject to skin lesions. Some lesions are caused by trauma (e.g., blisters), some by disease processes (e.g., tumors); others occur naturally (e.g., freckles and moles).

Lesions are primary or secondary, depending upon their severity; Figure 23-3 (p. 424) describes the various lesions. Note that several of the primary lesions (macules, papules, and nodules) occur normally in most people and thus do not necessarily constitute a state of disease.

Skin lesions, whether caused by trauma or disease or occurring naturally, fall into one of three stages: mild, moderate, or severe. Each stage can develop into the next stage, transforming a simple injury into a very serious one. Thus, to avoid this possibility, even mild injuries must be treated properly.

Wounds

Fortunately, the body's internal defenses are adequate to prevent most minor cuts, scratches, and abrasions from becoming major injuries. On the other hand, proper treatment for even these minor injuries greatly increases the chances for avoiding major infection. A good measure to prevent minor injuries from becoming more serious is to ensure that each athlete has a current tetanus injection.

Treatment. The basic treatment for minor cuts, scratches, and abrasions is to thoroughly clean the affected area with soap and water or hydrogen peroxide (see Putting It into Practice 23-1, p. 425). This cleaning is the most important step and should be performed even if nothing further is done because it removes any foreign bodies (dirt, etc.) from the wound. Then dry the area with a gauze pad (do not use cotton pads because they may leave cotton fibers embedded in the wound). If the wound is not too severe, apply an **antiseptic** spray to the area. Ioprep is often used because it does not burn the skin as some iodine compounds do.

With severe injury, do not apply any antiseptic to the injured area. An ice

Antiseptic: A substance that destroys germs.

Primary Lesions   **Secondary Lesions**

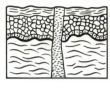 Macule   Flat area of color change (no elevation or depression; e.g., freckle)

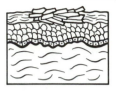 Scales   Flakes of cornified skin layer

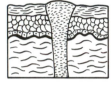 Papule   Solid elevation —less than 0.5 cm in diameter (i.e., wart)

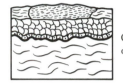 Crust   Dried exudate on skin

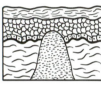 Nodule   Solid elevation 0.5 to 1 cm in diameter. Extends deeper into dermis than papule.

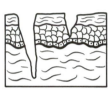 Fissure   Cracks in skin

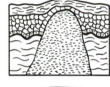 Tumor   Solid mass— larger than 1 cm

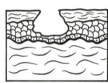 Erosion   Loss of epidermis that does not extend into dermis

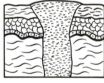 Plaque   Flat elevated surface found where papules, nodules, or tumors cluster together

 Ulcer   Area of destruction of entire epidermis

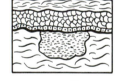 Wheal   Type of plaque. Result is transient edema in dermis

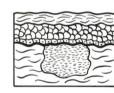 Scar   Excess collagen production following injury

 Vesicle   Small blister— fluid within or under epidermis

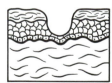 Atrophy   Loss of some portion of the skin

 Bulla   Large blister (greater than 0.5 cm)

Figure 23-3 Primary and secondary skin lesions. (Adapted from Sana, J. M., and R. D. Judge, eds. *Physical Assessment Skills for Nursing Practice*, 2nd ed. Boston: Little, Brown, 1975, fig. 6-14. Copyright © 1982 by Josephine M. Sana and Richard D. Judge. By permission of Little, Brown and Company.)

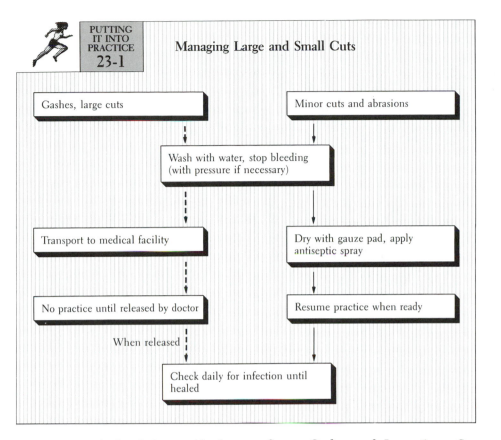

PUTTING IT INTO PRACTICE 23-1

Managing Large and Small Cuts

Gashes, large cuts → Wash with water, stop bleeding (with pressure if necessary) ← Minor cuts and abrasions

Transport to medical facility

Dry with gauze pad, apply antiseptic spray

No practice until released by doctor

Resume practice when ready

When released

Check daily for infection until healed

bag can be applied to help stop bleeding and prevent swelling, but leave the cleaning of the wound to the physician. The antiseptic itself may cause further skin damage or change the color of the wound, interfering with the physician's ability to correctly diagnose the severity of the injury.

Once training resumes, check the injury daily to make sure it is healing properly (Figure 23-4, p. 426). Watch for swelling and inflammation of the surrounding area, which indicate the beginning of infection (see Chapter 8 for the physiology of wound healing). In addition, do not apply any petroleum jelly or other non-water-soluble dressings to the wound because they cut off the air supply to the wounded area, leaving a moist, warm, anaerobic environment that is ideal for bacterial growth.

Severe Gashes and Lacerations. Severe gashes (caused by blunt instruments) and lacerations (caused by sharp instruments) requiring stitches should be treated by a physician as soon as possible. The athletic trainer should be interested only in stopping the flow of blood until the athlete can be transported to a medical facility. Apply a gauze wrap around the wounded area, using only enough pressure to stem the flow of blood. Use a tourniquet only in the rare instance when you cannot stop the bleeding; improper use of a tourniquet can result in the loss of a limb. Pressure applied by hand is usually sufficient to stop bleeding. Pressure with an ice bag sometimes helps slow the flow of blood. Again, the amount of pressure should be sufficient to stop the outward flow of blood but still allow deep circulation to continue.

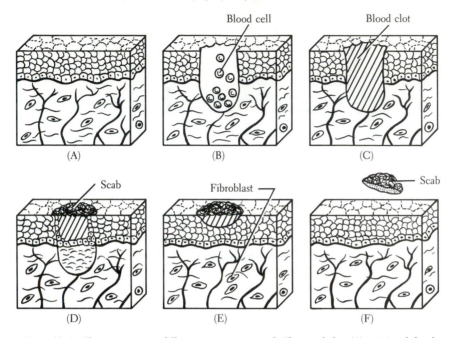

Figure 23-4 Skin regeneration following an open wound. If normal skin (A) is injured deeply (B), blood escapes from dermal blood vessels, and a blood clot soon forms (C). The blood clot and dried tissue fluid form a scab (D) that protects the damaged region. Later, blood vessels send out branches, and fibroblasts migrate into the area (E). The fibroblasts produce new connective tissue fibers, and when the skin is largely repaired, the scab sloughs off (F). (Adapted from Hole, J. W., Jr. *Human Anatomy and Physiology.* Dubuque, Iowa: Wm. C. Brown, 1978, p. 114, fig. 6-14.)

Contusions (Bruises)

Bruises or contusions damage the underlying dermal layer of the skin but the epidermis remains unbroken. The resulting capillary damage allows blood to leak between the cells in the dermis. As the blood collects under the skin, it takes on the common blue-black appearance of a bruise.

Treatment. Treatment of a bruise or contusion involves mostly protecting the area from further injury. Since the outer layer of skin has not been broken, no topical drug application will speed the healing process. Ice massage, commonly used to treat muscle contusion, will probably be of benefit to skin bruises. One preventative treatment is to pad the areas of the body that are susceptible to continuous bruising or that have been previously injured. This type of treatment is sport-specific; that is, each sport has its own inherent susceptible areas, so it is the athletic trainer's responsibility to determine the proper areas to pad for each sport.

Blisters

The blister is one of the most irritating minor skin injuries. Friction, irritation, and heating of the skin cause the outer layers to loosen. The resulting space is filled with fluid, creating a raised area on the skin. Blisters can lead to secondary infection if not properly treated.

Treatment. If a blister occurs, the best treatment is to leave it alone, especially if there will be no practice in the next twenty-four hours. If this is impossible to do, thoroughly clean the area with an antiseptic soap. Then, using a sterile needle, make a hole in one corner of the blister. The hole must be large enough so that it does not seal itself and become infected. Let the liquid drain, and lightly press the surrounding skin toward the hole to remove all the fluid. Use an antiseptic to clean the skin around the blister, pack it with Bacitracin or Neosporin, and tape a small donut pad over the area. Do not remove the skin from the blister unless it has been torn off because even loose skin provides some protection to the underlying tissue. The athletic trainer should then frequently check to catch any secondary infection that may occur. Remove and change the dressing if it becomes wet, to avoid bacterial or fungal infections. Blisters forming on top of blisters is another thing to watch for. The deeper the blister goes, the greater the possibility of infection.

If possible, try to catch a potential blister before it forms. Educate the athlete to detect the signs and symptoms of blister formation. Tape "hot spots" detected during practice, or place a pad on the area to avoid continuous rubbing. In many cases, further treatment is not needed if the underlying area becomes strong enough to endure the trauma it will receive.

Prevention. The best time to start preventing blisters is before practice begins. Each athlete should be made aware of how each piece of equipment is supposed to fit, and each equipment manager should see that each athlete has been provided with properly fitting equipment. Such equipment prevents the chafing of the skin that causes blistering. During long exercise periods, as in long distance running, frequently adjusting socks and shoes helps prevent formation of blisters. Athletes should undertake a preseason training program to toughen blister-prone tissues on the feet, toes, and hands.

Insect Bites

Insect bites, including bee and wasp stings, are usually more of a nuisance than a concern unless the person bit is **hyperallergic** to some of the toxins left by the bite or sting. Fortunately, the body's defenses usually destroy small amounts of toxic substances. The histiocytes remove foreign substances, and the mastocytes cause local edema in and increased blood flow to the injured area. The mastocyte reaction can cause some hyperallergic people to have an allergic response that, in severe cases, spreads over the whole body, affecting heart rate and respiration. Part of the preparticipation examination should include questions concerning allergic reactions to insect bites and stings. Another concern is the possibility of secondary bacterial infection from remnants of the insect part that caused the bite (bee stinger) or from continued scratching of the affected area, which breaks the skin and thus opens the way for bacterial invasion.

Treatment. Carefully remove any foreign bodies left in the wound to avoid further toxin injection. Then wash the area with a disinfectant. An ice pack usually helps control itching and keeps down swelling. If itching persists, apply an anesthetic or lotion over the bite to alleviate some of the symptoms. Some physicians recommend a **tetanus** injection following any injury in which the skin is broken; the athletic trainer might suggest this. With a hyperallergic person, immediately apply an ice pack to the area and have the patient treated by a physician as soon as possible.

Animal Bites

Insect bites are relatively common in athletics; animal bites are rarer. However, because animal bites can occur in athletics and are potentially serious, the athletic trainer should know how to

Hyperallergic: Exhibiting an extreme allergic reaction to specific substances.

Tetanus: A CNS infection, characterized by painful muscle contraction (initially in the jaw and neck) caused by the bacteria *Clostridium tetani* (found in soil). Can be prevented with a tetanus injection. Also called lockjaw.

deal with them. For example, cross-country runners may be bitten by poisonous snakes or dogs while on training runs. Nonpoisonous animal bites can be treated the same as any other wound, provided the animal can be captured and detained for observation for rabies by the proper authorities.

Treatment. If the animal cannot be captured, refer the injured person to a physician because of the possibility of rabies infection. Human bites may also cause infection and should not be treated lightly (see Putting It into Practice 23-2).

Poisonous animal bites require more first aid before the athlete is transported to a physician. Since most practice fields are within a reasonable distance of medical facilities, merely make the athlete comfortable and place an ice bag on the affected area to slow local metabolism. This will prevent more toxin from entering the bloodstream. If travel time to medical facilities is longer than an hour, use snake bite kits to remove some of the toxin before it gets a chance to enter the bloodstream. Then ice the bitten area and transport the victim to a medical facility for further treatment.

Calluses

Calluses are not usually a problem in athletics. A moist, supple skin can handle most of the stresses in athletic competition, but calluses can rip (gymnastics) or tear and blisters may form under the callus. The callus itself is merely a continuous buildup of the epidermis' stratum corneum layer. Since the area is receiving constant trauma, the cell division in the lower layers increases faster than the sloughing off of the outer layers. The resulting callus protects the lower dermal layer.

Treatment. The callus may have to be removed if the buildup restricts joint movement. See Putting It into Practice 23-3. This is most likely to occur on the fingers and toes. Callus removal is a simple process, involving light shaving or scraping of the skin's outer layer. In extreme cases, the skin may be removed with scissors or a scalpel. Do not remove too much skin or blisters may form when activity is resumed.

Bacterial Infections

One function of the epidermis is to protect the inside of the organism from invasion by pathological bacteria. It is important to remember that several species of bacteria reside on the skin (*Staphylococcus epidermidis*, Micrococcus genus, etc.), in the hair follicles (Corynebacterium), and on the mucous membranes (*Streptococcus salivarius*). The bacteria cause no harm unless their numbers increase too much or they are allowed to penetrate through the epidermis. In fact, some of these normal bacteria produce diffusible antimicrobial substances that help maintain the ecologic balance of the skin's flora. Removal of this "normal flora" may in itself increase the chance of secondary infection from some other bacteria. Table 23-1 describes common skin bacteria and their associated diseases (see p. 430).

The athletic trainer should be able to recognize several diseases. Treatment, however, should be left to a physician because most trainers do not have access to the proper drugs. These diseases are usually highly contagious, and if not properly treated, they could spread through the members of a whole team. Following is a description of the most common bacterial skin diseases.

Impetigo. Impetigo is a highly contagious disease caused by a Streptococcus infection followed by a secondary invasion of a Staphylococcus bacteria. Impetigo is marked by the formation of small red spots that become pustular

Managing the Human Bite

Cause: Human bites usually occur inadvertently when a player's hand or arm strikes an opponent's teeth.

Risks: Tissues injured by a human (or animal) bite are highly susceptible to serious infection. Refer the athlete to a physician if there is persistent bleeding, the wound is large and gaping (greater than two centimeters, which affects deep tissue), any sign of infection (body temperature greater than 100°F, persistent pain at site, redness radiating away from the wound, swollen lymph nodes), or if the wound was caused by an actual bite rather than a glancing blow.

Treatment: Apply direct pressure to the wound to stop bleeding. Wash the wound thoroughly with soap and water, clearing away any debris from the wound. Apply ice to control swelling. Apply an antiseptic and dressing. Watch for signs of infection. Refer the athlete to a physician if the wound is serious.

Identifying and Managing Calluses and Warts

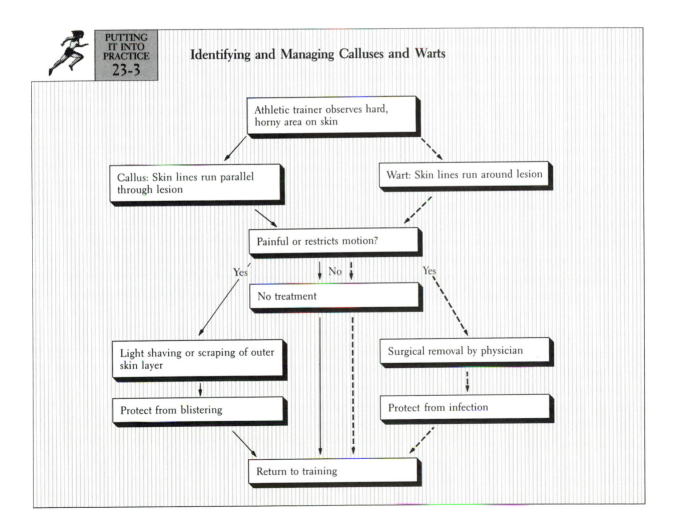

and finally burst. In later stages, a crust covers the area, and there is the possibility of deeper tissue involvement. The exudate seeping from the lesions is highly contagious.

Treatment. Treatment is performed by a physician and usually includes topical application of an antibiotic with a systemic antibiotic (penicillin or erythromycin) if the disease is severe.

Prevention. Preventative measures should include keeping the locker room clean, frequently washing clothing and equipment (including mats and pads), and educating all athletes about personal hygiene. Do not let athletes suspected of having impetigo practice until the physician releases them.

Ecthyma. Ecthyma is an advanced form of impetigo characterized by crusty skin over the infected area and ulceration of the tissues below. The ulcers can vary in depth and may extend well into the dermis. Treatment and prevention are the same as for impetigo.

Folliculitis. Folliculitis is an overall term for several diseases affecting the hair follicle. Folliculitis is a general Staphylococcus infection superficial in nature. If the infection is deep in the follicle and involves only one follicle, it is called a furuncle. During this stage a boil forms. Further infection involving many follicles and a large swollen area is a carbuncle.

Treatment and Prevention. If the infection is superficial or involves one follicle (furuncle), the athletic trainer or school nurse can apply treatment. Never squeeze the boils or infectious material may be pressed subcutaneously to other areas, thus spreading the infection. A hot compress reduces some of the discomfort and perhaps speeds draining. Once the infection has been drained, apply an antibiotic dressing like ichthammol ointment. If training is to continue, cover the area with a gauze dressing and protect it as you would a blister (see "Blisters" section, p. 426). If a carbuncle is suspected, the athlete needs immediate treatment by a physician. The infection is deep and

Folliculitis: Disease of the hair follicle, such as furuncle and carbuncle; caused by *Staphylococcus* infection.

Table 23-1 *Common Bacterial Skin Infections*

Disease	Causative Agent	Symptoms
Impetigo	*Straphylococcus aureus* *Streptococcus pyogenes*	Small, red, pustular lesions that burst, forming a crust over the lesion.
Ecthyma	*Staphylococcus aureus* *Streptococcus pyogenes*	Advanced impetigo. The crust is thicker, and there is ulceration of underlying tissue.
Folliculitis	*Staphylococcus aureus* *Streptococcus pyogenes*	Papules and pustules around the hair shaft, with local swelling and pain. Pus-filled exudate may drain.
Hidradentis suppurativa	*Staphylococcus aureus*	Pea-sized nodules affecting the apocrine gland may soften and drain. Similar to furuncle but affects a different area.
Acne	*Propionibacteria acnes*	Infects sebaceous glands around hair shaft, with local swelling and open (blackhead) or closed (whitehead) comedo.
Conjunctivitis	*Staphylococcus aureus* *Streptococcus pyogenes* *Streptococcus pneumoniae*	Edema, gritty feeling under eyelid. Sometimes occurs with mucous discharge.

involves a large area; in some cases a carbuncle has been fatal. Prevent folliculitis by having athletes wear clean clothing and equipment.

Intertrigo. Intertrigo is a nonbacterial skin eruption that occurs between two adjacent surfaces from the two surfaces continually rubbing. The constant chafing produces heat, which increases local sweating and results in a perfect bacterial-, fungal-, and/or yeast-growing medium. Intertrigo normally occurs on the inner thigh, the groin, between the toes, or under the armpits.

Treatment and Prevention. Treatment and prevention include frequently cleaning the area. Pay extra attention to drying the affected parts after showering. Reduce friction by placing cotton or wool padding over the area to allow air flow, reduce friction, and wick away moisture. Petroleum jelly or its equivalent has been used to relieve chafing, but it prevents air from reaching the affected area, thus providing a good medium for anaerobic bacteria to grow in. Thus, do *not* use lubricants.

Hidradentis Suppurativa. Hidradentis suppurativa is a chronic, infectious disease of the apocrine glands, usually occurring in the genital, perianal, or armpit area. It is characterized by several pea-sized nodules that undergo cycles of softening and draining. The disease looks like a furuncle, but its location helps discrimination between the two infections.

Treatment. Treatment is performed by a physician and includes draining the infection and applying an antibiotic.

Acne. Acne is one of the most common bacterial infections in the athletic training room. It is caused by a number of factors, including traumatic physical contact with equipment and other players, friction from clothing and equipment, skin hydration from excessive sweating, psychological stress, and androgenic-anabolic steroids (occurring naturally, as in puberty, or those taken by certain athletes to gain strength). The lesion is a closed comedo (whitehead) or open comedo (blackhead) found in association with a hair follicle. The puslike interior is composed of the metabolic by-products of the sebaceous gland (see "Glands" section, p. 420), with secondary infection by the Propionibacteria genus.

Treatment. Treatment of acne involves the good hygiene outlined previously. In addition, friction between the skin and athletic equipment should be minimized. If normal measures fail to clear up the problem, refer the athlete to a dermatologist for further treatment.

Small infections from minor cuts and scrapes can be treated by cleaning the area with soap and water and applying a topical antibiotic if one is deemed necessary. If the condition does not improve, encourage the athlete to seek the help of a physician to avoid future problems. Putting It into Practice 23-4 lists possible remedies for bacterial infections (see p. 432).

Conjunctivitis. One final important infection is conjunctivitis (see Chapter 14). The causative agents include *Staphylococcus aureus*, *Streptococcus pyogenes*, and *Streptococcus pneumoniae*. Conjunctivitis is characterized by edema, a sandy feeling under the lid (foreign body sensation), and mucous discharge.

Treatment. Conjuctivitis is highly contagious and should be treated by a physician. Treatment consists of topical erythromycin or penicillin, with systemic penicillin or cloxacillin in severe cases.

Fungal Infections

Fungal infections are a major problem for athletic trainers since the

PUTTING IT INTO PRACTICE 23-4

Managing Bacterial Infection by Antimicrobial Therapy
(Causative agents: *Staphylococcus aureus* and *Streptococcus pyogenes*)

Superficial Infection

I. Cleansing
  A. Tap water or physiological saline solution
  B. Debridement of scaly portion if present
  C. Antibacterial soaps
    1. Chlorhexidine
    2. Trichloro-carbanilide
  D. Improve personal hygiene and clean equipment and clothing
II. Topical antibacterial agents
  A. Corticoid/antibiotic combinations work the best
  B. Tetracycline cream (USP)—low skin sensitization

  C. Neomycin cream with Bacitracin and Polysporin
  D. Erythromycin cream
  E. Vioform: Some sensitive skin reactions
  F. Penicillin: Not used much in the United States because of skin sensitivity reactions

Severe Infection

I. Systemic application (oral or IV)
  A. Penicillin G: Some strains of bacteria are resistant, and some patients are allergic.
  B. Tetracycline
  C. Erythromycin
  D. Cephalosporin: For mixed bacterial infections
  E. Aminoglycoside: For mixed bacterial infections
  F. Oxacillin
  G. Methicillin
II. Surgery
  A. Surgical drainage for carbuncle, furuncle, and acne

warm, moist environment of locker rooms is the perfect growth medium for fungus and yeast. In addition, restrictive clothing or equipment limits the flow of air to the skin, improving conditions for fungal growth.

There are hundreds of fungal diseases, but most athletic trainers will never encounter most of them in the United States because of our more temperate climate. Many of the diseases occur in the more tropical areas of Africa and the Far East, although the deep south in the United States and the state of Hawaii have much higher incidences of a greater variety of fungal diseases.

Fungal infections are usually epidermal in nature and involve the dermis only if the skin is broken or if the infection enters through the hair follicles. There is some inflammatory response to the growth of the fungus, but in most cases it is not as pronounced as the inflammation associated with bacterial infection. The inflammation is greatest at the border of the infection, less in the middle, older areas. As the fungal growth advances in all directions, a characteristic ring or fan shape forms. The main fungal infections of interest to athletic trainers are ringworm, athlete's foot, and jock itch. (See Putting It into Practice 23-5 for treatment of athlete's foot. Table 23-2 describes common fungal diseases; see p. 434.)

Many ringworm infections are caused by species of the genus Trichophyton or Microsporum. Ringworm is a misnomer because the disease is caused by a fungus (usually *T. rubrum*), not by a worm. As the fungal growth advances, a red, ring-shaped lesion appears to enlarge in all directions, usually on the hands (tinea manus) or soles of the feet (tinea pedis), on the nails (tinea unguium), on the skin (tinea corporis), or on the groin (tinea cruris). It may remain many years without any appreciable growth, and it usually does not spread from one area to another. In fact, at least 90 percent of all adults have fungal growth between the webs of their toes, and 95 percent of these infections are asymptomatic.

If the infection involves the hair follicles (usually of the scalp or eyebrows), the disease is called tinea capitis. Scalp involvement is not as evident as it once was and occurs mainly in children. Resistance to ringworm fungus increases after puberty as the amount of saturated fatty acids increases in the secretions of the sebaceous glands. As with other fungal infections, poor hygiene and warm, moist environments increase the incidence.

Treatment. Treatment involves improving hygiene through bathing, cleaning clothes and equipment, and drying and improving air circulation around the affected areas. Do not use topical **fungicides** on mild infections because they may increase skin irritability and worsen the condition. Burow's solution applied with cold packs may provide some comfort. Many physicians feel that over-the-counter athlete's foot fungicides provide little or no improvement over the natural course of the disease; other physicians recommend nonprescription fungicides like Tinactin or Desenex or prescription drugs like Griscofulvin (see Putting It into Practice 23-6, p. 435).

Candidiasis. Candidiasis is often mistaken for ringworm because the two diseases cause similar skin lesions. However, candidiasis is caused by the yeast *Candida albicans*, whereas ringworm is caused by a fungus. *C. albicans* occurs naturally over much of the warm, moist parts of the body. It may not manifest itself as a disease organism unless some secondary infection changes the skin environment. Treatment should first concentrate on the underlying factors or causes of the disease. Topical application of nystatin cream or ointment also helps control

PUTTING IT INTO PRACTICE 23-5

Managing Athlete's Foot

- *Symptoms:* Cracking, itching, and burning skin around the toes.
- *Cause:* Fungal infection. Is mildly contagious.
- *Treatment:* Regularly clean and dry feet, and encourage athletes to change socks daily. Athlete's foot should be treated as soon as it appears because serious cases can be extremely debilitating. Over-the-counter medications sometimes help. Consult physician for severe cases.
- *Prevention:* Athletes should wash their feet with soap and thoroughly dry them after exercise. They should change their socks every day.

the spread. Since it is hard to differentiate between tinea and candidiasis, the team physician or family doctor should suggest diagnosis and treatment.

In addition to causing a skin disturbance, *C. albicans* is also responsible for urticaria (hives) in some people. Approximately 15 to 20 percent of the population suffers from this disorder, and 26 percent of these people are allergic to an antigen given off by *C. albicans*. The hives look like transient wheals, with erythema (redness) and pruritis (itching). The wheals may appear suddenly or over a long time.

Treatment. Treatment of Candida-caused hives is as simple as washing the affected area with one of the antifungal soaps listed in Putting It into Practice 23-6. Unfortunately, hives are caused by many other factors, including food allergy, emotional stress, exercise and heat, and insect bites. Different categories of urticaria demand different treatment. The best way to determine what is causing the skin disorder is to have a physician rule out various possibilities as soon as possible.

Viral Infections

Viral infections are commonly seen by the athletic trainer but should be treated only by a physician. The many types of viral infections range from

Fungicides: Substances that destroy fungus.

Table 23-2 *Common Fungal Infections*

Clinical Disease	Anatomy Affected	Symptoms	Etiologic Agent(s)
Tinea barbae	Bearded areas of face and neck; restricted to adult males	Mildly superficial to severe pustular folliculitis.	*T. mentagrophytes, T. rubrum, T. verrucosum, T. violaceum*
Tinea capitis	Scalp, eyebrows, eyelashes	Scaly, erythematous lesions; hair loss; deep ulcerative eruptions; endothrix or ectothrix invasion of hair shaft.	All *Microsporum* sp.; all common *Trichophyton* sp.
Tinea corporis	Stratum corneum layers of glabrous (smooth) skin	Ringworm infection, ranging from scaling, to erythema to deep granulomata.	Most commonly, *T. rubrum, T. mentagrophytes, M. canis;* most dermatophytes can produce the disease
Tinea cruris	Groin, perineum, perianal	Sharply outlined, raised, erythematous bordered with dry scaling center and pruritis (itching).	Most commonly, *E. floccosum, T. rubrum, T. mentagrophytes*
Tinea favosa	Scalp, glabrous skin	Formation of yellowish, cup-shaped crusts called scutula; vesicular and papulosquamous lesions may develop.	*T. schoenleinii*
Tinea manus	Interdigital and palmer surfaces of hand	Similar to tinea corporis.	Most commonly, *T. rubrum, T. mentagrophytes,* and *E. floccosum*
Tinea pedis	Infection of feet, particularly toe webs and soles	Lesions vary from mild and chronic scaling to acute inflammatory disease with pustules.	Normally, *T. rubrum, T. mentagrophytes,* and *E. floccosum*
Tinea unguium	Fingernails and toenails	A superficial infection restricted to patches or pits on nail surfaces (white onychomycosis) or chronic infection beneath nail plate, usually with hyperkeratosis and lifting of nail bed.	Normally, *T. rubrum* and *T. mentagrophytes*

SOURCE: Moore, G., and D. Jaeiow. *Micology for the Clinical Laboratory.* Reston, Va.: Reston Publishing Co., 1979, pp. 116–117.

small **warts** to highly contagious diseases such as measles and herpes. Trainers should be aware of the symptoms of the more contagious diseases, to prevent a teamwide outbreak (see Table 23-3, p. 436).

Warts. Viral warts are contagious and should be treated as such. They usually cause no problem if left alone; how-ever, they sometimes grow large, causing pain and discomfort, especially if they are located on a weight-bearing surface or on a finger or toe joint.

Wart virus may be spread from other warts, contaminated floors, clothing, etc. The **virus** can survive long periods in dry, exposed skin areas but must eventually find a vascular source to provide itself with nutrients. For this to

Wart: A rough, horny growth on the skin, typically caused by a virus.
Virus: An intracellular, infectious microorganism that can survive only within living cells. Viruses are extremely small and can be viewed only under an electron microscope.

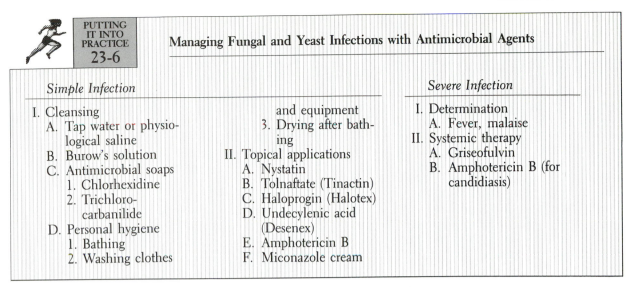

PUTTING
IT INTO
PRACTICE
23-6

Managing Fungal and Yeast Infections with Antimicrobial Agents

Simple Infection

I. Cleansing
  A. Tap water or physio-
    logical saline
  B. Burow's solution
  C. Antimicrobial soaps
    1. Chlorhexidine
    2. Trichloro-
      carbanilide
  D. Personal hygiene
    1. Bathing
    2. Washing clothes

    and equipment
    3. Drying after bath-
      ing
II. Topical applications
  A. Nystatin
  B. Tolnaftate (Tinactin)
  C. Haloprogin (Halotex)
  D. Undecylenic acid
    (Desenex)
  E. Amphotericin B
  F. Miconazole cream

Severe Infection

I. Determination
  A. Fever, malaise
II. Systemic therapy
  A. Griseofulvin
  B. Amphotericin B (for
    candidiasis)

occur, there must be a break in the stratum corneum. Warts are characterized by a raised papule with a gray, rough surface that is usually dry. Plantar warts (on the soles of the feet or palms of the hands) usually are not raised because of the thickness of the epidermal layer in these areas. Warts are sometimes difficult to differentiate from calluses. Calluses have thickened skin ridges running across the raised area; warts are not part of the skin and will push the epidermis out as the wart grows, leaving curved skin ridges.

Treatment. Treatment is usually removal by surgery. There is no evidence that any over-the-counter drugs shrink warts; warts may shrink on their own. Plantar warts may not be removed since the resulting scarring may cause more pain than the original wart.

Herpes Simplex. Herpes infections are the most painful and recurring of the viral infections. Herpes simplex is caused by the herpes virus hominus (HVH) and is usually seen as the common cold sore (caused by HVH type I). Cold sores may be found on any part of the body, but usually near the mouth. (If it is in the genital region, it is an HVH type II infection.) Cold sores are associated with respiratory infections (hence the name cold sores), menses, increased ultraviolet radiation (high altitude), or exhaustion and stress.

The disease manifests itself as a series of vesicles that rupture in one to two days. A serumlike exudate drains from the ruptured vesicles, forming a crust over the area. There may be bleeding if the area is scratched or stretched. The victim must be considered contagious for five days after the onset of eruptions and should be removed from competition for this period, especially if involved in a contact sport such as wrestling. The sores heal between ten and fourteen days, leaving a shiny "scar" that disappears a few days later.

Treatment and Prevention. Treatment usually consists of oil of camphor (10 percent) in alcohol, to dry the lesion. Prescription drugs are also available for herpes treatment (Idoxuridine or Vidarabine). Although there is no real preventative measure for those people sensitive to herpes virus, a sunscreen may prevent some lesions in sun-sensitive persons.

Herpes Zoster. Another type of herpes infection is herpes zoster (shingles), caused by the same virus as chicken pox (VZ). Shingles are usually found on the trunk as a series of vesicles on a red base. Inflammation varies from around ten days in young individuals to several weeks in adults. In adults, the disease usually starts with a slight tingling and progresses into very painful lesions.

Treatment. In mild cases, treatment consists of calamine lotion to dry up the lesions and prevent itching. Severe cases must be treated by a physician and include systemic steroid therapy. The steroid therapy does not increase healing time but does help control the pain.

Rubeola and Rubella. Other viral diseases are the highly infectious childhood diseases: rubeola and rubella. Even though these are considered children's diseases, many adults somehow manage to avoid them as children. Because of the diseases' highly contagious nature, any team member discov-

ered having rubeola or rubella should be removed from practice until the contagious period is over, to prevent the diseases from spreading to other team members. Rubeola is characterized by fever, conjunctivitis, blue-white spots in the mouth, and red eruptions that start on the forehead and spread over the face, trunk, and extremities. Rubella is characterized by pink macules starting on the head and spreading to the trunk in twenty-four hours. There are no spots in the mouth, and the body spots disappear in two to three days.

Treatment and Prevention. Treatment for rubeola is by a physician and consists of a gamma globulin injection. Rubella may now be prevented with a vaccination.

Sunburn

A final skin disorder of interest to athletic trainers is sunburn (see Putting

Table 23-3 *Common Viral Infections*

Disease	Symptom	Treatment
Rubeola (measles)	Fever, conjunctivitis, blue-white spots in the mouth, red skin eruptions.	Physician treatment: gamma globulin injection.
Rubella (German measles)	Pink macules starting on the head and spreading to the trunk in 24 h, then disappearing in 2–3 days; no spots in the mouth.	Physician treatment: vaccine for some types.
Warts	Raised papule rough- and gray-looking.	Surgical removal (over-the-counter drugs usually do not work).
Herpes simplex	Series of vesicles that rupture in 1–2 days; serumlike exudate drains, dries, and forms crust.	Simple treatment: (1) oil of camphor in 10% alcohol; (2) sunscreen for sun-sensitive lesions. Physician treatment: (1) Idoxuridine, (2) Vidarabine.
Genital herpes	Series of vesicles similar to those in Herpes simplex.	Simple treatment: (1) oil of camphor in 10% alcohol; (2) sunscreen for sun-sensitive lesions. Physician treatment: (1) Idoxuridine, (2) Vidarabine, and (3) systemic steroid therapy.
Herpes zoster	Series of vesicles on a red base, usually on the trunk.	Simple treatment: calamine lotion. Physician treatment: systemic steroid therapy.

It into Practice 23-7, p. 438). In mild cases sunburn is most often overlooked, but continued exposure can permanently damage skin and possibly cause skin cancer in sun-sensitive persons.

Sunburn is characterized by redness and edema beginning almost immediately upon exposure and increasing in intensity for about twelve hours after exposure. The redness disappears in seventy-two to ninety-six hours, usually with the loss of the outer layers of the epidermis (peeling).

Only certain wavelengths of light are responsible for damaging the skin: the shortwave, ultraviolet (UV) rays in the 4000- to 40-angstrom range of the light spectrum. Not all ultraviolet rays are harmful; vital UV rays in the 3200- to 2900-angstrom range promote calcium metabolism and vitamin D synthesis. The two types of UV light in the burning range are UVA, which occurs in late afternoon and northern latitudes, and UVB, which are the actual sunburn rays occurring during the heat of the day. UVB rays are also more prominent at the equator than in the northern hemisphere.

As the UVB rays hit the skin and penetrate the epidermal layers, prostaglandins are released, increasing local erythema and cell lability (instability). The lysosomes within the cells break, depositing powerful digestive enzymes that break up nearby cells. Continued exposure increases the damage as the rays penetrate to deeper layers. Once the skin has been damaged by the UVB rays, it is susceptible to UVA radiation, which increases the severity of the burn.

Skin sensitivity is an important consideration for the athletic trainer. There is a correlation between the amount of melanin in a person's skin and that person's susceptibility to sunburn. Generally, the darker the skin, the less chance of a burn with normal exposure. A number of drugs can increase skin sensitivity, including oral contraceptives, saccharin, Griseofulvin, some aftershave lotions, and lime juice (other citrus juices to a lesser extent). Topical applications of suntan oils, grease, and water increase the intensity of the burning rays as they contact the skin. Photosensitivity can be decreased with systemic drugs such as Indomethacin, which inhibits prostaglandin formation, and topical application of para-aminobenzoic acid (PABA) sunscreens. Since sunscreens come off easily with water or sweat, they should be reapplied at regular intervals.

Treatment. Treatment for sunburn includes one gram of aspirin every four hours to inhibit prostaglandin formation and application of Aloe vera lotion. Most over-the-counter sunburn remedies probably will not help alleviate the pain of sunburn. Second degree burns (characterized by blistered skin) may be treated as above, or in severe cases a physician may prescribe topical and/or systemic steroids along with the aspirin. Athletic trainers should check daily for infection by Pseudomonas bacteria.

Prevention. Preventative treatment should include regular, short exposure to the sun's rays, use of sunscreen in sun-sensitive persons, and if possible, rescheduling practice at times when the UVB rays are less abundant (morning and late afternoon).

References

Bluefarb, S. M. *Dermatology.* Kalamazoo, Mich.: Upjohn Company, 1972.

Emmons, C. W., C. H. Binford, J. P. Utz, and K. J. Kwon-Chung. *Medical Mycology*, 3rd ed. Philadelphia: Lea & Febiger, 1977.

Guyton, A. C. *Textbook of Medical Physiology*, 5th ed. Philadelphia: W. B. Saunders, 1976.

Hudson. A. How I manage acne in athletes. *The Physician and Sportsmedicine* 11(9):116–121, 1983.

Jawetz, E., J. L. Melnick, and E. A. Adelberg. *Review of Medical Microbiology*, 14th ed. Los Altos, Calif.: Lange Medical Publications, 1980.

PUTTING IT INTO PRACTICE 23-7

A Guide to Safe Sunning

If you are thinking about getting plenty of sun for a tan, here are some tips to avoid trouble, from *The Physician and Sportsmedicine* and the American Cancer Society.

1. Sun yourself before 10 AM and after 3 PM, when ultraviolet rays are weakest, or limit your exposure to short periods (10 to 20 minutes) at other times. Fair-skinned persons must be particularly careful about this.

2. It is possible to get burned through light, casual clothes, especially in a lengthy exposure to the sun. A beach umbrella does not offer full protection, because ultraviolet rays are only partially deflected by it, and the rays bounce toward you from other directions—off sand, water, or other surfaces.

3. A cloudy or foggy day can deceive the sunseeker, who might feel it would be safe to stay out longer. At least 70% of the burning power of the sun's rays penetrate clouds, and those who stay out for long periods could get severe burns. Also, water droplets or greasy preparations (such as baby oil) on the skin can cause a "lens effect," funnelling the rays onto the skin.

4. Very effective screening lotions are those that contain PABA (para-aminobenzoic acid), which absorbs much of the ultraviolet rays but allows gradual tanning. Ask your physician or pharmacist about preparations that contain PABA. However, no lotion or cream will "speed up" tanning, and limited, gradual exposure to the sun without any lotion is regarded by some authorities as the best way to get a tan.

5. Certain medications taken consistently can make you very sensitive to sunlight. These drugs include some diuretics (water pills), sulfonamides, antibiotics, and tranquilizers. If you are taking medicine on a long-term basis, check with your physician before starting your suntan plan.

6. Finally, remember that the sun is the leading cause of skin cancer. Anyone can develop skin cancer (and there are 300,000 cases in the United States each year), but those who have fair, ruddy, or sandy complexions and who are exposed to a great amount of sun get it most often. Fortunately 95% of skin cancer can be cured. Early warning signs for skin cancer include: a sore that does not heal, change in the size or color of a wart or mole, or development of any unusual pigmented (darkened) area. As a rule of thumb, any skin change that persists should be brought to the attention of your physician.

SOURCE: Stauffer, L. W. Coping with your patient's summer bummer—sunburn. *The Physician and Sportsmedicine* 5(7):42, 1977.

Kagan, B. *Antimicrobial Therapy*. Philadelphia: W. B. Saunders, 1980.

Nestor, E. W., C. E. Roberts, N. N. Pearsall, and B. J. McCarthy. *Microbiology*, 2nd ed. New York: Holt, Rinehart and Winston, 1978.

Nicolaides, N. Skin lipids: their biochemical uniqueness. *Science* 186:19–26, 1974.

Pillsbury, D. M., and C. L. Heaton. *A Manual of Dermatology*. Philadelphia: W. B. Saunders, 1980.

Stauffer, L. W. Coping with your patient's summer bummer—sunburn. *The Physician and Sportsmedicine* 5(7):26–43, 1977.

Stauffer, L. W. Skin disorders in athletes: identification and management. *The Physician and Sportsmedicine* 11(3):101–123, 1983.

Stedman, T. L. *Stedman's Medical Dictionary*. Baltimore: Williams & Wilkins, 1978.

PART
FOUR

Factors Affecting Performance

Disease and the Athlete

I llness and internal disability are unfortunate characteristics of the human condition, even among highly conditioned athletes. There is no evidence that fit individuals are less susceptible to infectious diseases. In fact, athletes involved in some types of sports (e.g., distance running) may have decreased immunity under certain circumstances.

The athletic trainer commonly encounters illnesses such as **flu,** colds, and **gastritis** that can cause problems for both individual athletes and teammates. Contagious diseases can spread and destroy the performance of an otherwise successful team. Likewise, a premature return to practice may worsen an athlete's condition or cause further complications.

Some otherwise healthy athletes suffer from chronic diseases such as asthma and diabetes. The athletic trainer should be aware of the nature of these disorders and any problems that may arise from them during exercise.

The extent of disease in humans is mind-boggling. Physicians with years of training and experience often have difficulty diagnosing illnesses because symptoms are unusual or they simply did not consider a particular disease when making the diagnosis. The athletic

World-class athletes such as Olga Korbut typify excellence of the human form, but no scientific data indicate that they are any more immune to disease than the average person.

Flu: A nonspecific viral illness characterized by fever, malaise, shivering, headache, and muscular discomfort.
Gastritis: Inflammation of the stomach.

trainer, who has little formal training in the pathology of disease, should take nothing for granted. Any unusual condition in an athlete, such as fever, uncharacteristic fatigue, persistent pain, or even a change in behavior, should be scrutinized. If the athletic trainer has even the slightest doubt about an athlete's condition, refer the case to a physician.

This chapter reviews certain major illnesses and chronic disorders the athletic trainer often encounters. The discussion also focuses on the principles of returning to competition after an illness. The topics of disease and exercise are broad and complex and mainly beyond the scope of this text, but here we do discuss the basic principles the athletic trainer needs to know.

Infection and Immunity

A variety of organisms can cause disease in humans. These organisms, called **pathogens,** include viruses, bacteria, fungi, protozoa, and parasitic worms.

Disease-Causing Organisms

Viruses are extremely small pathogens that can be seen only with an electron microscope. There are approximately 150 known types of viruses that cause infections in humans, and they are responsible for most contagious diseases. Viruses invade host cells, disrupting their normal function. Viruses tend to infect specific cells, causing the disease's characteristic symptoms. For example, when a cold virus infects the upper respiratory tract, the membranes in this area swell, resulting in sore throat, runny nose, and headache. A virus that enters the gastrointestinal tract may cause diarrhea. Viral infections include influenza, gastroenteritis,

herpes, **hepatitis, poliomyelitis,** infectious mononucleosis, and warts.

Bacteria are larger than viruses but still considerably smaller than the cells of the body. Bacteria usually cause problems by releasing toxins and harmful enzymes or by rapid growth, which interferes with normal physiological function. Bacterial infections include acne, strep throat, bronchitis, periodontal disease, appendicitis, food poisoning, and typhus fever.

The fungal infections the athletic trainer most commonly encounters are athlete's foot, jock itch, and ringworm (discussed in Chapter 23). Although only about fifty fungi cause diseases in humans, the disabilities can be extremely difficult to deal with. Systemic fungal infections, such as valley fever (coccidioidomycosis), can be life-threatening.

Protozoa are single-celled organisms that cause diseases such as malaria and amoebic dysentery. These diseases are more common in Asia, Africa, and Latin America, less so in most industrialized countries. However, because world-class athletes often tour countries where these diseases are prevalent, they could contract them. The parasitic worms that cause infection include tapeworms, hookworms, pinworms, and flukes. The athletic trainer rarely encounters these organisms.

The Body's Defenses

The body has a variety of mechanisms for combating pathogens. The first lines of defense are the *external* barriers that prevent pathogens from entering critical areas of the body: the skin; the mucous membranes of the respiratory, gastrointestinal, and urinary tracts; and the wax produced in the ear canal. The second lines of defense are *internal* barriers, including white blood cells and digestive enzymes.

The white blood cells consist of granulocytes, macrophages, and lympho-

Hepatitis: Inflammation of the liver.

Poliomyelitis: An infectious and contagious disease that affects the spinal cord. Usually occurs in children and paralyzes, atrophies, and deforms various muscle groups.

Pathogens: Organisms that cause disease.

cytes. The lymphocytes are capable of developing an adaptive **immunity** to specific pathogens by forming antibodies, which combine with the pathogens. This process renders the foreign substance harmless so that it can be removed from the body. Specific im- munity to a variety of dangerous pathogens can be partially or totally developed through a process called immunization. Table 24-1 lists the principal immunizations available in the United States.

Immunity: Ability of the body to recognize, neutralize, and eliminate foreign material without harming its own tissue.

Table 24-1 *Immunizations Available in the United States*

Type	Who Should Be Immunized	Effectiveness and Frequency of Booster Doses
Cholera	Foreign travelers	Only partial immunity; renew every 6 months for duration of exposure
Diphtheria	All adults in good health with no previous immunization; travelers	Highly effective; renew every 10 years
German measles	Mainly for children	Highly effective; need for boosters not established
Influenza	All adults of any age, especially those with chronic disease of the heart, respiratory tract, or endocrine system	Renew every year (because viral strains change easily)
Measles	Mainly for children	Highly effective; usually produces lifelong immunity
Mumps	Most helpful to children and young adults who have not had mumps	Believed to confer lifetime immunity
Plague	Anyone exposed; travelers to Asia, Africa, and Tibet	Incomplete protection; boosters necessary every 3 to 6 months
Polio	All adults, particularly travelers, those exposed to children, and those in health and sanitation industries	Long-lasting immunity; no booster necessary unless exposure anticipated
Rabies	Only those bitten by rabid animal	A vaccination each day for 14 to 21 days beginning soon after the bite
Spotted fever	. . .	Not very effective
Tetanus	Everyone	Very effective; renew every 10 years or when treated for a contaminated wound if more than 5 years have elapsed since last booster
Tuberculosis	High-risk people; nurses and children in contact with active tubercular cases	Highly effective
Typhoid fever	Anyone exposed; travelers	About 80 percent effective
Typhus	Anyone exposed	Renew every year (if exposed)
Whooping cough	Essential for children by age 3 to 4 months	Highly effective
Yellow fever	Anyone exposed; travelers	Highly effective; provides immunity for at least 17 years

SOURCE: Insel, P. M., and W. T. Roth. *Core Concepts in Health*, 4th ed. Palo Alto, Calif.: Mayfield Publishing Co., 1985, p. 436.

The Common Cold and Influenza

Almost all athletes get a cold or the flu at some time (see Putting It into Practice 24-1). Outbreaks of these illnesses can be as devastating to a team as a string of knee injuries. These illnesses are sometimes difficult to differentiate because they often have the same symptoms.

Colds are upper respiratory infections accompanied by runny nose, sore throat, headache, muscle aches, and clogged sinuses. Cold symptoms result from the viral inflammation of the membranes of the nose and throat and occasionally the chest and ears. Some colds are caused by any one of more than 120 different viruses; approximately 45 percent are caused by rhinovirus. Once infected, the cold sufferer is more susceptible to secondary bacterial infections, such as staphylococcus or pneumococcus, which can worsen the symptoms.

Millions of dollars are spent each year on various cold remedies. Many of the solutions are effective against some symptoms, but they have little, if any, effect against the virus itself. Antibiotics do not fight viral infections and are generally contraindicated because they create antibiotic-resistant strains of bacteria and may upset the resident bacteria in the intestinal tract, causing diarrhea.

Contrary to popular belief, chilly temperatures do not predispose an individual to the common cold. The cold virus is spread through sneezing, coughing, shaking hands, and touching contaminated articles. Individuals vary in their susceptibility to colds. The average person can expect to suffer two to three colds a year but may experience as many as five or six if exposed to a sufficient variety of cold viruses. Also, a person's susceptibility to colds may vary from one year to the next.

The athletic trainer should advise athletes suffering from colds. (See Putting It into Practice 24-1 to 24-3, pp. 445, 446.) First, warn athletes that overfatigue and exposure to excessively cold temperatures can place additional stress on the body's defense mechanisms. As discussed in Chapter 4, the body is less able to cope with a specific stressor when confronted with general stress, such as a bad cold (Selye's general adaptation syndrome). The athlete should go to bed if he or she has a fever. Aspirin helps the aches and pains, and lozenges, nose drops, and oral or nasal decongestants help shrink swollen membranes. Encourage consumption of fluids (at least eight ounces of juice or water every two hours). Megadoses of vitamin C are not presently recommended. Encourage athletes to be particularly concerned with personal cleanliness so that they are less apt to spread the cold to others.

Influenza is also a viral disease, characterized by aches, pains, and fever. The symptoms are often more serious than those of the common cold, and the fever can persist for several days. Influenza viruses are often identified before an epidemic occurs, so it is possible to specifically immunize against them. Recommendations for the flu are similar to those for the common cold, but a physician should be consulted if fever persists.

Viral infections are sometimes associated with **myocarditis,** an inflammation of the heart muscle. Exercising with myocarditis is contraindicated and can cause electrocardiographic arrhythmias and cardiomyopathy. A good practice to follow after an athlete has had a viral illness is to delay returning the athlete to practice for several days after the symptoms have gone. When practice is resumed, initially conduct the exercise training at reduced intensity.

Myocarditis: Infection of the heart muscle. A remote risk during febrile illnesses, so athletes should not exercise when they have a fever.

Cold and Flu
Symptoms: Fever

Fever is an above-normal elevation of body temperature. Normal oral temperature is 37°C (98.6°F), but there are individual differences. Rectal temperature tends to be about 1°F higher than oral temperature. Body temperature varies during the day, registering higher in the late afternoon and following exercise and lower in the early morning.

Although high fever can be dangerous, an oral temperature below 100°F is of little concern. Fever is an important part of the body's defense mechanism. The survival of various pathogens is optimal within narrowly defined temperatures. The raised body temperature disrupts pathogens' metabolism and checks their development. Additionally, fever facilitates the production rate of antibodies.

The athletic trainer should never overlook high fever. All athletes can expect to get several viral illnesses every year, but the potential for a catastrophic illness should not be treated lightly because the consequences are so severe. Aspirin or aspirin substitutes are useful nonprescription drugs for treating fever, but advise the athlete with significant fever (greater than 100°) to consult a physician (at least by phone) to rule out any serious illness.

Cold Symptoms:
Sore Throat and Coughing

Approximately 80 percent of sore throats (**pharyngitis**) are caused by viruses or irritations from shouting, smoking, coughing, and postnasal drainage (see Putting It into Practice 24-2). The remaining 20 percent are caused by bacteria, such as Streptococcus. Strep throat usually requires a prescription for an **antibiotic.**

Strep throats represent the minority of the total number of sore throats, but

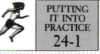

PUTTING IT INTO PRACTICE 24-1

Treating the Common Cold

- *Cause:* A virus (most commonly rhinovirus), most often in the early winter and late spring.
- *Symptoms:* Inflammation of the membranes in the nose and throat and sometimes those in the ears and chest; coughing, sneezing, and sore throat.
- *Treatment:* Rest; avoid cold temperatures; drink plenty of fluids; gargle with warm salt water; use nose drops, lozenges, and aspirin; and monitor body temperature.
- *Medical assistance:* Contact physician if body temperature exceeds 101°F or if there are chest pain, earache, increased sore throat, white spots on throat, dyspnea, and/or severe chills.

PUTTING IT INTO PRACTICE 24-2

Managing the Sore Throat

- *Cause:* A virus or bacteria (Streptococcus), irritation from yelling, coughing, or smoking.
- *Symptoms:* Throat pain, fever, runny nose, swollen lymph nodes.
- *Treatment:* Rest, gargle with warm salt water, drink plenty of fluids, take aspirin and lozenges, and check body temperature.
- *Medical assistance:* Contact physician if there is chronic sore throat, fever exceeding 101°F, severe headache, earache, dyspnea, or if symptoms do not improve within 2 to 3 days.

it is a good idea to refer the athlete to a doctor for a throat culture if the problem persists for three or more days. Suspect strep throat if there is yellow or white exudate in the throat, lymph nodes are enlarged, or the athlete has a fever.

The best advice to give an athlete with a sore throat is to drink plenty of fluids and to gargle every two hours with warm water. Fluids, such as juices, weak tea, and lemonade, soothe the throat membranes and replace fluid lost from sneezing, sweating, and nasal

Pharyngitis: Sore throat.

Antibiotics: Substances that destroy microorganisms like bacteria.

discharge. Throat lozenges, aspirin, and acetaminophen (Tylenol) may also help ease symptoms.

Coughing is not a disease but a symptom that accompanies colds, flu, and respiratory disorders. Coughing of course is also an important mechanism for clearing excess secretions, irritants, and foreign bodies from the lungs and throat. Coughs are dry or wet (loose and productive). The wet cough serves an important physiological function as it protects and helps clean out the respiratory tract. Caution athletes with a wet cough about overusing antitussive or anticough medication because either may interfere with the cough's cleansing function. Reliable methods for relieving the loose cough include sucking on a hard candy, drinking a hot beverage, or using an air vaporizer. Athletes with dry coughs can benefit from cough suppressants containing dextromethorphan or codeine.

Infectious Mononucleosis

Infectious mononucleosis occurs often among young adults and teenagers and can have devastating effects upon athletic performance. The disease is caused by the Epstein-Barr virus (EBV), a member of the herpes group, and characterized by sore throat, fever, enlarged lymph nodes in the neck, profound malaise, and general fatigue. It is estimated that 95 percent of college-age students are exposed to the "mono" virus. The acute phase of the disease lasts five to fourteen days, with complete recovery within six to eight weeks. Highly trained athletes may not achieve preillness levels of fitness for up to three months.

Once the individual is infected, the virus is present in the saliva for many months and is carried in the lymphocytoid cells for life. However, mono-

PUTTING IT INTO PRACTICE 24-3 · **Managing Sinusitis**

- *Cause*: Virus or bacteria, allergies.
- *Symptoms*: Runny nose, sneezing, headache, bad breath, facial edema, fever, muscular aches and pains.
- *Treatment*: Rest, hot-cold compresses, decongestants, aspirin, drink plenty of fluids, gargle with warm salt water, regularly check body temperature.
- *Medical assistance*: Contact physician if body temperature exceeds 101°F, facial edema increases, vision blurs, headaches become severe, or there is a thick nasal discharge.

nucleosis is not significantly contagious unless a person is repeatedly exposed to the infected person's saliva (which is why mono is sometimes called the kissing disease). The disease rarely recurs. Many individuals develop immunity to mononucleosis, but those who do not are more susceptible to the illness. Why there are individual differences in susceptibility to mononucleosis is not completely understood.

Mononucleosis is self-limiting and rarely fatal—there is approximately 1 death per 3000 cases. Most deaths have been due to complications such as bacterial sepsis, ruptured spleen, or asphyxia from airway obstruction. Mononucleosis is often accompanied by an enlarged spleen. The size of the spleen is an important consideration when determining if an athlete is ready to return to play. The spleen is a reservoir for blood. If it is enlarged, it can be easily ruptured in contact sports or during vigorous exercise. However, in approximately 50 percent of reported mono cases with ruptured spleen, there was no precipitating trauma or vigorous exercise. Ruptured spleens from mononucleosis occur most often in white males, rarely in blacks or females. The overall rate of spleen rupture in persons with mononucleosis is approximately 0.1 to 0.2 percent.

An athlete with mononucleosis and an enlarged spleen should be examined and cleared by a physician before being allowed to return to practice. For sports like football, basketball, ice hockey, lacrosse, rugby, wrestling, judo, karate, gymnastics, and diving, it is generally recommended that an athlete delay returning to practice for three to four weeks after symptoms disappear.

Gastroenteritis

Gastroenteritis (stomach flu) is extremely common in athletes (see Putting It into Practice 24-4 and 24-5). Symptoms include nausea, vomiting, diarrhea, abdominal cramping, back pain, muscular aches and pains, and fever. Approximately 90 percent of these cases are caused by viruses. Other causes include food poisoning by salmonella, Staphylococcus, or *Entamoeba coli* bacteria, or by other pathogens, such as *Giardia lamblia* and *Entamoeba histolytica*, which are involved in amoebic dysentery. Gastrointestinal problems can also be related to overindulgence in alcohol, emotional states such as pregame tension, or intolerance toward certain foods.

The athletic trainer can be extremely helpful by taking a careful history and reviewing pertinent symptoms. Always suspect appendicitis because of the impending danger of a ruptured appendix. The pain associated with appendicitis intensifies gradually and shifts to the lower right quadrant of the abdomen.

Food poisoning is of concern, particularly on team trips. The athletic trainer should determine if anyone else on the team is ill after eating the same individual foods. Determine if there have been similar outbreaks of gastrointestinal problems among people the athlete has come in contact with. If so, the problem is more likely viral in origin rather than bacterial (food poisoning). Other possible causes of the problem include infectious hepatitis (see

PUTTING IT INTO PRACTICE 24-4

Managing Gastroenteritis

- *Cause*: A virus or bacteria (food poisoning), alcohol, certain foods, appendicitis, hepatitis, diverticulitis, pancreatitis (see Chapter 20).
- *Symptoms*: Abdominal pain and spasm, back pain, fever, muscular aches and pains, constipation or diarrhea.
- *Treatment*: Rest, restrict food intake, treat diarrhea (see Chapter 27).
- *Medical assistance*: Consult physician if symptoms persist 2 to 3 days, there is blood in stools or vomit, body temperature exceeds 101°F, there are worms in stools, there is persistent pain in rectum or abdomen, or athlete had recent head injury.

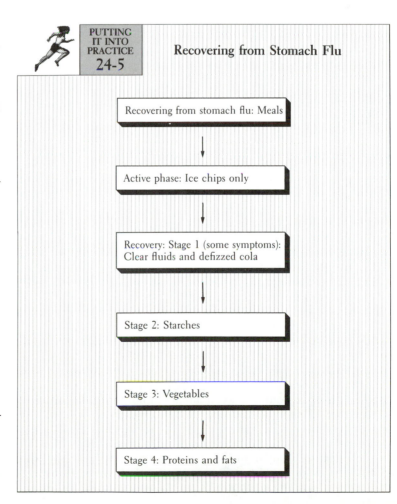

PUTTING IT INTO PRACTICE 24-5

Recovering from Stomach Flu

Recovering from stomach flu: Meals

↓

Active phase: Ice chips only

↓

Recovery: Stage 1 (some symptoms): Clear fluids and defizzed cola

↓

Stage 2: Starches

↓

Stage 3: Vegetables

↓

Stage 4: Proteins and fats

Putting It into Practice 24-6), **diverticulitis, cholecystitis,** and **pancreatitis.** Refer any severe gastrointestinal pain to a physician for evaluation because of the potentially severe consequences.

Viral gastroenteritis lasts approximately twenty-four to forty-eight hours. The athlete should rest in bed for a day until the diarrhea, nausea, vomiting, and fever are gone. The athlete should avoid alcohol, highly seasoned foods, and fruits. During the acute phase, the athlete should consume only ice chips, graduating to sweetened tea, ginger ale, or other soft drinks. After the symptoms have disappeared, the athlete should progress in stages to a normal diet: (1) clear fluids and defizzed cola, (2) starches, (3) vegetables, and (4) proteins and fats. Treatment for nausea and diarrhea may include administration of over-the-counter medication such as Emetrol.

Asthma

Asthma is not uncommon among young people. In the past, asthma excluded many people from competitive athletics, which was understandable because exercise is a major factor in precipitating an asthma attack. However, medications developed for asthma not only make exercise possible but actually decrease the incidence and severity of asthmatic attack. Now, almost all asthmatics can experience competitive athletics. Numerous asthmatics participate in professional athletics and at the highest levels of international competition. However, it is particularly important that asthmatic athletes gradually increase the intensity of their programs and avoid any environmental conditions (such as air pollution and extreme cold) that will complicate their asthma.

Asthma is a lung disorder characterized by edema and inflammation in the walls of the small **bronchi,** secretion of thick mucous into their inner lining,

PUTTING IT INTO PRACTICE 24-6

Managing Viral Hepatitis

- *Cause:* Viral liver infection.
- *Symptoms:* Early stages are characterized by flulike symptoms such as nausea, fever, vomiting, loss of appetite, sore throat, and muscular aches and pain. After a week, symptoms more characteristic of liver disease appear, such as jaundice and pain in the upper right part of the abdomen. The stools are usually clay-colored, and the urine is often dark yellow. The athlete may experience extreme fatigue and weakness for many months.
- *Treatment:* Rest, isolation from other team members, decreased physical activity, proper diet, and avoidance of substances such as alcohol and anabolic steroids, which disturb liver function. This disease is extremely infectious. Call the team physician or public health officials if you suspect this condition.

and spasm of their smooth muscle walls. During an attack, the asthmatic athlete may experience choking, shortness of breath (dyspnea), wheezing, tightness in the chest, increased production of mucous, and fatigue. When an asthma attack occurs, breathing becomes labored, particularly during expiration, because the diameter of the bronchi shrinks. An attack can be caused by such factors as emotional upset, dust, pollen, cold and damp weather, smoke, and exercise.

Asthmatics involved in athletic programs have shown improved lung function, muscle coordination, and emotional adjustment. Usually, there is also a decrease in the frequency and severity of asthmatic attacks (see Putting It into Practice 24-7).

Modify or curtail exercise if the asthmatic is too tired or under emotional stress or if it is too cold, humid, or smoggy. Under adverse environmental conditions, keep exercise bouts short, less than three minutes at a time (or as tolerated). Asthmatic athletes should avoid swimming in excessively cold water because doing so can induce an asthma attack. However, if the water

Diverticulitis: Inflammation of intestinal diverticula (herneations in the intestinal wall that are present in some people).
Cholecystitis: Inflammation of the gallbladder.
Pancreatitis: Inflammation of the pancreas.

Bronchi: Pulmonary airways that are extensions of the bronchiole and trachea.

Prescribing Exercise for Asthmatics

Warm-up: The patient should warm up before vigorous activity. This should consist of walking, progressing to jogging and other low-level activity, flexibility exercises, and some light mobilizing and strengthening activities. It should aim to increase the body temperature until mild sweating occurs.

Warm-down: The patient should warm down at the end of each exercise session. Vigorous work should not stop abruptly; a low level of activity (such as walking) should be maintained for about five minutes or until the heart rate returns to within 20 beats $\cdot$ min^{-1} of the resting level.

Duration: Sessions should last 30 to 40 minutes. (A very unfit subject may need to begin with 15-minute sessions.)

Frequency: Four to five times a week.

Intensity: Exercise should start at a low level of intensity and gradually increase in severity as fitness level improves. If using interval training, the work interval should be at an intensity that initially produces a heart rate of 70% of the maximum heart rate, gradually progressing to 90%. The rest interval should be short enough to reduce the heart rate to 50% to 60% of maximum. If using continuous training techniques the work intensity should progress slowly to 85% of the maximum heart rate.

Age: Regular exercise should be continued throughout life.

Mode: Activities and games of the subject's choice should be prescribed. If possible, the asthmatic should be involved in swim training at some time (preferably during his developmental years). Regardless of the activity selected, the program must aim at increasing the person's aerobic power.

Exercise loading: Programs should begin with walking. If the subject is regularly experiencing EIA [exercise-induced asthma], he should progress to low-level interval training using work intervals of 10 to 30 seconds followed by rest periods of 30 to 90 seconds, and then progress to high-intensity interval training. (However, if an asthmatic can "run through" his asthma or if he uses suitable preexercise medication, long-distance continous activity, despite its greater asthmogenicity, may be pursued with benefit. With suitable medication, either continuous or interval training is well tolerated by most asthmatics.)

Preexercise medication: This is essential for most asthmatics, and aerosol beta-2 agonists or cromolyn sodium are the preferred agents.

Medication to reverse EIA: If EIA occurs during the activity, it may be reversed by the appropriate aerosol agent.

SOURCE: Morton, A. R., K. D. Fitch, and A. G. Hohn. Physical activity and the asthmatic. *The Physician and Sportsmedicine* 9:51–64, 1981.

temperature is warm enough, the humidity near the pool's surface makes swimming an excellent sport for asthmatics.

An asthma attack can often be triggered by allergies to agents like dust, pollen, and specific foods. Some degree of allergic control is desirable before a vigorous endurance program is started. The incidence of allergic reactions can sometimes be reduced by allergy shots, which desensitize against the various aggravating substances. At the very least, asthmatics can prevent allergic reactions by avoiding things they are allergic to.

Athletes susceptible to exercise-induced asthma should take their prescribed medication before the workout. Modern medications have enabled asthmatics to participate in even the most vigorous sports, including endurance events in the Olympic Games. In the 1972 Games, an asthmatic won a gold medal in swimming (only to be disqualified for taking his asthma medication). These drugs can prevent exercise-induced asthma or reduce the effects once they have occurred. Chronic, recurrent wheezing is usually controlled by sympathomimetic drugs (they mimic the action of the sympathetic nervous system), such as ephedrine or epinephrine, in the form of an aerosol inhalant.

Encourage the asthmatic athlete to drink as much water as possible when participating in endurance exercises because ingesting water reduces the thickness of lung secretions, thus facilitating breathing. The athletic trainer should ensure that an inhaler and 100 percent oxygen are available for athletes with serious asthma. The asthmatic should be instructed in relaxation positions and breathing exercises to be used in the event of shortness of breath or distress.

Diabetes

In the past, there were few diabetic athletes. Although mild exercise has been part of the treatment of diabetes for centuries, the intensity of physical activity required in many forms of competitive athletics often proved harmful to the diabetic's condition. However, researchers have learned a great deal about the effects of strenuous exercise upon diabetes, and this has enabled diabetics to participate in sports. The athletic trainer should have a basic understanding of the possible problems confronting the diabetic athlete so that the athletic experience is a positive one. See Table 24-2.

Diabetes mellitus is a disease caused by a relative lack of production of the hormone insulin, which is produced by the pancreas' beta cells. Insulin is important because it is necessary for the uptake of glucose into the various tissues. Glucose in turn is an essential fuel for life. The brain, kidney, and red blood cells, for example, use glucose almost exclusively.

Diabetes is of both short- and long-term concern. Poorly controlled diabe-

tes can lead to diabetic coma or insulin shock, either of which can be life-threatening. Long-term effects include a higher risk of heart disease, kidney disease, stroke, blindness, and peripheral vascular disease. The athletic trainer can help the athlete avoid some of the serious short-term problems and instill the importance of a healthy life-style to minimize some of the long-term risks.

Diabetes, mainly a hereditary disease, is classified as type I (insulin-dependent) or type II (insulin-independent). There is no known cure for the disease, but usually it can be controlled. People with type I diabetes can survive if they are given injections of insulin and if they maintain a well-controlled diet. Type II diabetes is controlled by diet alone or diet and oral hypoglycemic drugs.

High blood sugar (**hyperglycemia**) is a prominent characteristic of diabetes. High blood sugar (glucose) results from a lack of insulin, which transports glucose into the tissue. There is a concommitant increase in the breakdown of fats and protein in an effort to meet the body's energy need.

Control of diabetes involves maintaining normal levels of blood glucose (by insulin injections in type I and diet, drugs, and exercise in types I and II). Diet is very important for the diabetic; food intake must be enough to satisfy the needs of growth (in children) and metabolism, but not so much as to produce obesity. The American Diabetes Association recommends that diabetics eat a balanced diet of about 50 percent complex carbohydrates, 35 percent fat, and 15 percent proteins. It is recommended that dietary cholesterol and saturated fats be curtailed to reduce the risk of heart disease.

An insulin injection is not physiologically the same as the natural secretion of insulin by the pancreas. In the nondiabetic, insulin is released both continuously and in response to blood sugar. After a meal, blood sugar rises and insulin is secreted to effectively utilize the

Hyperglycemia: High blood sugar.

fuel. In the diabetic, insulin is administered all at once (in an injection). Many of diabetes' side effects are caused by the chronic imbalance between insulin levels and glucose: Insulin levels may be too high after an injection and too low at other times. In other words, diabetes becomes very dangerous when it is not controlled.

Participation in athletics or an exercise program is not recommended unless the diabetes is under control, that

Table 24-2 *Characteristic Signs in Diabetic Emergencies*

	Diabetic Coma	Insulin Shock
History		
Food	Excessive	Insufficient
Insulin	Insufficient	Excessive
Onset	Gradual—days	Sudden—minutes
Appearance of athlete	Extremely ill	Very weak
Skin	Warm and dry	Pale and moist
Infection	May be present	Absent
Gastrointestinal system		
Mouth	Dry	Drooling
Thirst	Intense	Absent
Hunger	Absent	Intense
Vomiting	Common	Uncommon
Abdominal pain	Frequent	Absent
Respiratory system		
Breathing	Exaggerated air hunger	Normal or shallow
Odor of breath	Acetone odor usual (sweet, fruity)	Acetone odor may be present
Cardiovascular system		
Blood pressure	Low	Normal
Pulse	Rapid, weak	Normal, may be rapid and full
Vision	Dim	Diplopia (double vision)
Nervous system		
Headache	Absent	Present
Mental state	Restlessness merging into unconsciousness	Apathy, dizziness, irritability merging into unconsciousness
Tremors	Absent	Present
Convulsions	None	In late stages
Urine		
Sugar	Present	Absent
Acetone	Present	May be present
Improvement	Gradual, within 6–12 h following administration of insulin	Immediate improvement following oral administration of carbohydrates (glucose, candy, orange juice, ginger ale, sugar)

SOURCE: American Academy of Orthopaedic Surgeons. *Emergency Care and Transportation of the Sick and Injured.* Chicago: American Academy of Orthopaedic Surgeons, 1981, p. 241.

is, the blood sugar levels can be predictably regulated. Control problems have to be worked out by trial and error. The most immediate problem is **hypoglycemia,** low blood glucose (sugar). Glucose utilization is much greater during exercise than at rest. The diabetic who is taking insulin is involved in a daily and often hourly juggling act of trying to balance energy intake (food), energy output (exercise and resting metabolism), and insulin (energy regulator). A variation in any one of these three factors requires adjustment of the others.

Active diabetics often eat high-sugar foods, such as candy, orange juice, or graham crackers, before exercising to meet the increased glucose requirements of physical activity. This works particularly well if the time or amount of exercise is irregular. If exercise habits are more predictable, a change in the amount of insulin injected each day might help prevent hypoglycemia. Exercise at a given intensity and for a given amount of time has a predictable fuel requirement. Regular, predictable exercise habits make the control of diabetes much easier.

Hypoglycemia is particularly dangerous for the diabetic athlete because it can severely impair judgment and cause a loss of coordination, which could lead to injury. A person in a hypoglycemic state can easily overestimate personal capacity with potentially tragic results.

A diabetic in poor control of the disease and hyperglycemic (high blood sugar) may also be in a state of **ketosis,** a condition characterized by the accumulation of large amounts of ketones in the blood. Ketones make the blood more acidic, which disturbs the body's metabolism. Ketosis occurs when the availability of carbohydrates is severely diminished and fats must be used as the predominant fuel. If left to progress, ketosis can lead to diabetic coma. Exercise is not recommended when a person has ketosis or hypoglycemia.

Under certain conditions, exercise can make the problem worse by increasing blood sugar levels even higher. Thus, an athlete's diabetes should be controlled before the individual undertakes an exercise program.

The site of injection is very important in an exercising diabetic. Injections are usually given beneath the skin covering the thigh, upper arms, abdomen, or buttocks. If insulin is injected into an area of a muscle involved in exercise, then the insulin goes into the bloodstream much more rapidly and may lead to hypoglycemia. For example, if a runner were to inject insulin into a leg and then run, the insulin would begin to act more quickly and more powerfully than normal. The problem can be avoided by injecting the insulin into the abdomen or arm. However, some researchers have questioned whether this practice is really beneficial for the exercising diabetic.

Heart disease, which usually manifests itself in the nondiabetic population at about age thirty-five to forty-five, appears sooner among diabetics. Because of their increased risk of heart disease, diabetics of any age should take a treadmill test before participating in competitive sports or starting an exercise program.

The athletic trainer should be aware of any athlete who has diabetes so that the proper actions can be taken in an emergency. The most serious problems likely to be encountered are diabetic coma, insulin shock, and dehydration. Dehydration is more prevalent in the diabetic because of the chronically high levels of blood glucose that tend to draw fluid from inside the cells ("drying" them out). The higher risk of dehydration makes the diabetic athlete more susceptible to heat injuries and fluid-related fatigue. The athletic trainer should be particularly leery when working with a diabetic wrestler trying to "make weight."

Diabetic coma results from acidosis (pH of body fluids falls below 7.0 to

Hypoglycemia: Low blood sugar.

Ketosis: Metabolic condition characterized by an accumulation of ketones. Extreme ketosis, as in diabetic coma, can lead to dyspnea, low, rapid pulse, and coma if not treated.

6.9) and dehydration. A diabetic coma is usually fatal unless the athlete receives immediate medical attention. Emergency medical procedures include administration of massive quantities of insulin and infusion of sodium chloride and bicarbonate solutions.

Insulin shock results from an overabundance of insulin, which causes hypoglycemia. Insulin shock can lead to convulsions and coma. The coma from insulin shock may resemble diabetic coma except that the athlete will not have the characteristic acetone breath. Emergency medical procedures involve infusion of glucose solution. Diabetic athletes can prevent hypoglycemia by consuming a candy bar or orange juice before exercising.

Cardiac-Related Deaths in Athletes

Nothing in sport is as tragic as a young athlete who dies suddenly during a practice or competition. Fortunately, fatalities in athletics are rare. Cardiac-related deaths in young athletes (athletes younger than thirty-five) have been found to be principally caused by congenital disorders (abnormal heart conditions present at birth), coronary artery disease (hardening of the arteries), viral myocarditis (inflammation of the heart muscle), and coronary artery vasospasm (spasm of the coronary artery that results in coronary artery ischemia). Of these causes, congenital defects account for most cases of sudden death of young athletes during exercise.

Preventing such deaths is difficult because exercise and exercise training produce physiological changes that resemble disease states. Thus sophisticated tests, such as echocardiography, are sometimes required for diagnosis. Because athletes often have enlarged hearts and abnormal blood chemistries and electrocardiograms, the physician may be less suspicious when healthy athletes present these symptoms. For example, the doctor may confuse hypertrophic cardiomyopathy, a fibrous disease of the heart muscle implicated in many of the cardiac-related deaths among young athletes, with the enlarged heart common in many trained athletes. Fortunately, there has been a great deal of research into the causes of sudden death in athletes. The results of these studies help the physician differentiate between exercise effects that cause normal physiological variances in common medical tests and actual disease states.

As discussed in Chapter 19, always consider the unusual when faced with an athlete who is having health problems with no obvious cause. Symptoms that may be related to cardiac disease in young athletes include fainting, flu, unexplained fatigue, palpitations (rapid or forceful heartbeat at rest), skipped beats (caused by cardiac arrhythmias that the athlete can perceive), dyspnea (labored breathing), and chest pains. Refer athletes who are experiencing these symptoms to their physician.

Myocarditis—inflammation of the heart muscle—can occur in anyone and can cause ventricular fibrillation and sudden death. It tends to occur during febrile illnesses and can be worsened by physical exertion. For this reason, do not let athletes participate when they have a febrile illness such as the flu.

References

Amkraut, A. "Infection and Immunity," in *Core Concepts in Health*, 4th ed., P. M. Insel and W. T. Roth, eds. Palo Alto, Calif.: Mayfield Publishing Co., 1985, pp. 425–453.

Brodsky, A. L., and C. W. Heath. Infectious mononucleosis: epidemiologic patterns at United States universities. *American Journal of Epidemiology* 96:87–93, 1972.

Brooks, G. A., and T. D. Fahey. *Exercise Physiology: Human Bioenergetics and Its Applications.* New York: Wiley, 1984.

Brown, H. V., and K. Wasserman. Exercise performance in chronic obstructive pulmonary diseases. *Medical Clinics of North America* 65:525–547, 1981.

Campbell, J. A., R. L. Hughs, V. Sahgal, J. Frederiksen, and T. W. Shields. Asterations in intercostal muscle morphology and biochemistry in patients with obstructive lung disease. *American Review of Respiratory Disease* 122:679–686, 1980.

Frelinger, D. P. The ruptured spleen in college athletes: a preliminary report. *Journal of the American College Health Association* 26:217, 1978.

Green, R. L., S. S. Kaplan, B. S. Rabin, C. L. Stanitski, and U. Zdziarski. Immune function in marathon runners. *Annals of Allergy* 47:73–75, 1981.

Hanson, P. G., and D. K. Flaherty. Immunologic responses to training in conditioned runners. *Clinical Science* 60:225–228, 1981.

Hilsted, J., H. Galbo, B. Tronier, N. J. Christensen, and T. W. Schwartz. Hormonal and metabolic responses to exercise in insulin-dependent diabetics with and without autonomic neuropathy and in normal subjects. *International Journal of Sports Medicine* 2:216–219, 1981.

Holbreich, M. Exercise-induced bronchospasm in children. *Family Physician* 23:185–188, 1981.

Koivisto, V. A. Diabetes in the elderly: what role for exercise? *Geriatrics* 36:74–83, 1981.

Koivisto, V., and R. S. Sherwin. Exercise in diabetes. *Postgraduate Medicine* 66:87–96, 1979.

Ludvigsson, J. Physical exercise in relation to degree of metabolic control in juvenile diabetics. *Acta Paediatrica Scandinavica* supp. 283:45–49, 1980.

McFadden, E. R., and R. Ingram. Exercise-induced asthma. *New England Journal of Medicine* 301:763–769, 1979.

Maki, D. G., R. M. Reich. Infectious mononucleosis in the athlete: diagnosis, complications, and management. *American Journal of Sports Medicine* 10:162–173, 1982.

Patruno, D. Asthma and physical exercise. *Current Therapeutic Research* 32:257–264, 1982.

Petersen, G. E., M. Lorenzi, and T. H. Forsham. The effects of exercise upon platelet adhesion in diabetes mellitus. *Diabetes* 28:360, 1979.

Sergysels, R., A. van Meerhaeghe, G. Scano, M. Denaut, R. Willeput, R. Messin, and A. DeCoster. Respiratory drive during exercise in chronic obstructive lung disease. *Bulletin of European Physiopathological Respiration* 17:755–766, 1981.

Thompson, P. D. Cardiovascular hazards of physical activity. *Exercise and Sport Sciences Reviews* 10:208–235, 1982.

Thompson, P. D., and J. R. McGhee. "Cardiac Evaluation of the Competitive Athlete," in *Sports Medicine*, R. H. Strauss, ed. Philadelphia: W. B. Saunders, 1984, pp. 3–12.

Environmental Stress

E NVIRONMENTAL distress can affect the performance of even the most conditioned athlete. Athletic contests are often held in extremely hot or cold temperatures, at high altitude, or in smoggy air. It is not unusual for athletes to perform after a night with little or no sleep or when fatigued following air or automobile travel. The athletic trainer should be aware of the effects of these adverse environments upon performance and be familiar with techniques that maximize the health and well-being of athletes participating under these sometimes hazardous conditions.

Heat, particularly humid heat, is the most common and potentially most dangerous environmental condition the athlete faces. The athletic trainer should be aware of the basic physiology of heat stress and dehydration and know the factors, such as clothing and fluid and electrolyte replacement, involved in thermal disorders and physical conditioning.

Competition at high altitudes (above 6000 feet) is common in many parts of the country. Many athletes have the opportunity to visit and train in such an environment. The athletic trainer should be familiar with the process of **acclimatization,** decrements in perfor-

Endurance athletes, such as cyclists, are especially susceptible to environmental stressors like heat, cold, altitude, and air pollution.

Acclimatization: Physiological adjustment to a new environment.

455

mance at altitude, and the symptoms of the various altitude maladies, such as acute mountain sickness.

Air pollution can negatively affect athletes' physical performance, health, and emotional well-being. The athletic trainer should be aware of the physiological effects of poor air quality upon performance and health and know the techniques for minimizing athletes' exposure to air pollution.

Travel to a competition can have devastating effects upon athletic success. Jet lag, cramped muscles from prolonged sitting, and dehydration caused by pressurized aircraft can sometimes override the beneficial effects of even the most carefully planned training program.

This chapter explores the effects of environmental stress upon performance and discusses various strategies for coping with them. The athletic trainer should be well versed in this topic because there are many deaths and serious injuries from sports participation in adverse climates.

Temperature Regulation

Humans are able to function relatively independently of the environment because of their ability to maintain a fairly constant body temperature. Bodily processes such as **oxygen transport,** cellular metabolism, and muscle contraction remain unimpaired in hot and cold environments as long as internal temperature is maintained. But as soon as the body temperature rises beyond or falls below normal levels, physical performance deteriorates and well-being is threatened.

People experience a range of normal resting body temperatures, typically between 36.5 and 37.5°C (97.7 to 99.5°F). There is considerable temperature variation within the body. **Core temperature** is the temperature of the

hypothalamus, the body's temperature regulatory center. The internal temperature of the core remains relatively constant, whereas skin temperature varies dramatically according to that of the environment. Body temperature typically is expressed in terms of the core temperature.

The body regulates its temperature by controlling the rates of heat production and heat loss. When the rate of heat production exactly equals the rate of heat loss, the body is in heat balance. When out of balance, the body either gains or loses heat. The hypothalamus controls heat balance centrally, with feedback from peripheral heat and cold receptors in the skin.

The hypothalamus works like a thermostat by increasing the rate of heat production when the body temperature falls and increasing the rate of heat dissipation when the temperature rises. Temperature is regulated by physical and chemical processes. Temperature is regulated physically principally by the resistance to heat flow changing; temperature is regulated chemically by the body's metabolic rate increasing (Figure 25-1).

Metabolism is the body's source of internal heat production. Even during deep sleep, a certain amount of heat is produced. During exercise, there is considerable heat production. Heat production is enhanced when the metabolic rate is increased. Shivering (involuntary muscle contractions) is the main mechanism for increasing the metabolic rate when there is negative heat balance (net loss of heat). Maximal shivering can increase the body's heat production as much as five times.

Other means of increasing the metabolic rate include increased secretion of the hormones thyroxin and norepinephrine, and the Q10 effect, which is the tendency of the rate of chemical reactions to speed up as temperature increases. As temperature rises from shivering, thyroxin, and norepinephrine, the metabolic rate and heat production also increase.

Hypothalamus: A deep-lying brain structure responsible for visceral controls, including fluid balance, hunger, temperature regulation, and pituitary gland secretions.

Metabolism: The sum of all the chemical reactions that occur in the body.

Oxygen transport: Transportation of oxygen to tissue; determined mainly by cardiac output.

Core temperature: The temperature of the hypothalamus, the body's temperature regulatory center. Includes the temperature of vital internal organs like the heart and liver and the central nervous system.

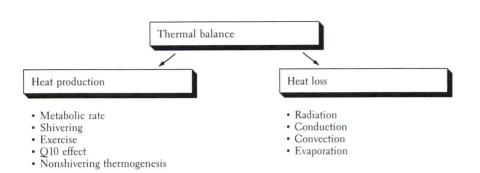

Figure 25-1 Factors contributing to thermal balance.

The body loses heat through **radiation, conduction, convection,** and **evaporation.** Radiation is the loss of heat in the form of infrared rays. Conduction is the transfer of heat from the body to an object; convection is the conduction of heat to air or water. Evaporation is the vaporization of water, which results in cooling. At room temperature, when skin temperature is greater than air temperature, most heat is lost by outward heat flow. In the heat, or during heavy exercise, evaporation of sweat is the dominant mechanism of heat dissipation.

Heat Stress

Heat stress is the athletic trainer's major environmental adversary. Fortunately, most episodes of thermal distress can be prevented by ensuring adequate fluid intake, minimizing practice sessions when it is excessively hot and humid, and recognizing early symptoms of dehydration, heat exhaustion, and heatstroke.

The extent of heat's effect upon exercise capacity is affected by the body's ability to dissipate heat and maintain blood flow to the active muscles. During exercise in the heat, muscle and skin's combined circulatory demands can effectively impair oxygen transport capacity. Additionally, during exercise there is a decrease in plasma volume that becomes increasingly acute as the

intensity of the effort increases. The decrease in plasma volume can be augmented by the loss of body fluids through sweating, which can be a particularly acute problem during dehydration.

Endurance capacity, as measured by the **maximal oxygen consumption** test conducted on a laboratory treadmill, is not impaired in the heat unless the subject is suffering heat stress when the test begins. For athletic contests, athletes rarely have the luxury of going from the comforts of normal room temperature into the heat of an environmental chamber; usually they have to sleep, eat, and train in the heat before performing. Dehydration, lack of sleep, and anxiety can combine to cause a high degree of physiological and psychological stress. Acclimatization is essential if the athlete is to perform optimally in the heat.

Heat Acclimatization

During its first week of exposure to heat, the body makes several adjustments that improve performance and make life more bearable: peripheral blood flow increases, for elimination of heat; plasma volume increases; sweating capacity increases; the threshold of skin temperature falls for the onset of sweating; and sweat is better distributed over the skin. These changes lower the heart rate, core temperature, and skin temperature at rest and during submaximal

Radiation: Projection of heat through infrared waves.
Conduction: Transmission of heat energy from one point to another.
Convection: Transfer of heat to air or water.
Evaporation: Sweating; the process of changing a liquid (sweat) into a vapor. The process requires heat, which results in heat loss from the body. Also called latent heat of vaporization.
Maximal oxygen consumption: The best measure of the fitness of the cardiovascular system; the heart's maximum capacity to pump blood and the tissues' maximum extraction and use of oxygen.

exercise. Acclimatization to heat is not complete unless the exposure is accompanied by exercise training. However, although exercise is essential for acclimatization to heat, training by itself is not a full measure of heat adaptation. An athlete from a temperate environment who must compete in the heat can become acclimatized for the effort by exercising (endurance training) in a hot room.

Thermal Distress

Thermal distress and heat injury occur relatively often in athletics and can cause death or permanently impair temperature regulatory capacity. Fortunately, heat stress is preventable if the necessary precautions are taken (see Putting It into Practice 25-1). Thermal distress includes dehydration, heat cramps, heat exhaustion, and heatstroke.

Dehydration. Dehydration is the loss of fluid from the body; it decreases sweat rate, plasma volume, cardiac output, maximal oxygen uptake, work capacity, muscle strength, and liver **glycogen.** Thirst results when the body loses 700 milliliters of fluid, or approximately 1 percent of body weight. At a fluid deficit of 5 percent of body weight, the athlete feels discomfort, goes through alternating states of lethargy and nervousness, becomes irritable, feels fatigued, and loses appetite. A dehydration of 5 percent is extremely common among athletes participating in sports like football, soccer, wrestling, and distance running. Dehydration levels greater than 7 percent are extremely dangerous and can cause thermal injury and even death.

Thirst, which is controlled by the hypothalamus, does *not* stimulate the athlete to drink sufficient amounts of water during physical activity to satisfy water deficits. Athletes can easily experience fluid depletion of 2 to 4 percent of body weight. It is very important that

dehydrating athletes take regular fluid breaks rather than relying upon only their thirst for fluid replacement.

The inadequacy of the thirst mechanism can be compounded by the type of fluid replacement. Fluids with a high amount of carbohydrate (concentrations greater than 2.5 grams per 100 milliliters) delay the rate of gastric emptying. Some commercially available fluid replacements with a high amount of sugar compound the problem of dehydration because they satisfy thirst but delay the replenishment of body water. Cold water is the best fluid replacement, but some commercial fluids have almost equal rates of gastric emptying and are also acceptable. Some athletes prefer the commercial fluids because they taste better. Honor the athletes' wishes as long as a *suitable* fluid is selected; the important thing is to get athletes to drink enough fluid.

Recent studies that used glucose polymer-electrolyte solutions (carbohydrate solutions that exert a lower osmotic pressure than glucose) as a fluid replacement found that the solutions emptied from the stomach at approximately the same rate as water. The use of glucose polymer-electrolyte solutions to replace fluids lost during exercise may help partially satisfy athletes' fluid and glucose needs. Glucose polymer solutions are available commercially from companies such as Unipro (Sunnyvale, California).

Heat Cramps. Heat cramps are characterized by sudden, involuntary, persistent cramping or spasm in muscles. The cause of heat cramps is unknown; they are thought to stem from an alteration in the balance between water and electrolytes caused by dehydration and salt depletion (fluid depletion is probably the most important factor). Cramps typically occur in people who have exercised and sweated heavily. They are most common in individuals unconditioned and unacclimatized to heat, but even extremely fit athletes can suffer from heat cramps.

Dehydration: Loss of body fluid.

Glycogen: A complex carbohydrate stored principally in the liver and skeletal muscle; an extremely important fuel during most forms of exercise.

PUTTING IT INTO PRACTICE 25-1

Preventing Thermal Distress

Thermal distress problems can be minimized by following a few simple principles:

- Ensure that athletes are in good physical condition. There should be a gradual increase in intensity and duration of training until the athletes are fully acclimatized.
- Schedule practice sessions and games during the cooler times of the day.
- Modify or cancel exercise sessions when the wet bulb/globe temperature is 25.5°C or greater. (Wet bulb temperature determines humidity; globe temperature is an indication of radiant heat.)
- Have regular water breaks.
- Supply a drink that is cold (8 to 13°C), low in sugar (less than or equal to 2.5 percent), with little or no electrolytes.
- Encourage athletes to "tank-up" before practice or games by drinking 400 to 600 milliliters of water thirty minutes before activity.
- Encourage fluid replacement particularly during the early stages of practice and competition. As exercise progresses, splanic blood flow tends to decrease, which diminishes water absorption from the gut.
- Weigh athletes every day before practice. Do not let any athlete showing a 3 percent or more decrease in weight participate until he or she is rehydrated. Identify and closely monitor those who tend to lose much weight in the heat.
- Prohibit salt tablets. However, encourage athletes to consume enough salt at mealtime.

SOURCE: Brooks, G. A., and T. D. Fahey. *Exercise Physiology: Human Bioenergetics and Its Applications.* New York: Wiley, 1984, p. 466.

The treatment for heat cramps is somewhat controversial. The classical treatment includes oral or intravenous salt replacement and rehydration. Unfortunately, most of the emphasis has been upon the salt replacement, which can actually compound the problem. Disproportionate salt intake leads to intracellular dehydration. The kidneys and sweat glands (particularly those of the acclimatized individual) have a remarkable ability to conserve sodium. During dehydration, potassium is not conserved to the same extent as sodium, so ample quantities of it must be provided in the diet to prevent potassium depletion. In most cases, electrolytes are concentrated during dehydration rather than depleted, so it is best to concentrate upon rehydration when treating heat cramps.

The athletic trainer dealing with an athlete suffering from heat cramps faces a dilemma: Are the cramps caused by salt depletion, dehydration without salt depletion, overexertion, or other factors (e.g., binding clothing, nerve irritability)? Even if salt depletion is a contributing factor, the problem may be localized to particular muscle groups. There is no guarantee that salt supplementation will positively affect the cramping muscles. More likely, giving salt pills or electrolyte solution to an athlete during physical activity will make the problem worse (salt pills also take up to two hours to dissolve in the gastrointestinal tract).

The most prudent course is to instruct the athlete to rest, drink fluids, and gently statically stretch the cramping muscles. Athletes should not take salt if they are to immediately return to participation. After athletes have practiced, instruct them to rest, increase salt intake, and drink plenty of water. This strategy is effective regardless of an athlete's fluid-electrolyte balance; with the stress of exercise removed, the kidneys (and their supporting hormone systems) will restore the balance to normal.

Most people consume more than

enough salt in their diets to prevent electrolyte depletion and heat cramps, even in extremely hot, humid climates. Present evidence suggests that in most instances copious quantities of fluid during and after exercise are sufficient for preventing this condition. To ensure adequate salt intake, encourage athletes to use extra salt with their meals.

Heat Exhaustion. See Putting It into Practice 25-2. Heat exhaustion and heatstroke are actually two points along a continuum. If untreated, heat exhaustion can become heatstroke. **Heat exhaustion** is actually hypovolemic shock (see Chapter 10) and is characterized by a rapid, weak pulse, low blood pressure, clammy skin, fatigue, nausea, headache, faintness, profuse sweating, and psychological disorientation. Heat exhaustion results from dehydration and the circulatory system's inability to concurrently supply blood to the skin (for cooling) and to active skeletal muscles (for exercise). Although core temperature may be elevated somewhat (usually less than 39.5°C or 103.1°F), it does not reach the extremely high level that occurs in heatstroke (greater than 41°C or 105.8°F). In addition to observing the above symptoms, the athletic trainer can accurately determine the degree of thermal distress by measuring rectal temperature, which should not exceed 39.5°C. A rectal thermometer should be part of every athletic trainer's field kit, to identify athletes with thermal disorders.

Treatment for heat exhaustion includes rest in a cool area (lying supine with feet elevated) and fluids. Intravenous fluid administration by medical personnel may be appropriate in some instances. The athlete should not participate in any further activity for the rest of the day and should be encouraged to drink plenty of fluids for the next twenty-four hours (athletes should consume salt in the diet, but do not overemphasize this point).

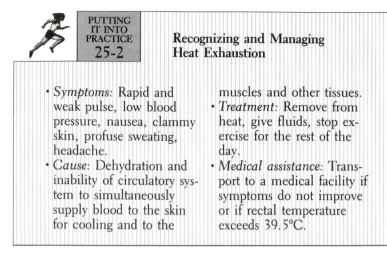

PUTTING IT INTO PRACTICE 25-2

Recognizing and Managing Heat Exhaustion

- *Symptoms*: Rapid and weak pulse, low blood pressure, nausea, clammy skin, profuse sweating, headache.
- *Cause*: Dehydration and inability of circulatory system to simultaneously supply blood to the skin for cooling and to the muscles and other tissues.
- *Treatment*: Remove from heat, give fluids, stop exercise for the rest of the day.
- *Medical assistance*: Transport to a medical facility if symptoms do not improve or if rectal temperature exceeds 39.5°C.

Heatstroke. This condition is also called hyperpyrexia or sunstroke; see Putting It into Practice 25-3. **Heatstroke** is characterized by damage to the hypothalamus (the temperature regulatory center), which impairs its ability to control internal body temperature. This disorder can result in death if not promptly treated. Athletes who sustain heatstroke are more susceptible to subsequent recurrence. Although heatstroke can occur even in relatively cool temperatures, it most commonly affects athletes exercising in the heat.

Heatstroke is caused principally by the hypothalamic center (temperature regulatory center) failing, thus increasing body temperature to dangerously high levels because of the lack of evaporative cooling. Heatstroke is characterized by a high core temperature (greater than 41°C or 105.8°F), hot, dry skin, dyspnea, and extreme confusion or unconsciousness. In exercise-related heatstroke, the individual may still be sweating. The cardiovascular effects are variable: Some athletes experience hypotension, but others have a full, bounding pulse and high blood pressure. This problem can result in shock and collapse and cook the cells. Heatstroke is a medical emergency and treatment must be prompt, aggressive, and lifesaving!!!

Heat exhaustion: A form of hypovolemic shock from dehydration and an inadequate amount of blood returning to the heart because it has been directed to the skin for cooling and, often, to the muscles to satisfy exercise's metabolic demands.

Heatstroke: Sunstroke; caused by a failure of the hypothalamic temperature regulatory center. This is a major medical emergency.

Reducing body temperature is the number one priority. Remove the athlete from the heat to a cool area or air conditioned room. Douse the athlete with cool water (not icy water because it may induce shivering, which could increase internal heat production), and instruct the individual to drink fluids to restore the body's fluids. Transport the athlete to a medical facility as soon as possible. If efforts to reduce body temperature are unsuccessful, pack the athlete in ice (use ice only as a last resort because it can cause frostbite). In the hospital, treatment includes submersion in an ice bath accompanied by massage to counteract shivering and shunting of blood toward the body's core. Rectal temperature is monitored to guard against rebound hypothermia. Fluids are intravenously administered to counteract shock and low blood pressure.

PUTTING IT INTO PRACTICE 25-3

Recognizing and Managing Heatstroke

- *Cause*: Failure of the hypothalamus' temperature regulatory center.
- *Symptoms*: High core temperature (exceeds 41°C), hot, dry skin (although athlete may be sweating), tachycardia (rapid heart rate), extreme confusion, or unconsciousness. Determine core temperature *rectally* rather than orally because oral temperature may register normal due to circulatory collapse.
- *Treatment*: Remove athlete from hot environment and call ambulance. Douse athlete with cold water and have the person drink cold fluids (preferably cold water). Pack in ice if body temperature fails to fall, but massage skin to prevent reflex vasoconstriction. Continue to monitor temperature to guard against rebound hypothermia.

Cold Stress

Maximal performance in the cold depends upon the proper amount of clothing and the extent of the awkwardness the numbing of exposed flesh induces. Too much clothing makes movement difficult; too little clothing causes heat loss, which impairs performance. Manipulative motor skills requiring finger dexterity, such as catching and throwing, are tremendously impaired in the cold because the cold effectively anesthetizes sensory receptors in the hands. Exposed flesh, particularly on the face, is susceptible to frostbite, which can become a serious medical problem.

Clothing is an important consideration during physical activity in the cold. The clothing's insulation value must be balanced with the increased metabolic heat production from exercise. If the athlete wears too much clothing, he or she risks becoming a tropical person in a cold environment. There have been instances of over-clothed persons exercising in extremely cold climates suffering thermal injury.

Clothes increase the body's insulation by entrapping warm air next to the skin and decreasing conductive heat loss. The best clothing for exercise in the cold allows sweat to evaporate while adding protection from the cold. Wool is excellent insulation against cold. Athletes should wear clothing in layers so that it can be removed as the metabolic heat production increases during exercise. In recent years, clothing manufacturers have made tremendous progress in developing lightweight clothing that provides both sufficient insulation and freedom of movement during exercise. Materials such as Gortex allow moisture to escape from the body while preventing moisture from penetrating from the environment.

Endurance performance is not impaired in the cold provided the clothing does not hinder movement. However, it is possible to impair exercise performance capacity, particularly in short-term, high-intensity exercise. Muscle functions best at a temperature slightly above 40°C. (104°F). In start-and-stop sports, such as football, it is very possible for muscle temperature to drop substantially while the player is on the sidelines if he is not adequately protected from the cold. In addition to impaired function, there may be an increased risk of injury from enhanced muscle tone or shivering. The athletic trainer should ensure that athletes are adequately protected from the cold after periods of heavy exertion.

Hypothermia (low body temperature) can also be a problem if the rate of heat production from exercise does not keep pace with the rate of heat loss induced by the cold environmental temperature. This is a serious problem in endurance races (particularly marathons) held in cold climates. There have been deaths from hypothermia in road races held in mountainous areas. Athletes at risk include those who are not properly conditioned, slow runners (who cannot generate sufficient heat through exercise, particularly during the later stages of running races), those who become wet, and those who become hypoglycemic (low blood sugar). The athletic trainer should have the proper supplies on hand, such as "space blankets" (blankets made of highly reflective material that prevents heat loss), blankets, and warm drinks, to prevent hypothermia.

Frostbite

Frostbite is the freezing of tissue. This injury is relatively common in extremely low air temperatures (−20 to −30°C or −4 to −22°F) or when excessive air movement causes low temperatures (windchill). Frostbite typically occurs in exposed protuberances, such as the tips of the nose, ears, and fingers. Wet feet (from improper footware) are also susceptible.

Frostbite can be categorized according to severity as (1) frostnip, or superficial blanching of the tips of the nose, ears, chin, cheeks, toes, and fingers; (2) superficial frostbite, which is freezing of

the skin and the immediate subcutaneous tissue; and (3) deep frostbite, or freezing of the skin, subcutaneous tissue, muscle, and bone. Types 1 and 2 are by far the most common in athletics.

Frostbite should be treated in a hospital. However, if immediate transport (within one hour) is not available, then the frostbitten body part must be rewarmed. To treat frostbite, place the frostbitten area in water heated to 100 to 105°F (37.8 to 42.2°C) until the tissue is thawed. Monitor the water temperature to prevent it from becoming too much above the recommended range or there may be severe tissue damage. The water bath must be clean and large enough so that the affected body part does not touch the side of the container. After the body part has thawed, keep it cool, to lessen metabolism and help convalescence. Cover the frostbitten part. Facilitate peripheral circulation by keeping the athlete warm with blankets. Do *not* rub or massage frostbitten tissue in an effort to restore circulation because of the danger of additional tissue damage. Do *not* thaw frostbitten tissue if there is the possibility that the tissue will refreeze—if the tissue refreezes, it will undergo even more damage.

Hypothermia

Hypothermia results when the body temperature drops below approximately 35°C (95°F) and is characterized by a failure of heat production mechanisms. It is becoming increasingly common in road races involving relatively untrained athletes whose rate of heat production from exercise cannot keep up with the rate of heat loss (e.g., running in cold environments). Hypothermia may also occur in skiers (sitting on chairlifts) and mountain climbers.

Symptoms depend upon the fall in core temperature. Shivering is initiated when body temperature falls even slightly below normal. At a body tem-

Hypothermia: Low body temperature. [Core temperature less than 35°C (95°F).]

perature of 95°F, the athlete loses coordination and has difficulty speaking and manipulating objects. At a body temperature of approximately 90°F, the athlete becomes lethargic, muscles stiffen, and the ability to shiver is lost. Unconsciousness and death ensue when body temperature drops below 80°F.

The hypothermic athlete must be transported to a hospital as soon as possible. Treat the individual as though she or he has a cervical spine injury: Rough handling may induce ventricular fibrillation. The athlete must be kept warm and dry (remove wet clothing). While waiting for transport, insulate exposed body parts from cold surfaces with blankets, towels, or other available material to prevent further heat loss. Keep the athlete out of the wind, to prevent heat loss by convection. The athletic trainer must not attempt to aggressively rewarm the severely hypothermic athlete because of the extreme danger of complications, such as ventricular fibrillation. Initiate CPR if appropriate (see Chapter 10).

Altitude

Athletic events seldom take place at altitudes above 10,000 feet, so the stresses of altitude in athletics are relatively moderate (compared to those of mountain climbers). However, there are numerous competitions at altitudes of 5000 to 8000 feet, and athletes in such competitions can expect a decrease in performance and an impaired sense of well-being.

Reactions to acute altitude exposure include increased resting and submaximal exercise heart rate and ventilation and decreased exercise capacity. Maximal oxygen consumption begins to deteriorate at about 1524 meters (5000 feet), further decreasing by approximately 3 percent for each 1000-foot increase in elevation. Acute altitude exposure can also induce a variety of

disorders that can make some athletes extremely ill.

Acute Mountain Sickness

Rapid ascent from sea level to high altitude in a car or plane can cause acute mountain sickness. Symptoms include headache, insomnia, irritability, weakness, vomiting, tachycardia, and disturbance of breathing. Although the condition typically is not experienced until 11,000 feet, it can affect some people at altitudes as low as 6000 feet (and be a factor in athletic contests). This condition usually disappears within a few days, but sometimes it can evolve into a serious medical emergency. A person may develop pulmonary or cerebral edema, which can be life-threatening unless the individual is moved to a lower altitude.

Acute mountain sickness is probably caused by disturbances in fluid regulation and depressed ventilatory control (see Putting It into Practice 25-4, p. 464). The condition can be minimized by a two- to three-day period of altitude acclimatization prior to heavy exercise and by encouraging athletes to drink water. Scheduling a practice immediately upon arrival may induce the problem in otherwise less susceptible athletes. Some athletes may benefit from acetazolamide or benzolamide (diuretics that promote the loss of bicarbonate and sodium, thus speeding up the acclimatization process).

Altitude Acclimatization

The body begins to acclimatize to altitude within the first few days of exposure. The initial adaptation includes changes in the acid-base balance, which improve the regulation of ventilation and oxygen binding. Long-term adaptations include increased oxygen carrying capacity, cellular metabolic efficiency, and pulmonary and muscular vascularity (increased blood vessel network). As expected, physically fit individuals acclimatize more readily than unfit people.

Athletes who must compete at altitude will benefit from an acclimatization period of one to eight weeks. Athletes involved in short-duration activities, such as sprints, jumps, and throws, need acclimatize only long enough to get over the effects of mountain sickness (see Box 25-1). Although short-term altitude adjustments (such as alterations in acid-base balance) take less than a week, the changes in oxygen carrying capacity (such as increased hemoglobin concentration) can take many months. Athletes in championship form risk losing their peak condition by too much acclimatization because they will be unable to train as hard at altitude as at sea level.

The effects of altitude training upon subsequent performance at sea level are controversial. Most studies show no improvement in maximal aerobic or exercise capacities when returning from altitude. In the studies that showed an improvement, the subjects may not have been in good condition at the start. It appears that subjects improve their exercise capacity when training at high altitude, but the improvement is no greater (and probably less) than they would have achieved by training at sea level. Altitude training is vital if the athletic contest is to be held at altitude, but it is probably counterproductive for sea level competition.

Athletes cannot train as hard or as long at high altitudes. Training intensity and duration are the most important factors for improving exercise performance. Even though athletes training at high altitude can reach the same relative percentage of maximum, their maximum is less. In addition, the physiological adaptations to altitude are not necessarily beneficial at sea level. The increase in hemoglobin is probably helpful, but the physiological changes from altitude acclimatization, such as

PUTTING IT INTO PRACTICE 25-4

Managing Altitude Sickness

- *Cause*: Low ambient oxygen tension leading to disturbed fluid regulation. Typically occurs at about 11,000-foot altitude but can occur as low as 5000–6000 feet in susceptible individuals. May occur among susceptible athletes riding in pressurized aircraft (airlines pressurize planes to a barometric pressure equivalent to an altitude of 8000 feet).
- *Symptoms*: Headache, insomnia, irritability, vomiting, weakness, tachycardia, dyspnea.

- *Treatment*: Rest. Symptoms usually disappear in 2–3 days. Prevent altitude sickness by physical conditioning, resting when first at altitude, and taking drugs like acetazolamide or benzolamide.
- *Medical assistance*: Consult physician and remove athlete from altitude if symptoms become worse. Serious altitude sickness may result in cerebral or pulmonary edema, which are medical emergencies.

decreased plasma volume and increased breathing responsiveness to carbon dioxide and alkaline reserve, are decided disadvantages.

Air Quality

Poor air quality is a characteristic of urban environments many days of the year. Smog can seriously affect athletes' performance, particularly those athletes suffering from pulmonary disorders, such as **asthma**. The effects of smog are often an additive to other environmental stressors, such as heat (in cities like Los Angeles or New York) and altitude (in cities like Denver or Mexico City).

Air pollutants are classified as primary if they are directly emitted from automobiles, energy plants, etc. and secondary if they are derived from the interaction of primary pollutants with ultraviolet rays or other agents in the environment. Primary pollutants include carbon monoxide, nitrogen oxide, sulfur dioxide, and particulate matter;

Asthma: Pulmonary disease characterized by narrowing of the airways (accompanied by wheezing and uncomfortable breathing) in response to particulate matter, infection, emotional stress, and exercise.

BOX
25-1

Altitude and Athletic Performance

Altitude causes marked improvements in short-duration, high-intensity events (sprints and throwing events) and deterioration in long-duration, lower-intensity events (endurance events). The accompanying table compares the Mexico City Olympics performances of the top three athletes in selected sprint events with their previous personal bests. High-altitude performances were much better in almost every instance. In the long jump and triple jump (not shown in the table), for example, the world records were surpassed by margins of 21¾ and 14¼ inches, respectively. It has taken athletes competing at sea level almost twenty years to approach or better these performances. In these types of events, much of the energy cost stems from overcoming air resistance, which is less at altitude.

In throwing events, altitude can help or hinder performances. In events such as the discus or javelin, air mass provides lift to the implements, so performance tends to be hampered. In the shot put and hammer throw, the implements have minimal aerodynamics, so performances improve marginally because of the decreased air resistance.

At altitude, performance declines in running events longer than 800 meters. At the Mexico City Games, many athletes who dominated distance running at sea level were soundly defeated by athletes native to high altitude. High-altitude natives placed first or second in the 5000-meter run, 3000-meter steeplechase, 10,000-meter run, and the marathon.

Comparison of Personal Best and Mexico City Olympics Performances of Selected Sprint Athletes

Event	Mexico City Olympics (s)	Previous Personal Best (s)
100 meters—men		
1st J. Hines (USA)	9.9	9.9
2nd L. Miller (JAM)	10.0	10.0
3rd C. Green (USA)	10.0	9.9
100 meters—women		
1st W. Tyus (USA)	11.0	11.1
2nd B. Farrell (USA)	11.1	11.2
3rd I. Szewinska (POL)	11.1	11.1
200 meters—men		
1st T. Smith (USA)	19.8	19.9
2nd P. Norman (AUST)	20.0	20.5
3rd J. Carlos (USA)	20.0	19.7[a]
200 meters—women		
1st I. Szewinska (POL)	22.5	22.7
2nd R. Boyle (AUST)	22.7	23.4
3rd J. Lamy (AUST)	22.8	23.1
400 meters—men		
1st L. Evans (USA)	43.8	44.0
2nd L. James (USA)	43.9	44.1
3rd R. Freeman (USA)	44.4	44.6
400 meters—women		
1st G. Besson (FRA)	52.0	53.8
2nd L. Board (GB)	52.1	52.8
3rd N. Burda (USSR)	52.2	53.1
400-meter hurdles		
1st D. Hemery (GB)	48.1	49.6
2nd G. Hennige (W. GER)	49.0	50.0
3rd J. Sherwood (GB)	49.0	50.2
110-meter hurdles		
1st W. Davenport (USA)	13.3	13.3[a]
2nd E. Hall (USA)	13.4	13.4[a]
3rd E. Ottoz (ITA)	13.4	13.5

SOURCE: Brooks, G. A., and T. D. Fahey. *Exercise Physiology: Human Bioenergetics and Its Applications*. New York: Wiley, 1984, pp. 483, 484.

[a]Previous personal best set at altitude.

secondary pollutants include ozone, peroxyacetyl nitrate, aldehydes, and nitrogen dioxide.

Studies of the effects of air pollutants upon exercise performance have tended to examine the effects of singular substances, principally ozone, peroxyacetyl nitrate, nitrogen dioxide, sulfur dioxide, particulates, and carbon monoxide. Few studies have examined the effects of *combinations* of these substances. In addition, there are few data about elite athletes. However, there is enough information about the effects of various pollutants upon young people to allow a few generalizations.

Air pollution can produce a number of adverse effects in the athlete, including tightening in the chest, difficulty in taking a deep breath, irritation of the eyes, pharyngitis (sore throat), headache, lassitude, malaise, nausea, and dryness of the throat. These effects are exaggerated when the athlete is physically active and are dose-dependent, the symptoms becoming more severe as the level of air pollution increases. Studies of athletes in competition show marked decrements in their performances when the air is significantly polluted. It has been suggested that the increased airway resistance in the lungs leads to discomfort, which limits the athletes' motivation to perform.

Smoking compounds the problem of a polluted environment. The carbon monoxide in smoke and polluted air competes with oxygen for hemoglobin in the blood, which decreases oxygen transport capacity. Breathing carbon monoxide results in a higher heart rate at any given exercise intensity and a reduced maximal work capacity.

Particulate matter in the atmosphere, such as dust and pollen, can have serious effects upon allergy-prone athletes. Antihistamines may cause drowsiness, which can negatively affect performance. Athletes with serious allergy problems may benefit from desensitization (the procedures are administered by allergy specialists).

Although air pollution is a fact of life in many areas, practices and competitions can be minimized during periods of peak concentrations. Air pollution levels tend to be higher during commute hours and during the middle of the day when the temperature is higher (particularly in areas of the country with frequent inversion layers: Cold air traps warm air near the surface of the earth). Curtail or cancel practices during smog alerts.

Travel Problems

Rapid travel is a fact of life in our society, which has encouraged the scheduling of athletic competitions at great distances from the home area. Prolonged airplane, bus, and automobile trips can adversely affect performance because they disturb normal living habits, require that athletes sit for extended periods, and alter biological rhythms.

Jet lag, characterized by fatigue, malaise, sluggishness, decreased reaction time, and disorientation, is a serious problem for athletes. This condition is caused by a combination of factors: loss of sleep from flying while keyed up and excited, irregular and unfamiliar meals, dehydration, and disturbance of the biological clock. Prolonged sitting can cause muscle stiffness and constipation in some people.

Eastbound travel seems to cause the most problems because it has the greatest effect upon sleep. If possible, time the journey for arrival in the evening so the athletes can get a full night's sleep. Several days before the trip, the athletes should attempt to gradually shift their eating and sleeping hours to the time schedule of their destination. Athletes should be well rested before beginning the journey.

Athletes often use travel as an excuse to eat too much. Fast food restaurants, which seem to be the most popular sites for team meals, often specialize in high-fat foods that can aggravate already queasy stomachs. Encourage athletes to eat *moderately*. Initially, the meals should be consumed at times close to the normal time zone; adjustment to the new time zone should occur over several days.

Dehydration can be a problem during prolonged air travel. Airplanes are pressurized to approximately 8000 feet, and the relative humidity is usually less than 20 percent. Under these conditions, the body loses fluid at an increased rate through evaporation. Encourage athletes to consume more water than normal to prevent this problem. In addition, constipation, which in some people occurs following prolonged sitting, can often be prevented by adequate fluid intake.

The athletic trainer can help diminish the effects of travel-related disorders, including jet lag (see Putting It into Practice 25-5) by ensuring that the trip is well planned. Although excitement and anticipation are part of any athletic contest, excessive disruption can be prevented if the outing runs smoothly.

PUTTING IT INTO PRACTICE 25-5

Preventing Jet Lag

- Make eastbound flights in daylight hours, leaving as early as possible—earlier as the distance increases.
- Make westbound flights late in the day, timing arrival as close to the athletes' usual retiring hour as possible.
- Ensure that athletes drink plenty of water during the flight.
- Encourage athletes to eat light meals; discourage fatty foods.
- Make sure the athletes regularly get up from their seats and stretch or walk around the cabin.
- Physical performance tends to be better later in the day than in the morning. Make sure that athletes traveling particularly long distances from west to east have time for adjustment so that they will not be at a disadvantage.

References

American Academy of Orthopaedic Surgeons. *Emergency Care and Transportation of the Sick and Injured.* Chicago: American Academy of Orthopaedic Surgeons, 1981.

Balke, B. "Variations in Altitude and Its Effects on Exercise Performance," in *Exercise Physiology*, H. Falls, ed. New York: Academic Press, 1968, pp. 240–265.

Baxter, C., and T. Reilly. Influence on time of day on all-out swimming. *British Journal of Sportsmedicine* 17:122–127, 1983.

Biological Rhythms in Psychiatry and Medicine. Washington, D.C.: National Institute of Mental Health, 1970.

Brooks, G. A., and T. D. Fahey. *Exercise Physiology: Human Bioenergetics and Its Applications.* New York: Wiley, 1984.

Convertino, V., J. Greenleaf, and E. Bernauer. Role of thermal and exercise factors in the mechanism of hypervolemia. *Journal of Applied Physiology* 48:657–664, 1980.

Coyle, E., D. Costill, W. Fink, and D. Hoopes. Gastric emptying rates for selected athletic drinks. *Research Quarterly for Exercise and Sport* 49:119–124, 1978.

Dempsey, J. A., and H. V. Forster. Mediation of ventilatory adaptations. *Physiological Reviews* 62:262–346, 1982.

Drinkwater, B., L. J. Folinsbee, J. F. Bedi, S. A. Plowman, A. B. Loucks, and S. M. Horvath. Response of women mountaineers to maximal exercise during hypoxia. *Aviation Space and Environmental Medicine* 50:657–662, 1979.

Elliott, P. R., and H. A. Atterbom. Comparison of exercise responses of males and females during acute exposure to hypobaria. *Aviation Space and Environmental Medicine* 49:415–418, 1978.

England, A. C., D. W. Fraser, A. W. Hightower, R. Tirinnanzi, D. J. Greenberg, K. E. Powell, C. M. Slovis, and R. A. Varsha. Preventing severe heat injury in runners: suggestions from the 1979 Peachtree road race experience. *Annals of Internal Medicine* 97:196–201, 1982.

Folk, G. *Textbook of Environmental Physiology.* Philadelphia: Lea & Febiger, 1974.

Greenleaf, J., and F. Sargent II. Voluntary dehydration in man. *Journal of Applied Physiology* 20:719–724, 1965.

Hanson, P. Heat injuries in runners. *The Physician and Sportsmedicine* 7:91–96, 1979.

Horvath, S. M. Exercise in a cold environment. *Exercise and Sport Sciences Reviews* 9:221–263, 1981.

Horvath, S. M. Impact of air quality in exercise performance. *Exercise and Sport Sciences Reviews* 9:265–296, 1981.

Hultgren, H. Circulatory adaptation to high altitude. *Annual Review of Medicine* 19:119–130, 1968.

Kilbourne, E. M., K. Choi, T. S. Jones, and S. B. Thacker. Risk factors for heatstroke: case-control study. *Journal of the American Medical Association* 247:3332–3336, 1982.

Kollias, J., and E. R. Buskirk. "Exercise and Altitude," in *Structural and Physiological Aspects of Exercise and Sport*, W. R. Johnson and E. R. Buskirk, eds. Princeton, N.J.: Princeton Book Co., 1980, pp. 211–227.

Lahari, S. "Physiological Responses and Adaptations to High Altitude," in *Environmental Physiology* II, D. Robertshaw, ed. Baltimore: University Park Press, 1977, pp. 217–251.

Lenfant, C., and K. Sullivan. Adaptation to high altitude. *New England Journal of Medicine* 284:1298–1309, 1971.

Lenfant, C., J. D. Torrance, R. Woodson, and C. A. Finch. "Adaptation to Hypoxia," in *Red Cell Metabolism*, G. J. Brewer, ed. New York: Plenum Press, 1972, pp. 203–212.

Luce, J. Respiratory adaptation and maladaptation to altitude. *The Physician and Sportsmedicine* 7:55–69, 1979.

Malhotra, M. S., K. Sridharan, Y. Venkataswamy, R. M. Rai, C. Pichn, U. Radhakrishnan, and S. K. Grover. Effect of restricted potassium intake on its excretion and on physiologic responses during heat stress. *European Journal of Applied Physiology* 47:169–179, 1981.

Nadel, E. Circulatory and thermal regulations during exercise. *Federation Proceedings* 39:1491–1497, 1980.

Nadel, E., I. Holmer, U. Bergh, P. O. Astrand, and J. Stolwijk. Energy exchanges of swimming man. *Journal of Applied Physiology* 36:465–471, 1974.

Nunneley, S. Physiological responses of women to thermal stress: a review. *Medicine and Science in Sports and Exercise* 10:250–255, 1978.

O'Donnell, T. F. Management of heat stress injuries in the athlete. *Orthopedic Clinics of North America* 11:841–855, 1980.

Patajan, J. H. The effects of high altitude on the nervous system and athletic performance. *Seminars in Neurology* 1:253–261, 1981.

Pirnay, F., R. Deroanne, and J. Petit. Maximal oxygen consumption in a hot environment. *Journal of Applied Physiology* 28:642–645, 1970.

Rennie, D., B. Covino, B. Howell, S. Song. B. Hang, and S. Hang. Physical insulation of Korean diving women. *Journal of Applied Physiology* 17:961–966, 1962.

Roberts, M., and C. B. Wenger. Control of skin circulation during exercise and heat stress. *Medicine and Science in Sports and Exercise* 11:36–41, 1979.

Rowell, L. Human cardiovascular adjustments to exercise and thermal stress. *Physiological Reviews* 54:75–159, 1974.

Seiple, R. S., V. M. Vivian, E. L. Fox, and R. L. Bartels. Gastric emptying characteristics of two glucose polymer-electrolyte solutions. *Medicine and Science in Sports and Exercise* 15:366–369, 1983.

Sutton, J., A. C. Bryan, G. W. Gray, E. S. Horton, A. S. Rebuck, W. Woodley, I. D. Rennie, and C. S. Houston. Pulmonary gas exchange in acute mountain sickness. *Aviation Space and Environmental Medicine* 47:1032–1037, 1976.

Still, H. *Of Time, Tides, and Inner Clocks*. Harrisburg, Pa.: Stackpole Books, 1972.

Strauss, R. H. *Sports Medicine*. Philadelphia: W. B. Saunders, 1984.

West, J. B. *Respiratory Physiology—The Essentials*. Baltimore: Williams & Wilkins, 1974.

Nutrition and Body Composition

Research proves that a diet high in carbohydrates provides greater endurance than a mixed diet or one high in fat.

THE ability to run, jump, throw, and swim depends upon the body's ability to convert chemical energy into work energy, which is part of the biochemical process called metabolism. Metabolism, the total of all the chemical reactions occurring in the body, requires sufficient calories, vitamins, minerals, and fluids to accomplish the many chemical reactions that determine the athlete's state of well-being and performance capabilities.

Nutrition has achieved an almost mystical status among athletes. Every year, some new diet or dietary supplement promises to provide the extra edge leading to winning performance. Consequently, athletes are duped into spending their limited financial resources on dubious products that do nothing to improve their nutritional status or athletic performance.

To date, nutritional research has been unable to improve upon the normal, balanced diet for training, competition, or daily living. Although proper diet enables the athlete to perform at an optimal level, biochemical processes control the metabolism during exercise, so the previous diet has only indirect influence. Extreme dietary manipulation before competition is more likely to hinder than help performance.

The athletic trainer should be familiar with the principles of sound nutrition because of the importance of diet in performance and the susceptibility of athletes to dietary fads. This chapter explores many dietary-related topics, including the components of a balanced diet, food supplements, dietary manipulation, weight control, and body composition.

The Well-Balanced Diet and Ensuring Dietary Compliance

The **balanced diet** consists of at least three meals a day of foods from the four basic food groups (Table 26-1): dairy and milk products, cereal and grains, fruits and vegetables, and meat and other high-protein foods. A well-balanced diet from these food groups provides energy and the necessary vitamins and minerals.

The four food groups are composed of various combinations of proteins, carbohydrates, and fats. Proteins should comprise 15 to 20 percent of the total calories consumed daily, carbohydrates 45 to 55 percent, and fats 35 percent or

less. The consumption of fats and refined sugar should be kept to a minimum.

The well-balanced diet satisfies the nutritional requirements stipulated in the **Recommended Daily Allowances (RDA)** of the National Research Council of the National Academy of Sciences. The RDA are based upon present nutritional knowledge but obviously cannot account for nutrients whose requirements have not been established. Therefore, it is important to encourage athletes to consume a variety of foods from the basic food groups. Foods have considerable social and psychological significance, so when recommending a diet that will satisfy the RDA, keep in mind the athletes' dietary preferences.

The dietary requirement from the dairy and milk group depends upon the athlete's age. Athletes nine to twelve should consume three or more servings, teenagers four or more, and adults two or more. Milk is an important source of calcium, riboflavin, high-quality protein, carbohydrate, fat, and other assorted vitamins and minerals.

Do not encourage athletes to drink too much whole milk because of its high caloric and fat content. The roots of obesity and heart disease are in childhood and adolescence; excessive

Recommended Daily Allowances (RDA): Minimum nutrient requirements as recommended by the National Research Council of the National Academy of Sciences.

Balanced diet: A diet of the basic food groups (dairy and milk products, cereals and grains, fruits and vegetables, and meat and other high-protein foods), of approximately 15 to 20 percent protein, 45 to 55 percent carbohydrate, and 35 percent or less fat.

Table 26-1 *Basic Food Groups*

Group	Sources
Dairy and milk products	Whole milk, skim milk, cheese, yogurt, buttermilk, eggs
Cereals and grains	Whole-grain or enriched bread, cooked or cold cereal, cornmeal, rice, noodles, spaghetti, grits
Fruits and vegetables	Apples, oranges, grapefruit, bananas, potatoes, asparagus, broccoli, spinach, pumpkin, carrots, squash, cantaloupe
Meat and other high-protein food	Lean meat, fish, chicken, beans, peas, peanut butter, soy products

milk drinking may contribute to these problems. Urge athletes who like to drink great quantities of milk to use low-fat or skimmed milk.

The meat and other high-protein food group is the most important source of protein from foods but also supplies iron, thiamin, riboflavin, niacin, phosphorus, and zinc. Encourage athletes to consume lean meats, fish, chicken, and nonmeat high-protein alternatives. Discourage meats with a high fat content because they are associated with increased risk of heart disease.

The cereals and grains group supplies carbohydrate, protein, thiamin, iron, niacin, and cellulose. This group is extremely important in supplying athletes' energy needs. Do *not* confuse this group with candies, honey, jellies, and sugars, which are considered sweets.

The fruits and vegetables group is the most important for supplying vitamins, minerals, and fiber. Athletes should be particularly encouraged to eat dark green and deep yellow vegetables because of their high nutrient content.

Fluids are a particularly important part of the athlete's diet because they directly affect exercise capacity. Body water is an important component in most of the body's biochemical reactions and helps maintain blood volume and thermal balance.

As discussed in Chapter 25, special care must be taken to maintain adequate fluid intake in athletes. Often, the thirst mechanism is inadequate to ensure adequate levels of hydration. Daily weigh athletes in sports that are prone to cause dehydration, such as football, wrestling, and running, to ensure adequate **rehydration.**

To ensure dietary compliance, examine the athletes' training diaries. Athletes do not have to keep detailed nutritional records, but from time to time it may help to obtain a detailed report. The athletic trainer should be especially wary of athletes who have difficulty maintaining weight and whose performances seem to be deteriorating (see Put-

PUTTING IT INTO PRACTICE 26-1

Gaining Weight

- *Stress quality over quantity:* Carrying extra fat does little to improve athletic performance.
- *Weight training:* Stress exercises that work large muscle groups. Exercise programs should consist principally of presses (bench press, seated press, incline press, etc.), pulls (cleans, snatches, dead lifts, high pulls, etc.), and squats (squats, leg presses, hack squats, front squats, etc.). Lifts should employ heavy resistance and numerous sets (e.g., five sets of five repetitions for major lifts).
- *Stress long-term gains:* Athletes should not expect to increase their lean mass by more than 8–10 pounds per year.
- *Discourage drug use:* Avoid drugs such as anabolic steroids and growth hormone.
- *Diet:* Diet should be well balanced and slightly higher in calories. Protein requirement is approximately 1–1½ grams per kilogram of body weight.
- *Monitor body composition:* Make sure athletes are gaining *lean* weight. Underwater weighing is the most accurate measurement method, but skinfold or anthropometric techniques also suffice.
- *Medical assistance:* Consult physician if athlete does not progress. Physician may check family history, maturational level, or endocrine status.

ting It into Practice 26-1). Inadequate consumption of food energy is the biggest nutritional problem in athletics. Daily weighing of athletes helps identify those who are not eating enough as well as those who are dehydrated.

There are various computerized nutritional analyses that can help the athletic trainer properly evaluate athletes' diets. These analyses are relatively inexpensive and are available for most of the small computers used in the majority of high schools and colleges.

After inadequate caloric intake, iron deficiency is athletes' second nutritional problem. Clinical observations suggest that iron-depleted athletes experience poor performance until the problem is remedied. Populations such as women between twelve and forty-five, early

Rehydration: Restoration of normal fluid balance. Body weight is a good way to determine if an athlete has restored lost body water.

grade school children, and teenage males living in socioeconomically deprived circumstances are particularly prone to iron depletion. Biochemical assays for **hemoglobin, transferrin** saturation, erythrocyte **protoporphyrin** concentration, and plasma ferritin levels are available for determining the body's iron status and should be used for all athletes in the high-risk category. Such tests help the athletic trainer (working with the physician) identify athletes who need special diets or dietary supplements.

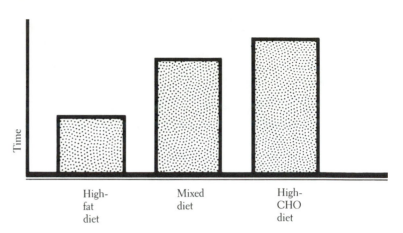

Figure 26-1 Length of time exercise was sustained on a bicycle ergometer following a high-fat, mixed, and high-carbohydrate (CHO) diet.

Diet and Performance

There is little that athletes can do to improve upon the balanced diet, but several principles of athletic nutrition, if followed, may make the difference between winning and losing. These principles concern maximizing and sparing muscle glycogen (particularly in endurance sports such as distance running) and preventing dramatic drops in blood sugar through a proper pregame meal.

Muscle Glycogen and Performance

Carbohydrates are the most important fuel for muscular work. Although fats and proteins are used for energy during exercise, carbohydrates' contribution toward supplying energy increases as the intensity of physical activity increases.

Glycogen, the principal carbohydrate used during exercise, is stored mainly in the muscles and liver. The amount of glycogen present when exercise begins can determine endurance time. Glycogen depletion is associated with fatigue, and if normal glycogen levels are not restored, physical performance levels will be impaired.

The deterioration in performance that many athletes experience during a competitive season often can be attributed to chronic glycogen depletion. Proper diet and training schedules are

the best remedies for this situation. Figure 26-1 demonstrates the importance of diet in determining endurance capacity. Notice the extreme negative effects of the high-fat-protein diet compared to the mixed and high-carbohydrate diets. Be careful to ensure that athletes are consuming enough calories, particularly in the form of complex carbohydrates. Overtraining, caused by excessively intense training programs, can also contribute to chronic glycogen depletion.

Carbohydrate Loading and Glycogen Supercompensation

The concentration of glycogen in the liver and muscle can be raised to levels two or three times greater than normal by a process called glycogen supercompensation (sometimes called **carbohydrate loading**). About a week before a competition, an athlete exercises to exhaustion by participating in prolonged endurance activities and interval training. Then the athlete rests or trains mildly two days prior to competition and eats a normal, balanced diet that contains substantial amounts of carbohydrates. This procedure has become very popular with athletes involved in activities requiring hard, continuous effort, such as marathon running and cycling.

Hemoglobin: A protein in red blood cells that carries oxygen.

Transferrin: A substance that facilitates the transportation of iron to the bone marrow and other tissue-iron storage areas.

Protoporphyrin: Part of the structure of hemoglobin.

Carbohydrate: Organic compounds, such as sugars and starches, composed of carbon, hydrogen, and oxygen.

Glycogen: A complex carbohydrate stored principally in the liver and skeletal muscle; an extremely important fuel during most forms of exercise.

Carbohydrate loading: A dietary technique that results in an unusual concentration of glycogen in the liver and skeletal muscle.

The practice of carbohydrate loading has not been universally successful; some individuals do not respond to the procedure. Additionally, after repeated attempts to glycogen supercompensate, the biochemistry "smartens up," and the supercompensation effect diminishes.

Carbohydrate loading can also result in **malnutrition.** When manipulating an athlete's diet immediately prior to competition, be sure to include necessary nutrients as well as calories. A carbohydrate-loading diet should be rich in whole-grain cereals and potatoes. Include fresh vegetables (for vitamins and minerals) as well as meats and meat substitutes (for protein). Too little protein or calories will atrophy lean tissue, and too much carbohydrate will result in fat gain. Have a preliminary trial to ensure that the diet is agreeable and palatable to the athlete.

Carbohydrate loading can also lead to excessive water retention, which is a disadvantage in sports where added weight is a liability, such as wrestling and gymnastics. Since each gram of glycogen requires almost three grams of water for storage, each gram in effect adds four grams of body weight. In endurance sports, such as running or cycling, the added water may help prevent dehydration.

A two-day period of carbohydrate starvation between the exercising to exhaustion and carbohydrate loading is often advocated as part of the carbohydrate-loading procedure. Supposedly this period, during which proteins and fats but no sugars or starches are allowed in the diet, leads to glycogen supercompensation. However, it has never been convincingly demonstrated that a carbohydrate starvation period is beneficial. To the contrary, carbohydrate starvation after exhaustive exercise often has been reported as producing serious side effects, such as depression, lethargy, and general malaise (conditions not conducive to championship performance). The body has a nat-

ural tendency to restore its glycogen reserves after exhausting exercise. If adequate carbohydrate is not supplied to accomplish this restoration, lean tissues will be broken down in an attempt to furnish the biochemical precursors necessary for the formation of glycogen. The dietary input of proteins may not be adequate to prevent this breakdown.

A general recommendation for maximizing muscle glycogen for competition is to maintain a relatively high amount of complex carbohydrate in the diet and to train vigorously early in the week, followed by several days of rest or diminished activity prior to the athletic contest. This dietary regime should culminate in a proper pregame meal.

Malnutrition: Inadequate nutrient status from poor diet or metabolic disorder.

The Pregame Meal

The pregame meal is a controversial subject, and the practice is particularly prone to faddism. Additionally, athletes are sometimes very emotionally biased about this meal; these biases have to be considered when the composition of the meal is being designed. For example, in the late 1960s, liquid meals were touted as the ultimate food source prior to competition. Liquid meal advocates cited the meals' digestibility, simplicity, and ideal composition as evidence of their superiority. Some athletes rebelled against the diet, feeling that they were not ingesting the substantial meal many of them associated with top-level performance. Any beneficial effect of the liquid meal was overshadowed by its negative psychological impact upon the athletes.

Nathan Smith, in his book *Food for Sport* (Palo Alto, Calif.: Bull Publishing, 1976, p. 118), summarized the goals that should be considered when planning the pregame meal:

1. Energy intake should be adequate to ward off any feelings of hunger or weakness during the entire period of the competition. Although

precontest food intakes make only a minor contribution to the immediate energy expenditure, they are essential for the support of an adequate level of blood sugar and for avoiding the sensations of hunger and weakness.

2. The diet plan should ensure that the stomach and upper bowel are empty at the time of competition.
3. Food and fluid intakes prior to and during prolonged competition should guarantee an optimal state of hydration.
4. The precompetition diet should offer foods that will minimize upset in the gastrointestinal tract.
5. The diet should include food that the athlete is familiar with and is convinced will "make him win."

Physiologically, the pregame meal should attempt to put the blood glucose (sugar) level in the high-normal range (100 milligrams per 100 milliliters of blood). Blood glucose plays an extremely important role in the function of the central nervous system, serving as the brain and nerves' preferred fuel. This is of obvious importance in athletic competition. Although blood glucose plays a smaller role than muscle glycogen in providing fuel for muscular work, it is nevertheless important for optimal muscle function.

The pregame meal should ensure that blood insulin levels are constant or falling slightly but not rising. Insulin is the principal regulator of blood glucose. A pregame meal high in simple sugars and refined carbohydrates, such as honey, candy, and pancakes, is rapidly digested, which causes an almost immediate rise in blood sugar, with a parallel rise in insulin, which then lowers blood sugar. The insulin clears the glucose from the circulation, but the hormone lingers, causing a continuous fall in blood glucose. This high-sugar pregame meal thus causes a lower blood glucose level than if no glucose were consumed. This is no condition to be in when entering competition!

The traditional pregame meal was a moderate portion of steak or eggs and pancakes, toast, or potatoes. This remains an excellent meal and is perhaps the best way to top off a carbohydrate-loading regime. A lean steak and eggs present minimal problems for digestion, and their digestion releases some fat and **amino acids** into the circulation. The fats are an immediate source of energy (thus sparing glycogen), and the amino acids maintain blood sugar during exercise.

Amino acids are used as fuel during exercise, but more importantly, in effect they are "glucose time-release capsules." A significant portion of the amino acids is broken down (deaminated) in the liver and converted into glucose (blood sugar). A protein meal is thus a way to supply glucose and avoid an exaggerated insulin response. It has long been recommended that people who suffer from hypoglycemia (low blood sugar) consume protein-rich meals and avoid sugars and simple, highly refined carbohydrates. People with hypoglycemia experience an exaggerated insulin response to elevations in blood sugar. The athlete who packs away sugar at the last minute will also experience this insulin response: The high amount of sugar triggers insulin, which decreases the blood sugar.

A problem with the steak-and-eggs breakfast is that the meat may be too high in fat and thus more difficult to digest. An alternative to this pregame meal is a high-protein milkshake along with a meal composed principally of complex carbohydrates (such as whole-grain bread, cereals, and potatoes). Table 26-2 lists the ingredients of the high-protein shake. Because complex carbohydrates are digested more slowly than sugars or simple carbohydrates, glucose is released more slowly from the gastrointestinal tract. A high-protein, low-fat, complex-carbohydrate pregame meal causes the blood glucose to slowly rise to a level that does not

Amino acids: The principal components of proteins. The acids contain one or more amino groups and a carboxyl group.

Table 26-2 *High-Protein Milkshake as
Part of a Pregame Meal*

8 ounces nonfat milk
2 tablespoons high-quality milk
    and egg-protein powder
1 banana (or other fruit)
2 noncholesterol egg substitutes

peak as high. The glucose will remain
elevated longer because of slower release and lesser insulin response. Also,
the milkshake is easily digested.

Nutritional Supplements and Aids

Athletes take a variety of food supplements, such as protein, vitamins, and
weight-gain formulas, to make them
better at their sport. Most of these
products are of little or no value in
improving performance or dietary status
if the athlete is eating a balanced diet.
However, if the athlete's diet is deficient in any essential nutrient, then
supplementation may very well be
beneficial.

Vitamins and Minerals

Vitamins are organic substances that
are vital in sustaining metabolism and
thus maintaining life. Minerals are inorganic substances also vital to metabolism. These substances are essential,
but the body requires only extremely
small quantities. Vitamin and mineral
supplements are extremely popular with
athletes.

Some evidence suggests that more
vitamins may be needed to support the
increased metabolic activity that occurs
in the trained athlete. However, vitamin deficiency in athletes in the
United States is extremely rare. Most
athletes take many times the minimum
daily requirement (even taking into
consideration any increased requirements) for these substances.

Vitamin C (ascorbic acid) is involved
in many important physiological functions: the regulation of amino acid, fat,
collagen, and steroid metabolism; the
formation of bones and teeth; immune
responses; and strengthening cell membranes and blood vessels. Although vitamin C has been used to improve both
cardiovascular and muscle endurance
and has been shown to speed up the
process of acclimatization to heat, most
studies have not demonstrated any effect upon factors important to physical
performance.

There are nine different B vitamins,
which help regulate and facilitate metabolism. B vitamins, such as thiamine,
riboflavin, and niacin, have become
extremely popular with athletes, who
take them in the hope of improving
endurance, strength, and recovery from
fatigue. In general, well-controlled
studies have failed to find any beneficial effects from the B vitamins upon
performance.

Vitamin C and B complex vitamins
are the most popular with athletes for
improving performance, but many athletes also take a variety of other vitamins and minerals for a supposedly
beneficial effect. Vitamin supplementation is usually harmless because many
vitamins are water-soluble, but overcon-
sumption of the fat-soluble vitamins A
and D can be toxic.

Pangamic acid, sometimes called
vitamin B_{15}, is the newest supplementation fad, being hailed by some people
as a miracle substance that improves
endurance and fights off fatigue. This
product has come under increasing
criticism from the Food and Drug
Administration because it has no established medical or nutritional usefulness.
It is said to increase oxygen utilization,
which could improve endurance, but
well-controlled scientific investigations
do not support the usefulness of this
substance as an **ergogenic** aid. In addition, B_{15} may be dangerous because it
has the potential to cause genetic
damage.

Vitamins: A group of organic substances essential
to metabolism.

Ergogenic aid: A substance
or technique used to im-
prove performance.

Nutritional Ergogenic Aids

Ergogenic aids are substances or practices (other than training) that improve athletic performance. The use of pharmacological substances such as anabolic steroids, amphetamines, and caffeine is discussed in Chapter 27.

Other than vitamins, protein is the most common nutritional supplement. Athletes take protein supplements to "bulk up" and improve strength. A dietary protein content from 0.8 to 1.0 gram of protein per kilogram body weight per day is recommended for most individuals (including those who are moderately active) to ensure nitrogen balance. The body is in nitrogen balance when protein intake matches protein utilization. Most athletes can easily achieve this level of protein intake.

Few studies have evaluated nitrogen balance in athletes during training. Studies by researchers like Gontzea et al. and Celejowa and Homa indicate that both endurance and strength athletes experience negative nitrogen balance during training (i.e., they are losing body protein). Athletes attempting to bulk up, or those in the early stages of training, may require two grams of protein per kilogram body weight. There is the possibility that consumption of high-protein, high-calorie diets coupled with extremely high resistance training can positively affect lean body mass. However, more research is needed to substantiate this hypothesis.

Precompetition carbohydrate (CHO) feeding, in the form of glucose, dextrose, or honey, has long been practiced by many athletes, who believe that CHO feeding increases strength, speed, and endurance. CHO feeding has no effect upon strength, power, or high-intensity short-term exercise and has been shown to decrease performance in endurance activities.

Foster et al. found a 19 percent decrease in endurance performance following glucose feeding. As discussed, CHO feeding causes an initial rise in blood sugar and then a feedback increase in the secretion of insulin from the pancreas, which also inhibits mobilization of free fatty acid. Thus, CHO feeding prior to endurance exercise accelerates depletion of muscle glycogen and reduces exercise capacity. An added problem is that the ingestion of high-carbohydrate fluids slows gastric emptying of fluids, which could increase the risk of hyperthermia in endurance exercise, particularly if the exercise is conducted in the heat.

Athletes have used wheat germ oil for many years in the hope of improving endurance. Vitamin E (alpha tocopherol) and octacosanol are purported to be the ingredients of this product, and cause it to render its beneficial effect. Supposedly wheat germ oil reduces the tissues' oxygen requirement and circulation in the heart. Some researchers have found beneficial effects from this substance, but these results have not been consistently replicated. However, a recent study found that vitamin E increased maximal oxygen consumption by 9 percent at 1524-meter (5000 feet) and 14 percent at 4572-meter (15,000 feet) altitude.

Buffering substances such as sodium bicarbonate have been suggested as an ergogenic aid in preventing fatigue during endurance exercise. Studies have been equivocal in determining a beneficial effect. Several recent studies suggest that alkalizing agents buffer the effects of metabolic acids and speed the movement of lactic acid from the muscles to the blood. This may be extremely significant because low muscle pH is suspected as causing fatigue in high-intensity exercise.

Numerous nutritional substances have been proposed as ergogenic aids: aspartate, bee pollen, gelatin, lecithin, phosphates, and organ extracts. Few studies support these substances' effectiveness, but because of wishful thinking by athletes, their use will remain widespread.

Weight Control and Body Composition: Energy Balance

Athletes often worry about weight control and body composition, and these subjects are of primary concern to the athletic trainer. Some athletes who compete in weight activities, such as wrestlers and weight lifters, are vitally concerned with weighing as little as possible without jeopardizing performance (see Putting It into Practice 26-2; Box 26-1, p. 478). Other athletes, such as football players and throwers, are concerned with developing large body masses. Still other athletes have problems either losing or gaining weight, and these problems may affect their performance.

The body's energy balance determines whether the amount of fat increases, decreases, or remains the same. The metabolism is in energy balance when energy intake equals energy expenditure (Figure 26-2). Fat gains occur when this balance becomes positive (more energy is consumed than expended). Once gained, body fat remains, unless there is also a period of negative energy balance. Individual differences in energy intake and expenditure are controlled by psychological and physiological factors. These factors are complex and outside the scope of this chapter. However, the athletic trainer should be familiar with the factors; see basic texts in physiology and obesity control.

Exercise

The amount of physical activity is probably the most significant and variable factor in energy expenditure. Basal metabolic rate is less than 1700 kilocalories per day (depending upon body size), but the additional caloric cost of physical activity can vary tremendously.

PUTTING IT INTO PRACTICE 26-2

Losing Weight

- *Stress fat loss*: Rapid weight loss from a fad diet is often caused by the loss of muscle mass and water. Therefore fat loss, not weight loss, should be the goal.
- *Restrict weight loss*: No more than 1½–2 pounds per week should be lost.
- *Diet*: Stress a balanced diet that is relatively high in complex carbohydrates and low in fat. Create a caloric deficit by a combination of caloric restriction and increased caloric expenditure.
- *Exercise*: Endurance exercise is best for losing weight. Have athletes exercise for a minimum of twenty minutes, four to six times per week, at an intensity above 70 percent of maximum. The best exercises for losing weight are running, cross-country skiing, cycling, swimming, and walking.
- *Monitor body composition*: Make sure that most of the weight loss is from a reduction in body fat rather than a reduction in lean body mass.

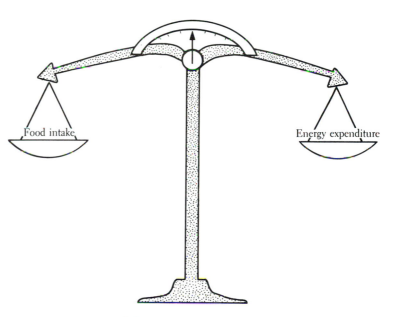

Figure 26-2 Energy balance.

BOX
26-1

The Right Way and the Wrong Way to Lose Weight

A professional football player's body composition was monitored monthly at a college exercise physiology laboratory. The athlete initially weighed 316 pounds and was 27 percent fat. The coach wanted him to reduce to 285 pounds by the time training camp began.

The athlete was advised to lose weight very slowly, at a rate of approximately 1½ pounds per week, and to lose most of the weight through exercise to help him maintain muscle mass while losing fat. During the first two months, he consistently lost weight without losing lean body mass. The weight-loss program was slow but effective.

Unfortunately, the head coach got impatient. He told the athlete that he was to be fined $25 per pound per day until he reached his target weight. The athlete proceeded to go on a popular liquid fad diet, which consisted of fewer than 800 calories per day. The next month, when he was underwater weighed, the athlete found that he had lost approximately the same amount of weight as before, but 50 percent of the weight loss was from lean mass.

The coach was informed. He instructed the athlete to return to his former weight-loss regime. The next month, the athlete again lost almost 8 pounds, but he increased his lean body mass. There is a right way and a wrong way for athletes to lose weight!

BOX
26-2

ACSM Position Statement on Weight Loss in Wrestlers

Despite repeated admonitions by medical, educational, and athletic groups, most wrestlers have been inculcated by instruction or accepted tradition to lose weight in order to be certified for a class that is lower than their preseason weight. Studies of weight losses in high-school and college wrestlers indicate that from 3 to 20 percent of the preseason body weight is lost before certification or competition occurs. Of this weight loss, most of the decrease occurs in the final days or day before the official weigh-in with the youngest and/or lightest members of the team losing the highest percentage of their body weight. Under existing rules and practices, it is not uncommon for an individual to repeat this weight losing process many times during the season because successful wrestlers compete in 15 to 30 matches per year.

Contrary to existing beliefs, most wrestlers are not "fat" before the season starts. In fact, the fat content of high-school and college wrestlers weighing less than 190 pounds has been shown to range from 1.6 to 15.1 percent of their body weight with the majority possessing less than 8 percent. It is well known and documented that wrestlers lose body weight by a combination of food restriction, fluid deprivation, and sweating induced by thermal or exercise procedures. Of these methods, dehydration through sweating appears to be the method most frequently chosen.

Careful studies on the nature of the weight being lost show that water, fats, and proteins are lost when food restriction and fluid deprivation procedures are followed. Moreover, the proportionality between these constituents will change with continued restriction and deprivation. For example, if food restriction is held constant when the volume of fluid being consumed is decreased, more water will be lost from the tissues of the body than before the fluid restriction occurred. The problem becomes more acute when thermal or exercise dehydration occurs because electrolyte losses will accompany the water losses. Even when one to five hours are allowed for purposes of rehydration after the weigh-in, this time interval is insufficient for fluid and electrolyte homeostasis to be completely reestablished.

(continued on next page)

ACSM Position Statement on Weight Loss in Wrestlers *(continued)*

Since the "making of weight" occurs by combinations of food restriction, fluid deprivation, and dehydration, responsible officials should realize that the single or combined effects of these practices are generally associated with (1) a reduction in muscular strength; (2) a decrease in work performance times; (3) lower plasma and blood volumes; (4) a reduction in cardiac functioning during sub-maximal work conditions which are associated with higher heart rates, smaller stroke volumes and reduced cardiac outputs; (5) a lower oxygen consumption, especially with food restriction; (6) an impairment of thermoregulatory processes; (7) a decrease in renal blood flow and in the volume of fluid being filtered by the kidney; (8) a depletion of liver glycogen stores; and (9) an increase in the amount of electrolytes being lost from the body.

Since it is possible for these changes to impede normal growth and development, there is little physiological or medical justification for the use of the weight reduction methods currently followed by many wrestlers. These sentiments have been expressed in part within Rule 1, Section 3, Article 1 of the *Official Wrestling Rule Book* published by the National Federation of State High School Associations, which states, "The Rules Committee recommends that individual state high school associations develop and utilize an effective weight control program which will discourage severe weight reduction and/or wide variations in weight, because this may be harmful to the competitor. . . . " However, until the National Federation of State High School Associations defines the meaning of the terms "severe" and "wide variations," this rule will be ineffective in reducing the abuses associated with the "making of weight."

Therefore, it is the position of the American College of Sports Medicine that the potential health hazards created by the procedures used to "make weight" by wrestlers can be eliminated if state and national organizations will:

1. Assess the body composition of each wrestler several weeks in advance of the competitive season. Individuals with a fat content less than 5 percent of their certified body weight should receive medical clearance before being allowed to compete.
2. Emphasize the fact that the daily caloric requirements of wrestlers should be obtained from a balanced diet and determined on the basis of age, body surface area, growth and physical activity levels. The minimal caloric needs of wrestlers in high schools and colleges will range from 1200 to 2400 kcal/day; therefore, it is the responsibility of coaches, school officials, physicians, and parents to discourage wrestlers from securing less than their minimal needs without prior medical approval.
3. Discourage the practice of fluid deprivation and dehydration. This can be accomplished by:
   a. Educating the coaches and wrestlers on the physiological consequences and medical complications that can occur as a result of these practices.
   b. Prohibiting the single or combined use of rubber suits, steam rooms, hot boxes, saunas, laxatives, and diuretics to "make weight."
   c. Scheduling weigh-ins just prior to competition.
   d. Scheduling more official weigh-ins between team matches.
4. Permit more participants per team to compete in those weight classes (119 to 145 pounds) which have the highest percentages of wrestlers certified for competition.
5. Standardize regulations concerning the eligibility rules at championship tournaments so that individuals can only participate in those weight classes in which they had the highest frequencies of matches throughout the season.
6. Encourage local and county organizations to systematically collect data on the hydration state of wrestlers and its relationship to growth and development.

SOURCE: *Medicine and Science in Sports and Exercise* 8(2):xi, 1976.

A sedentary person typically expends approximately 2200 kilocalories per day, but the endurance athlete (ultramarathon) may use as much as 6000 kilocalories.

In the past, exercise was not considered very important in controlling body composition. However, it is now apparent that chronic physical training may make the difference between obesity and relative leanness. Even small differences in caloric expenditure can become quite substantial when accumulated over many months and years.

Approximately ten calories per minute are consumed during an endurance exercise routine conducted at 75 percent of maximum effort. However, metabolic rate remains elevated after exercise because heat increases metabolic rate (exercise produces heat), and **anabolic** process elicited by the exercise stimulus can almost equal the caloric cost of the exercise itself. These post-exercise effects add to physical activity's potent effect in caloric expenditure.

Exercise is a particularly attractive form of caloric expenditure for the athlete. For example, distance running for the football player during the off-season not only helps take off fat but improves fitness for the sport (Box 26-2, pp. 478–479). Exercise acts as a protein sparer during periods of weight loss, which helps prevent muscle loss.

maintain for the rest of their lives. It is little wonder that rebound weight gain is so common.

Many fad diets promote low-carbohydrate intake. On the surface, these diets appear to be extremely successful. Weight loss of ten to twenty pounds in a few weeks is not uncommon. However, low-carbohydrate diets dehydrate muscle and deplete liver glycogen stores. Although the weight loss appears impressive, most of it is in the form of water, rather than fat. Additionally, glycogen depletion greatly diminishes exercise capacity, which almost eliminates physical activity as a source of caloric expenditure and leads to further decreases in lean body mass and impaired performance.

A successful diet must produce a negative energy balance (more energy expended than consumed). A pound of fat requires a caloric deficit of 3500 calories. Most athletes barely expend that many calories in a day, so it is impossible to lose more than a few pounds of fat in a week. Empirical evidence suggests that if weight is lost at a faster rate, the loss will be increasingly from muscle mass. Diets that promise large decreases in fat in a short time are misleading. The athletic trainer should help athletes with year-long weight-control programs so that they do not have to resort to crash diets that are potentially dangerous and impair performance.

Anabolic: Biochemical building processes.

Diet and Weight Control

Caloric restriction is an essential part of any weight-control program. Most quick-loss fad diets stress weight loss rather than fat loss and may seriously affect the athlete's performance because much of the lost weight comes from the **lean body mass.** The goal of a dietary program should be a loss of body fat and then maintenance of the loss. Unfortunately, the composition of fad diets is unpalatable and unhealthy and does not resemble a diet people could

Dehydration

Athletes (especially wrestlers and weight lifters—see Box 26-2) use diuretics and impermeable clothing to rapidly lose weight. These practices result in weight loss from fluid depletion and not fat loss, which can be extremely dangerous. Sauna belts and rubber suits are often used by the uninitiated in their quest to lose weight and inches. The resulting dehydration of the cells under the clothes does cause a temporary loss of circumference. However,

Lean body mass: Fat-free body weight.

the change is short lived because normal fluid balance is quickly restored. Again, encourage athletes to maintain a relatively stable body weight and to lose unwanted body fat very gradually.

Gaining Weight

A large body mass is an advantage in sports such as football, heavy-weight weight lifting, discus, and shot put (see Putting It into Practice 26-1, p. 471). However, if too much of this weight is fat, performance suffers. The principles are the same whether the athlete wants to gain or lose weight: Positive energy balance stores energy; negative energy balance depletes energy storage. Many underweight athletes can easily carry more fat without hindering their performance. In fact, lean body mass tends to increase with increasing body weight, even if the person is not involved in an exercise program.

Athletes should strive to gain "quality weight." This can be accomplished (to any significant degree) only through a vigorous weight-training program that stresses the large muscle groups in the legs, hips, shoulders, arms, and chest. Muscle weight takes many years to gain but is certainly preferable to the fat that is quickly added from high-calorie weight-gain supplements.

Body Composition

Body composition is categorized as lean body mass (fat-free weight) and body fat. Lean body mass is composed of all the body's nonfat tissues, including the skeleton, water, muscle, connective tissue, organ tissues, and teeth. Body fat includes both the essential and nonessential body lipids (fats). Essential fat includes lipid incorporated into organs and tissues such as nerves, brain, heart, lungs, liver, and mammary glands. The storage fat exists primarily within the fat cells (adipose tissue).

Body Composition of Athletes

Body composition is an important consideration in many sports. There have been many abuses in "weight class" sports like wrestling, boxing, and weight lifting when athletes try to lose significant amounts of weight in a very short time. Success and failure are sometimes dictated by an athlete's ability to "make weight." These practices can potentially compromise the athlete's health and have prompted the American College of Sports Medicine to issue a position statement on weight loss in wrestlers (see Box 26-2).

Athletes in various sports usually tend to have a characteristic body composition (Table 26-3, p. 482). A recent study found that among distance runners, body composition is as much related to success as a strong cardiovascular capacity. Variability in body fat seems to depend upon the metabolic requirement of the activity and the relative disadvantage of carrying an extra load. For example, successful male distance runners are almost always less than 9 percent fat; successful female distance runners are usually less than 12 percent fat. For these athletes, excess fat is a decided disadvantage. In addition, since running long distances expends tremendous calories, the prospect of obesity is very unlikely.

Football linemen, on the other hand, are almost always greater than 15 percent fat. This may be advantageous because of the added mass and padding the subcutaneous fat provides and the increase in lean mass that accompanies excess weight (as discussed, muscle mass accompanies gains in fat to support the extra weight). Unfortunately, many younger athletes gain too much fat in an attempt to attain the high body weights of the professional football player.

The daily weighing ritual on the athletic training room scale is really an attempt at estimating body composition. But body weight provides little information to help the athlete or athletic

Factors Affecting Performance

Table 26-3 *Typical Fat Percentages of Male and Female Athletes in Selected Sports*

Sport	Percentage of Fat	
	Males	Females
Football		
Linemen	16	—
Backs and receivers	8	—
Linebackers	14	—
Gymnastics	8	12
Baseball and softball	14	18
Distance running	8	10
Track—throwing	16	25
Tennis	13	18
Wrestling	7	—
Swimming	12	16

trainer determine if a fluctuation in weight is from a change in muscle, body water, or fat. The method can not differentiate between overweight and overfat. A 260-pound muscular hammer thrower may be overweight according to population height-weight standards yet actually have much less body fat than average. Likewise, a pudgy sixteen-year-old shot-putter may weigh the same as the Olympians yet be tremendously overfat.

More precise methods of estimating body composition have been developed. The most common ones available to the athletic trainer are skinfolds and underwater weighing. The skinfold method is probably the most accessible and practical. However, most universities and colleges, and even some high schools, have facilities for underwater weighing. These body-composition tools can help the athletic trainer educate athletes about the nature and importance of body composition in sports as well as provide good information about the ideal body composition for competition.

Skinfolds

A skinfold measurement is a simple, inexpensive, and practical way to assess body composition (Figure 26-3) and probably the most useful to the average athletic trainer. The basics of this method take little time to learn, but measurement reliability requires some experience. Skinfold equations are derived from a statistical technique called multiple regression, which predicts the results of a more precise laboratory technique, such as the hydrostatic weighing procedure, from the measurement of skinfolds taken at various sites. It is absolutely essential that a subject be measured using an equation derived from a similar population (although researchers are currently working on universally applicable equations).

Skinfolds are measured with a device called a caliper, which is composed of a pair of spring-loaded, calibrated jaws. Many companies make calipers of varying quality ($10 to $200). High-quality calipers are made of metal, have parallel jaw surfaces, and constant spring tension (regardless of the degree of opening). Many inexpensive, plastic calipers are available, but these should not be used because of their potential for error.

The athletic trainer should take great care when using the skinfold method because it is subject to considerable measurement error. Dehydration decreases a skinfold thickness by as much as 15 percent, most likely causing variability between morning and evening measurements. In addition, skinfold measurements have been shown to be useless in predicting changes in body composition following weight loss. Changes in body weight are not fully reflected in skinfold thickness, which is not true of the more precise underwater weighing technique. The accuracy of the skinfold method can be improved by having a single, experienced observer take multiple measurements.

Hydrostatic Weighing

Hydrostatic (underwater) weighing is considered the most accurate, indirect way to measure body composition and

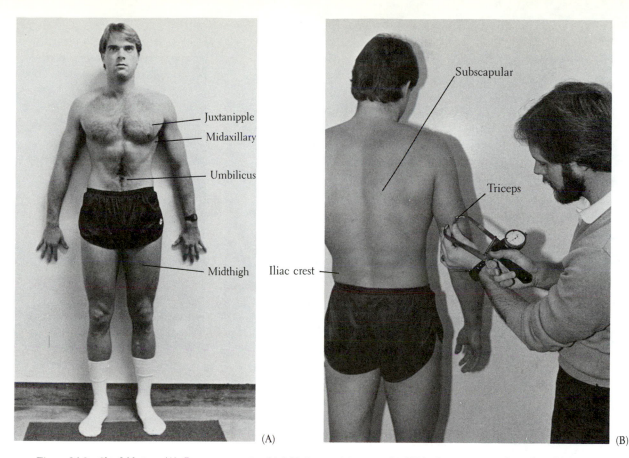

Figure 26-3 Skinfold sites. (A) Common anterior skinfold sites used in many skinfold body-composition formulas. (B) Location of common posterior skinfold sites.

is the "gold standard" for other indirect techniques, such as skinfold (Figure 26-4, p. 484). This technique is now an important tool in athletic training, exercise physiology, and medicine.

Underwater weighing calculates body density, which is a measure of tissue compactness. The percentage of fat and fat-free weight (lean body mass) are calculated from density using equations derived from reference cadavers. In this procedure, the subject is submerged and weighed underwater. Muscle has a higher density and fat a lower density than water (1.1 grams per cubic centimeter for muscle, 0.91 grams per cubic centimeter for fat, and 1 gram per cubic centimeter for water). Therefore, fat people tend to float and weigh less underwater, and lean people tend to

sink and weigh more underwater. At a given body weight, a fat person has a larger volume than a thin one and thus a smaller density.

Although somewhat cumbersome and expensive, this method is not beyond the budget of even some high schools (research-quality applications can be prohibitively expensive). A harness and autopsy scale (or even a supermarket fruit and vegetable scale) can be connected to a diving board and the school pool used as the underwater weighing tank. This method can be extremely educational: The visual sight of a light-weight wrestler outweighing a much larger but obese football player can be extremely instructive to a young athlete who stresses quantity of weight over quality.

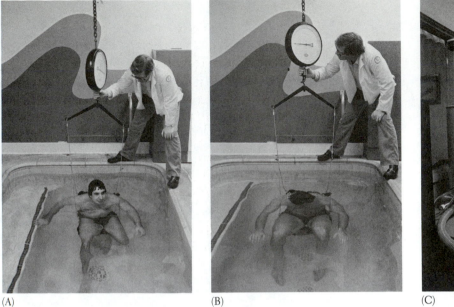
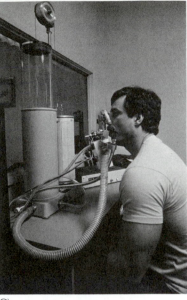

(A)   (B)   (C)

Figure 26-4 Estimating body composition by underwater weighing. (A and B) Body volume of an Olympic discus thrower is measured by taking his weight underwater. (C) Corrections are made for residual lung volume (amount of air in the lungs after a maximum exhalation). The O_2 washout technique is shown here.

References

Bailey, C. J. On the physiology and biochemistry of obesity. *Science Progress* 65:365–393, 1978.

Behnke, A. R., and J. H. Wilmore. *Evaluation and Regulation of Body Build and Composition.* Englewood Cliffs, N.J.: Prentice-Hall, 1974.

Brown, C. H., and J. H. Wilmore. The effects of maximal resistance training on the strength and body composition of women athletes. *Medicine and Science in Sports and Exercise* 6:174–177, 1974.

Buskirk, E. R. Obesity: a brief overview with emphasis on exercise. *Federation Proceedings* 33:1948–1951, 1974.

Buskirk, E. R. Some nutritional considerations in the conditioning of athletes. *Annual Review of Nutrition* 1:319–350, 1981.

Celejowa, I., and M. Homa. Food intake, nitrogen and energy balance in Polish weight lifters, during a training camp. *Nutrition and Metabolism* 12:259–274, 1970.

Clarke, H. H. Exercise and fat reduction. *Physical Fitness Research Digest* 5:1–27, 1975.

Consolazio, C. F., H. L. Johnson, R. A. Dramise, and J. A. Skata. Protein metabolism during intensive physical training in the young adult. *American Journal of Clinical Nutrition* 28:29–35, 1975.

Currey, H., R. Malcolm, E. Riddle, and M. Schachte. Behavioral treatment of obesity. *Journal of the American Medical Association* 237:2829–2831, 1977.

Epstein, L. H., and R. R. Wing. Aerobic exercise and weight. *Addictive Behaviors* 5:371–388, 1980.

Fahey, T. D., L. Akka, and R. Rolph. Body composition and VO_2 max of exceptional weight-trained athletes. *Journal of Applied Physiology* 39:559–561, 1975.

Foster, C., D. L. Costill, and W. J. Fink. Effects of preexercise feedings on endurance performance. *Medicine and Science in Sports and Exercise* 11:1–5, 1979.

Franklin, B. A., and M. Rubenfire. Losing weight through exercise. *Journal of the American Medical Association* 244:377–379, 1980.

Gontzea, I., R. Sutzescu, and S. Dumitrache. The influence of adaptation to physical effort on nitrogen balance in man. *Nutrition Reports International* 11:231–236, 1975.

Gray, M. E., and L. W. Titlow. B_{15}: Myth or miracle? *The Physician and Sportsmedicine* 10:107–112, 1982.

Himms-Hagen, J. Obesity may be due to a malfunctioning of brown fat. *Canadian Medical Association Journal* 121:1361–1364, 1979.

Ivy, J. L., D. L. Costill, W. J. Fink, and R. W. Lower. Influence of caffeine and carbohydrate feedings on endurance performance. *Medicine and Science in Sports and Exercise* 11:6–11, 1979.

James, W. P. T., and P. Trayhurn. Thermogenesis and obesity. *British Medical Bulletin* 37:43–48, 1981.

Katch, F., and W. D. McArdle. *Nutrition, Weight Control, and Exercise.* Boston: Houghton Mifflin, 1977, pp. 101–134.

Kindermann, W., J. Keul, and G. Huber. Physical exercise after induced alkalosis (bicarbonate or tris-buffer). *European Journal of Applied Physiology* 37:197–204, 1977.

Kleiber, M. *The Fire of Life.* New York: Wiley, 1961, pp. 41–59.

Krause, M. V., and L. K. Mahan. *Food, Nutrition, and Diet Therapy.* Philadelphia: W. B. Saunders, 1979.

Morgan, W. (ed.). *Ergogenic Aids and Muscular Performance.* New York: Academic Press, 1972.

Pernow, B., and B. Saltin (eds.). *Muscle Metabolism During Exercise.* New York: Plenum Press, 1971.

Pollock, M. L., E. E. Laughridge, B. Coleman, A. C. Linnerud, and A. Jackson. Prediction of body density in young and middle-aged women. *Journal of Applied Physiology* 38:745–749, 1975.

Smith, N. J. *Food for Sport.* Palo Alto, Calif.: Bull Publishing, 1976.

Stern, J. S., and M. R. C. Greenwood. A review of development of adipose cellularity in man and animals. *Federation Proceedings* 33:1952–1955, 1974.

Williams, M. H. *Nutritional Aspects of Human Physical and Athletic Performance.* Springfield, Ill.: Charles C Thomas, 1976.

Wilmore, J. H., C. H. Brown, and J. A. Davis. Body physique and composition of the female distance runner. *Annals of the New York Academy of Sciences* 301:764–776, 1977.

Wilmore, J. H., R. N. Girandola, and D. L. Moody. Validity of skinfold and girth assessment for prediction alterations in body composition. *Journal of Applied Physiology* 29:313–317, 1970.

Wilmore, J. H., and W. L. Haskell. Body composition and endurance capacity of professional football players. *Journal of Applied Physiology* 33:564–567, 1972.

27 Pharmacology

DRUGS are both a boon and a bane to athletics. On the one hand, drugs such as anti-inflammatory agents have allowed athletes to quickly rehabilitate their injuries or play with less pain. On the other hand, drugs used as ergogenic aids, such as anabolic steroids and amphetamines, have endangered athletes' health and possibly introduced a factor that places the athlete who does not use drugs at a disadvantage.

The abuse of drugs like alcohol, cocaine, and marijuana is rampant in many Western countries. Because athletics is a microcosm of society, it is not surprising that this problem exists, even among very young athletes. Drug abuse in athletes can have devastating effects upon performance, lead to tragic health consequences, and severely upset family and school environments.

The athletic trainer *must* have a basic knowledge of pharmacology. Although not legally permitted to dispense drugs, the athletic trainer must nevertheless be aware of drugs' effects because of their importance in athletic medicine. Diminished physical performance may be one of the earliest indicators of drug abuse by athletes. An aware trainer may be able to help athletes deal with the problem before it becomes overly destructive.

The athletic population has become much more diverse. An athletic trainer may have to deal with elderly or physically limited sportspersons (such as diabetics or asthmatics) who are taking medications much different than those commonly prescribed for younger athletes. Such drugs can have far-reaching effects upon the response to exercise. In some cases, the combination of certain medications and physical activity may produce side effects.

This chapter is an overview of pharmacology for the athletic trainer. Topics discussed include the action of drugs, commonly prescribed drugs in athletic medicine, drugs used as ergogenic aids, and drug abuse. (Specific drugs for specific problems, such as fungicides for skin disorders, are discussed in Chapters 14 to 23.)

Action of Drugs

Drugs are substances that alter the body's normal biochemistry. Clinically, drugs are administered to correct functional disorders, combat infections, and augment deficiencies. Drug effects depend upon type of drug, the dosage, interaction with other medications, and

In recent years, the International Olympic Committee's doping control program has discovered use of anabolic steroids among many athletes, including world-class female swimmers.

individual differences in response to the drugs. In many cases, determining the proper amount of the drugs to be administered is a trial-and-error procedure based upon the specific effects of the drugs. The athletic trainer can be of tremendous assistance to the physician by knowledgeably observing the effects of drugs in athletes.

The thousands of drugs can be classified according to their structure and basic effects. However, it is important to point out that even small alterations in structure can make very large changes in the drug's biological effect. The effects of a drug depend upon the drug's concentration at its target site. Concentration is directly affected by the drug's rate of absorption, its distribution within the body, its metabolism, and its rate of excretion. Because many of these processes are affected by blood flow, it is not surprising that exercise can alter them.

Drugs are administered orally, intramuscularly, intravenously, intraarterially, **subcutaneously, topically, sublingually, buccally,** and by inhalation.

The route of administration is determined by such factors as absorbency, patient cooperation, and local irritation.

Once a drug is administered, absorption is affected by blood flow, molecular weight of the drug, pH, water and fat solubility, and concentration. Once absorbed into the bloodstream, drugs readily enter the **interstitial fluid** and exert their effects at specific sites.

Many drugs resemble substances that are produced naturally in the body. Most drugs act upon tissue macromolecules (proteins, lipoproteins, or nucleic acids) by a "lock and key process" (Figure 27-1, p. 488). The drug is the key and the tissue receptor is the lock. The drug can either fit into the receptor and initiate a biological effect (as when the key opens the lock), or the drug can jam a receptor and block an effect (as when a key jams a lock).

Drugs administered simultaneously or sequentially may interact to either augment or diminish the expected effect or cause toxicity. Although the primary responsibility of drug interaction is the physician's, the trainer may be faced

Interstitial fluid: The fluid lying between the cells.

Subcutaneously: Underneath the skin.
Topically: Over the skin.
Sublingually: Under the tongue.
Buccally: In the cheek.

with an athlete consuming drugs from a variety of sources and of which the physician is unaware. The trainer should include in the records a list of all drugs consumed by the athletes; this helps the primary care physician determine possible negative drug interactions.

Commonly Prescribed Drugs in Athletic Medicine

A number of drugs are prescribed in athletic medicine. The most common are prescribed for musculoskeletal disorders, such as nonsteroidal analgesics, **anti-inflammatory agents,** and muscle relaxants. Other types of drugs the athletic trainer will encounter are antibiotics, disinfectants and antiseptics, drugs that affect the cardiovascular system, drugs that affect the pulmonary system, drugs used to treat metabolic disorders, and drugs used as ergogenic aids.

Drugs for Musculoskeletal Disorders

The most common drugs used to treat musculoskeletal pain and inflammation are nonsteroidal analgesics and anti-inflammatory drugs, such as aspirin, indomethacin (Indocin), ibuprofen (Motrin), naproxen (Naprosyn), fenoprofen (Nalfon), tolmetin (Tolectin), and sulindac (Clinoril); see Putting It into Practice 27-1. These drugs, which as a group are called nonsteroidal anti-inflammatants (NSAID), inhibit the synthesis of prostaglandins, which have been implicated in the development of inflammation.

NSAIDs can produce a number of side effects significant in athletics. They increase sweating and hasten dehydration, which could prove dangerous in endurance sports like running or sports conducted in weight classifications,

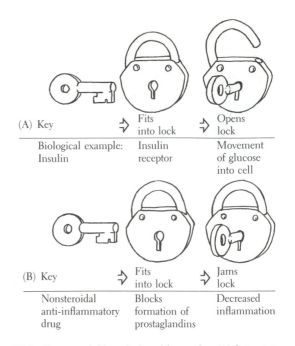

| (A) Key | Fits into lock | Opens lock |

| Biological example: Insulin | Insulin receptor | Movement of glucose into cell |

| (B) Key | Fits into lock | Jams lock |

| Nonsteroidal anti-inflammatory drug | Blocks formation of prostaglandins | Decreased inflammation |

Figure 27-1 Drugs work like a lock and key, either (A) fitting into a receptor and initiating a biological effect or (B) jamming a receptor and thus blocking an effect.

such as wrestling. **Dyspepsia** (upset stomach), a common side effect, can be prevented by taking the drug with food or liquid antacids. Aspirin is available in buffered form or coated with a substance to limit stomach upset. These drugs also affect blood clotting by inhibiting prothrombin synthesis and platelet aggregation, so they should be used sparingly when the athlete is suffering from a contusion.

Aspirin displaces a number of NSAIDs, such as naproxin and phenylbutazone (Butazolidin), from their protein-binding sites. For this reason, concurrently administering these drugs is not recommended. Phenylbutazone is a more potent and longer-acting anti-inflammatant, but it is also much more toxic. Although this is a commonly prescribed medication, athletes often obtain it illegally and by improperly using it subject themselves to possible severe side effects, including sodium retention and edema, dry mouth, nau-

Anti-inflammatory agents: Drugs that decrease inflammation.

Dyspepsia: Indigestion or upset stomach.

sea and vomiting, **peptic ulceration** and hemorrhage, **hypertension,** and fever. This drug is seldom prescribed for more than seven to ten days.

Corticosteroids, such as cortisone, are sometimes used as an anti-inflammatory agent to treat soft tissue disorders like tendinitis and bursitis. Cortisone injections limit the inflammatory process by decreasing capillary dilation and increasing membrane permeability following an injury and prevent the release of vasoactive kinins (polypeptides) and destructive enzymes. However, cortisone causes muscle atrophy and decreases tendons' and ligaments' tensile strength, so it tends to be a drug of last resort.

Athletes widely and covertly use dimethyl sulfoxide (DMSO), an anti-inflammatory agent. This substance is an industrial solvent and has not been shown to be medically beneficial in treating soft tissue injuries. DMSO typically is not available from medical sources, so athletes buy the potentially impure industrial source, which may increase the risk of infection. Discourage the use of DMSO because it affects the refractory power of the eye and may decrease the strength of tendons, making them more susceptible to injury. This substance may be **toxic** to the liver and carcinogenic. The athletic trainer can readily detect an athlete using DMSO by the odor of rotting fish on the athlete's breath and skin.

Muscle relaxants are sometimes prescribed to treat muscle spasm (see Putting It into Practice 27-2). Cyclobenzaprine (Flexeril), diazepam (Valium), carisoprodol (Soma), and methocarbamol (Robaxin) are among such drugs. These relaxants act as central nervous system depressants (rather than having a specific effect upon skeletal muscle), so they may negatively affect motor function.

Liniments and counterirritating drugs, containing substances such as oil of wintergreen, camphor, and ammonia, have long been part of almost every training room. These so-called

PUTTING IT INTO PRACTICE 27-1
Using Nonsteroidal Anti-Inflammatory Drugs

- *Examples:* Indocin, Motrin, Naprosyn, Clinoril, Feldene, and Nalfon.
- *Use:* Decrease inflammation.
- *Major side effects:* Stomach upset, heartburn, nausea, vomiting, and diarrhea.
- *Preventing side effects:* Take with meals, milk, antacids, or snack.
- *Medical assistance:* Consult physician if there are symptoms such as ringing ears, fever, dyspnea, edema, weight gain, hives, unusual bleeding, and sore throat.

PUTTING IT INTO PRACTICE 27-2
Using Muscle Relaxants

- *Examples:* Valium, Robxin, Romethocarb, and Metho-500.
- *Use:* Muscle spasms.
- *Major side effects:* Drowsiness, blurred vision, and dizziness. Athlete should not drive, operate machinery, or play contact sports while on this type of medication.
- *Medical assistance:* Contact physician if athlete exhibits allergic reaction or evidence of liver disease (jaundice).

analgesic balms irritate the skin, which in turn increases local superficial circulation. The use of liniments is fine for massages, but they should not be used in place of more effective **modalities,** such as ice. Counterirritant liniments may help decrease pain by overloading **sensory nerves** (see the gate theory of pain discussion in Chapter 8, p. 128), but this has never been effectively demonstrated.

Gastrointestinal Drugs

Gastrointestinal distress is common among athletes and can be caused by many factors, such as stress, unfamiliar or rich food, food allergies, bacteria, and viruses. Gastrointestinal distress can manifest itself in a number of ways, including "acid stomach," diarrhea, constipation, and dyspepsia.

Peptic ulcer: An ulcer of the inner lining of the stomach or duodenum.
Hypertension: High blood pressure.
Toxic: Poisonous.
Analgesic: A substance that reduces pain.

Antacids partially neutralize the acidic gastric secretion and are commonly consumed as sodium bicarbonate (baking soda) or aluminum and magnesium hydroxide tablets or liquid (see Putting It into Practice 27-3). Liquid antacids are considered superior to the tablet form because the smaller particles of the liquid chemical can neutralize stomach acid more readily. The use of antacids presents few side effects, other than occasional constipation or, in rare instances, mild alkalosis (a higher-than-normal blood pH).

Because exercise is a potent cathartic, young athletes rarely need laxatives. However, constipation is a common problem, particularly during prolonged travel or among older athletes. There are countless forms of laxatives, including irritants such as castor oil, which stimulate gastrointestinal motility; emodin alkaloids such as cascara and senna, which act locally on the colon to stimulate peristalsis (contraction); bulk laxatives, which distend the intestines; and fecal softeners.

Diarrhea can be a problem for athletes because it may dehydrate them. Drugs commonly used to treat this disorder are diphenoxylate and loperamide, which can be obtained without a prescription.

Antibiotics

The development of antibiotics is among the most important advances in medical science. These drugs work by interfering with the metabolism or synthetic process of specific microorganisms. Each type of antibiotic works upon a particular type of microorganism, so the physician should have a pretty good idea of the nature of an infection before prescribing a particular drug.

The trainer can help the physician judge the effectiveness of specific antimicrobial drugs prescribed to athletes. These drugs sometimes produce side effects or are ineffective if the wrong

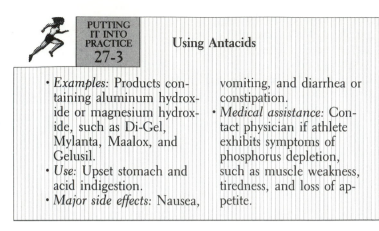

PUTTING IT INTO PRACTICE 27-3

Using Antacids

- *Examples*: Products containing aluminum hydroxide or magnesium hydroxide, such as Di-Gel, Mylanta, Maalox, and Gelusil.
- *Use*: Upset stomach and acid indigestion.
- *Major side effects*: Nausea, vomiting, and diarrhea or constipation.
- *Medical assistance*: Contact physician if athlete exhibits symptoms of phosphorus depletion, such as muscle weakness, tiredness, and loss of appetite.

drug is chosen. Negative consequences of improperly selecting an antibiotic include toxic reactions, hypersensitivity from repeated administrations, increased risk of more serious infection, and the creation of mutant bacteria that become resistant to the drug.

The literally hundreds of antibiotic drugs on the market fall into the following categories: sulfonamides, erythromycins and lincomycins, penicillins and cephalosporins, aminoglycosides, choloramphenicol, tetracyclines (see Putting It into Practice 27-4), and urinary antiseptics.

Antibiotics sometimes cause severe reactions in people who are allergic to one or more of these drugs. The trainer should keep a record of allergies to drugs, such as penicillins, to prevent hypersensitivity reactions. Encourage athletes who exhibit such allergies to wear a medical alert bracelet.

Disinfectants and Antiseptics

Although these two terms are often used interchangeably, a disinfectant is a substance that kills microorganisms in the inanimate environment (used to disinfect objects), and an antiseptic kills bacteria or inhibits their growth on living tissue. Alcohols, aldehydes, acids, halogens (iodine and chlorine), oxidizing agents, soaps, phenol, metals, and cationic surface-active agents are among the disinfectants and antiseptics. Heat is a major sterilizing agent. The effectiveness of disinfectants and antiseptics depends upon their concentration, temperature, and time.

The importance of these substances in the training room cannot be overemphasized. Athletic trainers regularly use disinfectants to keep the training room clean and antiseptics to treat athletes' many cuts and abrasions. The athletic trainer should ensure that the work area is as germ-free as possible; keep the whirlpool, refrigerator, sink, taping tables, and other areas as clean as possible.

PUTTING IT INTO PRACTICE 27-4

Using Tetracyclines

- *Examples:* Emeclocycline, doxycycline, minocycline, oxytetracycline, and tetracycline.
- *Use:* In the treatment of pneumonia, tonsillitis, bronchitis, ear or sinus infections, acne, syphilis, dysentery, and salmonella.

Often used when patient is allergic to the drug of choice.
- *Major side effects:* Allergic reactions, loss of appetite, diarrhea, nausea, vomiting, black discoloration of the tongue, and increased sensitivity to sunlight.

Cardiac Drugs and Exercise

With the increased popularity of masters athletics, the trainer can expect to come in contact with people suffering from various cardiac disorders. The drugs used to treat cardiovascular disease can alter many aspects of heart and circulatory function, including cardiac electrical conduction and the response to exercise. The drugs can also have far-reaching effects upon other physiological functions, such as temperature regulation and cerebral function. Exercise response can help gauge a drug's effectiveness, so it is important for people involved in exercise prescription and training to understand the interactions among physical activity and drugs. Table 27-1 summarizes the drugs used in heart disease, their actions, and their effects upon exercise and the electrocardiogram (see p. 492).

The most common drugs used to treat cardiovascular diseases are digitalis, diuretics, vasodilators, beta-adrenergic blocking agents, and **antiarrhythmic drugs**. Digitalis increases the heart's contractility and is not likely to be prescribed to a person involved in active athletic competition. Vasodilators, such as nitroglycerine, decrease the heart's oxygen consumption. Nitroglycerine can induce hypotension, which increases the risk of fainting during exercise. Beta blockers, such as propranolol, also decrease myocardial oxygen consumption by depressing heart rate and blood pressure; this often impairs exercise capacity and the ability to improve from an exercise-training program.

Diuretics are used primarily to treat hypertension (high blood pressure) and can be prescribed to an athlete of any age. The exercise capacity of people on diuretics may be impaired because these drugs decrease plasma volume. Particular care is necessary when exercising in the heat because severe fluid diuresis impairs the capacity to sweat. Healthy athletes sometimes use these drugs to lose weight; this dangerous practice should be discouraged.

Antiarrhythmic drugs, such as procainamide and quinidine, suppress ventricular arrhythmias, which can be particularly dangerous during exercise. These drugs can decrease myocardial contractility and cause slight muscle weakness.

Diuretics: Drugs or substances that promote fluid loss.

Drugs for Asthma

The athletic trainer will very likely encounter athletes of all ages who are suffering from asthma and taking medication to combat the problem. Asthma is a disease characterized by shortness

Antiarrhythmic drugs: Drugs that suppress abnormal electrical conduction patterns in the heart.

Table 27-1 *Cardiac Drugs and Their Uses*

Digitalis glycosides

Use: In heart failure to slow heart rate, increase the heart's contractile capacity, and control certain electrocardiographic abnormalities.
Examples: Digitalis, digitoxin, and digoxin.

Diuretics

Use: Hypertension, heart failure, fluid retention, pulmonary edema.
Examples: Chlorothiazide, hydrocholorothiazide, and furosemide.

Catecholamines (sympathomimetic amines)

Use: Regulate heart rate, rhythm, and arterial blood pressure, increase cardiac contractility, increase peripheral organ perfusion (particularly in the lungs). Clinically, used in treatment of chronic obstructive pulmonary disease, allergic reactions (anaphylaxis), low cardiac output, and cardiac arrest.
Examples: Epinephrine, norepinephrine, isoproterenol, dopamine, and dobutamine.

Vasodilators

Use: Angina, chronic congestive heart failure, hypertension, valvular heart disease, congenital heart diseases, chronic pulmonary hypertension.
Examples: Nitroglycerin, isosorbide dinitrate, hydralazine, Isordil, prazocin, phentolamine, phenoxybenzamine, and trimethaphane.

Beta-adrenergic blocking drugs

Use: Hypertension, angina, hypertrophic cardiomyopathy (enlarged intraventricular septum), congestive cardiomyopathy, cardiac arrhythmias, and thyrotoxicosis. Reduces heart rate and blood pressure.
Examples: Propranolol, alprenolol, Lopressor, tenformin, metoprolol, and atenolol.

Antiarrhythmic drugs

Use: Suppression of arrhythmias; type of arrhythmia dictates type of drug.
Examples: Quinidine, procainamide, lidocaine, phenytoin, mexiletine, tocainide, and aprindine.

Calcium channel blockers

Use: Angina, coronary spasm, some arrhythmias, and idiopathic hypertrophic subaortic stenosis.
Examples: Nifedipine, verapamil, and diltiazem.

of breath and is caused by temporary changes in the bronchial tubes or reflex spasm of the diaphragm. The most effective drugs for treating the symptoms of asthma are beta-**sympathomimetic drugs** (drugs that mimic the action of the sympathetic nervous system) administered as aerosols, such as metraproterenol, salbutamol, terbutaline, and fenoterol. Ingestion of these drugs orally is much less effective than by aerosol spray for preventing exercise-induced asthma. Also oral ingestion is often accompanied by such side effects as tachycardia (excessive beating of the heart), skeletal muscle tremor, and nausea.

The beta-sympathomimetic drugs are known effective bronchodilators and in many instances can effectively reverse asthmatic attacks. Prevention of the problem is perhaps the most important consideration, so the athletic trainer should encourage the use of these medications (when prescribed) before an asthmatic attack occurs. Asthmatic athletes may also use a variety of over-the-counter decongestants (see Putting It into Practice 27-5). Athletes should be warned about informing their physician about any drug they are taking besides the ones medically prescribed.

PUTTING IT INTO PRACTICE 27-5

Using Decongestants Containing Pseudoephedrine

- *Examples*: Sudafed, Cenafed, Novafed, D-Fed, and Actafed.
- *Use*: Nasal and sinus decongestant.

- *Major side effects*: Insomnia, restlessness, and nervousness. Decrease dosage if symptoms are present, and seek physician's advice for alternative medication.

Drugs Used as Ergogenic Aids

As discussed in Chapter 26, ergogenic aids are substances or techniques (other than training) used to enhance physical performance. Countless substances have been touted as ergogenic aids; Table 27-2 (p. 494) lists the more common ones. This section summarizes the more prominent drugs used to enhance performance among athletes.

Drugs Banned in International Competition

The International Olympic Committee (IOC) has banned the use of various substances that are ingested or consumed for the purpose of unfairly and artificially improving performance in competition; see Table 27-3, p. 495. Few of the substances in the table have been found beneficial; the IOC maintains the list to discourage any attempt or pretext of unfair competition.

Much money has been spent to control drug use in international competition. Doping control programs have escalated from the relatively modest effort during the 1960 Rome Olympics to the multi-million-dollar endeavor at the 1984 Los Angeles Olympics.

The athletic trainer who is fortunate enough to travel with a team competing internationally should be thoroughly familiar with banned substances. Many of the substances are in a variety of over-the-counter and prescribed medications, such as decongestants, throat lozenges, topical nasal decongestants, and eyedrops. Failure to pay proper attention to this problem could cause athletes to be disqualified if they inadvertently take a drug on the banned list.

Anabolic Steroids

Anabolic steroids are drugs synthesized in the laboratory to resemble male hormones, such as **testosterone**. Table 27-4 (p. 494) presents the most popular oral and injectable anabolic steroids. They are widely used by athletes involved in sports where size and strength are an advantage, such as football, weight lifting, discus throwing, and shot

Sympathomimetic drugs: Substances that mimic the action of the sympathetic nervous system.

Testosterone: The principal male hormone; produced by the testes and responsible for the development of secondary sexual characteristics; plays a role in muscle hypertrophy.

Table 27-2 *Substances or Techniques Used as Ergogenic Aids*

Alcohol	Epinephrine	Nitroglycerine
Alkalis	Electrical stimulation	Norepinephrine
Amino acids	Gelatin	Marijuana
Amphetamines	Growth hormone	Massage
Anabolic steroids	Heat	Mineral supplements
Aspartates	Human chorionic	Periactin
Bee pollen	gonadotropin	Protein supplements
Caffeine	Hypnosis	Sulfa drugs
Camphor	Organ extracts	Strychnine
Cocaine	Oxygen	Vitamin supplements
Cold	Negatively ionized air	Wheat germ oil
Digitalis	Nicotine	Yeast

SOURCE: Brooks, G. A., and T. D. Fahey. *Exercise Physiology: Human Bioenergetics and Its Applications.* New York: Wiley, 1984, p. 613.

put, to increase strength, endurance, weight, and speed.

The effectiveness of these drugs is unclear, in spite of their tremendous popularity. The American College of Sports Medicine has issued a position statement regarding the use and abuse of anabolic-androgenic steroids in sports: They state that any benefits from taking the drugs are likely to be small and not worth the health risks involved.

Anabolic steroids enhance anabolic properties (tissue building) and minimize androgenic properties (secondary sexual characteristics). Although the process is not completely understood, these drugs work by stimulating the synthesis of proteins and inhibiting the rate of protein breakdown.

Athletes may need to train vigorously with heavy weights for anabolic steroids to exert any beneficial effect (which may explain the discrepancy between negative experimental findings and the numerous personal testimonials attesting to the drugs' effectiveness). Some researchers have speculated that the real effect of anabolic steroids is the creation of a "psychosomatic state" that increases aggressiveness, which allows the athlete to train harder.

Scientific studies of anabolic steroids have rendered conflicting results. Most studies have shown only small increases in body weight, lean body weight, and strength; almost no study has demonstrated improvements in endurance. These studies typically have lasted six to eight weeks and usually have tested relatively untrained subjects. The gains athletes made in uncontrolled observations have been much more impressive. More research is needed to determine the effectiveness of these drugs.

The principal side effects of these drugs are attributable to (1) the normal physiological actions of male hormones that are inappropriate in the recipient and (2) toxic effects caused by the drug's chemical structure (principally "C-17 alpha alkylated" oral anabolic steroids). "Physiological" side effects include reduced production of testosterone, pituitary gonadotropin hormones, and **hypothalamic releasing factor** (all of which control testicular function and production of sperm cells). Libido may be increased or decreased. Anabolic steroids' structural similarity to aldosterone causes them to increase fluid retention. Steroid use by women and immature children may have masculizing effects, such as hair growth on the face and body, deepening of the voice, oily skin, increased activity of the apocrine sweat glands, acne, and baldness. In women, some of these masculine changes are irreversible. Women may also experi-

Hypothalamic releasing factors: Hormones produced by the hypothalamus; they control pituitary gland secretions.

Table 27-3 *Substances Banned by the International Olympic Committee*

Psychomotor stimulant drugs

Amphetamine	Premoline
Benzphetamine	Phenmetrazine
Cocaine	Phentermine
Caffeine	Pipradol
Ethylamphetamine	Prolintane
Methylamphetamine	Fencamfamin
Methylphenidate	Fenproporex
Norpseudo ephedrine	Related compounds

Sympathomimetic amines

Ephedrine	Methoxyphenamine
Methylephedrine	

Miscellaneous central nervous system stimulants

Amiphenazole	Leptazole
Bemegride	Nikethamine
Caffeine (greater than 15 mcg/ml in the urine)	Strychnine

Narcotic analgesics

Dextromoramide	Methadone
Dipipanone	Morphine
Heroin	Pethidine

Anabolic steroids

Methandienone (Dianabol)	Nandrolone phenylpropionate (Durabolin)
Oxandrolone (Anavar)	Nandrolone decanoate (Deca-Durabolin)
Oxymesterone (Oranabol)	Stanozolol (Winstrol)
Oxymetholone (Adroyd)	Testosterone

SOURCE: Brooks, G. A., and T. D. Fahey. *Exercise Physiology: Human Bioenergetics and Its Applications.* New York: Wiley, 1984, p. 614.

ence clitoral enlargement and menstrual irregularity. Children initially will experience accelerated maturation followed by premature closure of the epiphyseal growth centers in the long bones.

Oral anabolic steroids, such as methandrostenolone (Dianabol), are particularly toxic to the liver because their structure has been altered to make them digestible. This alteration causes the steroid to become concentrated in

Table 27-4 *Anabolic-Androgenic Steroids Athletes Use (listed in order of androgenicity)*

Orals	Injectables
Maxibolin	Deca-Durabolin
Anavar	Durabolin 50
Winstrol	Delatestryl
Dianabol	Testosterone proprionate
Anadrol	Depo-Testosterone
	Aqueous testosterone

the liver much earlier and in greater quantity than the injectable varieties.

Other side effects include muscle cramps, gastrointestinal distress, headache, dizziness, sore nipples, and abnormal thyroid function. These drugs have also been shown to decrease high-density lipoproteins, which protect against coronary heart disease. Thus, anabolic steroids produce severe side effects that are not worth the risk, particularly in women and adolescents.

Human Chorionic Gonadotropin

Human chorionic gonadotropin (HCG) is a relatively new ergogenic aid that acts like **luteinizing hormone** to stimulate testosterone production in the testes. Several studies have shown that HCG will increase serum testosterone, but no data about its effects upon performance are available. HCG has been used as an aid in weight loss, but its effectiveness for this use has not been substantiated.

Growth Hormone

Growth hormone (GH), a polypeptide hormone produced by the anterior pituitary gland, has been used by some powerlifters, bodybuilders, and throwers to increase muscle mass and strength. To date, GH's effect upon athletic performance has not been researched very much, but athletes have testified to weight gains of thirty to forty pounds in ten weeks. Nitrogen balance (a method of determining whether the body is gaining or losing protein) becomes highly positive when GH is administered to adult humans, which lends some credence to these observations.

Growth hormone is a potent anabolic agent that facilitates the transport of amino acids into cells. Increasing the rate of amino acid transport into muscle cells causes muscle hypertrophy. Growth hormone is also involved in the formation of connective tissue and stimulates somatomedin, which is an important hormone in chondrocyte metabolism. Growth hormone is also involved in carbohydrate and fat metabolism.

It has been well documented that GH has diabetogenic effects that could become permanent from large doses. GH can also cause symptoms of acromegaly, characterized by enlarged bones in the head, face, and hands; osteoporosis; arthritis; and heart disease. The skeletal changes are irreversible.

Serious weight-trained athletes have large heart walls. This condition probably has little (if any) effect upon health, but GH's ability to increase heart size may have severe consequences. Growth hormone-induced cardiac enlargement may be permanent. A larger heart has higher energy requirements that may not be adequately met as the athlete becomes older and begins to develop coronary artery disease.

In the past, growth hormone was very expensive and in short supply because it was obtained only from the pituitary gland of human cadavers or rhesus monkeys. However, recent advances in genetic engineering have increased the possibility that it will be more widely available. Even though it has severe side effects, GH is irresistible to some athletes, who hope it will dramatically increase their performance in a short time.

Amphetamines

Amphetamines are perhaps the most abused drug in sports, being particularly popular in football, basketball, track and field, and cycling. Athletes use the drugs to prevent fatigue and to increase confidence, cardiovascular endurance, muscle endurance, speed, power, and reaction time. Generic amphetamines include benzedrine, dexedrine, dexamyl, and methedrine.

Amphetamines stimulate the central nervous system (CNS) and act as sympathomimetic stimulants (sympathomimetic effects mimic the action of the

Luteinizing hormone: A pituitary hormone that is an important regulator of testosterone in males and ovarian follicle maturation in females.

sympathetic nervous system). Amphetamines stimulate the CNS by directly affecting the reticular activating system and postganglionic nerves. Effects include increased arousal, wakefulness, confidence, and the feeling of an enhanced capability to make decisions. Sympathomimetic effects include increased blood pressure, heart rate, oxygen consumption in the brain, and glycolysis in muscle and liver, vasoconstriction in the arterioles of the skin and spleen, and vasodilation in muscle arterioles.

The effectiveness of amphetamines in improving athletic performance is controversial. Many studies have been poorly controlled, used low dosages, and did not allow enough time for the drug to be absorbed. Studies have generally supported amphetamines' effectiveness as a psychotropic drug that masks fatigue, but results are equivocal about their ability to improve endurance performance. Many studies have demonstrated enhanced feelings of well-being and improved exercise capacity in fatigued subjects. Fatigued animal and human subjects improved endurance (time to fatigue) in marching, cycling, swimming, and treadmill exercise and improved simple reaction time; amphetamines had no effect upon reaction time in rested subjects.

Most studies have failed to demonstrate an effect upon cardiovascular function, even though exercise time to exhaustion was often improved. Maximal values for oxygen consumption, heart rate, minute volume, respiratory exchange ratio, respiratory rate, oxygen pulse, CO_2 production, and ventilatory equivalent were unaffected by amphetamines.

Amphetamines' effects upon strength and power seem determined by the number of motor units recruited. Chandler and Blair demonstrated a 22.5 percent increase in knee extension strength but no significant change in elbow flexion strength. In sprinting, the drugs enhance acceleration but not top speed. This fact points to an increased excitability in muscles but not to an increase in their maximal capacity. Most studies show increases in static strength but mixed results in muscle endurance.

Amphetamines' effects upon sports performance are also unclear. They appear to aid power-oriented movement skills in activities that employ constant motor patterns, such as shot put and hammer throwing. They are probably less effective in sports requiring the execution of motor skills in an unpredictable order, such as football, basketball, and tennis. In these sports, amphetamines are probably deleterious because they may interfere with the body's fatigue alarm system, cause confusion, impair judgment, and in high concentrations block neuromuscular activity and cause loss of effective motor control.

Amphetamines can have severe side effects. They increase the risk of hyperthermia because of their vasoconstriction effect upon the skin's arterioles. There have been numerous reported deaths in endurance sports of athletes competing in the heat while under the influence of these drugs. These drugs can also cause tremulousness, psychic distress, insomnia, dry mouth, addiction, and cardiac arrhythmias.

Caffeine

Caffeine is a xanthine (purine bases) that acts as a cerebrocortical stimulator and may stimulate the adrenal medulla to release epinephrine. It also stimulates the heart (both rate and contractility of the heart at rest), causes peripheral vasodilation, and acts as a diuretic by blocking renal tubular reabsorption of sodium. Caffeine is used in athletics as a **stimulant** and a fatty acid mobilizer. It is found in a variety of foods, such as coffee, tea, and chocolate.

Caffeine is a much weaker stimulant than amphetamine, yet it is widely used by weight lifters and throwers (discus,

Stimulant: A substance that excites the body to increase its activity.

shot, javelin, and hammer) to enhance strength and power. These athletes take the caffeine in the form of strong coffee or over-the-counter medications like Vivarin or No Doz. Some older, poorly controlled studies found that caffeine improved strength and power, but these findings have not been replicated in well-controlled studies.

Caffeine appears to enhance performance in prolonged endurance exercise by mobilizing free fatty acids and sparing muscle glycogen. A study by Ivy et al. found that a total of 500 milligrams of caffeine, administered before and during a two-hour ride on an isokinetic bicycle ergometer, caused a 7.4 percent greater work production. It appears that caffeine is an effective ergogenic aid in events such as marathon running.

There are risks in using caffeine as an ergogenic aid. The diuretic and cardiac stimulatory properties can combine to increase the risk of EKG arrhythmias, such as ventricular ectopic beats and paroxysmal atrial tachycardia. This is particularly alarming for older, less-conditioned individuals. Caffeine can also delay or lighten sleep and is addictive.

Cocaine

Cocaine is an alkaloid derived from the leaves of the coca plant and stimulates the central nervous system. It has become very popular with certain segments of the population. Cocaine has also become popular with some athletes, with reports often surfacing in the news media of its rampant use by professional football and basketball players.

The drug produces a feeling of exhilaration and an enhanced sense of well-being, and it depresses fatigue. It inhibits the reuptake of norepinephrine in sympathetic neurons and has a direct sympathomimetic effect. Several poorly controlled studies showed that cocaine increases work capacity. However, in rats, cocaine had no effect upon swim time to exhaustion. Cocaine is an extremely dangerous drug, particularly when it is administered intravenously or converted to its free base and smoked (these methods greatly increase the concentration of the drug). Cocaine's effects are similar to those of amphetamines, but more intense. This drug can induce paranoid and assaultive tendencies and withdrawal reactions. Overdoses can cause death, characterized by seizure, and cardiac and respiratory arrest.

Drug Abuse

Drugs such as alcohol and marijuana are more commonly used at the high school and college levels as "social" recreation than as ergogenic aids. Many forms of drug abuse can cause physical damage, impaired function, and behavior harmful to others. Apart from its destructive effects upon an individual's physiology and psychological well-being, drug abuse can be extremely disruptive to the athletic program.

People use drugs for a variety of reasons, including peer pressure, desire to alter self-physiology, poor self-image, boredom, depression, curiosity, and ready availability of drugs. The trainer may often be the first to know something is wrong in an athlete's life that may make him or her more prone to drug abuse. It is important that the trainer's line of communications with young people remain open. However, the athletic trainer is seldom trained in dealing with drug abuse, so he or she should seek help from experienced professionals rather than trying to deal with the problem personally.

References

Albrechtsen, S. J., and J. S. Harvey. Dimethyl sulfoxide: biochemical effects on tendons. *American Journal of Sports Medicine* 10:177–179, 1982.

American College of Sports Medicine. Position statement on the use and abuse of anabolic-androgenic steroids in sports. *Medicine and Science in Sports and Exercise* 9:xi–xiii, 1977.

Anderson, S. D. Drugs affecting the respiratory system with particular reference to asthma. *Medicine and Science in Sports and Exercise* 13:259–265, 1981.

Bender, K. J., and D. H. Lockwood. Use of medications by U.S. Olympic swimmers. *The Physician and Sportsmedicine* 5:63–65, 1977.

Brooks, G. A., and T. D. Fahey. *Exercise Physiology: Human Bioenergetics and Its Applications*. New York: Wiley, 1984.

Brooks, R. V., G. Jeremiah, W. A. Webb, and M. Wheeler. Detection of anabolic steroid administration to athletes. *Journal of Steroid Biochemistry* 11:913–917, 1979.

Chandler, J. V., and S. N. Blair. The effect of amphetamines on selected physiological components related to athletic success. *Medicine and Science in Sports and Exercise* 12:65–69, 1980.

Day, R. O. Effects of exercise performance on drugs used in musculoskeletal disorders. *Medicine and Science in Sports and Exercise* 13:272–275, 1981.

Fahey, T. D., and C. H. Brown. The effects of an anabolic steroid on the strength, body composition, and endurance of college males when accompanied by a weight training program. *Medicine and Science in Sports and Exercise* 5:272–276, 1973.

Frischkorn, C. G. B., and H. E. Frischkorn. Investigations of anabolic drug abuse in athletics and cattle feed. *Journal of Chromatography* 151:331–338, 1978.

Insel, P. M., and W. T. Roth. *Core Concepts in Health*, 4th ed., Palo Alto, Calif.: Mayfield Publishing Co., 1985.

Ivy, J. L., D. L. Costill, W. J. Fink, and R. W. Lower. Influence of caffeine and carbohydrate feedings on endurance performance. *Medicine and Science in Sports and Exercise* 11:6–11, 1979.

Meyers, F. H., E. Jawetz, and A. Goldfine. *Review of Medical Pharmacology*. Los Altos, Calif.: Lange Medical Publications, 1980.

Moncada, S., and J. R. Vane. Mode of action of aspirin-like drugs. *Advances in Internal Medicine* 24:1–22, 1979.

Morgan, W. (ed.). *Ergogenic Aids and Muscular Performance*. New York: Academic Press, 1972.

O'Shea, J. P. "Anabolic Steroids in Sport: A Biophysiological Evaluation," in *Relevant Topics in Athletic Training*, K. Schriber and E. J. Burke, eds. Ithaca, N.Y.: Mouvement Publications, 1978.

Percy, E. C. Ergogenic aids in athletics. *Medicine and Science in Sports and Exercise* 10:298–303, 1978.

Percy, E. C., and J. D. Carson. Use of DMSO in tennis elbow and rotator cuff tendonitis: double-blind study. *Medicine and Science in Sports and Exercise* 13:215–219, 1981.

Peterson, G. E., and T. D. Fahey. HDL-C in five elite athletes using anabolic-androgenic steroids. *The Physician and Sportsmedicine* 12(6):120–130, 1984.

Powles, A. C. P. The effect of drugs on the cardiovascular response to exercise. *Medicine and Science in Sports and Exercise* 13:252–258, 1981.

Richardson, J. H. A comparison of two drugs on strength increase in monkeys. *Journal of Sports Medicine* 17:251–254, 1977.

Rogozkin, V., and B. Feldkoren. The effect of retabolil and training on activity of RNA polymerase in skeletal muscles. *Medicine and Science in Sports and Exercise* 11:345–347, 1979.

Smith, G. M., and H. K. Beecher. Amphetamine sulfate and athletic performance. *Journal of the American Medical Association* 170:542–557, 1959.

Smith, G. M., and H. K. Beecher. Amphetamine, secobarbital and athletic performance. *Journal of the American Medical Association* 172:1502–1514, 1623–1629, 1960.

Sokolow, M., and M. B. McIlroy. *Clinical Cardiology*. Los Altos, Calif.: Lange Medical Publications, 1977.

Sutton, J. R. Drugs used in metabolic disorders. *Medicine and Science in Sports and Exercise* 13:266–271, 1981.

Sweeney, G. D. Drugs—some basic concepts. *Medicine and Science in Sports and Exercise* 13:247–251, 1981.

Williams, M. H. *Drugs and Athletic Performance*. Springfield, Ill.: Charles C Thomas, 1974.

Williams, M. H. *Nutritional Aspects of Human Physical and Athletic Performance*. Springfield, Ill.: Charles C Thomas, 1976.

Wright, J. *Anabolic Steroids and Sports*. Natick, Mass.: Sports Science Consultants, 1978.

Wright, J. Anabolic steroids and athletics. *Exercise and Sports Science Reviews* 8:149–202, 1980.

Problems in Child and Older Athletes

The increased popularity of masters athletics makes it imperative that the athletic trainer be familiar with age-related problems.

COMPETITIVE sports are no longer the private domain of high school and college athletes; now children and older adults participate in almost all sports. Children compete in their age-group sports that are often characterized by fierce competitiveness; masters sports for middle-aged and senior adults have reached the point where there are National and World championships that attract thousands of participants.

Children and older athletes are subject to injury for many of the same reasons: lack of physical capacity. Both groups are particularly vulnerable if their physical capacities are overextended. These people are often forced to practice or compete at substandard facilities, which make sports participation more dangerous. Individual differences in maturation or aging often create unfair and dangerous competitive situations; and professionals seldom coach these groups, so their training programs are often haphazard.

Always consider the growth process when working with child athletes. Although there are individual differences in diet, health, and physical activity, the developmental stages of growth are remarkably similar in all children. However, anyone working with children in sports should realize that the onset of the various growth stages varies from one athlete to the next. Each child matures at a slightly different rate and consequently varies in regards to readiness for certain activities.

Aging is often accompanied by myriad **degenerative** diseases and diminished capacity to adapt to various stresses. The masters-level athlete's program should be based upon a thorough assessment of individual capacity and should progress slowly.

This chapter examines the most important considerations when dealing with child and older athletes. Attention is on the growth and aging processes and their effects upon sports participation. In addition, we discuss the most prominent injuries these groups of athletes experience.

The Young Athlete

Growth is the development of the body in an orderly fashion; it is the predominance of anabolic over **catabolic** processes. Height and weight proceed along an S-shaped curve (Figure 28-1, p. 502). There is a rapid growth rate during the first two years, followed by a progressively declining growth rate during childhood, with an abrupt increase in the rate of growth at **puberty.**

Childhood is the period between about two years and the onset of puberty. During this time, height and weight steadily but gradually increase, with height increasing faster than weight. Males tend to be taller and heavier than females. However, females have relatively longer legs, which indicates a greater level of maturity (growth follows a cephalocaudal progression, i.e., from head to tail; longer legs indicate entry into the rapid adolescent phase of growth). Although the growth rate is faster in males, the relative changes are similar in both sexes. The skeletal age of girls is more advanced than boys throughout childhood.

Childhood is a period especially conducive for learning gross motor skills because of the relatively constant ratio between height and muscle mass and the gradual growth rate. Stress skills like running, jumping, hopping, throwing, and catching instead of overemphasizing competition.

Children have immature nervous, skeletal, and temperature regulatory systems and fragile epiphyseal bone-growth centers. Some forms of vigorous training, such as heavy weight lifting and marathon running, may be contraindicated for this age group. Definitive data about the relative risk of these activities during childhood are lacking, so it is best to be cautious.

Adolescence is a period of rapid growth accompanied by drastic changes in secondary sexual characteristics, muscle mass, fat deposition, and physical performance. The adolescent growth spurt generally begins at about 10½ to 13 years in females and 12½ to 15 years in males. The earlier maturing girls are often taller than boys of the same age, but the boys soon catch up and surpass the girls.

During the adolescent growth spurt, males' endurance, strength, speed, power, motor skills, and mass markedly improve. Females also experience a growth spurt, but their physical abilities tend to level off. Individual differences in maturation pose an increased risk to adolescent athletes. It is not unusual for prepubertal athletes to compete with those who are maturationally more advanced, even though they may be the same age.

The development of secondary sexual characteristics correlates well with the other developmental changes during puberty (Table 28-1, p. 503). Puberty is generally divided into five stages, based upon the development of pubic hair, genitalia, breasts, and facial hair. Stage 1 is the prepubertal or immature stage; stage 5 is the adult stage. Stages 2 to 4 are intermediate levels of development. Consideration of **pubertal stage** is a

Degenerative: A process of breakdown.

Catabolic: A biochemical process involving breakdown of compounds.

Puberty: The period of sexual development.

Pubertal stage: The status of sexual development as determined by the appearance and characteristics of primary and secondary sexual factors, e.g., pubic hair, breast development, and genital features.

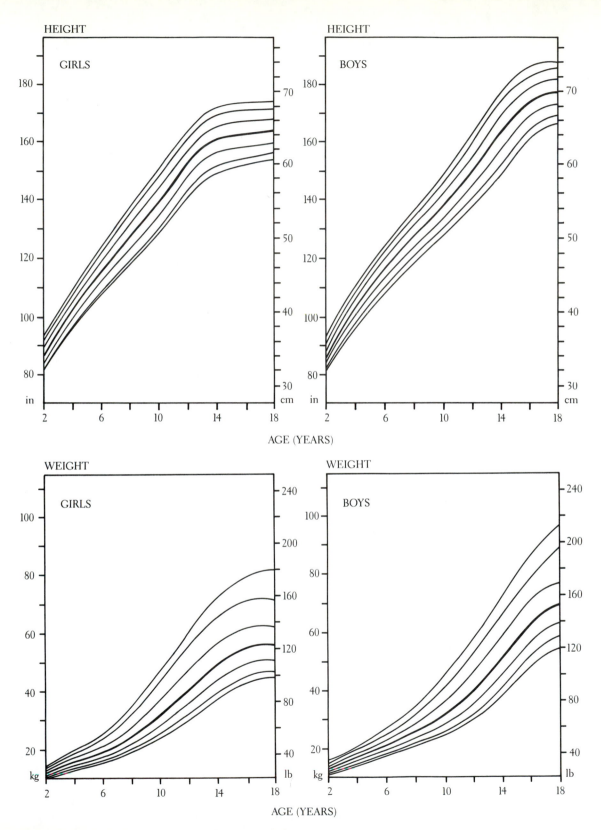

Figure 28-1 Growth charts for girls and boys two to eighteen.

Table 28-1 *Pubertal Stage Ratings for Boys and Girls*

Pubertal stage is rated on a scale of 1 to 5. Stage 1 is prepubertal development; stage 5 is the characteristics of the adult. Stages are determined by the degree of development of pubic hair in both sexes, genital development in boys, and breast development in girls.

Pubertal stage 1

Pubic hair: None.
Genital development: Testes, scrotum, and penis are of about the same size and proportions as in early childhood.
Breast development: Elevation of the papilla only.

Pubertal stage 2

Pubic hair: Sparse growth of long, slightly pigmented downy hair, straight or only slightly curled, appearing chiefly at the base of the penis or along the labia.
Genital development: Enlargement of the scrotum and testes. The skin of the scrotum reddens and changes in texture. Little or no enlargement of the penis at this stage.
Breast development: Breast bud stage; elevation of breast and papilla as small mound. Enlargement of areolar diameter.

Pubertal stage 3

Pubic hair: Considerably darker, coarser, and more curled. The hair spreads sparsely over the junction of the pubes.
Genital development: Enlargement of the penis, which occurs at first mainly in length. There is further growth of the testes and scrotum.
Breast development: Further enlargement and elevation of breast and areola, with no separation of their contours.

Pubertal stage 4

Pubic hair: Hair now resembles the adult in type, but the area covered by it is still considerably smaller than in the adult. No spread to the medial surface of the thighs.
Genital development: Increased size of the penis, with growth in breadth and development of the glans. Further enlargement of the testes and scrotum; increased darkening of scrotal skin.
Breast development: Projection of areola and papilla to form a secondary mound above the level of the breast.

Pubertal stage 5

Pubic hair: Adult in quantity and type, with distribution of the horizontal (or classically "feminine") pattern. Spread to the medial surface of the thighs but not up the linea alba or elsewhere above the base of the inverse triangle. In about 80 percent of Caucasian men and 10 percent of the women, the pubic hair spreads farther, but this takes some time to occur after stage 5 has been reached. This may not be completed until the midtwenties or later.
Genital development: Genitalia are adult in size and shape. No further enlargement takes place after stage 5 has been reached.
Breast development: This is the mature stage. There is projection of the papilla only, due to the recession of the areola to the general contour of the breast.

SOURCE: Adapted from Larson, L. *Fitness, Health, and Work Capacity.* New York: Macmillan, 1974, pp. 516–517.

reasonably accurate method of assessing relative maturation. Assessment of pubertal stage might be valuable in determining readiness for heavy training or contact sports.

The Nature of Children's Injuries

Are athletics a serious threat to young athletes? Although it is true that epiphyseal bone-growth centers are vulnerable and most aspects of a child's physiology are relatively immature, there is a surprisingly low risk of serious injury, even in contact and collision sports like football, basketball, and hockey. The injury rate for children is far less than that among high school or college athletes participating in the same sport.

There is a critical problem involved with treating injuries that do occur. Coaches are usually amateurs, with no training in first aid, and emergency medical care is often unavailable. There is also an alarming increase in the rate of overuse injuries, such as stress fractures, tendinitis of the shoulder, bursitis of the hip, and tennis elbow. The increased incidence of these overuse injuries implies overzealousness on the part of coaches and parents and poorly designed training programs.

The nature and causes of injury in children involved in competitive athletics vary with the sport. Soft tissue injuries, such as contusions, abrasions, and lacerations, are most common, followed by sprains, strains, fractures, tendinitis, and concussion. A study by Goldberg et al. showed that the knee, hand, wrist, foot, and ankle are the most common injury sites in boys and girls (Table 28-2). Boys tend to receive more head injuries than girls.

Table 28-3 shows the incidence of injury by sport in children belonging to a health maintenance organization. The largest number of injuries occurred

Table 28-2 *Distribution of Sports Injuries in Children*

Injury Site	Percentage
Knee	21.6
Hand/wrist	19.6
Foot/ankle	17.6
Head	13.7
Arm	11.8
Spine	9.8
Leg	5.9
	100.0

SOURCE: Adapted from data of Goldberg, B., P. A. Witman, G. W. Gleim, and J. A. Nicholas. Children's sports injuries: are they avoidable? *The Physician and Sportsmedicine* 7:93–101, 1979.
NOTE: Data are from boys and girls 6–16, who were treated at a sports medicine center.

in augmented speed sports, such as skateboarding; collision sports, such as football; and contact sports, such as basketball. The largest percentages of these injuries occurred in unsupervised recreational settings.

It appears that a large portion of childhood sports injuries are preventable. Goldberg and coworkers studied the problem and summarized several salient factors involved in childhood sports injuries: chance events, inadequate rehabilitation from previous injuries, poor and inadequate equipment, recklessness, environmental conditions (excessive heat or cold), inadequate supervision, and underlying predisposition (congenital anomalies). Approximately 35 percent of the injuries in their study were unavoidable, but the remainder stemmed from factors associated with the unprofessional and haphazard conduct of children's sports.

It is apparent from the injury statistics and the opinion of many experts in youth sports and **pediatrics** that a lack of concern for the individual child is an important part of the problem. Too often, the sport is considered more important than the child, as evidenced by coaches and parents who place too much emphasis upon winning, let children return to competition with injuries

Pediatrics: A branch of medicine dealing with diseases and disorders of children.

Table 28-3 *Incidence of Sports Injuries in Children*

Sport Category	Percentage
Speed sports	33.3
1. Skateboarding	
2. Ice skating	
3. Sledding	
4. Skiing	
5. Trampoline	
6. Bicycling	
Collision sports	29.4
1. Football	
2. Ice hockey	
Contact sports	27.5
1. Basketball	
2. Volleyball	
3. Soccer	
4. Baseball	
5. Field hockey	
Noncontact sports	9.8
1. Tennis	
2. Gymnastics	
3. Swimming	
4. Cross-country	
	100

SOURCE: Adapted from data of Goldberg, B., P. A. Witman, G. W. Gleim, and J. A. Nicholas. Children's sports injuries: are they avoidable? *The Physician and Sportsmedicine* 7:93–101, 1979.
NOTE: Data are from boys and girls 6–16, who were treated at a sports medicine center. Within each group, activities are listed in order of injury frequency.

that are not fully rehabilitated, let children participate when injured, and encourage an atmosphere where injuries may go unreported. Sports should be *fun* for the children!

Certainly, the services of an athletic trainer are necessary for athletic teams at this level. Currently, the only teams fortunate enough to have one are those to whom the athletic trainer has donated his or her services. Volunteer athletic trainers are only a temporary remedy; the long-term solution can only come from educating parents and physicians about the importance of these services. Ideally, funds for an athletic trainer should be incorporated into the budgets of all youth-sports teams.

Injuries and Conditions Unique to Young Athletes

The nature of specific injuries and diseases is similar in children and adults, but several conditions are unique, more prevalent, or of particular concern to children. Certain of these problems, such as asthma, mononucleosis, and chondromalacia, were discussed elsewhere. Conditions discussed here are Osgood-Schlatter disease, epiphyseal fracture, anorexia nervosa and bulimia, and menstrual problems.

Generally, children's lesser body size and muscular strength make them less susceptible to injury than older athletes. However, growth factors make children particularly susceptible to overuse injuries. The combination of immature bones and cartilage and muscle imbalances induced by the adolescent growth spurt may cause a higher incidence of overuse injury when the athlete is subjected to repetitive microtraumas. For example, patellofemoral syndromes, occurring in increasing numbers of child athletes, may be induced by this process. A laterally riding patella (see Chapter 21), softer cartilage, and training-induced overuse may combine to deform the patella. Relatively common overuse injuries in child athletes are plantar fasciitis, Achilles tendinitis, anterior leg pain, stress fracture, and patellofemoral syndromes. Treatment is the same as for adults and is discussed in the specific injury chapters.

Osgood-Schlatter Disease

Osgood-Schlatter disease—traction apophysitis of the tibial tubercle—is actually an overuse injury rather than a disease (see Chapter 21). The symptoms are pain, swelling, and tenderness around the tibial tubercle, the point of insertion of the patellar ligament. The tibial tubercle is frequently enlarged and often remains so into adulthood.

Osgood-Schlatter disease is caused by excessive stress upon and disruption to the attachment of the tibial patellar tendon. It is most common in sports involving repeated flexion and forced extension of the knee, such as soccer, weight lifting, surfing, and football. It usually afflicts girls between eight and thirteen and boys between ten and fifteen, although boys are about three times more susceptible than girls. The condition causes pain during such activities as kneeling, direct contact with objects, running, and climbing.

The athletic trainer should refer the athlete with suspected Osgood-Schlatter disease to a physician. Treatment includes rest and restriction from vigorous activities, although the condition probably will not disappear completely until after the child is fully grown. After a period of rest, the athlete may begin straight leg raises and isometrics and may benefit from electrical muscle stimulation. Mild quadriceps stretching may also be beneficial. Avoid vigorous knee extension exercises until the athlete is free of pain.

Epiphyseal Fracture

An epiphyseal fracture is a fracture to the growth plates of bones. Such fractures occur relatively infrequently, but they are particularly serious because they can lead to permanent disability from shortening and/or angular deformity of the bone. The epiphyses are particularly vulnerable in growing athletes; under experimentally applied stress, epiphyseal injuries occur before injuries to tendons, ligaments, joint capsules, or diaphyseal bone. These injuries tend to occur most frequently during the growth spurt: ten to thirteen years in girls and twelve to fifteen years in boys. Because of the possible serious consequences, suspect an epiphyseal injury whenever there is an acute injury near a joint (even if it does not appear on x-ray).

The fingers, thumbs, and great toe incur the most epiphyseal fractures; the long bones incur fewer fractures. The most serious fractures are those about the knee. Football produces the greatest number of growth plate fractures, followed by hockey, basketball, skiing, and baseball. Weight lifting causes these fractures when the weight lifted exceeds the growth plate's shear force tolerance.

Figure 28-2 depicts the Salter classification of epiphyseal fractures. Type I fractures involve only minimal epiphyseal slippage. Type II involves epiphyseal slippage accompanied by a fracture through the metaphysis. Types I and II rarely disturb growth. Type III fractures involve epiphyseal plate slippage, with an accompanying fracture through the epiphysis. Type IV fractures involve a fracture through the epiphysis, epiphyseal plate, and metaphysis. This injury requires open reduction and surgical fixation. The effects of types III and IV upon subsequent bone growth are mixed and unpredictable. These injuries seldom have an absolutely normal result. Type V epiphyseal fracture is a crushed growth plate and arrests growth.

Fortunately, about 98 percent of all epiphyseal fractures recover without complication. Rehabilitation involves minimizing inflammation and restoring range of motion, strength, and normal movement.

Anorexia Nervosa and Bulimia

Anorexia nervosa is an eating disorder characterized by a neurotic fixation upon body fat. The causes are unknown but may be from psychological stress resulting in an abnormal body image or perhaps an aberration in the appetite control center located in the

Anorexia nervosa: An eating disorder characterized by a neurotic fixation on body fat and food (not eating).

hypothalamus. Anorexia seems to occur most often in teenaged girls. This condition can be life-threatening. The resulting malnutrition causes hair loss, electrocardiographic arrhythmias, hypotension, bradycardia, and amenorrhea. Suicide is not uncommon in persons suffering from anorexia.

Some athletes with anorexia appear to eat normally but induce vomiting so that they do not absorb calories from the food. Others control energy intake by severe dietary restriction. Not surprisingly, a person with anorexia may also be a compulsive exercise enthusiast.

Steinbaugh suggested several symptoms that indicate an athlete is developing this condition: (1) dramatic weight loss, (2) amenorrhea, (3) single-minded commitment to physical effectiveness, (4) increasing but never attainable athletic goals, (5) denial of serious injury, and (6) depression if unable to exercise.

Anorexia is a very complex psychiatric disease that should not be taken lightly. The incidence of this problem is increasing, most likely from our society's emphasis upon leanness.

Bulimia, a condition characterized by eating binges followed by voluntary regurgitation of the food, is often classified as a subcategory of anorexia. However, there are marked differences between people with anorexia, who tend to shun food, and people who practice bulimia, who relish food. Anorexics who restrict dietary intake typically experience marked weight loss and amenorrhea and are obsessive about physical exercise. These people tend to be perfectionists, deny serious injury (e.g., they run even when in pain), and become extremely depressed when they cannot keep to their unrealistic diet and exercise plan. Bulimics, on the other hand, tend to be of normal weight, have more normal menses, often shun physical activity, and tend to not be as compulsive as the restrictive anorexics. Obviously, there are exceptions to these generalizations. For

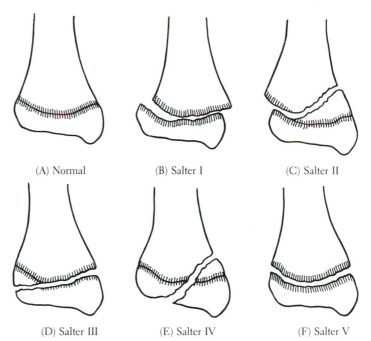

Figure 28-2 The Salter classifications of epiphyseal fractures. The crushed growth plate is usually not apparent radiologically. Within one year, part or all of the epiphysis is fused with the metaphysis. (From Benton, J. W. Epiphyseal fractures in sports. *The Physician and Sportsmedicine* 10:63–71, 1982.)

example, Kathy Rigby, the American Olympics gymnast, told the *Los Angeles Times* in an interview that she practiced bulimia for most of her athletic career. When competing, she was an extremely lean and hard-working athlete.

Menstrual Problems and Delayed Onset of Menarche

Menstrual problems, quite common in young female athletes, fall into three categories: delayed onset of menarche, amenorrhea, and dysmenorrhea. **Menarche** is the first menstruation; amenorrhea is the absence of menstruation; and dysmenorrhea is painful menstruation (see Putting It into Practice 28-1, p. 508). Amenorrhea and dysmenorrhea can occur in any premenopausal woman but are discussed here because they are often of great concern to child athletes.

Menarche is a benchmark for the

Menarche: The first menstruation.

onset of sexual maturation in the female. Menarche typically occurs after the adolescent growth spurt has peaked and pubic hair has appeared, breasts have developed, and mature patterns of fat deposition have formed. Menarche may be brought on by such factors as the attainment of a critical body weight or the concentration of a prerequisite amount of **gonadotropin hormones.**

Athletes, particularly those in high-energy sports like swimming and running, tend to reach menarche later than nonathletes. The average age for nonathletes' first menstruation is 12.9 years; for athletes', 13.1 to 14 years. Among both athletes and nonathletes, cultural differences affect menarche. Eastern European girls tend to attain menarche later than their Western counterparts; Latino-American females attain menarche earlier than Caucasian-Americans. These differences may be caused by such factors as genetics and diet.

Anorexia nervosa often occurs in athletes who participate in activities where low body fat is perceived as important, such as dancing, gymnastics, and figure skating. Malnutrition is a well-known cause of delayed menstruation. For example, the age of menarche occurred much later in European girls after both world wars because of periods of inadequate dietary protein.

Irregular menstruation is a common problem among young female athletes and has received much interest among sports medicine scientists. Amenorrhea and oligomenorrhea (reduced or irregular menstruation) with concomitant anovulation (failure to ovulate) may be related to low levels of body fat, weight loss, or chronically high energy expenditure.

The level of energy expenditure seems to be an important factor in irregular menstruation. In a study of track and cross-country runners, for example, 45 percent of women who ran more than eighty miles a week had irregular menstrual cycles. The mileage

PUTTING IT INTO PRACTICE 28-1   **Recognizing Dysmenorrhea**

- *Symptoms*: Painful menstruation.
- *Cause*: Prostaglandin F secretion from uterus; may be caused by uterine tumor, endometriosis, fibroid tumor, or pelvic inflammatory disease.
- *Treatment*: Suggest that athlete use aspirin.
- *Medical assistance*: Consult physician if symptoms persist. Physician may prescribe anti-inflammatory drugs, birth control pills, or discover and treat less obvious causes of the symptoms.

run per week seems to be an important factor in determining the degree and incidence of menstrual dysfunction. This condition is also common in women experiencing body fat losses from other causes, such as dieting and anorexia nervosa. Menstrual irregularities associated with rigorous physical training appear to be benign and reversible; the long-term effects upon fertility are not completely understood.

Irregular menstruation seems to be caused by the depression of estrogen secretion. A popular theory is that exercise training causes a reduction in fat, which may decrease the peripheral production of the estrogen hormones, which play an important role in controlling the menstrual cycle.

Painful menstruation (**dysmenorrhea**) is of more practical concern than oligomenorrhea or amenorrhea to women athletes (see Putting It into Practice 28-1) because as many as 90 percent of female athletes suffer from it. Symptoms are irritability, backache, abdominal cramps, headache, nausea, and vomiting. Because dysmenorrhea detracts from feelings of well-being, it very probably negatively affects physical performance (negative effects upon endurance and strength performance are probably caused by psychological factors).

Physical training seems to have no effect upon painful menstruation, although it appears to be less common

Gonadotropin hormones: Pituitary hormones that control reproductive function in men and women.

Dysmenorrhea: Painful menstruation.

among women athletes and physical education professional students than among physically inactive females. Various exercises have been suggested as a remedy for dysmenorrhea, but many physicians successfully use antiprostaglandin drugs, such as Motrin, to treat this disorder.

Prostaglandin F has been implicated in dysmenorrhea because it initiates gastrointestinal and uterine contractions. Some experts feel that the incidence and severity of this condition depend more upon psychological factors. In most cases, dysmenorrhea should not prevent a young woman from competing in sports. The athletic trainer can do little to prevent or treat dysmenorrhea but can suggest aspirin, provide psychological support, and refer the athlete to a physician if symptoms are severe.

Preventing Injuries in Young Athletes

Young athletes are particularly susceptible to a variety of injuries, including overuse syndromes, hyperthermia, hypothermia, and epiphyseal damage (Figure 28-3). The principles of injury prevention and treatment apply to all ages, but the following basic principles are particularly important for younger athletes:

- Closely monitor the intensity and duration of the young athlete's training program. Seriously consider complaints of fatigue, aches and pains, and feelings of depression and psychological pressures. Young athletes often go to great lengths to impress coaches and parents, and they may not complain about an ailment until the discomfort is severe (see Box 28-1, p. 510).
- Do not initiate serious weight training until the child is sixteen

Figure 28-3 Heavy weight training is contraindicated in children because of a possible increased risk of epiphyseal injury, even among children with obvious athletic talent.

or seventeen (recommendation of the American Academy of Pediatrics). Heavy training before this age may cause epiphyseal damage. This is a controversial position, with little experimental or clinical evidence to support it. Certainly athletes can improve strength through resistive exercise before they are skeletally mature, but the possible risks make vigorous weight training contraindicated.
- Children's temperature regulatory capacity is not as well developed as that of adults (see Chapter 25). When children are exercising in the heat, take extra care to ensure that they receive plenty of fluids and that the intensity and duration of exercise are not excessive.
- When exercising in the cold, children should wear enough clothing to keep warm. An adult should be careful to *not* judge whether a child is cold by the way the adult

BOX 28-1   Long-Distance Running Risks for Children

The American Academy of Pediatrics has not yet established guidelines for distance running for children. Medical documentation of injury to children running long distances is limited and largely anecdotal. The long-term psychological consequences of unrealistic goals in distance running, as well as other aerobic exercise, are not fully documented (though they can be expected to approximate the consequences of other parental- and peer-pressure situations). Yet some things are known, and even without established guidelines and extensive documentation, physicians can give children, parents, and coaches advice that fosters healthy physical and psychological growth.

Reports on a limited number of patients have suggested that children may acquire heel cord injuries, epiphyseal growth plate injuries, and other chronic joint trauma from long-distance running. Children have been shown to tolerate hypothermia or hyperthermic environmental extremes poorly during training or long-distance running. However, cardiovascular adaptation similar to that occurring in adults has been shown to occur in growing children training for long distances.

Lifetime involvement in a sport often depends on the type of early participation and gratification gained. Psychological problems can result from unrealistic goals for distance running by children. A child who participates in distance running primarily for parental gratification may tire of this after a time and quit, or the child may continue, chafing under the parental pressure. In either case, psychological damage may be done, and the child may be discouraged, either immediately or in the long run, from participating in sports. A prepubertal child should be allowed to participate for the enjoyment of running without fear of parental or peer rejection or pressure. A child's sense of accomplishment, satisfaction, and appreciation by peers, parents, and coaches will foster involvement in running and other sports during childhood and in later life.

Long-distance competitive running events primarily designed for adults are not recommended for children prior to physical maturation. Under no circumstances should a full marathon be attempted by immature youths (less than Tanner Stage 5 sexual maturity rating). After pubertal development is complete, guidelines for adult distance running are appropriate.

SOURCE: American Academy of Pediatrics. Risks in long-distance running for children. *The Physician and Sportsmedicine* 10(8):82, 86, 1982.

feels; a child may be experiencing significant cold stress while the adult feels fine. Children have a higher body-surface-to-tissue ratio than adults, so they tend to lose body heat at a faster rate. In addition, children do not have the same capacity to generate heat through shivering as do adults.

• Do not let an injured player participate until the injury has healed and has been rehabilitated. No athletic contest or practice is important enough to jeopardize a young athlete's health. Follow the guidelines in Chapter 12 for returning to participation after an injury.

• Discourage unsafe athletic practices. Many coaches of youth sports are untrained and unqualified and sometimes recommend unsafe practices, such as spear tackling, excessive training programs, and forced dehydration. The athletic trainer should insist that these unsafe practices be stopped. Encourage youth coaches to improve their knowledge through participation in programs such as the American Coaching Effectiveness Program (contact

Human Kinetics Publishing, Champaign, Ill. for more information).

The Older Athlete

The popularity of masters sports has increased the athletic trainer's exposure to older athletes. In general, their injuries are no different than those of the high school or college athlete. However, the athletic trainer should be aware of certain problems:

1. Masters athletes often have a number of inadequately rehabilitated injuries that have developed over a lifetime. These injuries may profoundly affect the athlete's training and injury-management programs.
2. Older athletes may be suffering from degenerative diseases such as atherosclerosis and arthritis that may demand a modification of the competitive training program (see Putting It into Practice 28-2 and 28-3).
3. Aging definitely affects the adaptation rate to training. Often the older athlete must be protected from overzealous training programs (usually self-induced).
4. The "healing time" following an injury is often longer.

The Effects of Aging

Aging is characterized by the body's diminished capacity to regulate its internal environment. It appears that no matter how well people take care of themselves, their physiological processes eventually fall prey to the ravages of old age. Even the most conscientious athletes can expect slowed reaction time, impaired resistance to disease, diminished work capacity, prolonged recovery from effort, and increased risk of musculoskeletal injury.

PUTTING IT INTO PRACTICE 28-2 — **Recognizing Osteoarthritis**

- *Symptoms*: Chronic progressive stiffness in one or more joints. Joint pain is most prevalent with overuse.
- *Cause*: Degeneration of cartilage and articular surfaces from injury, wear and tear, and aging. Older athletes should consult physician.
- *Treatment*: Rest and heat during active phases. Mobility must be maintained, or condition tends to worsen at a faster rate. Control pain with aspirin or anti-inflammatory drugs.

PUTTING IT INTO PRACTICE 28-3 — **Recognizing Myocardial Infarction**

- *Symptoms*: Angina, dyspnea, nausea, vomiting, sweating, syncope. Results in death of myocardial cells.
- *Cause*: Relative lack of blood flow to myocardium from atherosclerosis, coronary thrombosis, or coronary vasospasm.
- *Treatment*: Call ambulance and administer CPR if appropriate (see Chapter 10).

Peak physiological function generally occurs at about thirty years, with most factors declining 0.75 to 1 percent a year. The decline in physical capacity is characterized by a decrease in maximal oxygen consumption, maximal cardiac output, muscle strength and power, neural function, and flexibility, and increased body fat. Although remarkable levels of performance can be achieved throughout life, even the most diligent athlete can expect a continuous decline during middle and old age. Exercise does not retard the aging process; it just allows the individual to perform at a higher level of performance.

Maximal oxygen consumption drops approximately 30 percent between the ages of twenty and sixty-five because of decreases in the heart's ability to pump blood and the tissues' ability to extract oxygen. This decrease is also evident in the chronically active individual (the active individual will continue to have a higher maximal oxygen consumption than the sedentary person). However, even though cardiovascular fitness deteriorates with age, a person who begins training in middle age can expect to improve.

Aging is associated with demineralization of bone (see Chapter 6), which is a serious problem, particularly among postmenopausal women. Exercise that places longitudinal stress on the long bones, such as walking and running, has been shown to slow down or reverse this process. Bone may become thicker with exercise. **Osteoporosis** is of concern in the elderly because of the increased risk of fracture. With the increased participation of women in their sixties and seventies in masters sports, osteoporosis may be a problem.

Joints become more unstable with age. Aging tends to degrade collagen fibers and fibrous synovial membranes, deteriorate joint surfaces, and decrease the viscosity of synovial fluid. It is absolutely essential that the older athlete maintain range of motion through stretching and mobility exercise.

Characteristics of Masters Athletes

Masters athletes, particularly the successful ones, are considerably more fit than other men and women of their age. They tend to have less fat, more muscle, lower resting and submaximal exercise heart rates, lower resting blood pressure, and fewer abnormalities as revealed on an electrocardiogram. However, injuries are a significant problem with these older athletes. Shephard and Kavanagh surveyed track and field athletes participating in the masters World championship and found that 57 percent had suffered an injury sufficient to interrupt training during the previous year. Of those injured, one-third were affected for more than four weeks.

Sprinters and middle-distance runners tended to have a slightly higher rate of injury than distance runners. Although the incidence of abnormal electrocardiograms was less than that for sedentary persons of the same age, the results of approximately 12 percent of those tested suggested the presence of coronary artery disease.

Safeguarding the Masters Athlete

Although masters athletes tend to be healthier than sedentary persons of the same age (with respect to performance characteristics), they are certainly not immune to degenerative diseases and the impaired function that accompanies aging. The safety and enjoyment of sports and exercise can be enhanced for older athletes by ensuring that the athletes are properly evaluated before training, have rehabilitated old injuries before pursuing vigorous training for competition, understand the importance of gradual and consistent conditioning, and adhere to the basic principles of training.

The older athlete should obtain a thorough medical and physical performance evaluation before beginning the training program. This evaluation should include an exercise stress test, during which the electrocardiogram and blood pressure are monitored. The test can be used to determine appropriate training heart rates, which will minimize the risk of injury when the training program begins. It is well known that strenuous exercise in an older, coronary-prone, deconditioned individual can precipitate a myocardial infarction or sudden death. A thorough evaluation before the onset of serious training may prevent a tragedy.

Any existing injuries the participant has should be identified and rehabilitated. If rehabilitation is not possible (because of severe degeneration or other causes), modify movement patterns to prevent further injury. This process re-

Osteoporosis: A bone disease characterized by loss of bone matrix; most common in postmenopausal women.

quires a careful analysis of the specific movements that produce the symptom. For example, encourage an athlete suffering from deterioration of the patello-femoral articular surfaces to follow the patellar-protection program discussed in Chapter 21 (straight leg raises, restricted-range knee extensions, electrical muscle stimulation, avoiding patellofemoral compression, etc.).

The athlete should understand the importance of year-round conditioning. Too often, the masters athlete enters a competition without properly preparing for it, which can be dangerous. A training diary is a good tool for instilling habits of consistent and systematic conditioning (see Chapter 4). Encourage athletes to plan the training program in advance rather than training by whim.

Older athletes should be particularly diligent about warm-up and stretching. It has been shown that inadequate warm-up increases the incidence of abnormalities recorded on the electro-cardiogram. Stretching is important for maintaining joint range of motion, which tends to decrease with age.

References

Adams, G., and H. DeVries. Physiological effects of an exercise training regimen upon women aged 52–79. *Journal of Gerontology* 28:50–55, 1973.

Albinson, J. G., and G. M. Andrew. *Child in Sport and Physical Activity*. Baltimore: University Park Press, 1976.

American Academy of Pediatrics Committee on Sports Medicine. Risks in long-distance running for children. *The Physician and Sportsmedicine* 10:82, 86, 1982.

Astrand, P. O. Human physical fitness with special reference to sex and age. *Physiological Reviews* 36:307–335, 1956.

Barnard, J., G. Grimditch, and J. Wilmore. Physiological characteristics of sprint and endurance runners. *Medicine and Science in Sports and Exercise* 11:167–171, 1979.

Barnes, L. Preadolescent training—how young is too young? *The Physician and Sportsmedicine* 7:114–119, 1979.

Benton, J. W. Epiphyseal fractures in sports. *The Physician and Sportsmedicine* 10:63–71, 1982.

Bortz, W. M. Effect of exercise on aging—effect of aging on exercise. *Journal of the American Geriatric Society* 28:49–51, 1980.

Clarke, H. H. (ed.). Individual differences, their nature, extent and significance. *Physical Fitness Research Digest* ser. 4 (4), 1973.

Daniels, J., N. Oldridge, F. Nagle, and B. White. Differences and changes in VO_2 max among young runners 10 to 18 years of age. *Medicine and Science in Sports and Exercise* 10:200–203, 1978.

Dehn, M. M., and R. A. Bruce. Longitudinal variations in maximal oxygen uptake with age and activity. *Journal of Applied Physiology* 33:805–807, 1972.

DeVries, H. Physiological effects of an exercise training program regimen upon men aged 52 to 88. *Journal of Gerontology* 25:325–336, 1970.

DeVries, H. Tips on prescribing exercise regimens for your older patient. *Geriatrics* 35:75–81, 1979.

Dressendorfer, R. H. Physiological profile of a masters runner. *The Physician and Sportsmedicine* 8:49–52, 1980.

Eriksson, B. Muscle metabolism in children—a review. *Acta Paediatrica Scandinavica* supp. 283:20–28, 1980.

Eriksson, O., and B. Saltin. Muscle metabolism during exercise in boys aged 11 to 16 years compared to adults. *Acta Paediatrica Belgium* supp. 28:257–265, 1974.

Fahey, T. D. *Good-Time Fitness for Kids*. New York: Butterick Publishing, 1979.

Fahey, T. D. *What to Do About Athletic Injuries*. New York: Butterick Publishing, 1979.

Fahey, T. D., A. DelValle-Zuris, G. Oehlsen, M. Trieb, and J. Seymour. Pubertal stage differences in hormonal and hematological responses to maximal exercise in males. *Journal of Applied Physiology* 46:823–827, 1979.

Harvey, J. S. Overuse syndromes in young athletes. *Pediatric Clinics of North America* 29:1369–1381, 1982.

Kasch, F. W. The effects of exercise on the aging process. *The Physician and Sportsmedicine* 4:64–68, 1976.

Klissouras, V. Prediction of athletic performance: genetic considerations. *Canadian Journal of Applied Sport Science* 1:195–200, 1976.

Klissouras, V., F. Pirnay, and J. Petit. Adaptation to maximal effort: genetics and age. *Journal of Applied Physiology* 35:288–203, 1973.

Komi, P. V., and J. Karlsson. Physical performance, skeletal muscle enzyme activities, and fibre types in monozygous and dizygous twins of both sexes. *Acta Physiologica Scandinavica* supp. 462, 1979.

Larson, L. (ed.). *Fitness, Health, and Work Capacity.* New York: Macmillan, 1974, pp. 435–450, 516–524.

Legwold, G. Does lifting weights harm a prepubescent athlete? *The Physician and Sportsmedicine* 10:141–144, 1982.

Macek, M., J. Vavra, and J. Novosadova. Prolonged exercise in prepubertal boys. I: Cardiovascular and metabolic adjustment. *European Journal of Applied Physiology* 35:291–298, 1976.

Malina, R. M. Growth and development: the first twenty years in man. Minneapolis: Burgess, 1975.

Malina, R. M. "Growth, Maturation, and Human Performance," in *Perspectives on the Academic Discipline of Physical Education*, G. A. Brooks, ed. Champaign, Ill.: Human Kinetics, 1981, pp. 190–210.

Micheli, L. J., K. Kassabian, E. Grace, J. Kirkpatrick, L. LeChabrier, and E. Lincoln. Sports in childhood: a roundtable discussion. *The Physician and Sportsmedicine* 10:52–60, 1982.

Mital, M. A., and R. A. Matza. Osgood-Schlatter disease: the painful puzzler. *The Physician and Sportsmedicine* 5:60–73, 1977.

Moller, P. Skeletal muscle adaptation to aging and to respiratory and liver failure. *Acta Medica Scandinavica* supp. 654:1–40, 1981.

Murase, Y., K. Kobayashi, S. Kamei, and H. Matsui. Longitudinal study of aerobic power in superior junior athletes. *Medicine and Science in Sports and Exercise* 13:180–184, 1981.

Nicholas, J. A., and M. J. Friedman. Orthopedic problems in middle-aged athletes. *The Physician and Sportsmedicine* 7:39–46, 1979.

Niinimaa, V., and R. J. Shephard. Training and oxygen conductance in the elderly. *Journal of Gerontology* 33:354–367, 1978.

Ogden, J. A. *Skeletal Injury in the Child.* Philadelphia: Lea & Febiger, 1982.

Orlander, J., and A. Aniansson. Effects of physical training on skeletal muscle metabolism and ultrastructure. *Acta Physiologica Scandinavica* 109:149–154, 1980.

Rarick, G. L. "The Emergence of the Study of Human Motor Development," in *Perspectives on the Academic Discipline of Physical Education*, Brooks, G. A., ed. Champaign, Ill.: Human Kinetics, 1981, pp. 163–184.

Rarick, G. L. (ed.). *Physical Activity: Human Growth and Development.* New York: Academic Press, 1973.

Saltin, B., and G. Grimby. Physiological analysis of middle-aged and former athletes. *Circulation* 38:1104–1115, 1968.

Saltin, B., L. Hartley, A. Kilbom, and I. Astrand. Physical training in sedentary middle-aged and older men. *Scandinavian Journal of Clinical & Laboratory Investigation* 24:323–334, 1969.

Shangold, M. "Gynecological and Endocrinological Factors," in *Sports Medicine for the Female Athlete*, C. E. Haycock, ed. Oradell, N.J.: Medical Economics, 1980, pp. 315–329.

Shepard, R. *Physical Activity and Aging.* Chicago: Year Book Medical Publishers, 1978.

Shephard, R. J., and T. Kavanagh. The effects of training on the aging process. *The Physician and Sportsmedicine* 6:33–40, 1978.

Sidney, K., and R. J. Shepard. Frequency and intensity of exercise training for elderly subjects. *Medicine and Science in Sports and Exercise* 10:125–131, 1978.

Smith, E., and R. Serfass (eds.). *Exercise and Aging.* Hillside, N.J.: Enslow Publishers, 1981.

Steinbaugh, M. Nutritional needs of female athletes. *Clinic Sports Medicine* 3:649–670, 1984.

Suominen, H., E. Heikkinen, T. Parkatti, S. Forsberg, and A. Kiiskinen. Effects of lifelong physical training and functional aging in men. *Scandinavian Journal of Social Medicine* supp. 14:225–240, 1980.

Timaris, P. S. *Developmental Physiology and Aging.* New York: Macmillan, 1972.

Appendix:
Athletic Uses of
Adhesive Tape

Adhesive tape in the prevention and treatment of athletic injuries

Introduction

There is no doubt that there are a number of broad and varied uses for athletic adhesive tape not all related to injury prevention or treatment. We have all seen athletic adhesive tape used for: name tags on lockers, shirts, football helmets; to tie down lids on boxes; to seal the twisted end of a trash bag; to improve the grip on a baseball bat; to prevent socks from sliding down; as a temporary splint on a cracked crutch or cane; and as a patch over the tear on the fabric of a tackling dummy or a small hole in the toe of a sock. These are but a few items in an almost endless list of imaginative and innovative uses. However, athletic adhesive tape is also used quite effectively for:

1) a technique for the temporary or permanent closure of lacerations

2) the prevention of blisters on areas of skin exposed to repeated friction

3) holding bandages, protective pads, dressings, and splinting devices in place

4) secure splinting for small fractures

5) support of the bony anatomy and relieving stress on adjacent or supportive soft tissue

6) restriction of motion to support and eliminate stress on ligamentous tissue

7) restriction of motion and compression to support muscle, tendon injuries or stress.

The latter group of uses incorporate the basic "tenet of taping" and that is that all taping is based on common sense with a sound understanding of the anatomy and kinesiology of the parts involved and an accurate assessment of the problem and/or injury. Therefore, it's then easy to understand what must be protected, restricted or supported. With this information, the basic taping procedure can be applied with adjustments and refinements being made through trial and error and assisted by feedback from the athlete.

Small lacerations may be repaired by using commercially available preparations that are known as butterfly dressings or tape sutures. One variety has a latex base adhesive mass, and the second, a hypoallergenic acrylic adhesive mass. The edges of skin surrounding the wound are prepared by applying tape adherent in a wide area around the wound. When the tape adherent is dried, the tape sutures are pulled across the laceration bringing the edges of the wound together. The first strip should be applied in the middle of the laceration and then subsequent strips applied by working out toward the periphery. Diagonal tape sutures can be applied across the wound for additional support and a sterile dressing applied over the tape sutures.

The blister is a not infrequent and an annoying injury in sport, and there are certain areas that are more predisposed to blister formation as a result of friction over the surface of the skin. Many of us have experienced the blister on the thumb as a result of raking leaves in the garden. Blisters occur on the heel of the hand in squash, tennis, and baseball players, on the fingers and hands of crewmen, and on the toes and feet of runners, and in those athletes involved in soccer, basketball, and football.

The blister may be prevented on those susceptible areas by preparing the skin in advance. To do this: *1) paint the area with tape adherent, and 2) apply a piece of adhesive tape to cover the entire area.* This piece of tape may be left in place or reapplied daily, and moleskin may be substituted for the adhesive tape.

The discomfort and disability of a new or existing blister may be eliminated completely, allowing the blister to heal and still permitting the athlete to participate. A very simple procedure to use is as follows: *1) clean the area thoroughly, 2) apply a quantity of specially prepared skin lubricant or petrolatum directly over the denuded blistered area, 3) paint the area of skin around the blister with tape adherent, 4) place a pledget of cotton over the skin lubricant to completely cover the area, 5) use moleskin or elastic or nonelastic adhesive tape to cover the cotton pledget and seal the edges.* This then provides a friction-free surface by keeping the lubricant and padding in place. Some might like to use a doughnut of moleskin, foam rubber or felt on top of the pledget or around the blistered area.

Securing sterile dressing or bandages in the athletic setting. The dressings for wounds in sport must be held down firmly enough to withstand the effects of the vigorous motion and perspiration that will attempt to pull them away. Many times circumferential taping is necessary to hold a dressing in place, and in these instances, elastic tape is an ideal anchor for it allows the expansion of muscles as they contract. It is equally important to exercise the same precautions when fitting and applying protective padding and/or splints. Certainly a protective pad is going to be of little value if it shifts from the site it's intended to protect. It is always best to tape directly to the skin, and in this case a tape adherent is applied to the skin before the pad or splint is taped in position. An alternative method is to use an adhesive tape underwrap to hold the pad in position, and then use adhesive tape over top of the underwrap.

When underwrap is used, it is important that tape adherent also be used on the skin so that the underwrap adheres to the skin and, in fact, acts as a second skin. Elastic tape is again a very useful tool in holding down the protective pads and/or splints. This allows for movement and expansion of muscle on contraction. There is one precaution, however, and that is that the free end of elastic tape tends to peel so it is necessary then to secure this end with a circumferential piece of non elastic cloth tape. It's also important to bear in mind that contact and the abrasion of synthetic surfaces are much harder on tape procedures than natural grass surfaces. Therefore, what might be considered a satisfactory taping procedure to hold down a pad or splint in a natural turf setting would be inadequate on a synthetic surface, and additional taping must be used.

Small fractures (incomplete or avulsion) of the metacarpals and/or phalanges can be supported by adhesive tape procedures. These are applied in such a manner as to be effective splints with little or no motion occurring at the fracture site. Certainly, if the fracture cam be controlled in this manner, it is a useful procedure in those sports where any hard or unyielding substance applied to the part is illegal. Adhesive tape is used in the treatment of nasal fractures before and/or after reduction, and it is also effective in taping stress fractures of the metatarsals. In this procedure successive strips of tape applied longitudinally along the dorsum of the foot, carried around the lateral border to the plantar surface, a diagonal pattern of the interlocking reinforcing strips, and an arch support taping. For many, this taping procedure has proved to be effective in reducing the discomfort associated with a stress fracture of the metatarsal to an acceptable level and allowed participation. Thus, the athlete may be functional while his fracture is, in fact, healing.

The support of the bony anatomy and architecture as well as the control of the stresses in adjacent connective and supportive soft tissue is directed primarily to the bones of the foot and ankle. The stresses associated with running cause marked tissue overuse with resultant myositis, tendonitis, fasciitis, and synovitis. An adhesive strapping for the plantar fascia can reduce the discomfort associated with plantar fasciitis, as well as reducing the pull on its attachment to the calcaneus (plantar calcaneal spurs). This same arch taping can also reduce the stresses on the posterior tibialis

tendon and control the discomfort associated with the tendonitis of this muscle tendon unit (shin splints). An adhesive strapping for the Achille's tendon (pictured later in the text) can reduce and overcome the discomfort associated with an Achille's tendonitis, and allow participation within the level of the symptom-complex. A heel-lift and ankle taping to restrict full plantar flexion can reduce the symptoms associated with myositis of the anterior tibialis muscle.

Frank sprains of the ligaments of the foot and ankle can be treated and protected by supportive adhesive strapping. Although sprains of the joints of the fingers and thumb are most common in sports, ankle taping procedures seem to be given most of our attention. This is probably because of the degree and extent of disability after injury. A significant degree of protection can be afforded by protective taping and/or wrapping. The ankle is usually the only joint protected by regular and routine preventive taping and wrapping, although we do see a great deal more being done on fingers, thumbs and wrists as a preventive action. The adhesive taping does not eliminate motion but limits the excessive motions that overcome the elastic limits of the ligament and produce the injury. For this reason it is possible to allow parti-cipation while ligament is healing due to injury, and still protect the part. It is said that adhesive taping can be so expertly applied that in essence it can result in a flexible cast. It is in this area of the use of adhesive tape that the "tenet of taping"applies most strongly.

Supportive strapping for sprains is a universal supplement to the treatment and re-habilitation programs of joint injury. The support allows a maximization of functional activity in a graduated program so that adequate healing and a return of functional capability are achieved at the same time. It is important here to point out that during the rehabilitation program, there should be no activity that produces pain, either immediate or delayed.

There is a feeling that some muscle tendon strains can be made more comfortable or functional through the use of routine taping procedure. A snug taping around the forearm may reduce the discomfort of a lateral epicon-dylitis (tennis elbow). A snug taping around the leg may reduce discomfort of anterior or posterior tibial tendonitis or myositis (shin splints). A snug taping around the upper thigh may reduce the symptoms of a hamstring strain and allow participation. A snug wrapping and taping around the groin and back (hip spica) will reduce the discomfort of a "groin strain" (a strain of the rectus femoris, sartorious, iliopsoas, or hip adductors).

The supposition is that a tight wrap will reduce the pull at that point of the muscle belly or at its attachment and will reduce the level of discomfort. A trial taping will dictate which procedure will be used and if, in fact, it proves to be helpful, will continue to be used.

Supportive and specialty tapes are the two prime categories of adhesive tapes used by the athletic trainer. Uses for the specialty tapes have already been described. The adhesive tape used for supportive procedures is a two-component material consisting of a backcloth and an adhesive mass. The backcloth may be elastic or nonelastic, and the adhesive mass may be a latex base or an acrylic base. The tapes vary in tensile strength with some, elastic as well as nonelastic, able to be hand torn while others, always elastic, need to be cut by scissors. The specialty tapes that are used from time to time by the athletic trainer are plastic or a synthetic fiber with acrylic adhesive masses or of a cellulose backing commonly referred to as paper tape. Most of these specialty tapes will have a hypoallergenic adhesive mass.

Supportive adhesive tapes are available in a variety of widths so it is a matter of choice for the athletic trainer to select the type of adhesive tape that will be required for the support, as well as the various sizes that will be utilized. It should be pointed out here that the adhesive tape should be stored in a cool, relatively dry place. High temperatures above 70-75°F will start to alter the character and consistency of the latex adhesive masses, increasing the unwind tension on the roll, and making the tape very difficult to work with. Therefore, tape should be kept in a cool place and in its containers for as long as possible and not exposed to direct or constant airflow and high temperature.

The best stabilization is achieved when the tape is applied directly to the skin. The application of tape adherent to the skin enhances adhesion and increases the length of time the taping is effective. It is important to inspect and check the tape procedure at the conclusion of the practice session or game to ensure that stability and control are present. If not, then there is a question as to when the tape procedure became ineffective. All too often, poor work or skimping on material will result in inadequate stabilization. This is a waste of time and materials and can also give misleading statistics if record keeping indicates that a player was injured while taped. If for some reason it is necessary or desirable to use a tape under-

wrap, apply the tape adherent liberally to the skin. The underwrap will then adhere and act as a second skin to maximize adhesion in this compromised situation. Additionally, tape pads, with a bit of lubricant applied, may be placed in areas of stress or irritation to reduce the incidence of skin irritation or abrasion.

Tearing adhesive tape is a very simple procedure to learn that is often complicated by an appearance that the tape is twisted, or that a fingernail is used to start the tear. Neither of these techniques is useful. The adhesive tape is held firmly on each side of the point of the proposed tear line and the free end is pulled away at an angle so that the force crosses the lines of the fabric of the backcloth at a sharp angle (figure 1). The tear then occurs sequen-

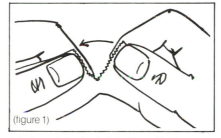

(figure 1)

tially through the backcloth (figure 2). The more quickly and deftly this maneuver is done, the more even will be the edges of the torn tape.

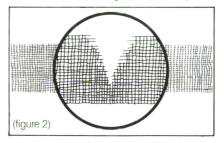

(figure 2)

Increased tensile strength of tape may be achieved by one of three techniques. The first is to fold over the leading edge of the tape (figure 3). This increases the tear resistance on

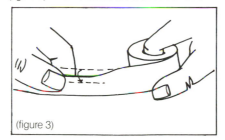

(figure 3)

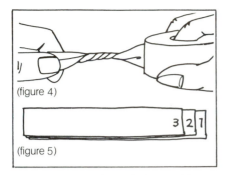

(figure 4)

(figure 5)

that edge. A second is to twist the tape into a cord (figure 4). The third method is layering and that is to use successive pieces of tape in exact overlap to increase the tensile strength in an area of stress (figure 5). This layered strip of tape can be then used as a basic support strip.

Some pitfalls the novice taper can avoid. One is that the folding of an edge as a positive action to increase the tear resistance of tape can be done inadvertently by the taper by twisting the tape as he attempts to execute a tear. Nothing is more embarrassing than to tug away and have nothing happen to the tape. If this should occur, use scissors or merely roll out another inch or two of tape and attempt the tear at a fresh point on the edge. A second is that turning corners over irregular anatomy with nonelastic tape is a difficult task for the novice and to have the tape smooth and wrinkle free. The nonelastic tape cannot be used to turn contour corners abruptly. The turns must be anticipated and gradual changes in the angle of pull effected. This becomes more apparent as the width of the adhesive tape used is greater. Additionally, the novice concentrates on the pattern of the procedure and applies uneven or inadequate pressure thus producing wrinkles. The effect of too little or too loose an adhesive taping procedure has already been pointed out.

Excessive pressure over bony prominences may not be felt immediately, but will give rise to an aching discomfort as the time that the tape is on is extended. Similarly, excessive tightness around soft tissue parts may cause impedence of venous and lymphatic return, restriction of arterial flow, and a concomitant reduction of neural transmission (the part goes to sleep).

Blisters may be caused by excessive traction on a portion of the skin for a prolonged period of time. This is most common at the upper and lower limits of an adhesive taping procedure of the ankle, the knee, and even the thorax (ribs). The reason for this is that excessive tension is applied to the tape beginning with the edge of attachment causing an ischemia at that point. It is better to adhere the first few inches before traction is applied to the tape and to utilize anchor strips for help to minimize this effect. A special caution to those who tape over prewrap. Remember that the best adhesion is between skin and tape. If the taping procedure extends beyond the prewrap, the traction will be greatest there, and the risk of blister formation is increased. Therefore, apply the adhesive tape procedure within the limits of the underwrap.

Easy removal of adhesive tape is accomplished by using bandage scissors or a specially constructed tape cutter. A bit of lubricant (petrolatum or skin lubricant) on the blunt edge of the scissors or cutter will allow it to slide under the edge of the tape with ease. Move the scissors or cutter along the natural channels or in areas of greatest soft tissue cushion, and avoid bony prominences. Peel the tape off directly back against itself at an angle as close to 180 degrees as possible. Careful observation while removing the tape will allow one to stop if there appears to be evidence of blistering or skin being pulled off with tape. Cut around these areas and remove the tape carefully. This is especially true on the sole of the foot where the adhesion of the tape can be quite strong and the callous tissue may be stripped away with the tape. If this should begin to occur, stop, and pull the tape from the opposite direction. Alcohol will remove the residue of tape adherent, and tape remover will remove any of the adhesive mass that remains on the skin. An ordinary skin cream may be used to keep the skin in good condition. If irritation due to repeated tapings does, in fact, occur, various topical ointments and preparations may be prescribed and prewrap may be used until the skin is healed.

Before beginning any taping procedure, put the athlete in a comfortable position so that he can maintain his position until the procedure is finished. Do not allow the athlete to test the taping before it is completed or immediately after taping, for the interlocking of pieces and the adhesion is increased with time, pressure and an increase in temperature. The fresh tape procedure is easily loosened; consequently, some athletic trainers will cover the taping procedure with an elastic pressure bandage to enhance the "set" until it is time to go to the field or court.

One last precaution; select a comfortable table height and position yourself to be in a good postural alignment to minimize strain and fatigue.

Basic Ankle Strapping

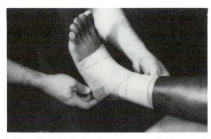

1 - The athlete's skin has been prepared in the usual manner and a layer of underwrap material has been applied. 1½" width tape will be used, although as the taper becomes more proficient, 2" may be used on individuals with larger ankles. The athlete is positioned comfortably on the table, the leg extended, the foot in neutral (neither turned in or out) and dorsiflexed (toes to nose) slightly to approximately a 90° angle.

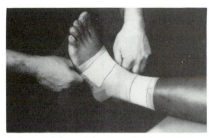

4 - Care must be exercised here that the tension is not so great as to cause discomfort to the athlete when walking, during running, in practice or a game situation. The overlap in adhesive taping is usually one-half to two-thirds of the previous strip. The two upper anchors and two lower anchors have been applied. This delineates the area of the preventive ankle taping.

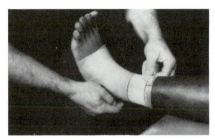

2 - The first strip of tape is applied around the leg above the ankle. This is the first of two anchor strips. The leg at this point is not cylindrically shaped; therefore, the tape must be angled slightly. This slight angling allows the tape to conform smoothly to the shape of the leg.

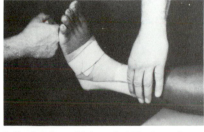

5 - The first stirrup strip is applied. It begins on the medial (inside) aspect of the ankle and continues down, over and behind the medial malleolus, under the foot and arch, up the lateral (outside) aspect of the foot, over and behind the lateral malleolus, and torn off at the upper anchor.

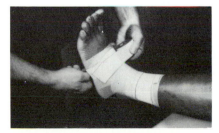

3 - Two more anchors are applied at the arch; the first is applied over the hook of the fifth metatarsal. The tape is applied quite snugly, but not so tightly as to compromise circulation, or exert undue pressure on the hook of the fifth metatarsal.

First Stirrup Begins Here...

and Ends Here

6 - This illustration demonstrates the first stirrup application.

Basic Ankle Strapping
(continued)

7 - The first horizontal strip is started on the medial (inside) aspect of the lower anchor, carried over and below the medial malleolus, behind the Achilles tendon...

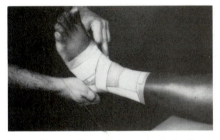

8 - brought around the ankle to over and below the lateral malleolus, carried across the dorsum (upper part) of the foot, and torn off where the strip was started.

9 - We now have one stirrup and one horizontal strip applied.

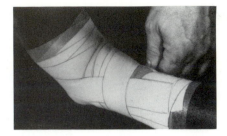

10 - Successive sets of interlocking stirrups and horizontal strips are applied, again overlapping the tape one-half to two-thirds of its width. The tape should be in smooth conformity with a little wrinkling, with snug tension, all pieces overlapped and joined.

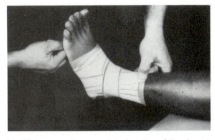

11 - We see now the completed portion of the closed basket weave with four sets of interlocking stirrups and horizontal strips.

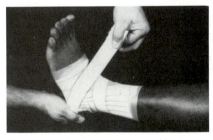

12 - The heel lock strip is begun by attaching the tape to the lateral (outside) aspect of the heel, coming across the dorsum (top) of the foot...

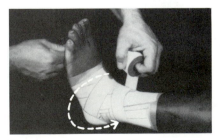

13 - angling underneath the arch to come up on the outside of the heel, progress behind the heel to come up over and above the medial malleolus...

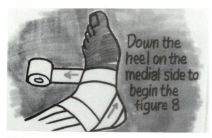

14 - traverse around the ankle and then come down the inside of the heel to come under the arch up just anterior to the lateral malleolus which is the beginning of the figure-eight pattern.

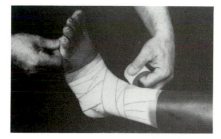

15 - Continue around the ankle and back to our starting point, which then has completed the figure-of-eight.

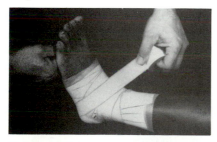

16 - The figure-eight pattern has been completed, the tape pulled up the heel on the outside to begin the spiral up the leg.

17 - The spiral is completed and the tape is torn off. What we have done with this strip of tape is given a lateral heel lock and a figure-of-eight support to our closed basket weave. The tape then is continued up in spiral fashion until we have passed the portion of the lower leg that is a cylinder.

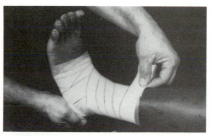

18 - A new strip is applied in the angle fashion at the upper end of the taping procedure. This is a finish strip that ties in all of the ends.

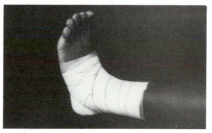

19 - For additional support, more heel locks may be applied. In fact, a medial heel lock may be utilized, beginning on the medial aspect of the heel and using the same pattern as the lateral heel lock but in a reverse manner.

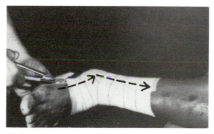

20 - To remove the tape, a scissor or tape cutter may be used, following the natural contours of the ankle and, in this case, a natural tunnel is on the medial aspect where the scissor or tape cutter can be run along the medial border of the foot, behind the medial malleolus and up the leg, care being taken not to press too hard over bony prominences.

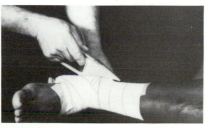

21 - A bit of lubricant on the blunt edge of the scissor or on the tape cutter described, facilitates the sliding of the instruments underneath the tape, between the underwrap and the skin.

Combination Elastic and Nonelastic Tape Ankle Strapping

A second method of ankle taping is being demonstrated and that is the use of a combination of elastic tape and nonelastic tape. This taping procedure is useful where a great deal of control is not necessary. It is used for an overnight compression period or for the normal activities of daily living.

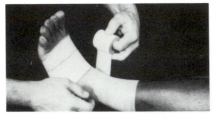

1 - The skin has been prepared as usual, the tape adherent applied and a layer of underwrap material wrapped over the extremity for the entire course of the taping procedure. An elastic tape is begun at the lower portion of the foot, carried around the ankle ...

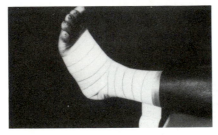

2 - and spiralled up the leg to the top of the underwrap where the tape is left dangling. We have, in effect, wrapped the extremity in a pressure bandage which, in fact, is elastic tape. When this is done, one must be certain that the pressure gradient is one that is reduced as we progress up the leg, that is, most of the pressure is along the foot and around the ankle. Once the tape progresses above the foot, the tension on the tape is slightly reduced. If the tape is applied too tightly, circulation may be impaired.

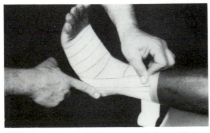

3 - We then use nonelastic tape, beginning on the medial aspect and applying a series of three or four stirrups. Care was exercised that the stirrup strips did not come over the hook of the fifth metatarsal, and we see also that the last two stirrup strips were angled slightly forward to fit the contours of the leg and allow the tape to be applied smoothly.

4 - Transverse strips are now being applied from behind the lateral (outside) malleolus to the medial (inside) malleolus. There is snug tension given to these strips when they are applied. This will help support the involved ligaments. A series of two or three of these transverse strips is used.

5 - After the transverse strips are applied, an additional stirrup is begun on the medial (inside) aspect of the leg to cover the ends of these transverse strips to help prevent them from peeling away.

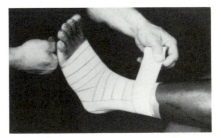

6 - After the application of this tie-down strip, the elastic tape then is wound down over the ends of the stirrups.

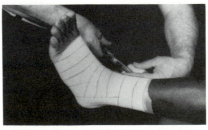

7 - This tape, then, is cut with scissors and we have completed the procedure.

Arch Taping

Useful for supporting the ligaments, small muscles and plantar (sole) aspects of the foot. It is also useful in a great percentage of those people suffering from shin splints on the medial (inside) aspect of the leg, a term given to what is believed to be posterior tibialis tendonitis. This is usually a result of overuse, through excessive running and pounding. The skin is prepared in the usual manner, cleansed and tape adherent is applied from the heads of the metatarsals to well up over the heel.

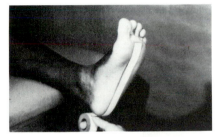

1 - The first strip of tape is applied from beyond the heads of the metatarsals, comes over the heel to approximately 1 to 1½" over the rounded contour of the heel. There is a bit of tension applied to this strip of tape and you will note that the foot is held in a semirelaxed position. Subsequent strips of tape are applied in a similar manner; however, they are fanned to the medial and lateral borders of the foot, respectively, and we have, in effect, created a fan appearance in the taping.

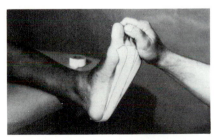

2 - The fan extends from the head of the first metatarsal to the head of the fifth and all strips converge at the heel where they go over the rounded contour into a single unit. Usually, six strips of tape are used, five in the fanning procedure and one additional supporting strip over the center of the fan. This reinforcement lends strength and the ability to withstand the forces that are going to be applied to it while running.

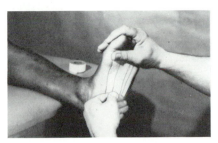

3 - The foot is then relaxed and the adhesive tape pressed up and contoured to the skin. What we're doing here, in effect, is "stringing the bow," whereby tightening the tape, we are attempting to increase the height of the arch.

4 - The next strip of tape begins just beyond the head of the first metatarsal, runs diagonally across the plantar aspect of the foot to the lateral portion of the heel where it traverses around the heel to lock in the end of our fan strips.

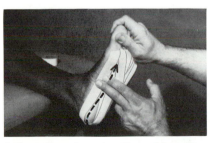

5 - Then we come forward over the medial aspect of the foot to the origin of the tape.

Arch Taping (continued)

6 - Additional and overlapping strips of tape are used in a similar manner from head of first. Additional support strips may be applied in the same manner from head of fifth metatarsal and returned to head of fifth metatarsal. These strips of tape lend reinforcement to the arch support as well as tie in the ends so that there is no slipping of the tape procedure.

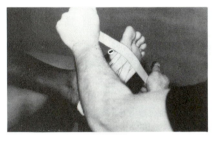

7 - Because of the unusual contour of the forefoot over the heads of the metatarsals, it is easy to anchor these down by using short strips of 1″ tape, and usually two strips will suffice, covering the distal end of the taping to anchor them in place as well as give the taping a very neat appearance. The ends are carried singly to the dorsum of the foot and tacked down.

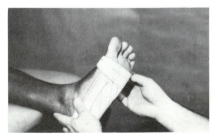

8 - A second strip is applied in an overlapping and like manner.

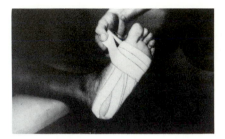

9 - Once we have applied these two strips, the forefoot and midfoot then resume more regular contours where a 1½″ tape can be used as an arch support or arch lifting. This tape is begun on the dorsum of the foot, carried over the lateral border under the plantar surface and then carried over the medial border of the foot to its origin, where the strip is torn off.

10 - Three or four of these overlapping strips complete the arch support taping procedure.

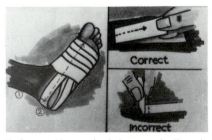

11 - Care must be exercised when removing the arch support taping. An easy method of removal is to cut the support strips just distal to the medial aspect of the heel, and then run the cutter or scissor down the medial aspect of the foot. *Remember the caution about removing tape from the sole of the foot.* Remove the tape slowly, close to a 180° angle to the skin, and if there is any evidence of callous tissue being pulled away from the plantar aspect of the foot, stop and reverse the direction of the pull.

Shin Splint Taping

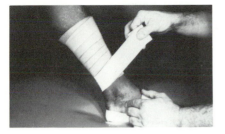

1 - Runners may obtain relief of their medial shin splint or posterior tibialis tendonitis through the use of circumferential elastic adhesive taping. For this procedure, the tape adherent is applied circumferentially on the leg from just above the malleoli line to just below the muscle tendon junction of the calf. Underwrap is then applied and elastic tape is then begun from the midline.

2 - Continue spiraling the elastic tape up the leg to just below the muscle of the calf, where the elastic tape may be cut with scissors.

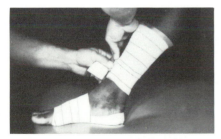

3 - When elastic tape is used, it is necessary to tie down the end of the elastic tape to prevent peeling. A circumferential strip of 1" tape is applied to the lower portion and to the upper portion of the elastic taping procedure.

Stirrup Taping

This is support taping for the lateral or medial aspect of the ankle. It is used when minimal control is necessary or, in fact, when the injury is mild enough to allow dorsiflexion and plantar flexion in those activities where this motion is essential and necessary, that is, in soccer, and for a punter in football. This is a taping procedure that certainly is effective in controlling some subtalar inversion (the inward ankle sprain).

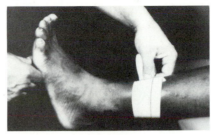

1 - The skin is prepared in the normal fashion and the two proximal anchor strips applied.

2 - We then apply a series of stirrups, however, without the interlocking horizontal strips. The stirrups are overlapped one-half to two-thirds of their width. As we progress forward on the lateral aspect of the foot, we are careful that we do not cross over the hook of the fifth metatarsal. As we cross the dorsum of the foot, you will note that the tape is angled forward slightly in order to be applied smoothly and meet the contours of the ankle and leg.

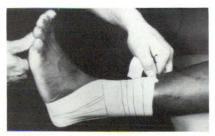

3 - This taping procedure is then completed by beginning a series of tie-down strips beginning proximally and working down the leg to just above the malleoli. These strips are angled slightly in order to meet the contours of the leg, and care is exercised that they do not come down the leg so far as to interfere with the hinge action of the ankle and act as an irritant to the skin on the dorsum of the foot.

Achilles Taping (Tendonitis)

The effect of this taping will be to restrict the degree of dorsiflexion at the ankle joint. In effect, the tape will tend to act as a second Achilles tendon and take some of the stresses of walking and/or running to allow participation. This, of course, would only be used with that individual who can demonstrate that he is, in fact, functional with the taping procedure applied. It certainly would be of no value on an individual who is incapacitated both by his injury and by the taping procedure.

4 - The first support strip of nonelastic tape is applied, going from the proximal to the distal anchor. You will note that the slight knee flexion and plantar flexion is maintained so that there is a small degree of tension across this first support strip and it is not adhered at this time to the skin and underwrap.

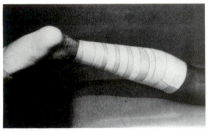

1 - The underwrap is applied from the knee to the ankle. We will have a slight bend in the knee for this tape application as well as a degree of plantar flexion at the ankle.

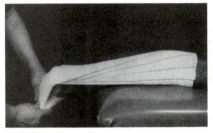

5 - Additional pieces of tape are applied in the manner of the fan; that is, they are fanning on the heads of the metatarsals as well as fanning over the calf, coming to a common point over the heel and increasing in strength as the tape is layered at this point. The tape is contoured to the plantar aspect of the foot.

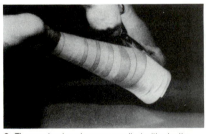

2 - The proximal anchors are applied with elastic tape. This is done smoothly and snugly, avoiding excessive tension to compromise any venous or lymphatic flow.

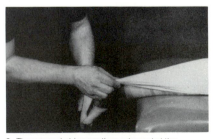

6 - The support strips are then crimped at the Achilles. This crimping wrinkles the tape and, in so doing, increases the tensile strength. At this point we are, in fact, constructing a second Achilles tendon.

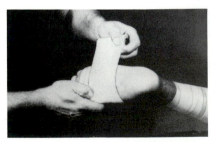

3 - Similarly, elastic anchors are applied over the heads of the metatarsals and the midfoot.

Basic Knee Strapping

7- We then use elastic tape, beginning at the heads of the metatarsals, and wrapping upward in a spiral fashion with a figure-eight around the ankle and tying down the nonelastic portions of the taping procedure.

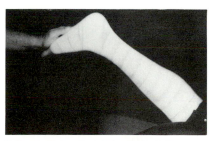

8- The elastic tape is carried up the leg to the proximal anchors where it is cut with scissors. We then use a nonelastic circumferential strip to anchor the end of our elastic tape.

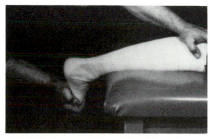

9- What we now have is the ankle supported in a position of plantar flexion and, in fact, we can see and demonstrate that the degree of dorsiflexion, the position and motion that will cause stretch and strain on the Achilles tendon is, in fact, restricted. We can press firmly on the plantar aspect of the foot and demonstrate that the angle is effectively limited to 90° dorsiflexion.

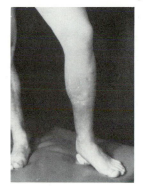

1- The next series will demonstrate a basic strapping for support of the knee joint for medial and/or lateral sprains of the knee. The athlete is positioned standing on a table so that the knee is at a comfortable height for the athletic trainer. The skin is prepared in the usual manner, being shaved and prepared with tape adherent. A lift is put under the heel so that an angle of approximately 20° of flexion is at the knee joint.

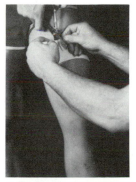

2- The first strip of tape applied is a 3″ elastic circumferential strip at mid-thigh. A second anchor strip is applied in an overlapping manner at this point.

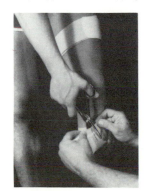

3- Two distal anchor strips are applied at just above mid-calf.

Basic Knee Strapping

(continued)

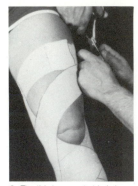

6 - The third support strip is begun on the medial aspect of the calf, crosses the knee joint at the joint line, goes above the patella, crosses the thigh and is attached to the proximal anchors on the lateral aspect of the thigh.

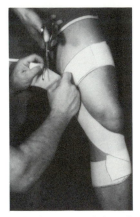

4 - The first support strip is applied by beginning at the lateral aspect of the leg, coming under the patella (knee cap), over the medial aspect of the knee to the proximal anchor on the medial aspect of the thigh. The tape is tacked down first, and a few inches run off before the firm tension is applied. We tack down the tape at the proximal anchor in a similar manner. The athlete cuts the tape at this point. We allow the end to retract before it is tacked down. By allowing the end to retract, we will reduce the probability of traction blisters at these points in our taping procedure.

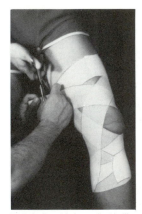

7 - A similar strip is applied in like manner from the lateral aspect of the leg and is completed at the medial aspect of the thigh on the proximal anchor.

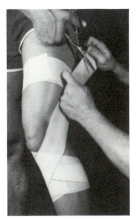

5 - The second support strip is begun on the medial aspect of the calf, carried under the patella and over the lateral aspect of the knee to the proximal anchor strip on the lateral aspect of the thigh.

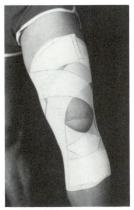

8 - We have now completed one set of medial and lateral support strips. It is easy to see that the taping procedure can be called an "X" method of taping for, in fact, we have created an "X" across the medial and lateral joint lines.

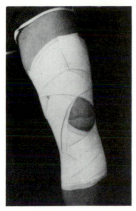

9 - Subsequent and overlapping strips of elastic tape are applied over the medial and lateral aspects of the leg. Two to three sets of these overlapping elastic strips usually suffice.

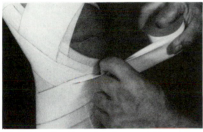

10 - We now begin a series of support strips, using nonelastic tape applied in a similar pattern. You will note that the first strip was applied on the medial knee. We fold the leading edge of the tape over so that it crosses the knee. We have the folded edge at a point of stress. This increases the tensile strength at this point to resist tearing, as the knee is flexed and extended.

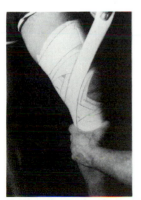

11 - We apply a number of sets of the nonelastic tape in the same manner as that described with the elastic tape, folding the leading edge of the elastic tape as it crosses the joint line.

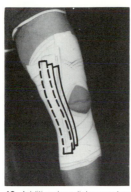

12 - Additional medial support can be given by a series of overlapping vertical strips, traversing from the calf to the thigh, with the leading edge of the tape folded. Three such overlapping strips have been applied to the medial aspect of the knee. To maintain good tension and stability at the joint line where it is most critical, we need to keep these support strips in good approximation and to allow no sliding.

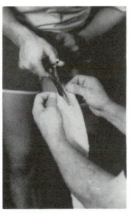

13 - We now take a strip of elastic tape that is cut long enough to go around the knee joint. A small slit is cut into each end of the tape.

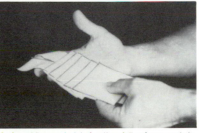

14 - A padding material of cotton, felt or foam pads is applied to the center of this elastic tape. This will act as a cushion as the tape is applied and pulled behind the knee in the popliteal space.

Basic Knee Strapping

15 - The padded portion of the tape is put behind the knee; just tack the medial tails temporarily while the lateral tails are split and stretched.

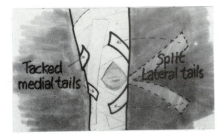

16 - The split ends are then brought above and below the patella (knee cap), with a fair degree of tension. Care must be exercised that tension is not so great as to compromise blood flow by pressing too hard too greatly in the popliteal space behind the knee where, in fact, the major vessels and nerves lie.

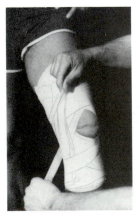

17 - The lateral tails are in place and now the medial portion of the popliteal band is picked up, split,

Tails are secured above and below patella

18 - and its tails are brought forward to above and below the patella.

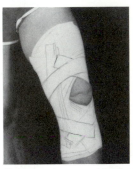

19 - We now have completed the popliteal band and the support strips are, in fact, well anchored at the points of most stress at the joint line.

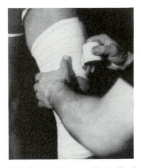

20 - Cover is then applied with elastic tape, beginning proximally and working downward. This is not necessary in all athletes, however, only for those who must put on a tight pant, as in football. If this cover tape is applied from distal to proximal, the elastic tape will roll and then slide the pant up the leg. However, if the tape is applied proximal to distal, this effect is minimized.

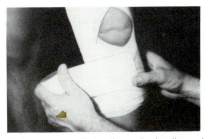

21 - The tape is applied on the proximal portion and is then cut as it crosses just above the patella. It is begun again just below the patella and carried to the most distal portion of the taping procedure.

Shoulder Strapping (Acromioclavicular)

Support of the acromioclavicular joint is a taping procedure that will certainly lend a degree of comfort and support to the individual who has a first or second degree sprain of the acromioclavicular joint, very much in the same manner that a sling would support the extremity. However, this does allow full function of the upper extremity while support is being exercised.

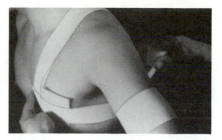

3 - Nonelastic tape is applied around half of the thorax from the anterior edge anchor to the posterior edge of the anchor.

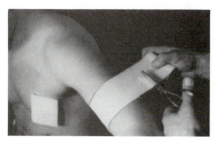

1 - The skin of the chest, thorax and back is prepared in the usual manner, being cleansed, shaved and tape adherent applied over the chest, back and arm on that side of the involved acromioclavicular joint. Protection can be given to the nipple, covering with a small piece of foam, felt or gauze held in place. The first anchor is applied to the arm just at about mid-biceps or mid-arm level. This is an elastic tape to allow for the expansion of the muscle as it contracts.

4 - We now begin a series of support strips from the arm to the anchor strips on the chest and back. An upward pull is exerted on the tape as we go from the arm to the anchor strips. This tends to support the extremity and helps to reduce any displacement of the acromioclavicular joint. These support tapes are applied diagonally from anterior to posterior, and then from posterior to anterior in the "X" or fanning pattern.

2 - A second anchor strip (nonelastic tape) is applied from the chest at its midline, over the shoulder and trapezius to the back, just below the tip of the scapula.

5 - Anchor strips are applied alternately to the chest and back with support strips on the arm. This ties the taping procedure together and reduces the incidence of pulling away from the skin.

Shoulder Strapping
(continued)

6 - These strips are anchored on the arm with elastic tape and...

7 - circumferentially around the chest.

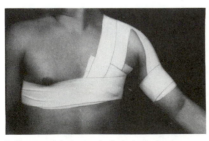

8 - The completed acromioclavicular taping is shown to demonstrate the upward pull of the arm and the downward pressure over the clavicle to support this joint.

Rib Taping

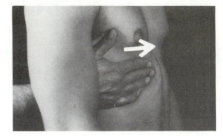

1 - The first photo illustrates forward pressure of the hand over the involved rib area. The athlete is asked to demonstrate a move that normally causes discomfort with the forward pressure. If, in fact, his discomfort is reduced with the forward pressure of the hand, we know then that the tape should be pulled from posterior to anterior.

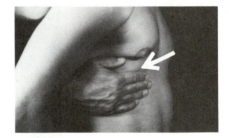

2 - If, in fact, the discomfort is reduced more with posterior pull of the hand on the involved site, we know then that the taping procedure should be pulled from anterior to posterior in support of the involved rib area.

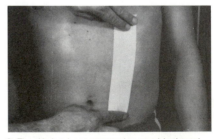

3 - The skin has been prepared as usual, is shaved and tape adherent applied. We are assuming that the area of injury is on the right side at the costo-chondral junction. An anchor strip of nonelastic tape is applied beyond the midline on the anterior abdomen and chest.

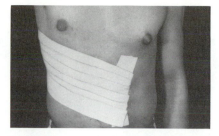

7 - We now have completed our first set of diagonal strips being pulled from anterior to posterior.

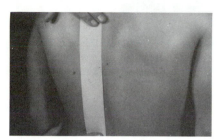

4 - A similar strip is applied to the back.

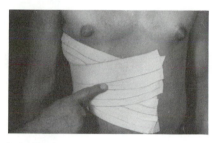

8 - Additional support is given by crossing the original set of strips in a diagonal manner, again from posterior to anterior. We can see how it indents, supports and limits the motion of the rib cage in this area. The finger points to the site of injury, which is in the center of our taping procedure.

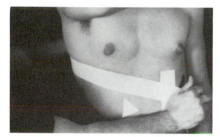

5 - We begin a series of diagonal support strips from posterior anchor to anterior anchor since our demonstration proved that anterior pull reduced the discomfort in the rib area. The angle of pull is an attempt to be at the same angle as the rib. The small arrow indicates the area of discomfort. We begin our taping procedure proximal to that area and will continue distally so that it is in the center of the taping procedure.

9 - In order to maintain the nonelastic tape in this position, and to keep it from peeling as the athlete moves and perspiration accumulates, an elastic tape is applied circumferentially over the entire taping procedure.

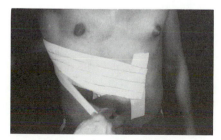

6 - A series of overlapping diagonal strips is pulled from posterior to anterior, completely covering the area of injury.

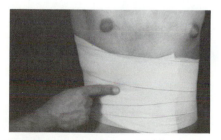

10 - The taping procedure is completed, the support strips have been anchored down by the elastic tape, and we have the finger pointing to the involved area.

Elbow Taping

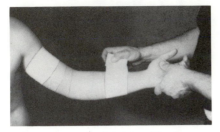

1 - The taping procedure is for injury of the elbow, which is, in fact, a sprain of the elbow joint occurring when the elbow has been forcibly extended beyond its limits. The skin is prepared in the usual manner, tape adherent has been applied and a layer of J-WRAP*material applied over the limits of the taping procedure. Elastic tape is used as proximal and distal anchors.

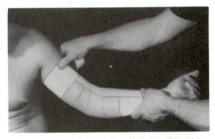

2 - The angle at which the elbow is held will be trial and error. We must realize that there is always a bit of slippage in the tape so the angle selected will be slightly more acute than that angle where discomfort begins so as to allow for that slight slippage. A series of support strips is then applied between the two anchors.

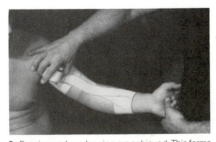

3 - Fanning and overlapping are achieved. This forms an "X" or a butterfly pattern with the strips overlapping in the anticubital space.

4 - We apply a sufficient number of strips, usually seven to nine.

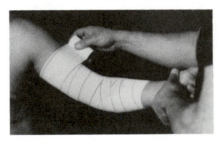

5 - Elastic tape is used to circumferentially spiral the support taping. The elastic tape must be anchored, however, with one strip of nonelastic tape.

Taping of Wrist & Fingers

The thumb may have been sprained in one or more directions. Passive movement of the joint will determine which directions or which motions are painful and have to be protected against excessive motion.

1 - Demonstration of the thumb being extended...

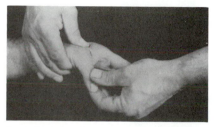

2 - passive flexion of the thumb.

3 - By holding the metacarpal still with one hand and pushing the thumb away from the metacarpal, we abduct the thumb...

4 - conversely, pulling the thumb toward the fingers of the hand adducts the thumb.

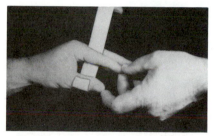

5 - The simplest protection for the sprained thumb is merely to tape it to the adjacent index finger. Here a strip of 1" tape is being circumferentially wrapped around the thumb and index finger.

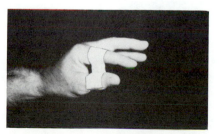

6 - After one or two turns have been taken around the thumb and index finger, a strip of ½" tape is wrapped around the space between the thumb and index finger. The shape of the taping then gives us the name, the butterfly taping for the thumb.

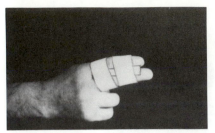

7 - Similarly, a sprained joint of one of the fingers may be protected by taping that finger to its neighbor. A piece of foam has been placed between the two fingers, and 1" tape has been circumferentially wrapped between the index finger and the middle finger. The only time the little finger would be taped to its neighbor is when itself is injured, for tying the little finger to the ring finger reduces full hand span.

8 - If it is necessary to maintain the useful function of each of the fingers, the taping of a single joint may be carried out. In this procedure, two anchor strips of ½" tape are then placed across the sides of the joint in an x-pattern very much like the taping for the knee joint.

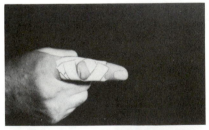

9 - The strips of tape are overlapping and fanned.

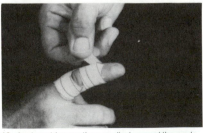

10 - Anchor strips are then applied around the ends of the x-taping to secure them in position. This taping procedure reinforces the collateral ligaments of the interphalangeal joint of the finger.

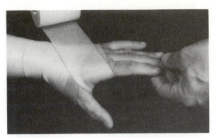

11 - If the athletic activity is such that it is necessary to protect the injured thumb but still have it be useful, we then can use a strip taping procedure. The hand and wrist are wrapped with J-WRAP* Underwrap material. The skin has been prepared in the usual manner and tape adherent applied.

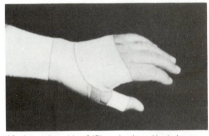

12 - An anchor strip of 1" tape is placed just above the first joint of the thumb, just above the knuckles of the hand and approximately 4" above the wrist bones. We are assuming that the thumb has been injured in such a way that causes flexion and abduction to be painful.

13 - The first strips of tape traverse across the back of the thumb, the hand and the wrist.

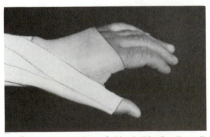

14 - Successive overlaps of strips in this direction will reduce the amount of flexion to the thumb.

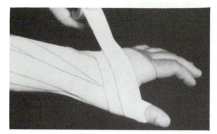

15 - Similarly, strips applied from the back of the thumb, across the dorsum of the hand, will reduce the amount of abduction that the thumb may go through.

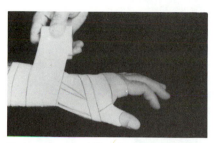

16 - An anchor strip of 1" tape is placed around the ends of tape on the thumb, and then 2" elastic tape is used as a cover, beginning proximally above the wrist joint, working down across the hand in a figure-8 pattern around the thumb and the back of the hand.

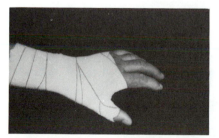

17 - Care is exercised not to pull the tape too tightly in the web space between the thumb and the first finger. Tape applied too tightly in this area will compromise the blood flow to the thumb.

Wrist Strapping

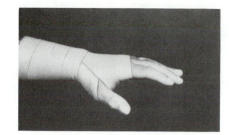

1 - To protect the sprained wrist, the same principle of strip taping may be used by applying strips across the dorsum, the back of the hand, and the volar, or palmar, aspect of the hand. The most secure taping is done by taping directly to the skin. However, the skin may be prepared in the usual manner, tape adherent applied and J-WRAP* Pretaping Underwrap applied from the knuckles to well above the wrist joint, approximately 5" up the forearm.

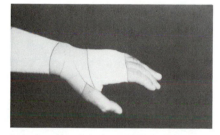

2 - Anchor strips of elastic or nonelastic tape are used at the base of the knuckles and at the upper portion of the taping procedure.

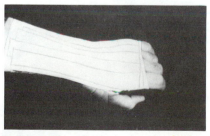

3 - A series of four or five overlapping strips of 1½" tape are placed on the dorsum of the hand, between the two anchor strips.

Wrist Strapping (continued)

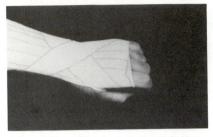

4 - Two additional strips are placed in an x-fashion in order to reinforce these longitudinal strips.

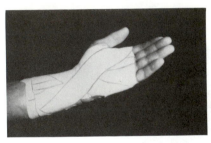

5 - Similarly, a series of longitudinal strips and reinforcing x-patterns are applied to the volar, or palmar, aspect of the wrist.

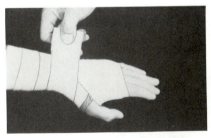

6 - All of these strips are held in position by a circumferential wrapping of 2″ elastic tape, beginning proximally and working down toward the base of the knuckles. Again, care is exercised not to pull the tape too tightly in the web space between the thumb and the first finger to compromise the blood flow in this area.

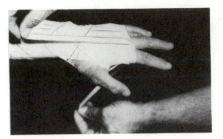

7 - Additional support for the wrist taping may be achieved through the use of longitudinal strips of ½″ tape, placed between the fingers and pulled up on the dorsal and the volar aspect of the tape procedure. First, small pieces of foam material are placed between the fingers and the web space in order to provide cushioning and reduce chafing or abrasion between the web space and the fingers. Mild tension is applied but not so tightly as to compromise the blood flow or irritate the web space between the fingers.

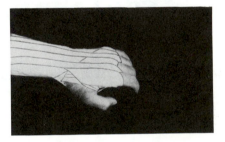

8 - This photo shows three of the longitudinal reinforcement strips in position. These strips will hold the taping procedure in place at the knuckle line.

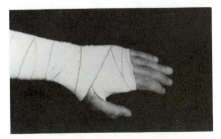

9 - The procedure is completed by circumferentially wrapping with 2″ elastic tape.

Index

Benzolamide, 463, 464
Beta-adrenergic blocking drugs, 491, 492
Beta-sympathomimetic drugs, 493
Biaxial joint, 110
Biceps curls, 71
Bicondylar joint, 111, 113
Bilateral comparison, 52
Bilateral visual comparison, 137, 138, 141
Biomechanics of back, 253–254
Bites, 427–428, 429
Black cat exercise, 265, 266
Bladder injuries, 325–326
Bleeding
    external, control of, 150–152
    facial, 228–229
    internal, emergency care for, 152–153
    nose, 227
Blisters, 426–427, 517
Blocker's exostosis, 301
Blood poisoning, 154
Blood pressure, measurement of, 171
Blood supply
    to bones, 95
    to foot, 405
    to inflamed tissue, 125, 126
    to lower leg, 382
    to shoulder, 273–274
    to skeletal muscles, 85
    to skin, 421–422
    and therapeutic manipulation of body
        temperature, 192, 205
    to upper extremity, 296, 300
Body composition, 481–483, 484
    measurement of, 171
    and weight control, 477, 478, 480
Body language, evaluation of, 182, 188
Body survey, 150
Body temperature
    elevation of, 445
    regulation of, in adults, 191–192, 421–
        422, 456–457
    regulation of, in children, 509–510
    therapeutic manipulation of, 192–194,
        205
Bone
    abnormalities of, 101–102
    adaptation of, to stress, 100–101
    aging of, 102–103
    composition of, 94–96
    demineralization of, 512
    formation of, 99–100
    fractures of, 102–109. *See also* Fractures
    of hand and wrist, 299
    structure of, 96–99
Bone marrow, metabolic function of, 94
Bone spurs, 404

Boron, 423
Boston brace, 211, 255, 264
Boutonniere deformity, 312
Bowstring sign test, 257, 259, 261
Boxing, 35
    injuries from, 39
Brace, tennis elbow, 303
Brachial plexus, 273
Bracing, 211
    of back injuries, 264
    of knee injuries, 376, 378
    of knee sprains, 360, 362
    of knee strains, 363
    of lower leg contusions, 396
    as protection for knee, 379
    as rehabilitative technique, 187
    of soft-tissue injuries, 91
    of unstable joints, 120
Breast injuries, 318
Breathing. *See* Respiratory arrest
Bronchitis, 442
Bruises. *See* Contusions
"Bucket handle" displaced tear, 366
Bulimia, 507
Bunions, 413
Burns, Art, 67
Burrow's solution, 433, 435
Bursae, 114–115
    subacromial, 272–273
Bursitis, 91–92, 281, 285, 290, 364, 367
    of foot, 411–412
    greater trochanteric, 347
    iliopsoas, 347
    treatment of, 92

Caffeine, 497–498
Calcaneus, fracture of, 405–406
Calcium, 95–96
Calcium channel blockers, 492
Calf muscle strain, prevention of, 54
Calf raises, 378
Calluses, 428, 429, 435
Calomine lotion, 436
Calvé's disease, 102
Can-Am derotation brace, 362
Cancellous (spongy) bone, 96, 99
    fracture of, 103
    healing of, 105, 106
Cancer. *See* Skin cancer; Tumors
Candidiasis, 433
Capital femoral epiphysis, fracture of, 337
Capsulitis, adhesive, 278, 293–294
Carbohydrate loading, 472–473
Carbohydrates
    and athletic performance, 469, 472–473,
        474